Handbook of Research on Hybrid Learning Models:
Advanced Tools, Technologies, and Applications

Fu Lee Wang
Caritas Francis Hsu College, Hong Kong

Joseph Fong
City University of Hong Kong, Hong Kong

Reggie C. Kwan
Caritas Francis Hsu College, Hong Kong

Information Science REFERENCE

INFORMATION SCIENCE REFERENCE

Hershey · New York

Director of Editorial Content:	Kristin Klinger
Senior Managing Editor:	Jamie Snavely
Assistant Managing Editor:	Michael Brehm
Publishing Assistant:	Sean Woznicki
Typesetter:	Carole Coulson, Kate Griffin, Sean Woznicki
Cover Design:	Lisa Tosheff
Printed at:	Yurchak Printing Inc.

Published in the United States of America by
Information Science Reference (an imprint of IGI Global)
701 E. Chocolate Avenue
Hershey PA 17033
Tel: 717-533-8845
Fax: 717-533-8661
E-mail: cust@igi-global.com
Web site: http://www.igi-global.com/reference

Library of Congress Cataloging-in-Publication Data

Handbook of research on hybrid learning models : advanced tools, technologies, and applications / Fu Lee Wang, Joseph Fong and Reggie Kwan, editors.
p. cm.

Includes bibliographical references and index.
Summary: "This book focuses on Hybrid Learning as a way to compensate for the shortcomings of traditional face-to-face teaching, distance learning, and technology-mediated learning"--Provided by publisher.

ISBN 978-1-60566-380-7 (hardcover) -- ISBN 978-1-60566-381-4 (softcover) 1. Distance education--Computer-assisted instruction. 2. Educational technology--Computer-assisted instruction. 3. Blended learning. 4. Virtual reality in education. I. Wang, Fu Lee. II. Fong, Joseph. III. Kwan, Reggie.
LC5803.C65H365 2010
378.1'734--dc22

2009047891

British Cataloguing in Publication Data
A Cataloguing in Publication record for this book is available from the British Library.

List of Reviewers

Kanishka Bedi, *Universitas 21 Global, India*
Raj Boora, *University of Alberta, Canada*
Giuliana Dettori, *ITD-CNR (Institute for Educational Technologies), Italy*
Wolfgang Halang, *FernUniversität in Hagen, Germany*
Yoko Hirata, *Hokkai-Gakuen University, Japan*
Diana Rosario Pérez Marín, *Universidad Rey Juan Carlos, Spain*
Iwona Miliszewska, *Victoria University, Australia*
Sabine Moebs, *Dublin City University, Ireland*
Barbara O'Byrne, *Marshall University, USA*
Zhiyong Peng, *Wuhan University, China*
Stephan Repp, *University of Potsdam, Germany*
Minjuan Wang, *San Diego State University, USA*
Shudong Wang, *Hiroshima Shudo University, Japan*
Marc Zhichang Xu, *The Hong Kong Institute of Education, Hong Kong*

List of Contributors

Table of Contents

Section 2
E-Learning Models

Section 3
Hybrid Learning Models

Detailed Table of Contents

This chapter proposes the hybrid inquiry-based learning (HIBL) model, a novel pedagogical model based on inquiry-based learning (IBL). In IBL, learning is achieved by questioning and learners are encouraged to invent new hypotheses instead of investigating questions posed by the instructor. This chapter first provides a holistic description of IBL. It begins with a brief history and survey on learning perspectives, pedagogical background of IBL is also provided. The IBL model, its implementations and variations, as well as the comparison of its pedagogical features against traditional teaching approaches are also given. This chapter further contributes the hybrid inquiry-based learning (HIBL) model, a new IBL model that integrates traditional and ICT-based implementations of IBL. By leveraging on the advantages of both classroom-based and web-based learning, the best sides of IBL can be elicited. A detailed example in Information Security education is also provided to illustrate the HIBL model.

This chapter seeks to highlight the unique characteristics of blended learning communities and the special design consideration they call for. The blended nature of a community is reflected through the interplay of the online and offline dimensions of a community and the mix of various media in support of community-wide interaction. The authors introduce the notion of blended learning community based on related literature on learning community and blended learning and put forward design guidelines for building such communities. Further, a pilot study was conducted to test out the proposed design principles in the context of pre-service teacher education with blogs as the main vehicle for online communication. The authors' work can contribute to a deepened understanding of learning communities situated in the blended media environment and provide a set of design principles for their development.

This chapter examines why despite decades of research and overwhelming evidence questioning the pedagogical effectiveness of lecturing as a teaching and learning strategy, it remains the dominant pedagogical mode in most higher education institutions worldwide. The authors explore further why lectures are not the most appropriate teaching strategy in the current higher education climate for three main reasons: the way we now view 'knowledge'; the information society in which we are currently immersed; and the diverse background and experience of today's student population. The authors offer an alternative to the lecture which can achieve what a lecture aims to, but in a more student-centred way. Their alternative is informed by the contributing student approach, devised by Collis & Moonen (2001), whereby students collaboratively find, explore, share, and engage with the content which they would have otherwise received passively via a didactic lecture.

This chapter describes a conceptual framework that aims to augment existing eLearning systems with a 3D virtual classroom environment to provide geographically dispersed online learners with a sense of being together and part of a natural class. The virtual classroom model the authors present is based on a combination a 'massively multi-user' games technology system from Sun Microsystems Research Labs, a distance learning platform based at Shanghai Jiaotong University and a mixed reality environment developed at Essex University. Learning is, to some extent, a social activity as it involves relationships between people (between students, between students and teachers). Networked technology has a global reach bringing not just new opportunities but also complex multi-cultural and pedagogical issues. Thus, in this chapter the authors discuss both the technology and the socio-educational aspects of designing online Mixed Reality Hybrid Learning systems.

This chapter is based on a research project on hybrid teaching and learning. This emerging hybrid mode is gaining popularity in tertiary institutions because the new technologies have integrated the classroom and online teaching and learning into an organic productive environment. The research project adopts a discourse analysis approach and intends to investigate issues arising regarding the hybrid mode in a higher education institute in Hong Kong. These issues include 1) the discourse features of teaching and learning in the classroom face-to-face (FTF) and online computer-mediated communication (CMC); 2) the changing roles of teachers and students in the emerging hybrid environment; and 3) the implications of the hybrid mode on the effectiveness of teaching and learning. In addition, this research project also adopts questionnaire surveys among the teaching staff of a language education faculty and students of three courses offered in the hybrid mode to discover their attitudes towards the hybrid teaching and learning mode. The research findings suggest that in the hybrid environments, the traditional roles of the teachers as information providers, knowledge transmitters, supervisors and assessors, and the students as learners, participants, and respondents are still dominant. However, the teachers are also increasingly putting on new 'hats' as expert learners, facilitators, course designers and organizers. Apart from being learners, the students are also taking on new roles as topic contributors, meaning negotiators, information providers, strategic communicators and monitors.

Section 4
Hybrid Learning Systems

Distance learning has come a long way since Sir Isaac Pitman initiated the first correspondence course in the early 1840s. Today the growing role of globalization calls for new and innovative learning systems for management education. To meet these challenges the traditional classroom model for delivering executive business education is giving way to a more holistic learning paradigm in which both the pedagogical and andragogical focus are on knowledge acquisition and management decision-making. The one-size-fits-all educational approach of the past is being supplanted by customized, web-based learning systems. The purpose of this chapter is to introduce a blended learning system that combines the best of both web-based learning and time-honed classroom practices for delivering cost-effective graduate management education.

This chapter describes original modalities of combining traditional methods and technologies in medical learning with good results. The electronic tool is TESYS, a non-commercial e-learning platform designed for completing and improving traditional medical learning by using new methods. Traditional learning is thus blended together with e-learning, offering the students and teachers the possibility to permanently evaluate the learning and teaching process. Besides the usual functions of an e-learning platform, TESYS includes elements of originality. The first one is a database with medical images collected during the process of diagnosing patients, which also include other useful information (diagnostic, treatment, evolution) in order to complete the currently limited number of images found in university courses and medical books. The second element of originality is the content-based visual query module designed for this multimedia medical database, which uses features that are automatically extracted from images (color, texture, regions). The content-based visual query used both in the e-learning and e-testing process stimulates learning by comparing similar cases along with their particularities, or by comparing cases that are visually similar but with different diagnosis.

This chapter explores how educators can harness the potential of a new wave of social software to respond to the challenges of tertiary education in the new millennium, by combining the interactivity and immediacy of face-to-face instruction with the openness, connectivity, and flexibility afforded by

The merging of knowledge management and hybrid learning has gained more and more attraction and has been put in the focus of interests lately, for the simple reason that both areas can benefit from each other. As a result, this chapter deals with knowledge management for hybrid learning.

Who being a Hybrid Learning teacher in the Web 2.0 era has not made him/herself ask this question: "*Are students working effectively while they are not in face to face class?*" Sometimes the questions are asked but he/she does not have the knowledge to create an Interaction Assessment Strategy that could provide this information. The authors present in this chapter a Model that provides the steps and data that should result in a much better teaching/learning process. Thus, the Model presents the questions that should be made, the data model that should be worked on, the visualizations that should better fit each type of data and the process of analysis teachers could make to improve different features, such as: the way of presenting information to the students through the year, prevent students' dropping outs and failures, and generally improve the pace of teaching.

This chapter presents a model for hybrid and collaborative learning based on an analogy with musical polyphony, starting from Bakhtin's ideas of dialogism. The model considers different voices (participants) inter-animating and jointly constructing a coherent tune (a solution, in problem solving), enabling other voices to adopt differential positions and to identify dissonances (unsound approaches). This chapter introduces also software tools, which visualize the discussion threads in a chat and the influences that an utterance has on the subsequent ones. Such tools help both teachers and learners to evaluate and enhance the learning process. The model helps to understand how learners inter-animate when they participate to collaborative chats for problem solving or other learning activities, including Hybrid Learning.

Teaching and learning computer programming has created significant difficulties to both teacher and student. Large class size is one of the major barriers to effective instruction. A well-designed pedagogy can make the instruction most effective. Hybrid teaching and learning combines face-to-face instruction and computer-assisted instruction to maximize students' learning. This chapter will share the authors' experiences in City University of Hong Kong (CityU) as they teach computer programming courses with large class size by hybrid learning model. Evaluation has showed that hybrid teaching and learning provide great flexibilities to both teaching and learning of computer programming. The students' academic results have been significantly improved in computer programming courses.

Foreword

Educational technologies are changing constantly. Part of the reason is due to the development of new media technologies. Throughout history, it is clear to see how technologies influence education. The printing press was started in 1436. Eventually, mass duplication and distribution of information led to schooling. In 1922, Thomas Edison predicted that motion pictures would replace textbooks. Although textbooks are still required today, film was the first true modern learning technology being used in military training during the World War II. With the development of satellite TV in the 80's, the military worked with leading universities and brought in behavioral and cognitive psychology, and eventually led to commercial educational films. In early 90's, multimedia technology with CD ROMs gave another highlight of using modern technologies in education. Shortly, with Internet and Web browsers, the notions of distance learning, virtual university, e-learning, m-learning, and u-learning (i.e., ubiquitous learning) were widely discussed and realized in high level education as well as in K-12.

In the blooming of this virtual university era, someone predicted that teachers will be partially replaced by distance learning systems. Yet, evidence shows that face-to-face instruction is still the most efficient way of teaching. The question comes to the fundamental meaning of education – to transfer information from experienced teachers to less experienced students. Technology is helpful but should never drive the education process. And people are the center of the process. Hybrid Learning or Blended Learning combines face-to-face instruction with computer-mediated instruction. This paradigm of instruction relies on modern media technologies, with serious considerations of their pedagogical implications. Hybrid learning models, although not well-defined with fundamental requirements such as instructional design principles and assessment methods, take notices of educational professionals, researchers, and engineers.

This handbook collects research contributions from both educational and engineering professors. Education theories and models are addressed, as well as practical software implementation and usage case studies. The interesting part of this book includes several good chapters discussing hybrid learning models with a few other chapters demonstrating practical software systems. Some of these chapters discuss advantages of Hybrid Learning over traditional education. Yet, others point out the fundamental issues of educational theories needs to cope with the technology changes. The discussion will benefit graduate students and young professors who are looking for research issues in e-learning and virtual university.

Timothy K. Shih
National Taipei University of Education, Taiwan
May 2009

Preface

Advances in technology continue to affect the way we learn and teach. Most practitioners embrace new tools, models, and systems stemmed from technological advancements while theorists are still hesitant at the moment. Our ability to harness the new technologies and blend them with appropriate pedagogical approaches could have profound impact on the effectiveness of learning and teaching. Even the best lecturers cannot tell for sure if learning is a result of a lecture. Lecturing has long been criticized as the least learner-centered approach in learning while many e-learning platforms have also been condemned as using technology for technology's sake. Hybrid Learning is a way to compensate for the shortcomings of traditional face-to-face teaching, distance learning, and technology-mediated learning.

This book is an attempt to compile the most recent research works done by prominent practitioners in the field from all over the world. As we are indebted to the army of reviewers, we would like to take this opportunity to thank them from the bottom of our heart for their insightful comments and suggestions. We would also congratulate all contributors to this book for their excellent work that made this book possible. The models, tools, and applications they built and put to practice are opening the door for the new frontier of learning and teaching.

Fu Lee Wang
Joseph Fong
Reggie Kwan
November 2009

Acknowledgment

The Handbook of Research on Hybrid Learning Models would not exist without the effort of many people whose names may not appear on the cover of the book. However, their hard work, cooperation, friendship and understanding are very important to the preparation and production of the book. Firstly, the editors of this book sincerely thank IGI Global to publish this book. In particular, we would like to thank Christine Bufton, Dave DeRicco, Lindsay Johnston, Kristin M. Klinger, Julia Mosemann, Heather A. Probst and Jan Travers, for their efforts to bring this book into existence. On the other hand, Prof. Timothy Shih supports a lot to this book. We thank him sincerely for all his help, valuable comments, and for writing a foreword to the book. The success of this book depends on the high quality chapters submitted. The editors wish to express their deep appreciation to the chapter authors who have significantly contributed to this book. Last but not least, the Editorial Advisory Board plays an important role in this book. They have reviewed the manuscript submitted and provided a lot of feedback to enhance the quality of this book. The editor would like to thank the following individuals in the Editorial Advisory Board, Kanishka Bedi, Raj Boora, Giuliana Dettori, Wolfgang Halang, Yoko Hirata, Diana Rosario Pérez Marín, Iwona Miliszewska, Sabine Moebs, Barbara O'Byrne, Zhiyong Peng, Stephan Repp, Minjuan Wang, Shudong Wang, and Marc Zhichang Xu, for their generous commitment of time and effort.

Section 1
Education Theories

Chapter 1
In Love and War:
Blended Learning Theories for Computer Scientists and Educationists

Esyin Chew
University of Glamorgan, UK

David A. Turner
University of Glamorgan, UK

Norah Jones
University of Glamorgan, UK

ABSTRACT

Blended learning involves the combination of two fields of concern: technological and instrumental considerations are, to a greater or lesser extent, combined with pedagogy and educational theory. The result of this is that blended learning suffers from considerable difficulties of definition, and its theoretical foundation is correspondingly weak. For this reason it is desirable to expose the philosophical and theoretical foundations of blended learning to critical scrutiny. Creating a foundation for blended learning will involve an examination of the gap between the paradigms and practices of educational theory and educational technology. The result should be a space within which academics from the diverse disciplines involved may be able to discuss and resolve their problems. This chapter will explore the contrasting disciplinary perceptions and suggest a sketch for blended learning theory.

INTRODUCTION

Blended learning involves the combination of two fields of concern: technological and instrumental considerations are, to a greater or lesser extent, combined with educational theory. There is general consensus that pedagogical considerations should be given priority over technical issues. However, technicians and educationists have different vocabularies, and even where they appear to use the same terms, the context that each gives to the term means that there is ample room for misunderstandings. For example, computer specialists and educationists use the term 'ontology' to mean entirely different and mutually exclusive areas of concern, so that even when they seem to be talking about the same topic, the concerns of one may be ignored by the other. Such misunderstandings may extend to areas of

DOI: 10.4018/978-1-60566-380-7.ch001

'learning theories', where computer specialists may be more instrumental, or tactical, than educationists. Consequently, terms such as 'efficiency' or 'efficacy', which may seem perfectly natural to the computer specialist, may seem problematic or inappropriate to the educationist.

The result of this is that blended learning suffers from considerable difficulties of definition, and its theoretical foundation is correspondingly weak. For this reason it is desirable to expose the philosophical and theoretical foundations of blended learning to critical scrutiny. Creating a foundation for blended learning will involve an examination of the gap between the paradigms and practices of educational theory and technology. For example the term "technology" for educational technologists is referring to VLE (Virtual learning Environment), web 2.0 or ICT used for education whereas educationists perceive the same term as any technology, including laser pen and whiteboard marker. The result should be a space within which academics from the diverse disciplines involved may be able to discuss and resolve their problems. Therefore, we would like to affirm that the term "technology" or "educational technology" as used in this chapter means ICT used education.

This chapter will explore the contrasting disciplinary perceptions and suggest a sketch for blended learning Theory. This will be accomplished by: (1) Identifying and exploring how educationists (possibly pedagogy classicists) and computer scientists (possibly blended learning romantics) differ in terms of what they think needs to be accounted for, and how, when blended learning is based on scholarly evidence. The paradigms of educationists and computer scientists will be examined through a philosophical examination, in part illustrated by a survey of the opinions of specialists who work in blended learning in a number of settings. (2) Offering an idiom for discussing a set of issues both pressing yet beset by confusion. And (3) Presenting a preliminary sketch for blended learning Theory on the basis of (1) and (2), together with educational practices and theories drawn from the authors' personal experiences.

In the field of computer science and engineering, efficiency, effectiveness and experimental results are the main focus, whereas, in education, the variety of social contexts and the complexity of educational purposes must be taken into consideration. The authors assert that technology and effectiveness by itself does not necessarily improve the teaching and learning experience. On the other hand, learning theories need to be grounded in such mundane concerns as whether resources are available for use. This requires that attention be paid to issues of access and allocation. Only through mutual understanding can initial principles for the grounding of blended learning Theory be established. Educational theory provides the basis for a coherent and stringent critique of blended learning practices, and by that means provides a framework for grounding its theories.

IN LOVE AND WAR: PERCEPTIONS FOR BLENDED LEARNING

The Scholarly Definitions and the Debates of Blended Learning

We are not sure which type of learning to use so we will use lots and hope that the whole is greater than the sum of its parts... blended learning gave way to 'blurred learning.' (Morrison, 2003, pp. 1)

In earlier work we found that researchers and practitioners consider that blended learning is currently embryonic in its development and many of the related concepts remain debatable (Chew et al., 2006). Most often, e-learning in higher education today refers to web-based learning and teaching materials and e-tivities (Salmon, 2002). Put very crudely, blended learning simply means a mixture of instructor-led teaching with some

Table 1. Definition of blended learning by various researchers

Researchers	Definitions of Blended Learning
Thorne (2003)	Represents an opportunity to integrate the innovative and technological advances offered by online learning with the interaction and participation offered in the best of traditional learning.
Graham, Allen and Ure (2003); Graham (2006)	(1) combination of delivery media and tools employed (Singh and Reed, 2001; Orey, 2002); (2) combination of a number of pedagogical approaches or instructional methods (Driscoll, 2002; Rossett, 2002); and **(3) combination of face-to-face traditional learning with online instruction** (Reay, 2001; Rooney, 2003; Ward and LaBranche, 2003). The first two positions above dilute the definition of blended learning and do not clearly define what blended learning is. The first two definitions provide an amorphous idea that almost anything can be defined as blended learning. It would be difficult to find any learning system that did not involve more than one media and tools; similarly, it would be difficult to find any teaching and learning scenarios that did not embrace multiple pedagogies or multiple instructional approaches. Graham (2006) argues that the third stance specifies more precisely the meaning of blended learning.
Vaughan and Garrison (2005)	The thoughtful integration of face-to-face classroom (spontaneous verbal discourse) and Internet based (reflective text-based discourse) learning opportunities is neither an add-on to a classroom lecture nor an online course. It is the fundamental redesign and an optimal (re)design approach to enhance and extend learning by rethinking and restructuring learning and teaching to create blended learning.
Littlejohn and Pegler (2007)	The "blend" which may refer either to the combination of e-learning with other approaches such as face-to-face instruction, or the mixture within the e-learning mix of media.
Sloan-Consortium (Vignare, 2007, pp.38)	(1) the integration of online with face-to-face instruction in a planned, pedagogically valuable manner and (2) do not just combine but trade off face-to-face time with online activity (or vice versa).
Allan (2007, pp.4)	(1) The use of different internet-based tools including chat rooms, discussion groups, Podcasts and self-assessment tools to support a traditional course and (2) A mixture of face-to-face and e-learning
Garrison and Vaughan (2008)	No more about reshaping and enhancing the traditional classroom than it is about making e-learning more acceptable. It necessitates that educators question what is important and consider how much time should be spent in the classroom.

online activities. Bielawski and Metcalf (2003) argue that this definition adds little new meaning to the term e-learning. Blended learning researchers and practitioners, however, argue that blended learning is distinctive from e-learning, and in some ways preferable to it. Table 1 presents a number of definitions of blended learning.

Oliver and Trigwell (2005) echoed the criticisms of Bielawski and Metcalf (2003), and suggested that the phrase 'blended learning' is meaningless, and that it has gained considerable currency in both commercial and educational contexts because of its ambiguity. As can be seen from Table 1, Graham (2006), Allan (2007) and Littlejohn and Pegler (2007) have offered definitions of blended learning that try to overcome this difficulty. Sharpe et al. (2006) tried to overcome the difficulty of the lack of consensus over a definition of blended learning by proposing that the concept has a number of dimensions, and that a multi-dimensional concept can accommodate the various different definitions. Blended learning would thus involve mixtures along the following dimensions:

1. Delivery – different modes (face-to-face and distance education);
2. Technology – mixtures of (web based) technologies;
3. Chronology – synchronous and a-synchronous interventions
4. Locus – practice-based vs. class-room based learning;
5. Roles – multi-disciplinary or professional groupings;

Figure 1. The landscape of blended learning (Allan, 2007)

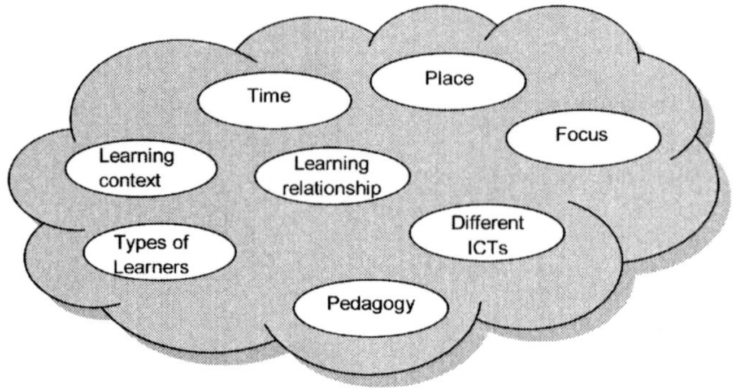

6. Pedagogy – different pedagogical approaches;
7. Focus – acknowledging different aims; and
8. Direction – instructor-directed vs. autonomous or learner-directed learning.

Allan (2007) adopts the same strategy as Sharpe et al. (2006). She recognises the amorphous nature of blended learning but by-passes the criticisms of Oliver and Trigwell (2005) by going straight into the study of the features of blended learning without further discussion or argument (Chew, 2008a). Built on the work of Sharpe et al. (2006), Allan refines those dimensions as "the landscape of blended learning" (Figure 1).

Both Sharpe et al. (2006) and Allan (2007) have made a reasonable attempt to present a general account of blended learning. The dimensions and landscape of blended learning remain broad and complex. One of the difficulties is that the dimensions are not orthogonal, and it can be argued that one dimension may embrace another. Even so, there may be some argument about which dimensions subsume which. Some dimensions are overlapping and confusing as they again, include almost everything in education, as Graham (2006) argued in a slightly different context. Littlejohn and Pegler (2007: 75-6) offered an attempt to simplify the confusing dimensions into four general areas as follows:

- The *space* blend: face-to-face or technology mediated communication;
- The *time* blend: based on geography and availability, synchronicity or asynchronicity;
- The *media* blend: tools, technologies and resources;
- The *activity* blend: learning and teaching activities, individual or group.

Similarly, Kim (2006) argued that the definition of blended learning can, and needs to, be made more precise than "the combination of classroom and e-learning". He suggested three dimensions to define blended learning: (1) physical – class-based or virtual, (2) formal or informal, and (3) scheduled or self-paced. He claims that there are possibly 8 combinations from the above 3 dimensions, for example, the informal physical class-based; or scheduled informal virtual learning space. These efforts go some way to eliminate the confusions introduced by the mix of pedagogies and the style of learning. One can frequently be confused by the complexity of pedagogies and learning behaviours and this has the capacity to provoke endless debates. Such simplified schema may be more easily accepted and put into practice. These definitions, dimensions, landscapes and frameworks provide a general setting and boundary to blended learning. More importantly, they present the idea of what blended learning is.

From an instrumental perspective, all the arguments discussed above may be well founded and avoid the criticisms raised by Oliver and Trigwell (2005) And certainly the blended learning practitioner or technologist would continue to "enjoy" blended learning practice within that boundary. We might, therefore, label them as "blended learning romantics". (The characteristics of this group will be the subject of discussion in Section 2.2 below).

However, it should be noted at this point that the definitions of blended learning that were presented above were firmly focused on a technological viewpoint. The dimensions of space, time and media, at the very least, deal with technical issues ancillary to pedagogy. Even the dimension of teaching and learning activities, which may be informed by pedagogy, does not deal with pedagogy with any depth or sophistication. Educational theorists and philosophers may therefore be relatively uninterested in debates about blended learning, which appear to focus on what is being blended than on any concern over learning.

The Conflicts and the Differences

The title of this chapter refers to the mixture of sweet and bitter experience which is part of any engagement with blended learning, and which is perhaps yet another dimension to it. Many pro-technology academics consider technology to be a key driver or necessarily trend in modern learning and teaching. Blacker (1995) described them as "computer romantics", who hold that technology will break down traditional barriers to effective and successful educational reform. In the context of this research, we borrow Blacker's terminology to label a group of academics and researchers in higher education as "blended learning romantics", who assert that the face-to-face instruction mediated by technology will break through traditional teaching and learning in the classroom. Blended learning romantics are a group of people who in a naively or unsophisticated way believe in all the "wonders" of modern technology. They may view themselves as evangelists who reveal the persistence of traditional settings and produce creative and effective efforts to develop modern learning.

On the other hand, in direct opposition to the "blended learning romantics", there is a group of academics who disagree with anything that involves technology. We shall call this group "pedagogy classicists". Technology is sometimes regarded as no more than a tool, a mere vehicle or information carrier (Luppicini, 2005). Pedagogy classicists, however, stress the negative aspects of that tool. They concentrate on the constraints imposed by the technology, while mumbling, "This system is useless", or "The VLE will not let me do this". They believe in pedagogy and learning theory rather than the "tool" or "vehicle". In the worst cases, they may not regard blended learning as a scholarly, educational or social science research activity at all. Pedagogy classicists would normally label blended learning romantics as the idealists, those who are correspondingly "weak" in theoretical grounding and lack educational insights. On the other hand, blended learning romantics may argue that pedagogy classicists are conservatives who having "the spirit of past" and that they react against change and new opportunities.

From a historical viewpoint, it is possible to wed certain classical and romantic element in the same piece of art, as happens in music or painting. This may be challenging, but it could be possible to draw a parallel with blended learning romantics and pedagogy classicists. Both groups hold to concepts that are simultaneously simple and complex.

Simple and Complex

From the above discussion, it may be seen that the idea of blended learning is too simple and not simple enough at the same time. It is simple in the sense that blended learning is a combination of face-to-face instruction and instruction mediated by technology. At the same time it is too complicated in the sense that it is neither a simple model nor a framework for designing successful blended learning. The complexity arises from the complex nature of educational behaviour. At one level the idea of blended learning is intuitively obvious and simple, but its application is more complex.

Allan (2007) argues that the success of blended learning lies in the possibility of responding to research and to the practical demands of the parent organisation and individual learner's needs. One of the authors of this chapter has noted, however, that, in the context of educational institutions, knowing and capturing how many people will follow a particular route through the educational system is more useful than being able to predict the behaviour and needs of each individual learner (Turner, 2007). Similarly, Littlejohn and Pegler (2007) affirm that there is no perfect blend for a specific context, just as there is no one perfect blends of coffee for all occasions. In this sense, many blended learning models suggested may be seen as a compromise in the same way as "3-in-1 coffee mix" is a compromise between ease of use and matching personal tastes. Blended learning mixes may be the equivalent of instant coffee for novice blended learning practitioners (Chew, 2008b). In this sense, we would like to assert that a professional educationist is unlikely to be satisfied by a simple mechanism to model learning and teaching. This is in some way parallel with a professional coffee lover will never be satisfied by instant coffee, which the connoisseur thinks is too simple and lack the 'real' taste of coffee.

Garrison and Vaughan (2008) capture this complexity as follows:

Blended learning, in short, is a coat of many colours. It took many reforms, many meanings, and many expressions. It means different things at different times to different people. It was simple as well as complex, pure as well as adulterated. In such ability to absorb such diversity of roles and meanings may well lie the secret of its historical success – defined rather modestly as its establishment as an institution and an idea that lasted beyond its own time. (p.5)

Therefore, professional educationists (or pedagogy classicists) who reject blended learning may be basing their judgment on a simpler idea of blended learning than that described by Garrison and Vaughan. Likewise, some naive blended learning romantics may not be aware of the intriguing and complex nature of education. The debate between blended learning romantics and pedagogy classics will never end. The former highlight the advancement of educational technology and its practical benefits, while the latter worry about the shallow perception of blended learning romantics, who always neglect the complexity of education and the integral nature of the learning and teaching experience. The following sections explore such simple and complex thoughts for blended learning romantics and pedagogy classicists, and the "war" between the extreme positions of romantics and classicists. Based on a deeper understanding of educational theory and its relationship with educational technology, an attempt is made to show how blended learning can be grounded in educational theory through such reflections.

THE SIMPLE: AN OVERVIEW OF BLENDED LEARNING FROM AN INSTRUMENTAL PERSPECTIVE

Available Technology for Learning and Teaching

The idea of blended learning is simple and exciting for blended learning romantics. However, the technology used for learning and teaching evolves over time. What once was new and on the cutting edge will one day become old technology and be challenged by the generation that follows. The

Table 2. The summary for face-to-face settings and technology in blended learning

Face-to-face (Live)	Technology (Virtual)		
	Synchronous (In community)	**Asynchronous (In community)**	**Self-Paced Asynchronous**
Instructor-led classroom (lectures) Tutorials Hands-on lab Workshops Seminars/ Conferences Coaching / mentoring Field works / Site Visits Work-place learning / Placements Examinations	Virtual Classroom / Online Lecture Online chat / Instant Messaging E-Conference Online assessment Interactive Whiteboard	Discussion board / e-Forum Announcement / Bulletin Board Offline message in online chat Emails Search engine User groups / News groups Polling and questionnaire or webforms Blog Wiki	Online Learning Materials Online Tutorials Online self-assessment Podcasts DVD/CD
	VLE or PLE that consist of more than one element of the above.		
	Online video and photo sharing such as youtube.com, video.google.co.uk and flickr.com.		
	Social Networking such as myspace, friendster, facebook and Ning.		
	Immersive virtual world such as secondlife.com		
	Proprietary software packages and simulations for different disciplines such as programming simulator, Matlab and etc.		
	Other general tools such as Power Point, flashcard, Camstudio and etc.		

concept of blended learning is not restricted to consideration of a specific technology, as it is meant to enable the appropriate use of current technologies in higher education. The focus in blended learning by extreme romantics is always "how to blend" rather than the learning itself. The issue of "how to blend" would normally lead to a variety of educational technologies – how to blend various technologies and face-to-face instruction in order to enhance learning? Many researchers and practitioners introduce a pool of technologies for blended learning through the discussion of case studies (Harrison, 2006; Shank, 2007; Allan, 2007; Littlejohn and Pegler, 2007; Sharpe, 2008). The classification of the technology in the "blend" is, however, varied. Most often, authors categorise the technology into asynchronous or synchronous; formal or informal; online or offline. Based on their work, we consolidate and summarise the current face-to-face settings and technology used in blended learning as shown in Table 2.

A VLE consists of online learning materials, announcements, emails, discussion boards, chat rooms and so on, are becoming ubiquitous in higher educational institutions. In an extensive survey of environments to support UK higher education, JISC (2005) reports that Blackboard is the VLE that is most widely used across the 63 surveyed universities, followed by VLEs developed in-house, WebCT, Moodle, FirstClass and Bodington. Online assessment is currently widespread in the UK. It is claimed that it offers the "potential of productivity gains in terms of more efficient authoring, publication, delivery, marking and reporting" and "effective reduction in paperwork" (Warburton, 2006, p.425). Various Computer-Assisted Assessment (CAA) applications on the market are designed to complement the assessment process. One of them, Question*mark* Perception assessment management system, claimed to be at the forefront of e-assessment technology (Shepherd, 2007). It enables educators to create questions and organise them into exams, quizzes, tests or surveys. In addition to large-scale CAA systems, e-assessment developed by individual institutions is also flourishing (Chew and Jones, 2006; Perez-Marin et al., 2007; Amelung et al., 2007; Mackenzie and Stanwell, 2007;

Schmid et al., 2007). All of these systems aim to facilitate the assessment process using innovative technology. There is some software that allows educators to create learning materials in a cost-effective, simple, attractive and professional way. Examples of this might be Power Point, Flashcard and Camstudio. These materials can be repurposed and reused to avoid spending valuable time when delivering the same content over and over again. Technology, such as programming simulators, can provide learners with a clearer understanding of the abstract reasoning and concepts involved.

Allan (2007) examined some of the aspects of technology set out in Table 2, and discussed some of their strengths and weaknesses. Garrison and Vaughan (2008: 153) assert that blended learning is not only about technology. They argue that looking at the technology should inspire teachers to completely change their whole approach to designing the curriculum in ways that are positive for the learner. The literature includes any number of rhetorical claims that new technology will inspire a renewed confidence and an "I can do it" attitude, but relatively little empirical evidence that this actually happens (e.g. Parker, 2007).

We are not arguing against the research into "how to blend", or discussion of which technologies to use. However, we incline to the view that this is trivial if educators do not know what they wish to teach and have a clear understanding of what promotes learning – or even worse if the educators divide learning content and pedagogical knowledge. From our experience, many extreme blended learning romantics and extreme pedagogy classicists comprehend learning content (what is to be learn) and pedagogy (how to learn or how to deliver the learning content) into two independent elements. They are perceived as separate aspects in blended learning practice and this result in the misunderstanding of education being made of two parts.

Available Blended Learning Activities and Design

Education is a structured learning experience designed to achieve intended outcomes effectively and expeditiously. The role of the educational leader is to provide the teaching presence that will structure, support and shape a meaningful and worthwhile learning experience. Hence, considerable thought and care must be devoted to the design, facilitation and direction of the learning experience. (Garrison and Vaughan, 2008, pp.32)

Many prominent writers on blended learning arrive at a consensus on at least one matter - the design issues for blended learning are challenging. Littlejohn and Pegler (2007) argue that, "One of the biggest challenges for educators is to design blended learning activities that motivate students and capture their imagination" (pp.5). Garrison and Vaughan (2008) also caution blended learning practitioners: "Designing a blended learning experience is a daunting challenge" (p.33). There are many face-to-face and learning activities mediated by technology listed in Table 2. At this point, two concerns in the design issues of blended learning we would pose are: (1) Which technologies and learning activities listed in Table 2 should be used for a particular lesson, a particular module or a particular discipline? (2) How does this blend work in maximising the effective learning? Such concerns involve technological and pedagogical concerns in learning and teaching.

Koehler et al. (2007) introduced a theoretical model to blend the technological, pedagogical and content knowledge (TPCK) in order to obtain the "sweet spot" (Figure 2).

According to Koehler et al. (2007), *Content (C)*, is the subject matter that is to be learned/taught. The content to be covered in social studies or journalism is very different from the content to be covered in a graduate course on computer science or nano-technology; *Technology (T)*, broadly

Figure 2. TPCK model for blended learning (Koehler et al., 2007, p.742)

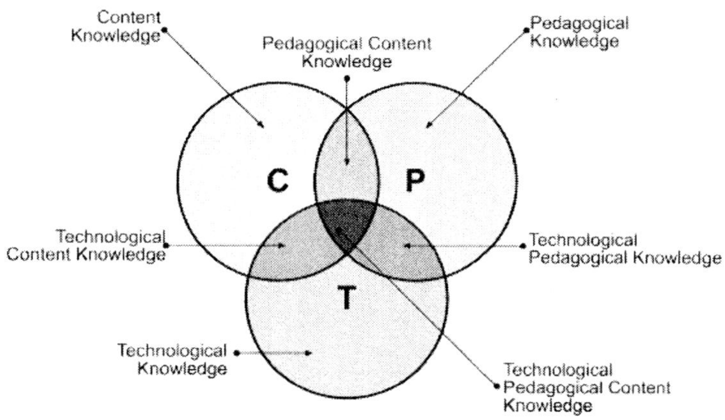

encompasses standard information communication technologies such as the VLE; *Pedagogy (P)*, includes the process and practice or methods of teaching and learning, including the purposes, values, techniques or methods used to teach, and strategies for evaluating student learning. This approach emphasises the connections and interactions *between* these three elements. For example, a consideration of *P* and *C* together results in *Pedagogical Content Knowledge*, which means the knowledge of pedagogy applied in content delivery. This would include representation and formulation of concepts, pedagogical techniques and knowledge of what makes concepts easier to learn. Similarly, *T* and *C* together produce *Technological Content Knowledge*. This kind of knowledge involves understanding the manner in which technology and content are reciprocally related to each other. Technology often affords newer and more varied representations and greater flexibility in navigating across these representations. Teachers need to know not just the subject matter they teach but also the manner in which the subject matter is transformed by the application of technology. A consideration of the overlap between *T* and *P* results in *Technological Pedagogical Knowledge.* This knowledge emphasises the existence, components and capabilities of various technologies as they are used in teaching and learning settings. This might include an understanding that a range of tools exist for a particular task as well as knowing what pedagogical strategies to employ to get the most out of a piece of technology. Finally, a consideration of all three elements *T, P,* and *C*, results in *Technological Pedagogical Content Knowledge (TPCK).* Koehler et al. (2007) argue that technology integration in teaching and learning requires understanding of the dynamic, transactional relationship between these three knowledge components. In this respect, good teaching with technology for a given content matter is complex and multi-dimensional". It requires understanding of the representation and formulation of concepts using technologies; pedagogical techniques that utilise technologies in constructive ways to teach content; knowledge of what makes concepts difficult or easy to learn and how technology can help address these issues" (Koehler et al., 2007, p.743).

While the model presented by Koehler et al. is helpful in that it stresses the interconnectedness of different aspects of the pedagogical process, it is unhelpful in that it suggests that the different spheres are simply additive. It is not the case that somebody who knows about the content of their subject and can work confidently with ICT will necessarily have any idea at all about how to use ICT in their specialist subject. Paradoxically, such a model reinforces the notion that the different spheres of understanding can be successfully disconnected and recombined.

Littlejohn and Pegler (2007) address the question of blended learning in greater detail. They offer practical advice to enable educational professionals to design a blended learning lesson within a framework called "LD_lite". This framework allows educators to plan and design blended learning activities, and document these activities for reuse and re-implementation by others. Littlejohn and Pegler suggest that there are four types of blends: (1) the *space* blend: face-to-face or technology mediated communication; (2) the *time* blend: geographically and availability; synchronously or asynchronously); (3) the *media* blend: tools, technologies and resources; and (4) the *activity* blend: learning and teaching activities, individual or group. They suggest that certain blends will result in different outcomes and that changing the elements will have different implications for educators and learners. The key elements of the LD_lite are: (1) the activities or tasks that students complete to attain one or more learning objective(s) or outcome(s). During these activities, students receive feedback from a variety of sources (peers or tutors); (2) People, including students and tutors, who are assigned roles within these activities, and (3) Resources including content materials and software support required to carry out the activities (p.83). The below figure illustrates a lesson plan in LD_lite that relates the four types of blends.

LD_lite represents a simple "start-up kit" for educators who wish to practise blended learning and also encourages them to revisit and redesign their curriculum frequently. The role of educators and students are clearly indicated. In this framework, there is no distinction of "what to learn" and "how to learn" but learning and teaching are seen as a whole. Littlejohn and Pegler (2007) also suggest an extensive design agenda and the ethical debates in blended learning development. This will stimulate blended e-learning practitioners to ponder and to incorporate re-usable and re-purposed object with ethical consideration in a coherent way. While this is clearly an approach from the technical perspective, and is a poor substitute for incorporating pedagogical theory, it may stimulate some blended learning romantics to address a broader range of concepts than they otherwise would (Figures 3 and 4). However, Littlejohn and Pegler provide little evidence that the blended learning experience will be improved by developing the complexity of blend using LD_lite, and such evidence would have been helpful (Chew, 2008a).

Figure 3. Blended learning lesson plan (Littlejohn and Pegler, 2007, pp.86)

Time	Mode	Tutor roles	Student roles	Resources (content)	Resources (courseware)	Feedback and assessment
Day 1	Online	Divide students into groups; introduce students to task and article	Review task and download article	Online article – link to university library (.pdf file)	Electronic learning environment	
Day 2	Face to face	Moderate discussion; offer feedback and encouragement to students	Group discussion face to face; one group member summarizes discussion online		Online conferencing discussion board	Feedback from peers within the group
Days 3–6	Online	Comment on summaries; post feedback to discussion board	Submit summary to discussion board. Group should comment on summaries of two other groups	Summaries generated by each group (.doc): feedback comments from tutor can be reused across student groups	Online conferencing discussion board	Group summaries are formatively assessed. Feedback from peers and tutor

THE COMPLEX: LEARNING AND EDUCATIONAL TECHNOLOGY IN HIGHER EDUCATION

...there has been little theorisation of the roles played by technology, despite widespread recognition of its importance and effectiveness. This omission has hampered a critique of the implications of technology within the university, and produced a plethora of crude ideas about its potential. (Pelletier, 2005, pp.11)

There are many educational technologies available in higher education and we have discussed the simple perception of blended learning romantics in relation to blending those educational technologies. However, as shown in the above quote, Pelletier (2005) argues that educational theory has been overlooked. Not surprisingly, professionals who are immersed in the practice of educational technology today might have a difficult time seeing the connection between the study of educational theories and practice of educational technology. Blended learning, however, involves the combination of two fields of concern; educational technology and educational theory (what to learn and how to learn). There is a general consensus that pedagogical considerations should be given priority over technical issues. However, technicians and educationists may have different vocabularies, and even where they appear to use the same terms, the context that each gives to the term means that there is ample room for misunderstandings. For example, computer specialists and educationists use the term 'effectiveness' or 'learning' to mean entirely different and mutually exclusive areas of concern. Such misunderstandings may extend to areas of 'learning theories', where computer specialists may be more instrumental, or tactical, than educationists. Consequently, terms such as 'efficiency' or 'effectiveness' in the educational context, which may seem perfectly natural to the computer specialist or e-learner practitioners, may seem problematic or inappropriate to the educationist.

The result of this is that blended learning suffers from difficulties of definition, and its theoretical foundation is correspondingly weak. For this reason we will develop here a philosophical discussion that scrutinises the foundations of blended learning.

Figure 4. Blended learning design sequence map documenting (same scenario above)

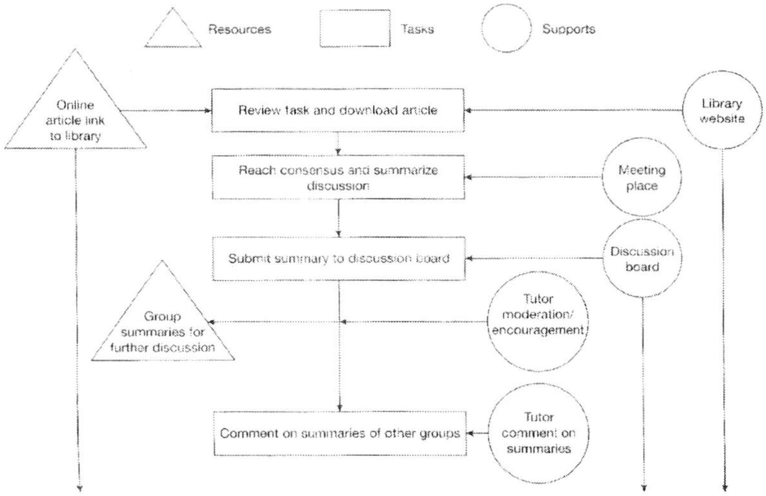

The Divergence of "Technology in Education" or "Education in Technology"

The debates date back to 1980s, when Richard Clark (1983) criticised the research on learning with media. Blended learning romantics have assumed that the use of any medium such as computers and television for instruction has no direct influence on students' learning. He argued that the role of the media is nothing more than a vehicle that delivers instruction. In an instructive metaphor, he argued, "Will the truck that delivers our groceries cause changes in our nutrition?" (pp. 445). Clark suggested that only the content of the instruction will influence students' achievement, not the vehicle, "the truck". In order to maintain this position, Clark has to ignore the entire area of media studies, from McLuhan (1964) onwards, including, in the sphere of education, authors such as Postman (1992). Even so, blended learning romantics have persisted in this myopic view that the technology is merely the vehicle, and has no effect on learning (Kulik, 1985; Russel, 1999; Perraton, 2000). One researcher, Arbaugh (2004) coincides with Clark and others. He conducted a research which showed that the educational technology packages, such as WebCT and Blackboard, have little effect and impact to the students' learning (Arbaugh and Stelze, 2003). While we agree with Clark and Arbaugh that the most important element in education is the content and context of learning, we do not think that technology can be bracketed off as separate to the degree they imply. Along with technology, other educational factors, such as socio-cultural conditions, support from peers, educators' communication skills and educational passion, curriculum resources and an emphasis on the learner as an active and constructive learner (Santrock, 2004) are essential elements to improve the learners' ability to learn.

Brabazon (2002) puts the question of emphasis in the educational design process very concisely. She stated:

> ***Money is being thrown at technology in education, not education in technology...*** *(pp.145).*

By this she means that where technology and education meet in educational design, priority is give to technology. This is normally conceived as a transmission model, with the technology being used to 'deliver' content. Thus "technology in education" has three general functions: (1) to present learning materials, (2) to permit an interaction between learner and text, and (3) to facilitate communication between learners and teachers – for operational purposes (Brabazon, pp.105). Brabazon draws a distinction between technology for education and for operational purposes. Different educational strategies are required to enable each of the above functions. The selection of technology must be related to the aims of teaching and learning and pedagogy, not the limits of the technology – for education purposes. When the emphasis is placed on meeting the educational purposes, the result is, Brabazon argues, "education in technology".

A philosopher of technology, Mitcham (1994), argues that there are differences in approach which have their roots in the epistemological bases of different disciplines. He suggests that the philosophy of technology consists of two discourses – the engineering philosophy of technology (EPT) and the humanities philosophy of technology (HPT). This classification maps quite readily onto Garrison's and Vaughan's notion that "different discipline provides different mindsets to engage with the same thing". From this idea, we expand the notion of Technology in Education and Education Technology as shown in Table 3.

Most often, the focal point of social scientists is in "education in technology" whereas technologists or scientists have spent more effort in "technology in education". At this point, we notice that Brabazon's warning raises a critical question related to blended learning: is research into blended learning today focused on "technology in education" or "education in technology"? We

Table 3. Technology in education versus education in technology

	"Technology in Education"	"Education in Technology"
Priority	Technology is the main focus in blended learning.	Education is always the highest priority in blended learning.
Design consideration	Which technology and how to blend are the main considerations.	Learning and teaching, pedagogy and educational theory are the main considerations.
Philosophy *Being with Technology* *Mitcham (1994, pp.62-63)*	EPT - engineering philosophy of technology	HPT - humanities philosophy of technology
	Begins with the justification of technology or an analysis of the nature of technology itself – its concepts, its methods, its cognitive structures and objectives manifestations.	Seeks by contrast insights into the meaning of technology – its relation to the trans-technical: art and literature, humanities and socio-cultural issues – begins with non-technical aspect of the human world (in this case education) and considers how technology may (or may not) fit in or correspond.
Consequences	Recognises blended learning as a "blanket solution", ONE solution for all disciplines; stereotypical mindsets related to blended learning and causes extreme pedagogy classicists consistently to reject blended learning. E.g. Kim (2007)'s 8 combinations and 14 learning types for blended learning and Koehler et al. (2007)'s TPCK model.	Recognise disciplinary differences; learning and teaching mediated with/without technology; integrates what to learn and how to learn; greater possibility of being accepted by both mild blended learning romantics and mild pedagogy classicists. E.g. perceptions from Brabazon (2007) and Littlejohn and Pegler (2007)
	Educational technology is design and used and "decorated" by pedagogical theory. Educators and students may find blended learning "excellent" or "terrible" depending on disciplinary needs and technological competence.	The thoughtful revisiting and redesign of learning and teaching **may or may not** lead to the uses of certain educational technology. Blended learning occurs with passion and impressive experience if it is the former.

would certainly assert that the latter should be the case, and blended learning researchers should be increasingly mindful of this issue.

Consider the above claim in Clark's and Arbaugh's terminology: one may prioritise the truck rather than the groceries, or emphasise the educational technology packages, such as WebCT and Blackboard, over the learning content! We would agree with Clark (1983) and Arbaugh (2004) that technology by itself does not necessarily improve the teaching and learning experience, especially where blended learning is "technology in education" or the mere "vehicle". We would argue, however, what we learn and how we learn in the process of learning and teaching, should reshape all of the other knowledge that we hold. This is a completely different idea of from merely the "truck and the groceries"!

Nevertheless, some researchers support the idea that educational technology will help to improve the ability to learn with evidence (Alavi, 1994; Kozma, 1994; Salmon, 2000; Price and Oliver, 2007). One of them, Kozma (1994) revisits Clark's argument and states that,

> *Educational technology is a design science, not a natural science. The phenomena that we study are the products of our own conceptions and devices. If there is no relationship between media and learning it may be because we have not yet made one. If we do not understand the potential relationship between media and learning, quite likely one will not be made...if we preclude consideration of a relationship in our theory and research by conceptualising media as 'mere vehicles', we are likely never to understand the potential for such a relationship. (p.7)*

We agree with Kozma's argument that, unless we understand the potential of such a relationship, most e-learning research will be devoted to technological-centred development. We do not view educational technology as a mere "deliverer" or "vehicle" as Clark (1983) describes it. It can be seen in this way only if researchers do not understand the potential relationship between educational technology and learning, and therefore focus on the "innovative", "effective" and "intelligent" design of the technology rather than on education and people. Less attention has been paid to educational theory and a pedagogical perspective or, "education in technology". In the worst case, the educational system developed by the technological scientist may not fulfil the educators or learners' real needs. O'Toole and Absalom (2003) researched the impact of blended learning on learning outcomes. They concluded that educational technology is unlikely to be effective if it is merely a replacement for traditional settings such as lectures or is seen as an alternative mode of delivery. Blended learning, however, will impact on learning outcomes only if both educational technology and face-to-face learning are "carefully blended, operating in tandem and both facing the same direction" (p.189). This raises the question of which direction they are facing.

Clark (1983) urges researchers to desist from investigating the relationship between media and learning unless a novel theory is propounded. However, based on substantial research findings from the past, Kozma (1994), argues that the theories that have been applied to blended learning have been constrained by the behavioural roots from which the disciplines sprang. For example, how engineers' and social scientist's use of the term educational technology creates confusion and constrains its development. In this way, we would link Kozma's claim to the possible cause of the debate between blended learning romantics and pedagogy classics, which is the divergent disciplinary, or even philosophical, roots. From a similar position, Simsek (2005) asserts that the literature related to the educational technology includes various definitions which draw upon different epistemological concerns.

Garrison and Vaughan (2008) also state that, "discipline provides the mindset to engage in critical discourse and reflection" (p.17). We would further expand Garrison's and Vaughan's statement to "different disciplines provide different mindsets to engage with the same thing". For example, Hunter and Carr (2000), from a technological position, said:

Universities are in the information dissemination business and computers are changing the way they work. (p.122)

Brabazon (2007), from a perspective provided by media studies, contends Hunter and Carr's statement is punchy but wrong, because academics do not only disseminate information, but are involved in the creation of knowledge through research. In the field of computer science and engineering, efficiency, effectiveness and experimental results are the main focus, whereas, in education or social sciences, the variety of social contexts and the complexity of educational purposes must be taken into consideration. Pedagogy classicists are more likely to be in sympathy with Brabazon's position. Luppicini (2005) indicates this disciplinary difference with a noteworthy insight:

Engineers, technologists and technicians are closely related in their view of technology as the process of material construction based on systematic engineering knowledge of how to design artifacts. This conception associates technology very closely with machines or physical systems of some sort.

Social Scholars typically view technology in broader terms, extending what is understood of material construction to take social significance into consideration. First, social science scholars' employment of the term "technology" refers to material construction uses as well as the intellectual and social context. It refers to the organisation of knowledge for the achievement of practical purposes as well as any tool or technique of doing or making, by which capability is extended. (p. 104)

We completely agree with Luppicini's view based on our personal experience. One of the authors was involved in computer science research from 1998 to 2005. Seven years of such applied science and systematic training had shaped her entire reasoning and she conceives of educational technology as being associated with physical and technical system design as Luppicini describes. Her skills of analysis were grounded on a purely "digital concept", the principle of right or wrong; black or white; a "zero or one" mechanism without educational reflections. The focus is merely on "the right", "the best", "the innovative", "the effective" solution as opposed to the traditional, the slow and the old, the theoretical and impractical one. Most often, the author was in agreement with certain superficial claims such as "the cornerstone of successful education is the effective use of assessments" (Shepherd, 2007, p.399) or "blended learning consists of 8 combinations and 14 learning types" (Kim, 2007). With technological advancement, she tended to get caught in technology in education instead of education in technology as Brabazon (2007) describes. The author had the engineering philosophy of technology rather than the humanities philosophy of technology as Mitcham (1994) described it. The author designed and developed curricula with Power Point, online assessment, websites, and a full array of online support materials. However from time-to-time, there was no substitute for getting into the lives of the students. It has to be recognised that education is about people not the design of educational technology. After a few years of cross-disciplinary research in the social sciences and education, her perception has increasingly extended to broader consideration in the intellectual and social context. In terms of Brabazon's and Mitcham's terminology, this author's focus has shifted from technology in education to education in technology; and from the engineering philosophy of technology to the humanities philosophy of technology.

In order to understand what "education in technology" is and how technology contributes to learning, we borrowed Kozma's (1994) assertion, that is the understanding of "their underlying structure and the causal mechanisms by which they might interact with cognitive and social processes" (pp.11) is the essential rather than the surface feature of technology. On the other hand, learning theories need to be grounded in such mundane concerns as whether educational technology is being used effectively and in the best possible way in order to interact with cognitive and social processes. Based on McGinn's (1978) work, Luppicini (2005) relates technology with the broader concerns of the social processes and context. Luppicini concludes technology is a value-laden human activity connected to socio-cultural and environmental influences in its conceptualisation, and there are five ways in which technology is value-laden:

1. The value of a technique reflects the values of those who make it and use it.
2. Technology is optimistic in assigning value to "technological progress".
3. Technology is value-laden insofar as use of resources for advance may preclude their use in other work that may improve life.
4. The institutionalisation of modern technology allows the direction of technology to be influenced externally by organisations rather than by practitioners.
5. Products of technology are expressions of individual and cultural values of designers. (pp.104)

However, the technological scientist may not be concerned with the agenda on which sociologist and educationalist focus as described by Luppicini (2005) – technology as a value-laden human activity connected to socio-cultural and environmental concerns. Koehler, et al. (2007) further contend that most research on educational technology has been criticised as being a theoretical in nature but driven more by the imperatives of the technology rather than sound theory (p.759).

Such educational technology may undermine the principles of education. Therefore, the design of "education in technology" must address all the activities essential for learning and teaching (Laurillard, 2002). Such design processes must acknowledge the nature of academic learning and seek to promote blended learning that beyond the flash and hype. On the other hand, research on e-learning environment based on pedagogical concern has gradually increased (Jonassen et al., 1999; Mehrotra et al., 2001; Simonson et al., 2006). The social scientist, however, may not consider that what and how of state-of-the-art technology contributes to education.

Overall, we would assert that, only through mutual understanding of both contrasting disciplines can initial principles for the grounding of blended learning theory be established. Educational theory provides the basis for a coherent and stringent critique of blended learning practices, and by that means provides a framework for grounding its theories.

The University of Google

The term, *The University of Google* is from Brabazon (2007). In that work Brabazon goes further than much previous research to identify how the introduction of different media is changing what is learned and how. Most often, academics and researchers in the UK emphasise reflection - "reflect on the materials you have read" or "reflect on the seminar or lecture you have attended". We opine that Brabazon's book is a true reflection on the problem caused by "technology in education". The Education Coordinator of Oxford University Library Service, Judy Reading (2008) strongly recommends this book as it critically discusses what education is, its purpose, and what academics should be doing to safeguard the quality of education, and how technology should be academics' servant not the servant of academics' masters. Brabazon (2007) claims the relationship between lecturers, students and curriculum is complex and intricate. Inserting technology into that relationship adds even greater intensity. Curriculum design is a key factor in students' learning experience. Less time and credit is being given to those academics who spend effort on their curriculum design and teaching yet policy makers keep pushing "strategies on technology in education". Rapid pressure has been exerted from management on academics.

This is why technology has become the servant of academics' masters, as described by Reading (2005). Brabazon further explains her experience as an academic in the modern university, that she feels powerless when she is responsible for events over which she has no control. We believe that an autonomous academic would rather be the one driving than the one driven – "it is my purpose and direction that counts, and I do not want to be pushed around passively by forces beyond my control". Hence, one would rather be a hammer than a nail as the nail that stands up get hammered down. This is a true reflection of the frustrations of those who are passionate about education. Although such expression may be extreme, it reveals the circumstances of "powerlessness" and helplessness that educational technology brings to academics from certain disciplines. Perhaps, this is also why pedagogy classicists consistently hold a negative view of educational technology.

We believe that Brabazon is not an extreme pedagogy classicist as her academic position is in a Faculty of Computer Science. Brabazon does not reject technology but considers a variety of social contexts and the complexity of educational purposes behind technology. She clearly states,

The computer is not the fount of educational troubles. Google is not the facilitator for neo-liberalism. The goal of this book is to embed computer-mediated communication and applications into other media and social structures. I look for the continuities and alliances between the analogue and the digital, past and present. (Brabazon, 2007, pp. 9)

In this sense, Mitcham (1994) expresses an interesting opinion: *"Technology is necessary but dangerous."* (pp.276)

Technology is a developmental trend and is necessary according to Mitcham. Brabazon would seem to agree with this view, as when she stresses "education in technology" is necessary but "technology in education" is dangerous because education always comes before technology, rather than the other way about. Learning and teaching is always the central focus, not technology. Her view is a reflection upon response Jaspers' (1960) perception - higher education should not leave behind social trends and technology - and Pelletier's (2005) view of the identity crisis of higher education. Brabazon cautions that flexible learning (simplified and reduced to internet-mediated education) must be introduced carefully and critically. Otherwise, it easily falls into the "culture of fast food". In a fast food, fast data environment, the web transforms into an information drive-through. It encourages a "type in-download-cut-paste-submit" educational culture (Brabazon, 2007, p. 22). Brabazon elaborates on this with an example e-mail from a student (Figure 5).

In response to the above email, Brabazon (2007) critically reflects upon the incident, and a tone of anger enters her reflection:

I was wondering in the first two lectures why some students were sitting in the lecture theatre with no paper, pen or bag and staring at me... the notion she expected notes would be available online means that technology has become a crutch and a replacement for learning... The 'reading' they determine to be sufficient is off PowerPoint slides, derived from a lecture... Such assumptions are corrosive of effective learning and reading. (pp.107-108)

This is a picture that we recognize from our own experiences of lecture theatres, where many students merely sit in the lecture with no paper and pen but expecting the PowerPoint slides from the lecturers. Brabazon further contends this kind of attitude results from the idea of flexible learning:

Consider this definition from Macquarie University: "flexible learning aims to meet individual needs by providing choices that allow students to meet their own educational requirements in ways suiting their individual circumstances." Such an ideology is more relevant to shoe shopping than education.... the language choice is crucial here. The emphasis is on individuals and choice, not communities and context. The roles and function of groups and collectives – sharing a time and place – discussing the issues of the day is no longer a priority. Students become consumers, selecting generic competencies for their shopping trolley, dodging around the issues and ideas that might require more than a passing glance. Yet this truth is masked as flexibility, becomes confused with access. Brabazon (2007, pp. 80)

Figure 5. Email from a student (Brabazon, 2007, pp. 107)

From: Yuanetta
Sent: Thursday, 4 August 2005 6:04PM
To: Tara Brabazon
Subject: Te: lecture notes

Hi Tara, just wanted to know if you post any notes online from the lectures? I assume you would so I made no attempt to write anything down from the previous lectures, so I'm having a bit of panic, now that I can't find anything on the web.

If you don't, could I access to the overheads you used so that I could make some notes, please? I'll come to your office at a time that's convenient for you.

Thank you.

Yuanetta

Due to the globalisation and increasing market demand, university has become a business organisation "shopped" by students. Convenience, flexibility and accessibility are the key considerations rather than, as Flexner (1930) described it, an "autonomy organism". Neumeier (2005) states that blended learning is as easy as a child shopping in a toy shop but correspondingly difficult because academics are confronted by a vast variety of "toys" (technologies) and complex task that they are not familiar. If one was "lost in the shopping mall", not familiar with the technology, or completely disagreed with education as in shopping mall, a feeling of powerlessness, helplessness and frustration may possibly aroused, as described by Brabazon.

If we think of this in Mitcham's (1994) terms, of a separation of the philosophy of technology into two discourses – the engineering philosophy of technology and the humanities philosophy of technology – the technologist may see blended learning as flexible and convenient learning mediated by technology while the humanist may believe there is more to education than convenience and flexibility. There are consequences of making education convenient and flexible, both good and bad. To take a phrase from Brabazon (2007), "In teaching you will come to grief as soon as you forget that your students have bodies" (pp.109). This may be a provocative claim but we would argue that it reveals the possible ignorance of blended learning romantics and technologist.

Brabazon acknowledged educational technology but stressed the humanistic and social considerations that lay behind the technology. Mitcham (1994) affirms that technology is so broad that only a humanities philosophy of technology (rather than the engineering philosophy of technology) can meaningfully engage it. Long time ago, AECT (1972) already illustrated this perception:

I firmly believe that the future of educational technology is now in the hands of thinkers. *What is needed is a handful of experienced people who have thought widely and deeply, and who are literally obsessed by the problems posed.* (pp.103)

From a philosophical perspective, Mitcham (1994) suggests three ways of using technology in a philosophical manner (see Table 4).

The basic attitudes that Mitcham listed are closely linked with discipline and philosophical stance adopted, and the epistemology and ontology that underpin them.

CONCLUSION

The future of educational technology is in the hands of thinkers not in the hands of technicians, of educational philosophers not computer technologists. Does it enhance the learning experience? If the answer is yes, then how does this happen (and on the basis of what evidence)? This tallies with Kozma's (1994) perception that, "If there is no relationship between media and learning it may be because we have not yet made one" (p.7). A thinker would propose an appropriate link after careful and profound thought, evidence-based investigation and careful consideration of the many problems posed. As a conclusion, ontological and epistemological differences will cause conflict and debates between blended learning romantics and pedagogy classicists. We have argued here that educational technology is necessary but at the same time dangerous if (1) there is no mutual understanding of the multi faceted nature of the curriculum development process, and (2) there is no relationship between learning theory and technology or an absence of the wider social considerations underpinning learning theory.

We suggest that blended learning must be grounded in educational theory with understanding of both disciplinary needs and diversity. Educationists and technologists, blended learning romantics and pedagogy classicists, lecturers and developers or instructional designers must use pedagogical theory to inform their passion for

Table 4. Three ways of being-with technology (Mitcham, 1994)

	Basic Attitudes		
Conceptual Elements	**Suspicious of Technology**	**Ambivalent about Technology**	**Promotion of Technology**
Activity (ethics)	*Personal*: Technical affluence undermines individual virtue *Societal*: Technical change weakens political stability	Personal: Technology engenders freedom but alienates from affective strength to exercise it *Societal*: Technology weakens social bonds of affection	*Personal*: Technical activities socialize individuals *Societal*: Technology creates public wealth
Knowledge (epistemology)	Technical information is not true wisdom	Imagination and vision are more crucial than technical knowledge	Technical engagement with the world yields true knowledge (pragmatism)
Objects (metaphysics)	Artifacts are less real than natural objects and thus require external guidance	Artifacts expand the process of life and reveal the sublime	Nature and artifice operate by the same mechanical principles

education (and not merely for a market or for business). Pedagogical theory must be linked with the thoughtful integration of blended learning – the decision as to whether to use educational technology or not, and if so how – grounded in "education in technology".

REFERENCES

AECT. (1972). The field of Educational technology: A Statement of Definition. *Audiovisual Instruction*, *17*, 36–43.

Alavi, M. (1994). Computer-mediated Collborative Learning: an Empirical Evaluation, Computer-mediated discussion. *Journal of Educational Computing Research*, *8*, 291–309.

Allan, B. (2007). *Blended learning Tools for Teaching and Training*. London: Facet Publishing.

Amelung, M., Piotrowski, M., & Rosner, D. (2007). Large Scale Computer-Assisted Assessment in Computer Science Education: New Possibilities, New Questions. In J. Fong & F. L. Wang (Eds.), *Blended learning* (pp. 257-266). Singapore: Pearson Prentice Hall.

Arbaugh, J. B. (2004). Learning to Learn Online: A Study of Perceptual Changes between multiple Online Course Experiences. *The Internet and Higher Education*, *7*, 169–182. doi:10.1016/j.iheduc.2004.06.001

Arbaugh, J. B., & Stelzer, L. (2003). Learning And Teaching Management On The Web What Do We Know? In *Educating Managers with tomorrow's Technologies* (pp. 17-51).

Bielawski, L., & Metcalf, D. (2003). *Blended eLearning: Integrating Knowledge, Performance, Support and Online Learning*. MA: HRD Press Inc.

Blacker, D. (1995). Philosophy of Technology and Education: an Invitation to Inquiry. In . *Proceedings of the Philosophy of Education, 1994*, 320–328.

Brabazon, T. (2002). *Digital Hemlock*. Sydney: UNSW Press.

Brabazon, T. (2007). *The University of Goolge: Education in the (post) Information Age*. Hampshire, UK: Ashgate Publishing.

Chew, E. (2008a). Book Review for Allison Littlejohn and Chris Pegler Preparing for Blended e-Learning: Understanding Blended and Online Learning. *Journal of World Education*.

Chew, E. (2008b). Book Review for Barbara Allan: Blended learning Tools for Teaching and Training. *Journal of Educational Technology & Society, 11*(2), 344–347.

Chew, E., & Jones, N. (2006). Generic Model of Computation for Intelligent Computer Aided Progress Assessment (iCAP). In *Proceeding of the 10th International Computer Assisted Assessment (CAA) Conference: Research into E-Assessment*, Loughborough University (pp. 107-121).

Chew, E., Jones, N., & Blackey, H. (2006). Embedding Blended learning Across a Higher education Institution. In *Proceedings of the First Annual Blended learning Conference: Blended learning – Promoting Dialogue in Innovation and Practice* (pp. 64-73). Hatfield, UK: University of Hertfordshire Press.

Clark, R., E. (1983). Reconsidering Research on Learning from Media. *Review of Educational Research, 52*(4), 445–459.

Flexner, A. (1930). *Universities: American, English, German*. New York: Oxford University Press.

Garrison, D., & Vaughan, N. D. (2008). *Blended learning in Higher education: Framework, Principles and Guidelines*. San Francisco: Jossey-Bass.

Graham, C. R. (2006). Chapter 1: Blended learning systems: Definition, current trends, future directions. In C. J. Bonk & C. R. Graham (Eds.), *Handbook of Blended learning: Global Perspectives, Local designs*. San Francisco, CA: Pfeiffer Publishing.

Graham, C. R., Allen, S., & Ure, D. (2003). *Blended learning environments: A review of the research literature*. Unpublished manuscript, Provo, UT.

Harrison, M. (2006). *Blended learning II: Blended learning in Practice*. Brighton: An Epic White Paper. Retrieved January 14, 2007, from http://www.epic.co.uk

Hunter, M. G., & Carr, P. (2000). Technology in Distance Education: a Global Perspective to Alternative Delivery Mechanisms. *Journal of Global Information Management*, (April-June): 50.

Jaspers, K. (1960). *The Idea of the University*. London: Peter Owen.

JISC. (2005). *Study of Environments To Support E-Learning In UK Further and Higher education: A Supporting Study for the Joint Information Systems Committee (JISC), Education for Change Ltd, The Research Partnership Social Informatics Unit, University of Brighton*. Retrieved January 10, 2008, from http://www.jisc.ac.uk/media/documents/programmes/buildmlehefe/elearning_survey_2005.pdf

Jonassen, D. H., Peck, K. L., & Wilson, B. G. (1999). *Learning with technology: A Constructivist Perspective*. Upper Saddle River, NJ: Merrill, Prentice Hall.

Kim, W. (2006). Towards a Definition and Methodology for Blended learning. In J. Fong & F. L. Wang (Eds.), *Blended learning* (pp. 1-8). Singapore: Pearson Prentice Hall.

Koehler, M. J., Mishra, P., & Yahya, K. (2007). Tracing the Development of Teacher Knowledge in a Design Seminar: Integrating Content, Pedagogy and Technology. *Computers & Education, 49*(3), 740–762. doi:10.1016/j.compedu.2005.11.012

Kozma, R. (1994). Will Media Influence Learning? Reframing the Debate. *Educational Technology Research and Development, 42*(2), 7–19. doi:10.1007/BF02299087

Kulik, J. A. (1985). The Importance of Outcome Studies: a reply to Clark. *Educational Communications and Technology Journal, 42*(6), 437–448.

Laurillard, D. (2002). *Rethinking University Teaching: A Conversational Framework for the Effective Use of Learning Technologies* (2nd ed.). London: Routledge.

Littlejohn, A., & Pegler, C. (2007). *Preparing for Blended e-Learning: Understanding Blended and Online Learning (Connecting with E-learning)*. London: Routledge.

Luppicini, R. (2005). A Systems Definition of Educational technology in Society. *Educational technology & Society, 8*(3), 103-109.

Mackenzie, D., & Stanwell, M. (2007). Quick-Trl A Visual System for the Rapid Creation of e-Assessments and e-Learning Materials. In *Proceeding of the11th International Computer Assisted Assessment (CAA) Conference: Research into E-Assessment* (pp. 301-302). Loughborough University.

McGinn, R. (1978). What is Technology? *Research in Philosophy and Technology, 1*, 179–197.

Mcluhan, M. (1964). *Understanding Media: The Extensions of Man*. London: Routledge & Kegan.

Mehrotra, C. M., Hollister, C. D., & McGahey, L. (2001). *Distance Learning: Principles for effective design, delivery and evaluation*. Thousand Oaks, CA: Sage.

Mitcham, C. (1994). *Thinking Through Technology*. Chicago: The University of Chicago Press.

Morrison, D. (2003). *The Search for the Holy Recipe. Library Blended learning, e-learning Centre*. Retrieved June 15, 2006, from http://www.e-learningcentre.co.uk/eclipse/Resources/blended.htm

Neumeier, P. (2005). A Closer Look at Blended learning – Parameters for Designing a blended learning Environment for Language Teaching and Learning. *ReCALL, 17*(2), 163–178. doi:10.1017/S0958344005000224

O'Toole, J. M., & Absalom, D. J. (2003). The Impact of Blended learning on Student Outcomes: is there Room on the House for two? *Journal of Educational Media, 28*(2-3), 179–190. doi:10.1080/1358165032000165680

Oliver, M., & Trigwell, K. (2005). Can 'Blended learning' Be Redeemed? *E-Learning, 2*(1), 17–26.

Parker, J. A. (2007). Book review: Blogs, Wikis, podcasts, and other powerful tools for the classrooms. *The Internet and Higher Education, 10*(4), 289–291.

Pelletier, C. (2005). *New Technologies, New Identities: The University in the Information Age*. London: RoutledgeFalmer.

Perez-Marin, D., Pascual-Nieto, I., & Alfonseca, E. (2007). A Study on the Impact of the Use of an Automatic and Adaptive Free-text Assessment System during a University Course. In J. Fong & F. L. Wang (Eds.), *Blended learning* (pp. 186-195). Singapore: Pearson Prentice Hall.

Perraton, H. (2000). Choosing Technologies for Education. *Journal of Educational Media, 25*(1), 31–38. doi:10.1080/13581650050001221

Postman, N. (1992). *Technopoly: The Surrender of Culture to Technology*. New York: Knop.

Price, S., & OLIVER, M. (2007). A Framework for Conceptualising the Impacts of Technologies on Teaching and Learning. *Educational technology and Society, 10*(10), 16-27.

Reading, J. (2008). Book Review: The University of Google: Education in the (Post) Information Age. *Ariadne, 54*. Retrieved March 3, 2008, from http://www.ariadne.ac.uk/issue54/reading-rvw/

Russel, T. (1999). The No Significant Different Phenomenon. *Office of Instructional Telecommunication pg the CAM, 36*(5), 37-41.

Salmon, G. (2000). *E-Moderating: The Key to Teaching and Learning Online.* London: Kogan Page.

Salmon, G. (2002). *E-tivities: The Key to Active Online Learning.* London: Kogan Page.

Santrock, J. W. (2004). *Educational Psychology.* New York: McGraw-Hill Higher education.

Schmid, F., Mitchell, T., Whitehouse, J., & Broomhead, P. (2007). Exam online: e-Enabling "Traditional" HE/FE Examinations. In *Proceeding for 11th International Computer Assisted Assessment (CAA) Conference: Research into E-Assessment* (pp. 381-396). Loughborough University.

Shank, R. (Ed.). (2007). *The Online Learning Idea Book: 95 Proven Ways to Enhance Technology-based and Blended learning.* San Francisco, CA: Pfeiffer, John Wiley & Sons.

Sharpe, R., Benfield, G., Roberts, G., & Francis, R. (2006). *The Undergraduate Experience of Blended e-learning: a Review of UK Literature and Practice.* UK: The Higher education Academy.

Shepherd, E. (2007). Blended Delivery Meets e-Assessment. In *Proceeding for 11th International Computer Assisted Assessment (CAA) Conference: Research into E-Assessment* (pp. 399). Loughborough University.

Simonson, M., Smaldino, S., Albright, M., & Zvacek, S. (2006). *Teaching and Learning at a distance: Foundations of distance education* (3rd ed.). Upper Saddle River, NJ: Merrill Prentice Hall.

Simsek, N. (2005). Perceptions and Opinions of Educational Technologies Related to Educational Technology. *Educational Technology and Society, 8*(4), 178–190.

Thorne, K. (2003). *Blended learning: How to Integrate Online & Traditional Learning.* London: Kogan Page.

Tuerner, A. D. (2007). *Theory and Practice of Education.* London: Continuum International Publishing Group.

Vignare, K. (2007). Review of Literature Blended learning: Using ALN to Change the Classroom – Will It Work? In A. G. Picciano & C. D. Dziuban (Eds.), *Blended learning: Research Perspectives.* MA: The Sloan Consortium.

Warburton, B. (2006). Quick Win or Slow Burn? Modelling UK HE CAA Update. In *Proceeding for 10th International Computer Assisted Assessment (CAA) Conference: Research into E-Assessment.* (pp. 425-439). Loughborough University.

KEY TERMS AND DEFINITIONS

Blended Learning Romantics: Blacker (1995) labelled those who hold that technology will primitively break down traditional barriers to effective and successful educational reform as "computer romantics". In the context of this research, we borrow Blacker's terminology to label a group of academics and researchers in higher education as "blended learning romantics" - represents pro-technology academics who naively consider technology as will breakthrough traditional classroom or necessarily trend to the modern learning and teaching.

Blended Learning: The combination of face-to-face learning and teaching mediated by technology. The thoughtful integration of face-to-face classroom and web-based learning opportunity by fundamental redesign and an optimal (re)design approach by rethinking and restructuring teaching and learning.

Education in Technology: Education is always the highest priority in blended learning. Learning and teaching, pedagogy and educational theory are the main considerations but winged by educational technology. Seeks by contrast insights into the meaning of technology – its relation to the trans-technical: art and literature, humanities and socio-cultural issues – being with non-technical aspect of the human world (in this case is education) and considers how technology may (or may not) fit in or correspond. The thoughtful revisiting and redesign of learning and teaching **may or may not** lead to the uses of certain educational technology based on disciplinary needs.

Higher Education: Universities or tertiary education.

Pedagogy Classicists: The opposition to the "blended learning romantics" who disagree with anything that involves technology. Technology is sometimes regarded as no more than a tool, a mere vehicle or information carrier (Luppicini, 2005). Pedagogy classicists, however, stress the negative aspects of that tool. They concentrate on the constraints imposed by the technology and believe in pedagogy and learning theory rather than the "tool" or "vehicle". In the worst cases, they may not regard blended learning as a scholarly, educational or social science research activity at all.

Technology in Education: Technology is indirectly the main focus in blended learning and which technology and how to blend (for operational purposes) are the main considerations. The philosophy behind is being with the justification of technology or an analysis of the nature of technology itself – its concepts, its methods, its cognitive structures and objectives manifestations. Educational technology is design and used and "decorated" by pedagogical theory. Educators and students may find blended learning "excellent" or "terrible" depending on disciplinary needs and technological competence.

The University of Google: A term invented by Brabazon (2007) referring to the education in the (Post) Information Age. The impact of Google on education, teaching and learning is similarly to instant food and fast data environment, a mere mouse-click away. Students in the University of Google lose the capacity to sift, discard and judge.

Chapter 2
Hybridizing Online Learning with External Interactivity

Donna Morrow
University of Canterbury, New Zealand

Richard G. Bagnall
Hong Kong Institute of Education, Hong Kong

ABSTRACT

One approach to hybrid learning is to hybridize online learning through recognizing and including external interactivity. This chapter examines that possibility. After reviewing the nature of interactivity and individual learner experience in online learning communities, it presents a recent study of interactivity in online professional development learning by practising teachers. From that study emerges the importance and scope of external interactivity between the learner and his or her local community of colleagues, friends, and family in a learning community beyond the traditional online class. Building on that case study, and indications from the literature that its implications may be generalizable, the chapter suggests ways in which external interactivity can be recognized and included in the online learning environment – as a way of hybridizing on-line learning through its inclusion of learners' interactive engagements in the external learning communities that they bring to their studies.

INTRODUCTION

Interactivity in education and learning is a topic that is attracting renewed attention in education, especially with the increasing importance of online learning (Garrison & Cleveland-Innes, 2005; Giguere, Formica, & Harding, 2004; LaPointe & Gunawardena, 2004). It is seen as being important to the processing of content and the creation of new understandings (de Bruyn, 2004; Hawkes, 2006; Williams & Humphrey, 2007). What is not so clearly understood, however, are the ways in which interactivity functions for individuals and groups whose learning is increasingly taking place outside the traditional face-to-face methods, supported and managed by information and communication technologies in online learning environments. Such learners, crucially, are still located by time and place within their local communities.

DOI: 10.4018/978-1-60566-380-7.ch002

The notion of interactivity here captures those actions and impacts by and on the elements of an educational or learning event that influence the nature and outcomes of the engagement (Anderson, 2004; Garrison & Anderson, 2003; Wagner, 1997). The perspective taken in studying and managing interactivity is, correspondingly, commonly centred on the learner – focusing particularly and variously on: interactions between and among learners; those between the learner and the educator, teacher, tutor, or instructor; those between the learner and the content; and, especially in online or hybrid learning engagements, those between the learner and the educational interface (Hillman, Willis, & Gunawardena, 1994; Hirumi, 2002; Moore, 1993).

These dimensions of interactivity focus singularly on components of the educational event itself. They exclude possible influences that are located beyond the traditionally recognized boundaries of the event – influences such as the learner's family, work, and friendship communities and relationships. Such influences tend to be externalized in educational planning and management. Their potential influence on learning processes and outcomes, though, raises the question of whether and how they might usefully be recognized and engaged in educational planning and management. This question is, perhaps, particularly pertinent to educational events that are essentially online, since it is arguably in such events that learners are most likely to face limitations from traditional forms of educational interactivity, especially those involving other persons.

The question is addressed here by firstly examining the nature and role of interactivity in learning. The chapter then presents a case study which challenges traditional concepts of educational interactivity as being essentially internal to educational events. The implications of that case study for educational design and management are then articulated as an approach to the hybridization of educational engagements, before drawing out conclusions from the analysis.

BACKGROUND: THE NATURE AND ROLE OF INTERACTIVITY IN LEARNING

The role of interactivity in learning encompasses differing perspectives, due to epistemological assumptions about the role of human interaction in education and learning. Salomon and Perkins (1998) have described two conceptions of learning: first, the concept of the individual learner, which emphasizes the acquisition of knowledge and cognitive skill and, second, the socio-cultural concept of learning, which emphasizes the participatory aspects of context, interaction, and situation. In both conceptions, interaction is seen to be essential but present in different forms. As early as 1933, John Dewey described the interaction for the individual learner as internal interaction, and saw it as necessary to the process of transforming inert information into meaningful knowledge (Dewey, 1933). Holmberg (1983, p.115), speaking particularly to distance education, referred to this process as the "guided didactic conversation" that occurs as a student interacts with content. While not denying the value of individual interactivity, the more participatory, socio-cultural concept of learning encompasses and depends on a broader range of interactivity between learners, instructors, and other learners (Jonassen, 2002). This social definition of learning has been supported by Wenger (1998, 2000) who argued that the act of knowing is a matter of displaying competence defined within a social community, but always in interplay with individual experience.

Until recently, interaction between learner and content, and to a lesser degree interaction between learner and teacher, have been the mainstays of distance education (Anderson, 2004). Web-based technologies and Internet access have increased markedly in the last 10 years and distance learning, infused with information and communication technologies, has evolved into a medium of exchange that allows for faster and better communication between learners and educators, and between and among learners. This evolution has changed the way in which content is delivered and constructed (Wagner, 1997). This evolution makes possible types of interactivity that support social learning and constructivism, where learning is seen to be a socio-dialogical process (Duffy & Cunningham, 1996) that requires communication and feedback from fellow learners as meaning is explored and constructed (Jonassen, 2002; Salomon & Perkins, 1998). Garrison (1993), taking this new functionality of emerging technologies into account, defined interactivity as "sustained two-way communication among two or more persons for purposes of explaining and challenging perspectives" (p. 16). Anderson and Garrison (1998), defining more clearly the purpose and outcomes of the interactions, described interactivity in terms of reciprocal, consensual, and collaborative communication that furthers and facilitates the making of meaning.

Much of the study of interactivity in the online learning environment builds on the work of Moore (1993), who defined interaction between (and among) learners, between learner and instructor, and between learner and content; and on the work of Hillman, Willis, and Gunawardena (1994), who identified the interaction between learner and the interface as a critical aspect of the online environment. Using these interactions identified in online environments, researchers have attempted to define the quality, impact, and outcomes of interactivity on the learner and on learning. In this work they have: expanded the models of interactivity to encompass interactions beyond the confines of the online environment (Hirumi, 2002; Wise, Duffy, & Padmanabhan, 2008); examined the purposes behind interactivity (Sims, 2003); and explored outcomes such as student satisfaction (Lin, Lin, & Laffey, 2008), academic self-concept (Gibson, 1998), social presence (Kehrwald, 2008; Tu & McIsaac, 2002; Williams & Humphrey, 2007), patterns of engagement (Guldberg, 2008; Pawan, Paulus, Yalcin, & Chang, 2003), and cognitive presence (Garrison & Cleveland-Innes, 2005).

Thoughtful and specific comment is evident in the debate about how interactivity is to be defined and utilized in the online environment. Rose (1999, p. 43) made the point that attempts to define the term have resulted in "exhaustive taxonomies of interactions" that focus on outlining and naming while avoiding the thoughtful criticism and discussion required to understand, apply, and build on the implications for learning inherent in the construct. Berge (1999) cautioned that it is possible to design poor interactivity into a course and that increasing the quantity of interaction does not necessarily mean an improvement in its quality. Yacci (2000) argued that interactivity viewed from the students' perspective is a psychological construct of each student, which further increases the challenge for those who design online instruction. Shearer (2003) questioned the importance of interactions in meeting learning outcomes and argued that adult learners, normally highly motivated and self-directed, may require only minimal online interactivity to be successful in meeting the learning outcomes of the course. He cautioned that all interactions should be meaningful and authentic and should be analyzed according to how well each interaction assists the learners in meeting the course objectives.

Online learning and how it may be hybridized through responding to an extended conception of interactivity in education and learning are the focus of attention in this chapter. For the purposes of this analysis, the following conceptions of key terms have been adopted. Firstly, interactivity itself is being viewed just from the learner's perspective as action or impact by or on the learner. It is thus learner-centric in that sense. With that qualification, it is being taken broadly as action or impact by or on the learner involving other elements with which the interactions are at least in part driven by the educational or learning intentions of the learner. Those elements may this include both the traditional elements of the educator, other learners, educational processes, educational content, and the communicative interface. They may also, though, include elements beyond the traditional boundaries of the educational event, so long as the interactivity with those elements is driven, to some extent at least, by the learner's educational or learning intentions related to the event. Secondly, following Moore (1993), interactivity of the former, more traditional, type may then be regarded as 'internal interactivity', in the sense that it is internal to what has traditionally been regarded as the educational event. Interactivity of the latter type is correspondingly 'external interactivity' in the sense that it involves one or more elements that are outside the traditionally perceived boundaries of the event. Such external interactivity may be seen as involving local communities of support, such as members of family and friends. These are communities in the traditional sociological sense of a bounded, interactive association of individuals (Jary & Jary, 2000), and they function in the educational or learning engagement by contributing to the learning outcomes in some way. External interactivity may also involve more formal communities of practice – especially, in the case of professional development learning engagements, communities of *work* practice – in the Wengerian sense of a social conception of learning where, through processes of participation and reification, community members both support and challenge one another, and where interaction with peers is seen as a critical process in the development of new understandings and negotiated meaning, within the community (Wenger, 1998, 2000).

A CASE STUDY OF EDUCATIONAL INTERACTIVITY

This analysis draws on research into a semester-long, professional development course for practising teachers, delivered entirely online and focused on the use of information and communication technologies in the participants' teaching. The case study course included 14 participants. It involved the sharing of ideas through asynchronous discussions and the sharing of and feedback on work that was completed within the course. The research focused on the learner-centric interactivity present in the online environment. It specifically sought to discover how that interactivity supported the students' learning (Morrow, 2007).

Dealing with Technical Issues in the Online Environment

In the online environment the technical interface is the gatekeeper to the content, both because it allows access to the content itself and because it mediates how other interactions about the content occur. Students in the study found the interaction required with the technical interface to have both positive and negative aspects. On the one hand, it provided organized content and access to other learners and the lecturer. On the other hand, it required of the students a weekly commitment of time and energy and dictated to them the form and method of their interaction with the content. Initially finding the interface unfamiliar and stressful to use, the students reported struggling with the technical skills required to log into the course site, download content, and upload their own materials. However, as interaction with the interface was required to access the content, the students showed a strong sense of commitment to working out the technical issues. Solving these technical problems stimulated interactivity with others outside the class as students sought help from colleagues and family to solve technical problems.

Students' comments concerning their experiences with the interface revealed that initially they felt a distinct lack of control. For some students, the lack of control was centred on their inexperience with the course management software and their lack of the technical skill and understanding needed to solve the problems they encountered.

The processes involved in gaining access to the course site included getting a connection to the Internet from their own computer, navigating to the correct address on the World Wide Web, putting in the correct username and password to access the site, and then navigating to the proper class link. Once in the course site, students needed to access the appropriate folder containing the week's work. This folder included such tasks as viewing hyperlinked materials, accessing content placed on the site by other students, and placing their own comments and other work on the site. In the beginning, the students, many of whom were traditional distance learners, found the process unfamiliar and complicated. A response from Catherine is typical of such experiences in the online class and points out her need for help in dealing with the technical aspects of studying online –

I struggled, I think initially I got quite stressed on this course, everybody else seemed to be super efficient and I was challenged by just the task of logging on. We sat as a group in room five and that was tremendous because they gave me support to show me how to go through things; but the thing was they are such busy people that often I'd be the last one left sitting in there typing in and then thinking how am I going to drop box this, and I'd make a mistake and I don't know where I'd put it and it would be out in cyberspace and I wouldn't know where it had gone and I'd try to retrieve it and I'd lose it and I'd have to retype it because I didn't know the system had saved it. So I was very stressed initially. But I got into the hang of it. A colleague actually sat down with me and helped me with some of the things and so that collegial support was really important.[1]

Some students sought technical help from their spouses and children. This help included assistance with specific software programs, in solving problems with downloading or uploading files, and in locating things on the World Wide Web. Elaine described the assistance she received from her daughter –

Well my daughter, who's very computer savvy, but she isn't what you would call a patient person, so support is probably not a good word for it. But because she knows – she knew how to do it – she had to help me to send my first assignment.

In these statements we receive an insight into the local communities and how they functioned to scaffold Catherine's and Elaine's educational engagement as they sought assistance from more knowledgeable members. Stemming from their membership in the online class, which constituted a new community in which they felt inept and unqualified, Catherine sought help from *super efficient* and *busy people,* and Elaine braved the impatience of her daughter in getting the help needed from local communities to which they both belonged.

Previous studies have found that confidence in using both a technical interface and a course management system is essential to a student's success with other types of interactions required by the online environment (Hillman et al., 1994; Tsui & Wing, 1996), allowing them to work online more efficiently and effectively (Shih, Munoz, & Sanchez, 2006). The experiences of the students in this course were consistent with those findings and a catalyst for seeking the help they needed. In gaining this confidence, it appears that students sought help first from those in their own communities, where they could sit with another person to work through their problems.

Negotiating the Textual Nature of the Online Environment

Participants in the online environment interacted in what was primarily a textual setting. While some multimedia elements did exist, it was generally through the written word that most exchanges took place. In the online environment, a student's words represented him or her; to be 'present' the student had to write and submit that writing, which then became a textual persona. In such a situation, where the instant feedback, body language, facial clues, and tone of voice that normally inform a face-to-face discussion of ideas are lacking, students find themselves presenting their ideas and opinions for the scrutiny of a group of individuals whom they often know only through their respective online personas and for whom they may have developed little trust (McConnell, 2005; Tu & McIsaac, 2002). Shy or reticent students, or those lacking confidence in their ability to interpret the content or express this interpretation in writing, find this exposure to be especially problematic (Russo & Campbell, 2004; Stephens & Hartman, 2004).

It is clear that the textual environment of the online class was a source of concern for the students, who were anxious about posting their own writing to the class site. This apprehension showed as they interacted with the content, with other learners, and with others outside the class. Students' comments on the impact of communicating by writing in the online environment included concerns about a lack of confidence in their writing abilities, expressed either as a worry about their use of grammar, syntax, and spelling, or a concern about finding the right words to articulate what they wanted to say. While the level of comfort and skill in expressing themselves in writing differed among the students, all had reservations about the textual environment. Their concerns, while varied, pointed out some important ways in which the textual environment stimulated interactivity within their local communities.

Brenda, who described herself as someone who *wrote things in very everyday language*, was concerned about how her writing would compare with that of others in the class. She described getting feedback from two staff members in her school who had taken the class previously, often asking them to read through assignments before they were submitted. In her words, she wanted them *to have a look and see if they thought it was alright*. Her colleagues read her work and gave her their feedback, which was incorporated into her work before she uploaded it to the class site. Even though the worry over comparing herself to others lessened as she gained more experience, she remembered her initial fear of not wanting to *sound thick* to others in the class and credited her colleagues with helping her achieve confidence in the online class.

Other students in the class also reported seeking and accepting support from colleagues. Diane, meeting in *weekly get-togethers* with a colleague who was also enrolled in a distance course, described the mutual support given and received, which helped them to maintain their motivation for studying at a distance. Nancy mentioned that she was able to discuss issues with a colleague and that sharing problems was beneficial to them both.

Some students relied on spouses to get feedback on their ideas before responding to weekly discussions and uploading assignments. From proofreading to advice on phrasing and content, students relied heavily on input from their families. Students sought this help because of their anxiety about posting a written response in sharing areas in discussion forums. Elaine described relying on her husband's help –

I never have any trouble saying anything but when it comes to writing it down – my gosh, it's all of those forgotten skills, your grammar and your, you know your syntax and all of that and it's not one of my strengths. My husband's been an English teacher for a few years and he's a bit of a perfectionist about writing and things like that. So at the beginning I had to get him to check it for me. It was this big adult stuff here!

In addition to help with proofreading, Elaine described the influence of her husband on her growing belief in her ability to make a valuable contribution to the class. Initially she was worried about formal matters, such as spelling and punctuation, as well as the content of her writing. She felt that she had lost her writing skills, and depended heavily on her husband to proofread and give her feedback on the content of her writing before she submitted her work to the class. She felt that this support was important and allowed her to regain her confidence as a writer –

I needed him to check and his comment was "you have really improved during this course." He said, "you have really got your skill honed – your skills back again" and a couple of times he even said to me, "I really like the way you said that; I couldn't have said that better myself." It was – that was real – you know.

Elaine's experience points to the support she received locally and highlights the way in which this scaffolding increased her confidence and made the online experience richer and more meaningful.

Katie, another student who worried about her ability to express herself in writing, described herself as *threatened* and *insecure* as she prepared her weekly contributions to the class discussions –

I'm not a linguist, as such. I mean language doesn't – as you probably noticed already – language doesn't flow out easily and I found it very hard to um put my thoughts into the computer. And every time I did I thought – oh no you know my, my comments are nowhere near, not as well done as everybody else's. I don't have the vocab that a lot of other people have and yeah, I found that very threatening.

A theme that ran through all the students' comments was that of comparison with others. The impetus behind the apprehension was the public forum in which the students' thoughts and opinions would be on display. The fact that the text was archived and available for others to view and review was also a factor that created anxiety for some students. Brenda expressed her fears of the public display of her writing –

It's the idea of putting it into print you know. Because if you say it and it was a silly idea then people can sort of go "hahahaha – where is she coming from?" – and it's over. But when you've got it written in print then people can go back you know. And then you think well if that's in print some clever person's going to come along and say "Well that's a load of rubbish."

It is clear that interacting in a textual environment was a catalyst for seeking support from the local community, as students worked on getting to an acceptable level of comfort in self-expression and submitting their opinions and ideas to the course site. That the writing was displayed in a very public arena where it was read by others and archived so that it could be re-read at other times, and where it was perceived as being available for comment or disagreement by other students and the lecturer, was initially reported by the students as a barrier to their engagement. Although students' comfort with submitting their writing did increase over time, they never progressed beyond the bulletin-board type of posting – described by Pawan et al. (2003) – where students upload their carefully constructed comments and reflections, but fail to follow through the exchanging or challenging of ideas. The online environment, textual and mediated through a technical interface, demands a level of individual participation that both isolates and exposes the student in a way that most face-to-face classes do not. Tu and McIsaac (2002) found that the more public the students perceived a medium to be, the lower the social presence, and this finding was supported by the present study.

On the positive side, the textual nature of the online environment did mean that each student had the opportunity to read and process the ideas and thoughts of the other students, allowing them to reflect on and process material and messages before submitting their own responses. All students noted this to be a positive feature of the online class and credited it with an important part of their own learning. Although evidence is contradictory that participating in an online course increases students' writing skills (Picciano, 2002; Stephens & Hartmann, 2004), students in this class reported that they gained confidence in expressing themselves through this medium as the course progressed. Importantly, though, in achieving that increased confidence, it is clear that they were drew on help from local communities. By the end of the course, they had become more comfortable with operating in the online textual environment, finding increased confidence in their ability to express themselves in writing and creating a comfortable level of response.

Interactivity Between the Learners and Their Local Environment

Evidence that students made connections between the course and the environment in which they worked was found in the comments made by students in the discussion forums and sharing areas. The course required that students plan and implement a lesson that used some of the content and techniques relating to the use of ICT found in the course content. It was clear from the students' comments that their use of ICT within their own environments was a useful and effective aid to their learning, and that it was also ongoing and extended beyond this one assignment. Frequent mention of the use of software, hardware, and teaching strategies in their own classrooms showed that students in the course were using this type of interactivity to help them understand and process the course content. Comments from post-course interviews also demonstrated the point that learner-environment interactivity was a motivating factor for the students in the class.

Involvement within their own communities of practice took different forms as students attempted to put the ICT strategies from the course into place in their own classrooms. Some students worked with small groups in their own classrooms. Diane remarked that she was using a *target group* of four children with whom to trial her ideas. Some students implemented a less formal approach. Margaret described a *queue at the computers each morning before school, since we have begun our weekly ICT learning/ exploring time.* Some students reported overall attempts to integrate ICT into their teaching. Brenda described an instance where she looked around her classroom and realized that she had created a situation where *all the resources at my disposal were being meaningfully used.*

Comments made by the students indicated that the interaction in their own classrooms and schools resulted in new awareness and insights. Students reported observations made as they attempted to put the theories, strategies, and skills in place within their own classroom environments. They mentioned that they were surprised by the motivation and interest shown by children in their classrooms, were pleased with how quickly and how much the children learned, and that children were taking the initiative and going beyond what the teacher had introduced. Several students mentioned that children in their own classrooms learned from one another through experimentation and collaboration.

Discussing things with colleagues was mentioned frequently as a way to help students process and understand content. Brenda remarked on her discussion of course content, including new ideas and new skills, in staff rooms and with other teachers in her school –

You could exchange ideas and talk about the different things that you came across and then the conversation would digress like "oh look, I've used that and it worked really well" and "oh have you tried this?"

It is apparent that these conversations were important to the students' learning, by extending the discussion beyond the members of the class and providing opportunities to gain knowledge locally through the sharing of ideas and practical examples.

The students also mentioned that these interactions within their local environments were an important part of their learning. Testing ideas and theories in their own classrooms helped them to process and understand the content and provided a relevant context for the theoretical and practical applications introduced in the course. Catherine described the growing confidence resulting from her work within her own teaching practice –

I think I can learn a great deal in terms of applying that as a teaching tool with the kids. As we progressed through, I definitely became more confident as I got feedback – I definitely gained confidence. I feel much happier about using the computers now in the room than I did at the end of last year.

Increased confidence and understanding of how the children reacted to the introduction of ICT into the classroom, as well as a growing awareness of how the ICT changed the dynamics within the classroom, were also evident. Lawrence found that some students were more advanced in their knowledge than he was, but he also made the discovery as he worked with ICT in his own classroom that this phenomenon was acceptable and worked to the advantage of both the teacher and the students –

They learn so much from each other and if you have one expert in your room then that can quickly turn to 8 or 10. When doing assignments, three of the children are far more advanced than me and that's okay.

This type of discovery, which resulted in a perceptual change for this student, could not have happened without the interactivity within his own community of practice.

Students also commented on their goals for the future, such as increasing the size and number of the groups of children using ICT, or branching out into a broader use of ICT strategies within their classrooms. Among these comments, students remarked on the use of software, hardware, and learning strategies that they saw themselves implementing in the future. Students liked an assignment that required them to plan, implement, observe, and reflect on a classroom activity that incorporated the use of ICT to support teaching and learning. They noted that the increase in their experience, self-confidence, and personal expertise encouraged them to engage in further learner-environment interactions of this kind.

Putting ideas into practice within their own communities was an important part of the interactivity that contributed to the students achieving the learning goals of the class, and it was actively sought by the students. It appears that the students in this course used their professional, friendship, and family communities as a resource on which they drew for emotional, technical, and academic help – seeking out and creating interactions that existed within these multiple environments in support of their online learning, although those interactions were outside the online environment.

The nature of an online professional development class would also imply that practical applications of the content may be expected in the students' own classrooms as they attempt to integrate and apply the material presented in the course. Consistent with findings of Conrad (2008), who found that participants in online professional development courses were interested in information they saw as relevant to their own classroom situations, students in the present study reported that they used skills and techniques in their working environments which provided them with an opportunity to make the content meaningful on a personal and practical level. Interaction about the content with others in their communities of practice was another important aspect of their processing and mastering of the material.

That the online community did not become a vibrant, reciprocal community of its own may be due to the fact that the students were strongly situated in local communities of practice and other communities and did not see the online community as essential to their learning, or that their meaningful and involved participation resided in local communities rather than in those to which they belonged online. They could and did take from the online community that which they saw as being useful to them. Students commented on the usefulness of reading the comments posted by others and the ideas they developed through viewing the work of others, but this was for the most part a one-way flow of information.

Impact of the Case Study on the Hybridization of Online Learning

It thus became apparent in the case study outlined here that support structures operating within the course were divided into two main areas: those that functioned within the online environment and those that were found outside the online course environment. Support for learning described by students as functioning inside the online environment is closely aligned with Moore's (1993) conception of interactivity. It includes interactions with other learners, the educator, and the content. However, while the support that students recognized from these internal types of interactions was interesting in its application to this study, it was the support that students described as functioning outside the online environment that was unexpected and significant. When asked after the course to identify what supported their learning, students generally remarked first on some aspect of their local community: help from family, collaboration and discussion with colleagues, and trying things out in their own classrooms. They drew support from their local communities, which helped shape their contributions, the way they interacted, and the artefacts they produced and contributed within the online environment. This local participation directly contributed to and shaped the online community in which they were required to participate to complete the course. The support was seen as an important element as students progressed through the course content. They used members of their local communities to give technical aid or to act as a 'dry run' for work they planned to submit to the class site. The motivation for these interactions was presented by the participants as stemming from three major sources: (1) a need for help in dealing with the technical requirements of online learning; (2) a need for help in negotiating the textual nature of the online environment; and (3) a need to explore and understand the content within the community in which they lived and worked.

The case study outlined here thus highlights the importance of external interactivity in online learning. While it involved a professional development course for teachers, the work and theorization of others suggests the potentially more general importance of external interactivity in online educational engagements. Gibson (1998) has commented on the importance of considering the multiple environments in which online learners are located and engage, noting that these micro-systems can have positive or negative effects, and suggesting that enhancing communication between the online and the local community would allow both learners and teachers to access a rich resource. Hirumi (2002) has argued that interactions which allow learners to access and acquire knowledge from sources external to the online environment exert a positive influence on learning, creating a connection between environments that allow learners to link theory and practice. Recognising that the increase in online learning has made it possible for such online communities of learning and workplace communities of practice to exist in the same time and space, Stacey, Smith, and Barty (2004) sought to explore possible disruptions or disturbances that might occur as a result of multiple memberships in such communities. These researchers found that the participants regarded dual membership as having a positive impact overall, even when some disruption did occur. Schlager and Fusco (2003) asserted that informal learning occurs as new and less skilled members of a group participate peripherally with more experienced members of the group and take on new roles themselves which in turn take them on a path to greater expertise. They suggested also that it is important to step outside the online world to study the socio-cultural processes of local communities of practice – noting that online professional development is often created in isolation from the local community of practice in which the practicing teachers work.

This phenomenon thus needs to be understood and addressed within the design of the online learning environment. Wenger (1998, p. 216) noted that this "potentially difficult work of reconciliation can be facilitated by communities that endeavour to encompass, within their own practice, an increasing portion of the nexus of multi-membership of their members." The result of this reconciliation becomes part of a shared learning practice of such communities, which will thereby "not only gain the allegiance of their members; they will also enrich their own practices" (p. 216). That such interactivity may happen in local communities rather than in the online environment is perhaps not surprising when we consider that students commonly come to online educational engagements from established local communities encompassing persons who may have greater skills and experience and who may effectively, efficiently, and less threateningly be called on for help and support. It is not impossible for online communities to function to support each other in this way, but it takes time for those who are more experienced or more skilled to become apparent and, more importantly, to become trusted.

It is important to see the learner in context and to realize the complexity and richness of the local communities in which the he or she lives. Although stimulated by the online class, these local alliances function outside it. Yet this 'behind the scenes' support from the students' families, friends, colleagues, and local work environments makes contributions that increase the effectiveness of the individual student's experience, while at the same time enriching the experience for others in the course.

DESIGNING A COURSE THAT RECOGNIZES AND INCLUDES EXTERNAL ACTIVITY

The rapid increase in the online delivery of instruction in higher education has provided the opportunity and highlighted the need for more in-depth examination of the design, not only of the interface used for delivery, but also of interactivity that is embedded in that design. This study has shown that there is compelling evidence to recognize and include the external interactivity that supports learners in an online environment. We suggest that the design of online spaces for learning should provide frameworks that recognize, facilitate, and encourage such interactivity as a valid dimension of students' learning.

The design of online learning environments has historically been influenced by two major frameworks of instruction. The first, a transmissional framework, is sustained by a belief that a set body of knowledge exists to be transmitted to the learner. It relies on text-based lectures, textbooks, and videotapes, and is based on positivist and behaviourist theorizations. The second, a transformational framework, understands the learner as transforming information by generating hypotheses, making decisions, and constructing knowledge either individually or through social interaction with others. It is based on constructivist theorizations (Bates, 1995). Cautioning that we must be aware of the paradigms that we are using to develop, implement, and evaluate online opportunities for learners, Twigg (2002, p. 3) suggested that "the higher education paradigm, honed and perfected for hundreds of years, [that] has served us well," is a factor in maintaining traditional academic practices and the more traditional transmission of content. Contrasting these frameworks as, respectively, teacher-centred versus learner-centred, Bates (1995) cautioned that the transmissional model no longer meets the changing educational needs of knowledge economy workers, who need to communicate effectively and to work collaboratively to analyze information and generate new knowledge.

Transformational, constructivist online environments use collaborative activities to engage learners, embed learning in authentic contexts, and encourage reflection based on conversations with other learners. Jonassen, Davidson, Collins, Campbell, and Haag (1995) outlined a framework of context, construction, collaboration, and conversation to facilitate the making of meaning for learners. They suggested that the design of online instruction needs to shift from prescriptive, directed learning situations to environments that allow learners to solve real-world problems and engage in dialogues with a community of practitioners. Within the online learning environment, this interactive framework can be mediated by a variety of technologies such as electronic mail, computer-based discussion, and conferencing. Collaboration is available online through the ability of the technology to support groups across a distributed environment, where learners can actively work toward negotiated understanding. Using situated, case-based learning to give authentic contexts in which students can work is supported by both video and hypermedia environments and gives learners an opportunity to reflect, communicate, and negotiate a shared meaning within the group (Garrison, 1993; Jonassen et al., 1995; McLoughlin, 2002). Taking the viewpoint that learning is more than just a response to teaching, Olgren (1998) suggested that course design should: (1) include activities that foster mental involvement in the learning and draw on interactions between the student and instructor, other learners, and the content; (2) support emotional involvement in the learning by communication, collaboration, and support; (3) develop students' learning capacities by embedding support devices in the instruction; and (4) use assessment methods that allow students to demonstrate that they have developed knowledge structures and applied new skills.

Design of the online environment has been found to be a significant factor in successful online learning experiences for students. Swan, Fredericksen, Pickett, Pelz, and Maher (2000) found that three factors contribute to the success of online courses: a transparent interface, frequent and constructive interaction with the instructor, and the availability of dynamic and ongoing discussion. The interrelationship of these factors was argued to be significant in that they jointly support the building of a learning community within an immersive environment in which course content and interactions occur online and students generate the course content in a sophisticated, constructivist, learning community (Harmon & Jones, 1999). Relatedly, Garrison and Anderson (2003) have asserted that the value of online learning lies not in faster access to information, but rather in the capacity to facilitate communication, thinking, and the construction of meaning and knowledge.

Online technologies have the capacity and the potential to create student-centred learning environments where participants can share a sense of community, relate to one another, and pursue a common goal (Ng, 2001). Paloff and Pratt (2001) have suggested that course development should focus on interactivity, not on content, and that, for this to happen, the roles of faculty and students must change from a teacher-centred to a more learner-centred environment, where students take a lead in learning activities.

Drawing on these considerations, we suggest the following design elements in providing a structure that supports the students' membership in multiple communities, recognizing and valuing the ways in which local communities of practice contribute to the online environment.

1. Create a culture that values the existence of local communities that support and contribute to the students' knowledge. This may be done, for example, through –
    - Introductions that encourage students to share information about local situations and communities that impact on them as learners.
    - Discussions that encourage students to share experiences from their local communities of practice.

It is important to remember that, even though students live in a world where the relationship of people to time and space is changing, online students are still contextually situated in time and place and are still immersed in local communities with which they interact and through which they find meaning (Hodgson & Reynolds, 2005). Wenger (1998) has argued that membership of multiple learning communities is a critical source of learning, because it requires students to bring divergent perspectives together and to negotiate an engaged identity in each community. However, unless membership in multiple communities is acknowledged and valued, the experience and the learning will be private to the individual and will lack the capacity to enrich the community. Mann (2005) has suggested that it is a lack of communication, rather than a lack of community, that is a source of alienation in online environments. He has argued for the individual to have a stronger voice, and a correspondingly greater responsibility, in opening up and maintaining communication. Conversations that are inclusive of the learners' local communities of practice, and that acknowledge the impact of multiple community memberships, may help to bridge the gap between the local and the online worlds inhabited by the students.

2. Build-in structures that allow the students to choose the direction of their study, so that it is aligned with their interests and local communities of practice. This may be done, for example, through –
    - Providing a range of articles and/or topics from which students may choose those to be used in their analyses and reporting back to the online class.
    - Including a small action research project to be conducted in students' classrooms and shared with the online class.
    - Incorporating a student self-identified problem that is explored and shared with the online class.

Meaningful learning requires that students be able to make connections between the content in the course and the practically-oriented focus of their work in their own classrooms. Failure to see such connections may result in the dissociation of the online and the local environments (Stacey, Smith, & Barty, 2004). Lack of both interest and participation in the online environment has also been linked to the collegiality present in the participant's place of employment. If professional and pedagogical support is seen to be high in the local community, then students have less need to find this community of practice online (Hough, Smithey, & Everton, 2004). These points argue for the merging of the online content with interests, problems, and questions from the students' own local practice. Pointing out the importance of such an amalgamation, Schlager and Fusco (2003, p. 213) remarked that "Although we see a place for highly structured e-learning environments, we also see a need for teachers to have a set of online learning and collaboration capabilities that they can own and tailor to meet their own needs and the needs of the community."

3. Allow students to develop and build the content of the course through sharing artefacts

that they have created within the context of their own classrooms or schools. This may be done, for example, through –

- Reports of exploratory studies.
- Presentations of techniques that students have tested.
- The results of action research.

It is through the creation and sharing of artefacts that ideas and knowledge are communicated, giving students the opportunity to engage with one another and develop a group identity (McConnell, 2005; Wenger, 1998). The design of a constructivist online learning environment, where students are encouraged to share their knowledge, experiences, judgement, and initiative, will draw on their local practice and encourage connections across the boundaries of their local and virtual communities. Refering to these artefacts as "common referents," Wise, Duffy, and Padmanabhan (2008) suggested that this strategy will create a situation that allows students to make connections within the virtual world of the online environment and the world of their local practice.

4. Make sure that students reflect on and have the opportunity to share the processes of their learning, including interactions with local communities and how these interactions have helped to shape their perceptions and their learning.

Wenger (1998, p. 60) noted that reification can refer to both a process and its product, stating that "…the products of reification are not simply concrete, material objects. Rather, they are reflections of these practices, tokens of vast expanses of human meaning." In providing the opportunity for an examination of the processes of learning, learners have the opportunity to share how they have been supported and challenged by their local communities of practice, but also to contribute ways in which the local community may have been challenged and changed as a result. Cousin and Deepwell (2005), drawing on the work of Wenger, have pointed out that learner variation is a critical element that must be supported in the design of online learning environments. They have argued that network learning should blur the boundaries between enrolled students and other interested groups in the learning environment.

As educators, we should endeavour to include all stakeholders – not just seeing the individual in the context of an isolated online class, but rather examining how the local communities impact on and are themselves impacted on by those members of their own communities who are involved in the class.

CONCLUSION

An examination of the learner-centric interactivity in an online professional development course for practicing teachers has revealed that there may be recognized two main categories of interactivity that impact on the learners' experience in the online environment. On the one hand, there is interactivity that operates within the online environment between the learner and the other learners, the educator, the computer interface, and the content. On the other hand, there is that which operates outside the online class. It is clear that personal, learner-centric interactivity occurs between the learner and his or her local community of colleagues, friends, and family and that these communities function largely external to the online environment. This interactivity, normally invisible within the online learning environment, supports the online learner technically, academically, and emotionally and is an important element in success as an online learner. While this external interactivity does have an impact on the online class, it is not readily traceable or identifiable, because such types of interactions are not normally acknowledged or examined educationally and may not be valued for the contributions that they make to the overall functioning and development of the online environment. Because the venue for the online class is situated within the context of the students' professional, personal, and community lives, it is important in educational planning for online learning – particularly in online professional development programs – that we consider how to recognize, validate, incorporate, and encourage such support as a potentially important part of these educational engagements.

As individuals we may join different communities and create multiple identities as we interact within these communities. Those community memberships and interactions contribute to how we learn. It is important to explore the potential of online environments to support, not just the individual, but rather the individual in the context of the multiple and evolving communities in which they interact.

In recognizing the importance of external interactivity in online educational engagements, and through integrating it into the online educational planning and management, its educational benefits may be further enhanced. This may be seen as a form of hybridization of online learning – bringing external interactivity into the proximity of the internal with synergistic effect. It brings a further dimension to traditional considerations in online educational planning and management. It impacts on the quality of the educational and learning engagement. Its outcomes would seem, from the work examined in this chapter, to be significant and positive. The tentative suggestions advanced in this chapter for working towards such a hybridization may be taken as a starting point for both further research and experimental educational development on this topic.

REFERENCES

Anderson, T. (2004). Toward a theory of online learning. In T. Anderson & F. Elloumi (Eds.), *Theory and practice of online learning* (pp. 33-60). Athabasca, Canada: Athabasca University.

Anderson, T. D., & Garrison, D. R. (1998). Learning in a networked world: New roles and responsibilities. In C. C. Gibson (Ed.), *Distance learners in higher education: Institutional responses for quality outcomes* (pp. 97-112). Madison, WI: Atwood Publishing.

Bates, A. W. (1995). *Technology, open learning and distance education*. London: Routledge.

Berge, Z. L. (1999). Interaction in post-secondary web-based learning. *Educational Technology, 39*(1), 5–11.

Conrad, D. L. (2008). From community to community of practice: Exploring the connection of online learners to informal learning in the workplace. *American Journal of Distance Education, 22*, 3–23. doi:10.1080/08923640701713414

Cousin, G., & Deepwell, F. (2005). Designs for network learning: A communities of practice perspective. *Studies in Higher Education, 30*(1), 57–66. doi:10.1080/0307507052000307795

de Bruyn, L. L. (2004). Monitoring online communication: Can the development of convergence and social presence indicate an interactive learning environment? *Distance Education, 25*(1), 67–81. doi:10.1080/0158791042000212468

Dewey, J. (1933). *How we think*. Chicago: Henry Regency.

Duffy, T. M., & Cunningham, D. J. (1996). Constructivism: Implications for the design and delivery of instruction. In D. Jonassen (Ed.), *Handbook of research for educational communication and technology* (pp. 170-198). New York: Simon & Shuster McMillan.

Garrison, D. R. (1993). Quality and access in distance education: Theoretical considerations. In D. Keegan (Ed.), *Theoretical principles of distance education* (pp. 9-21). New York: Routledge.

Garrison, D. R., & Anderson, T. (2003). *E-learning in the 21st century: A framework for research and practice*. London: Routledge-Falmer.

Garrison, R., & Cleveland-Innes, M. (2005). Facilitating cognitive presence in online learning: Interaction is not enough. *American Journal of Distance Education, 19*(3), 133–148. doi:10.1207/s15389286ajde1903_2

Gibson, C. C. (1998). The distance learner in context. In C. C. Gibson (Ed.), *Distance learners in higher education* (pp. 113-125). Madison, WI: Atwood Publishing.

Giguere, P. J., Formica, S. W., & Harding, W. M. (2004). Large-scale interaction strategies for web-based professional development. *American Journal of Distance Education, 18*(4), 207–223. doi:10.1207/s15389286ajde1804_3

Guldberg, K. (2008). Adult learners and professional development: Peer-to-peer learning in a networked community. *International Journal of Lifelong Education, 27*(1), 35–49. doi:10.1080/02601370701803591

Harmon, S. W., & Jones, M. G. (1999). The five levels of web use in education: Factors to consider in planning an online course. *Educational Technology, 39*(6), 28–32.

Hawkes, M. (2006). Linguistic discourse variables as indicators of reflective online interaction. *American Journal of Distance Education, 20*(4), 231–244. doi:10.1207/s15389286ajde2004_4

Hillman, D. C. A., Willis, D. J., & Gunawardena, C. N. (1994). Learner-interface interaction in distance education: An extension of contemporary models and strategies for practitioners. *American Journal of Distance Education, 8*(2), 30–42. doi:10.1080/08923649409526853

Hirumi, A. (2002). A framework for analyzing, designing, and sequencing planned e-learned interactions. *The Quarterly Review of Distance Education, 3*(2), 141–160.

Hodgson, V., & Reynolds, M. (2005). Consensus, difference and 'multiple communities' in networked learning. *Studies in Higher Education, 30*(1), 11–14. doi:10.1080/0307507052000307768

Holmberg, B. (1983). Guided didactic conversation in distance education. In D. Sewart, D. Keegan, & H. Borge (Eds.), *Distance education: International perspectives* (pp. 114-122). London: Croom Helm.

Hough, B. W., Smithey, M. W., & Everton, C. M. (2004). Using computer-mediated communication to create virtual communities of practice for intern teachers. *Journal of Technology and Teacher Education, 12*(3), 361–386.

Jary, D., & Jary, J. (2000). *Collins dictionary of sociology* (3rd ed.). Glascow: Harper Collins.

Jonassen, D. H. (2002). Learning as activity. *Educational Technology, 42*(2), 45–51.

Jonassen, D. H., Davidson, M., Collins, M., Campbell, J., & Haag, B. B. (1995). Constructivism and computer-mediated communication in distance education. *American Journal of Distance Education, 9*(2), 7–26. doi:10.1080/08923649509526885

Kehrwald, B. (2008). Understanding social presence in text-based online learning environments. *Distance Education, 29*(1), 89–106. doi:10.1080/01587910802004860

LaPointe, D., & Gunawardena, C. N. (2004). Developing, testing and refining of a model to understand the relationship between peer interaction and learning outcomes in computer-mediated conferencing. *Distance Education, 25*(1), 83–106. doi:10.1080/0158791042000212477

Lin, Y.-M., Lin, G.-Y., & Laffey, J. M. (2008). Building a social and motivational framework for understanding satisfaction in online learning. *Journal of Educational Computing Research*, *38*(1), 1–27. doi:10.2190/EC.38.1.a

Mann, S. J. (2005). Alienation in the learning environment: A failure of community? *Studies in Higher Education*, *30*(1), 43–55. doi:10.1080/0307507052000307786

McConnell, D. (2005). Examining the dynamics of networked e-learning groups and communities. *Studies in Higher Education*, *30*(1), 25–42. doi:10.1080/0307507052000307777

McLoughlin, C. (2002). Learner support in distance and networked learning environments: Ten dimensions for successful design. *Distance Education*, *23*(2), 149–162. doi:10.1080/0158791022000009178

Moore, M. G. (1993). Three types of interaction. In K. Harry, M. John, & D. Keegan (Eds.), *Distance education: New perspectives* (pp. 21-24). London: Routledge.

Morrow, D. (2007). *Interactivity in an online learning environment: A case study of participant experience in professional development.* Unpublished doctoral dissertation, Griffith University, Brisbane.

Ng, K. C. (2001). Using e-mail to foster collaboration in distance education. *Open Learning*, *16*, 191–200. doi:10.1080/02680510120050343

Olgren, C. H. (1998). Improving learning outcomes: The effects of learning strategies and motivation. In C. C. Gibson (Ed.), *Distance learners in higher education: Institutional responses to quality outcomes* (pp. 77-95). Madison, WI: Atwood Publishing.

Palloff, R., & Pratt, K. (2001). *Lessons from the cyberspace classroom: The realities of online teaching*. San Francisco, CA: Jossey-Bass.

Pawan, F., Paulus, T. M., Yalcin, S., & Chang, C. F. (2003). Online learning: Patterns of engagement and interaction among in-service teachers. *Language Learning & Technology*, *7*(3), 119–140.

Picciano, A. G. (2002). Beyond student perceptions: Issues of interaction, presence, and performance in an online course. *Journal of Asynchronous Learning Networks*, *6*(1), 21–40.

Rose, E. (1999). Deconstructing interactivity in educational computing. *Educational Technology*, *39*(1), 43–49.

Russo, T. C., & Campbell, S. W. (2004). Perceptions of mediated presence in an asynchronous online course: Interplay of communication behaviors and medium. *Distance Education*, *25*(2), 215–232. doi:10.1080/0158791042000262139

Salomon, G., & Perkins, D. N. (1998). Individual and social aspects of learning. In D. P. Pearson & A. Iran-Nejad (Eds.), *Review of Research in Education* (Vol. 23, pp. 1-24). Washington, DC: American Educational Research Association.

Schlager, M. S., & Fusco, J. (2003). Teacher professional development, technology, and communities of practice: Are we putting the cart before the horse? *The Information Society*, *19*, 203–220. doi:10.1080/01972240309464

Shearer, R. L. (2003). *Interaction in distance education.* Madison, WI: Distance Educator, Inc.

Sims, R. L. (2003). Promises of interactivity: Aligning learner perceptions and expectations with strategies for flexible and online learning. *Distance Education*, *24*(1), 87–103. doi:10.1080/01587910303050

Stacey, E., Smith, P., & Barty, K. (2004). Adult learners in the workplace: Online learning and communities of practice. *Distance Education*, *25*(1), 107–123. doi:10.1080/0158791042000212486

Stephens, A. C., & Hartmann, C. (2004). A successful professional development project's failure to promote online discussion about teaching mathematics with technology. *Journal of Technology and Teacher Education, 12*(1), 57–73.

Swan, K., Shea, P., Fredericksen, E., Pickett, A., Pelz, W., & Maher, G. (2000). Building knowledge building communities: Consistency, contact and communication in the virtual classroom. *Journal of Educational Computing Research, 23*(4), 359–383.

Tu, C. H., & McIsaac, M. S. (2002). The relationship of social presence and interaction in online classes. *American Journal of Distance Education, 16*(3), 131–150. doi:10.1207/S15389286AJDE1603_2

Twigg, C. A. (2002). *Innovations in online learning: Moving beyond no significant difference.* Retrieved August 2003 from http://www.center.rpi.edu/PewSym/Mono4.html

Wagner, E. D. (1997). Interactivity: From agents to outcomes. *New Directions for Teaching and Learning, 71*, 19–26. doi:10.1002/tl.7103

Wenger, E. (1998). *Communities of practice: Learning meaning and identify*. Cambridge, UK: Cambridge University Press.

Wenger, E. (2000). Communities of practice and social learning systems. *Organization, 7*(2), 225–246. doi:10.1177/135050840072002

Williams, R. S., & Humphrey, R. (2007). Understanding and fostering interaction in threaded discussion. *Journal of Asynchronous Learning Networks, 2*(2), 129–143.

Wise, A., Duffy, T. M., & Padmanabhan, P. (2008). Deepening online conversation: How and why to use a common reference to connect learners with diverse local practices. *Educational Technology, 48*(4), 3–11.

Yacci, M. (2000). Interactivity demystified: A structural definition for distance education and intelligent computer based instruction. *Educational Technology, 40*(4), 5–16.

KEY TERMS AND DEFINITIONS

Communities of Support: (1) Communities in the traditional sociological sense of a bounded, interactive association of individuals that function in the educational or learning engagement by contributing to the learning outcomes in some way. (2) More formal communities of practice – especially, in the case of professional development learning engagements or communities of *work* practice – in the Wengerian sense of a social conception of learning where, through processes of participation and reification, community members both support and challenge one another, and where interaction with peers is seen as a critical process in the development of new understandings and negotiated meaning, within the community.

Hybridization: Bringing external interactivity into the proximity of the internal with synergistic effect.

Interactivity: Action or impact by or on the learner involving other elements with which the interactions are at least in part driven by the educational or learning intentions of the learner. May be either: (1) **Internal Interactivity** – internal to what has traditionally been regarded as the educational event; or (2) **External Interactivity** – in the sense that it involves one or more elements that are outside the traditionally perceived boundaries of the event.

ENDNOTES

1. Italicised text in this chapter is participant narrative.

Chapter 3
Using Metanotation as a Tool for Describing Learning Systems

Philip Barker
University of Teesside, UK

ABSTRACT

Metanotation is a powerful tool for describing systems, objects and processes. This chapter illustrates how this tool can be used to specify the nature and characteristics of learning systems and the various artefacts from which they are composed. It is suggested that messages and messaging systems are the fundamental building blocks from which learning artefacts are created. The chapter therefore discusses the nature of communication and messaging from an educational perspective and then outlines how various types of message artefact can be used to build hybrid learning systems that involve the use of Webs, Wikis, weblogs and electronic books.

INTRODUCTION

In keeping with Shannon's fundamental theory of communication (Shannon, 1948), this chapter regards communication as a process that involves the movement of information from one location to another. The process involves three types of agent: *sender*, *transmitter* and *recipient*. The sending and receiving of information can have important effects on the states and behaviour of the entities that are involved in a communication process. This is particularly so in the case of educational communication - the intent of which is to share ideas, skills and knowledge. It is therefore important to consider the role that communication and messaging systems play in relation to learning systems development.

Naturally, effective communication between individuals, groups of people and between people and machines is fundamental to human existence. It also underlies many important industries - such as those based on broadcasting, advertising, publishing, education and entertainment. Within each of these areas of activity, effective communication depends critically upon the existence of appropriate 'media'. The printing press was the first major

DOI: 10.4018/978-1-60566-380-7.ch003

step forward in the use of mass communication media (Eisenstein, 1980). Now, of course, we also have film, radio, television and the Internet. All of these are powerful vehicles for the transmission of material to widely disparate audiences. Never before, in the history of communication, have media been as important as they are today. Indeed, in his famous book, McLuhan (2001) coined the phrase '*the medium is the message*'. Nowadays, when using this phrase, we often employ it in order to reflect how dependent organisations, groups and individuals have become on the use of media for projecting an appropriate system image (or 'persona') from self across to others. This is particularly relevant in the case of online communities.

From an educational perspective, effective communication is an essential pre-requisite for virtually all forms of learning activity. This communication can involve both local and global interaction with other people or objects that are external to ourselves. It can also be based on various forms of personal reflection and introspection. Of course, it is important to remember that learning is a continuous process that takes place with different intensities during an individual's personal lifecycle. Naturally, the intensity of any given learning activity (and the level of motivation involved) is likely to be strongly influenced by the nature of the stimuli that are embedded within the communication events in which a person participates. Bearing in mind the implicit and fundamental importance of communication in relation to the design of learning systems, this chapter discusses the basic nature of this activity and then goes on to analyse the types of artefact that are used to support communication within learning environments.

As hinted at by McLuhan, fundamental to the idea of communication is the concept of a '*message*'. Essentially, communication takes place as a result of passing messages between two (or more) communicating entities using an appropriate '*channel of communication*' - the 'medium'. There are various ways in which this can take place and various issues that need to be considered when analysing a messaging system. Two fundamental points that have to be taken into account are: the physical content and transmission of a message (from one location to another); and the cognitive interpretation of a message within the mind of its recipient(s). Obviously, messages can be very short (as is the case in a SMS text message sent using a mobile phone) or much longer (as is the case of an article that is published in an electronic or paper-based journal). Books (both paper-based and in electronic form) may be regarded as composite or aggregated collections of many individual messages each of which is related to a particular topic of discourse - see, for example, Worstall (2005).

Increasingly, as the 'science and technology' of communication media has evolved, more and more ways of sending messages have become available. It is therefore often necessary to consider the best medium to use, or indeed, the optimal combination of media that might be employed in order to communicate, most effectively, the content of a message. Nowadays, people often become involved in using hybrid communication strategies that involve the '*blending*' of two or more communication channels either in sequence or in parallel. For example, an employee within an organisation might send an email message to a colleague; this message might have several attachments - a sound file, an image file and a text file. Similarly, a holiday-maker might use a 3G mobile phone to send to a friend a static picture (or a video clip) of a scenic place of interest - along with either a textual or a sonic message "*Having fun - wish you were here!*". From a recipient's perspective, the use of several different communication channels is illustrated schematically in Figure 1.

As can be seen from this diagram, each of the channels within a given communicative sequence can host a number of different '*modes*' of communication. Each mode, in turn, will require an

Figure 1. Blended communication in terms of multiple media channels

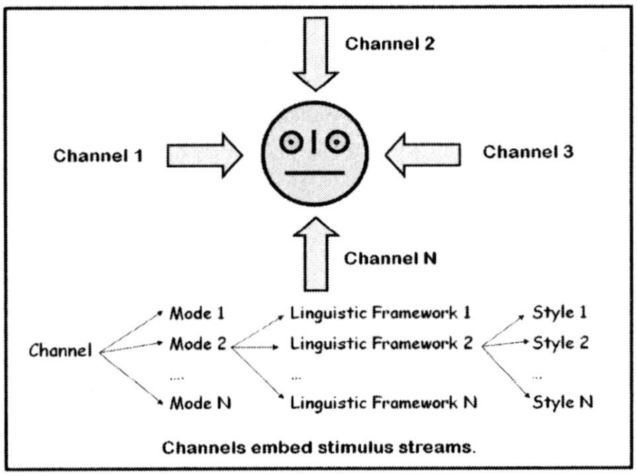

appropriate *linguistic framework* within which to encode the various messages that have been previously referred to. As can be seen in Figure 1, the messages that are embedded in a given channel can also employ many different *styles* or *genres* of communication. Of course, as was established by Claude Shannon (Wikipedia, 2007a), it is important to remember that the 'purity' of a message is often strongly perturbed by the level and quantity of extraneous noise that it embeds (Cherry, 1971). In mediated human-to-human communication systems this noise can arise from both physical and cognitive sources.

Naturally, it is hoped that the messages carried by the various channels depicted in Figure 1 will embed appropriate stimuli that will activate and motivate its recipients to assimilate the message content in an appropriate way. This content may be used: (1) to build new and/or augment existing cognitive structures; and (2) to take action in relation to some issue and/or to modify personal behaviour. Naturally, because a message consists of a stream of signs and symbols, an understanding of the principles and techniques of semiotics is an important asset in relation to designing messages and predicting their affect on human behaviour (Chandler, 2006; de Souza, 2005). The role of semiotics in relation to message transmission is illustrated schematically in Figure 2.

Within Figure 2, three different message sources are depicted: an *event* (such as an earthquake), an *object* (for example, a book); and a *human being* (such as a teacher). Each source acts as an origin of signals/data/information that is encoded in various ways into a message using an appropriate linguistic framework and a relevant genre. For example, if an earthquake happens, people might find out about it either *first-hand* (by directly experiencing the vibrations and aftermath of the event) or *second-hand* (by reading a newspaper article, watching a TV broadcast or by receiving a phone-call or a SMS text message). Similarly, someone might read a book (to extract its messages) or read a review of that book (to obtain a subset of the messages that are reported by a reviewer). Invariably, people will often be exposed to multiple messages arising from a wide variety of different sources (of symbol streams). In Figure 2, these messages are denoted by the labels M_1, M_2, M_3, and so on. The curved arrows in this diagram are intended to denote possible semantic connections between the content of the different messages. The contents of the messages shown in the diagram could positively reinforce each

Figure 2. A semiotic framework for messages

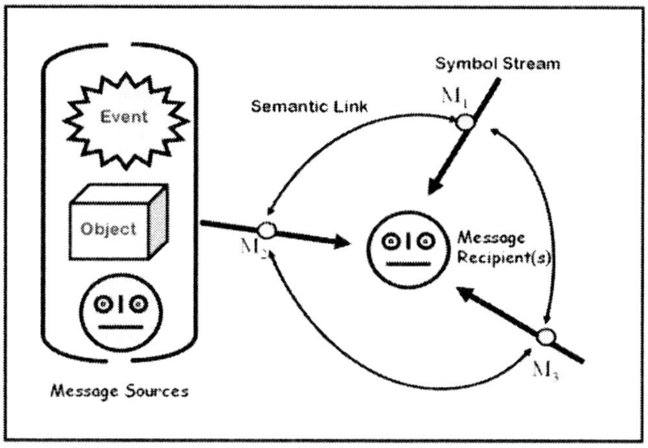

other or they might create 'dissonance' - in situations where they embed contradictory evidence. From a communication-design perspective, it is obviously important to consider how to embed appropriate stimuli in messages so that they can trigger relevant cognitive processes within the minds of their recipients - resulting in subsequent action-taking activities that are relevant to the message content. Naturally, these actions may be appropriate to the received message, or inappropriate to it - depending upon the recipient's understanding of the message, his/her cognitive make-up and the context in which the message is received.

Bearing in mind, the primal nature of messages, it is important to consider their basic characteristics and how they can be used to construct more complex communication artefacts - such as email systems, online conferencing environments, weblogs, wikis, 'participative' electronic books (Barker, 2007a) and hybrid learning environments. These topics are discussed in subsequent sections of this chapter. Within these sections, descriptive metanotation is used in order to define the basic structure and composition of the entities and artefacts that are presented and discussed. Further details on this approach are presented elsewhere (Barker, 1975; Barker and Jones, 1978; Alexander, 1987; Caplan, 2003; Foulonneau and Riley, 2007).

In subsequent sections of this chapter, descriptive metanotation will be used to describe various artefacts relating to the communication processes that were introduced and discussed in the previous section. An indication will also be given of how this approach to system definition is currently being used to specify the nature of hybrid learning systems.

HYBRID LEARNING SYSTEMS

This section briefly describes the essential structure of a learning system in terms of the types of resource needed to sustain its activities. Based on the types of 'media' involved, an attempt is made to define a typical hybrid learning system (HLS). An explanation is then given of the importance of a pervasive *messaging system* and an underlying *digital object repository.* These items form a solid foundation upon which to build such a learning system using various types of 'messaging artefact' as system components.

Most learning systems are complex human-centred organisational entities that provide a wide range of learning opportunities for their clients.

Naturally, the range and nature of the opportunities that are provided will depend critically on the characteristics of the clients and the types of environment in which they have to exist. Invariably, the provision of learning opportunities will also be strongly influenced by the type and extent of the resources which are available for their initiation and sustenance. In most cases, four broad types of generic resource are needed in order to create a learning system: human resources, conventional resources, digital resources and items related to organisational infrastructure. The relationship between these is depicted schematically in Figure 3.

Depending upon the types of resource needed to sustain the activities involved in any given learning system, it is possible to create a simple taxonomy that provides a mechanism for classifying learning systems. An *electronic learning* (e-learning) *system*, for example, will depend upon the use of resources that are essentially digital in nature; these will usually be delivered by means of some form of computer system. In a similar way, a *conventional learning system* will usually utilise human resources combined with the use of books, face-to-face classes and laboratory sessions that take place in a locally available purpose-built environment such as a school or a university. In contrast, a *distance learning system* will usually involve the distribution of resources (be they electronic or conventional) from one or more distribution units to a population of learners that are physically remote to each other and which are located in a wide variety of different study locations. Such a facility might use a virtual classroom for synchronous teaching/learning activities and a set of virtual laboratories in order to conduct various scientific experiments.

Bearing in mind what has been said above, it is possible to define a *hybrid learning system* as one in which the different types of resource depicted in Figure 3 are used in various ways in order to achieve particular types of learning outcome. As can be seen in Figure 3, within a typical learning system, communication (by means of appropriate messaging facilities) is of paramount importance. Indeed, the underlying contention of this paper is that people learn as a result of receiving messages from different sources - see Figures 1 and 2. The range of different message sources involved within any given learning environment can therefore be used to form the basis for defining a hybrid learning system.

Note that in Figure 3, the messaging systems form part of the infrastructure provided by the organisation that hosts the learning system. Obviously, although it is not shown explicitly,, there is an implicit link between the human resources shown in this diagram and the messaging systems that an organisation employs.

In its simplest of forms, a learning system is essentially an environment that enables an individual (or group of people) to acquire skills and knowledge. These important commodities will usually be needed in order to enable people to perform various tasks that are of interest to them - or which are imposed upon them by the demands of their employment. The acquisition of skills and knowledge is usually accomplished by means of some form of learning activity. Using descriptive metanotation it is possible to represent this requirement in the following way:

```
<learning-system>::= [<media-
mix><learning-activity>]{1:N}
                    & [<learner>]
{1:M} & <LAS-mapping>
<media-mix>::= [<medium>]{1|2:P}
<LAS-mapping>::= [<learner(j) has <activ-
ity-set(j)] for all j in <cohort>
<cohort>::= [<learner>]{1:M}
<medium>::= <human>|<electronic>|<paper>|
<film>| …
<electronic>::= <computer>|<calculator>|<
radio>|<television>| …
```

Bearing in mind the above description, a necessary requirement for a *hybrid learning system* is that at least two media are used in relation to

Figure 3. Schematic organisation of a learning system

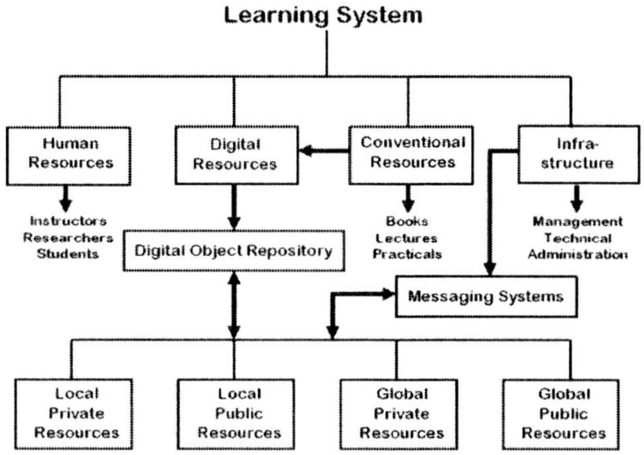

the available learning activities. In the above set of expressions, the *<LAS-mapping>* component represents a '*learner to activity-set mapping*'. That is, it is essentially an allocation structure that maps each individual student (that uses the learning system) onto an appropriate subset of the available learning activities. Each of the learning activities identified in the above expression can now be specified in terms of their important characteristics. The following expressions illustrate how this can be done:

```
<learning-activity>::= <objectives> &
<activity-chain> & <outcomes>
<activity-chain>::=[<doing-activity>]
{1:J} & <resource-set>
                    & <DAR-mapping>
```

Within the above expression, the *<doing-activity>* represents the sequence of events that need to be undertaken in order to achieve the required outcomes for the learning activity. Some examples of the types of activity that might be involved in a given learning event are listed below.

```
<doing-activity>::= <reading>|<writing>|<
listening>|<speaking>|
             <watching>|<reflecti
ng>|<communicating>|
             <collecting>|<resear
ching><calculating>|<drawing>|
             <practical-
activity>|<assessment>| ...
```

Each of the above generic types of activity can be expressed in terms of one or more different, but more specific, activities - for example:

```
<practical-activity>::= <experimenting>|<
observing>|<creating>| ...
<listening>::= <live-
lecture>|<radio>|<MP3-download>|<phone-
message>| ...
```

The list of activities given above is not exhaustive; its purpose is to illustrate rather then to define, in an exhaustive way, all the possibilities that exist. Naturally, each of the doing-activities involved in a learning event will probably require appropriate resources for their realisation. In order to accommodate this requirement, the *<DAR-mapping>* (that was introduced above) provides a mechanism for mapping the available resources onto the various doing activities that any given learner needs to participate in.

Within many learning systems there is an increasing tendency to make resources available in a digital format - primarily because of the ease with which they can be stored, manipulated, shared and controlled. For resources that are not created in a digital form, two important processes that are required to support this objective are *digitisation* and *virtualisation*. As depicted in Figure 3, digital objects created through these processes are normally stored within an organisation's (or, in some cases, an individual's) *digital object repository*. The importance of such a tool, as a mechanism for storing the substantial volume of digital resources that are involved in knowledge and skill management to support learning processes, is discussed later in the chapter.

Subsequent sections of this chapter will discuss the importance of messaging systems and digital object repositories as fundamental building blocks for the creation of a hybrid learning system. Other types of system component (such as webs, wikis, weblogs and e-books) that are based on the use of these underlying resources will also be introduced and discussed.

MESSAGING SYSTEMS

Depending upon the purposes for which they are designed, messaging systems vary both in complexity and capability. As has been discussed earlier in this chapter, fundamental to all such systems is the primitive concept of a message. Bearing this in mind, we can define a message as being a primitive communication event that facilitates the transfer of 'material' from an originator to one or more recipients. This basic requirement is embedded in the following expression:

```
<message>::= <originator><content>[<recip
ient>]{1:N}<attribute-list>
```

The *attributes* of a message could include a wide variety of possibilities - such as its date and time of creation, the medium upon which it was created, the transmission medium, the transmission route from source to destination, encryption parameters, importance, urgency, currency, semantic richness, level of ambiguity, and so on. Like all other entities, a message will have a lifecycle - that is, the time-based sequence of events to which it is subjected during the time that elapses between its creation and its ultimate destruction. During its lifetime, a message will probably reside in some kind of '*message store*'. Within electronic messaging systems, this will most likely be some form of '*digital object repository*' - as is discussed later in this chapter.

Although individual messages may be regarded as discrete entities, any given message may form part of a 'message sequence' (see Figure 2) that constitutes a (mediated) dialogue or conversation. In such situations, each message in a given set will normally have both a *temporal* (*<t-net>*) and a *semantic* relationship (*<s-net>*) with the other messages embedded within the communicative sequence of message exchanges. This idea is represented schematically in the following description:

```
<communication-event>::= [<message>]{1:N}
+ <t-net> + <s-net>
```

One of the most obvious realisations of the above idea of a communication sequence is probably embodied within an online conferencing system where a 'message space' is populated by contributions from different members of the parent forum. Other examples of online systems containing collections of electronic messages are weblogs and wikis. These are discussed in more detail in a subsequent section of this chapter.

Within a communication event, messages will normally be of two basic types: those which are sent by a given individual (we refer to these as instances of the class *<s-message>*) and those that are received by that person (denoted by *<r-message>*). The various types of communicative exchange that can now take place can be represented by various combinations of these two primitive message types. Two important categories of communication that need to be distinguished are those based on 'one-way' and 'two-way' message sequences. The two variants of a one-way sequence can be represented as follows:

```
<one-way-sequence>::= [<s-message>]{1:N}
| [<r-message>]{1:N}
```

Of course, when considering a two-way exchange, the relative 'balance' of the message flow needs to be considered - that is, the way in which sent and received messages are inter-leaved and their relative frequencies - that is the symmetry of message flow. A well-balanced message sequence (B) could be represented in the following way:

```
<B-two-way-sequence>::= [<s-message><r-
message>]{1:N}
                                    | [<r-
message><s-message>]{1:N}
```

The two options given in the above expression are needed to reflect the way in which the communication sequence is initiated - by sending a message or by the receipt of one.

In an unbalanced sequence of messages (U), the messages may not be synchronised with each other and will probably not have a regular pattern of interleaving. An attempt to capture this requirement is given in the following expression:

```
<U-two-way-sequence>::=
     <s-message> [[<r-message>]{0:1}[<s-
message>]{0:1}]{1:N}
     | <r-message> [[<s-message>]{0:1}
[<r-message>]{0:1}]{1:N}
```

In the above expression, the replication factor {0:1} is used to denote the presence or absence of the contained entity to which it refers. By choosing appropriate values for the coefficients, various patterns of message balancing can be achieved.

Within an online environment, a communication event can, in principle, involve any number of participants. This observation provides us with a useful way of discussing messaging in terms of the number of message originators or sources (S) and the number of recipients (R) that are involved. On this basis, some typical categories of messaging situation that could arise are: 1:1, 1:N, N:1 and N:M. Graphical depictions of these situations are illustrated schematically in Figure 4.

Within Figure 4, **Case A** depicts a situation involving message transfer between two individuals; notice how the 'roles' of sender and recipient can alternate depending upon the context involved. **Case B** shows a person sending a message to a mailing list that targets a large number of recipients. The situation shown in **Case C**, depicts a number of people all sending a message to a particular individual recipient - as would be the case of an online survey conducted by email or using a web-based form. **Case D** illustrates the use of a shared list-server facility in which the members of a group of authorised users can each send messages to a given target group of recipients.

As was suggested at the beginning of this section, as well as the people involved in a messaging system, the other important characteristic of a message is its *content*. There are various ways in which this can be expressed. The following expression can be used to identify seven different types of message based on different combinations (or blends) of text, audio and pictorial material:

```
<content>::= [<text-part>]{0:1}+[<audio-
part>]{0:1}+[<image-part>]{0:1}
```

Blended multimedia messages will contain various combinations of the three base resources listed above. A more precise specification of the different amounts of resource involved can be given using an expression of the following form:

```
<content>::= [<text-part>]{A:B}+[<audio-
part>]{C:D}+[<image-part>]{E:F}
```

Figure 4. Examples of simple online messaging systems

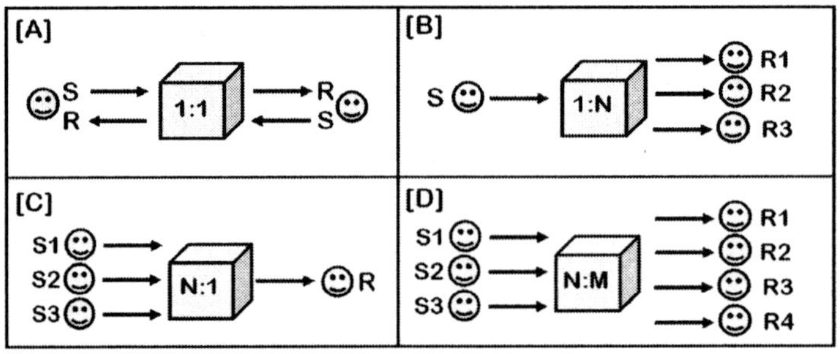

In the above expression, the replication factors {A:B}, {C:D} and {E:F} specify the upper and lower limits on the contributions that the different resources can make to a blended multimedia message.

The content of a message will, to a large extent, determine the type of message that is created. Some typical examples of different message types include: explicit, implicit and hidden. The latter category includes coded, encrypted and subliminal messages. This list of message types is by no means exhaustive but it does serve to illustrate the wide range of possibilities that exist. Naturally, different media will be able to embed different sorts of message. Indeed, returning to McLuhan's comment, which was cited earlier, the '*power*' of a medium will determine both the nature and the sophistication of the messages that it can embed.

An important aspect of the content of a message is its 'meaning'. Normally, this would probably be extracted by manual means and would involve applying an appropriate *context*, a suitable *linguistic framework* and relevant *semantic guidelines* to its interpretation (the relevance of this latter topic is discussed in more detail in the following section). Of course, in systems where there is a large volume of messages involved (such as in online conferencing situations) it may be more appropriate, or even necessary, to apply automatic methods for achieving the content analysis of messages. This topic is discussed in detail elsewhere (Leng, Huang and Liao, 2007).

DIGITAL OBJECT REPOSITORIES

Within a communication system, the various messages that 'move around' within it will have a lifecycle involving three basic phases: creation, existence and deletion. During the existence phase of their lifecycle, messages will need to be stored safely and securely until they are no longer needed. Within an electronic messaging system, messages, message components and/or message referents will usually be stored in a particular type of computer database facility known as a '*digital object repository*' (DOR) - as depicted schematically in Figure 5.

Within this figure, each of the communication artefacts that is depicted would be associated with a corresponding '*semantic framework*' (denoted by SF). In this context, a semantic framework is essentially a mechanism for adding structure and meaning to a collection of message objects extracted from the DOR. Typically, a practical implementation of such a semantic framework would produce a software constructor that would render a collection of message objects (and their associated artefacts) from the DOR into a format that is appropriate for the type of target application for which they are intended.

In its simplest form, a digital object repository is essentially a 'store-house' for a collection of digital objects along with a suitable management infrastructure for organising the objects and controlling access to them. Of course, there is no real requirement that a DOR has to reside at one particular geographic location. Indeed, for security and privacy purposes it may be distributed (as a 'DDOR' - distributed digital object repository) over several different locations - particular groups of objects then being retrieved from these different places as and when they are needed. In order to add 'meaning' to the clusters of objects embedded within them, some DORs also provide 'ready made' semantic frameworks (SFs) that enable retrieved objects to be combined (through a process of aggregation) into a form that represents particular types of artefact that are characteristic of a particular host domain.

The above ideas can be represented in terms of descriptive metanotation in the following way:

```
<digital-object-repository>::= [<digital-
object>&<digital-object-identifier>]{1:K}
<application(X)>::= <semantic-framework(X
)>&<constructor(X)>&<object-set>
<object-set>::= [<object>]{1:Q}: <object>
ISIN <digital-object-repository>
                              AND <object>
ISIN <selection(X)>
```

There are numerous examples of DOR systems and architectures available for the creation and management of digital assets - particularly, in the library domain. Probably one of the most well known of these is the '*Fedora*' system that was developed at Cornell University in the USA (Payette, and Lagoze, 1998). Fedora is an acronym for '*Flexible and Extensible Digital Object Repository Architecture*'; an overview description of this system can be found in (Wikipedia, 2007b). As this is a very active research area, there are numerous other examples of practical DOR systems described in the research literature - see, for example, the '*aDORe*' system (Van de Sompel et al, 2005) which was developed at the Los Alamos National Laboratory in the USA and the '*Pennsylvania Education Network Digital Object Repository*' (PEN-DOR) described by Fullerton et al (1999). DOR systems similar to these are currently widely used as the underlying basis for the creation of most digital library systems. A good example of this type of usage can be found in the use of a repository for building the digital collection hosted by the Australian National Library (http://www.nla.gov.au/digicoll/oai).

Although sophisticated DORs are required for organising large digital collections such as those cited above, the principles involved can be applied on a much smaller scale. For example, someone who has a large personal collection of digital images that have been captured using a digital camera could create a repository in order to store the various 'base' images along with different transformations of them. In an application such as this, a base image refers to the original photograph taken by the camera while the transformed images arise as a result of applying different types of image processing operation to this image - such as, resizing, cropping and the application of different types of 'special effect'. Obviously, the underlying principles of a digital repository can be applied to any kind of digital collection - for example, digital music in MP3 format (say), video clips, digitised text, digital text, and so on.

In our own work, we have been using repositories as supporting infrastructures for the creation of the system components needed to create hybrid learning systems (as depicted in Figure 5). Such components include various types of web, wiki and weblog structures. Other important components of our HLS include dynamic and flexible electronic book systems. For this latter type of application, the various components that make up an e-book (text fragments, images, application-orientated digital data, sound clips, video clips, and so on) are held in a DOR - being stored as discrete elements. When a particular page of a book (or the whole book) is needed for 'publication' in printed form or for display on a screen, the e-book SF constructor retrieves the relevant components from the DOR and builds the target objects (a page or the complete book) using an

Figure 5. The role of a digital object repository in messaging systems

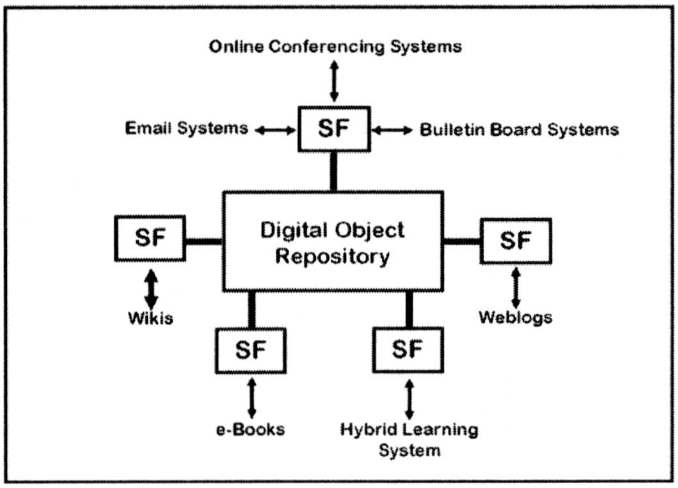

'on-demand' strategy. Of course, the primitive objects in the repository could be retrieved and put together in many different ways in order to create different variants of the book - or indeed, a different type of book. For example, a subset of the photographs in the DOR could be retrieved and published as a picture book or as a photo-album (by using different SF constructors). Similarly, the digital maps held in our DOR system could be retrieved and published as an atlas. Our use of a DOR for producing 'participative' electronic books is discussed later in the chapter.

Undoubtedly, digital object repositories provide a very powerful tool for the storage of collections of digital assets - be they for a large organisation or for individual, personal use. As is discussed elsewhere, for example, our '*PeDAL*' system provides an illustration of how such systems can be used for managing personal collections of digital assets within the context of a hybrid learning environment (Barker, 2007b).

MESSAGING ARTEFACTS: WEBS, WIKIS, WEBLOGS AND E-BOOKS

The underlying contention of this chapter is that messages, in one form or another, form the basis for all human-human communication - be this direct or mediated by artefacts such as books or electronic mail systems. Simple messages, as used in electronic mail or SMS texting may be very short and might only contain a single idea, fact or concept. More complex messages will usually be embedded within larger artefacts - such as poems, books, films, songs, research papers, and so on. Indeed, as has been suggested earlier, these larger communication artefacts will usually contain an aggregation of messages that are integrated into a larger entity (such as an email system or an on-line conferencing system) through the creation of appropriate <*t-net*> and <*s-net*> structures. The former denotes the temporal relationships between the ideas/messages embedded in a communication corpus. Similarly, the <*s-net*> is a structure that integrates the various semantic elements embedded within the corpus under consideration.

Bearing in mind what has been said in the previous parts of the chapter, this current section illustrates and discusses how webs, wikis and weblogs (as human-communication artefacts) fit into the framework of messaging systems that has previously been discussed. This discussion commences with a consideration of the conceptual composition of a conventional web page and then goes on to consider the other types of system component referred to in the previous section.

Using Conventional Web Structures

In terms of the notation that was introduced earlier in the chapter, the conceptual make up of a simple web site could be represented in the following way:

```
<web>::= [<page>]{1:N} + <link-set>
<page>::= [display-part]{1:P} + [<action-
part>]{1:Q}
                              + [<page-map-
ping>]{1:R}
<display-part>::= [<message> + <message-
wrapper>]{1:S}
<action-part>::= [<action-agent> + <ac-
tion-wrapper>]{1:T}
```

In the above description, the *<link-set>* describes the linkages between the different pages that make up a multi-page web object - thereby defining its overall structure. The individual web pages themselves consist of two basic parts: material for display and actions that a user can perform; the *<page-mapping>* describes how the basic page components (extracted from a repository) are physically organised on a display medium such as a CRT screen. The *<display-part>* of the page embeds one or more messages, each one of which may be 'wrapped up' within the conventions of the linguistic framework and modalities that are used for its representation (see Figure 1). Similarly, each of the allowed actions available on a given web page will be 'wrapped' within an appropriate action wrapper - such as an icon, scroll-bar, button, textual hyperlink, menu-item, and so on. The wrapper for a message (and/or an action) forms a number of different purposes. For example, it is likely to embed the motivational stimuli referred to earlier in the introduction to this chapter. Wrappers can also be used to fine-tune a primitive (or un-adorned) message to the particular needs of different audiences.

As is depicted in Figure 6, a conventional web site can be thought of as a 1:N communication system in which an organisation, a group or an individual author 'posts' material for some population of consumers to access. The major direction of message flow is thus from author to consumers. There is relatively little explicit message flow from consumers back to the author or owner of the web page. Small volumes of feedback that do 'go back' to the web and/or its author are denoted by small arrows in Figure 6.

Of course, there is no reason why the communication bandwidth available through a particular web site should not be shared by several authors or (within an organisation) several different departments - each with its own set of messages. In

Figure 6. A conventional web site interpreted as a 1:N messaging system

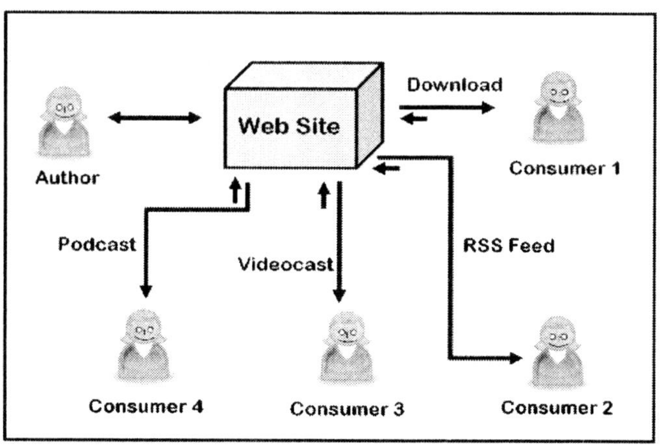

this situation the web site takes on some of the characteristics of a N:M messaging system - that is, N senders communicating in a one-way fashion with M recipients.

Using Weblogs

In order to shift the focus of control with respect to message creation within systems similar to that depicted in Figure 6, weblogs (also known as 'blogs') have emerged and have proven to be very powerful messaging facility within a variety of different application contexts (Clyde, 2004; Barker, 2005; Bruns and Jacobs, 2007; Wikipedia, 2007c). The mechanism by which a weblog functions is illustrated schematically in Figure 7.

As depicted in this figure, a weblog is a more explicit example of a messaging system that mixes both 1:N transfer (from author to participants) and N:1 flow (from participants to author). In Figure 7, the message set (M) that originates from the blog owner forms the vertical 'spine' of the diagram. Each message has associated with it a comment chain (C). Some of the important weblog components depicted in the diagram include: the message *archive* (this will probably be based on a digital object repository); a *search engine* (for locating messages that fit a particular description); and an *index* (to facilitate rapid access to specific entries in the blog).

In keeping with the approach used earlier in this section, it is useful to attempt to define and represent the various features of a weblog using descriptive metalanguage. The following ordered list of expressions documents one approach for achieving this (Barker, 2005):

```
<blog-space>::= <blog-set> + <link-set>
<blog-set>::= [<blog>]{1:N}
<link-set>::= [<link>]{0:M}
<link>::= <inter-blog-link> | <intra-
blog-link> | <external-link>
<inter-blog-link>::= <source-blog-entry-
address> to <target-blog-entry-address>
<intra-blog-link>::= <source-posting-en-
try> to <target-posting-entry>
<blog>::= [<posting><date-time-
stamp>[<comment-set>]{0:1}]
{1:P}<index><archive>
<comment-set>::= [<comment><date-time-
stamp>]{1:Q}
```

In the above definition, the 'blog-space' refers to the universe of all weblogs relevant to a particular situation or application space. Weblogs can be interlinked in various ways by cross-referencing messages in one blog with those in another. In the same way, messages (or postings) within a given blog can also be inter-linked in a variety of different ways. Within the definition of

Figure 7. A conceptual architecture for a weblog

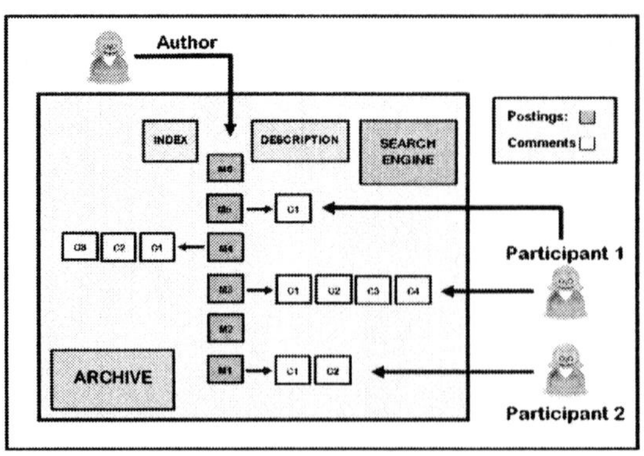

a <*blog*> (given in line 7 of the above listing), the term <*posting*> should be regarded as being synonymous to the term <*message*>. Similarly, a <*comment*> is essentially a message (or posting) sent by one of the blog participants in relation to a message posted by the blog author.

The importance of blogging as a shared community activity is reflected in the rapid growth of community weblogs in which people 'talk about' and discuss matters of interest and importance within their local communities. An example of this can be found in the '*TS20 Blog*' at http://TS20.gazettelive.co.uk. Within the local area that it serves, this is just one of a number of parallel ongoing blogs (organised in terms of their UK national post code) run by a local newspaper publisher. The system uses the *Movable Type Publishing Platform* (Wikipedia, 2007d) as an 'umbrella' system for hosting all the different types of blog (clubs, societies, gossip, news, comments and commentaries, etc) within the range of post codes involved. The blogs embedded within this system can contain a wide variety of digital resources. For example, my own weblog (which I run for a local rambling club) contains text, pictures, photographs, images (such as digital maps), diagrams, sound clips, video clips, and so on.

Using Wikis

Software of the type described above is often referred to as 'social software' because of the ways in which it allows online communities to communicate with each other through various types of 'message passing'. In this context, another very important category of social software is 'the wiki' (Klobas, 2006; Ebersbach et al, 2006; Barker, 2007c; Wikipedia, 2007e). A wiki can be thought of as a N:M messaging system in which a community of N authors (as creators of messages) provide material for consumption by an audience of M recipients (consumers of messages). Of course, within an open wiki system, it is possible for anyone to be an author as well as being a consumer of material. The basic concepts upon which a wiki structure is based are illustrated schematically in Figure 8.

This diagram is intended to portray a wiki as an interconnected collection of fully editable web pages (denoted by the labels $\boldsymbol{WP_1}$ through $\boldsymbol{WP_n}$) that could also embed further wiki webs (as indicated by the labels $\boldsymbol{WW_1}$ through $\boldsymbol{WW_n}$). Naturally, each page of a wiki can embed numerous different messages. The 'thick' broad arrows depicted in this diagram (connecting people to

Figure 8. A wiki interpreted as a N:M human-messaging system

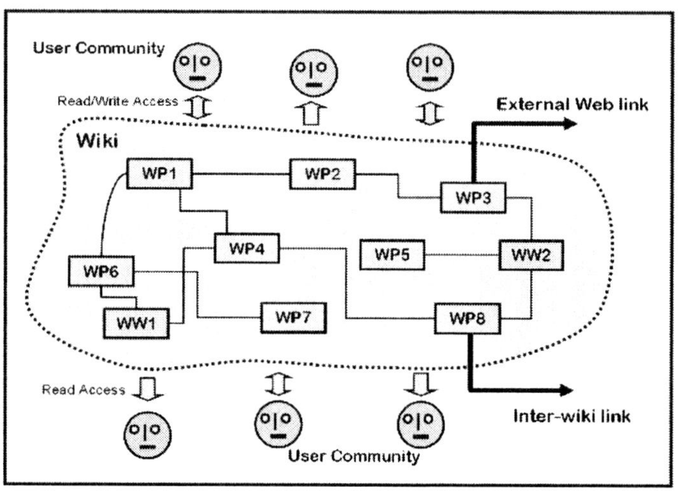

the wiki) represent the ability, on the part of a user, to create, read and/or modify selected pages within the structure. How these functions map onto individual user-capabilities will depend upon the access rights assigned to these users. Of course, there may also be pages within the wiki that are 'hidden' from ordinary users; such pages are normally associated with the various administrative processes associated with running the wiki and would usually only be seen by those who have 'admin' rights. As is the case with a conventional (or electronic book) each wiki page can be regarded as a collection of messages that are 'glued together' using the linguistic framework and semantic rules that are agreed upon for that page (or for the wiki as a whole).

In keeping with the approach that was used earlier in this section (for talking about conventional webs and weblogs), it is possible to use descriptive metalanguage to describe the concept of a 'wiki-space' (for a particular area of interest - say, chemistry or physics) in terms of an inter-related collection of wikis. Such a structure could be represented using the following expression:

```
<wiki-space>::= [<wiki>]{1:N} + <link-
set>
```

A simple wiki-space relating to the discipline of chemistry might therefore be represented as:

```
<chemistry-wiki-space>::= <organic-wiki>
+ <inorganic-wiki> + <link-set>
```

One of the attractive features of descriptive metalanguage is its ability to generalise situations of interest. The specific wiki structure depicted in Figure 8 could therefore be generalised using the following approach:

```
<wiki>::= <node-set> + <link-set> +
<link-mapping> + <properties>
<node-set>::= [<node>]{1:N}
<link-set>::= [<link>]{1:P}
<link-mapping>::= [<source-node><target-
node>]{1:Q}
<properties>::= <end-user-interface> +
[<functions>]{1:W}
<link>::= <intra-wiki-link> | <inter-wi-
ki-link> | <external-link>
<node>::= <RO-node> | <RW-node> | <hid-
den-node> | <wiki-web-node>
<wiki-web-node>::= <wiki>
```

In the above notation, the abbreviations **RO** and **RW** denote 'read-only' and 'read-write' capabilities, respectively. Naturally, these access capabilities would normally map (individually) onto the various members of the wiki's user community. Although they are not further discussed in this current treatment, the nature of the *<function>*s provided by a wiki and its *<end-user-interface>* also need to be defined. Another important issue that needs to be addressed is the characteristics of the various *<node>*s that make up a wiki. Because of its importance in relation to the different types of knowledge that a wiki embeds (for example, textual, graphical, executable, and so on) the *<mediality>* property of nodes needs to be introduced. In order to utilise this property, the definition of *<node>* that was given above would need to be modified in the following way:

```
<node>::= <node-type> + <node-content> +
<node-history>
<node-type>::= <RO-node> | <RW-node> |
<hidden-node> | <wiki-web-node>
<node-content>::= <monomedia-node> |
<multimedia-node>
<monomedia-node>::= <text-node> | <graph-
ic-node> | <audio-node>
<multimedia-node>::= [<text-part>]
{A:B}+[<graphic-part>]{C:D}
                    +[<audio-part>]
{E:F}
<node-history>::= [<version(J)>]{J=1,N}#
+ [<amendment(K)>]{K=1,M}#
```

In the fifth line of the above amended definition, replication operators have been introduced in order to describe the various blends of knowledge (as embedded messages) that a node might contain. Of course, the history of the knowledge nodes in a wiki web would also be another important property to consider - as this defines how a given page has evolved. These more involved issues of wiki definition are discussed in more detail in another paper (Barker, 2007d)

The wiki concept is an extremely important one. This is evidenced by the substantial interest shown in projects such as Wikipedia (http://en.wikipedia.org/wiki/), Wikitravel (*http://wikitravel.org/en/*) and Wiktionary (http://en.wiktionary.org). However, it is possible to apply the principles underlying a wiki to the more general domain of electronic books. The term 'wiki book' is often used in this context (http://en.wikibooks.org). An example of one particular type of wiki book that we have been designing and building (and the important role of messages therein) is briefly described in the following section.

Using Participative Electronic Books

As part of our research effort into the specification, design and fabrication of hybrid learning systems, we have been exploring the role that both conventional (*<p-book>*) and electronic (<e-book>) book artefacts might play within such a learning environment - along with the other types of system component that were described in the previous section. Bearing in mind the definitions that were presented earlier in this chapter, 'book' resources fit into the system in the following way:

```
<resource-set>::=
<book>|<web>|<weblog>|<wiki>| ...
<book>::= <e-book>|<p-book>
```

In their simplest form, books may be thought of as a structured collection of pages - each page containing one or more messages. For convenience, pages are often arranged within some form of organisational unit - such as a chapter or a section. The ideas inherent in this concept of a book can be represented using descriptive metanotation in the following way:

```
<book>::= <front-part>><body><back-part>
<body>::= [<chapter>]{1:N}
<chapter>:: [<page>]{1:P}
```

In the above definition, no mention is made of the medium upon which a book is published - this could be paper or it could be an electronic medium. Of course, electronic media provide many opportunities for creating new types of book (such as audio books) that embed facilities that are not available in conventional printed books.

The underlying basis for much of our ongoing research and development work within the domain of e-books has been described in detail elsewhere (Barker, 1996; 1997a; 1997b). As well as describing a basic conceptual model for electronic books, we also introduced a number of taxonomies for classifying different types of e-book. One of our taxonomies was used to categorise e-books into three basic types (static, dynamic and living) depending upon the characteristics of the material that they contained.

In essence, a wiki book is an electronic artefact arising from combining a book metaphor with a wiki structure. The underlying wiki is therefore 'made to look' like a book - thereby giving this type of 'book' manifestation many of the properties of a wiki. For example, pages of a wiki book can embed direct links to a dictionary, an encyclopaedia and various other types of online resource such as a digital library, a personal electronic archive, simulations, animations, and so on. Users can also make comments and ask questions about the content. Each page within a wiki book is essentially a node within the underlying wiki web structure upon which it is built (see Figure 8). Bearing in mind the tripartite e-book taxonomy that was introduced above, a participative book is thus an example of a 'living book' (Barker, 1996). Such books embed three basic types of message flow: control messages (between authors), informative display messages (from authors to readers) and participatory messages (from readers to each other and from readers to authors).

A sample page from one of our participative wiki books is depicted in Figure 9 (Barker, 2007e). This diagram shows how a dynamic page for an outdoor activity book can be constructed from relevant objects held in a digital object repository that contains walk descriptions, walk statistics, photographs, digital maps and coordinate data that can be downloaded to a personal GPS navigation system or a GPS-enabled mobile phone.

Within the menu-option list depicted at the bottom of the page (shown in Figure 9) there is a 'comment' option that allows users to send messages to the author of the page and/or other users. Of course, many different authors could be involved in the creation of this type of book. In order to facilitate communication between them, a dedicated 'message channel' is made available and devoted solely for message passing between authors and the publisher of the book.

The type of wiki book that is illustrated in Figure 9 can be represented using descriptive metanotation in the following way:

```
<wiki-book>::= <front><main-body><back>
<front>::= <front-page><[<index-page>]
{1:Q}
<index-page>::= [<index-entry>]{1:Q1}
<back>::= [<credits-page>]{1:Y}<back-
page>
<credit>::= [<credit>]{1:Y1}
<main-body>::= [<contents-page>]{1:W}
<content-page>::= <descriptive-
content><action-part><support-tools>
<action-part>::= [<action-option><option-
wrapper>]{1:Z}
<action-option>::= 'back' | 'download
route' | 'download-map' | 'comment'
```

Figure 9. Example of a page from a participative wiki book

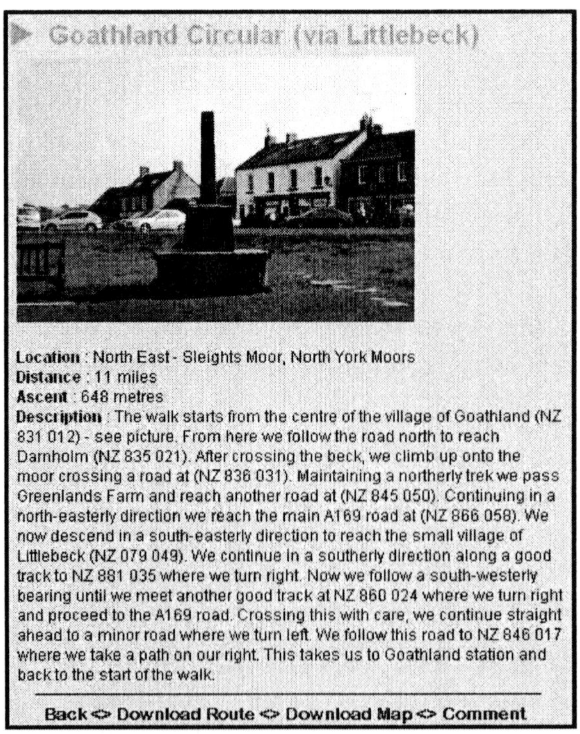

In the above description, the index entries are essentially textual descriptors that are hyperlinked to the book's contents. Each index entry leads to a particular page similar to that shown in Figure 9. The 'back' option depicted in this diagram leads the user back to the index pages of the book. The definition of the descriptive content of the pages in a book of this sort will be similar to the definition of the monomedia and multimedia nodes presented in the definition of a wiki.

FUTURE WORK

Learning is a never-ending ubiquitous activity. It takes place in both explicit and implicit ways; it can be both serendipitous and pre-planned. Of course, because people are 'mobile' agents, learning can take place in a variety of different contexts within a multitude of different types of location. This places considerable demands on both conventional 'fixed-location' learning environments and distance learning systems. As people move from one location to another, their learning needs are likely to change - as will their modes and styles of learning. Fortunately, hybrid learning systems that embed an architecture which is similar to that described in this chapter (see Figure 3) offer a useful mechanism for overcoming the limitations of conventional approaches to learning system provision. Indeed, a suitably designed hybrid learning system can offer the possibility for enabling dynamic and flexible allocation of learning resources using an 'on-demand' or an 'as needed' strategy. In our future work, in this area, we would hope to explore some of the important issues that underlie the realisation of this development - for example, the virtualisation of locally situated resources so that they can become globally accessible to communities of online, offline and mobile learners.

Another important future aspect of our work in the area of hybrid learning systems will involve the provision of tools and techniques to support a learner's knowledge and skill management activities (Barker, 2008). This work involves the development of a portable knowledge management facility that is capable of organising the multitude of digital objects that are involved in creating a personalised hybrid learning system for a mobile learner. Our work focuses on mobile learners since we believe that in the future most people will want to learn in a variety of different places (a university campus, at home, in a library, at work, and so on) using a wide range of different kinds of delivery platform (such as a desktop PC, a laptop computer, a pocket computer or a mobile phone). This work has involved the design and creation of a '*Personal Digital Archive for Learning*' (PeDAL) based on the use of a digital object repository (for storing learning objects) and a personalised wiki facility for managing the collection of knowledge objects that it contains (Barker, 2007b). We are now designing a *digital knowledge pocket book* as a new type of delivery platform that will facilitate access to portable and remotely located collections of information and knowledge.

CONCLUSION

Sharing ideas, thoughts and observations with others is fundamental to teaching and learning activities. It requires the creation (within the mind) of basic 'packets' of information which can be transmitted (in various ways) to those others with whom we wish to share. The term 'message' is commonly used to refer to these communication packets. Messages are usually generated as a result of some observational process that is made upon events that take place either within or without a system of observation. Simple messages can be aggregated and combined in various ways to create a wide range of different communication artefacts. Sharing (and hence learning) requires the transmission of messages via appropriate channels of communication (as was illustrated in Figure

1). Each channel requires the availability of a linguistic framework and a semantic infrastructure within which to 'wrap' the messages that are to be sent. Naturally, the impact of a message can be strongly influenced by its genre or communication style. Undoubtedly, messages and 'messaging' are of paramount importance within all areas of human activity.

Of course, it is important to remember that the generation of messages is not purely a human prerogative; animals, machines, and especially computers, can also generate messages. However, the intent of this chapter has been to concentrate on messages originating from humans as part of the human-to-human (machine-mediated) communication systems that underlie many learning processes. Various artefacts relating to this goal have been discussed and their similarities and differences briefly outlined in terms of the types of message that can be sent and the nature of the message flows (or protocols) that are involved.

The main thrust of this chapter has been concerned, primarily, with asynchronous modes of communication. However, much of what has been said will apply equally well to (or could be extended to cover) synchronous messaging systems - such as a telephone conversation, Internet chat and real-time online conferencing.

ACKNOWLEDGMENT

The author is indebted to *Anquet Technology Ltd* (UK), for providing access to its digital map collection and archive of walking routes. He would also like to thank the two anonymous referees who made some valuable suggestions for improving the original manuscript.

REFERENCES

Alexander, H. (1987). *Formally-Based Tools and Techniques for Human-Computer Dialogues*. Chichester, UK: Ellis Horwood Limited.

Barker, P. G. (1975). Syntactic Definition and Parsing of Molecular Formula. Part 1: Initial Syntax Definition and Parser Implementation. *The Computer Journal, 18*(4), 355–359. doi:10.1093/comjnl/18.4.355

Barker, P. G. (1996). Living Books and Dynamic Electronic Libraries. *The Electronic Library, 14*(6), 491–501. doi:10.1108/eb045515

Barker, P. G. (1997a). Electronic Libraries of the Future, In A. Kent & C.M. Hall (Eds.), *Encyclopedia of Library and Information Science* (Vol. 50, Supp. 22, pp. 119-153). New York: Marcel Dekker.

Barker, P. G. (1997b). Electronic Documents and their Role in Future Library Systems, In D. Raitt (Ed.), *Libraries for the New Millenium - Implications for Managers* (pp. 89-113). London, UK: Library Association Publishing.

Barker, P. G. (2005). Potential Uses of Weblogs in Electronic Course Delivery. In G. Richards (Ed.), Proceedings of the *E-LEARN 2005 World Conference on E-Learning in Corporate, Government Healthcare & Higher Education* (pp.515-522). Norfolk, Virginia, USA: Association for the Advancement of Computing in Education.

Barker, P. G. (2007a). *Designing and Building Electronic Books* (Research Seminar). Middlesbrough, UK: University of Teesside, Barker, P.G. (2007b). *Using PEAs and PeDALs for Personal Knowledge and Information Management* (Research Seminar). Middlesbrough, UK: University of Teesside.

Barker, P. G. (2007c). Using Wikis as a Teaching and Learning Resource. In C.P. Constantinou, Z.C. Zacharia, & M. Papaevripidou (Eds.), *Proceedings of the CBLIS 2007 International Conference on Computer-Based Learning in Science - Contemporary Perspectives in New Technologies in Science and Education* (pp. 12-23). Nicosia, Cyprus: Learning in Science Group, University of Cyprus.

Barker, P. G. (2007d). Blended Learning the Wiki Way. In *Proceedings of the 2nd International Conference on Blended Learning - Supporting the Net Generation Learner* (pp. 60-71). Hatfield, UK: University of Hertfordshire.

Barker, P. G. (2007e). *Published GPS Walking Routes*. London: Anquet Technology Ltd.

Barker, P. G. (2008). Blended Electronic Learning - Managing the Blend. In *Proceedings of the 3rd International Conference on Blended Learning -Enhancing the Student Experience* (pp. 45-53). Hatfield, UK: University of Hertfordshire.

Barker, P. G., & Jones, P. (1978). Syntactic Definition and Parsing of Molecular Formula. Part 2: Graphical Synthesis of Molecular Formula for Data Base Queries. *The Computer Journal, 21*(3), 224–233. doi:10.1093/comjnl/21.3.224

Bruns, A., & Jacobs, J. (2006). *Uses of Blogs*. New York: Peter Lang Publishing.

Caplan, P. (2003). *Metadata Fundamentals for all Librarians*. Chicago: American Library Association.

Chandler, D. (2006). *Semiotics: The Basics* (2nd ed.). London: Routledge.

Cherry, C. (1971). *On Human Communication - a Review, a Survey and a Criticism* (2nd ed.). Cambridge, MA: The MIT Press.

Clyde, L.A. (2004). *Weblogs in Libraries*. Oxford, UK: Chandos Publishing.

de Souza, C. S. (2005). *The Semiotic Engineering of Human-Computer Interaction*. Cambridge, MA: The MIT Press.

Ebersbach, A., Glaser, M., & Heigl, R. (2006). *Wiki Web Collaboration*. Heidelberg, Germany: Springer-Verlag.

Eisenstein, E. L. (1980). *The Printing Press as an Agent of Change*. Cambridge, UK: Cambridge University Press.

Foulonneau, M., & Riley, J. (2007). *Metadata for Digital Resources: Implementation, Systems Design and Interoperability*. Oxford, UK: Chandos Publishing.

Fullerton, K., Greenberg, J., McClure, M., Rasmussen, E., & Stewart, D. (1999). A Digital Library for Education: the PEN-DOR Project. *The Electronic Library, 17*(2), 75–82. doi:10.1108/02640479910334279

Klobas, J. (2006). *Wikis: Tools, Information Work and Collaboration*. Oxford, UK: Chandos Publishing.

Leng, J., Huang, R., & Liao, J. (2007). Research on FCA and its Application to Content Analysis of Online Learning. In *Proceedings of the E-LEARN 2007 World Conference on E-Learning in Corporate, Government Healthcare & Higher Education*. Norfolk, Virginia, USA: Association for the Advancement of Computing in Education.

McLuhan, M. (2001). *Understanding Media*. Oxford, UK: Routledge Classics, Taylor and Francis.

Payette, S., & Lagoze, C. (1998). Flexible and Extensible Digital Object and Repository Architecture (FEDORA). *Lecture Notes in Computer Science, 1513*, 41-59. Berlin, Germany: Springer-Verlag. Retrieved from http://www.cs.cornell.edu/payette/papers/ECDL98/FEDORA.html van der Sompel, H., Bekaert, J., Liu, X., Balakireva, L., & Schwander, T. (2005). aDORe: a Modular Standards-Based Digital Object Repository. *The Computer Journal, 48*(5), 514-535.

Shannon, C. E. (1948). A Mathematical Theory of Communication. *The Bell System Technical Journal, 27*, 379–423, 623–656.

Wikipedia. (2007a). *Claude Shannon*. Retrieved November 13, 2008 from http://en.wikipedia.org/wiki/Claude_Shannon

Wikipedia. (2007b). *Fedora (Software)*. Retrieved November 13, 2008 from http://en.wikipedia.org/wiki/Fedora_(software)

Wikipedia. (2007c). B*logs and Blogging*. Retrieved November 13, 2008 from http://en.wikipedia.org/wiki/Blog

Wikipedia. (2007d). *Movable Type Publishing Platform*. Retrieved November 13, 2008 from http://en.wikipedia.org/wiki/MoveableType

Wikipedia. (2007e). *Wikis*. Retrieved November 13, 2008 from http://en.wikipedia.org/wiki/wiki

Worstall, T. (2005). *2005 Blogged: Despatches from the Blogosphere*. London, UK: Friday Books.

KEY TERMS AND DEFINITIONS

Communication: Communication is a process by which signals, data, information or knowledge is transferred from one location to another. Usually this involves a *sending agent*, a *transmission mechanism* and one or more *receiving agents*. Communication can take place between people - for example, one person talking to another. It can also take place between people and the various other types of object that they use - such as computers and mobile phones. Often, the use of technology to support communication between people is often referred to as technology-mediated communication. Communication can also take place between different types of machine - particularly, computers.

Descriptive Metanotation: Within the context of studying systems, a metanotation is a *linguistic framework* that is used to describe the nature, structure and behaviour of different types of system. Metanotations usually consist of a pre-defined (axiomatic) set of *primitive objects*, *classes of constructed objects*, *rule sets* and *transformation operators* that can convert one type of object into another according to the rules specified in the set of rules.

Digital Object Repository: This is a digital storage facility upon which are stored various types of *digital artefacts* such as messages, images, sound clips, text, and so on. The repository provides mechanisms for *storing*, *retrieving* and *managing* the objects that are sent to it. This type of storage system usually requires various types of management processes in order to ensure that the contained objects are stored in a way that ensures their efficient retrieval as and when they are needed.

Dynamic Web-Based Artefact: A web-based artefact is an object that exists within the context of an electronic web structure. Web pages are the most common example; these can be of two basic types: *static* and *dynamic*. The latter are able to change their content and appearance as a result of various types of perturbation (or *change agent*) that are applied to them. Two of the most common types of dynamic web-based structure are *wikis* and *weblogs* - of course, there are many other types of dynamic web artefact such as bulletin boards and online conferencing systems.

Electronic Book: An electronic book is essentially a corpus of electronic information to which a *book metaphor* has been applied. This gives the corpus many of the structural and visual attributes that are normally associated with conventional paper-based books. There are many advantages associated with electronic books - for example, ease of distribution, updating and searching. Collections of electronic books are usually stored in a digital library facility along with other types of similar artefact such as electronic journals and electronic pamphlets.

Learning System: A learning system is essentially a collection of artefacts that are 'brought together', in an appropriate way, in order to create an environment that will *facilitate* various types of *learning process*. Learning systems can take a variety of different forms - for example, a book, a mobile form, a computer, an online forum, a school and a university. Most learning systems will provide various types of learning resource and descriptions of procedures for using these to achieve particular learning outcomes. They will also embed various strategies for assessing the levels and quality of the achievement of their users.

Messaging System: A message is a communication artefact that is used to *transfer information* from one entity to another. Messages can take a wide variety of different forms - for example, a gesture, a postal letter, a SMS text, an electronic message. A messaging system is an infrastructure that facilitates the *creation, transmission, delivery* and *storage* of messages. Electronic mail is an example of a messaging system since it provides facilities for creating sending, receibving and storing electronic messages.

Semiotics: This term is used to describe the scientific study of *signs* and *symbols* and the relationships that exist between them in relation to the creation of messages and the *meaning* that these messages embed. Signs and symbols can take many different forms - for example, textual, sonic and graphical. The meaning of symbols often depends upon their size, colour, proximity, order of presentation, and so on.

Chapter 4
A Tabular Approach to Outcome-Based Course Planning and Assessment

Oliver T. S. Au
City University of Hong Kong, Hong Kong

ABSTRACT

Many educational institutions are migrating towards outcome-based teaching and learning. Being true to criterion-referenced assessment, students' final grades are often determined elaborately on a set of complex rules. The author proposes a tabular approach to help instructors in course planning and assessment. The resulting course plan consists of tables that show learning outcomes, study topics, teaching, learning and assessment activities in rows and columns. Instructors can more easily spot misalignments between items on the tables. Though marks are assigned to learning outcomes, students' final grades are still assessed criterion-referenced rather than norm-referenced. This mark-based assessment is transparent and familiar to students. The tabular approach may reduce the OBTL migration effort of the instructors and improve the learning experience of the students.

INTRODUCTION

Outcomes are clear, observable demonstrations of student learning (Spady & Marshall, 1994; Towers, 1996). In outcome-based teaching and learning (OBTL), course intended learning outcomes (CILOs) are used to derive the teaching, learning and assessment (TLA) activities. When TLA activities are chosen to support student achievement of CILOs, they are said to be constructively aligned with the CILOs (Biggs, 2003). Constructive alignment is required to realize the benefits promised by OBTL. We advocate a tabular approach to facilitate visual inspection of constructive alignment. We also advocate the assignment of marks to CILOs for the calculation of students' final grades. Though this mark-based approach differs from the commonly used rule-based approach, it does not necessarily stray from the criterion-referenced assessments endorsed by OBTL purists.

First we discuss one of the challenges to implement OBTL, namely assessment. Our approach is

DOI: 10.4018/978-1-60566-380-7.ch004

Table 1. Action verbs based on Bloom's Taxonomy of Cognitive Learning

Class	Action Verbs
1. Knowledge	write, state, recall, recognize, select, reproduce, list
2. Comprehension	identify, illustrate, represent, formulate, explain, contrast, paraphrase, summarize
3. Application	predict, select, assess, find, show, use, construct, compute, solve
4. Analysis	select, compare, separate, differentiate, contrast, break down, classify
5. Synthesis	summarize, argue, relate, organize, generalize, conclude, design
6. Evaluate	judge, evaluate, support, recognize, criticize

illustrated with a simple example of a software design course. We then create the CILO table with weights assigned to learning outcomes. The weights reflect the relative importance of the various CILOs useful for the final grade determination. We then create the syllabus table to ensure that study topics align with CILOs. The TLA table is the last table we create that ensures the alignment of teaching and learning activities with the CILOs. It shows the marks of assessment activities distributed over the CILOs.

THE CHALLENGE OF ASSESSING STUDENTS IN OBTL

An early task in planning an OBTL course is to write the CILOs. The majority of courses do well with five to seven CILOs. A CILO begins with an action verb of a student's ability. Verbs like 'understand' or 'appreciate' are to avoid because their attainment cannot be objectively observed. Table 1 shows a list of verbs that may be used (Bloom, 1956). Note that some action verbs belong to more than one class.

Writing CILOs is actually easier than the subsequent challenge of assessing the students. A student may be better at one CILO but weaker at another. At the end of the course, we need to assign a percentage or a letter grade to every student. How do we amalgamate the performance of multiple CILOs into a final grade?

There are two main grading systems: norm-referenced assessment (NRA) and criterion-referenced assessment (CRA). In NRA, a student is graded in comparison to other students. A grade B performance last year may earn a student a grade A now just because he or she belongs to a weaker cohort. In CRA, a student is graded against predefined criteria. A grade B performance last year will still be grade B this year even if it is at the top of the class. The majority of educationists, most notably the OBTL purists, tend to advocate CRA (Frankland, 2009; Biggs, 2003).

As an example, we shall consider an OBTL course with 5 CILOs. Students may perform each CILO in one of four levels: excellent, good, pass and fail. The following rules may be used to grade a student.

1. Grade D for passing any 4 CILOs
2. Grade C for 2 good CILOs with 2 other passing CILOs
3. Grade B for 1 excellent CILO, 1 good CILO and 2 more passing CILOs
4. Grade A for 2 CILOs at the level of excellent and passing all other CILOs

Consider a student with an excellent CILO and 4 passing CILOs. According to the above rules, the student will only get grade C. If the extra passing CILO can substitute the missing good CILO, the student will get grade B. Should such a substitution be allowed? It is tedious to devise and use a

Table 2. CILO table

ID	CILO Description	Weight
1	Draw UML diagrams	15%
2	Create requirements specifications	15%
3	Create analysis models	20%
4	Create system design documents	20%
5	Select appropriate design pattern for reuse	10%
6	Write interface specifications in OCL	10%
7	Transform models to code and databases	10%
		100%

set of comprehensive rules to cover all possible scenarios. It is difficult to justify the rules and explain them to students. Our approach attempts to address this problem by assigning weights to CILOs. We will explain that the use of weights or marks do not necessarily mean that we have gone norm-referenced.

COURSE INTENDED LEARNING OUTCOME (CILO) TABLE

The benefits of OBTL are in part due to the focus on a few explicitly stated abilities. Not all CILOs are of equal importance. The importance of a CILO can be ranked as high, medium or low. In the determination of students' final grades, does a high importance CILO contribute the same as two medium importance CILOs? As far as the students are concerned, assessment defines the curriculum (Ramsden, 2003). Weights expressed in percentages eliminate their confusion and afford appropriate effort allocated by the students. Some instructors may not want to commit a specific percentage to a CILO at the beginning of the course. After the final examination, they will have room to play with different weight combination to yield a nicely distributed graph of final grades. But we advise against this practice that goes against the principle of CRA. As an example, we create a CILO table (Table 2) for a course with the aim to develop knowledge and skills in the students on the specification, design and implementation of software systems.

Why is the first outcome worth 15 percents not 14 or 16? Some outcome-based purists fault weight assignment for its arbitrariness. Several alternatives have been proposed that are supposedly less arbitrary (Biggs, 2003). As explained in the previous section, with enough scenarios considered, arbitrary decisions will have to be made. The mark-based approach to determine the final grade is no more arbitrary than the rule-based approach. The main difference is that the mark-based approach moves the potentially controversial decisions up front and is more transparent to students.

Instructors can associate a particular score with a performance level (Heywood, 2000). For the first outcome above, we may award 3% for the ability to choose the right kinds of UML diagrams for the given situations. If the student can also draw UML diagrams with errors, we award 6%. We award 9% for diagrams with insignificant errors, 12% for error-free diagrams for ordinary problems and a perfect 15% for error-free diagrams for complex problems. Each level of performance is assigned a score. We are still using criterion-referenced assessment despite the use of marks.

Table 3. Syllabus table

CILO Study Topic	1	2	3	4	5	6	7
Requirements Elicitation: problem statements, use cases and non-functional requirements	√	√					
Requirements Analysis: CRC, entity objects, boundary objects and control objects	√		√				
System design: subsystems, component diagrams, deployment diagrams and persistent data	√			√			
Reuse: delegation, Liskov substitution principle and design patterns					√		
Object design: types, signatures, invariants, pre-conditions, post-conditions and OCL						√	
Model transformation: refactoring, optimization, mapping models to code and databases							√

SYLLABUS TABLE

The learning outcomes represent one view and the syllabus represents another view. The later view is important because it is how most instructors look at their courses and how books are organized. The syllabus shown in Table 3 helps to ensure the agreement of the two views. The rightmost columns on the syllabus table correspond to the outcomes of the CILO table. A check mark in a cell indicates that the study topic directly supports the outcome.

When preparing the table, the instructor wants to be sure that there is at least one check mark on every row. Otherwise, the study topic does not contribute to any outcome. This may indicate that the study topic is irrelevant to the outcomes or an outcome has been omitted. The instructor should also ensure that there is a check mark on every column. Otherwise, the respective outcome is not supported by any study topic listed. If there is at least a check mark on every row and column and the check marks are placed correctly, we gain confidence that the outcomes and study topics are indeed aligned.

TEACHING, LEARNING AND ASSESSMENT (TLA) TABLE

Teaching, learning and assessments should all contribute to the learning outcomes. Therefore we list them in the TLA table. Lecturing and reading are not part of student assessments. All the outcome columns are check-marked for lecturing and reading. This is not necessarily the case for some courses.

The bottom right cell in Table 4 shows that three assessments add up to 100%. Each assessment covers a different set of learning outcomes. Two things are required to ensure alignment. First, every outcome has to be assessed at least once. For example, CILO 7 involves the creation of a computer program that is difficult to assess in an examination. Therefore we have chosen to assess it in the second assignment. Second, the subtotals on the bottom row have to agree with the weights assigned to the respective outcomes listed in the CILO table. For example, we have assigned 15% to outcome 1 in the CILO table. The three assessment actvities of CILO 1 must add to 15% as shown on the bottom row in the TLA table.

Many instructors would consider assessment separate from teaching and learning. However assessments are known to influence student learning (Ramsden, 2003). We find it appropriate to con-

Table 4. TLA table

CILO Activity	1	2	3	4	5	6	7	Total
Lecturing	√	√	√	√	√	√	√	
Reading	√	√	√	√	√	√	√	
First assignment	5	10	10					25
Second assignment	5			10		5	10	30
Examination	5	5	10	10	10	5		45
	15	15	20	20	10	10	10	100

sider assessment along with teaching and learning. We have limited ourselves to a few assessment activities to keep the example brief. The readers are encouraged to choose additional assessment activities such as tutorials, case studies, group projects, student presentations, class discussions, laboratory sessions, essays, reflective journals, and portfolios.

CONCLUSION

The CILO table captures the relative importance of the course outcomes. The syllabus table relates the study topics to the course learning outcomes. Non-empty rows and columns ensure the alignment of the study topics with learning outcomes. The teaching, learning and assessment (TLA) table ensures that the activities are aligned with the outcomes. Some alignment checks can be performed mechanically. Our approach does not eliminate the possibility of badly chosen TLA activities but the tables make them easier to spot. Misaligned and nonassessable outcomes are more readily caught. A colleague knowledgeable in OBTL can help the instructor to complete an OBTL course plan in which the three tables form a significant part.

CILO tables, expressing weights in percents, clarify the priorities of the outcomes. Syllabus tables relate study topics to course outcomes bridging the gap between OBTL and the prevalent content-based teaching. Finally, we combine teaching, learning and assessment activities into a TLA table to have a holistic view of various activities' contributions to the learning outcomes. We can verify that the assessments are consistent with the importance of the outcomes. Final grades can be determined criterion-based using the weights assigned to CILOs. Our tabular approach affords a cost-effective and pleasant migration to OBTL.

REFERENCES

Biggs, J. (2003). *Teaching for Quality Learning at University* (2nd ed.). Buckingham, UK: Open University Press.

Bloom, B. S. (1956). *Taxonomy of Educational Objectives – Handbook 1 The Cognitive Domain*. New York: David McKay Co Inc.

Frankland, S. (2009). Perspectives of Teachers and Students towards Assessment. In S. Frankland (Ed.) *Enhancing Teaching and Learning Through Assessment*. Berlin, Germany: Springer.

Heywood, J. (2000). *Assessment in Higher Education – Student Learning, Teaching, Programmes and Institutions*. London, UK: Jessica Kingsley Publishers.

Ramsden, P. (2003). *Learning to Teach in Higher Education* (2nd ed.). London: RoutledgeFalmer.

Spady, W., & Marshall, K. (1994). Light, not heat, on OBE. *The American School Board Journal, 181*, 29–33.

Towers, J. M. (1996). An Elementary School Principal's Experience with Implementing an Outcome-Based Curriculum. *Catalyst for Change, 25*(2), 19–23.

KEY TERMS AND DEFINITIONS

Assessment: An educational term refers to the process of measuring students' knowledge and skills.

Constructive Alignment: The notion assumes that students learn or construct meaning through appropriate teaching, learning and assessment activities.

Criterion-Referenced Assessment: Students' knowledge and skills are measured against predefined criteria. If all students in a class are exceptional, they can all get the top grade.

Learning Outcomes: Statements that specify what learners will know on the successful completion of a course or study program. Learning outcomes may be knowledge or skills. Whether attitudes should be learning outcomes is open to debate.

Norm-Referenced Assessment: Students' knowledge and skills are measured in relative terms. The score of a student is an indicator of where the student stands amid his or her peers. This kind of assessment is also known as "grading on the curve" because an effort is made to achieve a desirable distribution of student grades. Even if all students in a class are exceptional, for instance, they will not all get the top grade.

Outcome-Based Teaching and Learning (OBTL): Traditionally, teaching is conceived as a process of imparting knowledge to students. The planning of teaching activities is based on the question of what topics to teach and to what depth. OBTL, on the other hand, shifts the emphasis to the question of what abilities the students should possess on the completion of the course.

Section 2
E-Learning Models

Chapter 5
Driver or Drifter?
Two Case Studies of the Blended Learning Practices in Higher Education

Esyin Chew
University of Glamorgan, UK

Norah Jones
University of Glamorgan, UK

ABSTRACT

The emergence of blended learning has played a role as either driver or drifter to higher education (HE) in the modern world. This chapter explores the blended learning practices by investigating two higher educational institutions in the UK and Malaysia. First, the strategies and practices related to blended learning are clearly analysed and compared. A large amount of qualitative data extracted from academics' experience is discussed. Primarily, the findings firmly show that blended learning enables educators to revisit and to rethink their professional ethos and values, and redesign their learning and teaching where necessary. Such revisiting and rethinking facilitate the awareness and praxis of blended learning (or vice-versa: blended learning facilitates the revisit and redesign). The in-depth discussions based on academics' voices, and reflective matrix summary from the case studies described in this chapter will act as evidence of the blueprint for blended learning policy makers and practitioners.

INTRODUCTION, CONTEXT AND RESEARCH METHOD

Of all instructional methods in the modern day, the term "blended learning" is pervasive among higher educational institutions. 95% of higher education institutions in the UK are blending at least one Virtual Learning Environment (VLE) to scaffold the face-to-face classrooms (JISC, 2005). Outside the UK, Bonk and Graham (2006) capture a vast amount of methods and applications of worldwide blended learning case studies in universities and commercial training and development units. Other researchers such as Littlejohn and Pegler (2007), Allan (2007), and Garrison and Vaughan (2008) also provide comprehensive resources related to blended learning models in the context of higher education. The emergence of a digital culture has played a role as either driver or drifter to the higher education in the modern world. In the context of

DOI: 10.4018/978-1-60566-380-7.ch005

Table 1. Summary of some key facts (UoL, 2008; UM, 2008)

	University A	University B
Founded	1921	1905
Gain University Status	1957	1962
Country	UK	Malaysia
Background	Civic university	National university
Nature of the University	Old university, research-led	Old university, research-led
Number of Students (2007)	19,002	27,498
Number of Academic Staffs (2007)	1,186	1,921
Total Number of Staffs (2007)	3,355	5,053
National Ranking (Guardian University Guide, 2008; WDE, 2006)	21 (out of 120 universities)	1 (out of 53 universities)
The World Top 500 University Ranking (THES-QS, 2007)	185	246

this research, drifter refers to those swimmers who float in the pool of blended learning. To understand the richness of the term blended learning and its practices in higher education, it is necessary to revisit the research on educational technology and higher education. This research aimed to explore the blended learning experiences by investigating the blended learning practices in two higher educational institutions. Such case studies eventually highlight how blended learning contributes to the instrumental and pedagogical impacts on educators. A matrix summary and reflections from the comparative study will act as evidence of driver or drifter and blueprint for blended learning policy maker and practitioners.

This chapter presents a comprehensive investigation of blended learning strategy, practices, awareness and perception directly from the academics' voices. The confirming and disconfirming responses concerning blended learning in their institutions are discussed. A large amount of qualitative data about their blended learning experiences has been collected from the academic staff. Primarily, blended learning enables educators to revisit and to rethink their professional ethos.

BACKGROUND OF THE CASE STUDIES AND RESEARCH METHOD

This research was conducted based on Yin's (1989, 2003) method of case study. The case studies were selected from two countries, United Kingdom (UK) and Malaysia. Two HEIs were surveyed in this research: University A and University B. Tables 1 and 2 summarise some comparative facts and figures of both case studies:

The case studies research followed an exploratory and qualitative methodology. 18 in-depth interviews were conducted. Interviews were then fully transcribed and coded under four categories (1) Strategy and Perception; (2) Awareness and

Table 2. The World University ranking by Times Higher Education (THES-QS, 2007)

	2005	2006	2007
University A	273	239	185
University B	169	192	246

Table 3. Profile of the interviewees

Interviewees	*Uni A*	*Uni B*	*Total*	*%*
Gender				
Male	5	3	8	**44.44**
Female	4	6	10	**55.56**
Discipline				
Science-based	2	6	8	**44.44**
Social Science-based	6	3	9	**50.00**
Inter-disciplines of the above	1	0	1	**5.56**
Length of Experiences in Academic				
<5 years	3	1	4	**22.22**
5-9 years	2	2	4	**22.22**
10-14 years	1	3	4	**22.22**
15-19 years	2	2	4	**22.22**
20 years or more	1	1	2	**11.12**
Involvement in Management				
Yes	2	4	6	**33.33**
No	7	5	12	**66.67**
Duration of Interview				
Between 30 mins – 60 mins	6	6	12	
Between 61 mins – 120 mins	3	3	6	**33.33**
More than 120 mins	0	0	0	**66.67**
Academics (N=18)	**9**	**9**	**18**	**100**

Practice; (3) Confirming and Disconfirming experiences and (5) Future trends and wish list. Commentaries from different responses across the transcripts were extracted and organised into these categories. All qualitative data discussed below is the outcome of these commentaries. The participants were analysed as shown in Table 3.

CASE STUDY I: UNIVERSITY A

Strategy and Practices

It is a challenge for a traditional and old university such as University A to embed blended learning across the institution, especially as Salmon (2005) emphasises:

University A is typical of the traditional campus-based university keen to capitalise on the benefits of e-learning... In a 'research-led old' university, dominated by campus learning in traditional subjects, the process of strategy development needed to be one deep engagement of groups of management and staff, academics and support departments...I needed to develop insight into a range of fundamentals such as resources, control and autonomy and the power of commitment to disciplines and departments. (p.210)

Figure 1. The E-learning & Pedagogical Innovation Strategic Framework (UoL, 2005)

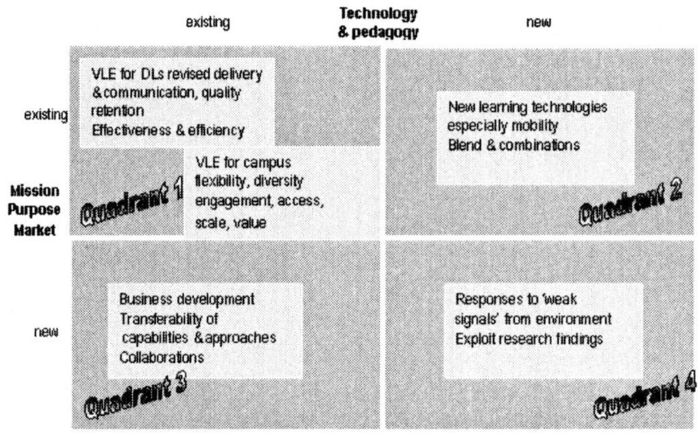

In July 2005, University A adopted an e-learning strategy (UoL, 2005) which was enforced by a centralised department, Beyond Distance Research Alliance (2008). Figure 1 depicts the E-learning and Pedagogical Innovation Strategic Framework. According to the e-learning framework, Quadrants 1, 2 and 3 represent the deployment of University A's existing core capabilities and capacity through incremental innovation. Quadrants 1 and 2 suggest deployment of the university key strengths in teaching excellence but with adjustments to new technologies. Quadrant 3 suggests deploying the understanding of technologies already in place to promote business development, solve problems and increase quality of all kinds. Quadrant 4 represents a more radical view of change using peripheral technologies, new products, new markets and missions (Salmon, 2005, p. 211).

Interestingly, these four quadrants were conveyed in a creative and colourful illustration, namely Media Zoo (2008) as shown in the following figure. These four quadrants, *Pet's Corner, Breeding Area, Safari Park* and *Exotics House* are supported by ongoing practical blended learning projects and research projects respectively:

Overall, the implementation of e-learning strategy of University A is grounded on the four quadrants in Figure 2.

Pet's Corner

Pet's corner (Quadrant 1) demonstrates what University A can achieve with the established technologies such as current VLE (e.g. Blackboard) and Macromedia Breeze. One of the major projects in this corner is ADELIE (UoL ADELIE, 2008). ADELIE enables the academics from different disciplines to embed blended learning in their teaching practice:

We do not encourage them but we enable them...*we try our best to understand the needs and requirements of the lecturer from different disciplines, and enable them via ADELIE project. ADELIE stands for Advanced Design for E-learning – Institutional Embedding. It is a two-day workshop which we run in a regular basis which is focuses on finding the best tools out of them. It is also called Carpe Diem, from the Latin for 'Seize the Day'. ~Academics D9*

Carpe Diem approach in English means 'Seize the Day'. You capture everything in a day or two days. So what they do is they bring a team in an environment to work on the design for e-learning, focusing on a particular module or what they are teaching. And ideally in those two days, they will go out with everything they need, the skills they

Figure 2. The E-learning & Pedagogical Innovation Strategic Framework (Media Zoo, 2008)

need, examples for blended learning activities they have designed. ~Academics D4

The central idea of ADELIE is to provide the practical and tailored blended learning workshop at least once a month built into as a staff development programme. To join this workshop, academics within the department have to be in a group of at least 4-5 in order to enable more peer support before and after the Carpe Diem:

...about once a month or two months. The purpose is to encourage all academics in all departments in the university attended at least once. ~Academics D3

Usually there are staff development programme in the university, a little bit of e-learning, but when you have done that kind of course, it would be a bit difficult for academics to go on and design their courses in blended learning way. It becomes even more difficult if you are working with a team because you were trained as an individual and sometimes you are going to teach in a team. So, what ADELIE was doing is provide an education process intervention into a whole team. The team will act as a team rather than individual. They are working focusing on the individual focused course. ~Academics D4

Other than the group Carpe Diem, individual sessions about e-moderation course or different current educational technology are available for all staff. We are impressed by the idea of working in group and disciplinary tailored workshop. A positive response from academic concerning ADELIE is clearly expressed here:

The best way for an academic is started with the ADELIE. It is encouraged that you may group your colleagues from the same department to join this workshop... we join the workshop and discuss with the ADELIE group, report your current stage and what do you plan to do. They will provide strategies and directions to us on how to make use of e-learning. ~Academics D3

Breeding Area

Breeding Area (represent Quadrant 2) demonstrates many mobile technologies available that have not been specifically developed for learning, but are prevalent among entertainment and business communication. Three research projects concerning with social networking and mobile devices in education in order to obtain a good understanding of potential educational applications to be successful for teaching and learning in University A. Informal Mobile Podcasting and Learning Adaptation project (IMPALA) is one of them:

This project was started by a professor in Engineering School, John Fothergill, who is also the vice chancellor of the university. He used Podcasting in his lectures for the first time. We used his project as a pilots study to apply for external funding. We got it…there are **many lecturers in this university and in the UK already use Podcasting and…***joined our project and the workshops. So, the project is growing. ~Academics D4*

The case study shows how a simple idea started with an academic used for an institutional serious research of new technologies adopted in teaching practice. We would certainly believe in the influences of exemplar – academics would possibly be attracted by a simple but practical idea on how technology can be embedded in teaching and learning.

Safari Park

Safari Park (Quadrant 3) demonstrates the use of technologies that University A has developed and applied them in new ways. New ways are in terms of new markets, new missions, and new levels and disciplines of learning and teaching through global alliance such as UN-Gaid:

Now down here, what we are looking at here is new mission that using the existing ideas. And this is where we have got our Un-Gaid network, and that's where we are transferring what we understand about that to the developing world… ~Academic D9

University A is one of the UK's largest providers of distance learning education. Safari Park is one of the strategies from research and implementation to introduce and to enhance its collaboration of research and education to the world.

Exotics House

Exotics House (Quadrant 4) is the most challenging, risky and potentially rewarding area of the zoo. Research on how second life can be embedded in higher education is the focus at the moment: Second Environment Advance Learning (SEAL, 2008). There is no comment from the interviewees in this area as it is still a developing idea and area associated with the introduction of innovative technology in learning and teaching.

Generally, University A has a clear, creative and research-led e-learning strategy (UoL, 2005) that recognises disciplinary differences (e.g. Carpe Diem is disciplinary tailored workshop). The university has, however, an eleven-page Learning and Teaching Strategy (UoL, 2007) that mentioned the e-learning strategy once:

6.5…the development and dissemination of good practice to ensure the promotion of high quality face-to-face, blended and distance learning, consistent with both this Strategy and the E-learning Strategy. (pp.10)

Interestingly University A has two independent learning and teaching strategies, one for traditional settings and the other one for the "e" environment. At this point, we would like to raise two questions: what is the definition or perception of "e-learning" or "blended learning" in University A? Are the process of learning and teaching the same when it occurs in a conventional class room or in an e-platform? From this sense, I would like to borrow Salmon's (2005) expression that, "it is typical of the traditional campus-based university keen to capitalise on the benefits of e-learning…"

(pp.210). It appears that the University has a certain level of prudence to the benefits and investment of e-learning by not completely integrating blended learning in the learning and teaching strategy.

Awareness and Perception of Blended Learning

Confusion over the Definition

Further from the strategy and practice implemented in the university, academics' awareness and experiences are the next research focus. From our observation during the data collection, academics' responses rarely use the term 'blended learning' but 'e-learning' instead. The confusion of the definition of blended learning is amongst some of the academics in University A:

Blended learning? ...I am not sure what it means. ~ Academic D6

...blended learning is a bit of fuzzy concept at the moment. What makes the blend? The technology? Or the facts is that the distance and face-to-face together? ~ Academic D1

Well I would like to think we are but I am not very sure are we practising blended learning. ~Academics D5

The concept of "blended learning" is hidden behind a term that is more commonly used such as "e-learning". I suppose this is the consequence of the vague nature of blended learning definition (Oliver and Trigwell, 2005) and of the institutional learning and teaching strategies that merely highlight e-learning instead of blended learning.

Learners' Expectations (e.g. Blended Assessment Feedback)

Academics often comprehend e-learning as a flexible way for the learners' convenience – availability of learning materials at anytime. Assessment feedback either in print, online or f2f is expected from learners to support the learning process. Consider the below voice,

An important part of what we do in terms of supporting learning is to provide feedback on the assessment... We do that online and we also do that face-to-face and in print. But we also do try to make sure that we are giving them opportunity to face-to-face teaching, which we don't make compulsory because we recognise that not everyone can find the time to take the advantage of that but we try to make sure that is available. And we also recognise increasingly online support is important...there are expectations. ~Academics D5

Recognising the expectation of both online and f2f instruction is crucial but on the other hand, the expectation of both worlds is not equivalent to the "best of the both worlds". The journey from "expectations" to realistically live up to the expectation is a challenge. The disciplinary and individual differences make it even more challenging:

The idea of hybrid and the idea of blend would vary from person to person. You can say this course is blended and provide the best of both worlds. It gives you the best of face-to-face and the best of online, rubbish! Because that blanket approaches take it for granted that everybody seems to be the same and they are not. Some people would perform and would enjoy and feel be rewarded, feel brave about being in the classroom much more so that online and the other way round. ~ Academic D1

From Blanket Approach to Tailored Approach: The Empowerment

Neither blanket approach would benefit all educators and learners, nor one type of blend that will feed everyone's taste. The superficial perception of a particular way of blended learning as blanket approach may emphasises technology rather than people and pedagogy. Promote technology without recognising disciplinary and individual differences, most often, may lead to the disappointments. Therefore, the enhancement of learning and teaching experience must lay on the deeper understanding of the nature of education. Education is complex and is a matrix. For this nature, a blanket approach, say "Podcasting plus f2f instruction will make the best learning experience", will not satisfy everyone at all stances. A major concern raised by an academic:

...I think the key is that: how to foster the meta information; **how to empower people** *to make their own choices...empower people to* **make that kind of decisions, of choices**. *~ Academic D1*

Empowerment is the important theme here – not only to promote "technology enhances learning and teaching experience" in words but **to practically empower educators to make their choices of blended learning**. There are two empowerment approaches obtained from this university. First, educators can learn from each other by actually "seeing" how educational technology was incorporated into teaching practices. The journey of a successful peer can be recorded and publicised for others to adopt and more importantly to adapt. Here is one of the exemplar that is well-known and frequently mentioned by interviewees.

There is a professor in engineering school - John puts his entire teaching module, each chapter of the learning material with Podcasting available online. He used e-moderation model, including discussion board. ~Academic D3

You have people (like John) have done the pioneering work before. I think it's also quite important to see what people have done, learn from people like John. ~Academic D4

With these "light bulb moments", peer would visualise and learn from the idea of a successful blended learning case study. Second, ADELIE is the disciplinary tailored workshop aimed to eliminate the impression of blanket approach for all disciplines. Academics in a group development can support and learn from each other from "seeing" to "experiencing" how educational technology could be incorporated into teaching practices and move on to practically do it with peer-support. Overall, ADELIE offers extensive workshops and successful case studies to both novice and expert of blended learning. It is not merely providing training courses but to empower the academics to practice in daily teaching practice:

There are many training courses in the Staff Development Centre in University A, for example, how to use Blackboard and how to transfer your course details and data to Blackboard, some technical skills. However if you wish to have an overall idea for blended learning, ADELIE is the choice. ~Academic D3

The Academics' Experience

In the section that follows, we report the many ways in which blended learning affected or impacted on learning and teaching practice in University A, both positively and negatively.

The VLE: Blackboard

Basically, Blackboard is the VLE used in University A to enhance face-to-face teaching and learning. The most valued aspect of Blackboard is the accessibility and flexibility it offers to students in terms of how learning and teaching materials can be delivered and accessed online in a structured manner. A positive response from the academics is clearly presented in the following:

I was quite impressed by the Blackboard when I came here. It's something new compared with when I was in undergraduate...if you didn't go to the lectures, you didn't get the notes, that kind of thing. Initially at the surface I saw Blackboard as a kind of place to put the notes for students. I was impressed by that and now by developing the distance learning, I have been even more impressed with the discussion board we can do and that's sort of thing really. ~Academics D6

Although all modules in University A are on the Blackboard, the usage of Blackboard among the academic is, however limited to uploading materials, linking to external websites and announcements. The degree of integration of face-to-face classroom and further online interactivities varied across the departments and is dependant on the competency of the academics:

Basically, our modules are 100% on the Blackboard. ~Academics D9

And now my usage of Blackboard is very basic. We use it occasionally for synchronise tutorials, not very often, hardly ever...I do like it but I think we have some problems using Blackboard in our department which I think it's partly our own approach to using Blackboard and partly what Blackboard could do for you. ~ Academic D2

Basic users merely upload the reading list, announcement and teaching materials. Advance users such as J F, would use online activities and more interactions. He is a technology competence person. He did the Podcast himself. ~Academics D3

Furthermore, an academic will have expectation if he or she has pleasant experience with other similar application(s). Thus, the constraint of Blackboard facilities and poor user guides are another two frustrations:

I do get frustrated by Blackboard. That is because it is not as smart as the other application I have been working with. And it's not as intuitive, it's not as user friendly and some of the ways they have been integrated at other product, they have integrated with the product turn into Blackboard but the user guide they provide is...basically useless because it doesn't tell you any screen shot that looks like what you have seen. ~Academics D7

For example creating online activities start by Blackboard, you can't preview it you have to preview it and then you have to go back to another route and then edit it, so you can't just flip between the two...I am so get use to the things like FrontPage, you can actually have the screen split and preview and you can edit at the same time... ~ Academic D8

Another constraint of Blackboard is that it does not support typing up mathematic symbols. This can be a major frustration for lecturers from the Mathematics department whereas this is not an issue for other departments. Again, to recognise the disciplinary needs and problems is necessary for designing a VLE. Almost everyone experiences the learning curve of picking up a new technology but it does not always fit to the disciplinary needs. Some frustrated voices of academics who experienced this state:

One frustration that I found with technology is getting the Maths into Blackboard because you can set the online assessment in Blackboard but you can't type in Maths. There is no ways for you to put in mathematical symbols. ~Academics D6

Often Blackboard hasn't really been working for our students. I am quite overhaul with Blackboard now. It seems now to be working a little bit better, so Blackboard started to take off in our department, initially it didn't work. ~Academics D8

Confirming or Disconfirming Experiences

According to Salmon (2000), the first and the most basic elements in online learning is accessibility. One will lose attention and not be able to learn well if accessibility is not well attended:

If you got password wrong once and they will not use it again. They would convince that it didn't works. ~ Academic D8

Academics in the university experienced the benefits of educational technology as described in Table 4.

The above voices clearly present several positive evidences and good examples of what and how educational technology could enhance learning and teaching experiences. As discussed before, accessibility is the first and major frustration. Most of the academics who are experienced in distance learning, report that there is confusion over several passwords, such as Blackboard, library and Athens, provided to the distance learners. Learning would be delayed and both learners and educators would be frustrated once accessibility was disrupted:

One of the biggest frustrations for all, is both Blackboard and the Athens...for the distance learning students...they are not on campus so they have different password...3 or 4 passwords for them, it's really really confusing...So, it's quite difficult for students to have more than one password and we often get email saying that "I can't access this", "My username is not working" and etc. So, that's been a real frustration... ~ Academic D8

Furthermore, comparison and expectations were made between the experience in industry and university. For example an academic who has an extensive background in industry was disappointed when entered higher education:

...the challenges I found now is that the system that we use in the teaching and learning environment are not as advance as those software I used to use when I was working in the industry. ~ Academic D7

Most often, HE are "chasing" or merely "following" the innovation and progression of industry in terms of technology. The step of HE is possibly slow and "plump" as educational technologies adopted in HE perhaps does not stand a competitive advantage with those prevalent in industry. This insight is described by an academic:

...the challenge I have with the teaching and learning in terms of electronic technology we have go with the university is that, is much what I call **'plumper'** *in terms of trying to do anything, it takes longer. ~ Academics D7*

CASE STUDY II: UNIVERSITY B

Strategy and Practices

The e-Learning strategy in Malaysia was enabled by the Ministry of Higher Education (MoHE). University B is a public university which is directly monitored and governed by the ministry. Hussain (2004) evidences that millions of Ringgit was spent to provide the ICT infrastructure and to develop e-learning delivery and management systems in HEIs, consequently, most of the public universities in Malaysia have some form of strategic plan with well-established infrastructure of e-learning. Many of them, however, have yet to draw and to implement an institutional-wide strategic plan specifically for the use of ICT in teaching, learning and assessment. The University B is a typical traditional and research-led university without the institutional-wide commitment to blended learning.

The culture of learning and teaching in an old university is campus-based, lectures delivered in

Table 4. Examples of what and how technology enhances learning and teaching experiences in University A

Technology Usage	Descriptive Experience
Email – used to improve communication between educators and learners.	"For the job that I am doing now, the main thing is obviously the emails that make things differently compared with ten years ago when I first started, we used to send lectures by post to Malaysia, to Hong Kong. We used to send those assignments and comments about them, sometimes they will telephone, but the time differences in Hong Kong make things difficult. So, a lot of these things have made a longer time, it's slow and etc. So, technology made a huge huge difference." ~ Academic D2
Podcasting - used as a flexible lecture (audio/ video guide) for independant learning; used as a tour guide and manual to enhance traditional teaching and learning setting.	"Students in Geography Studies need a lot of field trips. They need to go to the outdoors for observations. For example we brought the students to Thames River for research, to investigate that whether can it be an appropriate landscape or resource for water? Normally the students are required to visit different places along the Thames River. The students can listen to the Podcasting in one place, it says that you are now standing in XXX place along the river and you need to observe XXX and this XXX is what and etc. What is the next step that you need to perform? The students move to another place and listen to another Podcasting. We call this as location-specified information. It is something like an audio guide or video guide. The lecturer could bring them physically and tell them physically in that place. That is however, with the pre-recorded Podcasting, the students can listen repeatedly and do it accordingly by themselves without tutors' present. ~ Academic D3 "It's something like museum guide or tour guide. There is another thing is some students need to use a lot of equipment for research and for testing. You need to provide a video or audio guide on how to use that particular piece of equipment. Sometimes it can be quite complicated to use equipment. Benjamin recorded a video to teach the students how to use the equipment. They could listen to it when doing field trip." ~ Academic D3
Video - used in the traditional classroom.	"I was very much impressed by the use of video in the class. I thought that was fantastic at that time." ~ Academic D1
Tablet PC – used in the traditional classroom for better learning and teaching experience.	"I got a Tablet PC…I found it really impressive when I write on the Tablet PC, just sat down in front of the class and writing. So, without having my back facing the students, I can keep eye contacts with them all the time. **I really really enjoy** that and **I think I have done a better job, teaching on campus and the students were very impressed**." ~ Academic D6
Online Conference – used for communication remotely with learners.	"Our department was quite advance in using technology. In 1997 , we started to use online conferencing with our students. So I think we are the first department to use this." ~ Academic D2

big lecture hall with small group discussion, lab and tutorial sessions. Conventional classroom setting with the face-to-face interaction with lecturers are the major assets and practice. Such culture can be quite exclusive, and all about scholarly research, intellectual and research excellence. Blended learning could be an innovative idea but merely a complementing "tool" to many academics.

From our observation, most of the academics in the university understand and agree on the benefits of teaching mediated by technologies at certain levels. There is an in-house build VLE, UM e-Learning, implemented across the university. However, the idea of blended learning or e-learning to the policy maker of this institution is, perhaps, a mere alternative way of accessing learning and teaching materials. This is clearly stated on the introduction section of the website: "UM E-Learning is an alternative means of providing online notes to student at large" (UM e-Learning, 2008). Periodic emails will be sent out to all academics for the workshop and training for this newly established VLE:

Recently they developed this thing called UM e-learning system and they are conducting training. I received an email today saying that they are conducting training for this UM e-learning system. ~ Academic A8

Awareness and Perception of Blended Learning

Based on the statistic published on the official website on 8 April 2008, the statistic of users accessing the e-learning system is only 178 staff and 3456 students (UM e-Learning, 2008). The university has a total number of 1,921 academic staff and 27,498 students. It clearly indicates that the academics have not been keen to embed this facility in their teaching practice if we compared the statistic of user accessing with the figures of academics staff and students:

I never use the university system. ~ Academic A2

There is a course content management. It seems is workable but I have not tried yet. So, I don't know how sophisticated it is. ~ Academic A4

I have heard about this from a colleague from other faculty but I never use it. ~ Academic A8

In general, the academics in University B perceive that blended learning and e-learning are synonymous. They hold few perceptions and different attitudes towards blended learning:

1. *Disciplinary differences are recognised and therefore a fixed instructional method of e-learning will not be the total solution for every discipline.* An experienced academic has recognised the disciplinary differences for learning and teaching practice. We agree with the following view in the sense of - we believe that neither educational technology, purely e-learning nor the VLE will serve or satisfy all disciplines:

...things that are very difficult for example mathematic subject, engineering subjects, science subjects...I believe some type of learning is very suitable for certain area of study, but not encompassing all kinds of subject. For example probably blended learning is very suitable for history. Or probably blended learning is good for the language study where as face-to-face is very important to develop the people and to communicate with each other...As I said one style of learning is not encompass all. ~ Academic A9

I believe that neither one educational technology nor any VLE will serve or satisfy all disciplines. However, blended learning is not about technology. According to Vaughan and Garrison (2005), blended learning is an ideal - a thoughtful integration of face-to-face classroom and web-based learning opportunity. I would like to assert that such thoughtful integration by rethinking and restructuring teaching and learning can be encompassed by educators across disciplines. Blended learning is not about accessing learning material online. According to Vygotsky, the socio-cultural platform and language is essential in education (Jaramillo, 1996). Blended learning acts as a socio-cultural platform with personalised feedback, other than the traditional lecture hall for educator and student to communicate and to interact with each other.

Blended learning and e-learning are usually perceived as synonymous. An experienced academic in e-learning concludes this with an insight view:

To me, e-learning is not just a static website... this is just what they called information access. That is not e-learning! E-learning should be the platform for communication because we don't have enough time to really interact with the students here, right? We only have 2 hours lecture plus 1 hour tutorial, it's very limited. If our class is big, you don't know the students. At the end of the semester you can't even remember the students' names, unless the most outstanding one or the worst. So, two plus one is equal to three hours to meet with the students, so why not we make full use of the technology which is available - whatever is lacking here, we can give more information there. Not just to give more information, I mean feedback. The most important thing in the learning process is feedback. ~ Academic A2

2. *Educational technology is merely a tool to compliment but not to replace face-to-face; or to be seen as a symbiotic relationship:* Most of the interviewees agree that teaching and learning will be enhanced when they are mediated by technology. However, they claim that it emphatically plays as a supplementary tool to compliment face-to-face rather than replacing it. A lecturer teaches networking in computing subject uses different computing simulator to facilitate students in understanding complicated networking concept. His/her experience, however, made him/her affirm that traditional tutorial and lab setting can never be replaced by online learning:

The experience the students gain is very different when you compare with the flash simulation and the packet trace. The latter is much better than the former because the packet trace got a lot's of flexibility. When compare to the actual physical devices, the actual physical devices will actually build confidence within the students because they can touch and see and smelt the devices... Of course we can use technology compliment our teaching but not to replace our face-to-face teaching! ~ Academic A7

E-learning can never replace the face-to-face instruction. This perception is agreed by the other interviewees:

I am not encouraging this 100% without face-to-face, maybe a certain portion can be online. We still need face-to-face, we still need face-to-face! ~ Academic A4

I don't really believe in e-learning because...we were trying to make used of what we call a learning space, where lecturer can upload their lecture notes, and then they can have the chat room and so on...you can only use this to compliment but not to replace. ~ Academic A6

On the other hand, these two elements – face-to-face and technology-mediated instruction, rather than fall into dualism view that is either the former or the latter, they could be blended. They can be seen as a symbiosis or conflating for better teaching and learning experience:

Blended learning make use technology and also the humanity values, face-to-face...the technology alone is not enough, with the human alone is still also have certain constraint, as we are now in a technological world. So we need to combine both. ~ Academic A3

This is the reason that makes blended learning important – we need to combine both face-to-face instruction and educational technology. It also clarifies the confusion of the definition of blended learning with e-learning. The former means the combination of face-to-face learning and teaching mediated by technology where as the latter refers to learning with the uses of ICT.

3. *Interested and try it out by self-initiative and driven by impressive experience:* Interestingly University B has no clear institutional-wide policy to embed blended learning, however, most of the academic staff that we interviewed are aware of blended learning and recognise its benefits. Their awareness came from individual research interest, the culture and facilities at the faculty level, and above all, from the individual passion for enhancing the learning and teaching quality:

...when you get your hands on the digital one such as computer, I think you can't go back anymore. I mean you just have to use it...it is a so effective! I think I can do so many things with technology and with my students! ~ Academic A3

4. *Cultural barrier can be brought down by blended learning:* Confucius's values hold important implications for Asian education (Hawkins and Su, 2003). The 'divine' and authority of the educator has been rooted in the culture of teacher-speak-student-listen and take notes. The idea of active learning and of the educator as a facilitator is suffering from the ideal versus the realistic of such culture. It is signified that blended learning can promote active learning:

The new terminology, blended learning...as an educator, I would see more in terms of how does it helps the intellectual learning, helps the attitude changed better for a student. How does it help student to be motivated in learning? ~ Academic A9

Our problem here is the students' problem - the culture, which is called passive learning. They were trained since young: it is 'wrong' to ask question, negative impression if you were very out spoken or aggressive to ask question. So, we tend to be polite and quiet, listen to what the lecturer has to say. The culture has to be changed to active learning! After you have corrected their mind, make them aware, and then make them realise - you also have to change the culture. **Active learning can be promoted by blended learning!** *~ Academic A2*

THE ACADEMICS' EXPERIENCES

The Confirming Experiences

These are the several academics' experiences related to blended learning: (1) unspecific and unfamiliar with UM e-Learning system; (2) impressed by Power point but solely dependant on it; (3) luxurious research; (4) exemplar of technologies enhance learning and teaching: simulator, video conference, chat room and mobile coach.

1. *Unspecific and unfamiliar with UM e-Learning:* we asked academics from the University A which educational technology impresses them in their teaching practice and below are two of their responses:

CAL (Computer Aided Learning) setting because you can use tools associated with the computer to deliver teaching materials. ~ Academic A1

We also have the courseware design here, courseware packages from University B. I think University B provides Kursus (Course) Online. ~ Academic A4

The university provides in-house build CAL (or VLE in the UK context) and some lecturers demonstrated that e-learning system to us. This e-learning system is the one we suppose would probably enhance the academics' teaching practices across the university. However, the above responses presented an unsure and unspecific impression of UM e-learning.

2. *Impressed by Power point but solely dependant on it:* Most often, Power Point is one of the controversial technology used in teaching and learning. One lecturer may be impressed by its animation and usefulness where as another may prefer not to use it due to the serious lack of interaction and flexibility. We could imagine the strong criticism from educationists to an educator who "cannot teach without Power Point":

I think Power Point is something very useful because you can put up all the important points then after that you can explain from there. After using it for so many times and so long, I cannot imagine if I have to teach without Power Point. It would be much more difficult. ~ Academic A8

3. *Luxurious research:* This term "luxurious research" was used by a senior academic. Compared with "those were the days" without world-wide-web and digital library, the researchers today have more flexibility and accessibility when conducting research:

Compared to our older generation, I think today students and lecturers - their accessibility to various sources of information is much better. I remember when I did my master; I have to go down to Singapore National Library to get permission to photostat some of the journal article, or to do some research because it is the best library in Asia. But today we can do research almost anywhere, anywhere. For example in University of Malaya, we do subscribe to IEEE journal, which is a luxury compared to twenty years back. Now we have the entire set of IEEE. And these resources, web blog, wikipedia and whatever resources you mentioned or electronic journal... ~ Academic A7

4. Exemplar of different useful applications used in teaching and learning by academics, initiated by experience or peer's recommendation (see Table 5)

The Disconfirming Experience

An academic from strong technical background with more than ten years lecturing experience in higher education made the following statement:

However, I can't think of any impressive technology in learning and teaching. ~ Academic A5

This academic has no impressive experience with teaching and learning with technology. There are three possibilities behind the scene: first, he has vast experience in teaching and learning and holding a strong particular pedagogy. Therefore no educational technology could satisfy such pedagogical requirements. Second, he is a computer expert and no educational technology could impress him in terms of flexibility and intelligence. Third, he never uses any educational technology in teaching and learning due to first or second reason, or is trying to be in the comfort zone and do not care. At this point, we do not want to judge or draw any conclusion but this response provokes three critical issues related to the strategy of blended learning: (1) how does blended learning satisfy the pedagogical requirement by experienced educationist? (2) how does blended learning provide a flexible and intelligent setting for educators with technology competence? (3) how does blended learning enable an educator to revisit and redesign curriculum? This issue inform the disciplinary problems raised in previous case study.

Sometimes, academics do experience some frustration in blended learning such as: (1) network down or server down; (2) lack of interactions and educational designing issue; (3) blended learning is good: except time-consuming for the lecturer but benefit to the students' time; (4) age-constraint; (5) No frustration at all due to technology competence – "it is a matter of time; (6) No Culture of 'feedback' but this can be enabled by blended learning.

1. *Network down or server down* is the most common frustration for an academic as "there is nothing you can do with it until it is up again":

I think this happen when you have uploaded everything online, so you think you no need to bring your CD or pen drive and everything, but suddenly you want to access the site and it's down! So this is the most frustrating situation. It can be server down, not specifically on the courseware system is down. ~ Academic A4

...when the internet connection is disrupted during classes, it can be frustrating! ~ Academic A1

Table 5. Examples of what and how technology enhances learning and teaching experiences in University B

Technology	Descriptive Experience
Simulator - subject-related learning and teaching – used to demonstrate and visualise certain concepts in computer science subject.	"We have a simulator in our course, called packet tracer. We allow the students to download the tracer, from there they can actually draw the topology, switchers, hubs and router and they can actually do a real life configuration…The number of configuration is limited but this is enough to demonstrate lots of networking concept." ~ Academic A7 "Actually they created the simulation using the PowerPoint, so you can see the stack, the queue, so that the students can actually visualise. I think that is something very good." ~ Academic A8
Free Video conference and chat room – used for distance communication and discussion.	"When I was having sabbatical in South Korea, I couldn't see my students in Malaysia face-to-face except through online discussion and emails. At once, I actually ask one of the students using this skype to discuss about the problem. I think this skype is very useful when you are apart, when you need to do the discussion. You can have the voice, the communication and you can also show your software, captured it in camera and then send it over…they are very useful…So, it's free technology, just whether you adopt it or not." ~ Academic A4
Mobile Coaching (shared by peer's recommendation) – used to enhance language skill.	"I know everyone actually carries a hand phone. So, I have this friend who actually is the one who made me aware of this situation. She came to me and she said, "I have these materials on the Internet. Through sms the system, people can actually receive the information on your mobile and you can actually access it from anywhere and at any time." So, I thought of using this system with my students. As you know, Malaysia, we are on the transition period for delivering Maths and Science in English. And my students are mainly future science teachers. Their command of the language is rather weak. What we plan together was I gave my students a writing assignment on being a biology teacher. I gave them this sms number; they sms and they got 8 short messages, each giving a tip on how to write in English. A tip for example, 'keeps your sentences short'. Things like that, you know. My students sent the sms and they got the tips and I gave them reading material and they read it. And then they started writing why I would like to be a Biology teacher. And they wrote in short simple sentences, they actually got it done quite well. I told them just one page and they did it. They had grammatical errors but much lesser because they are guided by the tips. When I ask them to keep the sentence short it is easier and fewer mistakes. So, that how I use the **mobile coaching** in my lesson, it's working. So I have used this mobile coach for enhancing language skill of my students…I am using it and I can see the prospects for the hand phone is fantastic. " ~ Academic A3

Sometimes the server is down, so we can't really get the things up...if it is down, we can't do anything. This is the major problem that I face! ~ Academic A6

A thoughtful academic has prepared a backup plan in case the network is unavailable; however, we would assert that this is not the total solution. ICT infrastructure and technical support of an institution are the fundamental issues.

But I would normally have some important screen shots of what I want to show kept in a file in case this happen. ~ Academic A1

Luckily now the down time for the university site is quite short. It won't be down more than 1 minute... but sometimes it happens for few minutes, like 5 minutes...the university has improved in overall. ~ Academic A4

2. *Lack of interactions and educational designing issue:* Many VLE or educational technology was designed by technologists without being underlined by educational theory or mutual understanding of technical competence and pedagogical requirement between educationists and technologists:

It is not so much interactive, the interactivity is not there. For example, I plan to prepare a course, I want to put the content, all those images that I can adjust but I will not be able to do so. It's more like only upload your final slides. You can upload images but you can't do it like in the courseware... I still see there are many aspects to be improved. ~ Academic A4

The system is a failure. Why it's totally a failure? Because they never ask us: our user requirement as educators. That's why my website is only to put up notice but nothing else. ~ Academic A2

3. *Blended learning is good: except time-consuming for the lecturer but benefit to the students' time:* A practical problem of blended learning that faced by most of the academics across the institution – the time constraints.

...it will actually takes more times...the lecturer need to spend a lot's of times on it. ~ Academic A8

Actually I am very interested in that but I don't really have the time to read and try further about blended teaching. Now we have so many kinds of systems and choices of technologies, you don't know which one is good. And if you want to assess which one is the best then it takes time. ~ Academic A4

It takes up a lot's our time - the lecturers' time when we need to manage such learning space, in the electronic environment. ~ Academic A7

4. *Age Constraint:* Not only time constraint but age also is a constraint for some aged academics, especially when technology changes so fast:

Especially the academician in the older generation, they would like to pick up the new technologies but they have no time to sit down there just to try it out. ~ Academic A8

Yes, there are many technologies that would frustrate us. When we grow older, even though we are in computing field but many things are getting complicated. Although their usefulness is increased, for example Microsoft Word, it is very complicated. The things we use are probably only 15% out of what it can provide. We do not expose to the rest of the functions. When we know there are such facilities and we do not know how to use due to the learning curve, we would be frustrated. There are many new technologies arising from time to time and cause me frustration. And you need time to pick up and you would realise the time limit and our learning ability is much decreasing due to age. This is facts. ~ Academic A5

However, students will be the beneficiary if you put yourselves in their shoes, and willing to spend more times on the "thoughtful integration" of blended learning. From the following conversation, this academic prefer to mark on paper but she is willing to spend more time to pick up online assessment for the benefit of students:

Academic A4: You can save a lot's of students' time. Sometimes, you have to think from the students' perspective, like they are staying in Cyberjaya, so far for them to come here and traffic jam especially. If they have written few pages, they don't have to send the hard copy over here to let me read, I can do it online... for example we delete certain things, it's just like you cancel thing on paper, strike through...

Researcher: You are generous on your time.

Academic A4: Yes, it consuming a lot's of time.

Researcher: Comparing marking online and marking on paper, which one do you prefer?

Academic A4: Of course is on paper. If possible paper would be faster, I just mark and cross, it's faster that just cross something with pen...

5. *No frustration at all due to technology competence – "it is a matter of time": An* academic who is competent in technology has a frustrated experience with blended learning and views it as a learning curve that will be resolved over time. Most often, educators are willing to spend more time if they consider the benefits to the students as discussed above.

Most of the technologies that I have encountered personally impress me. And I don't have any bad experience." ~ Academic A2

So far no frustration caused by educational technology. It's just a matter of time. The first time when you use it may be difficult but after you get used to it you would find it is more efficient and effective than if you are doing it manually. ~ Academic A8

6. *No Culture of 'feedback' but this can be enabled by blended learning:* One of the practices of this university is that it does not reveal the marks of a module to students. They would only obtain the final grade and

Table 6. Summary of the blended learning strategy, perceptions and practices of case studies

	University A	University B
Blended learning Strategy and Practices	1. University A has two independent learning and teaching strategy for traditional setting and for e-learning. 2. The E-learning and Pedagogical Innovation Strategy: the Media Zoo. 3. Research is the key element to underpin the on going blended learning project and implementation of e-learning strategy. 4. The centralised e-learning team does not encourage academics but **enable** them by ADELIE project: working in group and disciplinary tailored workshop. 5. Impala project: simple idea, exemplar case study has great influences.	1. University B has some form of strategic plan with satisfied result related to the infrastructure of e-learning but yet to draw and to implement an institutional-wide strategic plan specifically for use of ICT in teaching, learning and assessment – therefore no institutional-wide commitment. 2. The blended learning practices are up to the faculty and individual academic interest.
Blended learning Awareness and Perception	1. Confusion on the definition of blended learning, more emphasis "e-learning" instead of blended learning. 2. Extensive use of Blackboard on basic facilities. Research-led innovative blended learning practice. 3. There are learners' expectation on assessment and feedback. 4. Recognise disciplinary differences - from blanket approach to tailored approach. 5. Empowerment is the important theme here – to empower or to enable academic to make their choices of blended learning is substantive.	1. Perceive blended learning and e-learning are as synonymous. 2. Recognise the disciplinary differences and therefore the instructional methods of e-learning will not be the total solution for all discipline. 3. Educational technology is merely a tool to compliment but not to replace face-to-face, or to be seen as a symbiotic relationship. 4. Interested in blended learning and try it out by self-initiative and driven by impressive experience. 5. Cultural barrier can be brought down by blended learning. 6. Academics' awareness came from individual research interest, the facilities at the faculty level, and above all, from the individual passion for education – to enhance the learning and teaching quality - driven by confirming experience.
VLE Implemented Across Institution	All modules on VLE - Blackboard. Basic usage such as learning and teaching materials, announcement and reading list. The degree of integration of face-to-face classroom and advanced online interactivities varied across the departments and is depending on the competency of the academics.	**Elearning,** an in-house built web-based learning management system but not well publicised to the academics and students. Many lecturers and students do not aware of or do not use such system.

normally without feedback of the assignments or essays being marked:

When I was in the US, each of my assignment that sent to my professor, I would get feedback in writing or in discussion. But here... at first I was very shock...not to reveal the marks to students? You can only reveal their grade... it's really important that students submit the assignment either in the form of soft copy or hard copy and then we can provide feedback to students, we can communicate with students, we can let them know what are your weaknesses through the technology. However, that is not the culture here. ~ Academic A2

Other than the above major confirming and disconfirming experiences related to blended learning, it could actually change educators' attitude and values on teaching and learning practice, or even their epistemology! Such personal experience offered from an academic is described next:

CASTLE, stands for Classroom Assessment System for Teaching and Learning. This is a very impressive system we have developed. Why I said it is impressive because we actually change the wrong mind set of teachers, maybe. Because teachers thought assessment is always like: we are teaching the students, and then we are assessing them. We give them test and exam at the end of the semester or the end of the term or at the end of the year. This was what my understanding...the wrong mindset in the earlier years of my teaching.

I got 'enlightenment' in the sense that assessment actually can be done continuously by using this system - we are trying to assess our students in the process of teaching and learning and not assess them towards the end of the semester. CASTLE is actually adopting assessment from learning principles and this assessment from learning principles is actually started by the assessment reform group in the UK – formative assessment.

I am very happy because CASTLE actually helps me and enlightens me a lot's on how to build up the holistic learners. While we are building, we are also building ourselves. Because we as the lecturers we are not only teach...we motivate students along the way. ~ Academic A6

Table 7. Summary of the confirming and disconfirming experiences of case studies

	University A	**University B**
Major Confirming Experience on blended learning	1. Impressed by Blackboard. 2. Impressed by the accessibility and flexibility of learning materials. 3. Impressive experience of how each following technology being used in learning and teaching: Email, Podcasting, Tablet PC, Video and Video Conferencing.	1. Impressed by Power point but solely dependant on it. 2. Luxurious research compared with the old days. 3. Exemplar of different applications used in teaching and learning: simulator, video conference, chat room and mobile coach.
Major Disconfirming experiences or problems in blended learning	1. Frustrated by the problem of accessibility. 2. Do not support Math symbol. 3. Expectation from the previous experience and background. 4. Learning curve. 5. Does not meet specific disciplinary needs. 6. Problems with Mature Students to study online. 7. Issue for distance learners, e.g. time zone and confusion of several passwords. 8. Technology in HE is "plumper" than industry.	1. Network down or server down, 2. Lack of interactions and educational designing issue. 3. Blended learning is good: except time-consuming for the lecturer but benefit to the students' time. 4. Age-constraint. 5. No frustration at all due to technology competence – "it is a matter of time 6. No Culture of 'feedback' but this can be enabled by blended learning.

Table 8. Driver or drifter for blended learning practices

Driver	*Drifter*
(1) Institutional-wide commitment and a clear institutional blended learning strategy and definition that recognise disciplinary differences. (2) Peer recommendation, successful case studies or exemplar. (3) Funded research project. (4) Recognise disciplinary differences, needs and requirement - learning and teaching-focused rather than technology-focus. (5) Awareness raising and knowledge dissemination for good practices via general and disciplinary-tailored seminar, workshop and resourceful project website. (6) Awareness before change – to answer what, why and how types of questions. (7) Thoughtful consideration from students' perspective. (8) Firm and clear individual definition on blended learning – a thoughtful integration for the face-to-face learning, teaching, assessment and educational technology – a symbiotic relationship. (9) Individual passion in learning and teaching or educational theory.	(1) No institutional-wide commitment or clear strategy. (2) Centralised support team or management do not recognise and value disciplinary differences and needs. (3) Lack of resources and support. (4) Pre-perception of face-to-face learning and teaching is the main stream and technology is only considered as supplementary tool – not a symbiotic relationship. (5) Time-consuming yet without educational passion or student-centered thoughtfulness. (6) Innovative educational technology is flashy and exaggeration but not stable.

THE CROSS UNIVERSITIES COMPARISON

Tables 6 and 7 summarise the comparative qualitative discussions in both case studies.

In the light of the comparative study, a list of driver or drifter for blended learning practice is highlighted from the academics' voices (see Table 8)

The list of driver above such as institutional culture and supportive environment for blended learning will make a "natural reason" for academics to embed blended learning. On the other hand, On the other hand, blended learning would acts as drifter if one or more issue in the drifter list happened.

CONCLUSION AND FUTURE TRENDS OF BLENDED LEARNING

The findings presented in this chapter contribute to the growing debates of blended learning in two ways. Firstly, the term blended learning lacks definitional clarity and consensus among academics from both case studies. Both blended learning and e-learning are often perceived as synonymous although we do not agree with this. The definitions of blended learning are (1) the thoughtful integration of online with face-to-face instruction in a planned, pedagogically valuable manner and (2) do not just combine but trade off face-to-face time with online activity (or vice versa)" (Vignare, 2007, p.38). Thus, we would assert that in the process of blended learning, face-to-face and educational technology can be seen as a symbiotic relationship for better teaching and learning experience. Secondly, the superficial perception of blended learning as a "blanket approach", emphasising technology rather than people without recognising the complexness of education, the disciplinary and individual differences, may lead to the grave of the "blended learning romantic" (who represents pro-technology academics who naively consider instrumental blended learning is the only key driver or the technology is the necessarily trend that break down traditional barriers of classroom instruction (Chew, Tuner and Jones, 2009).

The main lessons learnt from the case studies include the following:

1. Creative, simple but complete blended learning strategy by a traditional university presented in case study I. The idea of disciplinary tailored workshop and working in groups is an excellent way to enable academics to

adopt blended learning in their learning and teaching practice. Empowerment by peers and working in teams are the key drivers enabling academics across the institution in making their choices of blended learning.

2. Disciplinary needs and differences are necessary for designing a VLE. One educational technology, one VLE or one method of pedagogy may not fit into all disciplinary needs. Many VLEs or educational technology were designed by technologists without being underlined by educational theory or mutual understanding of technical competence and pedagogical requirement between educationists and technologists.
3. The influences of exemplar would empower blended learning practices – academics are more attracted by a simple but practical idea or by successful applications by peers on how technology can be embedded in teaching and learning. Most academics who are interested in blended learning would try it out by self-initiative and driven by experience. However, time consuming and age constraint are two major obstacles. These obstacles may be resolved if educators hold a passion in education and emphasis on the needs and benefits of students.
4. These case studies provoke three main challenges related to the strategy of blended learning: (1) how does blended learning satisfy the pedagogical requirement by experienced educationists? (2) how does blended learning provide a flexible and intelligent setting for educators with technology competence? (3) how does blended learning enable an educator to revisit and redesign curriculum?

The following show the general "wish list" and future trends suggested by academics from both case studies related to blended learning:

1. A "blended learning day"- a similar idea of research day, a day or space off only for blended learning - revisit and redesign learning and teaching.
2. An all-in-one blended learning system, which is an upgrade version of what current VLE (e.g. Blackboard and Moodle) could offer with improved facilities – Personalised Learning Environment (PLE) with integrated ability such as (i) learning object or application plug-in; (ii) FAQ or knowledge-based system to avoid irritating students' email and appointments by asking the same questions on related subject; (iii.) integrate with administrative system such as student registration, attendance and timetabling system.
3. Prefer comfort and stable old technology rather than flashy but not stable new technology.

Bonk and Graham (2006) predict that in the future, the term "blended learning" will fade when the educational technology becomes maturing and stable, and everyone learns and teaches in a blended mode. The educational theories, however, remain the fundamental foundation for any educationalist as well as educational technologist. Thus, we would assert that further research to investigate more possible educational theory which related to the principles of blended learning, especially the meaningful ways of configuring teaching and learning mediated by technology in different disciplines is necessary.

REFERENCES

Allan, B. (2007). *Blended learning Tools for Teaching and Training*. London: Facet Publishing.

Beyond Distance Research Alliance. (2008). *The Beyond Distance Research Alliance, University of Leicester*. Retrieved April 11, 2008, from http://www.le.ac.uk/beyonddistance/index.html

Bonk, C., & Graham, C. R. (Eds.). (2006). *The Handbook of Blended learning: Global Perspectives, Local Designs.* San Francisco, CA: Pfeiffer Publishing.

Chew, E., Tuner, D., & Jones, N. (2009). In Love and War: Blended learning Theories for Computer Scientists and Educationists. In F. L. Wang, J. Fong, & R. C. Kwan (Eds.), *The Handbook of Blended learning*. Hershey, PA: Information Science Reference.

Garrison, D., & Vaughan, N. D. (2008). *Blended learning in Higher Education: Framework, Principles and Guidelines.* San Francisco: Jossey-Bass.

Hawkins, J. N., & Su, Z. X. (2003). Asian Education, In F. R. Arnove & C. A. Torres (Eds.), *Comparative Education: The Dialectic of the Global and Local* (2nd ed.). Lanham, MD: Rowman & Littlefield Publishers.

Hussain, R. M. R. (2004). eLearning in Higher Education Institutions in Malaysia. *E-mentor, 5*(7), 72–75.

Jaramillo, J. A. (1996). Vygotsky's sociocultural theory and contributions to the development of constructivist curricula. *Education, 117*(1), 133–141.

JISC. (2005). *Study of Environments To Support E-Learning In UK Further and Higher Education: A Supporting Study for the Joint Information Systems Committee (JISC), Education for Change Ltd, The Research Partnership Social Informatics Unit, University of Brighton.* Retrieved January 10, 2008, from http://www.jisc.ac.uk/media/documents/programmes/buildmlehefe/elearning_survey_2005.pdf

Littlejohn, A., & Pegler, C. (2007). *Preparing for Blended e-Learning: Understanding Blended and Online Learning (Connecting with E-learning).* London: Routledge.

Media Zoo. (2008). *University of Leicester Media Zoo.* Retrieved April 17, 2008, from http://www.le.ac.uk/beyonddistance/mediazoo/

Oliver, M., & Trigwell, K. (2005). Can 'Blended learning' Be Redeemed? *E–Learning, 2*(1), 17–26.

Salmon, G. (2000). *E-Moderating: The Key to Teaching and Learning Online.* London: Kogan Page.

Salmon, G. (2005). Flying not Flapping: a Strategic Framework for e-learning and Pedagogical Innovation in HEIs. *ALT-J. Research in Learning Technology, 13*(3), 201–218.

SEAL. (2008). *Second Environment Advance Learning.* Retrieved April 11, 2008, from http://www.le.ac.uk/seal/

THES-QS. (2007). *The World University Ranking by Times Higher Education.* Retrieved April 1, 2008, from http://www.topuniversities.com/worlduniversityrankings/results/2007/overall_rankings/top_400_universities/

UM. (2008). *Official Website for University of Malaya.* Retrieved February 11, 2008, from http://www.um.edu.my

UM e-Learning. (2008). *Official Website for UM e-Learning.* Retrieved February 11, 2008, from http://elearning.um.edu.my/login.php

UoL. (2005). *E-Learning Strategy.* Retrieved April 15, 2007, from http://www.le.ac.uk/strategies/elearning/

UoL. (2007). *Learning and Teaching Strategy 2007.* Retrieved April 15, 2008, from http://www.le.ac.uk/teaching/strategy.html

UoL. (2008). *Official Website for University of Leicester.* Retrieved April 15, 2008, from http://www.le.ac.uk/portals/university.html

UoL ADELIE. (2008). *ADDELIE Project in University of Leicester*. Retrieved April 15, 2008, from: http://www.le.ac.uk/adelie/

Vaughan, N. D., & Garrison, D. R. (2005). Creating Cognitive Presence in a Blended Faculty Development Community. *The Internet and Higher Education*, *8*(1), 1–12. doi:10.1016/j.iheduc.2004.11.001

Vignare, K. (2007). Review of Literature Blended learning: Using ALN to Change the Classroom – Will It Work? In A. G. Picciano & C. D. Dziuban. (Eds.), *Blended learning: Research Perspectives*. MA: The Sloan Consortium.

Yin, R. K. (2003). *Application of Case Study Research* (2nd ed.). Thousand Oaks: Sage Publications.

Yin, R. K. (1989). *Case Study Research: Design and Method* (rev. ed.). Newbury Park, CA: Sage Publications.

KEY TERMS AND DEFINITIONS

All-in-One Blended Learning System: An ideal combination of VLE and PLE with all facilities in one system - learning and teaching materials, social networking technologies, PLE, learning object or application plug-in; FAQ or knowledge-based system and integrated facilities such as be able to integrate with student registration, attendance and timetabling system.

Blended Learning: The combination of face-to-face learning and teaching mediated by technology. The thoughtful integration of face-to-face classroom and web-based learning opportunity by fundamental redesign and an optimal (re)design approach by rethinking and restructuring teaching and learning.

Higher Education (HE): Universities or tertiary education.

Personalised Learning Environment (PLE): An upgraded version of VLE where such environment is learner-centred, powered by web 2.0 technology and learners be able to take control of and manage their own learning.

Podcasting: From the words iPod and broadcasting. In the educational context, it means the learning and teaching materials is delivered and shared in audio content to iPods, other portable media players or computers, so that it can be listened and learnt at the learner's convenience at anytime at anywhere.

Virtual Learning Environment (VLE): Pervasive terminology in the UK which represents a web-based system designed to support teaching and learning in an educational setting, a well-designed learning and monitoring space for educators and student such as Blackboard and Moodle.

Chapter 6
The Clustering of Large Scale E-Learning Resources

Fei Wu
Zhejiang University, China

Wenhua Wang
Zhejiang University, China

Hanwang Zhang
Zhejiang University, China

Yueting Zhuang
Zhejiang University, China

ABSTRACT

E-learning resources increase vastly with the pervasion of the Internet. Thus, the retrieval of e-learning resources becomes more and more important. This chapter introduces an approach to retrieve e-learning resources from large-scale dataset. The basic idea behind that method is, the authors cluster the whole resources into topics first, and only search from those clusters which are the most tightly relevant to the query. To make the clustering feasible to large-scale dataset, the authors adapt affinity propagation in MapReduce framework and therefore the so called parallel affinity propagation is proposed. The proposed approach could improve the retrieval of e-learning resources by understanding users' underlying intentions.

INTRODUCTION AND RELATED WORK

With the pervasion of the Internet, e-learning is more and more popular, which provides a brand new way for people to learn without attending face-to-face class. With e-learning, the student and the teacher use online technology to interact, which profits from a combination of techniques including computer networks, multimedia, content portals, digital libraries, search engines, etc.. The worldwide e-learning industry is estimated to be worth over 38 billion euros according to conservative estimates. With the prevalence of e-learning, the amount of learning resources also grows exponentially, which makes it not feasible to access them only by clicking links. Thereby, an effective

DOI: 10.4018/978-1-60566-380-7.ch006

mechanism is needed to locate the resources, with which people could find the e-learning materials they want with facility. To accurately locate the e-learning materials a user is seeking for, system has to guess the user's underlying intentions from the text typed in, rather than merely return the results from literally matching, particularly when the user is not familiar with the terminologies of the field which he/she is trying to learning. Thus, leveraging the data mining technology to locate the resources semantically related to the querying text becomes meaningful. Nowadays, the e-learning resources comprise texts, images, videos, audios and materials in other modalities, however, text materials are the best choice to be analyzed and understood, in that texts account for the biggest part and only the text resources reflect the information most directly. Besides, taking efficiency and the expensive mining cost into account, it's reasonable to focus only on the text materials and to neglect materials in other modalities. Therefore, e-learning materials and e-learning resources in this chapter mostly mean e-learning text documents.

In data mining technology, clustering is to partition a data set into subsets, so that the data in each subset share some common trait. See (Jain et al.,1999; Xu et al., 2005) for details. Therefore, clustering is an effective method to discover clues when little is known about the data. Besides, e-learning resources are intrinsically appropriate to be clustered, in that fields of materials concerning likely overlap fields of others, and materials concerning similar fields probably use the same words, particularly the same terminologies. For example, two physics books will likely use words such as 'energy', 'force', 'mass', and 'charge' repeatedly, which consequently strengthens the correlation between the books . So we adopt the clustering method to preprocess the e-learning resources to mine the correlations among the materials.

Traditionally, measures of text similarity have been used for a long time in applications in natural language processing and related areas (Corley & Mihalcea, 2005) .One of the earliest applications of text similarity is perhaps the vector model in information retrieval, where the document most relevant to a user's query is determined by ranking documents in a collection in reversed order of their similarity to the given query (Salton & Lest, 1968). In the vector space model, a document is represented by a vector indexed by the terms of the corpus, so two documents that use semantically related but distinct words will therefore show no similarity (Kandola et al., 2002). Many methods were proposed to explicitly or implicitly discover the similarity between different terms, such as (Landauer, Foltz & Laham, 1998; Corley & Mihalcea, 2005; Kandola et al., 2002), as well as other WordNet based methods (Budanitsky & Hirst, 2001) .

Those information retrieval technologies work well with toy data. However, because of memory limitations of stand-alone computers and the expensive computation cost of matrix operations such as singular value decomposition, the situation becomes intractable when they are applied to large-scale data, taking an unendurably long time or even being interrupted due to out of memory. To tackle the unavoidable problem, usually two categories of methods are used. The first kind is to use matrix factorization and to merge the results using a mathematic method, such as (Pauca et al., 2004; Xu et al., 2003). The other kind is to parallelize the learning procedure and to compute each part on distributed computers in parallel, such as (Graf et al., 2005; Collobert et al., 2004). In this paper, we take advantage of MapReduce framework (Dean & Ghemawat. 2004), which helps to run a specially designed program on distributed computers. After the original large dataset is clustered, we then construct semantic spaces on the resultant relatively small-scale datasets to carry out semantic retrieval on e-learning materials.

In this paper, we proposed a method to manage the e-learning resources and to retrieve the semantically related materials according to users' underlying intentions. To tackle the problem induced by the large scale of data, we devise a parallel clustering method in MapReduce framework to preprocess the e-learning materials.

E-LEARNING RESOURCES RETRIEVAL

Typically, information is retrieved by literally matching terms in documents. However, this kind of methods can be inaccurate to match a user's query. Since a given concept can be expressed by in many different ways, the literal terms in the query may not match those of a relevant document, particularly when the user is not familiar with the terminologies of the field he/she is learning about. In addition, most words have multiple meanings, so lexical matching may mistake an irrelevant document as relevant as long as the document contains the same term. A better approach would allow users to retrieve information on the basis of a conceptual topic or meaning of a document (Berry, Dumais & Obrien, 1995).

Conceptual Topic Clustering

As we mentioned in the introduction section, e-learning materials are intrinsically appropriate and straightforward to be clustered into conceptual topics. It's reasonable to think that e-learning materials belonging to different topics have little resemblance. For instance, if the query is "Algorithms and Data Structure", obviously, the results belong in the topic of computer science and materials belonging in other topics such as physics needn't to be searched. In addition, varying from literally matching, methods employing semantic information are time-consuming and use a lot of memory. Therefore, e-learning resources are required to be preprocessed and partitioned into topics before semantic retrieval.

In this paper, we adopt a method called affinity propagation to cluster the e-learning resources. Affinity propagation takes as input a collection of real-valued similarities between data points, and outputs the clustered data by identifying a representative example called exemplar for each data point. Instead of using the original affinity propagation directly, we adapted it in MapReduce framework to make it applicable to large-scale data. The adapted parallel affinity propagation is elaborated on in later section.

Semantic Retrieval by Topic

After e-learning resources are clustered, each cluster has an exemplar which can represent the topic of resources in this cluster. Hence, we construct a two-layer retrieval model using latent semantic indexing (LSI).

LSI is used to overcome the problems of lexical matching by using statistically derived conceptual indices instead of individual words for retrieval (Berry, Dumais & Obrien, 1995). In LSI, truncated singular value decomposition is used to estimate the structure in word usage across documents (Berry, Dumais & Obrien, 1995). To use LSI, a term by document matrix $\mathbf{A}_{t \times d}$ is constructed first, where the value a_{ij} reflects frequency of term i in document j. The matrix $\mathbf{A}_{t \times d}$ is factored into the product of three matrices using the SVD. The SVD of $\mathbf{A}_{t \times d}$, denoted by $SVD(\mathbf{A}_{t \times d})$, is defined as

$$\mathbf{A}_{t \times d} = \mathbf{U\Sigma V}^T \qquad (1)$$

The SVD derives the latent semantic structure model from the orthogonal matrices $\mathbf{U}$ and $\mathbf{V}$ containing left and right singular vectors of $\mathbf{A}_{t \times d}$, respectively, and the diagonal matrix $\mathbf{\Sigma}$. These matrices reflect a breakdown of the original relationships into linearly independent vectors or factor values. The use of k factors or k-largest singular triplets is equivalent to approximating the original term-document matrix. In some sense, the SVD can be viewed as a technique for deriving a set of uncorrelated indexing variables or factors, whereby each term and document is represented by a vector in k-space using elements of the left or right singular vectors (Berry, Dumais & Obrien, 1995). LSI represents terms and documents in the same semantic space, and see references (Berry, Dumais & Obrien, 1995; Deerwester et al.,1990; Landauer, Foltz & Laham, 1998) for details. Most of LSI processing time is spent in computing the truncated SVD of the large term by document matrices (Berry, Dumais & Obrien, 1995).

The retrieval process is as follows. When a query is submitted, it is analyzed implicitly and the most relevant topics are returned, which is done by construct a semantic space using the exemplars, since the number of clusters is much smaller than that of e-learning materials, thus, the dimension of the exemplar semantic space is much lower.

For each cluster, topic semantic space is built, and the semantic retrieval is processed with LSI within the several most relevant topics which are returned in the topic retrieval step. Thus, we don't have to do the expensive singular value decomposition step with all the data at one time, and the cost of semantic retrieval is alleviated accordingly.

PARALLEL AFFINITY PROPAGATION

In this section, we propose a clustering method called parallel affinity propagation, implemented in MapReduce framework. We first introduce the MapReduce programming model, and then apply the programming model to parallelize the standard original affinity propagation. With the proposed parallel affinity propagation, it is feasible to cluster the vast amount of e-learning resources.

MapReduce Framework

MapReduce is a programming model and an associated implementation for processing and generating large datasets (Dean & Ghemawat. 2004). Users specify a map function that processes a key/value pair to generate a set of intermediate key/value pairs, and a reduce function that merges all intermediate values associated with the same intermediate key. Programs written in this functional style are automatically parallelized and executed on a large cluster of commodity machines. The run-time system takes care of the details of partitioning the input data, scheduling the program's execution across a set of machines, handling machine failures, and managing the required inter-machine communication (Dean & Ghemawat. 2004).

The computation takes a set of input key/value pairs, and produces a set of output key/value pairs. The user of the MapReduce library expresses the computation as two functions: Map and Reduce. Map, written by the user, takes an input pair and produces a set of intermediate key/value pairs. The MapReduce library groups together all intermediate values associated with the same intermediate key *I* and passes them to the Reduce function. The Reduce function, also written by the user, accepts an intermediate key I and a list of values for that key, which makes sure that values with same key are processed at one time on the same computer. Reduce function merges together these values to form a possibly smaller set of values. The intermediate values are supplied to the user's reduce function via an iterator. This allows us to handle lists of values that are too large to fit in memory (Dean & Ghemawat. 2004).

Adaptation of Affinity Propagation

Affinity propagation is a clustering method, which starts by considering all the data points as potential exemplars, and then recursively transmits real-valued messages along edges of the network whose nodes are data points. At any point in time, the magnitude of each message reflects the current affinity that one data point has for choosing another data point as its exemplar (Frey & Dueck, 2007). After certain number of iterations, a good set of exemplars and corresponding clusters emerges. The input of affinity propagation is a collection of real-valued similarities between data points, where the similarity $s(i,k)$ indicates how well data point k is suited to be the exemplar for point i. In affinity propagation, the number of clusters is not required to be specified, which could be influenced implicitly by adjusting values of $s(i,i)$ called "preference". Usually, all data points are equally suitable as exemplars, the preferences should be set to a common value—this value can be varied to produce different numbers of clusters. The shared value could be the median of the input similarities (resulting in a moderate number of clusters) or their minimum (resulting in a small number of clusters). The data point with larger value of $s(i,i)$ is more likely to be chosen as an exemplar, which means a data point cannot be made an exemplar explicitly. There are two kinds of messages are exchanged between data points, namely "responsibility" $r(i,k)$, sent from point i to point k and "availability" $a(i,k)$, sent from point k to point i. The update is according to the following rules:

$$r(i,k) = (1-\lambda)\times r(i,k) + \lambda \times \left(s(i,k) - \max_{k' s.t. k' \neq k}\left\{a(i,k') + s(i,k')\right\}\right) \quad (2)$$

$$a(i,k) = (1-\lambda)\times a(i,k) + \lambda \times \left(\min\left\{0, r(k,k) + \sum_{i' s.t. i' \notin \{i,k\}} \max\{0, r(i',k)\}\right\}\right) \quad (3)$$

$$a(k,k) = (1-\lambda)\times a(k,k) + \lambda \times \sum_{i' s.t. i' \neq k} \max\{0, r(i',k)\} \quad (4)$$

In the three equations above, λ is the damping factor used to avoid numerical oscillations. To begin with, the availabilities are initialized to zero: $s(i,k) = 0$. The "responsibility" $r(i,k)$, sent from point i to point k, reflects how well-suited data point k is to serve as the exemplar for data point i. According to equation 2, the "responsibility" $r(i,k)$ varies directly with $s(i,k)$, which means data point i tends to choose a close point as its exemplar. In the first iteration, because the availabilities are zero, $r(i,k)$ is set to the input similarity between point i and point k as its exemplar, minus the largest of the similarities between point i and other candidate exemplars. In later iterations, when some points are effectively assigned to other exemplars, their availabilities will drop below zero. These negative availabilities will decrease the effective values of some of the input similarities $s(i,k')$ in equation 2, removing the corresponding candidate exemplars from competition. The "availability" $a(i,k)$, sent from candidate exemplar point k to point i, reflects the accumulated evidence for how appropriate it would be for point i to choose point k as its exemplar, taking into account the support from other points that point k should be an exemplar (Frey & Dueck, 2007). Let's look at equation 3, the "availability" $a(i,k)$ is set to the self-responsibility $r(k,k)$ plus the sum of the positive responsibilities candidate exemplar k receives from other points, which intuitively means the availability of point k as an exemplar can be increased if some other points have positive responsibilities for point k being their exemplar.

We give some intuitively explanations here, and the detailed explanations to these equations could be found in reference (Frey & Dueck, 2007). In this paper, we focus on how to parallelize the updating process now that the computation of "responsibility" and "availability" depend on each other recursively and tightly. If we represent the "responsibility" and "availability" in the form of matrix, we can find by analyzing three equations above that the value of $r(i,k)$ depends on the entire row of similarity matrix and "availability" matrix, namely $s(i,:)$ and $a(i,:)$. Similarly, the value of $a(i,k)$ depends on the entire column of "responsibility" matrix, namely $r(:,k)$. Therefore, it's not possible to split data points into several partitions and compute their "responsibility" and "availability" values respectively, which corresponds well to the fact that the computation of "availability" of each data point need to collect the support from all other points. The same situation is also applicable to "responsibility".

There are some constraints to be considered when parallelizing affinity propagation:

1. The entire row of "responsibility" should be calculated on the same computer, in respect that each value of $r(i,k)$ takes the same entire i^{th} row of similarity and "availability" as input.
2. Similarly, the entire column of "availability" should be calculated on the same computer, since each value of $a(i,k)$ depends on the entire k^{th} column of "responsibility".
3. Considering every value should to be damped, it is necessary to make sure the corresponding value calculated in the last iteration should be kept for the current iteration.

Since it's not possible to parallelize the global computation by splitting input data into pieces and calculating each piece respectively, we intend to parallelize computation within each iteration.

Figure 1 shows the process of parallel affinity propagation. Each box represents a step respectively corresponds to step 1 to step 4. Each step mainly comprises a mapper class and a reducer class in Hadoop implementation. If mapper class or reducer class takes little effect in some step, it is ignored when we elaborate. The whole process is comprised of four steps; step 2 and step 3 are iterated for certain times or until convergence. Here are the details of each step as below.

Step 1: Initialize the input similarities using class called InitMapper and then output the similarity, responsibility and availability in the form of "*i*: **flag***k* value". Here, colon is used to separate the key and value in MapReduce framework. **Flag** is used to tell the type of the value, which could be one of the values in '**s**', '**r**', and '**a**', representing similarity, responsibility and availability correspondingly. In step 1, all the values of responsibility and availability are initialized to zero.

Step 2: Compute the "responsibilities" according to equation 2, and the output of responsibility is a little tricky, by which we mean, the output of "responsibility" and "availability" of step 2 is in the form of "*k*: **flag***i* value". For instance, $r(i,k) = 0.5$ is represented as "*k*: **r***i* 0.5", and similarly $a(i,k) = 0.1$ is represented as "*k*: **a***i* 0.1". The reason is shown in step 3. To calculate $r(i,k)$, all the values of $a(i,k')$ and $s(i,k')$ are needed as input. Though computation is distributed on different computers, all the values taking *i* as key are passed into the reduce function in class SA2RReducer as a list. In reduce function, it is easy to tell the type of the value according to the flag, and to figure out the correct value of $r(i,k)$ after looking over all the values with *i* as key.

Step 3: Compute the "availabilities" according to equation 3 and equation 4, then output "responsibilities" and "availabilities" in normal order as the input of step 2 of the next iteration. Similarly to step 2, the calculation of $a(i,k)$ needs all the values of $r(i',k)$ as input. Since after step 2, all the key/value pairs are indexed by the column, all the values in the kth column are organized as a list; it's possible to calculate $\sum_{i' s.t. i' \notin \{i,k\}} \max\{0, r(i',k)\}$, which is part of equation 3 and equation 4.

Step 4: Figure out the exemplars for all the data points using the result of iteration of step 2 and step 3. First, reduce function in class CleanReducer finds the candidate exemplars whose summation of "availability" and "responsibility" is larger than zero. Second, for each data point *k*, it chooses from candidate exemplars with largest similarity to *k* as the real exemplar for *k*. It is worth noting that the task number of step 4 has to be set to 1, by which we mean this step can't be distributed. Because each choice of exemplar for data point can only be made after all the candidate exemplars are looked up, which makes the step can only be processed on the unique computer.

Figure 1. Flow chart of parallel affinity propagation

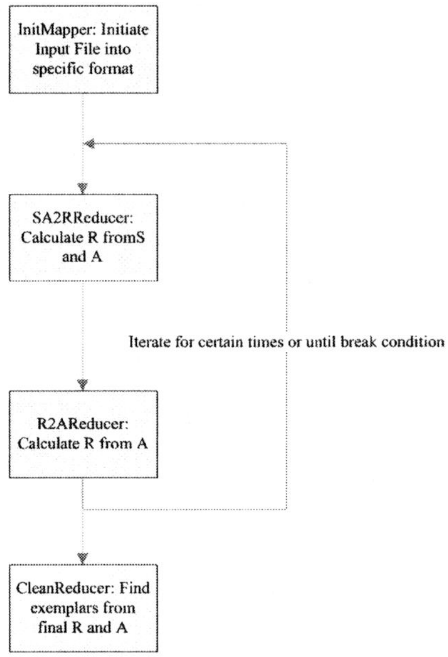

EXPERIMENTS

To evaluate the effectiveness of our approaches, we experimented with 1425 e-learning documents. The 1425 documents are divided into 150 conceptual topics, and generally each conceptual topic contains less than 20 documents. In our experiments, we evaluate the precision of our method, which is defined as:

$$precision = \frac{the\ number\ of\ correctly\ returned\ objects}{the\ number\ of\ total\ objects\ returned} \quad (5)$$

Besides, to evaluate how effective our approaches are to retrieve e-learning materials a user want to find, we define coverage as:

$$coverage = \frac{the\ number\ of\ correctly\ returned\ objects}{the\ number\ of\ relevant\ objects\ in\ database} \quad (6)$$

Conceptual Topic Clustering

In this section, we mainly evaluate the performance of the conceptual topic clustering of e-learning resources. In our experiment, each document is assigned to a conceptual topic in advance. After the unsupervised clustering by affinity propagation, every document in each cluster is looked up in the digital library and its real conceptual topic is found. Then, we assign the most common topic to the cluster, calculate the ratio of the number of documents in the cluster that belonging in the most common topic over the total number of documents in the cluster and regard it as a clustering accuracy percentage.

Figure 2 shows the accuracy of clustering when the number of clusters is changed. From figure 2, we can see that the number of clusters produced by affinity propagation ranges from 151 to 191, and the accuracy percentage is around 0.87. The result of clustering is crucial to the final retrieval results, since by clustering, irrelevant documents are excluded and will not be searched. According

Figure 2. The accuracy of clustering with different number of clusters

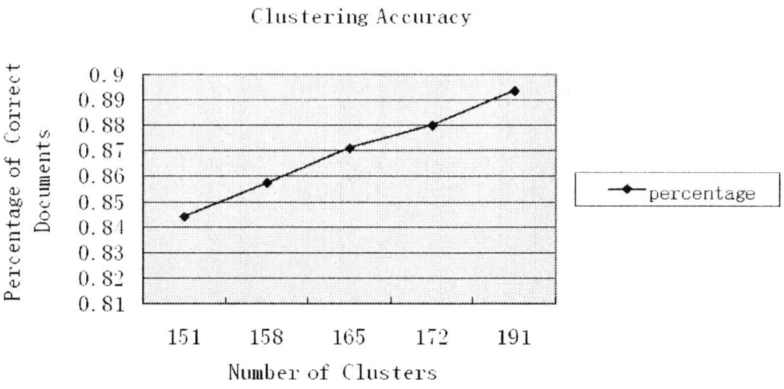

to this experiment, we can see that less than 20 percent of irrelevant documents are clustered into the not so relevant topic, which could satisfy the need of excluding most irrelevant documents.

Query Relevant E-Learning Resources

In this section, we do some experiments to test the performance of the proposed method. Before the retrieval with LSI, e-learning documents have been clustered into 165 conceptual topics. When a query is arrived, several target clusters are chosen to search from, which are determined according to similarities of query and exemplars. Obviously, if the query is a document in database, it will choose right the cluster it is clustered to as the first target cluster. The standard LSI is used to search the target clusters then. In our experiment, for each query, top 24 results are returned. If the total number of documents in target clusters is less than 24, then all the documents in target clusters are returned. Usually, we return top several documents as results in each target cluster averagely.

Figure 3 shows the accuracy and coverage of proposed method. Figure 3 reflects the influence caused by number of target clusters. When only one cluster serves as the target cluster, the precision is best, since most of documents in the only cluster is relevant to the query; the coverage is not good enough though, because part of this conceptual topic is clustered into other clusters; besides, in some cases, the query semantically relates to several topics, which makes the coverage low with only one target cluster. As the number of target clusters increase, the coverage grows up at first due to more target clusters are took into account, and the precision falls because more less relevant documents in new introduced clusters are returned as results. It is worth noting that when the number of target clusters grows to six, the coverage also falls relative to the situation when number of target clusters is four. This is caused when the total number of documents in all target clusters exceeds 24, then less results in the best several clusters could be returned. According to our experiments, we can see that over 50% of relevant documents are in one cluster, and we could choose two or three clusters as target clusters, taking coverage into consideration.

CONCLUSION

In this paper, we adapted affinity propagation in MapReduce framework which is implemented by project Hadoop to make the clustering method applicable to large-scale data, since the proposed

Figure 3. The accuracy of retrieval with different number of target clusters

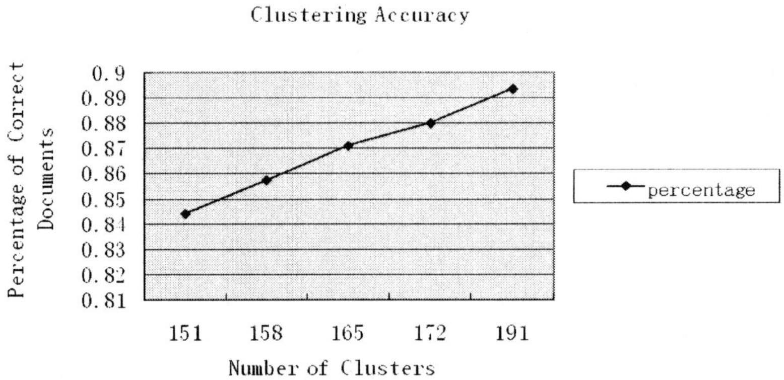

parallel affinity propagation could run in the distributed way. We also introduced a method to retrieve e-learning resources according to conceptual topics efficiently, utilizing the proposed parallel affinity propagation. Experiment shows this method retrieves relevant resources relatively accurate and takes little time, which benefits from the off-line clustering limiting the target clusters to search from.

REFERENCES

Berry, M. W., Dumais, S. T., & O'Brien, G. W. (1995). Using linear algebra for intelligent information retrieval. *SIAM Review*, *37*, 573–595. doi:10.1137/1037127

Budanitsky, A., & Hirst, G. (2001). Semantic distance in wordnet: An experimental, application-oriented evaluation of five measures. In *Proceedings of the NAACL Workshop on Word-Net and Other Lexical Resources,* Pittsburgh.

Collobert, R., Bengio, Y., & Bengio, S. (2004). A Parallel Mixture of SVMs for Very Large Scale Problems. In *Neural Information Processing Systems* (Vol. 17). Cambridge, MA: MIT Press.

Corley, C., & Mihalcea, R. (2005). Measuring the semantic similarity of texts. In *Proceedings of the ACL Workshop on Empirical Modeling of Semantic Equivalence and Entailment,* Ann Arbor, MI (pp. 13-18). Association for Computational Linguistics.

Dean, J., & Ghemawat, S. (2004). Mapreduce: Simplified data processing on large clusters. In *Operating Systems Design and Implementation* (pp.137-149).

Deerwester, S., Dumais, S. T., Furnas, G. W., Landauer, T. K., & Harshman, R. (1990). Indexing By Latent Semantic Analysis. *Journal of the American Society for Information Science American Society for Information Science*, *41*, 391–407. doi:10.1002/(SICI)1097-4571(199009)41:6<391::AID-ASI1>3.0.CO;2-9

Frey, B. J., & Dueck, D. (2007). Clustering by passing messages between data points. *Science*, *315*, 972–976. doi:10.1126/science.1136800

Graf, H. P., Cosatto, E., Bottou, L., Dourdanovic, I., & Vapnik, V. (2005). Parallel support vector machines: The Cascade SVM. In L. Saul, B. Schölkopf, & L. Bottou (Eds.), *Advances in Neural Information Processing Systems* (Vol.17). Cambridge, MA: MIT Press.

Jain, A., Murty, M., & Flynn, P. (1999). Data clustering: A review. *ACM Computing Surveys*, *31*(3), 264–323. doi:10.1145/331499.331504

Kandola, J. S., Shawe-Taylor, J., & Cristianini, N. (2002). Learning semantic similarity. In [NIPS]. *Advances in Neural Information Processing Systems*, *15*, 657–664.

Landauer, T. K., Foltz, P. W., & Laham, D. (1998). Introduction to Latent Semantic Analysis. *Discourse Processes*, *25*, 259–284. doi:10.1080/01638539809545028

Pauca, V. P., Shahnaz, F., Berry, M. W., & Plemmons, R. J. (2004). Text mining using non-negative matrix factorization. In *Proceedings of the 2004 SIAM International conference on Data Mining (SDM 2004),* Lake Buena Vista, FL (pp. 452-456).

Salton, G., & Lesk, M. E. (1968). Computer evaluation of indexing and text processing. *Journal of the Association for Computing Machinery*, *15*, 8–36.

Xu, R., & Wunsch, D. (2005). Survey of clustering algorithms. *IEEE Transactions on Neural Networks*, *13*, 645–678. doi:10.1109/TNN.2005.845141

Xu, W., Liu, X., & Gong, Y. (2003). Document clustering based on non-negative matrix factorization. In *Proceedings of the 26th annual international ACM SIGIR conference on Research and development in information retrieval*, Toronto, Canada (pp. 267-273).

KEY TERMS AND DEFINITIONS

Affinity Propagation: A clustering method, which starts by considering all the data points as potential exemplars, and then recursively transmits real-valued messages along edges of the network whose nodes are data points.

Clustering: Clustering is the classification of objects into different groups, or more precisely, the partitioning of a data set into subsets (clusters), so that the data in each subset (ideally) share some common trait - often proximity according to some defined distance measure. Data clustering is a common technique for statistical data analysis, which is used in many fields, including machine learning, data mining, pattern recognition, image analysis and bioinformatics.

E-Learning: A type of technology supported education/learning (TSL) where the medium of instruction is computer technology. In some instances, no in-person interaction takes place. E-learning is used interchangeably in a wide variety of contexts. In companies, it refers to the strategies that use the company network to deliver training courses to employees. In the USA, it is defined as a planned teaching/learning experience that uses a wide spectrum of technologies, mainly Internet or computer-based, to reach learners. Lately in most Universities, e-learning is used to define a specific mode to attend a course or programmes of study where the students rarely, if ever, attend face-to-face for on-campus access to educational facilities, because they study online.

Hadoop: A free Java software framework that supports data intensive distributed applications. It enables applications to work with thousands of nodes and petabytes of data. It is inspired by Google's MapReduce.

Latent Semantic Indexing: A technique in natural language processing, in particular in vectorial semantics, of analyzing relationships between a set of documents and the terms they contain by producing a set of concepts related to the documents and terms.

MapReduce: A software framework introduced by Google to support distributed computing on large data sets on clusters of computers. The framework is inspired by map and reduce functions commonly used in functional programming, MapReduce libraries have been written in C++, Java, Python and other programming languages.

Singular Value Decomposition: In linear algebra, the singular value decomposition (SVD) is an important factorization of a rectangular real or complex matrix, with several applications in signal processing and statistics. Applications which employ the SVD include computing the pseudoinverse, least squares fitting of data, matrix approximation, and determining the rank, range and null space of a matrix.

Chapter 7
E-Assessment as a Learning Tool

Reggie Kwan
Caritas Institute of Higher Education, Hong Kong

Kenneth Wong
Hong Kong Institute of Education, Hong Kong

Philip Tsang
The Open University of Hong Kong, Hong Kong

Francis Yu
Po Leung Kuk Tang Yuk Tien College, Hong Kong

ABSTRACT

Using virtual and physical resources to enhance learning and teaching is the cornerstone of Hybrid Learning. This chapter deals with how an online assessment system, as part of a hybrid learning initiative, can be used for learning and not just assessment. A system has been built based on the Item Response Theory (IRT) model. The system helps teachers to gauge the competency level of each individual student and at the same time provides students with feedback and an individualized study path right after a sequence of multiple choice questions attempted by each student.

INTRODUCTION

Gauging students' learning progress is an integral part of learning and teaching. Various forms of conventional assessment seem happen in every course at every level. With the advances in Web technology, this task has been done through web-based discussion board in higher education (Lui, Kwan & Lai, 2004) and online assignment submission system (Ng, etc., 2006), for example.

The migration to web-based teaching and learning has been an ongoing process since the mid-90's (Kwan, 2005; Kwan, 2001; and Kwan & Wong, 2001). We believe that web-based education has the potential not only to provide savings in time and money, but, more importantly, it's flexibility and convenience may also revolutionize the way to live and play. Assessment for learning can be one of the ways of improving learning by gauging students' competency, e-assessment should be an integral part of any e-learning system. As a matter

DOI: 10.4018/978-1-60566-380-7.ch007

of fact, the Curriculum Development Council published a report entitled "*Learning to learn: The Way Forward in Curriculum Development*" in 2001 to urge schools to put more emphasis on assessment for learning (CDC, 2001). It is a process in which teachers seek to identify and diagnose student learning problems, and provide quality feedback for students on how to improve their work.

Assessments in any form are, however, not viewed favorably by students. The conventional paper and pencil tests are still the most common form of assessment in Hong Kong. Students are bound by the restricting time and place. Thus, having assessment through the web is appealing to say the least. The process, on the other hand, may not be an easy task and not all assessments can easily be turned into a learning tool (Kwan & Wong, 2001).

Owing to the nature of Mathematics, quite a number of digital learning materials have been developed for learning and teaching. This is especially true at the primary and secondary level because multiple choice format tests if designed probably can not only gauge students' competency level, but also detect students' misconception on the topic being tested. That is why creating a learning platform through the use of assessment is nothing novel. However, most online assessment systems do not provide immediate feedback or recommend study path to make use of the assessed result to help students learn. We are building an online assessment system to enhance learning by helping teachers teach Mathematics from Secondary 1 to 3 (Key Stage 3) in Hong Kong. The system is built based on the concept domain model and the Rasch model (Linacre, 2000; Keeves & Alagumalai, 1999; and Umar, 1997). The two integrated models are used for providing adapting features to students, such as, navigation support, optimal study path and direct guidance.

AN ADAPTIVE MODEL

Taking tests could be a tedious task even though students in Hong Kong are very well versed in this activity. To expedite this gauging process, an adaptive model based on the Rasch model is employed. This Item Response Theory (IRT) approach, can be classified as objective measurement, has been proven to be effective. IRT can overcome some of the problems and assumptions associated with Classical Test Theory (CTT) and to provide information for decision-making that is not available through CTT. It is based on the probability that an examinee with a given ability level will correctly answer a question representing a given difficulty (Wright & Stone, 1979). We also use the Rasch model to estimate students' ability, attitude, and personality traits. The Rasch model can be used as an interval scale of scores for both the difficulty of items and the ability of the examinee tested. Interval scores are constant differences along the scale which can be mapped to the ability of individual student. For example, the difference between 3 and 2 is equal to the difference between 2 and 1, but still a student with 4 is not twice as good/bad as that of 2. These scores are reported in units called logits. Since logits unit can be manipulated, it helps us understand students' strengths and weaknesses. It also provides an objective way to make comparisons between groups. Rasch model presents a simple relationship between the examinee and the difficulty of items. The relationship can be described as:

$$\theta_{j\,-}\, b_i = \log (P_i / (1 - P_i))$$

where:

$\boldsymbol{P_i}$: Probability for an examinee responding correctly

$\boldsymbol{\theta_j}$: Ability parameter of an examinee

$\boldsymbol{b_i}$: Difficulty parameter of an item

Figure 1. The Rasch Model Test Characteristic Curve (Linacre & Wright, 1994)

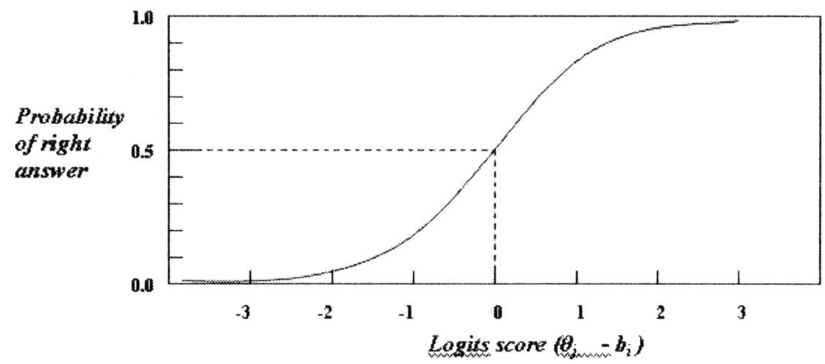

Figure 1 is the Rasch Model Test Characteristic Curve (Wright, 1996). It shows the relationship between the probability P(i=1) and (θ_j - b_i), the difference between the examinee's ability level θ_j and the item difficulty b_i .

Assuming an examinee's ability level exactly equals to the difficulty level b_i of the item, he/she will have a 50% chance of passing the item. Similarly, if the examinee's ability level is greater than the difficulty level of the item, he/she will have over a 50% chance of responding correctly to the item. Conversely, if the examinee's ability level is less than the difficulty level of the item, he/she will have less than a 50% chance of responding correctly to the item. The best design for the selection algorithm of items is that the difficulty level of an administrated item is close to the current ability level. The examinee ability level parameter and item difficulty parameter can be estimated iteratively through application of a process such as Conditional Maximum Likelihood estimation.

Using the Rasch model, we can collect two chi-square fit statistics, namely outfit and infit statistics (Linacre & Wright, 1994). Outfit statistics are more sensitive to extreme scores and infit statistics are more sensitive to unexpected patterns. Use of this two fit statistics information, the Rasch model helps the user identify any items that are not fitting the model, and any examinee whose scores do not appear to be consistent with the model.

To put it in a nutshell, Computer Adaptive Test (CAT) works like a viva exam. The examiner can ask questions based on his/her assessment of the examinees perceived ability. Most followed up questions are the result of particular responses. In our model, if an answer is correct, the next question generated will be an item of higher difficulty. If the answer is incorrect, the procedure will be reversed. The examinee's ability level can be estimated during the testing process (Rudner, 1998). Since the item selected next for obtaining ability estimates is based upon one's previous item performance, an algorithm must be chosen for sequencing the set of test items administered to the examinees. Therefore, using the Rasch model to design such algorithm is very suitable.

QUESTION SELECTION PROCESS

Though CAT can determine an individual's overall ability level, it does not assure content balance nor guarantee that one could obtain subtest scores. To overcome this concern, the algorithm should develop a set of construction rules to select the best questions. To optimize the online assessment system, the research team decided to construct a set of construction rules based on a concept domain model. The concept domain model consists of two parts: skillful tree and curriculum tree. The skillful tree can viewed as a relationship between

Figure 2. A skillful tree

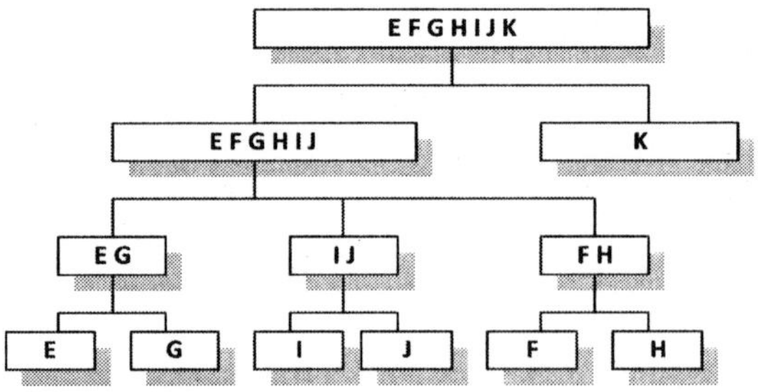

different skills interconnected together to form a network. Figure 2 is an example.

BUILDING AN ITEM BANK

Every CAT is associated with a test bank or item bank in which questions are drawn from. "An item bank is a large collection of test items organized and catalogued to take into account the content of each test item and also its measurement characteristics." (Umar, 1997). In a way, an item bank is a database of items. The size of an item bank should be big enough to cover the wide range of test content. The great advantage of an item bank is its flexibility. Tests can be long or short, easy or difficult depending on the aim of the test. Normally, the questions in CAT are drawn from an item bank. All individual items are carefully calibrated and ranked in the level of difficulty. However, there are several disadvantages of building an item bank. No item bank is perfect. The items in an item bank must be continually re-calibrated. Therefore, an item bank's standard has to be continually maintained. This could be the most tedious part of an assessment system and it has be done by content experts.

We started with just scores of items, preferably a critical mass of the past examinations. We must calibrate them by assigning with difficulty levels based on our intelligent guesses. It so happens that the researchers of this project are computer scientists and mathematicians, the initial estimates were found to be right on. In addition, inspection of individual items gives indications of their relative difficulty. Initially, items are stratified into 10 different difficulty levels and related topic areas. Each research member gives his/her scale first, then an average will be derived accordingly. This process of constant revamping and re-calibrating is a key part of any automated assessment system. All the difficulty scale will be converted to Rasch scare which generally falls within the range of -3.0 to +3.0 logits on the log-linear scale (the mean of the scale is zero). An item with a -2 to -3 logits value tends to be relatively easy, while an item with a +2 to +3 logits value tends to be relatively hard. The distribution of the difficulty levels of the items is shown in figure 3.

THE SYSTEM

Since there is no single tool that can handle adaptive online testing with a tutoring feature. We first define the distinctive features for this online assessment system and it should have:

- A knowledge mode that provides knowledge elements
- A skilful mode for practice purposes
- A set of questions with distinct level of difficulties
- A selection mechanism based on the Rasch model
- The ability to classify students competency level

Figure 3. Distribution of item's difficulty level in logits with 134 items

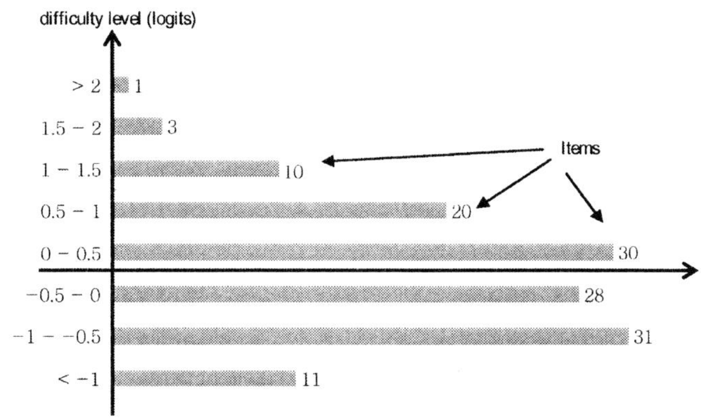

- Instant feedbacks with individualized study path
- A concept domain model to map knowledge elements in the information space
- A report generating ability

Users who want to attempt the CAT should access thought the Internet. The system will identify the status of users (teachers or students) by the login user name and password. If the users are students, they will attempt the Test. If the users are teachers, they will able to access the group and individual record of their students. If the system cannot identify the status of user, it will ask the users to re-enter but it only allows three attempts.

When a student has completed the first question, the system will immediately analyse the student's answer and estimate his/her current ability level and standard error (SE). Then, the system will automatically generate a new item to the student according to his/her current estimated student's ability level and a set of instruction rules. The test will end when one of stopping criteria is met, the details will describe at next section. Furthermore, the student has to complete at least 5 questions before the test end.

When the test is finished, the system presents a report to the student and summarises a report to teachers. The reports will reflect strengths and weaknesses of students' ability.

The Selection Algorithm

The ability to select the best possible item at any given point when the online assessment system is administrated is crucial in this project. The Rasch model gives very favorable estimate of the examinee's ability based on the current response as well as all the past responses. As far as we are concerned, the faster the system converges to a competency level the better. We use the simple CAT algorithm described by (Linacre, 1999) to estimate an examinee's ability. The next item generated will give an appropriate level of difficulty corresponding to the examinee's estimated ability. This iterative process is part of the Rasch Model. Similarly, to estimate an appropriate content of next item, the algorithm uses a set of construction rules. We employ the concept domain model. If the user selects the Knowledge mode, the construction rules will focus on the content balance based on different knowledge elements. If the user selects the Skilful mode, the construction rules will focus on the content balance based on a different skill type. The steps are shown on figure 4.

As an examinee answers a question (Figure 5a), the tally is updated and a new question (Fig-

Figure 4. The algorithm of the online assessment system

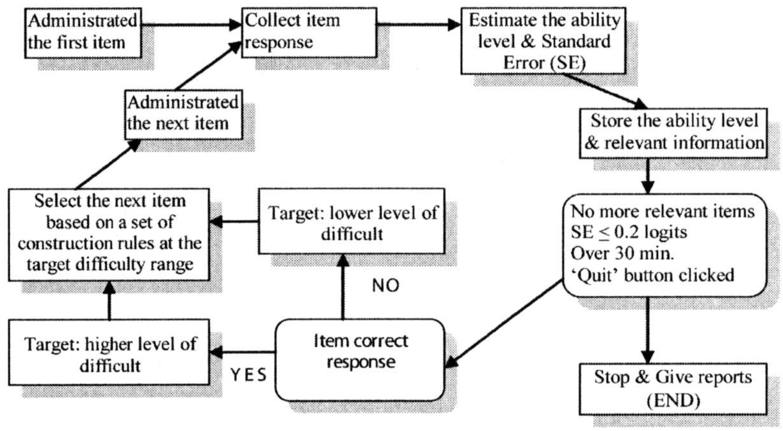

Figure 5. A sample sequence

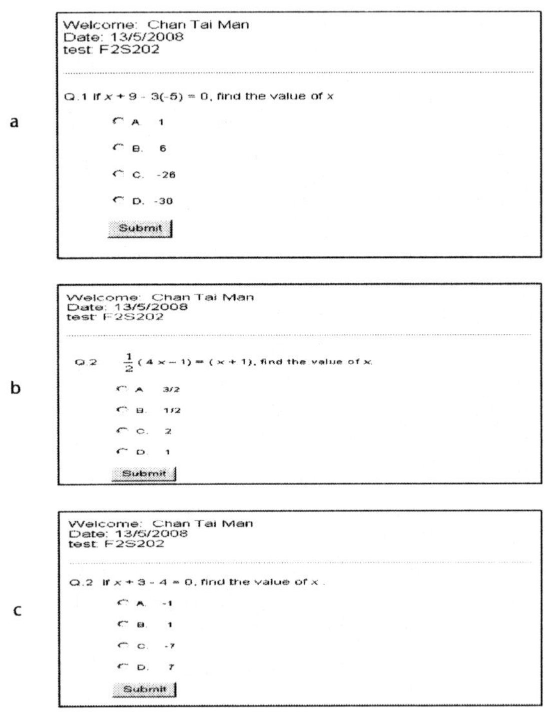

ure 5b) is picked based on the current response together the history of previous responses. If the examinee gets the item wrong, the process is similar, however the next item received will be easier like in Figure 5c.

In short, this process continues until the end of the testing session, the test item administration is shown in Figure 6. The confidence level rises as the examinee's ability level is closed to a particular level.

The more items that are administered, the more precise this ability estimate becomes. When the Stopping condition is met, the testing session ends. The stopping conditions are crucial factors for our system, they are when:

1. No more relevant questions are left in the item bank; or
2. The ability measure is estimated with sufficient precision, i.e. the standard error (SE) is less or equal to 0.2 logits; or
3. A pre-determined time-limit was reached; or
4. The examinee decided to quit the test.

The last estimated ability level was the final ability level of the examinee. The examinee will be given an immediate feedback, study guides if any and score on her/his performance and examinees' performance (Figure 7). Performance information of individual students is also collected at this point.

Figure 6. Test items administration

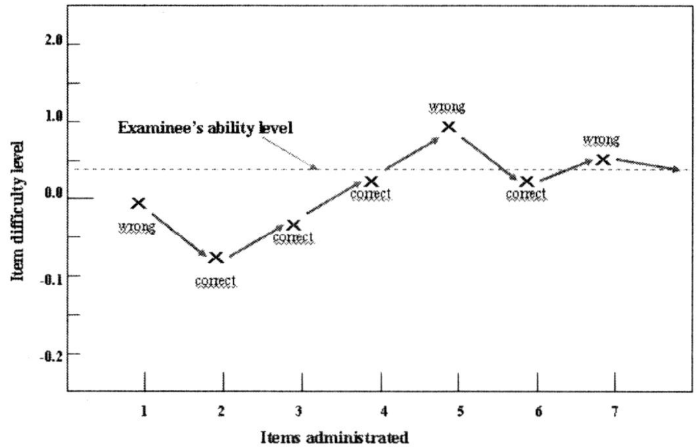

Figure 7. A student's assessment report

Student: Chan Tai Man
Class: 2B02
Ability level: 1.92
Test ID: F2S202
Topic: Linear Equations in One Unknown

Question ID	Response	Answer	Diff Level
1	C	C	0.1
2	A	A	0.5
3	A	A	0.95
4	D	D	1.5
5	C	A	2
6	B	B	1.75
7	A	A	1.95

Skill	Ability	Description
E	100%	Simplify +− on one side
F	100%	Simplify ×÷ on one side
G	100%	Moving +− terms
H	100%	Moving × ÷ terms
I	100%	Grouping
J	100%	Removal of brackets
K	100%	Simplification
M	50%	Technique of substitution

The Database

The system contains several main records: the item record, the item frequency record, the student record, the student response record, student test record, student ability record, knowledge domain record, and skill domain record. Details are elaborated below.

Item records stores all relevant item information, e.g. the item ID (*Qid*), content topic (*Qtype*), skill type(*Stype_A, Stype_B,...*), date of upload (*Qdate*), question statements (*Stem, Alt_A, ..., Alt_D*), keys (*Key_A, ..., Key_D*) and difficulty level (*Rindex*).

The item frequency record contains the item ID (*Qid*), the number of right (*R_freq*) and wrong (*W_freq*) responses by students, total operation time (*Total_time*) by the students).

The student record stores all relevant student information. The record consists of student ID (*SID*), first name (*F_Name*), last name (*L_Name*), class (*Class*).

The student response record stores student information regarding particular examined item, e.g. student ID (*SID*), test indicator (*Tid*), item ID (*Qid*), student response on item(*R_time*), login date and time (*Date_test*).

The student test record stores student's information during the test, e.g. student ID (*SID*), test indicator (*Tid*), executive time on item (*Ex_Time*), and executive time for the whole test (*Finish_Time*).

The student ability record stores student's ability information during the test, e.g. estimated ability level (*Ability_L*), standard error (*SE*), knowledge_domain(*K_1, K_2,K_3, ...*), skill_domain(*S_1, S_2, ...)*

Knowledge domain record and skill domain record store information of knowledge elements and skill type respectively.

The System at Work

Figure 8 shows the overall architecture of the system which consists of a Web Interface, a Main system, Database, Rasch Model and Concept Domain Model. The Web interface provides a communication channel between the system and examinees. It operates in conjunction with examinees and the online assessment learning system.

The brain of the system lies in the main operation which is the core module controlling all tasks in the system: database connection, authentication, estimating the ability level and standard error, selecting the next item, determining the end of the test, giving feedback and generate summary reports. The Database contains item bank which contains all the pre-calibrated items and examinee's response record. The Concept Domain Model contains a set of relationships between different knowledge domains and different skill domains.

We picked the web over the localized online system to provide anywhere access through the Internet. The Linux platform running Apache is the system of choice for its stability and cost. We naturally use PHP and JavaScript to build the front pages and CGI. As for the backend database, mySQL was used.

Project Checkup

We have selected one school to conduct two pilot tests. A single-group pretest-posttest evaluation design is used to evaluate the effectiveness of the system. This design compares the same group of participants before and after the programme. The purpose of the single group pretest-posttest design is to determine if students improved after receiving such online assessment learning system. Students do both tests. The two tests are in traditional PAPT format that is in the form of multiple-choice questions; all items are selected from the item bank. In both pretest-posttest pilot tests, each participant has to answer all questions

Figure 8. Architecture of the online assessment learning system

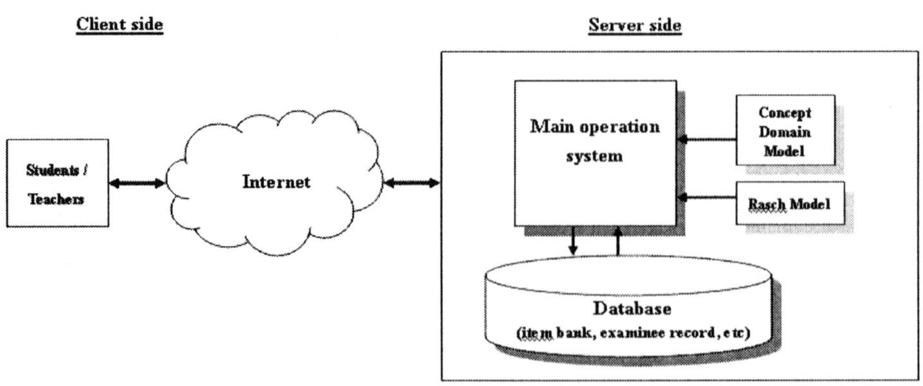

within the test period. They are not be allowed to leave the test until test session ends. The result of the test will be analysed, items will be verified and the difficulty level of each item will be re-calibrated. Then, all re-calibrated items will be used as a part the regular item bank. After the students conducting the pretest pilot test, they are told to try the online assessment learning system at home. Then, a posttest pilot test is scheduled a few weeks after the students have completed the prototype of the online assessment learning system. The research team asks students to give feedback on the system by filling in a questionnaire at the end of the posttest pilot test (Wong, 2000).

The result of the pilot tests is being analyzed. We hope to measure the internal reliability and the content validity (Wong, Kwan, & Chan, 2002) and (Wong & Kwan, 2002). The preliminary result shows the online assessment learning system fulfills all the requirements set forth by the research team.

FUTURE WORK

As the project has been implemented for students at the high school level, the research team has invited other members who are interested in using the e-assessment system to help students enhance their language skills. Initially, the team has decided on providing e-assessment for learning both English and Putonghua (the most popular spoken form of Chinese). The new team has pretty much followed the roadmap and it is at the building up of the MC bank stage. As the new system can be run on the same server based on the same design, the launching of the new system is relatively straightforward. As a matter of fact, a longitudinal study of e-assessment in learning is being planned on multiple disciplines.

CONCLUSION

Assessment for Learning was one of the goals of this project. The continuous feedback to students when they are engaged in the pilot test could be a by product that is welcomed by the teachers. We have confident in the model, and thus, the system built should provide a good indicator of students' collective as well as individual abilities. The nest step of this project is to quantify the effectiveness of such a system. A fine-tuning process has been carrying out to improve the interface as well as the quality of the items in the test bank.

REFERENCES

CDC. (2001). Learning to learn: The way forward in curriculum development. *The Curriculum Development Council, Hong Kong SAR.*

Keeves, J. P., & Alagumalai, S. (1999). New approaches to measurement. In G. Masters & J. P. Keeves (Eds.), *Advances in Measurement in Educational Research and Assessment* (pp.23-48). Oxford, UK: Pergamon.

Kwan, R. (1999). *A virtual laboratory in a Web-based programming course.* Missoula, MT: Montana Academy of Sciences.

Kwan, R. (2001). Using the Web to conduct computer labs. *WebNet Journal, 3*(4), 45–49.

Kwan, R., Chan, J., & Lui, A. (2004). Reaching an ITopia in distance learning—A case study. *AACE Journal, 12*(2), 171–817.

Kwan, R., Tsang, P., & Lui, A. (2005). Presenting a course entirely through the Web. *IACIS (International Association for Computer Information Systems) Pacific 2005*, Taipei.

Kwan, R., & Wong, T. M. (2001). Migrating to the on-line environment: The experience of OUHK's School of Science & Technology. In *International Conference on Learning and Teaching On-line*, Guangzhou, China.

Linacre, J. M. (1999). Individualized testing in the classroom. In G. Masters & J. P. Keeves (Eds.), *Advances in Measurement in Educational Research and Assessment* (pp. 186-194). New York: Pergamon.

Linacre, J. M. (2000). Computer-adaptive testing: A methodology whose time has come (memo #69). *IOM Research Memoranda, Institute for Objective Measurement, Inc.* Retrieved from http://rasch.org/memo69.pdf

Linacre, J. M., & Wright, B. D. (1994). Chi-square fit statistics. *Rasch Measurement Transactions*, *8*(2), 350.

Lui, A., Kwan, R., & Lai, C. F. (2004). A learning thermometer: Improving visibility of learning activities in online discussion forums. In *The Proceedings of the International Conference of Distance Education (ICDE 2004)*, Hong Kong SAR, China.

Ng, S. C., Choy, S. O., Kwan, R., & Tsang, Y. C. (2006). Integrated assignment management system with plagiarism detection for programming courses. In *Enhancing Learning through Technology* (pp. 136 -146). Hackensack, NJ: World Scientific.

Rudner, L. M. (1998). An on-line, interactive, computer adaptive testing mini-tutorial. *ERIC Clearinghouse on Assessment and Evaluation*.

Umar, J. (1997). Item banking. In J. P. Keeves (Ed.), *Educational Research, Methodology, and Measurement*. New York: Pergamon Publishing.

Wong, K. (2000). *Web-based tool for a computerised adaptive test system*. Master Thesis, University of Victoria, Wellington, New Zealand.

Wong, K., & Kwan, R. (2002). Building a Web-based computerized adaptive testing system. In *International Conference on Information and Communication Technologies in Education*, Badajoz, Spain (Vol. 1, pp. 62-66).

Wong, K., Kwan, R., & Chan, J. (2002). A preliminary evaluation of a computerized adaptive test system on the Web. In R. Kwan et al. (Eds.), *Web-based Learning: Men & Machines* (pp. 123-134). Hackensack, NJ: World Scientific Publishing.

Wright, B. D. (1996). Reliability and separation. *Rasch Measurement Transactions*, *9*(4), 472.

Wright, B. D., & Stone, M. K. (1979). *Best test design*. Chicago: MESA Press.

KEY TERMS AND DEFINITIONS

Computer Adaptive Test (CAT): A method that gauges the level of ability of the examinee based on the responses and decides to level of difficult of the next question until the ability of the examinee converges. It is sometimes called tailored testing.

E-Assessment: The use of Information and Communication Technology in any assessment activities.

Item Response Theory (IRT) Model: A mathematical model to objectively measure the abilities or attitude based on responses to questions.

Chapter 8
Performance and Agility in Orchestrating Learning Online

Lai Yung Yuen
The Hong Kong Polytechnic University, Hong Kong

Eric Tsui
The Hong Kong Polytechnic University, Hong Kong

ABSTRACT

Hybrid learning is taking centre stage and the conductor, by means of visible gestures, directs performances on the e-learning platform. Real-time personalized communication takes place as it does in a harmonious ensemble. Intellectual agility ensures that bottom-line contributors to the performance are in good shape and are fit to contribute in this participatory theatre. In the new knowledge era, everyone gets connected, everything is personalized, and adapted to the digital world. Orchestrating the music on the e-learning platform, the conductor and individual performers are joining forces with the artists to produce the desired response or near perfect performance. The technological world enhances the bottom-line contributions with the latest Web 2.0 instruments which make it increasingly effortless for a conductor to access a world of information both which is comprehensive and yet personal. Furthermore, Web 2.0 applications often help to bring novelty to the stage. In this chapter the authors will adopt an empirical approach to explore how the new but less hyped Web 2.0 instruments will be helping the next generation to make full use of an e-learning platform. They will also explore the strengths and ascertain the suitability of the instruments and demonstrate the process of making such a performance a reality on the platform. This scenario is in support of the Hong Kong SAR Government's initiative of its implementation of the Government Wi-Fi Programme, under the 2008 Digital 21 Strategy.

INTRODUCTION

In May 2005 in Hong Kong, the Special Administrative Region Government published a report on *"The New Academic Structure for Senior Secondary Education and Higher Education – Action Plan for Investing in the Future of Hong Kong (the Action Plan)"*. The HK government has found that the introduction of Career-oriented Studies (COS) is generally welcomed by the school sector. As part

DOI: 10.4018/978-1-60566-380-7.ch008

and parcel of the New Senior Secondary (NSS) curriculum, the COS has been formulated. It is based on one of the key principles, namely the "learning platform". Its aim is to facilitate the learning of those topics which will enable true life-long learners to reach their goals. The framework helps learners to get inspiration from new ways of thinking and acquire the knowledge which matches their learning needs, values and attitudes. The linking of the curriculum at the senior secondary level with their future studies/careers reflects the importance of cross-curricular links. "Globalization in higher education and other sectors is characterized by expanded cross-border flows of people, messages, knowledge, ideas, policies, technologies and money." (Marginson, 2007) The prevailing trend apart from traditional teaching and learning practices is to expand learning opportunities, in a form of educational globalization that enables learners to acquire knowledge and skills across a variety of disciplines.

Learners everywhere today are having the chance to see, hear, and try out new things. From home schooling to kindergarten, kindergarten to primary school, primary school to secondary school, post-secondary school to the University, University to workplace, learners have an irresistible desire to grow and learn according to their needs. The ongoing practice of teaching activities such as lectures, seminars, tutorials or workshops have long been established, facilitating interaction and discussion between peers and peers or students and teaching faculty. Education is indispensable to life and students are ready to get well-equipped. They prefer to keep up-to-date with knowledge and information of the outer world, motivating themselves to do better and generating ideas to benefit themselves and others in the real world. The question is: What makes the difference between non e-learning and e-learning? The popularity of the personal computer has made it a dominant partner in every student's learning history; it is their main source of connections to knowledge of the world. With the advent of internet space, information and communication technology (ICT) is enhancing communication all over the world at an incredible pace. The speed at which information can travel using vehicles provided by ICT and the vast storage space available, makes possible the free flow of information and knowledge. This is creating a paradigmatic shift in the history of education. The world is changing and learners can take advantage of this surge of knowledge resources and tools. Humans have countless ideas and now they have the tools to make their dreams a reality. "The school is not the privileged locus of learning. It is not a self-contained, closed world in which students acquire knowledge to be applied outside, but a part of a broader learning system", Wenger (2005) says. The world is not static - learners are no longer just surfing, searching and browsing on the Internet. The Internet facilitates the construction of architectural designs for new faster and better connections. A new perspective derives from a new paradigm. Sharing and collaboration are taking a prominent position thanks to the Internet.

The advances in ICT are transforming the world and that allows us to rush in, pick up, get involved, travel, move forward at high speed. Ehlers (2007) says, "The focus in the discussion about how e-learning can make a difference, moved from e-learning as a *technological innovation* to e-learning as a *pedagogical innovation* and today has arrived at a discussion about the strategic level—how e-learning can make a difference through stimulating a new learning and organizational culture." A new start can now be made using web-based education. This can drive and train learners globally taking them to a higher level of education than ever before as they can have access to various systems of knowledge in government, business, science and professional services. This advances the application of ICT and prepares learners to get marvelous educational experiences. In a knowledge era of stunning diversity of all kinds, fascinating sources of knowledge are available. Every single source from cell phone, digital camera, PC, portable device, etc. is involved in this process. In the prevailing trend, learning can take place within/beyond traditional classrooms, at anytime the learner is available offline/online. Such learning with the help of a mixture of these components creates ideas and invisible assets. Knowledge can be instantaneously captured, accessed, retained and shared. This helps to shape the intellectual agility of each individual via the virtual environment on the learning platform. "The result is an integration of human capabilities and learning sub-processes beyond mere intuition that excludes other cognitive processes and forms of conscious learning." (Castaneda & Rios, 2007, pp. 363) Learners are motivated by knowledge resources through a web-based educational environment. An internet platform is an arena to serve the purpose of making these resources available to everyone (Miller, 2007). In particular, the platform of a virtual environment with interoperable applications plays a great role in stimulating creativity, imagination and originality. Agility is the power of moving quickly and easily. Nimble wits allow us to exercise our ability to think and draw conclusions quickly. What is needed in this new environment is intellectual sharpness, acuteness, keenness and acuity of vision and mind.

Hybrid learning has started to make its mark on and contribution to the educational world. Downes (2006) says, "E-Learning... is the core to numerous business plans and a service offered by most colleges and universities." In the virtual world, facilitators are directing groups of learners with sound body language i.e. visible tools and applications to shape ones' learning objectives, goal awareness and outcome. "Characteristics of self-directed learners include independence, willingness to take initiative, persistence in learning, self-discipline, self-confidence, and the desire to learn more", says Cercone (2008). Learners gain satisfaction via the effective use and adoption of tools and applications with a well-designed framework of learning infrastructure. With a novel collection of tools and applications in supplement to a class-mode delivery service of a physical environment, the learning infrastructure enhances our growing needs. O'Reilly (2005) introduces web 2.0 to the world and says, "You can visualize Web 2.0 as a set of principles and practices that tie together a veritable solar system of sites that demonstrate some or all of those principles, at a varying distance from that core." Web 2.0 "is the network as platform, spanning all connected devices; Web 2.0 applications are those that make the most of the intrinsic advantages of that platform: delivering software as a continually-updated service that gets better the more people use it, consuming and remixing data from multiple sources, including individual users, while providing their own data and services in a form that allows remixing by others, creating network effects through an "architecture of participation," and going beyond the page metaphor of Web 1.0 to deliver rich user experiences." (O'Reilly, 2005) Web 2.0 defines its position with a great diversity of applications, for example, blogging, tagging, quintessential search engines, Wikipedia, RSS/XML, mashups that can be harnessed to produce network effects in accomplishing a great deal. It serves as a landmark for locating the pathway forward to web-based education. In the 21st century, every one of us enjoys contributing as a writer, publisher, and weaving together our ideas as if we are adapting to a play for performance on the 'stage' of the internet. The technology facilitates our performance at all levels enabling us to participate with rich internet applications (RIAs). According to Bielski (2008), RIAs "offer the promise of a web environment with easier-to-place links, buttons, tables, and pop-out dialogue boxes among other such features, which can engage customers with their sheer niftiness, not to mention, their utility." RIAs encompass a diversity of applications that empower users and enrich users' experience and satisfaction in a functional shift through the internet. This makes it relatively effortless for us to access a world of information both comprehensive and increasingly personal. Web 2.0 applications also create novelty value. Web based instruments are playing a significant role, serving the purpose of enabling individual learners to provide value-added services and allowing our performances to take place in collaboration with others. Learning in this way weaves folk tunes into this symphony of education from every corner of life from entertainment to work… It adds an element of fun to whatever takes place whenever it happens. Environment creates no barrier at all! "An essential aspect of this kind of inquiry is to engage collaboratively in improving shared knowledge objects; hypotheses, theories, explanations, or interpretations." (Ryymin, Lallimo & Hakkarainen, 2008) This is a leading paradigm providing universal solutions to education throughout the world.

The remainder of the chapter looks into the traditional views and the gradual shift of the e-learning platform with new but less hyped Web 2.0 instruments on stage that help learners to realize their learning goals. We will also summarize the main points, and draw a conclusion to stimulate additional thoughts.

CURRENT POSITION AND ENVIRONMENT

Traditional setting of teaching and learning mostly held in the classroom in early days and it continues nowadays in Hong Kong while we are in a learning life that classes are not a primary event. In a region with advanced ICT like Hong Kong, school, classrooms, training, teaching and learning should not be singled-out as sources of primary learning entry point while they should be found as partners of broader learning systems. Bob Fox (Associate Professor and Deputy Director of the Centre for Information Technology in Education, HKU) says "Educators in Hong Kong should integrate information and communication technology into teaching and learning by adopting new methods." (So, 2008) Educators are developing systems which have tools with the capacity to easily link and manipulate data across the world through the web. The curriculum design caters for a distributed community and empowers learners with new capabilities which they can use for decision making. Everything is attracted to the internet space. People's appetite for this newly available knowledge is rapacious.

One of the major initiatives under the 2008 Digital 21 Strategy of the Hong Kong SAR Government is to build Hong Kong into a wireless city with its Government Wi-Fi Programme - "GovWiFi aims to provide free and convenient Wi-Fi Internet access to the general public of Hong Kong." (GovHK, 2008) There are more people worldwide completing postsecondary schooling than ever before. "In the 30 OECD member nations, 50% of all young adults attended some form of tertiary education, with an average of 32% completing a first-level university degree." (Thomas, 2006) An unprecedented tide of learners flooding into the institutions has given rise to an array of new challenges and global trends in higher education. Marginson (2007) says, "Globalisation breaks down barriers and connects institutions across the world making universities in every country visible to each other, facilitates knowledge flows, values global learning, creates new opportunities for advanced graduates." In today's globalized economy, countries worldwide are rushing into the internet to take advantage of the mass movement for innovation. E-readiness is gaining momentum especially "those countries that have advanced in the top 10 — the US, Hong Kong, the Netherlands and Australia—have largely done so on the back of improvements in connectivity—both in fixed and wireless broadband access, as well as in their innovation environments." (eiu.com, 2008) Those cities and countries are advancing vigorously and are forging ahead in the world factory. In this regard, Hong Kong is ranked the second (loc. cit.). One of the eight elements that determines global competence in higher education as highlighted by Marginson (2007) is "Connectivity: languages and technologies". A widening, deepening and speeding up of connectivity has been advantageous to Hong Kong enabling her to gain second position (scored 8.91 out of 10) in the ranks of the leaders of global e-readiness in 2008. Well-facilitated by a capability of continuing effectiveness and by Hong Kong's practical environment, higher education embraces the network and helps shape the economy and those institutions which are key players in developing the education system. "Higher education is the core to emerging global systems of knowledge and culture/language and trains globally mobile labour in business, the professions and science... not only produces knowledge and skills; along with government it sustains national identity and the capacity to be self-determining in the global environment." (Marginson, 2007) The digital world enhances a virtual environment which is well-received by learners and facilitators and which helps the implementation of a blended mode of teaching. The bringing together of functionalities is an exceptional aid to the active learners on the internet.

The internet gives educators flexibility in the field of curriculum design and planning which leads to a broad and integrated approach to suit the learners' need and develop their potentials in support of "the emerging global system of communications, knowledge and culture/language, partly sustained nation-by-nation in the form of state-financed public good (e.g. education, research, communication grids, etc.) and partly by global market forces in the culture and communication industries." (Marginson, 2007) An e-learning platform serves "to provide an entry point or desktop to functionality for collaboration, content supply chains, search and retrieval, taxonomy or category construction and management, analytics, application integration, personalization, and performance-based metrics." (Collins, 2003) The stronger the motivation, the quicker the group in an open space will learn and spread ideas of enlightenment with the blooming of health and beauty in the knowledge world. Downes (2005) says, "e-learning is evolving with the World Wide Web as a whole and it's changing to a degree significant enough to warrant a new name: E-learning 2.0." In the knowledge era, knowledge is built up with knowledge work throughout a person's lifetime. "The knowledge that we consider knowledge proves itself in action. What we now mean by knowledge is information in action, information focused on results – Peter F. Drucker" (Allen, 2001). E-learning is the silver bullet that helps us to approach a digital world of knowledge. An Educator is a conductor, who thinks of himself as conducting an orchestra on stage. He continuously restructures, redesigns and revamps an old symphony. After the symphony has been restructured it becomes a new piece that the performers, as learners, can use to exhibit their talents while they themselves will enjoy a new experience!

GRADUAL SHIFT AND THE OVERALL TREND

E-learning is gaining popularity because the telecommunication devices/equipment let learners go into space for adventure. Smart (2008) reports, the "Most wired country per capita: South Korea; twenty-nine per cent of its population are broadband subscribers." The development trend of connectivity results in E-learners in South Korea playing a key contribution to the economy. Jin (2008) reports, "South Korea's 'E-learning' market grew 6.8 percent to 1.73 trillion won in 2007, boosted by a sharp increase in the number of users." Al Bawaba (2008) also reports, "The strong support of key government officials for the adoption of eLearning programs is evident in the considerable increase in KSA's (King Abdullah University of Science and Technology) budget appropriation for education and manpower development, which has grown from SR 96.7 billion in 2007 to SR 105 billion in 2008." E-learning is not new these days. Jin (2008) says, "Electronic learning, or e-learning,

Figure 1. The release of an accumulation of creative force to the audience

is a term that refers to computer-enhanced learning that uses networked multimedia technologies in cyberspace." With the internet, learners can be 24-hours online. They decide their own learning pattern for studying materials that are designed to be interactive at any time. Educators should "choose a series of strategies and tools that can be used to guide and direct students in a blended learning course." (Garrison & Vaughan, 2008) Working simultaneously in different areas, the Web 2.0 is now touring kindergartens, schools, training centres, and tertiary institutions in many countries including Hong Kong. It is similar to watching an orchestra playing, on a plasma screen. A conductor makes visible gestures from behind the music stand directing the performers "symphony" (Figure 1)

Learners in possession of the capability of basic and computer literacy hold conversations with others and will benefit greatly from the wisdom of the crowds and will obtain what they need. Hybrid learning is growing in popularity these days because it is a combination of physical presence and wire/wireless contacts. Ramirez (2008) says, A 'Hybrid class' has been proved to be more successful for students than traditional class settings." The world is flat, interconnected and flowing, and knows how to learn. Learning activities cover most topics by direct instruction complemented with questions, by lectures/tutorials, by group activities in a workshop format. Theme-based learning, project-based learning and embedding the decision-making processes in a case study are among other popular methods now being used. The real situation now-a-days is that a range of human teaching activities, learning systems and administrative resources have been deployed to enhance student learning. Those systems are made up entirely of work composed by the facilitator him/herself. These activities and ideas are completely new and not previously heard in public. This work is continuous, constantly being supplemented by the production of an astounding series of other weighty compositions with the help of Web 2.0 and making it a World/Web 2.0 series of educational initiatives. Educators are enjoying the all-classical series while adding to it some fabulous orchestral numbers. The performance is not conducted by Herbert von Karajan! However, it is an orchestral version of a popular video, audio, multi-media, large-scale symphonic movement. An important feature of which, apart from the features inherited from the classical tradition, is the free combination of heterogeneous "Web 2.0 Heroes." Whatever your choice, enjoy the orchestral platform. Make it a wonderland and welcome learners at many performances!

REAL-LIFE EXPERIENCE: LEARNERS AND EDUCATORS

Downes (2005) says, "E-Learning today is characterized not only by greater autonomy for the learner, but also by a greater emphasis being placed on active learning, with creation, communication and participation playing key roles, and on changing roles for the teacher, indeed, even a collapse of the distinction between teacher and student altogether." With the popularity of personal computers, e-learning is proving its attractiveness by showing a ubiquitous trend. Learners embrace e-learning in a spontaneous gesture of affection. Cross (2002) pays a high tribute to Peter Henschel on "the 7 principles of learning" and greatly emphasizes the importance of the following guide lines for learning processes and activities:

1. **Learning is fundamentally social**. The significance of the encounter springs not so much from the decision of a single individual learner. But from the learners associative discussions within a structural platform and from gatherings, meetings, functions, events, etc.
2. **Knowledge is integrated in the life of communities**. Social life is integrated with study, work, and family. In this way shared values, interests and practices are developed. The learner keeps in touch with peers, mentors, coaches, trainers, etc.
3. **Learning is an act of participation**. The desire to learn is a motivational factor. The learner's desire to learn is reflected in is/her continued support, consistent input, and participation as a club members, a participant in learning communities, circles, open forums, etc.
4. **Knowing depends on engagement in practice**. The amount of participation and contribution reflect the degree of investment in the perceived value. The learner observes, learns and practices in real situations. Learning activities are carried out in a dedicated environment.
5. **Engagement is inseparable from empowerment**. This refers to empowerment as the "Role" that communities should play. Learners play individual roles when they add their small contribution to make a whole. Learners from all walks of life take responsibility/act in their different capacities.
6. **Failure to learn is often the result of exclusion from participation**. Separation from learning demonstrates a lack of concern for preserving a status which helps to form the learning cycle. Students' motivation to learn and to participate reflects their perceived value of the activities.
7. **We are all natural lifelong learners**. Learning and the initial sense of know-how take us for at first gentle, reflective, pacific, jubilant and exultant. Learners weave their life together with work, study, entertainment, living, etc.

The pivotal issues here are learners' profiles in playing a significant part in the development of literary course via codification of language, taste, and behavior, and discussions on the dedicated platform. The web serving as an e-learning platform is well-facilitated with a series of activities, but not limited to, master classes, workshops, demonstrations, forum, talks and the "meet-the-professor" sessions. Higher education with a global domain is flourishing flags on campus by way of encouraging the adoption of new technologies. Web 2.0 applications are well-known of its loyalty in performance pledge (in terms of reliability and pervasiveness) to facilitators of all disciplines and are causing a revolution in teaching and learning of web-based education. Through participation, learners are also joining knowledge communities where 3 dimensions of educational practices (Table 1) are being affected:

Endless fine-grained differentiation of instructions should be considered before any deployment

Table 1. Dimensions of educational practices (source adapted: Wenger, 2005)

Dimensions	Questions	Answers
Internally	How to organize educational experiences that support school learning in practice through participation in communities around subject matters?	Shape learners' mind, ideas transformation
Externally	How to connect the experience of students to actual practice through peripheral forms of participation in broader communities beyond the walls of the school?	Connect with ICT tools and applications on the platforms of the internet world
Over the lifetime of students	How to serve the lifelong learning needs of students by organizing communities of practice focusing on topics of continuing interest to students beyond the initial schooling period?	A natural, happy home environment with harmony, ecosystem and social responsibility

and leverages. "The idea that humans possessed certain virtues formed a common thread in Socrates' teaching." (Wikipedia, 2008) Leading a person to develop the potential to take advantage of the valuables i.e. the philosophical or intellectual virtues in an ideal learning environment, Garner (2008) discovers that there are "possible models for embedding Socratic Learning within web-based education are focusing in particular, on the potential for enhancing Blended Learning using Socratic discourse within Web 2.0 Services." Web 2.0 brings to the world wide web by offering features like, among others, blogs, RSS, Wikis, podcasts, collective preferences, social bookmarking/networking, and mashups. Through these tools, people-based or bottom-up knowledge sharing is greatly facilitated. Such a platform is increasingly becoming a personalized, specific-designed, and adaptive around e-learning. The purposes of the platform are designed to enrich the learners' experience, enhance the contact between facilitators, learners and audiences. These parties form a joint venture based on trust, mutual respect and understanding in sharing thoughts, experience, and insights relating to the repertoire and communication channels as desired. Together, they enjoy great happiness in performance with the powerful and fabulous creatures in appreciation of the open space via the internet. The key role players on this platform are:

- **Conductor:** Taking a role as an instructor or a facilitator
- **Individual performers/audiences:** The learners connected via various agents (web 2.0 tools) operating in a co-learning environment
- **Reinforcing agents:** Content and pedagogy within the collaborative and cooperative framework especially with Web 2.0 tools

The adoption of web 2.0 applications has emerged as a leading practice in the education sector and one that enables a new set of tools and applications to the web learning platform. "Moodle" is one leading E-learning system with pedagogical activities from open-source helping educators in such a launching platform. Facilitators do not necessarily possess technological savvy skills and the environment allows them to learn during the course of interaction in recognizing the prior knowledge of the learners, their interests and the complexity of the content. Angel (2006) recalls the concept of Web 2.0 by O'Reilly (2005) and outlined the core competencies required to be successful in building Live Web sites, which are value, collaboration, self-service, and abstraction. With Web 2.0 technology, the design tools/applications provide a greater degree of autonomy and academic freedom rendering the platform to be more applicable worldwide. It is time to change for a technological world with Web 2.0!

DIVERSITY FROM UNITY: WEB 2.0 SYMPHONY

Advances in technology and an understanding of e-learning have spawned a new perspective. Web-based applications are intrinsically multi-platform and Web 2.0 has a novelty value. A Web 2.0 platform facilitates the curriculum design for the target group to enhance mutual understanding by allowing discussion and communications to be systematically integrated into personal development, thereby facilitating individuals to develop all-rounded thinking and be well-trained and well-prepared for future challenges. Keengwe, Onchwari & Wachira (2008) say, "To achieve the full benefits of education technology requires strategic planning and integration of these tools into instruction that only a sense-making and skilled teacher can provide." Technology helps to provide the Web 2.0 tools and enlarge the scale where a leading paradigm provides a universal solution to education the world. Distinguished examples of e-learning collaborative applications are wikis, blogs, online-storage, services and directories, bookmarking and tagging, calendar and event, search, messaging and email, content management, feeds, widgets, etc. Angel (2006) says, "Web 2.0 employs the idea the "the Smartest Guy in the Room is Everybody," by endlessly eliciting user feedback and then leveraging the input to drive constant improvement." The idea is to let shape a platform by choosing values, building unique workplaces, sharing creations with co-learners online. It is real time personalized communications between a conductor (the facilitator) and individual performers (co-learners) to shape an ensemble to make a live broadcast in creating value-added services by integrating Web services from multiple sources in innovative ways. The boundary shift to a unique and innovatory quality of web-based education is particularly in evidence on display. There is only one word to describe every aspect of the realization of Web 2.0 symphony: "BRAVO!"

A facilitator starts a new game for those who often dream of leading an orchestra on stage. There is a new exhibit that offers a taste of that experience. The internet offers would-be conductors "SHAPES" - the chance to lead a virtual orchestra with a remote control baton. SHAPES is

> Stage: The e-learning platform of a participatory theatre
> Hybrid: A combination of face-to-face and wired/wireless contact
> Applications: Effective and efficient processes of delivery
> Profit: Yield from the teaching and learning processes
> Excel: To show quality output in knowledge and strength that surpass others
> Superiors: Personnel scale up to new heights through life-long learning

The unique, stupendous composition, which burst the bounds of instrumental functionalities for the first time in the history of the symphony, has been the object of controversy form the very first symphony orchestra with a harmonious combination of Web 2.0 instruments (Figure 2). Start bringing the world for web-based education to higher education as a continuing journey and in a co-learning environment!

LEARNING 2.0: PROFESSIONAL DEVELOPMENT/FACILITATION STRATEGIES

Li Chen et al. (2003) state that "in 2003, 1,373,000 university students in China were studying via modern 'information and communications technologies', involving a combination of satellite and terrestrial communications, and including in most cases some elements of Web-based teaching." (Bates & Bates, 2005) The unique display and innovatory quality of Learning 2.0 is evident of in the first movement of professional development

Figure 2. A symphony orchestra with a harmonious combination of Web 2.0 instruments

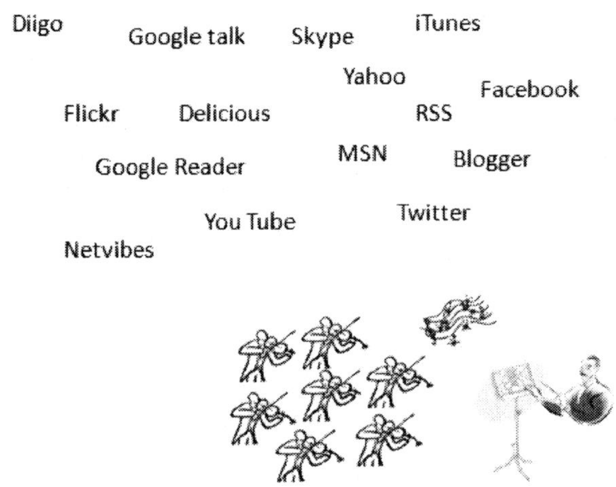

and facilitation strategies of higher education in the global world. The Web-Based Education (WBE) 2008 Conference – Globalization of Education in March 2008 marked a change in form and character from generation to generation, reflecting the changes in popular feelings and ideas in shaping e-learning development.

Masie (2008) interviewed some CEO of the key Learning Systems companies e.g. ACS, Adobe, Blackboard, Meridian, NetDimensions, Q2Learning, Skillsoft, etc. on 4 key questions, namely, "Learning Changes? Technology Changes? Future Plans for Your Organization? Impact of the Economy on Learning Field?" Technology soars to heaven above all rivals. Uskov (2008) reported that the group of 182 WBE experts from 146 universities/colleges in 47 countries ranked "Courseware" and "Quality" as the first and second most important strategic issues of web-based education for 2008-2015. It is certain that educators would surely have acted more to the purpose if they had followed the well-meant and trustworthy advice of co-learners and done what they learnt in the case of their plan. In order to make a magnificent composition of them as practicable as possible, even on those occasions when a large group and reliable learners are not available, educators have choices, according to circumstances, either to practice or in adoption of the instruments. Miyata (2008) says, "In the educational world, the Internet has created a new learning environment called "E-learning" and "Ubiquitous Learning". This ubiquitous setup enables education delivered to home, office, libraries, etc. that breaks the boundaries of a traditional classroom and knowledge exchange and idea sharing stay round-the-clock. An e-learning platform may include some common e-learning tools and applications that facilitate a variety of learning activities.

An e-learning platform incorporates Web 2.0 online tools facilitates an effective e-learning environment without programming required. Desirable features, among others, include blog reader, web-based calendar, conferencing services, content management systems, database management system, free-content encyclopedia, image sharing/storage, instant messenger, internet telephone, knowledge commons, online surveys, open source emails, photo sharing/storage, portable multimedia player, project management tools, quintessential search engines, RSS aggregator, social bookmarking, social networking, TV shows, word processor, and spreadsheet tool.

Table 2. Examples of e-learning tools / applications

Learners		**Facilitators**	
Web 1.0	Web 2.0	Web 1.0	Web 2.0
Alert Assignment drop box Bookmarks Directories Discussion board Email system Online Calendar Online presentation Password authentication Search engine Site map Vote / Rating Web page creation	Joint calendars Content Management System File/Image Storing and Sharing Forums Instant Messenger Quintessential search engines RSS RSS aggregator Social bookmarks Social Networks Tagging To-Do Lists Video conferencing Visual Search Engines Web 2.0 Start Pages Weblogs Webslides Wikis	Assignment drop box Content repository Database for class management Electronic Survey Image Database Interactive quiz Internal email system Online Calendar Online discussion board Online Glossary Online tutorial Password authentication Search engine Student performance tracking	Joint calendars Content Management System File/Image Storing and Sharing Forums Instant Messenger MashUps Online Surveys Podcasting Presence Management Quintessential search engines RSS RSS aggregator Social bookmarks Social Networks Tagging To-Do Lists Video conferencing Visual Search Engines VoIP Web 2.0 Start Pages Web-based job tracking Webcasts Weblogs Webslides Wikis

Suggestions in table 2 are not exhaustive while there are more emerging with advanced technological supports. Applying Web 2.0 concepts, we are everywhere and work gets done when everyone is connected, personalized, and adaptive.

Aldridge (2008) reminds educators to facilitate the environment and design details to meet the students' needs:

- Navigate comfortably from one virtual room to another
- Participate in threaded group discussions
- Efficiently search the Internet

Garrison & Vaughan (2008) say, "Three items, in particular, must be addressed: a description and rationale for strategies of blended learning, structure and expectations for the course, and support and resources." In order to appreciate the sensation that the use of Web 2.0 in the new era produces the creative boldness inspired platform with the tools, educators should draw attention on a plan with the virtue of being practical at the beginning. As noted by Aldridge (2008), there are four key components for implementing the application of tools to succeed in e-learning:

1. **Online paralanguage:** Capitalization, punctuation, and other expressions
2. **Social networking:** Cohorts of diverse students with compatible learning preferences
3. **Online communities:** Organized by common profession or research area
4. **Localizing classrooms:** Familiar icons and terms

1. Online Paralanguage

Social software serves as the instrument of online paralanguage in visualizing "capitalization, punctuation and other expressions". Rosenberg (2006) says, "Social software is to enable a dynamic exchange of ideas, knowledge, and viewpoints among participants, making their collective wisdom greater than individual wisdom." Several introductory interactive applications may help to play delicately to achieve primarily by social and dynamic means and not solely by individual teaching/learning.

"A **podcast** is a digital media file, or a related collection of such files, which is distributed over the Internet using syndication feeds for playback on portable media players and personal computers." (Wikipedia, 2007) Podcast allows any electronic text to learning with free high-quality text to speech! OEDb (2008) says, "The Apple-developed music player now features all kinds of accessories to help you study better, and now other companies are in a rush to get their designs in sync with the iPod." Podcasting has become a popular technology in education, in part because it provides a way of pushing educational content to learners. Stanford took its first step to go onto the iTune U – it is leading the education world!

Weblogs is "an open forum allows free flow of ideas, inputs, create 'friends' networks… The modern blog evolved from the online diary, where people would keep a running account of their personal lives." (Wikipedia, 2007) The instrument reacts with new, very tuneful motifs which may be fragmented into valuable resources well suited to the environment. Gillmor (2004) says, "The rise of the citizen journalist will help us listen." This genuine "open-air" instrument was blown to the world mainly by the huntsmen and their attendants.

Forum specifies dynamic shows societies within its community. It turns out to be a complex dialogue, in which inversions and other devices are used. New comers do not need to struggle against single-out from the special interest groups but accompanying by the body of the orchestra in conducting a dialogue within the community. Cross (2007) says, "Conversations carry news, create meaning, foster cooperation, and spark innovation." The others play energetic roles on the input, where open discussions through forum setting spread co-creative dialogue and relationships that sometimes create some unusual academic synergy.

E-mail – Messages in the open space are strongly delineated and normally questions, distributed information, and updates to each other i.e. learners/facilitators. It is a true keyboard interaction in the history of the internet. At the end of the 20th century, email received the large scale adoption in the internet as a global standard and became the most popular of all instruments. "It is an excellent vehicle to notify people (provide alerts) of the availability of new information or distribute knowledge to entire communities or organizations." (Rosenberg, 2006) It can sometimes be used with full RSS support.

"**RSS** is a format for syndicating news and the content of news-like sites, including major news sites like Wired, news-oriented community sites like Slashdot, and personal weblogs." (Pilgrim, 2002) This chromatic step is emphasized in the most excited way, by giving it the dynamic "really simple syndication" and a particular attraction of which is unchanged scoring of RSS, XML, ATOM that can be identified only by their dynamics, and the different manner of playing. The GovHK web site uses RSS extensively to provide news to citizens or learners in various communities of the society.

Google Reader – Learners/facilitators share the recommend articles to each other or friends with just one click. Hunting of blog is principally used in hunting, different horn signals serving to keep the widely scattered groups informed on the progress of the hunt. "With your Google Reader public page, you can share your favorite items with your friends, simply by sending them to relevant links." (Google Reader (Labs), 2008) Allotting articles to the horn which belong to the same category in design, seems reasonable, the more so since then they were created and played by the same performer! Tsui E. (a co-author of this book chapter) is the subject leader in MSc Knowledge Management is using tagged content in Google Reader and sharing them with the class thereby not only to complement the often static online learning content with up to date information on the topics but also fostering a co-learning environment in 2008.

Instant messaging – "The instantaneous nature of IM allows single or multiple conversations to begin at the moment of need, making it much more convenient than telephone or e-mail communications." (Rosenberg, 2006) It is a synchronous approach to electronic conversations that learners, facilitators or groups can find each other online. Instant communication immediate goes online in a particular time for collaboration and learning. All possible dialogues between learners/ facilitators can be exploited and presented using this instrument, via the accompanied learner(s) in the various groups.

File repositories – Great mobile store creates convenient services, e.g. Box.net. Rosenberg (2006) says, "For anyone who has worked with huge binders of outdated documentation and has tried to keep up with color-coded page updates, new approaches to managing documents and other physical knowledge assets have been nothing short of a revolution in information management and distribution, as well as a revolution in learning, because of the enhanced ability to update a broadly distributed workforce and keep content-up-to-date in real time." Online storage and sharing service provide access point to learners to store files from anywhere with internet connections. With online storage, learners can access documents from their desktop computer, laptop, or even mobile phone. Learners can also share them with anyone, anytime when files are uploaded to the online storage box. This makes online web file sharing simple!

Webslides - The construction of Webslides as a relentless, goal-directed event that can be narrated as a "story". The ideal subject and the objectified posts to which learners give a form to those who happened, in real life, create as a thought of as existing but independent of the knowledge construct. A fundamental feature "on demand" of this movement is the perfect symmetrical arrangement, which is comparable with the architecture of a "Baroque palace", by which learners use time and time again in their works. A new way of organizing, sharing, and publishing one's work!

Social Bookmarks - "Social bookmarking is a method for Internet users to store, organize, search, and manage bookmarks of web pages on the Internet with the help of metadata." (Wikipedia, 2008) A collection of elements of personalization in an online space – all of us are empowered with tools in composition. The works of learners' and various groups' composition develop different ensembles to be executed by all the performers simultaneously of which style and genre for the repertoire of their works are performed personally. All possible permutations and combination of a learner are exploited and presented via some accompanied, often open source, software e.g. del.icio.us.

Quintessential Search Engines – Search is one of the earliest works in cyberspace history in which a search engine is employed as an instrument across the entire breadth of its capabilities. The hunting instrument is principally used in locating relevant signals. Even a novice in the first performance may well have been travelling "search" at all events, made very clear to learners in their debut, a real hunting at a spectacular public display should be adapted to the quintessential characteristics of the hunt.

Electronic performance support systems – Collins (2003) says, "Reference information, expert systems, online job aids, application help, online analytical processing, integrated tracking and reporting and task performance tools" are features that support knowledge management. It is sure to be great value if they are enhanced to assist the learning progress for individual review.

These have a much louder effect than ordinary recorders. The systems would then be the "echo" and the echo effect may have been important that facilitators included it in the title of the collaborative work.

2. Social Network

Apart from social software, the other instrument play energetic chord on the beat - Social network brings in a large web of connections and we are aggregating relationships that may come back with rewards one day. MacManus (2007) says, "Note that this type of e-learning social network is similar to "smart" social networks, in which you can put access controls around your personal details, so that only people you trust can see them. Facebook, imbee, Vox, and Multiply are all examples of smart social networks." This is unique and basic in regard both to instrumentation and style as networking to every tradition it is scored only for the personal network. Learners/facilitators could have deliberately link these two representatives of separate families who complement each other so as to associate people for every collaboration opportunities.

3. Online Communities

"It is time for the academic world to recognize **Wikipedia** for what it has become: a global library open to anyone with an Internet connection and a pressing curiosity." (Wilson, 2008) The concerted play can be by a single learner, group of learners as a dialogue or contest with an open group (in a case small string is occasionally reduced to a purely formal, only recognizable idea). This represents in every respect the maximum possible differentiation and variety. Diversity takes precedence over uniformity and wikis continue to assert its precedence as the world's leading position to empower learners to create and control community websites.

4. Localizing Classrooms

Traditionally, learners receive their education in a school environment. A school is a traditional, dominated place designed for acquiring knowledge. Questions arise may cover, but not limited to, nature of activity, date, time, place, resource allocation, frequency of activity, etc. that are possible in a more free style learning environment. Different form of delivery means different things to learners/facilitators. Facilitators request the stimulus artifacts to active processing from learners in involvement and active participation. Thus, the learners also get their share of their solo work. Responded with a smile in front of the group, facilitators conduct and show them the way through in situations where issues may affect learners. Facilitators need have to be a good understanding, balance the various concerns and be sensitive to the different situational needs. "The ORID method is effective in helping diverse groups all over the world to address simple to complicated issues, and it certainly can play an important role in the classroom through a logical progression of questions." (Wee, 2006) Sample questions of the 4 levels of ORID method are:

- **Objective**: What's happened?
- **Reflective**: How did you feel?
- **Interpretive**: What did you learn?
- **Decisional**: What will you do to benefit from this course?

The checklist with elements of "questions" for planning helps student understand in better details, e.g. objective/outcome, target audience, type of interaction, rules/guideline/governance, etc. In localizing classrooms, facilitators should pay great care to arouse the enthusiasm of performers to better appreciate the interactions in between.

WEB 2.0 FOR E-LEARNING IN HONG KONG

The 2008 Digital 21 Strategy of the Hong Kong SAR Government is an initiative by which the government can transform the way the education does with learners/educators. In real situation, if the educators as conductors wave it too slowly, the learners as performers play at a crawl. If it is moved fast, the transformation speeds up, too. As well as the fast movement by the production of an astounding series of the weighty composition with the help of Web 2.0 making it some fabulous orchestral series in the education world, educators/learners are motivated to share their knowledge with others and participate actively.

The city is highly networked, both personally and technologically. Learners are beginning to progress on to Web 2.0 instruments with their predecessors (Web 1.0). Relationship building with or without selection changes individual's contribution to various knowledge communities. As the present situation allows, the gentle natural ICT blends well with the ensemble of Web 2.0 instruments with a moderate pitch. Learners read and write and find no big difference in operating the modern instruments while it is natural to cope with the classical, fascinating, and modern repertoire which does not call for such very high attention.

What facilitators need is an all-new, revolutionary feature set like *SimCity Societies* act to allow learners to create their own kinds of cities and shape their cultures and environment. In view of a marvelous collection of contemporary resources, there is no question the facilitators accompany other instruments in entirely willing to take sides. The idea is to let learners and facilitators shape their platform by choosing their own values, building unique workplaces, sharing creations with friends online i.e. in combination of ICT irrespective of an expertise and a tutoring component. Obviously, there is a distinction between a center and focus of great activity or intense concentration.

CONCLUSION AND FUTURE WORKS

In this paper we have reviewed some significant issues regarding the change of the state of the art of ICT's on e-learning. Web 2.0 heroes highlight the victory of the ICT by having a weighty deposition, and in presence as a swift runner at the platform for self-development and collaboration that greatly brightened up the performance with read-write applications. In particular, we have identified the importance of technological applications in the field supported by social source with a background support of 2008 Digital 21 Strategy of the Hong Kong SAR Government which is crucially to promote globalization in higher education. However, we should look beyond the boundaries of traditional training, and go beyond the boundaries. Technology is just a lever by faculty members. Chickering and Ehrmann (2007) introduce an article that "describes some of the most cost-effective and appropriate ways to use computers, video, and telecommunications technologies to advance the Seven Principles", "Good practice":

1. Encourages Contacts between Students and Faculty
2. Develops Reciprocity and Cooperation among Students
3. Uses Active Learning Techniques
4. Gives Prompt Feedback
5. Emphasizes Time on Task
6. Communicates High Expectations
7. Respects Diverse Talents and Ways of Learning

Learning contributes to great importance to one's goal and new technologies can dramatically improve time on task, collectivity and connectivity for learners and faculty members. In the near future, with e-learning, we aim to continue the adaptation of different tools and applications on the platform. We are implementing them on the platform for lifelong education in a form of pedagogy which often accompanied e-learning. Conducting a performance with agility is a great privilege to facilitators and learners on stage for hybrid learning with applications to gain profit and propel others to excel. Gradually, present-day performances are required to cope with the classical and modern repertoire consisting of competent members and the reinforcing agents within the big e-learning family:

- **Conductor:** Traditionally the instructor/facilitator, gradually shift to the learner
- **Individual performers:** The learners, originally they are discrete and not teamed up, gradually they are connected via various agents (web 2.0 tools) enabling to share views, knowledge, and operate in a co-learning environment (with the reduced role of the conductor)
- **Reinforcing agents:** Content and pedagogy, originally a 1-1 interaction, closed system (no external input), gradually moving towards collaborative and cooperative framework especially with Web 2.0 tools

A desired response or performance makes a good show of strength for:

- This is the way that Web 2.0 realizes our learning goal
- This is the way that Web 2.0 shifts our boundary
- This is the way that Web 2.0 (re-)clarifies our roles
- This is the way that Web 2.0 points us to the direction of true learners

This is the way that Web 2.0 shapes our learning life. We agree with Downes (2008) on his prediction of "De-schooling" and that is advantageous with the presence of an extensive networking via inexpensive ICT. The learning infrastructure is highly innovative and market-driven. From Web 2.0 onwards, technology development starts a transformational history of education and taking a great chance to go "mobile" in the near future!

Mobile learning focuses on the use of wireless Internet and GovWiFi in Hong Kong facilitates access to the general public so learners can enjoy learning anytime, anywhere. We should go further on e-learning development into primary schools, secondary schools, and universities locally, and across the borders to benefit the real world. This expansion view of learning delivery offers exciting concerto new approaches to movement on blended learning.

ACKNOWLEDGMENT

The authors gratefully acknowledge the support of The Hong Kong Polytechnic University (under grant account 8CBX) for the carrying out of this piece of research.

REFERENCES

Aldridge, S. (2008). *Proceedings of the 2008 international conference on Web-Based Education (WBE-2008)* – Innsbruck congress Center, Innsbruck, Austria. Retrieved April 18, 2008, from http://www.interlabs.bradley.edu/wbe2008/

Allen, D. (2001). *Getting Things Done: The Art of Stree-Free Productivity*. New York: Viking Penguin

Angel, M. (2006). *A Modern Approach to Improving Customer Support: Leveraging the Concepts of Web 2.0 for Self-service and in the Contact Center. KNOVA*. Retrieved April 14, 2008, from http://www.knova.com/products/learnmore.html

Bates, T., & Bates, T. (2005). *Technology, e-learning, and distance education* (2nd ed.). London: Routledge.

Bawaba, A. (2008). *Saudi Arabia's eLearning industry to touch US$125 million in 2008*. Retrieved April 30, 2008, from http://www.menareport.com/en/business/226175

Bielski, L. (2008). 2008: year of rich internet apps? (April 08). *ABA Banking Journal*. Retrieved January 11, 2009, from http://www.nxtbook.com/nxtbooks/sb/ababj0408/index.php?startpage=0

Castaneda, D. I., & Rios, M. F. (2007). From Individual Learning to organizational Learning. *Electronic Journal of Knowledge Management, 5*(4), 363-372. Retrieved March 30, 2008, from http://www.ejkm.com/volume-5/v5-i4/v5-i4-art3.htm

Cercone, K. (2008). Characteristics of adult learners with implications for online learning design. *AACE Journal, 16*(2), 137–159.

Chickering, A., & Ehrmann, S. (2007). *Implementing the Seven Principles: Technology as Lever*. Retrieved March 22, 2008, from http://www.tltgroup.org/programs/seven.html

Collins, H. (2003). *Enterprise knowledge portals: Next generation portal solutions for dynamic information access, better decision making, and maximum results*. New York: American Management Association.

Cross, J. (2002). *Internet Time Blog. Peter Henschel, RIP*. Retrieved April 14, 2008 from http://internettime.com/blog/archives/000228.html

Cross, J. (2007). *Informal learning: Rediscovering the natural pathways that inspire innovation and performance*. San Francisco: Jossey-Bass.

Curriculum Development Council and the Hong Kong Examinations and Assessment Authority. (2007). *Technology Education Key Learning Area: Business, Accounting and Financial Studies – Curriculum and Assessment Guide (Secondary 4 - 6).*

Downes, S. (2005). E-*Learning 2.0. Stephen's Web*. Retrieved April 10, 2008, from http://www.downes.ca/post/31741

Downes, S. (2006). *E-learning 2.0. eLearn magazine*. Retrieved March 22, 2008 from http://www.elearnmag.org/subpage.cfm?section=articles&article=29-1

Downes, S. (2008). *The OECD Schooling Scenarios in Brief. Stephen's Web*. Retrieved April 25, 2008, from http://www.downes.ca/cgi-bin/page.cgi?post=41340

Education and Manpower Bureau. (2006). *Action for the Future: further Consultation on Career-oriented Studies and the New Senior Secondary Academic Structure for Special Schools*.

Ehlers, U. (2007). A new pathway for e-learning: From distribution to collaboration and competence in e-learning . *AACE Journal, 16*(2), 187–202.

Garner, B. (2008). *Embedding Socratic Learning within Web-based Education (WBE)*. Hong Kong Polytechnic University

Garrison, D. R., & Vaughan, N. D. (2008). *Blended learning in higher education: Framework, principles, and guidelines* (1st ed.). San Francisco: Jossey-Bass.

Gillmor, D. (2004). *We the Media*. Retrieved March 22, 2008, from http://www.authorama.com/we-the-media-1.html

Gov, H. K. (2008). *Wi-Fi Facilities at Government Premises. Usage Guide*. Retrieved April 14, 2008, from http://www.gov.hk/mobile/en/wifi/guide/index.htm

Jin, R. (2008). *S. Korea's 'e-Learning' Market Tops W1.7 Tri*. Retrieved April 1, 2008, from http://www.koreatimes.co.kr/www/news/include/print.asp?newsIdx=20526

Keengwe, J., Onchwari, G., & Wachira, P. (2008). The use of computer tools to support meaningful learning. *AACE Journal, 16*(1), 77–92.

MacManus, R. (2007). *e-learning 2.0: All You Need To Know. Read/WriteWeb*. Retrieved November 13, 2007, from http://www.readwriteweb.com/archives/e-learning_20_all_you_need_to_know.php

Marginson, S. (2007). *Going Global: Trends in higher education and research in the APEC region*. Retrieved from http://www.cshe.unimelb.edu.au/people/staff_pages/Marginson/APEC_HRDWG_Symposium_170407.pdf

Miller, P. (2007). *Marc Andreesen digs into the Platform. Web 2.0 Explorer: Guest bloggers*. Retrieved April 25, 2008, from http://blogs.zdnet.com/web2explorer/?p=402

Miyata, H. (2008). Mobile & Collaborative Learning Development by a Concept of "Mobile-As-Participation-Platform". In *Proceedings of the 7th International Conference on Web-Based Education (WBE-2008),* Innsbruck, Austria

O'Reilly, T. (2005). *Web 2.0: Compact Definition? O'Reilly Radar*. Retrieved April 30, 2008, from http://radar.oreilly.com/archives/2005/10/web-20-compact-definition.html

O'Reilly, T. (2005). *What is Web 2.0: Design Patterns and Business Models for the Next Generation of Software. O'Reilly*. Retrieved March 22, 2008, from http://www.oreilly.com/pub/a/oreilly/tim/news/2005/09/30/what-is-web-20.html

OEDb. (2008). *100 Ways to Use Your iPod to Learn and Study Better*. Retrieved March 22, 2008, from http://oedb.org/library/beginning-online-learning/100-ways-to-use-your-ipod-to-learn-and-study-better

Pilgrim, M. (2002). *What is RSS? O'Reillyxml.com*. Retrieved March 22, 2008, from http://www.xml.com/pub/a/2002/12/18/dive-into-xml.html

Ramirez, M. (2008). *UH report shows college students making the grade online, in class. Back to EurekAlert!* Retrieved March 30, 2008, from http://www.eurekalert.org/pub_releases/2008-03/uoh-urs032408.php#

Reader, G. *(Labs)*. (2008). Retrieved April 18, 2008, from http://www.google.com/help/reader/tour2.html

Rosenberg, M. J. (2006). *Beyond e-learning: Approaches and technologies to enhance organizational knowledge, learning, and performance*. San Francisco: Pfeiffer.

Ryymin, E., Lallimo, J., & Hakkarainen, K. (2008). Teachers' professional development in a community: A study of the central actors, their networks and web-based learning. *E-Learning and Education (Eleed) Journal*, (4). Retrieved December 14, 2008, from http://eleed.campussource.de/archive/4/1251/

Smart, A. (2008). Tim Berners-Lee: a very British boffin. *Telegraph.co.uk*. Retrieved April 6, 2008, from http://www.telegraph.co.uk/connected/main.jhtml?xml=/connected/2008/03/30/sv_timbernerslee.xml

So, P. (2008). Getting with the programme. *South China Morning Post*.

Thomas, R. (2006). Global Trends in Higher Education. 2006 Britannica Book of the Year. In Joe (Ed.), *Encyclopaedia Britannica*. Retrieved November 7, 2007, from http://www.gather.com/viewArticlePF.jsp?articleId=281474976776571

Uskov, V. (2008). *Proceedings of the 7th International Conference on Web-Based Education (WBE-2008),* Innsbruck, Austria

Wee, L. C. (2006). The ORID in IS Classes. In *Proc ISECON 2006, v23 (Dallas): §3732 (refereed)*. Retrieved April 25, 2008, from isedj.org/isecon/2006/3732/ISECON.2006.Wee.pdf

Wenger, E. (n.d.). *Communities of Practice*. Community of Practice – a brief introduction. Retrieved April 1, 2008, from http://www.ewenger.com/theory/index.htm

Wikipedia. (2008). *Electronic Learning*. Retrieved March 22, 2008, from http://en.wikipedia.org/wiki/E-learning

Wikipedia. (2008). *Socrates*. Retrieved April 21, 2008, from http://en.wikipedia.org/wiki/Socrates

Wilson, M. (2008). Professors should embrace Wikipedia. *Inside Higher Ed*. Retrieved April 1, 2008, from http://insidehighered.com/layout/set/print/views/2008/04/01/wilson

KEY TERMS AND DEFINITIONS

E-Learning: The integrated use of various tools and online resources to provide an environment for learning development and assessment free of the time and location constraints imposed on the instructor(s) and learners.

Hybrid Learning: Combines a range of human teaching activities, learning systems and administrative resources that educators have been deployed a significant amount of online activities strategically to enhance student learning.

Learning Platform: An infrastructure that supports, among others, the authoring, matching, tracking, delivery and assessments of learning in an online environment.

Reinforcing Agents: Content and pedagogy within the collaborative and cooperative framework to reward a desired response or performance.

Social Software: Computer applications that harness, maintain and sustain the growth of social capital, trust and relationships among individuals in a networked environment.

Web 2.0: Defined as "...the network as platform, spanning all connected devices; Web 2.0 applications are those that make the most of the intrinsic advantages of that platform: delivering software as a continually-updated service that gets better the more people use it, consuming and remixing data from multiple sources, including individual users, while providing their own data and services in a form that allows remixing by others, creating network effects through an "architecture of participation," and going beyond the page metaphor of Web 1.0 to deliver rich user experiences." (O'Reilly, 2005)

Web 2.0 Online Tools: Facilitate an effective e-learning environment without programme required which make it relatively effortless for all to access a world of information comprehensive and personal increasingly.

Chapter 9
Using Podcasting and Digital Audio in Higher Education

Jogesh K. Muppala
The Hong Kong University of Science and Technology, Hong Kong, China

Sean McMinn
The Hong Kong University of Science and Technology, Hong Kong, China

David Rossiter
The Hong Kong University of Science and Technology, Hong Kong, China

Gibson Lam
The Hong Kong University of Science and Technology, Hong Kong, China

ABSTRACT

Audio and spoken word has always been an important component of teaching and learning in higher education. However this remained an ephemeral component given that it is rarely captured for later use. Digital audio production and distribution has given a new means for facilitating the capture and preservation of this learning component for reuse. This chapter reports the authors' experience with the use of digital audio in teaching and learning in higher education. The use of podcasting as a means of delivering online recorded audio of classroom lectures to enhance the course materials is discussed. Podcast production as a means of learning by students is then highlighted. Finally, the use of audio discussion forums as a means of communication is presented. Results from student surveys and reflections of the authors on their experiences with digital audio usage in the classroom to illustrate its advantages and disadvantages are then presented.

INTRODUCTION

The spoken word has long been the primary medium for learning and disseminating information and knowledge (Clark & Walsh, 2004). The emergence of other forms of communication and information dissemination including the printed word and electronic media has not diminished the primacy of aural communication. We need to look no further than the higher education environment where the face to face style of teaching still dominates as the primary means of instruction.

Podcasting has emerged as the premier push technology for delivering online audio content.

DOI: 10.4018/978-1-60566-380-7.ch009

Listeners interested in automatically receiving updated content subscribe to a podcast, and, whenever new content becomes available, it is unobtrusively delivered to the users without their explicit involvement. Podcasting does not mean just putting audio content online. The advantage of podcasting is in its ability to automatically deliver content to listeners without their explicit intervention. Increasing availability of sophisticated and inexpensive audio recording and processing technologies has made it easy for individuals to produce and make available audio content online. The ubiquitous PC with its ability to capture audio and the increasing prevalence of audio (e.g., MP3) players with audio recording capability makes this process very convenient. Once the content is captured, it can easily be made available online for downloading in a few simple steps. This has significantly contributed to the growth of individuals making a large amount of audio content available through podcasts. Podcasting has also found increasing application in the higher education environment for many different purposes such as making available lecture audio recordings, audio and music clips relevant to a course. This chapter summarizes our experience with the use of digital audio podcasting in different courses and in different ways at the Hong Kong University of Science and Technology (HKUST). In particular experience in:

- developing and using tools for podcasting,
- using podcasting as a means of delivering online recorded audio of classroom lectures to enhance the course materials,
- using podcasting as an integrated tool across a curriculum,
- using podcasting as a means of motivating, stimulating and engaging students with rich resources and activities, and
- using podcasting to extend the classroom and create a mobile learning environment,

are highlighted.

The terms *hybrid learning* and *blended learning* have been used to mean the integration of learning styles, tools, techniques and mechanisms, especially in the context of e-learning. Heinze and Procter (2004) define blended learning as *learning that is facilitated by the effective combination of different modes of delivery, models of teaching and styles of learning, and founded on transparent communication amongst all parties involved with a course*. This chapter discusses the pedagogical uses of digital audio combined with traditional classroom environments, thus fitting the general definition of a hybrid learning environment. The chapter includes the methodology, implementation and evaluation of this form of hybrid learning environment, which provides a useful case study for future research in the field.

First the use of audio in higher education is reviewed. Then some discussions on pedagogical aspects related to the use of audio and podcasting in higher education is presented. Then the authors' experiences at HKUST which have involved the use of podcasting are presented. Finally conclusions and suggestions for future research are presented. This experience sharing is intended to provide an example of how the new technology can be adopted in teaching and learning.

BACKGROUND

The Importance of Audio in Learning

One question that begs examining in detail is why auditory learning is a useful approach. Gardner's theory of multiple intelligences (Gardner, 1983) divides the way people learn into eight categories: musical, rhythmic, spatial, mathematical, interpersonal, intrapersonal, and natural. Audio definitely addresses many of these intelligences. A related issue is the three learning styles: visual, auditory and kinesthetic. See for example (Wikipedia, Learning Styles). Indeed, auditory learning is recognized as one of the most basic forms of learning and predates the written form of communication. Clark and Walsh (2004) delve in depth into this issue in their report. Another detailed discussion on auditory learning can also be found in Chan and Lee (2005). To quote Morales and Moses (2006), auditory learners learn best through verbal lectures, discussions, talking things through and listening to what others have to say. Similarly, Durbridge (1984) highlights the advantages of using audio in learning. In his words, the spoken word can influence both cognition (adding clarity and meaning) and motivation (by conveying directly a sense of the person creating those words), as compared to written text.

Similarly, the constructivist conditions for learning (Driscoll, 2005, p. 399) suggest that using multiple modes of representation can be juxtaposed to deliver the same content through visual, auditory and tactile sensory modes, with the content complementing one another. Driscoll (2005, pp. 399-400) also cites an example of how the production of learning content can help students take ownership for their own learning, in the process promoting their own understanding of the subject matter.

One more distinct advantage of podcast audio is the time-shifting ability that it affords to the listeners. Users are no longer restricted by time and space in terms of their learning activity (Clark & Walsh, 2004). Auditory learning is the most "portable" form of learning, and can be used anytime, anywhere. Morales and Moses (2006) point out that podcasting is not a means of replacing in-class lectures. They emphasize that recording an in-class lecture without giving due consideration to the visual cues that are delivered in class may result in an incomplete learning experience to the students. This observation can indeed be corroborated by the authors' own experience with recording in-class lecture audio, as discussed later. According to Morales and Moses (2006), for podcasting to become popular, several challenges including rights management, production and maintenance of the content, integration with learning management systems, and end-user experience need to be addressed.

Related Work

Alexander (2006) reports that social software, like blogs, wikis, podcasting etc. have emerged as the new components of what has now been labeled as Web 2.0™ (O'Reilly, 2005), the next generation of web technologies. He discusses several emerging technologies and their impact and implications to higher education.

Several authors have suggested the use of the emerging technologies in the teaching and learning process. In particular D'Souza (2006) has written an interesting article on the use of web feeds in education. He explains the use of various emerging web technologies in the classroom. Similarly, Richardson (2006) gives a detailed description of how these new technologies can be used for education. He also maintains an online resource wiki on the application of these emerging technologies in education at http://webloggedlinks.pbwiki.com/.

Podcasting as a new e-learning technology has attracted attention in the academia in the recent past. One of the earliest reports detailing the potential of podcasting was by Clark and Walsh (2004). They give detailed analysis of why listening is a good way of learning. They point out the virtues of auditory learning and delineate the advantages of using an audio device as a means of delivering learning content. A recent report by Morales and Moses (2006) examines podcasting in detail. In particular, they survey the podcasting arena, give reasons why this is a good medium of delivery, point out the advantages and shortcomings of this technology. They also speculate on the future evolution of this technology and its application in higher education.

Chan and Lee (2005) report on the use of podcasting in an information technology course. They do a comprehensive survey of the advantages and disadvantages of the use of audio in learning.

They specifically studied the use of short audio clips delivered to students in order to alleviate the pre-class anxiety encountered by the students. They give a comprehensive background on the use of audio as an aid in the learning process from the tape recording era to the (now) podcasting era. It must be emphasized that while the use of audio or multimedia content in courses is not new, what is particularly noteworthy about the new technologies is that podcasting provides an excellent channel of delivering this content through subscription to the users' computers or portable media players. The delivery mechanism is the new innovation that has revolutionized the use of audio in education because it now provides an inexpensive medium for delivering the content to end-users.

Podcasting is considered part of m-Learning. Tynan and Colbarn (2006) identify m-Learning as "a different form of eLearning, as it takes the learner away from a fixed point and 'respects that a user would like to interact with educational resources whilst away from a normal place of learning-classroom or computer'" The idea is that podcasting creates a borderless classroom. By extending the classroom, making it mobile, educators are able to increase the time students allocate to studying. But podcasting as used in education is more than this. It enhances the potential outcomes of a course for today's tech-savvy students. As Campbell (2005) explains in *There's Something in the Air: Podcasting in Education,* more students are aware of this technology and know how to use it: "More and more students come to school with these skills. This is a language they not only understand but use often and on a daily basis. These are the tools of their native expressiveness, and with the right guidance and assignments, they can use these tools to create powerful analytical and synthetic work". Barnnes, Marateo and Ferris (2007) categorize these students as Net Geners (that is, from the Net Generation) and suggest that "the challenge of evolving pedagogy to meet the needs of Net-savvy students is daunting, but educators are assisted by the fact that this generation values education. These students learn in a different way than their predecessors did, but they do want to learn".

Hartigan et al. (2006) describe several examples of the use of podcasting at Brandeis University. In particular they describe the use of podcasting by students to contribute audio content to the courses. They describe both the technical and educational challenges that they encountered. Brittain et al. (2006) present their experiences with using Podcasting at University of Michigan School of Dentistry. In particular they adopt the formative evaluation strategy to appraise the use of appropriate technology to meet the students' need for access to lecture recordings. Through a series of three pilot studies, they concluded that lecture audio content made available to students through podcasting is the best solution. Similarly Osswald and Dugdale (2006) describes the use of podcasting to engage the students in course content.

Similarly many universities have deployed institution-wide infrastructure to provide podcasting and elearning support for their instructors. See for example (iLecture, 2006) (Berkeley, 2006) (Purdue, 2006) (UW-Madison, 2006) (ELI-Duke, 2006). Such systems provide many facilities including automated recording and upload of audio and podcast of the lecture audio without the explicit involvement of the faculty. It must be noted that many of these initiatives require the setting up of large IT infrastructure together with dedicated IT support staff.

Apple is offering support for the use of podcasting in universities through its iTunesU program (Apple, 2006). One successful use of iPods in education at Duke University is described in (ELI-Duke, 2006). This project involved distributing iPods to students and studying the various uses of the technology in the education process. Podcasting was one component of the overall research study.

Technology Overview of Podcasting

Podcasting is a type of Push Technology in which the request of a transaction originates from the content publisher. Webcasting describes an Internet-based content delivery system where information is delivered from a central server to a client computer based upon a predefined set of request parameters outlined by the client computer. The client computer would subscribe to various information topics provided by a content provider and as that content is created and made available online it is "pushed" or delivered across the Internet to the user. Push Technology differs from normal Web usage, where a user has to request for content from a website through a Web browser.

Podcasting is an automatic mechanism whereby multimedia files are transferred from a server to a client, which pulls down XML files containing the Internet addresses (or URL) of the digital files. In general, these files are audio or video files, but they could also be image files, text files or PDF files. Podcasting can be divided into four sequential stages: producing the content, publishing the content in RSS format, subscribing to the RSS feed, and consuming the content. Figure 1 illustrates the concept of podcasting using the steps in the process of making an audio podcast.

Producing the Content

This is stage A in Figure 1. The producer (or Podcaster) produces a multimedia file. After planning the topic and content he wants to speak, the speaker records the audio into a sound file (like mp3). There are multiple audio formats like wave and mp3. Sometimes, post-production activities like removing noise, adding sound effects and mixing sounds are done on the file.

Figure 1. Process of making an audio podcast

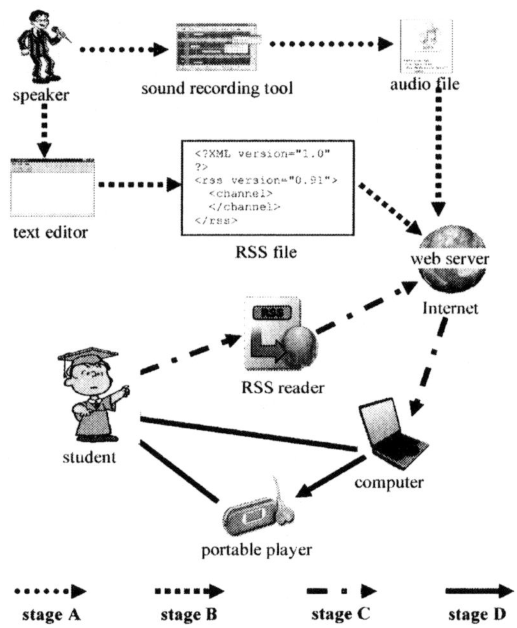

Publishing the Content in RSS Format

This is stage B in Figure 1. After the producer updates an RSS file, he uploads it and the previous produced audio file(s) to the Internet. RSS is a family of Web feed formats. "RSS" is variously used to refer to the standards: Really Simple Syndication (RSS 2.0), Rich Site Summary (RSS 0.91, RSS 1.0), and RDF Site Summary (RSS 0.9 and 1.0). RSS delivers its information as an XML file called an "RSS feed", "webfeed", "RSS stream", or "RSS channel". An RSS reader makes use of the information provided by an RSS file to perform automatic download.

Subscribing to the RSS Feed

This is stage C in Figure 1. Using a RSS reader, users subscribe to a RSS channel by specifying the URL, the universal resource locater, of an RSS feed file in an RSS reader. After the subscription, multimedia files from this channel are automatically downloaded to their computers. An aggregator (also called news aggregator or feed reader) is client software that uses a feed to retrieve syndicated Web content.

Consuming the Content

This is stage D in Figure 1. After downloading the audio file, students listen to it either on their computers, PDAs, iPods or mp3 players. By using mp3 audio players, students can enjoy listening to the audio recording anytime and anywhere.

LEARNING THROUGH AUDIO

Learning through Reception

This section describes the use of podcasting in some university courses at the authors' university to deliver lecture audio. For many years students have been requesting the authors to make course lecture recordings (either audio or video) available for their use in revising and reviewing the course materials. Technological constraints and the prohibitive cost of providing such a service proved to be impediments in making this feasible in the past. With the advent of digital audio/video, the cost factor became less significant. However there still existed technological constraints in terms of efficiently and cost-effectively capturing and processing the audio/video and making it available online. The growing availability of inexpensive MP3 players with recording capability made it quite simple to capture, process and make the audio available through the Internet. In addition, podcasting provided a simple mechanism of delivering the content to users through subscription.

The course lectures were recorded while being delivered in the traditional classroom setting. A simple MP3 player (a Samsung Yepp YP-T6 MP3 player) was used to record the audio during the lecture. The quality of the recorded audio was quite clear and acceptable to the students. This player records the audio in WAV format (32 Kbps mono audio). Thereafter the recorded WAV audio was converted to MP3 format. The typical MP3 file size was about 15 Mb for a one hour of audio.

The audio files were made available online either for download directly from a website, or through a podcast that students could subscribe using their favorite podcatcher software like iTunes (Apple, 2006) or Juice (Juice, 2006). This enables them to automatically download the lecture audio and listen to the lectures at their convenience either using a MP3 player or a PC. Post-processing of the recorded audio and making it available online took about 15 minutes.

For podcasting the audio files, the department web server which hosts our course web pages was sufficient. No additional infrastructure to support podcasting was required. Podcasting required the setting up and editing of a simple XML (extended markup language) file containing the podcast information. This was accomplished by directly editing the file containing the XML syntax. Whenever a new audio file was uploaded, the podcast XML file was edited to add in the information pertaining to the newly uploaded audio file.

Learning through Production

Creating audio is becoming increasingly easier to do and at lower costs, paving new ways for using audio technology in education. As a result, podcasting as an educational tool need not only come from the educator; students, too, can benefit significantly from producing and publishing their own audio through podcasting. By learning through podcast production, students are able to participate in constructivist learning, situated learning, problem-based learning, context awareness learning, collaborative learning, and conversation learning situations. This section discusses how podcasting enhances learning through production, and a language course, Campus Beat, where podcasting has been integrated into the curriculum will be used as an example to show how podcasting technology can be used. In addition the following questions will be considered.

- Does podcasting assist with student motivation?
- Is learning more flexible, easier or successful?
- Does producing a podcast provide opportunities to students for self improvement and continued learning outside of the classroom?
- Are skills adapted from producing a podcast transferable to other disciplines?

Integrating podcasting into the curriculum allows for a constructivist learning framework; that is it helps transform learners from being passive recipients of information to active constructors. As a result, an environment where students participate in the learning process occurs. Furthermore, the tool allows the possibility of embedding students into a realistic context. For example, language instructors can develop creative ways of encouraging students to practice their language skills outside the classroom through the use of student-produced podcasts. Podcasting should not, however, be the centre of attention in an English language course. Instead, it should be integrated into the curriculum, and, essentially, be invisible (O'Bryan and Hegelheimer, 2007).

Campus Beat

Campus Beat is two things: a magazine podcast produced by students at the authors' home institution, the Hong Kong University of Science and Technology, and a course module offered by the HKUST Language Centre. Segments of the Campus Beat podcast are written and recorded by a student volunteer staff and students from the Language Centre's Campus Beat course. The volunteer staff writes stories related to entertainment, academics and current events at HKUST, in Hong Kong and worldwide. Students enrolled in the Campus Beat course write two news segments, one related to Hong Kong current events and one to HKUST, as an assessed task for the podcast. All stories are broadcast on the Campus Beat podcast. In addition to campus current events, Campus Beat provides an English language learning segment called "Word Power".

Campus Beat: The Course

The Campus Beat module is offered by the HKUST Language Centre. The purpose is to help them become better critical readers of English, to introduce them to the various styles of writing, and to write more effectively. Students are taught basic news writing skills and theory, such as news values, and they practice their own writing skills through two assigned tasks. The first assessed task requires students to work in groups of 3 or 4, find a newsworthy story in Hong Kong, paraphrase it if it is taken from a newspaper, record it and submit it to the teacher who will include it in an episode of Campus Beat. This task is a part of their participation mark and is used primarily to allow students to become familiar with podcasting and news writing. The second task is an individual assignment. Students must write a newsworthy story about something occurring on campus, record the story and submit it to their teacher who will include it in an episode of Campus Beat. In addition to language skills, students have the chance to develop technical skills as they are required to record and edit their voice using Audacity, a free audio recording tool. Because Campus Beat has a real audience, that is, an audience outside the classroom, these tasks give students a chance to work in a real life situation.

Campus Beat: The Podcast

The Campus Beat podcast is a platform for students to practice their English writing, speaking and listening skills. In addition to the stories written by students taking the course, it has other segments marketed towards a university audience. These include commentaries, entertainment news, English language tips and English-language music. Each episode is approximately 30 minutes long, and students and staff are invited to contribute stories for, or comment on, the podcast. The goal of this podcast is to develop an English speaking community on campus and to provide interesting, entertaining, and newsworthy information for students and staff. To date, the average download rate has been over 700 per episode. This includes listeners from HKUST and other countries, such as Japan and the United States (students and instructors from a university in Japan have left comments about Campus Beat on the Campus Beat website http://campusbeat.libsyn.com/).

Interactivity

The Campus Beat module was designed to encourage interactivity among students and staff within the university community through podcasting. For the purpose of language acquisition, this increase in interactivity adds to the time a student spends practicing a second language.

For example, a group assignment in the Campus Beat module requires students in small groups to conduct research and write a story in English about something newsworthy occurring on campus. Most of the information needed to write the story will come from the university community, peers or review of literature. Once the students have gathered their information and written the story, they produce an audio segment for the Camus Beat podcast, which is then published for the university community and, in fact, the entire world community, to listen to. The flow of information is mainly one way at this point; a student has taken data, written something and then produced an audio for an audience. However, the flow of information does not stop there. Potentially, the story will be listened to by the target audience (university students and staff), a worldwide audience, and the teacher (for grading); and the listeners can contribute back by leaving comments on the Campus Beat blog, or through an interactive flash player that allows listeners to place text, audio, or video comments anywhere on the timeline of an episode. Students will then see (or listen, or watch) the comments that have been added. This type of interaction could go on for as long as listeners and the students want.

Figure 2 shows the interactions that can take place in a collaborative and conversational learning environment with podcasts.

As mentioned earlier, podcasting allows for a collaborative and conversational learning environment. In an ESL course, students are collaborating with their peers, teacher and audience though podcasting, learning how to report and discuss information, such as campus news. In addition, the interactivity allows for a conversational language learning environment; a student could learn formal language during the writing process of a news story, and then learn informal language during discussion through the commenting system.

It should be noted that this type of interactivity need not only be used for language acquisition. The same sort of interactivity with podcasting can be applied to any learning process and promote

Figure 2. Campus Beat

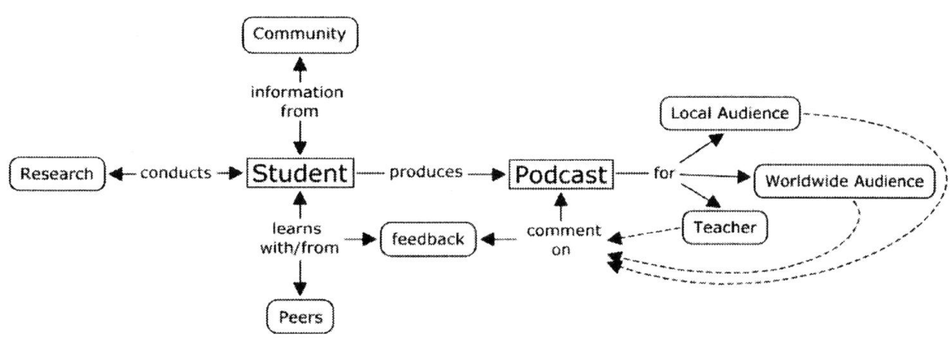

different learning outcomes. For example, instead of focusing on language, teachers could adapt the integration of podcasting into a lesson with a focus on the content or critical analysis of a subject. The possibilities are numerous.

Motivation Factors

Motivating students to practice English outside classroom time is often difficult to do, and podcasting may assist with this problem. There is a potential for podcasting "to foster a more seamless integration of in-class and out-of-class activity and materials, in addition to the wealth of authentic foreign language material freely available for download" (Thorne & Payne, 2005). O'Bryan and Hegelheimer (2007) also suggest that podcasting has the potential for creating intrinsic and extrinsic motivation in students. Stanley (2005) suggests that students who produce podcasts for assessed tasks "will probably take more care with the preparation, knowing that it could be potentially listened to by people all over the world. After discussing and planning the contents, the learners should be involved in writing and rewriting scripts which they will revise with their classmates (and later their teacher) ensuring that the content is understandable and there are no mistakes. They will then rehearse the show before finally recording it." The Campus Beat course attempts to create both intrinsic and extrinsic motivation in students through listening and writing activities (see Table 1).

Learning through Communication

The Gong system is a free Web-based voice communication tool created by two of the authors (Gong, 2007). Data entered by people when they download the system together with email and forum interaction with users show that the system has been employed by many institutions around the world since it was freely released, involving thousands of students.

The primary use of the Gong system is for the creation and management of a collection of voice boards where people can communicate with each other over the Internet. Inside a voice board people can post their own text/voice messages as well as read, listen to and reply to messages created by others. The system can be used as an applet in a web page, or as a stand-along program.

Gong has many advanced and interesting features that increase the pedagogical value of the voice boards. For example, a voice message can be played faster or slower without losing its quality and voice messages can be 'indexed' so

Table 1. Use of podcasts in the Campus Beat module

	Integrated listening podcast	Integrated writing podcast
Type of task	Short-answer response, comprehension	News story or commentary
Type of student activity	Frequent interaction with students. Some interaction with computer through the lesson.	Frequent interaction with students. Some interaction with university community.
Type of feedback	Interpreting, evaluating, commenting, stimulating thought	invention, content, grammar, revision, peer, and formative
Teacher's roles	Facilitator Manager	Facilitator Manager
Position of podcast in curriculum	tool for learning; normalized integration into syllabus; adapted to learners' needs	tool for practicing; normalized integration into syllabus; adapted to learners' needs
Position of podcast in lesson	Assigned as homework; smaller part of every lesson.	Assigned as homework; assessed tasks.
Motivation	Intrinsic and extrinsic	Intrinsic and extrinsic

that people can selectively playback only one word or a phrase inside the text of a message (Rossiter, Lam, & Mak, 2006). Furthermore, a group of teachers and students can participate in recordable voice chat. The Gong system can also be configured to provide a voice board feature within the Moodle system, one of the most popular learning management systems (LMS) (Lam, Rossiter, & Cheung, 2006).

Using Gong for Podcasting

The Gong system can be used to easily generate podcasts (Rossiter & Lam, 2006). By simply selecting an option in the system, an administrator can enable the podcasting of any voice board. Subsequently, a podcast of the voice board is automatically generated by the system. It contains all the text and voice components of recordings in the board. Any changes to the voice board are immediately reflected in the podcast. Instructors and students only need to record and submit messages to the Gong board, which is a very simple process, and can ignore any technical issues concerning podcasting. Figure 3 provides a high level illustration of the way in which the system operates.

When broadcast as a podcast, a voice board may be accessed in a number of ways, as follows.

1. By using the Gong software to access the voice board.
2. By subscribing to the voice board podcast using an RSS reader, such as iTunes, possibly with upload to a portable device for later access.
3. By using a web browser, such as Internet Explorer or Firefox, to access the podcast RSS feed.

KEY FINDINGS AND OBSERVATIONS

Students' Feedback on Lecture Podcasts

One to two student surveys were conducted for each course to give a better understanding of the overall comments on the lecture recordings, the students' behavior with respect to listening to the audio lecture recordings, the students' understanding of Podcasting, and further enhancements about the provision of online lectures. The studies involved about 160 students. This section summarizes the survey results.

Figure 3. A high-level illustration of Gong voice board access via the Gong applet/application, and via a podcast

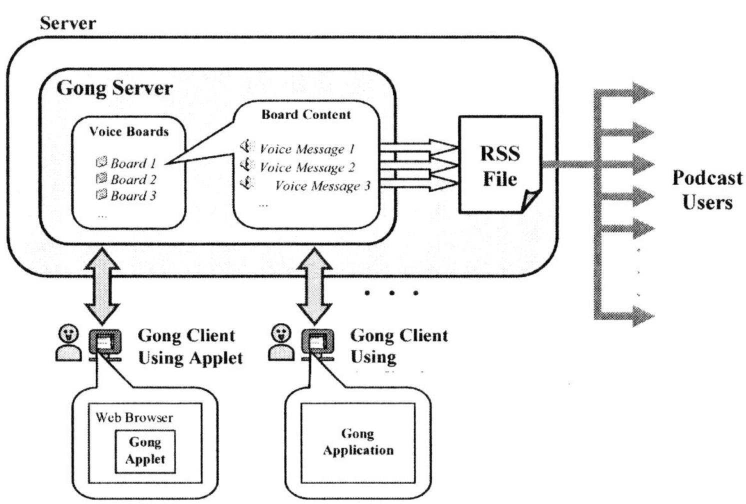

Overall Comment about the Lecture Recordings

Since the Spring Semester in 2006, recorded mp3 lectures were provided online. Since the Spring Semester in 2007, in addition to mp3 lectures, video recordings and online viewing of indexed presentations were also provided. The students were asked whether they had accessed the recorded lectures. The results reveal that 59% students accessed to the recorded lectures.

Several potential advantages of providing lecture recordings were listed and students were asked to make multiple selections on the choices. The survey results indicate that the major advantages of providing lecture recordings as perceived by the students were: it is convenient (55.24%), it makes students less worried about missed classes (48.95%), it aids students in studying for examinations (41.26%), it provides a written record of lecture content (37.41%), it perverse information accurately (30.42%), and it frees students from copying everything (30.42%). The availability of recorded lectures provides a written record of lecture content and preserve the information accurately. This gives students the confidence that they can always review a difficult concept again just in case they do not understand it in the first time. This also relieved their pressure from having to take detailed notes during the lecture which might detract their attention from the lecture.

Several potential disadvantages of providing lecture recordings were listed and students were asked to make multiple selections on the choices. In the students' view the major disadvantages of providing lecture recordings were: it is time consuming to find information within the audio (39.86%), it encourages students to skip lectures (37.68%), and it is difficult to find information within the audio file (36.23%).

After selecting the advantages and disadvantages of providing recorded lectures, the students were asked for the overall comment on providing audio lectures. To a large extent (19%) and to some extent (37%), which summed up to 56%, students found that audio lectures are effective in enhancing course content. Furthermore, to a large extent (29%) and to some extent (25%), which summed up to 54%, students prefer a class which provided recorded lectures.

Student Behavior with Respect to Listening to the Audio Lectures

The surveys included questions about students' behavior with respect to listening to the audio lectures. The factors that were investigated include how many times did the students listen to and how long did the students listen to each audio lecture; why did students listen to the lecture recordings; what devices did they use to play the audio lectures; will the provision of recorded lectures encourage skipping classes, and will the provision of recorded lecture help non-native English speaking students to understand the lecturer's spoken language.

Most students (91%) listen to each of the recordings once. The total length of a recorded lecture is about 80 minutes (which is the duration of a class). On average, most students (65%) listen to only about 5-30 minutes of the audio file.

Several reasons for them accessing the recorded lectures were listed and students were asked to make multiple selections on the choices. According to the students, the major reasons were: to review a lecture that was missed (63.10%), to study for an examination (45.83%), and to review a lecture after attending it (39.68%). From the results, many students prefer to listen to the lecture as a way of reviewing the materials covered in class. This provided them additional reinforcement for the understanding of concepts as they could always revisit the lectures and review materials that they found difficult to understand the first time around. Also, students found recorded lectures to be very useful especially when they were reviewing the materials for examinations. Further evidence corroborating this fact is that most students mentioned that more often they listened to the audio files just before examinations.

One advantage of providing lecture Podcasting is that students can learn at their convenient time and place. To facilitate this, portable devices seem to be the favored options for listening to the audio lectures. Students were asked to identify the devices they used to listen to audio lectures. About 76% of the students used only PC to listen to audio lectures, 11% of the students listened to the audio files using both PC and portable devices, and, surprisingly, only 6% of the students used portable devices to listen to the audio lectures.

The surveys did indicate the prevalence of portable media players, especially mp3 players among the students (Over 65% of the students used mp3 players). However, most students consider portable audio players as entertainment devices and do not envisage the devices as being useful in education. The survey results reveal that using portable devices, 79.31% of the students listen to music, 27.59% of the students listen to radio, but only 10.34% of the students listen to lectures.

One concern related to the provision of lecture recordings is whether it decreases class attendance. To understand this issue, the students were categorized into two groups: the first group was students who feel guilty if they skip a class; the second group was students who do not feel guilty if they skip a class.

For the first group of students, one potential reason for decreasing class attendance was that the provision of recorded mp3 lectures has made lecture skipping less guilty. The surveys indicated that: not at all (36%) and to a limited extent (19%), which summed up to 55%, students decreased class attendance because of such a reason. Another potential reason causing a decrease in class attendance was the decrease in lecture attendance might prompt a student to skip class. The surveys indicate that not at all (36%) and to a limited extent (19%), which summed up to 55%, students skip class because the decrease in class attendance prompts them to skip class. For the second group of students, the provision of recorded lectures and/or online lecture notes may prompt them skip a class. As a result, the class attendance decreases. To sum up the above two results, the general conclusion is that the provision of recorded lectures does not encourage the first group of students to skip classes. For the second group of students, the provision of recorded lecture does make them less worried about missing classes and may encourage them to skip classes.

Making available audio lectures is beneficial to students who are non-native English speakers. In the classroom, they may not be able to keep up with the pace of the lecturer's teaching in English. HKUST offers an excellent experimenting ground for this theory. All courses in HKUST education are taught exclusively in English. However most of the students entering the university have received their schooling mostly in their mother tongue. They do find some difficulty in adjusting to being taught in English. Very often the students' command of English is not very good. Added to this, they are now faced with being taught in English by faculty members who hail from all over the world, some of whom are not necessarily native English speakers. With recorded audio, students can listen to the lectures again to fill in the parts they found difficult to follow in the first place.

Questions concerning non-native English learners were asked in one course in the Fall Semester 2006. All students enrolled in the class were non-native English speakers. Two surveys were conducted: the first was done in the middle of the semester and the second was done at the end of the semester. The results indicate that students got used to the lecturer's spoken language as the lecture went on. In the second survey, the results show that to a large extent (17%) and to some extent (40%), which summed up to 57%, students think the audio lectures have help them understand the lecturer's spoken language.

Students' Understanding about Podcasting

The audio recordings were distributed using Podcasting but the concept of Podcasting is not well understood by students. Internet browsers like Internet Explorer allow students to view a Podcast file as if it is a normal webpage. Students can manually download the audio files or listen to the audio files on the same webpage. The surveys showed that 61% of the students manually downloaded the audio lectures, 22% of the students listened to the audio online, but only 13% of the students used RSS reader/podcatcher to subscribe to the Podcast channel. Students were asked the reasons why they did not use RSS readers to subscribe to the RSS feed. The three main reasons were: I was satisfied with the way I access the audio lecture and didn't want to try out alternative methods; I was using computers in computer laboratories or barns with no RSS reader/podcatcher provided; and I didn't use the same PC to access the audio lectures, so setting up an RSS subscription for automatic download is useless.

Further Enhancement to the Provision of Online Lectures

In each survey, students were asked to provide suggestions to improve the effectiveness of recorded lectures. The suggestions are summarized into 4 main points in Table 2.

1. Students want to have a video recording of the lecture so that they see the notes and listen to the audio at the same time
2. Students want to have a way to index the recorded lectures into sections to facilitate them to locate the part of the lecture which they are interested in
3. Students want the quality of the audio recording improved

Table 2. Suggestions to improve the effectiveness of recorded lectures

Points	Related suggestions collected by the surveys
Provide video recording	Synchronous recording of audio and switch of PowerPoint Use SMIL to provide notes Provide video recording Include images, notes Maybe use RealPlayer to embed the page of PowerPoint taking about Use videocasting Video are better than audio
Index the recording into sections	Index the audio by slide number Organize the audio by topic or FAQ Mark the topic in time Split the audio into sections according to the page numbers
Improve the quality of the audio recording	Prefer instructor speak British-accented English Improve the quality of the audio by removing background noise Speak slower and clearer Avoid using the word 'this' when describing something. A listener does not know what you are talking about
Record materials written on the board	Take photos of the diagram on the board and put online As instructor may draw or write something on the white board, which might not be found in the lecture notes. The instructor can include some description of the item in the recording It may be better if we can always refer to diagrams drawn on the board, that is which part of the recorded mp3 refers to it
Other	Want RealPlayer to play the audio Provide instructions on how to use Podcasting

4. Students want to record the materials written on the board

An interesting point made by Morales and Moses (2006) about making recordings of in-class lecture audio available was that many of the visual elements of the in-class lecture cannot be captured. Indeed this was clearly observed in the authors' own experience. This point was brought home by some interesting student comments in the surveys which are quoted here: "Avoid using the word 'this' when describing something. The listener does not know what the speaker is talking about", "As the instructor may draw or write something on the white board, which might not be found in the lecture notes, the instructor can include some descriptions of the item in the recording", "It may be better if we can always refer to diagrams drawn on the board, that is which part of the recorded mp3 refers to it. We suggest taking photos of the diagram and making it available online." Indeed these comments bring out the limitations of the audio format. However, all is not lost as long as supplementary material can be provided in a form that students can print and use in conjunction with the audio recordings. Indeed when the lecture notes are made available online, the lecturers can make references to the specific page numbers within the lecture notes while delivering the lecture. While this requires some adaptation on the part of the instructor, it will be a beneficial change.

Gong: An Investigation into Podcasting

An investigation into student's perception of podcasting when used as support for a course taught in face-to-face mode was carried out. This course was offered as part of a Masters degree in Information Technology offered by the author's institution. There were 56 students in the study, who were taking the course in a part-time mode. The primary method of delivery was a 3 hour face-to-face lecture each week, for a period of 14 weeks. All lecture material was handed out in hard copy form during the lecture. After the lecture, the course web site was updated to include soft copies of all material covered. The majority of students had a further incentive to attend lectures, which was to attain at least a minimum attendance quota in order to qualify for a refund of course fees under the Hong Kong Government CEF grant.

Each lecture was 2.5 hours duration. The sound of the lecture while it was delivered was first recorded in its entirety. It was then transferred into the Gong system as a series of 15 minute long recordings. This was done to enable better navigation of the lecture audio and to reduce demands on transmission and storage. Approximately 10 messages were created for each 2.5 hour lecture. After each class students could access the lecture podcast using any of the methods described at the end of the previous section.

Gong Survey Results

The survey was conducted in the last lecture of the course. Of the 56 students registered for the course, a total of 43 responded to the survey. About 39.5% of the students who responded accessed the recorded lectures. The main reasons were reviewing a lecture that was missed (70.6%), reviewing a lecture after attending it (41.2%) and studying for an exam (35.3%).

A summary of students responses concern their perceived helpfulness of the recorded audio lectures. Approximately a third of students thought they were very helpful, with a mean of 3.18 indicating a solid level of appreciation.

Students were asked what method they used to access the voice recordings. By far the most popular method to access the voice recordings was via the podcast, accessed through a browser, with the second most common method being the use of the Gong program. Interestingly, not one of the students used software to subscribe to the RSS feed, indicating that RSS reader, such as on an iTunes, is not popular. One of the main reasons was that they thought clicking on the links in the browser was sufficient (47.1%). In the survey, students were further asked why they did not use software to subscribe to the RSS feed to maintain up-to-date information. The students kept up-to-date with the podcast either by checking the podcast webpage regularly (47.1%) or from their friends informing or sending them the updated one (35.3%).

Students had diversified opinions about their level of preference for taking a class that provides recorded lectures compared to a class which does not provide recorded lectures. The mean rating of 3.44 shows that students tend to prefer to take a class with recorded lecture support.

Students were queried further on the reasons they prefer recorded lecture support. The top two advantages of recorded lectures selected, were "It provides students with a record of the lecture content for review at a later time" (66.7%) and "It makes students less worried about missing class" (61.9%). Around 40% of the students also thought that the recorded lectures helped them in studying for exams and preparing for assignments. One student mentioned in the 'comments' section that it frees students from copying everything down in class, especially for important notes.

The possibility that students may attend lectures less due to the availability of the recorded lectures has been an issue of concern since multimedia recording of lectures began. Students in our survey were asked to rank the extent to which they would be likely to reduce their attendance of lectures as a result of the availability of the audio recordings. Students made their selection from a scale of 1, meaning no skipping of lectures, to 5, meaning much more likely to skip. More than 50% indicated that they would not skip lectures as a result of the audio recordings. However, some 22% of students selected a 4 or 5, indicating that providing audio recording of lectures may lead to less attendance of the lectures for a significant, although not substantial, portion of students.

Miscellaneous written comments from students included some observations that podcasting was a good concept but the quality of the recording was also important. Furthermore, some comments mentioned that the indexing of recordings should also be addressed so that learners can efficiently access the relevant audio and match it with the notes.

Students Attitudes towards Campus Beat

Pilot Run

The Campus Beat module, which ran for 7 weeks, was first offered to year-three Science students in 2006 to 62 students. After the module completed, students were asked to complete a questionnaire to measure their attitudes towards the course. The questionnaire consisted of 7 questions related to the interests, strengths and weaknesses of the course. Fifty-one students completed the questionnaire. Students were asked if they found the course interesting, where 1 was "Very Uninteresting" and 5 was "Very Interesting". A large majority of the students said that they found the course interesting (mean = 3.9216). Students were also asked if they would recommend the module with 48 responding "Yes".

Students were asked to write what they think the main strengths and weakness of the module are. Fifty-six responses were given for strengths. Thirty-one responses were given for weaknesses. Within the results, 11 responses state that the introduction of podcasting was a strength; 11 responses state that the module is interesting and new; six responses state that the module enhanced critical thinking; five responses state that the module improved comprehension skills; and 4 responses state that the module was very interactive. In addition, 11 responses state that the module was not useful for final year students and that a module about job seeking skills would be preferred; 5 responses state that there was not enough practice during classroom time; and three responses state that there was not enough time for classroom discussion.

The responses suggest that the introduction of podcasting has had some impact on the students' attitudes towards the course. While the results of the questionnaire do not measure whether podcasting has an effect on student motivation, they do suggest that students have a positive attitude towards the technology and that students consider the podcasting a strength of the course.

After Two Years

Eighteen sections of the Campus Beat module were offered to students during the Spring term, 2008; each section averages 18 students. The learning outcomes and the length of the module are the same as the pilot module, as is the integration of podcasting. Only minor adjustments to course content were made. Five classes taught by three different instructors were randomly chosen and asked to complete a questionnaire. The questionnaire consisted of 10 questions related to interests, strengths and weaknesses of creating podcasts and language learning. Fifty-five students completed the questionnaire.

Students were asked if creating a podcast was enjoyable, where 1 was "Strongly Agree" and 5 was "Strongly Disagree". A large majority of the students felt that creating a podcast was enjoyable, with 54 per cent stating "Agree" and 2 per cent stating "Strongly Agree". Only 16 per cent stated "Disagree" and 24 per cent said that they were uncertain. An open-ended question asking students to list three things that they enjoyed about using podcasts to learn English was also given. According to the responses, there were 25 indicating that students found podcasting has some form of entertainment value, such as having enjoyment, interest, and creativeness in using podcasting to learn; and 21 answers indicated that students found educational value in podcasting, such as reviewing, reflecting, practicing and sharing their English skills.

In addition, a large majority of the students stated that they agree that podcasting is an effective way to practise their English skills, with over half of the students agreeing or strongly agreeing; only 15 percent disagreed. In an open question asking students to list three things that they enjoyed using podcasts to learn English, there were 21 answers related to the usefulness of podcasting for reviewing, reflecting, practicing and sharing English skills.

Students were also asked to comment on the motivational value of creating podcasts. A large majority are uncertain about whether creating a podcast motivated them to complete the assignments, but a significant number did agree that it does, with 31 per cent stating that they "Agree" and 4 per cent stating that they "Strongly Agree".

Similar results were also given for the question asking whether students are motivated to perform better on the assignment knowing that it will be published in a podcast. Less than half stated that they "Disagree" or "Strongly Disagree".

In English language teaching (ELT), educators are exploring how podcasting can assist with language acquisition. Diem (2005), McCarty (2005), and Stanley (2006), in particular, have discussed in great detail the potential benefits of podcasting for students of English as a second language (ESL). And a new term, podagogy, meaning "the act or practice of delivering instructional content or academic support content via podcasting", has emerged (Meredith, 2006). Exploration of how podcasting can be used in ELT is still in its infancy, but some potential uses discussed by these authors so far are: for distance learning; to facilitate self-paced learning; for remediation of slow learners; to allow faculty to offer advanced and or highly motivated learners extra content; to offer a richer learning environment; to assist auditory learners; to provide feedback for learners; and to motivate students. Rosell-Aguilar (2007) also provides a useful taxonomy for understanding the uses of podcasting for language learners, including teacher developed, student developed and authentic podcasts.

Yet, while there has been a lot of discussion on the topic of using podcasts to assist with language acquisition, empirical data on the subject is still lacking. The little research that has been conducted is related to other disciplines and focuses mainly on teacher produced podcasts and student attitudes towards the technology. In ELT, aside from the in-depth discussions, very little research is available for review. Furthermore, there is very little data available on how having student produce podcasts can assist with learning in general. Still, because the technology is relatively new, the available data about student attitudes towards podcasting is valuable. There is still much to be done in terms of researching student attitudes towards creating podcasts and learning. Measuring motivation is difficult to do, and a questionnaire does not provide substantial evidence that podcasting may or may not motivate students to learn.

CONCLUSION

This chapter reviewed the use of digital audio in teaching and learning in higher education. Three ways in which audio was used for enhancing the traditional teaching environment, viz., through podcasting of lecture recordings, production of podcasts, and an audio discussion board was illustrated. The authors' experience and findings from the previous section indicate that digital audio indeed provides an important enhancement to traditional classroom environment and must play an important role in a hybrid learning environment. In particular, this study indicates that:

- Students are very receptive to digital audio as a means of receiving instructional content to enhance their learning experience
- Students access the content as a means of reviewing their lecture materials
- A personal computer seems to be the preferred means of accessing digital audio rather than portable devices
- Students prefer indexed audio so that they can easily locate the specific content required for their review
- The availability of recorded lectures does not seem to have any significant impact on classroom attendance
- The availability of digital audio provides additional benefit for non-native English speakers by enabling them to review the lectures again at their convenience
- Podcast production is perceived as enabling students to express their creativity and motivate them in their studies
- Digital audio by itself should be viewed as yet another channel to enhance the learning opportunities, rather than as a replacement for the traditional learning environment
- The ease of production and distribution of digital audio, with the availability of convenient tools, makes it an attractive addition to the existing learning environment

The authors view the addition of digital audio to a hybrid learning environment as yielding significant benefits at a reasonable cost and effort. Thus, they are very positive about the adoption of this technology in the near future.

REFERENCES

Alexander, B. (2006, March/April). Web 2.0: A New Wave of Innovation for Teaching and Learning. *EDUCAUSE Review*, 33–44.

Apple. (2006). *iTunes U at Apple.* Retrieved from http://www.apple.com/education/solutions/itunes_u/

Barnes, K., Marateo, R., & Ferris, S. (2007). *Teaching and Leaning with the Net Generation.* Retrieved November 4, 2007, from http://www.innovateonline.info/

Berkeley. (2006). *Webcast.Berkeley.* Retrieved from http://webcast.berkeley.edu/

Brittain, S., Glowacki, P., Ittersum, J. V., & Johnson, L. (2006). Podcasting Lectures. *EDUCAUSE Quarterly*, (3): 24–31.

Campbell, G. (2005). There's Something in the Air: Podcasting in Education. *EDUCAUSE Review*, *40*(6), 33–46.

Chan, A., & Lee, M. J. (2005). An MP3 a day keeps the worries away: Exploring the use of podcasting to address preconceptions and alleviate pre-class anxiety amongst undergraduate information technology students, Good Practice in Practice. In D. H. Spennemann & L. Burr (Eds.), *Proceedings of the Student Experience Conference*, Wagga Wagga, NSW (pp. 59-71).

Clark, D., & Walsh, S. (2004). *iPod-Learning.* Epic Group Plc.

D'Souza, Q. (2006). *RSS Ideas for Educators.* Retrieved from http://www.teachinghacks.com/wp-content/uploads/2006/01/RSS%20Ideas%20for%20Educators111.pdf

Durbridge, N. (1984). Media in Course Design, No. 9, Audio Cassettes. In *The Role of Technology in Distance Education.* Kent, UK: Croom Helm.

ELI-Duke. (2006). *The EDUCAUSE Learning Initiative, DukeCapture: Automated Classroom Lecture Recording.* Retrieved from http://www.educause.edu/ir/library/pdf/ELI5011.pdf

Gardner, H. (1983). *Frames of Mind: The theory of multiple intelligences.* New York: Basic Books.

Gong. (2007). *The Gong Project*. Retrieved from http://gong.ust.hk

Hartigan, T., Hill, J., Lewis-Faupe, S., & Springsteen, A. (2006). iPods and Podcasting: Too Cool for School? In *Proceedings of the NERCOMP.*

Heinze, A., & Procter, C. (2004). Reflections on the Use of Blended Learning. In *Proceedings of the Education in a Changing Environment Conference,* University of Salford, Salford, Education Development Unit. iLecture. (2006). *iLecture system*. Retrieved from http://lectopia.uwa.edu.au/

Juice. (2006). *Juice, Cross-platform podcatcher*. Retrieved from http://juicereceiver.sourceforge.net/

Lam, G., Rossiter, D., & Cheung, R. (2006). Web Content Development and Integration Using the Gong System. In Proceedings of the *The 4th AEARU Workshop on Network Education*, Taipei, Taiwan (pp. 125-138).

Morales, C., & Moses, J. S. (2006). *Podcasting: Recording, managing, and delivering the classroom experience.* Retrieved from http://www.educause.edu/LibraryDetailPage/666?ID=DEC0604

Muppala, J. K., & Ha, T. S. (1998). Effectiveness of Web-based Instructional Support in Teaching and Learning Process. In *Proceedings of the IEEE International Conference on Multimedia Engineering and Education (M2E2 1998),* Hong Kong.

O-Bryan, A., & Hegelheimer, V. (2007). Integrating CALL into the Classroom: the Role of Podcasting in an ESL Listening Strategies Course. *ReCALL*, *19*(2), 162–180. doi:10.1017/S0958344007000523

O'Reilly, T. (2005). *What is Web 2.0.* Retrieved from http://www.oreillynet.com/pub/a/oreilly/tim/news/2005/09/30/what-is-web-20.html

Osswald, T., & Dugdale, T. (2006). *Podcasting: Portable Knowledge for New Opportunities in Teaching and Learning.* Retrieved from http://academictech.doit.wisc.edu/workshops/epedagogy/sessions/epedagogyPodcasting06.htm

Purdue. (2006). *Purdue University Boilercast.* Retrieved from http://boilercast.itap.purdue.edu:1013/Boilercast/

Richardson, W. (2006). *Blogs, Wikis, Podcasts and Other Powerful Web Tools for Classrooms.* Thousand Oaks, CA: Corwin Press.

Rossiter, D., & Lam, G. (2006). Integrated Learning with Podcasting Import and Export in the Gong System. In *Proceedings of the International Conference on ICT in Teaching and Learning 2007*, Hong Kong (pp. 27-36).

Rossiter, D., Lam, G., & Mak, B. (2006). Automatic Audio Indexing and Audio Playback Speed Control as Tools for Language Learning. In *Proceedings of the 5th International Conference on Web-based Learning,* Penang, Malaysia (LNCS 4181, pp. 290-299). Berlin, Germany: Springer-Verlag.

Stanley, G. (2005). *Podcasting for ELT.* Retrieved November 10, 2007, from http://www.teachingenglish.org.uk/

Stanley, G. (2006). Podcasting: Audio on the Internet Comes of Age. *TESL-EJ, 9*(4). *The EDUCAUSE Learning Initiative, 7 Things You Should Know About Blogs.* (n.d.). Retrieved from http://www.educause.edu/ir/library/pdf/ELI7006.pdf

The EDUCAUSE Learning Initiative, 7 Things You Should Know About Podcasting. (n.d.). Retrieved from http://www.educause.edu/ir/library/pdf/ELI7003.pdf

The EDUCAUSE Learning Initiative, 7 Things You Should Know About Wikis. (n.d.). Retrieved from http://www.educause.edu/ir/library/pdf/ELI7004.pdf

Thorne, S., & Payne, J. (2005). Evolutionary Trajectories, Internet-mediated Expression, and Language Education. *CALICO, 22*(3), 371–397.

Tynan, B., & Colbran, S. (2006). *Podcasting, Student Learning and Expectations.* Retrieved November 4, 2007, from http://www.ascilite.org.au/

UW-Madison. (2006). *Podcasting at University of Wisconsin-Madison.* Retrieved from http://engage.doit.wisc.edu/podcasting/teachAndLearn/

Wikipedia, Learning Styles. (n.d.). Retrieved from http://en.wikipedia.org/wiki/Learning_styles

KEY TERMS AND DEFINITIONS

Digital Audio: An audio content that has been converted into a digital form such as an MP3 file and stored on a computer

Podcast: A set of digital audio files made available online in a syndicated form so that they can be downloaded automatically without user intervention.

Podcasting: The process of providing digital audio online such that it can be downloaded automatically by the users by subscribing to the podcast

Podcatcher: Software used to subscribe to a podcast and automatically download new items. Examples include iTunes, Juice. Sometimes it is referred to as feed aggregator

Portable Media Player: A hardware device capable of downloading, storing and playing back digital audio files

Push Technology: The approach used by a media server to alert/deliver content to the user without waiting for the user to explicitly request for the content.

RSS: One of the many data formats used for providing meta-information about available digital content to podcast reception software to enable automatic download

ENDNOTE

™ Web 2.0 is now a trademark of O'Reilly.

Chapter 10
Adaptive Computer Assisted Assesment

Diana Pérez-Marín
Universidad Autónoma de Madrid and Universidad Rey Juan Carlos, Spain

Ismael Pascual-Nieto
Universidad Autónoma de Madrid, Spain

Pilar Rodríguez
Universidad Autónoma de Madrid, Spain

ABSTRACT

This chapter introduces the reader in the fields of automatic assessment of free-text students' answers, student modeling and adaptive educational hypermedia. Traditionally, these fields have been studied separately missing the benefits of their synergic combination (i.e., free-text scoring systems which do not keep any student model, and adaptive educational hypermedia systems which do not use any natural language processing technique). In particular, a procedure to automatically generate students' conceptual models from their answers to a free-text adaptive computer assisted assessment system will be fully described, together with its implementation in the will tools. Furthermore, the authors will explore how useful this new possibility of hybrid learning is both for teachers and students in two case studies carried out during the 2006-2007 and 2007-2008 academic years, in which traditional lessons were combined with the use of the Will Tools both in technical and non-technical domains.

INTRODUCTION

E-learning can be defined as the use of Information and Communication Technologies (ICT) to improve the quality of learning by facilitating access to resources and services as well as remote exchanges and collaboration (Page, 2006). In the last decades, given the increasing acceptance and use of ICTs by the population (Hopkins, 1998), there has been a great deal of research devoted to E-learning, and in particular to web-based learning.

The main benefits of web-based learning are well known: students having more control over their learning process, being able to study from any computer connected to Internet at anytime; and, in some cases, even receiving the contents and navigation of the course adapted to their particular features such as with Intelligent Tutoring Systems

DOI: 10.4018/978-1-60566-380-7.ch010

(Shute & Torreano, 2002), or Adaptive Educational Hypermedia systems (Brusilovsky, 2004).

On the other hand, web-based learning has also presented some problems of sociological and legal nature. For instance, Chung & O'Neill (1997) discussed about the negative effects of losing the student-teacher relationship. Furthermore, Ford (2000) warned that scores achieved with electronic media instead of traditional exams might not be legally defensible.

Therefore, Blended Learning (Graham, 2006) or Hybrid Learning has recently appeared to combine the traditional teaching methods with the application of ICTs for education. That way, it is possible to take advantage of the benefits of e-learning without bearing its disadvantages.

A possible scenario of Hybrid Learning could be as follows, a teacher who has 200 university students enrolled in a course. The teacher would like to give personalized tuition to each student. Moreover, s/he would like to be able to solve collaboratively exercises in class, and set partial exams. However, the teacher is overwhelmed by the number of students and tasks s/he has to accomplish. Therefore, s/he decides to impart lectures, ask the students to use an automatic evaluation system to get more training, and set a final traditional exam.

Furthermore, the students can ask the teacher the doubts they have not been able to solve with the automatic system. That way, students can practise more and receive a personalized tuition. At the same time, the teacher-student relationship is not lost. On the contrary, students ask more doubts to the human teacher as they have been trying to solve the exercises on their own, or collaboratively, with the computer after class.

Computer Assisted Assessment (CAA) is the field that studies how computers can effectively be used to assess students' learning progress (Knowles, 1999). This field has also received a long-lasting attention because assessment is essential to learn (Dewey, 1933; Berry, 2003). Originally, CAA was limited just to Multiple Choice Questions (MCQs) and fill-in-the-blank exercises (the so-called objective testing). The reason can be found in the easiness of implementation of objective testing. It is only necessary to provide the computer with the correct item answer, and the evaluation will consist of checking whether the student option matches the one previously stored.

The general CAA community opinion is that only evaluating the students' learning progress with MCQs and fill-in-the-blank exercises is not enough to measure the higher cognitive skills (Birenbaum, Tatsuoka & Gutvirtz, 1992; Sigel, 1999; Mitchell, Aldridge, Williamson & Broomhead, 2003). Therefore, a shift from the "evaluation" culture to the really "assessment" culture was done and, new kinds of assessments were developed such as the assessment of free-text answers. The subfield of free-text CAA was created to focus on how to automatically assess free-text students' answers. Free-text CAA has been able to progress by using several Natural Language Processing (NLP) resources, techniques and tools.

However, despite the advances of free-text CAA systems, most educational systems keep relying the evaluation of the courses only on the basic objective-testing items (Dougiamas & Trust, 2004; Barchino et al., 2006). At the same time, most free-text scoring systems do not take any advantage of the advances of other fields such as Student Modeling (i.e. to keep static and dynamic information from the student) or Adaptive Educational Hypermedia systems (i.e. to adapt the free-text assessment) (Valenti, 2003).

Hence, a natural evolution of free-text CAA systems could be free-text Adaptive CAA (ACAA) systems (Pérez-Marín, 2007). Free-text ACAA systems keep a student model containing static and dynamic information about the student to adapt the assessment of open-ended questions to these features. For instance, these systems can change the order of the questions according to how difficult the questions are, and also they can change the level of difficulty that students are able to pass according to the stored model (Pérez-Marín, 2007; Aguilar & Kaijiri, 2007).

The models of free-text ACAA systems may contain an automatically generated submodel focusing on the conceptual knowledge of the students. This is called the student's conceptual model, and it can be defined as a simplified representation of the concepts and relationships among them that each student keeps in his or her mind about an area-of-knowledge at a certain instant (Pérez-Marín, 2007).

The automatic generation of the students' conceptual models from their answers provided to the free-text ACAA systems is one of the many benefits that the synergic combination of techniques from Natural Language Processing, free-text Computer Assisted Assessment, Student Modeling and Adaptive Educational Hypermedia can bring. In this chapter, some of these new possibilities will be explored for Hybrid Learning.

In particular, we will focus on the procedure to automatically generate students' conceptual models as implemented in the set of Hybrid Learning tools called the Will Tools (Pérez-Marín, 2007). The Will Tools consist of: Willow that is the free-text ACAA system; Willed that is the authoring tool; Willov that is the monitoring tool; and, Willoc that is the configuration tool. They can be accessed on-line[1] and process courses written both in Spanish or in English.

Two case studies carried out during the 2006-2007 and 2007-2008 academic years, in which traditional lessons were combined with the use of the Will Tools both in technical and non-technical domains, are described in the chapter.

The chapter is organized as follows: Section "Background" briefly reviews the state-of-the-art of free-text Computer Assisted Assessment, Student Modeling, and Adaptive Educational Hypermedia fields independently and the attempts of convergence; Section "Benefits of the convergence for Hybrid Learning" outlines the benefits of the combination of techniques from the previously mentioned fields for Hybrid Learning; Section "Exploiting the benefits of the convergence with the Will Tools" focuses on the possibility of automatically generating the students' conceptual models from the free-text answers to a free-text ACAA system as implemented in the Will Tools; Section "Case studies" gives the results of the experiments performed; and, finally Section "Conclusions and future trends" ends with the main conclusions and lines of future work.

BACKGROUND

Automatic Assessment of Students' Free-Text Answers

The first free-text CAA systems were based on simple features of the text, such as counting the number of different words, the length of the words, etc. (Page, 1966). It provoked the criticism of the research community that considered unacceptable to base the assessment of students' learning progress in such basic features.

Hence, the research on free-text CAA was nearly stopped until the Natural Language Processing (NLP) field started to offer a number of resources, tools and techniques that permit the research in free-text CAA to advance (Valenti, 2003).

Some of the NLP resources used are: electronic dictionaries to check the spelling of the written answers and their definitions; or, ontologies such as WordNet for English and EuroWordNet for European languages (Vossen, 1998) that help testing the similarity between two words, not because they appear one next to the other in a document, but because the two of them are semantically related according to some relationship registered in the ontology.

Some of the NLP tools used are: stemmers to transform each word to its canonical format (e.g. roses to rose); removal of closed-class words to filter meaningless words for the global content of the student's answer (e.g. filtering prepositions or interjections); or, Word Sense Disambiguators to find out the sense used in the text for a polysemous words (e.g. looking up in an electronic dictionary from all the senses which ones make more sense with the context in which the word has appeared in text under assessment).

Some of the NLP techniques used are: Information Extraction (IE), which skims the text to find out general information according to a predefined template; Latent Semantic Analysis (LSA), which uses a mathematical formulation of the text to find meaning similarities between words; and, statistical techniques that are based on the automatic extraction of frequencies, and other information from the annotation of a big corpus (i.e. a big set of documents).

As can be seen in Figure 1, there are currently more than twenty different free-text CAA systems (Pérez-Marín, 2007). The core idea of most of them is to compare the student's free-text answer to a set of correct answers (references) previously stored in the system. Hence, the more similar the student's answer is to the references, the higher the score given to the student will be.

Free-text CAA systems are both academically and commercially available. However, the results that they are achieving are not completely comparable since they are based on different NLP resources and techniques (Cucchiarelli, Faggioli, & Velardi, 2000) and metrics (Whittindgon & Hunt, 1999).

Notwithstanding, if we consider the Pearson correlation between the automatic and the human's scores as one of the most used metrics, the results range from 45% (Christie, 2003) up to 95% (Mitchell, Russell, Broomhead, & Aldridge, 2002). Some authors even say that the correlation between their system and the teacher scores is higher than between two human teachers for the same set of answers (Ishioka & Kameda, 2006).

Putting these debates aside, if these systems are not meant to replace the teachers with summative purposes, but rather to support them with formative purposes in Hybrid Learning contexts, then it could be concluded that the tools are performing well enough to be used.

Student Modeling

Student modeling is concerned with the task of keeping a record (i.e. a student model) of several aspects of a student such as how much and what the student has learned to date, his or her misconceptions and problem solving strategies. Student models can be classified according to many different points of view. Some of them are regarding: the information they keep, their openness, and the granularity of the model (i.e. how many students are considered in the model).

According to Jameson (1999), the information of a student model can be classified as static or dynamic. Static properties are constant through

Figure 1. Time line of research in free-text CAA

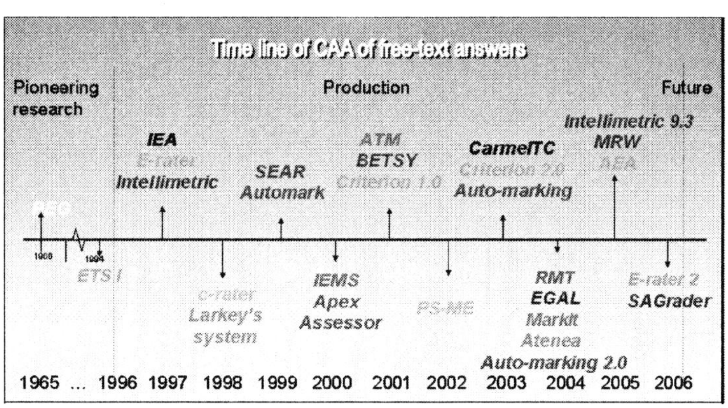

the learning process, while dynamic properties involve information about the student interaction with the system and thus, they change during the learning process.

Regarding their openness, models can be shown to instructors, students, both or any of them (Hartley & Mitrovic, 2001). In particular, open student models are shown to students and/or instructors. In this way, students may get actively involved in their diagnostic process by looking at how they are understanding the concepts in the learning domain. Besides, educators can be provided with more feedback about their students' knowledge assimilation state and help them to improve it (Bull & Nghiem, 2002). On the other hand, closed student models are shown neither to instructors nor to students as their aim is just to modify the behavior of the educational system to be adapted to the student.

According to the number of students modeled (Gouli, Gogoulou, Papanikolaou, & Grigoriadou, 2004), the models can represent information of just one student, or information of a group of students.

Currently, there are many different educational systems that keep a student model (Pérez-Marín, 2007). If we focus on the most related systems to the work described in this chapter, that is, educational systems that keep some kind of open student conceptual model, three systems can be highlighted. They are: STyLE-OLM (Dimitrova, 2003), VisMod (Zapata-Rivera, 2004) and E-TESTER (Guetl, Dreher, & Williams, 2005).

STyLE-OLM (Dimitrova, 2003) interactively builds the student model through a dialogue based on conceptual graphs between the student and the system. The resulting negotiated student model can be visually depicted as a cognitive matrix, in which the students are mapped onto the x-axis and, the concepts of the course are mapped onto the y-axis. The performance values are mapped onto the colour of the square corresponding to a student and a concept. Representation of the dependencies among the concepts is also included.

VisMod (Zapata-Rivera, 2004) is an interactive tool for inspection and reflection on Bayesian collaboratively built group student models. It allows students to complain about the level of knowledge estimated by the system about a certain concept and to prove that s/he has a more complete knowledge about it. VisMod has been tested with a group of 110 school students and 6 teachers. Students seemed to understand the behavior of the system and all were able to interact with the model. They appreciated the difference between traditional assessment and continuous negotiated assessment using VisMod. Teachers valued VisMod as a tool that supports self and negotiated assessment.

E-TESTER (Guetl, Dreher, & Williams, 2005) identifies the main concepts in a text, generates questions from these concepts such as "*What is xxx?*" or "*Explain yyy*", and evaluates the free-text answers provided by the students against a set of correct answers. The models are inspectable and with one student granularity. In fact, the feedback generated is a histogram per student in which each concept has two bars: one with the frequency of the concept in the student's answer and the other one with the frequency of the concept in the model answers. That way, the two bars can be compared to detect whether irrelevancies have been introduced in the student's answer (higher frequency of the concept in the student's answer) or there has been deficit of knowledge (higher frequency of the concept in the correct answers).

Adaptive Educational Hypermedia

Adaptive Educational Hypermedia (AEH) systems can be used in any situation in which several students with different learning styles and backgrounds have to access common information (Paredes, 2002). This approach has proven to be effective since learners using AEH systems have demonstrated faster learning, more goal-oriented attitude and take fewer steps to complete a course (Conlan, 2003). Brusilovsky (2001) distinguished two main types of adaptation: adaptive presentation and adaptive navigation.

Adaptive presentation comprises changes to the contents of the course. For instance, in a programming course, for a beginner, some initial information could be provided about data structures, and additional explanations should be given for new algorithms. On the other hand, if the user is a senior programmer, this information would be unnecessary, and s/he should be provided with more advanced information instead, e.g. where to learn more about an algorithm or what improvements can be applied to it in order to augment its performance.

Adaptive navigation comprises changes to the structure of the course. For instance, beginner students should be presented with only a few links so they do not get lost in the course; while advanced students may have all links activated since they know the required knowledge to fully understand the course contents and structure.

AEH systems that have been used both in academic and commercial environments include: ELM-ART (Brusilovsky et al., 1996), TANGOW (Carro et al., 1999), and AHA (de Bra et al., 2002). A more extensive overview can be found in Brusilovsky (2004).

Attempts of Convergence

The enhancement of the assessment process with adaptive capabilities is worthwhile for at least two reasons (Gouli, Papanikolaou, & Grigoriadou, 2002): to make it dynamic and individualized as it is adapted to each student's performance, and to reduce the number of questions required to estimate the student's knowledge level.

The first attempts of making CAA systems adaptive have included: to adapt the problem selection (Mitrovic & Martin, 2004), to permit adaptive navigation through the problems (Sosnovsky, 2004), Computer Adaptive Testing (CAT) (Wainer, 2000) that modifies the order in which the MCQs items are presented to the students according to their performance during the test; and, adaptive assessment of concept maps (Anohina, Graudina, & Grundspenkis, 2007), that bases the adaptive assessment on concept maps.

Furthermore, various systems have proved the feasibility of the synergic combination of AEH and NLP techniques including: Welkin (Alfonseca, Pérez, & Rodríguez, 2004), which automatically selects the contents of the course to show the student using NLP techniques based on the student's profile; CarmelTC (Rosé, Gaydos, Hall, Roque, & VanLehn, 2003), which complements the Carmel tutoring system to permit the assessment of free-text students' answers; and, SPEBC, a free-text Adaptive Computer Based Assessment (Aguilar & Kaijiri, 2007) focused on the adaptive evaluation of essays, and designed to be used in class together with the teacher.

BENEFITS OF THE CONVERGENCE FOR HYBRID LEARNING

Figure 2 shows how the NLP, CAA, Student Modeling and E-learning fields can be related. Firstly, NLP techniques are necessary for free-text CAA to automatically assess students' answers. That way, the advances of NLP can be applied to more domains, and free-text CAA systems can progress.

Secondly, Student Modeling techniques together with NLP techniques permit the extraction of information from the free-text students' answers, not only to keep a student model but to keep it automatically updated. That way, the advances of Student Modeling permit to have a more detailed and useful model, and free-text CAA systems can be more effective and adapt the assessment of open-ended questions according to the information stored in each student's model (e.g. asking questions with a level of difficulty more adjusted to the real knowledge of the students so

Figure 2. How several fields can be synergically combined with a common goal

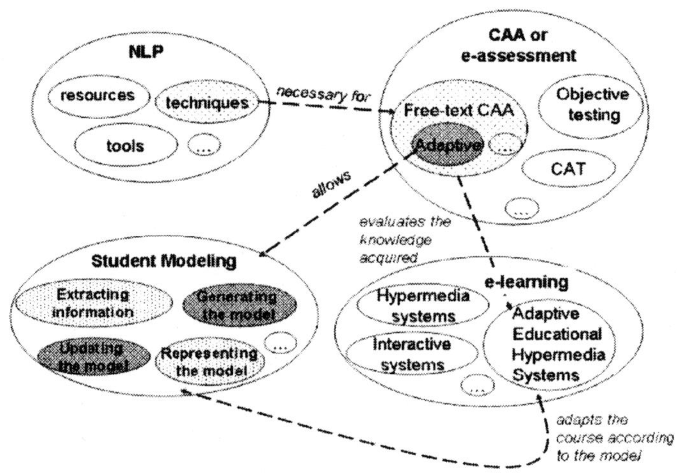

that the questions are not too complex or too easy; or, focusing on the misconceptions discovered by each student).

Thirdly, e-learning can get benefited from the possibility of free-text scoring the students' answers. That way, the assessment is able to reach higher cognitive skills and more conceptual errors can be discovered (Sigel, 1999). Furthermore, whenever the assessment detects some misconception or ignorance of concepts, a particular link to the theoretical explanation can be automatically generated.

Finally, if we take up again the scenario previously described in which the teacher wanted to combine his or her traditional lectures with the automatic assessment system, it can be seen that one ultimate goal of exploiting the synergic combination of the already existing NLP, Student Modeling, Adaptive Hypermedia and free-text scoring techniques is providing teachers with new procedures such as the automatic generation of students' conceptual models from students' free-text answers.

By using that procedure, the teacher needs to provide less information to the system. In fact, given that the student model is automatically generated, not only s/he has to provide less information, but s/he has only to create it just once at the beginning of the first course year. Moreover, since the model is automatically updated, the teacher can focus on his or her lectures, and still s/he will have access to an always updated representation of each one of his or her student models and the whole class model. Incidentally, by looking at the model several times during the course, s/he will have access to his or her students' knowledge evolution.

EXPLOITING THE BENEFITS OF THE CONVERGENCE WITH THE WILL TOOLS

In this section, the possibility of automatically generating students' conceptual models from their answers to free-text ACAA systems is going to be described as implemented in the Will Tools. The goal is to show in a practical procedure how the techniques previously mentioned can work together for a common goal. In fact, each technique used will be highlighted in bold.

It is also important to indicate that the procedure permits not only the automatic generation of individual conceptual models, but the automatic generation of the whole class conceptual model (as an average of each particular student's conceptual model).

Students are allowed to see their particular model and the whole class conceptual model. Whereas teachers can see both each student's conceptual model and the class conceptual model.

In brief, the steps of the procedure are the following ones:

1: Setting up a course
2: Finding the concepts
3: Finding the relationships between the concepts
4: Calculating the confidence-value associated to each concept
5: Updating the model and showing it both to teachers and students

Setting a New Course in the Will Tools

To set up a new course in a certain language (the languages currently implemented are Spanish and English), it is necessary to ask the teachers to fill in a template like the one shown in Figure 3.

The template can be completed by using any text editor or the Will Tools authoring tool. As can be seen, first of all it is necessary to specify the language, name of the course, an optional brief description of the course, and for each lesson (topic), its name and one or more open-ended questions.

A question is defined by its statement, level of difficulty, lesson to which it belongs, score to pass the question, maximum score that can be achieved by the student if his or her answer is perfect, and one or more references (i.e. correct short answers, not longer than one paragraph each, written in natural language). The experiments performed suggest that around three references per question is the optimum number (Pérez-Marín, 2007). In courses imparted by several teachers, it is advisable that each teacher writes a different answer to have more lexical variability in the answers and thus, to gather more points of view in the answer.

Given that the core idea of the Will Tools free-text ACAA system is the same that most free-text CAA systems, that is, to compare the student's free-text answers to the references, teachers can include any open-ended question provided that it is not too ambiguous and does not have any mathematical calculation.

Teachers are also requested to mark in the references of each question, the key concepts that they consider essential for the students to know in order to pass the question. All the same, it is also possible to automatically identify the concepts in the references, without asking the teachers to mark them, by using a **Term Identification** algorithm (Cabré, Estopá, & Vivaldi, 2001). Furthermore, it is possible to combine both approaches, and firstly

Figure 3. Sample template for teachers

LANGUAGE: *English or Spanish*

COURSE: *name of the course*
DESCRIPTION: *a paragraph explaining the goal of the course*

TOPIC: *name of a lesson of the course*

Question. [maximum-score level-of-difficulty]

- Correct answer written by one teacher.
- Correct answer written by a different teacher.

apply the automatic algorithm to have an initial list of key concepts and, secondly give the list to the teachers so that they can modify it according to their particular preferences for the course.

Finding the Concepts

Three different types of concepts have been distinguished following the criterion of keeping the basic structure of the course in the free-text ACAA system as similar as the structure of a traditional course as possible. They are:

- Area-of-knowledge Concept (AC): It refers to the global course.
- Topic Concept (TC): It refers to each lesson in the course.
- Basic Concept (BC): It refers to each key concept marked by the teachers in the correct answers or identified by the **Term Identification** algorithm.

All of these concepts are associated a value that indicates how confident the free-text ACAA is that the student knows them. This value is called the Estimate of the Level of Competence (ESLOC) or confidence-value (CV), and it is calculated according to a set of metrics that will be explained later. The CV associated to a concept is always in the scale 0 (complete lack of knowledge) to 1 (full understanding of the concept).

As provided by the teacher, from the name of the course, the AC is fixed. Similarly, from the name of each lesson of the course, the name of each TC is fixed. The AC and TCs are equal to all students. On the other hand, BCs are particular to each student. Hence, it is possible not to consider the BCs until the students actually start using them in their answers to the free-text ACAA system. This could be called the AC-TC-reset (ATRET) possibility. The AC and TCs are associated a 0 CV as the system does not assume any previous knowledge of the student in the course, but will adaptively adjust the level of difficulty of the course to each student according to his or her answers to the free-text ACAA system.

Other possibility (the all-concepts-reset, ACRET, possibility) is to create a basic hierarchical model with all AC, TCs and BCs extracted from the information provided by the teacher, and marked them as unknown by the students (CV=0). That way, whenever a student starts answering questions in the free-text ACAA system, the Will Tools will modify the level of confidence that this student knows the BC used.

The ATRET possibility permits a better visualization of the conceptual evolution of each student. Therefore, although both options are possible and have been tested, we recommend the ACRET possibility to better follow the students' conceptual evolution.

Finding the Relationships Between the Concepts

Following the same criterion than in the previous step, that is, to follow the structure of the course as faithfully as possible, three different types of links have been devised:

1. Type 1 link (AC-TC): It relates the AC with each TC to capture the relationship between each lesson and the global course.
2. Type 2 link (TC-BC): It relates each TC to the BCs, marked in the correct answers of the questions of the TC lesson, to capture the relationship between each BC and the lesson to which it belongs to.
3. Type 3 link (BC-BC): It relates two BCs to capture the relationships between two key concepts in a student's answer.

Each link is associated with some linking words. We have not used the traditional "is-a", "has-a", etc. relationships, because we wanted to be more specific in the linking words to the educational courses. Thus, given that the courses talk about concepts to be taught to students, we have chosen as the linking words: "talks about".

Therefore, if the ATRET possibility has been chosen, in this step only type 1 links are created (only the AC and TCs have been extracted from the domain model). On the other hand, if the ACRET possibility has been chosen, in this step, type 1 and 2 links are created (AC, TCs and BCs have already been extracted and can be linked).

Calculating the Confidence-Value Associated to Each Concept

Once the basic architecture of the conceptual model has been generated, students can start using the free-text ACAA system. As previously stated, the Will Tools will start asking the easiest questions for each topic, but if the student answers correctly a certain number of questions (as indicated by the teacher), s/he will be promoted to a higher level of difficulty in this topic. On the other hand, if the student fails a certain number of questions of a topic (as indicated by the teacher), s/he will be demoted to a lower level of difficulty in this topic. This **promotion-demotion difficulty level** procedure is our proposed adaptive technique for changing the order of the questions according to the level of knowledge of the student.

The benefits of the promotion-demotion difficulty level procedure is to keep asking questions to the student that are not too easy (i.e. boring) or too complex (i.e. impossible to answer). This increases the possibilities that the student keeps engaged answering questions of the free-text ACAA system (Pérez-Marín, 2007).

Each time a student answers a question, the text provided to the system is processed by several NLP techniques. The first NLP techniques applied to the text can be **stemming** and/or **removal of class-closed words.** During this phase, the free-text ACAA system is also looking for which BCs are using the student in his or her answer. Whenever the system finds one BC, the Will Tools updates the confidence-value associated to it according to a weighted combination of two internal metrics called *ScoreConfidence* and *RateConfidence*.

The *ScoreConfidence* metric (Equation 1) is focused on the idea that the higher the automatic score provided by the Will Tools to the student *i* is, the higher the CV associated to the BC *c* labeled by the term *t* as the student is correctly using *t*. In fact, its value is the mean of the weighted scores for the set of questions *Q* whose references (i.e. correct answers) contain *t*.

$$ScoreConfidence(t,i,Q_i) = \frac{\sum_{q \in Q_i} score(answer(q)) \times f(t, refs(q))}{f(t, \sum_{q \in Q_i} refs(q))} \quad (1)$$

The *RateConfidence* (Equation 2) metric is more related to the comparison of the frequency of *t* in the answer provided by *i* and the frequency of *t* in the correct answers taken as references. In fact, it is calculated as the mean of the ratio between the frequency of *t* in the answers provided by *i* and the references of all the questions in the area-of-knowledge to assess.

$$RateConfidence(t,i,Q_i) = \frac{\sum_{q \in Q_i \wedge f(t, refs(q)) \neq 0} \frac{f(t, answer(q))}{f(t, refs(q))}}{\|Q_i\|} \quad (2)$$

To calculate the CV of a BC in the class conceptual model, it is necessary to calculate the average value of the CV associated to that BC in each student's conceptual model. The confidence-values associated to the TCs and the AC are not recalculated until the student or the teacher asks to see the conceptual model, to avoid doing too many unnecessary mathematical calculations. The same rule is applicable for the class conceptual model.

Additionally, the **pattern recognition** template *"BC linking words BC"* to extract type 3 links in the students' answer is applied to complete the student model created following the ACRET possibility. Please, note that in the case of the class conceptual model, the type 3 links are extracted not only from the answers of one student, but from the answers of all students in the class.

If the student model was created following the AC-TC possibility, not only type 3 links but also type 2 links are established. Next, the processed student's answer is compared with the references using the statistical technique called **Evaluating Responses with Bleu** (ERB, Pérez-Marín, 2007) and/or **Latent Semantic Analysis (LSA).** The combination of techniques is chosen by the administrator of the Will Tools depending on which configuration has been determined as optimum for that course and language (Pérez-Marín, 2007).

The free-text ACAA always provides as immediate feedback to the student the numerical score achieved in the scale indicated by the teacher. However, the student is not allowed to see the references (i.e. teachers' correct answers) if s/he has not passed the question. This is to foster reflective thinking and avoid that students start answering in blank just to memorize the teachers' correct answers.

On the other hand, the Will Tools automatically generates new questions, called **clarification or compensation questions,** to try to guide the student towards the correct answer. These questions are based on the conceptual model. In fact, the procedure to automatically generate the student's conceptual models from their free-text answers is cyclic: not only the model is generated from answers given by the student to the free-text ACAA system, but the model modifies the questions asked by the system. In particular, the clarification questions ask about BCs associated a low CV in each student's conceptual model.

Updating the Model and Showing It to Teachers and Students

As students keep answering new questions in the systems, the CVs of BCs are recalculated according to the *ScoreConfidence* and *RateConfidence* metrics. The fact that this process is automatic permits to have an always updated model without human supervision.

Whenever teachers and students want, they can look at one of the visual representations of the conceptual model. Originally, both teachers and students have to access the Will Tools conceptual model viewer to look at the models. However, to make the Will Tools easier to use so that each role has a different system to log in, the access to the models has now been separated.

Students can look at each particular model and the whole class conceptual model in the Will Tools free-text ACAA system. Whereas, teachers have access to all students' conceptual models and the class conceptual model in the Will Tools teacher monitoring tool with more statistical information: how many questions the students have answered, how long they have been using the system, the overall progress they have made, etc. The only information teachers are not provided is the score achieved by the students in the questions. This is because the Will Tools is not intended for summative purposes, and students can feel safe that the automatic scores are only a guide for them.

Furthermore, to reinforce the formative assessment possibilities of the Will Tools, **the free-text assessment has been combined with self-assessment** in the Will Tools free-text ACAA system (Pérez-Marín, 2007). That way, students who do not agree with the automatic score given by the system can change it. All the same, teachers should warn their students that by unfairly changing the Will Tools automatic scores, the Will Tools might "believe" that unknown concepts are already learnt.

Moreover, according to the promotion-demotion difficulty-level procedure, the system will start asking more and more difficult questions to the students until they may be considered apt in the course and do not get more training before their real final exam in class.

Figure 4. A snapshot of one of the topics of a generated student's conceptual model represented as a concept map

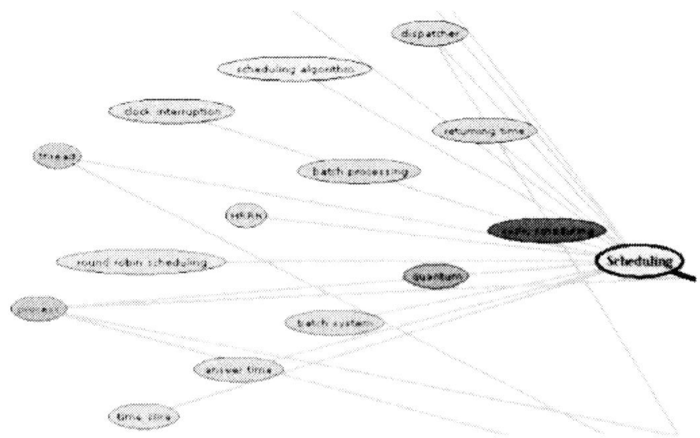

Five different representations of the conceptual model have been implemented: a concept map, a conceptual diagram, a bar chart, a table, and a textual summary. Each of them focuses on a different aspect of the model. For instance, the concept map, as shown in Figure 4, shows a general view of how well the student seems to know each concept according to a color schema in which a red (dark) color means lack of knowledge, while green (light) color means good knowledge. The relationships extracted between the concepts are also shown as grey lines.

The conceptual diagram hierarchically represents the concepts with the AC at the top, and TCs and BCs below. That way, relevancy and organization by topics are highlighted.

The rest of the knowledge representation formats are focused only in the BCs given that they are key concepts of the course. The bar chart is ordered according to the relative percentage of CV of the BCs with the aim of comparing BCs. The table provides the exact values for the ScoreConfidence, RateConfidence and frequency of use for each BC in the model. The textual summary contains three ordered lists indicating the ten best and worst understood BCs and their relevancy (i.e. relative importance according to the frequency it has in the references, Pérez-Marín, 2007).

We propose the following taxonomy of conceptual errors that can be identified by looking at these representation formats of the generated conceptual model:

- **For concepts:**

Ignorance: Whenever a student does not use a certain concept, the concept is associated a CV of zero, and it may indicate that the student ignores that concept

Misconceptions: Some concepts may seem to be known by students as sometimes they use those concepts. However, the students might have wrongly used the concepts in their answers. Thus, these concepts are associated a CV below 0.5 in a 0 (no knowledge) to 1 (perfect knowledge) scale of estimation

- **For links:**

Ignorance: Whenever a student does not relate two concepts, the teacher can notice the lack of links between these two concepts, and it may indicate that the student ignores that the concepts are related

Erroneous links: Sometimes students erroneously relate two concepts in their answers. This evidences an error in the cognitive structure of the student as s/he believes that the concepts are related in a wrong way. It is fundamental to correct this situation to allow the student to continue **learning meaningfully** and linking correctly new concepts to the existing ones (Ausubel, 1963)

Once the procedure has been described, in the next section it will be analyzed the results of two case studies in which the procedure was applied both to technical and non-technical domains using the Will Tools.

CASE STUDIES

Using the Will Tools in Technical Domains

First of all, in the 2005 year, we set up a course in Spanish for the Operating Systems subject of an Informatics degree. The course consisted of five lessons with four questions per lesson. The ACRET possibility was chosen to generate the model because it was the first time the procedure was going to be tested. Thus, we wanted to see each student's conceptual model global architecture since the very beginning of the study. On the other hand, in order to test the goodness of the automatic procedure of Term Identification, we used the C4.5 (Quinlan, 1993) algorithm to classify each term in the references as BC or not BC. We achieved a 0.74 f-Score value, which is a state-of-the-art result (Pérez-Marín, 2007).

The accuracy of the free-text scoring techniques in the Will Tools was also measured to find out how the system compares to the other currently available free-text CAA systems, and which combination of the NLP techniques was optimum. It was found out that the optimum combination for Spanish and the Operating Systems course was to use stemming and ERB, achieving a 54% Pearson correlation between the Will Tools and a human teacher's scores (Pérez-Marín, 2007). Taking into account that current state-of-the-art results range from 45%-95% Pearson correlation, this is an average result, in our opinion, good enough to be used with formative purposes, always as a support to the teacher instead of trying to replace him or her.

Next, we asked a group of 32 volunteer Informatics degree students in the 2005-2006 academic year to use the Will Tools. The system was initially used in a class, rather than at home, so that we could observe the students using it. We found out that students liked the feature of the Will Tools to interactively answer questions and have immediate feedback. We also proved our hypothesis that adaptive assessment allows students to answer more questions (Pérez-Marín, 2007).

These results encouraged us to repeat the experiment in the 2006-2007 academic year in the same subject, during the whole course. 24 out of the 59 students enrolled in the subject (41%) volunteered to use the Will Tools. We observed that 10 out of these 24 volunteers (42%) made regular use of the system, while the rest used the system only in the days prior to the final exam. Figure 5 shows a graph indicating the average number of questions answered by the students to the free-text ACAA system.

As can be seen in Figure 5, students did not use the Will Tools on a regular basis. The reason provided by the students was unanimous: lack of time due to the rest of compulsory activities they have. In any case, students seemed to have considered the Will Tools useful as they kept using the Will Tools after the mid-term exam. In fact, more questions were answered after the mid-term exam to practise for the final exam.

We also wanted to see if the Pearson correlation achieved the previous year could be improved. Hence, we repeated again the tests but, using the best correct answers of the 2005 students as references of this year course. It turned out that the correlation increased up to 63% (Pérez-Marín, 2007).

Regarding the opinion of these students about the Will Tools, they mostly appreciated having an alternative way of reviewing the concepts in the lessons from any computer connected to Internet, at their own rhythm and with immediate feedback

Figure 5. Number of questions answered by the students of the 2006-2007 study

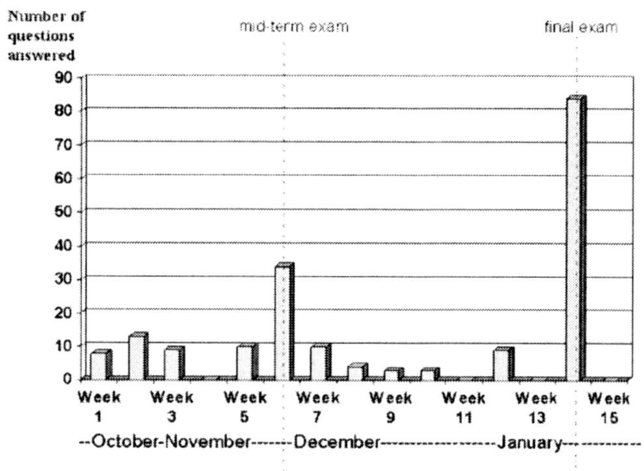

(particularly, with the teachers' correct answers). Some students even claimed that reviewing with the Will Tools was fun.

Using the Will Tools in Non-Technical Domains

In the 2007-2008 academic year, our hypothesis was that the procedure to automatically generate the students' conceptual models could also be applied to non-technical domains, and that students without computer training could use the Will Tools without any difficulty. Therefore, we asked for the collaboration of the rest of faculties of our university. The English Studies faculty took notice of our petition. In particular, the Pragmatics teachers were willing to test the Will Tools with their students.

All the same, the first necessary step to implement the procedure was to set up the Pragmatics course. In order to do that, and given that Pragmatics is not our area of expertise, we asked the teachers to provide us with some questions they usually ask their students and the correct answers for those questions.

We found out that Pragmatics have a defined set of concepts that should be learnt by the students. It makes to apply the Will Tools easier as the focus of the assessment is on concepts. On the other hand, we also found out that answers to Pragmatics definitions are not so determined as answers in Operating Systems. The problem with that is that the core idea of the Will Tools is to compare the student's answer to the set of teachers' correct answers and, in the case of some concepts, many possible definitions were possible.

We solved that problem by modifying the way in which some questions were expressed. That is, instead of directly asking for a concept that may be difficult to automatically evaluate as the answer is too open, the question can be formulated to let the student less choices of answer. For instance, for the concept "relation maxim" instead of asking "What is a relation maxim?", a more appropriate question would be:

Imagine the following conversation extracted from a Garfield's cartoon:

A: Do you like ice-cream?

Garfield: Is the Pope a Catholic?

A: Yes.

Garfield: Bingo!

Explain whether the relation maxim is being observed or flouted and why.

This last question keeps being an open-ended question, but less ambiguous and, involves the knowledge, understanding and application competence of Bloom's taxonomy (1956). The question requires that the students know what the relation maxim is, and apply this knowledge not only to identify whether it has been observed or flouted (and to know what to observe or flout a maxim is), but to explain the reason for their answer.

We explained these guidelines to Pragmatics teachers and asked them whether they would like to use the Will Tools authoring tool or a text editor to fill in the template of the course. They chose the text editor because they already have material in electronic documents and they thought it would be easier for them to start creating the questions and the answers from that material. Similarly, when we had to choose between using the automatic Term Identification module, or asking the teachers to provide us with the list of BCs, the second option was chosen. Incidentally, in this study, the ATRET possibility was selected.

After one month of non-full time work, the Pragmatics teachers came up with 49 English questions that covered the 4 first topics of Pragmatics. Each question addressed a particular key concept of the subject. Given that the Will Tools was modified to include self-assessment features, we did not repeat the tests to calculate the correlation for this course. Besides, from the experiments performed in the 2005-2006 year, we knew that the optimum combination of NLP techniques for English is: stemming, removal of closed-class words, ERB and LSA achieving 56% Pearson correlation.

The first day of the study, we asked the Pragmatics teachers to allow us to go to one of the lessons, so that we could briefly explain the Will Tools to the non-technical students. Additionally, by going to the lab, we could immediately solve any technical difficulty and, we could also observe how these students interacted with the system.

From the 45 students enrolled in the subject, 22 (49%) volunteered to take part in the experiment. We could see how any of the non-technical students had any technical difficulty in using any of the Will Tools features. On the contrary, all of the students were able to answer questions with very little explanation (just a 5-minute Powerpoint presentation of the Will Tools interface). In fact, 123 students' answers were recorded, and 15 students looked at more than one of the knowledge presentation formats available in the system.

Thus, once we had proved that the students could start using the Will Tools alone from any computer connected to Internet at any time, we let them freely use the system during the rest of the semester. Figure 6 shows the graph indicating the average number of questions answered by the students since November 16th 2007 until January 8th 2008 (the date of the final Pragmatics exam).

As can be seen, non-technical students have also not regularly used the Will Tools as already

Figure 6. Average number of questions answered by the students when using the Will Tools

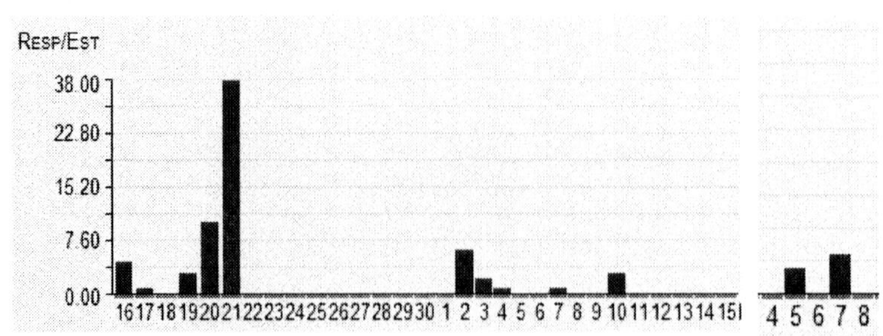

happened with the technical students. In fact, the reason provided by the non-technical students has been the same than the reason given by the technical students: lack of time due to the rest of compulsory activities they have. Nevertheless, these students have also valued this new possibility by using the Will Tools again in the days previous to the exam. Some students have even thanked us and their teachers for giving them this opportunity.

Regarding the use of the generated conceptual models, 32% of the 19 students have looked again at them. Moreover, in some cases, students have entered the Will Tools just to look at their concept map representation and the class concept map representation without answering any questions.

CONCLUSIONS AND FUTURE TRENDS

In this chapter, the reader has been briefly introduced into three different research fields that have traditionally been separately studied: free-text Computer Assisted Assessment (CAA), Student Modeling and Adaptive Educational Hypermedia (AEH).

Up to date, free-text CAA systems have used NLP techniques to improve the accuracy of the assessment of the students' free-text answers. On the other hand, AEH systems have traditionally adapted the content and navigation of the course, relying the evaluation on the so-called objective testing (i.e. MCQs or fill-in-the-blank exercises) that according to the general opinion of the CAA field are not enough to assess the higher cognitive skills of the Bloom's taxonomy (1956). Moreover, the full potential of the synergic combination between the techniques devised in all these fields kept being unexploited for Hybrid Learning.

Therefore, our goal has been to explore the benefits of the synergic combination between free-text CAA, Student Modeling and AEH, focusing on one of its possibilities: to automatically generate students' conceptual models from students' free-text answers. Two case studies have been provided to prove the feasibility of the procedure as implemented in the Will Tools. Additionally, if we look back to the Hybrid Learning scenario described in the Introduction and extended in Section "Benefits of the convergence for Hybrid Learning", we can now complete it with the use of the Will Tools.

That way, the teacher with the 200 students and without enough time to set all exams and exercises s/he would like because of lack of time, is helped with the use of the new ICTs for education. In particular, the teacher has only to work harder the first year the course is set up to be used with the Will Tools. In particular, s/he has to complete the template of the course indicating the name of the subject, lessons and a set of questions per lessons with their correct answers.

Next, the students can start using the Will Tools free-text ACAA system to get more training before their final exam. The system automatically and adaptively assesses their questions and, immediately provides the students with the score. The rest of the feedback is provided when the student passes the question to foster reflective thinking. Moreover, the doubts that the student may have when practising with the Will Tools, should be asked to the teacher. That way, the teacher-student relationship is not lost.

Whenever the students or the teachers want to access a report of which concepts seem to be better understood and which ones should be reviewed more, they can look at the generated conceptual model. It is possible to generate it automatically thanks to the combination of NLP, AEH and Student Modeling techniques. Moreover, given that it is automatically generated, it is always updated, and a taxonomy has been provided to identify the main misconceptions and conceptual errors so that students can organize their study, and teachers can check whether students have understood the concepts exposed in the lessons.

Finally, regarding future trends, the authors believe that the benefits of the synergic combination of techniques from several fields should be researched more. By including a student model in more free-text CAA, more students could take advantage of an adaptive assessment. That way, the students will be asked questions more adequate to their level of knowledge and, the feedback will be personalized focusing on each student's misconceptions.

Furthermore, by combining these new free-text Adaptive CAA (ACAA) systems with the current AEH systems, both fields would progress. AEH systems widening the assessment to cover higher cognitive skills in the Bloom's taxonomy (1956), and free-text ACAA systems providing not only formative assessment but also personalized tuition.

ACKNOWLEDGMENT

The work described in this chapter has been sponsored by Spanish Ministry of Science and Technology, projects number TIN2004-03140 and TIN2007-64718.

REFERENCES

Aguilar, G., & Kaijiri, K. (2007). Design Overview of an Adaptive Computer-Based Assessment System. *Interactive Educational Multimedia, 14*, 116–130.

Alfonseca, E., Pérez, D., & Rodríguez, P. (2004). Welkin: Automatic Generation of Adaptive Hypermedia Sites with NLP techniques. In *Proceedings of the International Conference in Web Engineering (ICWE)* (LNCS 3140, pp. 617-618). Berlin, Germany: Springer-Verlag.

Anohina, A., Graudina, V., & Grundspenkis, J. (2007). Using Concept Maps in Adaptive Knowledge Assessment. In *Advances in Information Systems Development* (pp. 469-479). Berlin, Germany: Springer.

Ausubel, D. P. (1963). *The Psychology of Meaningful Verbal Learning*. New York: Grune and Stratton.

Barchino, J. M., Gutiérrez, S., Otón, J. J., Matínez, J. R., Hilera, J. A., & Gutiérrez, J. A. (2006). E-learning model for assessment. In Proceedings of the *IADIS Virtual MultiConference on Computer Science and Information Systems*, Portugal (pp. 59-63).

Berry, R. (2003). Alternative assessment and assessment for learning. In *Proceedings of the 29th IAEA Conference, theme: Societies' Goals and Assessment,* USA.

Birenbaum, M., Tatsuoka, K., & Gutvirtz, Y. (1992). Effects of response format on diagnostic assessment of scholastic achievement. *Applied Psychological Measurement, 16*(4), 353–363. doi:10.1177/014662169201600406

Bloom, B. (1956). *Taxonomy of educational objectives: The classification of educational goals. Handbook I, cognitive domain.* New York: Longmans, Green.

Bra, P. D., Aerts, A., Smits, D., & Stash, N. (2002). AHA! version 2.0, more adaptation flexibility for authors. In *Proceedings of the AACE ELearn Conference*, Canada (pp. 240-246).

Brusilovsky, P. (1996b). Methods and techniques of adaptive hypermedia. *User Modeling and User-Adapted Interaction, 2-3*(6), 87–129. doi:10.1007/BF00143964

Brusilovsky, P. (2001). Adaptive Hypermedia. *User Modeling and User-Adapted Interaction, 11*, 87–110. doi:10.1023/A:1011143116306

Brusilovsky, P. (2004). Adaptive Educational Hypermedia: From generation to generation. In *Proceedings of the 4th Hellenic Conference on Information and Communication Technologies in Education*, Greece (pp. 19-33).

Bull, S., & Nghiem, T. (2002). Helping learners to understand themselves with a learner model open to students, peers and instructors. In *Proceedings of Workshop on Individual and Group Modelling Methods that Help Learners Understand Themselves, International Conference on Intelligent Tutoring Systems*, Spain (pp. 5-13).

Cabré, M.T., Estopá, R., & Vivaldi, J. (2001). Automatic Term Detection: a review of current systems. *Recent advances in computational terminology, 2*, 53-87.

Carro, R., Pulido, E., & Rodríguez, P. (1999). TANGOW: Task-based adaptive learner guidance on the web. In *Proceedings of the Second Workshop on Adaptive Systems and User Modeling on the Web en la Eight International World Wide Web Conference*, Canada (pp. 23-24).

Christie, J. R. (2003). Automated essay marking for content - does it work? In *Proceedings of the 7th International Computer Assisted Assessment Conference*, UK (pp. 85-92).

Chung, G., & O'Neill, H. (1997). *Methodological approaches to online scoring of essays* (Technical Report 461). UCLA, National Center for Research on Evaluation, Student Standards, and Testing.

Conlan, O. (2003). *State of the art: Adaptive hypermedia* (Technical report). Waterford Institute of Technology.

Cucchiarelli, A., Faggioli, E., & Velardi, P. (2000). Will very large corpora play for semantic disambiguation the role that massive computing power is playing for other AI-hard problems? In *Proceedings of the 2nd Conference on Language Resources and Evaluation*, Greece.

Dewey, J. (1933). *How We Think: A Restatement of the Relation of Reflective Thinking to the Educative Process*. DC Heath.

Dimitrova, V. (2003). STyLE-OLM: Interactive Open Learner Modelling. *International Journal of Artificial Intelligence in Education, 13*(1), 35–78.

Dougiamas, T., & Trust, M. (2004). *Moodle*. Moodle Trust.

Ford. (2000). *Automated scoring of writing assessments* (Powerpoint presentation for the Assessment Council).

Gouli, E., Gogoulou, A., Papanikolaou, K., & Grigoriadou, M. (2004). COMPASS: An adaptive web-based concept map assessment tool. In *Concept Maps: Theory, Methodology, Technology. Proceedings of the First International Conference on Concept Mapping*, Spain.

Gouli, E., Papanikolaou, K., & Grigoriadou, M. (2002). Personalizing assessment in adaptive educational hypermedia systems. In *Proceedings of the Adaptive Hypermedia and Adaptive Web-based Systems, Second International Conference* (LNCS 2346, pp. 153-163).

Graham, C. (2006). *The Handbook of Blended Learning: Global Perspectives, Local Designs*. San Francisco: Pfeiffer.

Guetl, C., Dreher, R., & Williams, R. (2005). E-tester: A computer-based tool for auto-generated question and answer assessment. In *Proceedings of the AACE E-Learn Conference*, Canada.

Hartley, D., & Mitrovic, A. (2001). *The effectiveness of open student modelling on learning*. Unpublished master's thesis, Intelligent Computer Tutoring Group, Department of Computer Science, University of Canterbury, UK.

Hopkins, C. (1998). Web + qmark + humanities = ? a case study. *Computers and Texts, 16-17*.

Ishioka, T., & Kameda, M. (2006). Automated Japanese Essay Scoring System based on Articles Written by Experts. In *Proceedings of the Association for Computational Linguistics*, USA (pp. 233-240).

Jameson, A. (1999). *User-adaptive systems: An integrative overview*. Tutorial presented at the seventh International Conference on User Modeling, Banff, Canada.

Knowles, J. (1999). *Booklet 3*. Learning and teaching on the web: Computer Assisted Assessment.

Mitchell, T., Aldridge, N., Williamson, W., & Broomhead, P. (2003). Computer based testing of medial knowledge. In *Proceedings of the 7th Computer Assisted Assessment Conference*, UK.

Mitchell, T., Russell, T., Broomhead, P., & Aldridge, N. (2002). Towards robust computerised marking of free-text responses. In *Proceedings of the 6th Computer Assisted Assessment Conference*, UK.

Mitrovic, A., & Martin, B. (2004). Evaluating adaptive problem selection. IN *Proceedings of the Adaptive Hypermedia and Adaptive Web-Based Systems conference* (LNCS 3137, pp. 185-194). Berlin, Germany: Springer-Verlag.

Page, E. (1966). *The imminence of grading essays by computer*. Phi Delta Kappan.

Page, K. (2006). A preliminary study on the current state of e-learning in lifelong learning. In *Cedefop Panorama series, Official Publications of the European Communities* (pp. 5-7).

Paredes, P. (2002). *An attempt to incorporate learning styles in adaptive web-based courses*. Advanced Studies Diploma, Escuela Politécnica Superior, Universidad Autónoma de Madrid.

Pérez-Marín, D. (2007). *Adaptive Computer Assisted Assessment of free-text students' answers: an approach to automatically generate students' conceptual models*. Unpublished doctoral dissertation, Escuela Politécnica Superior, Universidad Autónoma de Madrid. Retrieved from http://www.eps.uam.es/~dperez/index1.html

Quinlan, J. R. (1993). *C4.5: Programs for Machine Learning*. San Mateo, CA: Morgan Kaufmann Publishers.

Rosé, C., Gaydos, A., Hall, B., Roque, A., & VanLehn, K. (2003). Overcoming the knowledge engineering bottleneck for understanding student language input. In *Proceedings of the 11th International Conference on Artificial Intelligence in Education*, Australia.

Shute, V. J., & Torreano, L. A. (2002). Formative evaluation of an automated knowledge elicitation and organization tool. In *Authoring Tools for Advanced Technology Learning Environments: Toward Cost-Effective Adaptive, Interactive, and Intelligent Educational Software*.

Sigel, I. E. (Ed.). (1999). *Development of mental representations: Theories and Applications*. Mahwah, NJ: Lawrence Erlbaum Associates.

Sosnovsky, S. (2004). Adaptive navigation for self-assessment quizzes. In *Proceedings of the Adaptive Hypermedia and Adaptive Web-Based Systems* (LNCS 3137, pp. 365-371). Berlin, Germany: Springer-Verlag.

Valenti, S., Neri, F., & Cucchiarelli, A. (2003). An overview of current research on Automated essay grading. *Journal of Information Technology Education, 2*, 319–330.

Vossen, P. (1998). *EuroWordNet - A Multilingual Database with Lexical Semantic Networks*. Amsterdam: Kluwer Academic Publishers.

Wainer, H. (2000). *Computerized Adaptive Testing: A Primer*. Mahwah, NJ: Lawrence Erlbaum Assoc Inc.

Whittingdon, D., & Hunt, H. (1999). Approaches to the computerised assessment of free-text responses. In *Proceedings of the 3rd International Computer Assisted Assessment Conference*, UK.

Zapata-Rivera, J. D. (2004). Interacting with inspectable bayesian student models. *International Journal of Artificial Intelligence in Education, 14*(2), 127–163.

KEY TERMS AND DEFINITIONS

Adaptive Educational Hypermedia (AEH): It is a subfield of Adaptive Hypermedia (i.e. the combination of hypermedia-based techniques with adaptive and user-model-based interfaces) whose application is on the educational field.

Concept Map: One powerful knowledge presentation format, devised by Novak, to visualize conceptual knowledge as graphs in which the nodes represent the concepts, and the links between the nodes are the relationships between these concepts.

Conceptual Diagram: A knowledge presentation format to visualize conceptual knowledge as hierarchical diagrams in which each cell is a concept of a certain area-of-knowledge.

E-Assessment or Computer Assisted Assessment (CAA): It is the research field that studies how computers can effectively be used to assess students' knowledge.

Formative Assessment: A type of assessment in which the goal is not to score the students but to support them. For instance, by giving them detailed feedback. That way, students could progressively improve their understanding of the lesson.

Free-Text Adaptive Computer Assisted Assessment: It is a subfield of CAA in which the assessment is automatic and adaptive. That is, the computer system asks open-ended questions to the answers, automatically evaluates the students' free-text answers, and provides adaptive feedback to the student. Furthermore, the free-text ACAA system keeps a student model to adapt the type and order of the questions to each particular student.

Natural Language Processing (NLP): It is a subfield of Computational Linguistics (i.e. the field that researches linguistics phenomena that occur in digital data), whose focus is on how to build automatic systems able to interpret/generate information in natural language.

Open Learner Modeling: Show the model kept by an educational system such as an AEH or a free-text ACAA system to the students so that they can reflect on it.

Student's Conceptual Model: Simplified representation of the concepts and relationships among them that each student keeps in his or her mind about an area-of-knowledge at a certain instant.

Summative Assessment: A type of assessment in which the goal is to evaluate the students by giving them a score, and finding out whether they have enough level to pass the subject or not. For example, by testing the students with an exam.

ENDNOTE

1 The Will Tools are available at http://www.wisdicor.com/willtools/

Chapter 11
Just-in-Time Knowledge and User Interface Design for Effective Hybrid Learning

Michel C. Desmarais
Polytechnique Montreal, Canada

ABSTRACT

The means for hybrid learning take on many forms. In this chapter, the author looks at learning facilitators that can be embedded within the user interface. He argues that these learning means can be even more effective than formal training. The author describe different features of the user interface that can provide just-in-time knowledge and fosters learning: immersing the student into a rich environment where he can readily have access to the information for the task at hand.

INTRODUCTION

The European Commission is devoting over 50M Euros annually in recent years to fund projects that are aimed at developing new means of learning and new means of creating and managing digital content[1]. Few of the funded research, if any, aim to develop technologies intended for the classroom. Instead, the emphasis is on developing technologies to make the delivery of learning content more individualized, interactive, and embedded into our everyday environment. In this chapter, we look at how the issue of enriching our everyday environments with just-in-time knowledge delivery technologies that can foster autonomous and highly effective forms of hybrid learning.

DOI: 10.4018/978-1-60566-380-7.ch011

LEARNING WITHIN TASK-ORIENTED ENVIRONMENTS

Why are just-in-time learning technologies the focus of such interest? One of the reasons is that it draws upon factors that naturally foster learning.

Looking at the learning phenomena in general, we know that most of what we learn occurs outside of a structured context such as a classroom. Any researcher in Artificial Intelligence can attest that most cognitive tasks that humans perform involve a phenomenal amount of knowledge that was acquired throughout life. Much of this knowledge has to do with problem solving skills and ``common sense" inference, which is mostly acquired in a semistructured or non structured environment, through practice.

Language is a good example of our ability to learn in an unstructured context. Learning a language starts with the imperative need to communicate, and with the environment in which that language is omnipresent. The combination of need plus environment is sufficient to incur the learning of a complex skill.

Now, this is not to say that we should aim to ultimately replace structured learning with unstructured learning. The point is that when we get the co-occurrence of the *need to know*, or the *need to perform* some task, and an environment that provides the elements to learn and perform, then learning will effectively and efficiently occur.

What makes unstructured learning so powerful, is that learners often have a constant need to know or to perform. It is up to us to provide them with the proper environment that can foster that learning. The constant availability of that environment and the prevalence of the need to know and perform can far outweigh the time and the attention the learner can devote to learning in a structured context, such as a classroom.

Furthermore, learning in the context in which one performs a task is also more effective. The influence of contextual cues greatly increase the ability to recall knowledge and to act appropriately when needed (Bouton, 1993). This phenomena stems from the fundamental nature of human associative memory and the statement that we learn better in the context where our knowledge is put to practice should not be considered as a mere belief in one of many flavor of learning. That statement is rooted in the notion of associative learning which is a well studied and accepted phenomena (Wasserman and Miller, 1997).

JOB AIDS IN WORK ENVIRONMENTS

The advantages of just-in-time learning in the context of doing a task have been recognized by many, in particular in the domain of professionnal training. Gloria Gery is probably the best known proponent of the approach known as Electronic Performance Support System (EPSS) which aim at providing on the job training electronic aids. The concept is not totally new and, as Rossett and Shafer (2006) notice, job aids have been around since prehistoric times. But the availability of electronic devices to deliver this aid is giving this old concept a new life. Not only are computers more readily available, in all forms, from PDAs to large display workstations, and in all contexts with the advance of wireless networks, but they are also more and more instrumental to do our tasks.

Kasvi (2003) picks a compelling example of how the computer has become instrumental with a modern lumberjack cockpit which, nowadays, is filled with several computer and communication screens and control devices (see figure 1). Here, the computer can become a far more efficient tool in providing job aids than, say, a checklist or a user manual. In principle, such device could provide highly context sensitive aid and can even volunteer relevant information or recommentations.

As long as the machine's operations are entirely controlled through a computer, then all kinds of means can be deployed to assist the user in performing a given task, from reminders of what operations need to be performed, to highly context sensitive help and information, warnings for dangerous or apparently abnormal operations, automation of repetitive operations, etc.

Performance and learning aids for forestry machine operation is currently limited because the computer has limited information about the objects being manipulated and the outside environment in general. As more sophisticated sensors such as cameras and object recognition features become

Figure 1. Modern lumberjack cockpit equipped with multiple screens and computers. A view of the Timbermatic 300 system (www.deere.com/en_US/cfd/forestry/deere_forestry/harvesters/wheel/1070d_flash.html, last accessed 2009.01.31).

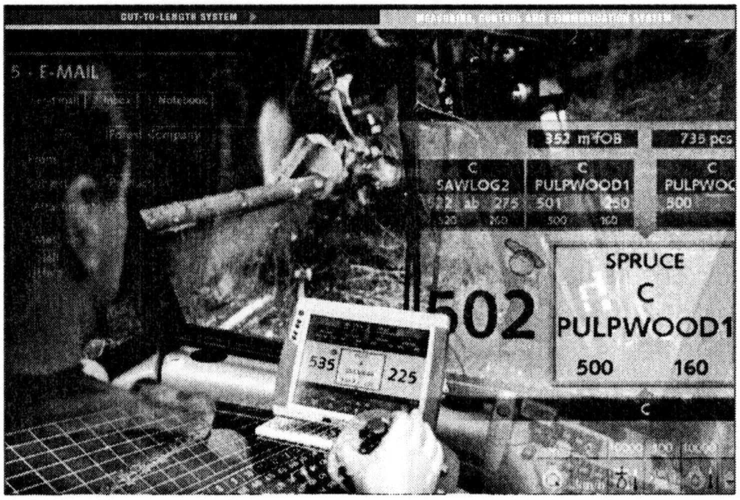

readily available for such machinery, better means to provide performance and learning aids will become possible.

Although that vision leads to a futuristic view of how job aids will appear, but Rossett and Schafer (2006) report on an existing application of that vision:

> *Information Weeks' 2005 annual survey of 500 innovations revealed a stunning example of information delivered to the worker and workplace, exactly where the work gets done. JM Family Enterprises Toyota Dealership is devoted to cutting the time it takes to repair a vehicle. According to Chabrow (2005), the company is testing a wireless headset with a flip down screen from Microvision, Inc. Using retinal scanning display technology, pages of an auto repair manual are cast onto the working mechanic's retina. The mechanic searches and changes pages using a belt mounted touchpad. The technology VP admitted that mechanics are not initially keen on the idea, but noted that they adjusted swiftly. He anticipated the performance support will increase technician productivity by more than 30% because they do not have to stop work, put down tools, and search for what they need in a manual.*

However, the technological requirements for these applications are paramount and can falsely lead to the impression that they will remain applicable only to very specific context for the time being. That is not so. Sophisticated job aids have been around for some time and, currently, one can argue that nowhere is performance aids better put to practice than in the field of programming, where the object being manipulated (softare code) is fully transparent to computer analysis without any special sensors, and well understood by the designers of software development environments who can rely on this analysis to design clever job aids. These features transform the programming environments into rich learning environments as we explain in the next section.

Interactive Development Environment Examples

The power of embedding, within the user interface, job aids and different means to help the user learn complex tasks has now been recognized within some communities. One of the most notable example is in the computer programming community where IDE (Interactive Development Environment) have evolved into highly sophisticated interfaces to support computer program development. These environments allow the programmer to have access to a large array of contextual tips, documentation, and other interface features that help them not only in doing the task more efficiently, but also to better learn the programming language and more advanced programming techniques.

There are many examples that could be mentioned here, and we name but just a few for brevity.

Project Template Skeletons and Examples

The typical software project development types (GUI, library, etc.) are provided as template code that is complete with default structure and configuration, relieving the programmer from the initial effort of finding sample code to start from, and providing a useful and well designed example for the novice programmer.

Syntax Correction

When typing, all syntactically incorrect lines are as well as other more complex errors automatically detected are highlighted and, when possible, their corrections are suggested.

Auto-Completion and Context Sensitive Information

A powerful feature is the ability of the IDE to analyse the code and display a list of possible completions to the expressions as the user is typing them, such as the list of all methods that can be called upon a given object. Not only does this feature relieve the load on the user's memory, it also allows him to explore and learn the possibilities of the library.

Source Code

All of Java's source code base is available by clicking over the corresponding function call in the user's program. Exploring the inner architecture of Java's source code helps the programmer understand the framework and learn advanced programming tips and patterns.

The result of these features is two fold:

- The user has fewer things to remember, and thus fewer things to master before being able to perform useful tasks
- The learning occurs naturally as the user performs the tasks

The case of *auto-completion* is a clear example of how this result can occur (Figure 2). It is taken from the NetBeans IDE[2]. The two popup windows of the NetBeans interface screendump show the auto-completion feature in action (refer to the two popup windows pointed to by the "completion and documentation" bubble text in Figure 2). The user is typing the name of the "System" class and the top window shows the applicable methods for that class, whereas the bottom window shows some details about the highlighted choice.

In this example, the cognitive load of remembering the name of the methods is reduced to a task of recognition and, in the case where the method is actually unknown, it provides immediate documentation to find and learn the method that should be used for the intended goal.

All the other features mentioned above serve the same purposes of reducing the amount of learning, providing examples, highlighting errors at the very moment the user makes any and of providing highly precise and context sensitive documentation to learn to do a task.

When compared to performing the same task without such aid, we find that not only is the IDE

Figure 2. Some features of the NetBeans IDE interface such as auto-completion as when the user is typing the name of the class "System", syntax correction, and code template skeleton

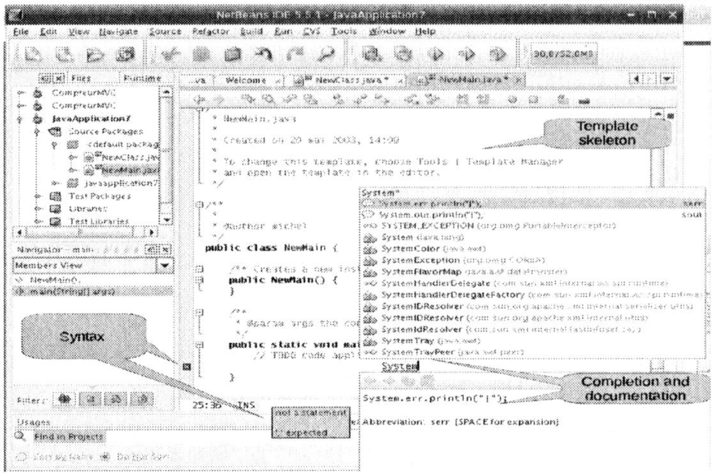

allowing for a much more efficient, error-less and overall more pleasant experience, it also fosters knowledge acquisition. The user becomes more prone to consult help tips, documentation, and examples of good programming practice because she does not have the burden and perceived waste of production time incurred by the effort of searching for such content in a user manual or a textbook.

In turn, the availability of this just-in-time knowledge also affects how programming should be taught as well: there is no advantage to spending time in class over knowledge that can be made available to the learner at the very time he needs it. Time in class is much better spent over teaching concepts that are harder to communicate through job aids. Moreover, this approach also implies that teacher time must be spent in choosing the relevant tasks and the relevant environment where knowledge can be acquired and concepts can be put to practice.

In the next section, we look at how effective just-in-time knowledge aids can be used in training.

Formal Use of Just-in-Time Knowledge Aids in Training

An instance of how to use just-in-time knowledge delivery as a pivotal means of providing training is found in the THEO EPSS project, where embedded job aids provide just-in-time knowledge (Desmarais et al., 1997).

THEO is a system designed for the customer support centers at a large utility company with millions of clients. The original interface is a standard GUI interface to access client file information.

The tasks that the user can perform with THEO are quite diversified and sometimes non trivial, such as explaining how a fixed monthly payment is derived from year to year, or making a diagnostic of a sudden increase of electricity consumption in a household. As a consequence, the classroom training for a new employee required three weeks.

In order to reduce the training period, we integrated a number of additions to the original THEO interface that are meant to provide a kind of just-in-time training, often referred to as an Electronic Performance Support System (EPSS). These features are accessible from the original interface and are not intended to replace it. Their intent is to allow learning through the user interface.

Letter

The first and simplest mean of support consists in providing access to the most recent letter sent to the client by the company where the numbers are highlighted (Figure 3). This is in general what the client has in hand when he calls the CSR (Client Support Representative). It gives the CSR a common point of reference in the exchanges with the client.

Hyperlink

The second means consists in making expandable each of the highlighted number in that letter, akin to hyperlinks (Figure 3). As most questions refer to these numbers, that mechanism allows easy, access to the details of how each amount on the letter is derived. The user clicks on a number and a window shows how this number is derived. The numbers in the explanation window can be further explored this way.

Another feature of the interface is its ability to facilitate access to the relevant information by inferring the most likely causes of a CSR call. It allows direct access to the part of the system that is needed to answer the client's question. For example, Figure 4 shows the three most likely causes of a CSR call based on a statistical analysis of the client's profile. If the reason for the call is, say, the first item shown (a 26% increase of annual electricity consumption), the plausible causes are reminded to the CSR and can be discussed with the client. When applicable, all numbers shown are computed to reflect the actual impact in dollars

Figure 3. Two examples of hypertext-like expansions of amounts that provide explanation on how they are derived

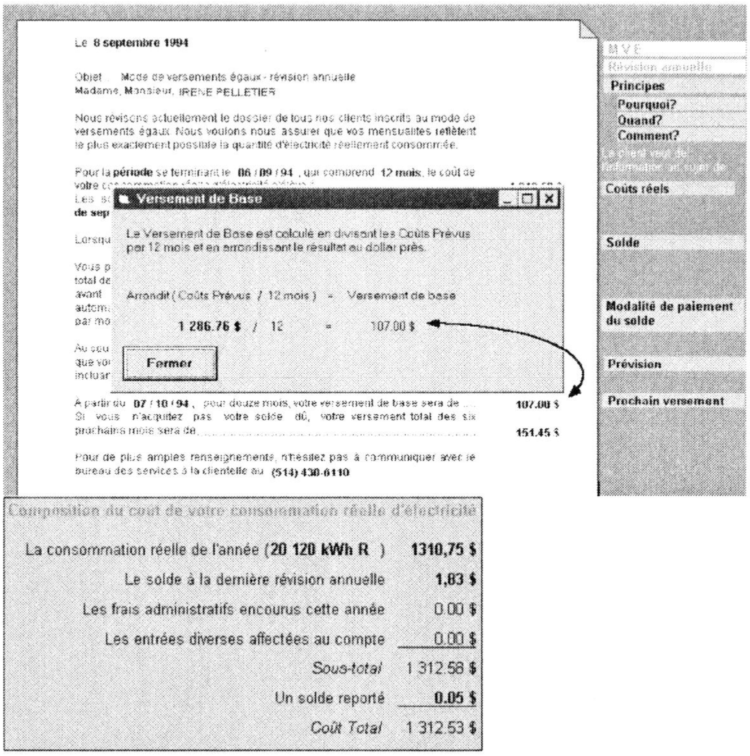

for that particular client to make the information more relevant.

Evaluation Results

The impact of introducing the EPSS to the original THEO interface were investigated in an informal experiment (see Desmarais et al., 1997, for details). The results of this experiment show that two out of three users with no training at all were able to perform the standard 15 out of 15 tasks relating to the topic chosen for the experiment (the *equal payment plan* that normally requires three weeks training). The other subject was able to perform 10 out of the 15 task. In comparison with the original interface without the EPSS, only one of the tasks was succeeded by a person without training. However, the trained CSR representatives were able to do almost all of them, as expected.

These results form a compelling argument for the effectiveness of the EPSS enhanced user interface. Considering that two out of three subjects were able to complete all of the 15 CSR tasks without training, it is quite reasonable to consider that the original three weeks training could be substantially reduced given the EPSS.

INTERFACE DESIGN, LEARNING, AND PERFORMANCE

The observations from the THEO and NetBeans interfaces bring us to a larger understanding of the interactions between interface design, learning, and performance. These interactions are illustrated in Figure 5.

The learning curve of Figure 5(a) is typical of the evolution of performance. If performance is expressed as the inverse of task completion time, then that curve would follow the well known Power law of practice Newell and Rosenbloom (1981). As the user gets familiar with the tasks and the application, he develops strategies to perform better. The performance increases from an initially low level to an expert level and then levels off. However, this curve is not necessarily the best that can be achieved. Often, interface designers settle for a design that allows the user to perform at an acceptable level quickly, but that design may not be optimal for expert users. Moreover, expert users tend to stop their learning process too early because they lack the incentive to make the effort of consulting the necessary documentation, or the time to explore new and complex functionality that could him to new levels of performance.

Figure 5(b) depicts the "Ideal" learning curve (top line). Long term performance reaches a greater level of performance and the initial performance also starts off at a higher level. This goal is difficult to reach because there often is a tradeoff between initial performance and the potential performance that can be reached with an interface. Some interfaces can have a steep learning curve but, once the user has gotten over the initial effort of mastery, the performance can be much greater than with a simpler interface to start with. On the

Figure 4. Inference of the three most likely causes of a CSR call (left) and a corresponding explanation of cause 1 (right). Each tabbed text display in the explanation windows highlights, for that particular customer, the amount that corresponds to the different causes.

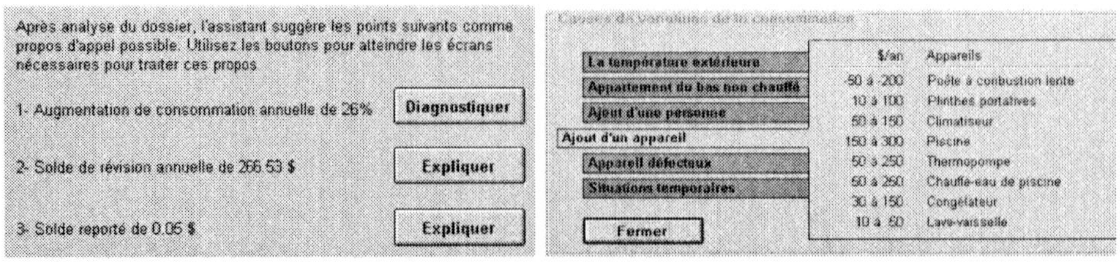

Figure 5. (a) The learning curve, and (b) interface design issues

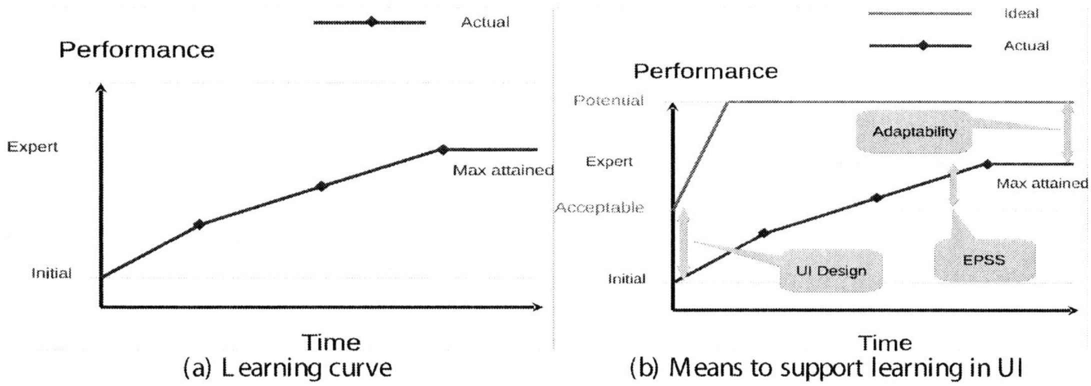

contrary, interfaces that are very easy to use for novice users often do not meet the needs of high performance for expert users.

Three means can be deployed to avoid this tradeoff between initial ease of use and the optimal performance for experts, and, thus, to transform the "actual" performance curve into the "ideal" one:

User Interface Design

The first one is the best known and consists in good User Interface (UI) design. Proponents of the user-centred approach to developing interactive software know that a good UI design can make a substantial difference in the user productivity. Studies have shown that a gain of 35% in productivity is what can be expected (Landauer, 1995) by properly applying a user-centred approach to UI design. One of the key element of the design here is to support the diversity of users, namely experts as well as novices.

EPSS

The second means consists in using Electronic Performance Support Systems (EPSS). This is what is depicted in the THEO and NetBeans examples. As argued above, it enriches the user environment with embedded mechanisms to foster learning in a just-in-time, context sensitive and on-demand fashion. The user can learn to gradually perform more complex tasks, more efficiently, in a naturally occurring manner that is akin to how most of our learning is acquired.

Adaptability

Finally, the third mean refers to the ability of an interface to adapt to its user. For the purpose of training and learning, one of the most important adaptation is the ability to adapt the interface help, documentation, and guidance to what the user knows and his level of skills for a given task. Another is the ability to infer what is the current user's goal. The auto-completion is such an adaptation feature. This feature is the most difficult to implement and the advances in the field are slow, in spite of substantial research efforts in the field during the last two decades[3]. However, in the long term, it should yield significant returns. As an example, we mention the work of Garcia et al. (2009) as an interesting case of a system which recommends changes to an online course content based on data mining logs of learner behavior. The system attempts to identify problems in the current content and learns from the feedback of course authors.

CONCLUSION

Our daily environment is becoming more computerized than ever before. We argue that we need to think of the user interface of our computerized environment not only as a tool to perform tasks, but as a tool to help increase our skills and learn through that very interface. We have outlined different means of doing so and shown that they can prove very effective towards that goal.

The prospect of user interfaces designed for knowledge intensive applications centered around providing just-in-time performance and learning accelerators can have a major impact in training as well as in academia. It implies that the teacher should focus on choosing and making available the tools that offer the most appropriate learning environment. Such environment shold provide easy access to information when needed, and provide templates, rich examples of good practice, and even volunteer recommendations. It also implies that the teacher should keep the time in class for what cannot be learned in ajust-in-time context, such as synthesis of concepts and providing feedback to students over their work.

Hopefully, this approach to designing learner-centered user interfaces will also enjoy greater emphasis on the part of application designers too. In spite of the examples mentioned in this chapter, there might be too much of a tendency in the human-computer interaction area to focus on making the application readily usable by novices, at the expense of making the interface a learning environment in which the user can acquire the knowledge and skills to learn to perform better.

The potential of reaping the benefits of enriching our computerized environments with learning facilitators is great. The opportunity for teachers to leverage on such learner centered environments is something to consider.

REFERENCES

Bouton, M. E. (1993). Context, time, and memory retrieval in the interference paradigms of Pavlovian learning. *Psychological Bulletin, 114*(11), 80–99. doi:10.1037/0033-2909.114.1.80

Chabrow, E. (2005). Wireless revs up vehicle production. *Information Week*, p.100.

Desmarais, M. C., Leclair, R., Fiset, J.-Y., & Talbi, H. (1997). Cost-justifying electronic per formance support systems. *Communications of the ACM, 40*(7), 39–48. doi:10.1145/256175.256183

Garcia, E., Romero, C., Ventura, S., & de Castro, C. (2009). An architecture for making recommendations to courseware authors using association rule mining and collaborative filtering. *User Modeling and User Adaptive Interfaces, 19*(1-2), 99–132. doi:10.1007/s11257-008-9047-z

Kasvi, J. J. J. (2003). *Knowledge support in learning operative organisations*. Unpublished doctoral dissertation, Helsinski University of Technology.

Landauer, T. K. (1995). *The Trouble with Computers*. Cambridge, MA: MIT Press.

Newell, A., & Roosenbloom, P. (1981). Mechanisms of skill acquisition and the law of practice. In J. R. Anderson (Ed.), *Cognitive Skills and their acquisition* (pp. 1-55). Hillsdale NJ: Erlbaum Associates.

Rossett, A., & Schafer, L. (2006). Job aids and performance support: the convergence of learning and work. *International Journal of Learning Technology, 2*(4), 310–328. doi:10.1504/IJLT.2006.011337

Wasserman, E. A., & Miller, R. R. (1997). Wath's elementary about associative learning? *Annual Review of Psychology, 48*, 573–607. doi:10.1146/annurev.psych.48.1.573

KEY TERMS AND DEFINITIONS

Electronic Performance Support Systems: Assistance and information provided through the user interface in a timely manner.

Just-in-Time Learning: Learning that occurs in a timely fashion, on an as needed basis, based on the delivery of appropriate information and knowledge within task environment.

User-Centered and Learner-Centered Design: User-centered design is a philosophy and development process in which the needs and limitations of end users of an application or device are given extensive attention at each stage of the design process. Learner-centered design builds upon this concept to address the need to support user skills evolution and diversity.

ENDNOTES

1. http://cordis.europa.eu/fp7/ict/telearn-digicult/telearn_en.html (last consulted on 2001.01.30)
2. See http://www.netbeans.org/. The same could be said of most popular IDEs such as Microsoft's .NET, Borland's Turbo series, or IBM's Eclipse
3. See, for example, the User Modeling and User Adaptive Interfaces Journal.

Section 3
Hybrid Learning Models

Chapter 12
Eight Educational Considerations for Hybrid Learning

Philip P. Alberts
Brunel University, UK

Linda A. Murray
Brunel University, UK

Julia E. Stephenson
Brunel University, UK

ABSTRACT

This chapter sets out educational considerations (pedagogic principles) that can be used to guide the design of hybrid learning. Eight educational considerations have been determined from a review of education theories according to their relevance to teaching in higher education. The origin of each consideration is described and evidence from the literature of their application in e-learning is provided. The way in which this set of educational considerations has been used by the authors to enhance the design of hybrid learning at a UK higher educational institution is described. It is anticipated that those who need to design pedagogically-valid hybrid learning programmes will find the information provided here helpful. Furthermore, those engaged in helping others to combine the advantages of face-to-face teaching and e-learning will be assisted in developing a methodology for changing the approaches of teachers, thus achieving maximum impact on student learning.

INTRODUCTION

The fundamental premise on which this chapter is based is that it is the purpose of higher education to add value to the learning experience of the students. Adult learners are generally able to learn on their own and do so more or less successfully depending on inclination, need and opportunity. However, learning through programmes provided by educational institutions including universities must add something to the learning experience. What exactly is - or should be - added is a matter of debate. Our starting point, based on contemporary (and classic) educational theory is that teaching

DOI: 10.4018/978-1-60566-380-7.ch012

should not be conceived of as the transmission of knowledge. Rather, the added-value of structured higher education programmes lies in the facilitation of the learning process in the learners.

Conceptions of Teaching in Higher Education

The idea that teaching consists of the transmission of knowledge from an expert to a learner is a misconception that is manifested in an over-reliance on the face-to-face lecture format. Research has shown that this teaching method does have advantages; for instance, one person can present information to a large audience, it is an ideal format for auditory learners, and the action of note-taking during lectures aids concentration (Badger, White, Sutherland & Haggis, 2001). Good lectures are tailored to meet the requirements of the students, the content of the lecture can be easily updated and it can also provide human interaction (D'Alessandro, Kreiter, Erkonen, Winter & Knapp, 1997). However, it has also been argued that it is not always an effective method of teaching (Bligh, 2000; Costa, Van Rensburg & Rushton, 2007). Disadvantages explored in the literature include the fact that the students' role is rather passive (Feldberg, 1999; Tomaska, 2000) as they sit listening to the lecturer and then decide what they want to write down possibly in their own words or in shorthand (Bligh, 2000). The traditional lecture is also constrained by location and time (D'Alessandro et al., 1997), tends to be teacher-centred, the lecturer is required to have good delivery and communication skills, and enrolment is limited (Rosenkoetter, 2006). There is no hard-wearing record of the interaction (D'Alessandro et al., 1997) and this method assumes that all students learn at the same pace as their peers.

The notion that knowledge is simply passed from teacher to student originated from assumptions created between the 7th and 12th centuries from the Monastic and Cathedral schools (Knowles, 1990). This particular process of acquiring knowledge, where the teacher takes the responsibility for all learning decisions, was the sole pedagogic model and continued to be the favoured method of instruction well into the 20th century. Rather intriguingly however, during the ancient times of the great teachers such as the Chinese philosophers of Lao-Tse and Confucius (5th century) and later Socrates, Plato and Aristotle, teaching was antithetical in that it was predominantly active and enquiry-based and not so authoritarian (Clark, 1999). Ironically, in today's society, it is the style derived from the *ancient* times that dominates current educational thinking. The teacher is indeed evolving from a 'sage on the stage' to a 'guide on the side' (Chung, 2005).

Role of Information and Communication Technologies

Now that we are embedded in the digital age, this thinking applies just as much to considerations of how to use information and communication technologies (ICT) in learning as it does to face-to-face teaching. Thus, the recognition that teaching is best conceived of in terms of the facilitation of learning, provides an impetus to the design of programmes of study which include substantial elements of e-learning. Along with Lu, Ma, Turner & Huang (2007), we argue that the increased use of ICT has created a technology-enhanced student-centred learning setting as opposed to a traditional teacher-centred environment. For instance, the new learning environments might include online lectures maintaining the advantages outlined above. However, in addition - and importantly - the use of technology also permits the mitigation of some of the lecture's disadvantages. This will be explored further in later sections. There are many other approaches to the facilitation of learning besides providing good lectures and our purpose here is to explore these in some detail in the context of hybrid learning.

Role of Pedagogy

The effective facilitation of student learning must bear some relationship to the processes by which students learn. In many cases, teachers engage in activities which help their students to learn without those activities being *explicitly* based on appropriate theories or evidence. It may be that only when teachers are asked to examine their methods closely that they identify their approach and can make the assumptions underlying it explicit. Many teachers may still be unaware of theories and evidence that validate their assumptions. One indirect advantage of the growth of ICT and its introduction into education stems from the need to decide on the beneficial aspects of various existing face-to-face teaching approaches. This is necessary to determine the most effective ways to use the new technology – either in hybrid learning, or in a distance learning scenario. In our view, this examination itself may well have benefits for the way that face-to-face teaching is conducted.

As will be seen in later sections, other advantages of hybrid learning lie in the fact that technology can be used to provide a wide range of learning experiences for students that are based on sound pedagogic principles derived from theories and evidence. This extends the range of facilitation methods that can be used by the teacher/designer. Furthermore, it will be argued that the combination of face-to-face teaching and e-learning provides a richer learning experience than either mode on its own. As a Gestaltist would say, "The whole is more than the sum of the parts".

E-Learning

E-Learning can be defined as "learning which is supported and delivered through the use of information and communication technology" (Clarke, 2004). It is evident from research that e-learning provides an impressive learning arrangement which provides many advantages to the learner (Liao, 2007). Furthermore, it offers a unique selling point; namely accessibility (Blass & Davies, 2003) and also provides a meaningful response to the challenge of widening access to higher education and the increasing size and diversity of the student population.

Claims in the literature propose that the advantages of well-designed e-learning include providing the student with easier access to more information (Salter, 2003), allowing learning to take place anytime/anywhere (Race, 1994), being student-centred (Griffin & Stephenson, 2005), and allowing for self-pacing (Cantoni, Cellario & Porta, 2004; Pilcher, 2001), and interactivity (Barfield, 2004). It is also claimed that e-learning has the ability to promote higher-order learning outcomes (Kekkonen-Moneta & Moneta, 2002).

However, researchers have also reported that the e-learning experience can be perceived of as inferior to the face-to-face on-campus learning experience. Disadvantages might include feelings of isolation (Salter, 2003) and loneliness (Martínez, Mílans del Bosch, Henar Pérez Herrero, & Sampedro Nuño, 2007), lack of a sense of community (Rovai, 2002) and increased student drop-out rates (Levy, 2007). Furthermore, a study by Sapp & Simon (2005) suggested that students partaking in an online course tend to "thrive or dive" as the students' grades were clustered at the extremes very good or very poor. However, in face-to-face teaching, students either "thrived" or "survived". Other disadvantages of e-learning might include higher performance anxiety leading to less enjoyment (Cybinski & Selvanathan, 2005), access/server problems (Pilcher, 2001), lack of hands-on experience (Rosenkoetter, 2006). e-Learning is thought to require more self-discipline and self-motivation (Mullen & Tallent-Runnels, 2006) and the availability of online notes can lead to students using them as a complete replacement for attending lectures (Grabe, 2005).

From this generalised list of potential advantages and disadvantages, it is clear that the use of e-learning needs to be carefully planned with sound pedagogic underpinnings so that the advantages can be realised and the disadvantages minimised. For e-learning however, there is a danger that lecturers might jump on the "e-learning bandwagon" (Darbyshire, 2005) and just produce the equivalent of electronic page turners (Nielsen, 1998) or use a virtual learning environment (VLE) as a simple document repository (Badge, Cann & Scott, 2005). In order to avoid the growth of such scenarios, we believe it is important to put pedagogic principles or educational considerations at the heart of the design of e-learning. This will ensure that it does add value.

Hybrid (Blended) Learning

Although e-learning is being used to deliver whole programmes of study, this is generally the case where students are geographically dispersed and at a distance from the teachers, i.e. distance learning. Expanding Clarke's (2004) definition set out above, we would define e-learning as learning which is *entirely* supported and delivered through the use of information and communication technology. However, our focus is on the use of e-learning combined with face-to-face teaching in those contexts where students undertake higher education programmes by attendance at a university campus. This is now referred to as hybrid learning (Olapiriyakul & Scher, 2006), although, in the United Kingdom at least, the term "blended learning" is more widespread. At a simple level it is the combination of e-learning experiences with face-to-face teaching (Garrison & Kanuka, 2004). However, a more in-depth view is provided by Sharpe, Benfield, Roberts & Francis (2006). They suggest that blended (hybrid) learning can take one of three characterisations:

- Supplementary resources for learning programmes, through institutionally supported VLEs
- Transformative course level practices underpinned by radical course designs, making significant use of technology to replace other modes of teaching and learning
- Holistic view of technology and learning, including learners' own technologies to support their learning.

This paper addresses the second characterisation of hybrid learning. This has the potential to offer many practical advantages as opposed to one 'stand-alone' teaching mode. For instance, the literature has demonstrated that it has the ability to reduce commuter time and provide greater flexibility (Olapiriyakul & Scher, 2006), eliminate distance barriers, provide regular interaction, reduce costs and maintain a large student audience whilst maintaining personal rapport. However, it may be that what is of *particular* importance is the fact that blending "provides a stable transition of familiar and new features" (Boyle, Bradley, Chalk, Jones & Pickard, 2003). Moreover, empirical research has shown that the hybrid approach, as opposed to one stand-alone (or "un-blended") mode, is more effective and efficient and is also preferred by students (Dewhurst & Norris, 2003; Laurillard, 1996; Sapp & Simon, 2005; Stephenson, Brown & Griffin, 2006).

The technology available to support hybrid learning is continuously and rapidly evolving, allowing teachers to do more and be more creative in their approach. However, it is important that the teaching approaches implemented with the technology are driven by educational considerations rather than by the power of the technology itself. In the next section, we present eight educational considerations which should inform how the technology is used. The section draws on a booklet produced at Brunel University: "Educational considerations for blended learning" (Stephenson, J.E., Murray, L.A., Alberts, P.P., Parnis, N.G., Sharma, A., Fraser, J.E., Zammit, M.J., 2008). These considerations are derived from theories about the nature of student learning. In presenting these considerations, reference is made to schools of thought and/or theorists from whom they are derived. We do not go into great theoretical detail as our focus is on the considerations and their application in hybrid learning. In the next section we also refer to studies which provide evidence of the effectiveness of their application because we believe that such evidence is more important than detailed theoretical analysis in promoting course designs that will facilitate student learning effectively and achieve the intentions of the teaching. The final section will provide a case study of how the eight educational considerations were used in a project to identify sound e-learning practices within the contexts of decentralised Schools at a university. The results of the project provided an evidence-base of the effectiveness of the e-learning practices.

EIGHT EDUCATIONAL CONSIDERATIONS FOR HYBRID LEARNING

Here we discuss eight educational considerations which should be taken into account when designing hybrid learning. These particular considerations emerged from discussions among Brunel University's team of educational leaders and e-learning technologists during a major project to ensure pedagogic effectiveness of the hybrid learning implemented at the institution. It is not claimed that this is the *only* set of considerations that might be identified. We also recognise that they are not mutually exclusive in their definition, nor in their implications for teaching. We do not believe that determining a definitive list is a feasible objective. We do, however, argue that it is a comprehensive set of considerations which is defensible as an aide to the design of e-learning elements of an effective hybrid approach to learning facilitation. The eight considerations are that learning should be outcomes-based; learning programmes should require students to be active; and to be collaborative. Teaching should be student-centred; recognise differing learning styles; and provide feedback to students on their learning. It should assist learners in becoming independent; and reflective. We now discuss each of these in turn.

Outcomes-Based Learning

At the minimum, this consideration refers to the need to provide students with a clear statement of what is expected from them in their learning. This not only guides their studies, but also helps to prepare them for assessment. One origin of this seemingly common-sense idea is the neo-behavourism school of thought underpinned by the work of the American educational psychologist Robert Gagné. In his "Nine Events of Instruction" (Gagné, 1985), he includes "Inform the learner of the objectives" as the second. Of course, all nine events should be incorporated into learning situations according to neo-behaviourists (Gredler, 2005 and Kruse, 2005).

A learning outcome may be defined in terms of course content (such as topics to be covered), but the learning outcomes identified for each course of study should also include a range of cognitive skills, e.g. a selection of components from Bloom's taxonomy of educational objectives (see also Anderson et al., 2001). He proposed a hierarchy of cognitive levels consisting of knowledge, comprehension, application, analysis, synthesis and evaluation (Bloom, 1956). Making the higher levels of cognitive skill explicit in this way promotes a 'deep' approach to learning rather than a 'surface' one as defined by Marton & Saljo (1976) and others. This consideration also suggests the need to ensure 'constructive alignment' of learning outcomes, content and assessment as advocated by Biggs (2003). In addition, cognitive theory, or cognitivism, implies that there is value in breaking the learning task into meaningful sub-goals. This assists in keeping less motivated students on task and can be managed in a computer-based tutorial. For example, information can be organised into a hierarchical structure through the use of child and sibling menus (Evans & Edwards, 1999). Similarly, the use of selective release of material and tasks (conditional on the achievement of an earlier step) enables the online learning experience to be closely managed according to the teacher's analysis of the task. On the contrary, in a face-to-face setting, the planned order can be ignored by the students as they can choose to miss a teaching session, thus disturbing the organisational framework for the module and overriding the pre-determined learning experience.

Taking these aspects of the outcomes-based consideration together, it is clear that courses including e-learning need to be highly structured. A study by Young & Norgard (2006) illustrates this. They carried out a survey to explore student perceptions about different aspects of online courses. They found that 85% of the students commented that it was important that courses are designed so that they are appropriately structured with set due dates for student input, similar to face-to-face courses. Badly designed courses can discourage the students and consequently affect the achievement of learning outcomes. Furthermore, 97% of those surveyed agreed that the online material supported the course goals and 95% believed that implementing assignments in the online course facilitated mastering the content.

Active Learning

An effective learning experience requires active involvement by the students. This pedagogic principle was, in recent history, derived from Piaget's classic theory of cognitive development (see Beard, 1969). The work of this Swiss epistemologist was instrumental in the development of the theory of learning known as "constructivism". He proposed that learners cannot be "given" information, which they immediately understand and use. Instead, learners must actively "construct" their own knowledge rather than be passive participants (or empty vessels into which knowledge is poured). Learners, like children, build their knowledge through experience. Experiences enable them to create schemas - mental models - in their minds. Therefore, the teacher's role is to be a provider of learning experiences rather than an imparter of information. For instance, actively providing answers to questions allows learners to engage with material, creating their new knowledge for themselves and improving comprehension. e-Learning examples of such active learning experiences include online quizzes and interactive multimedia programs. They might include the use of case studies and role playing using virtual reality. In fact, VLEs provide excellent platforms for applying constructivist principles because of the range of tools provided (Moreno, Gonzalez, Castilla, Gonzalez & Sigut, 2007). A study by Perry (2006), which was based on the constructivism framework, demonstrated that using digital photographic images combined with a reflective question had the ability to promote active learning; it grasped the students' attention and stimulated the students to think "outside of the box". Similarly, according to Wong, Ab Jalil, Fauzi Mohd Ayub, Abu Baker & Sai Hong (2003), infusing a course with constructivist approaches offered considerable benefit to the students because it enhanced their positive attitudes towards IT and furthermore, it facilitated active learning.

The pedagogic concepts associated with constructivism can be applied in both face-to-face and online contexts with the potential for positive learning experiences in each case. Take, for example, applying the notion of active learning in lectures. Just as traditional face-to-face lectures can be listening-intensive and provide little opportunity for the student to engage with the material, so online lectures can be reading-intensive (Mullen & Tallent-Runnels, 2006). However, both can encourage active learning by involving beneficial student interaction with the material. Although the same principles can be applied in each case, practical application in the face-to-face setting is inherently more difficult than in the online situation. Issues of "crowd management" can present themselves in large classes as soon as the students are encouraged to be less passive and differences between students in their pace of work are also limiting. These difficulties are not apparent in the online setting.

Collaborative Learning

An effective learning experience promotes collaboration between students. Collaboration and communication are fundamental learning skills and, in a collaborative environment, learning is socially constructed. Salmons (2007) defines collaboration as, "an interactive process that engages two or more participants who work together to achieve outcomes they could not accomplish independently". Collaboration involving teachers and students, or peers alone, can be the means by which students further their understanding. However, it is interesting that, anecdotally, someone who only just understands something can be more effective as a teacher than an expert. Thus peer-to-peer interaction is the key feature in the use of this pedagogical principle. Meaningful collaboration or peer-peer interaction can be achieved in a variety of ways, including undertaking authentic tasks (Woo & Reeves, 2007).

With increasingly widespread technologies and increased bandwidth, methods of communicating, and thus collaborating, online are becoming readily available e.g. e-mail, internet relay chat/instant messaging, video conferencing, blogs and wikis. Using the internet now provides an excellent means of both synchronous and asynchronous communication (Gillespie, Boulton, Hramiak & Williamson, 2007). This allows for the embedding of online learning in a social experience. One of the most valuable of the communication tools is the asynchronous discussion function (Kennedy, 2005). This allows for two-way communication to be spread out over time providing the basis for a community as it further develops student-student relationships. The effectiveness of online discussion was shown by Campbell et al. (2007) who set out to determine the effects of face-to-face discussion seminars and online asynchronous discussion seminars on educational attainment. They concluded that increased *online* activity was associated with higher assignment marks. Nevertheless, it is important not to presume that students know how to engage in discussions effectively (face-to-face or online) to gain the maximum benefit from the experience (Ellis, Goodyear, O'Hara & Prosser, 2007).

Research has also shown that weblogs (or more simply blogs) can be used as a 'middle space' between face-to-face contexts and forms of structured online instructional delivery. The weblog is a malleable and fluid medium through which individuals can develop an individualised voice that reflects facets of their personal style and idiosyncratic intellectual approaches" (Oravec, 2003 page 225). Similarly, peer-to-peer networking through tools such as wikis is another method by which a social constructivist approach may be manifested in course design.

Social constructivist pedagogic concepts have their associated practical advantages and limitations depending on delivery mode. Take peer-to-peer interaction for example. If a face-to-face seminar group is unstructured and unplanned it can quickly turn into a mini lecture and the students become disengaged and consequently gain nothing from the experience. It would be erroneous to assume that the facilitation skills necessary to run an effective face-to-face discussion are ubiquitous. In an online setting, (e.g. using a discussion board) there is a certain amount of anonymity (which is advantageous for less confident students). However, at another level, students might feel isolated and unsure about how to use the system. They may also be happy not to contribute but just watch and become a "lurker" (Salmon, 2004), particularly if they lack competent typing skills. Furthermore, face-to-face settings allow students to see emotions, facial expression and gestures and these are facilitative of effective discussions. These tend to be lacking in an online setting.

However, if the user is competent at talking online (having "Netspeak" to use David Crystal's term) then there are solutions to the lack of non-verbal communication channels; for instance, using emoticons (ComputerUser, 2004; Derks, Bos & Von Grumbkow, 2007) - ASCII glyphs which represent expressions and attitudes within a piece of text. Furthermore, in the medium term, it is likely that technologies that enable the transmission of speech and video images will mitigate some of these current disadvantages.

Student-Centred Teaching

An effective learning experience creates a student-centred environment. From a psychology of learning perspective, this refers to the fact that new knowledge and skills can more easily be learnt if clear connections are made to what the students already know or can do. This has implications for the content of courses and the way new material is introduced. More generally, and with regard to e-learning, a student-centred environment is one that recognises the nature and needs of today's students. They are very different from their predecessors. We are embedded in the information age and today's students have spent their lives surrounded by technology e.g. computer games, mp3 players, mobile phones, the internet, instant messaging and e-mails. They are used to sitting in front of a personal computer or laptop and receiving information instantly on demand. They expect to be able to access their education in the same way. Implementing a virtual learning environment allows students to access their work anytime and anywhere, thus accommodating these characteristics, needs, experience, expectations and choices of the learner.

An investigation of student responses to a specific e-learning facility was undertaken by Bridge & Appleyard (2007) when they required online submission of assignments. Forty-seven students submitted their essay-style assignments online using a commercially available e-learning platform (Blackboard™ Virtual Learning Environment) and received feedback. Using a questionnaire, students were then asked to compare this method of submission with that of paper submission methods which they had previously performed in another course. The survey results indicated that students saw numerous advantages in Online Assignment Submission Management (OSAM). 88% of students felt it was considerably time-saving and, as it reduced printing burden, was environmentally friendly.

There are also examples of teachers introducing innovative e-learning designs that seek to build on the sorts of activities that students engage in spontaneously. A study by(Cai et al. (2006) explored the use of gaming with designs based on extreme sports to learn the 3D structures of proteins. This type of gaming application with virtual reality could provide learners with close interaction with the "virtual bio-molecular world". It has the potential to create a fun learning environment which would be risk free and it would also allow the students to play the game repeatedly.

Feedback to Students

One of the most significant components of learning on a structured programme compared with learning alone is the provision to the learner of feedback on their progress in understanding. Timely and constructive feedback adds great value to the learning process. The notion is embedded in the behaviourism school of thought where the power of "knowledge of results" is recognised as a fundamental element of learning. Feedback consists of information regarding the correctness and/or quality of individual performances. The quality of feedback itself can vary: to add maximum value it needs to be timely, helpful and encouraging. Furthermore, positive feedback can have the power to motivate the student.

In the context of e-learning, online feedback can be implemented to provide information automatically and instantly. For formative assessments, students can be provided with short on-line quizzes where the feedback allows them to actively test their understanding. In addition, the provision of more qualitative and/or personalised feedback can be managed online, avoiding issues of handwriting illegibility. Computers do not get tired and can display feedback in a variety of formats (e.g. graphical, audio, video).

In Bridge and Appleyard (2007) referred to above, students were also surveyed about the receiving of feedback online. 93% of students commented that feedback was received *faster* electronically than by the traditional method. Overall, 56% preferred online feedback whilst a mere 6% preferred paper-based feedback (32% had no preference). Other practical advantages to online feedback (in addition to its timeliness) were identified. Students liked the 'safety' of having an online copy in case it got mislaid and furthermore, the issue of illegible handwriting was solved. Electronic feedback software is now available and a study by Denton et al. (2007) found that students rated the electronic feedback as "superior" to "traditional red pen annotation". Furthermore, "students appreciate the structured word-processed feedback produced by the software as it clarifies the mark scheme employed and is easier to read than handwritten annotation".

An example of providing formative assessment tasks with feedback is the study conducted by Stephenson et al. (2007). They created a computer-based assessment bank (incorporating mini tutorials and formative and summative feedback) for a cohort of sixteen students to practise the higher learning skills of analysis and application in the field of genetics. Question types included text entry, drag and drop and MCQ radio buttons. Feedback was constructive and supportive and displayed in a variety of media. The authors concluded that such programs allow students to answer questions repeatedly and receive instant feedback. Such repetition in this study led to the majority of students (11/16) gaining a mark of 85% or more and 5 students a mark of 98% or greater. Computer-based formative and summative feedback also eliminates problems often associated with tutor marking in the face-to-face mode.

Learner Independence

An effective learning experience encourages independence in the learner. Metaphorically, learning can be likened to a staircase, where the steps represent increasing learning capability. The teacher's role is to design a staircase which will be proportional to the learner, and it is the learner's role to climb the stairs. In designing the staircase, the teacher uses their knowledge of the task, analysing it into achievable chunks. Each new stage of learning builds on the student's prior knowledge and experiences, and where necessary support can be provided in the form of (temporary) scaffolds.

This metaphor is based on ideas from developmental psychologists, Bruner and Vygotsky. The American cognitive psychologist and educationalist Jerome Bruner, as well as advocating learning by discovery, advanced the notion of scaffolding (Bruner, Goodnow & Austin, 1956). This idea is in turn related to the work of Russian psychologist and philosopher Lev Vygotsky (Daniels, 2005). He introduced the notion of the Zone of Proximal Development (ZPD). This is the discrepancy (or gap) between what the learner can do aided and un-aided.

In this conception of how learning programmes should be designed, personal responsibility and initiative are always required by the student. This is increasingly so as learners progress through the learning programme but assistance in the form of guidance, suggestions and access to resources is always to hand. Providing suggestions for resources such as journals (instead of, always, a specific article) is an example of gradually increasing student independence and eventually eliminating the need for scaffolding. It perhaps goes without saying that e-learning provides for easier access to more information through the internet. Access to resources is essential for independent learning and electronic access should be of benefit to students, but the sheer amount of information now available to everyone makes the development of "information literacy" in students a matter to be addressed in higher education.

In order to support independent learning in the e-learning mode, Drozd & O'Donoghue (2007) designed, implemented and evaluated a WebQuest (web inquiry) for a cohort of undergraduate nurses. They found that student attitudes were encouraging. Comments included: "references at hand", "reinforced my understanding", "allows private time at home...can go back to it at my leisure", "all the information was there...good links to other sites", "easy to locate", and "good way of working". Furthermore, incorporating a WebQuest into the course has the power to promote inquiry-based learning, leading to active and deep learning.

Learning Styles

Learners perceive and process information in different ways (e.g. visual, auditory, kinaesthetic and tactile). Individuals differ in their preferences for different styles of learning. Consequently, effective learning is promoted when teachers provide diverse teaching environments to accommodate this. This in itself provides a rationale for hybrid learning providing as it does alternative modes with which students can engage according to what suits them best. Recognising and understanding learning styles (and the related 'multiple intelligences' (Gardner, 1983)) helps to create both more successful and more versatile students. Virtual learning environments, with rich multimedia options, allow us to embrace the varying student learning styles. Material can be presented in a variety of formats such as graphic, video, audio, animation, simulation and text. This is also thought to minimise cognitive load.

According to Thorne (2007), using the opportunity provided by ICT to accommodate individual learning characteristics is important for meaningful learning to occur. Evidence of the potential power is provided by a study by Kekkonen-Moneta & Moneta (2002). Students were delivered a course on "computing fundamentals" either via PowerPoint lecture notes or via web-based, multimedia-rich highly interactive equivalents. These included short videos, hyperlinks, still and interactive graphics, narrated and non-narrated animations, narrated screen capture recordings and interactive exercises. The results indicated that, if interactive learning modules are designed correctly, they can foster higher-order learning outcomes across a variety of student learning styles. It is worth bearing in mind that e-learning experiences can range from a minimum interpretation of multi-media to the more sophisticated use just described. A recognition of different learning styles might be manifested by adding a second channel of input. The student appreciation of adding voice to a textual online presentation was reported by Ridgway et al. (2007) when they delivered a web-based surgical lecture series to eighty-eight medical students. HTML lecture slides were delivered to the students via a Virtual Learning Environment (Blackboard™). However, half of the cohort experienced the addition of voice-over (consisting of reinforcement of text and further reading). They found that there was considerable student support for the incorporation of voice over files. Furthermore, it enhanced knowledge transfer and significantly improved exam performance compared to the text only web-based lecture group.

Reflection

Our final educational consideration states that an effective learning experience provides encouragement and time for reflection. This is the fundamental process of metacognition. A prominent advocate of metacognition as a significant domain within theories of cognitive development is John Flavell (1977; 1985). He refers to the definition provided by Masters (1981, page 129): "the individual's own awareness and consideration of her or his cognitive processes and strategies". Its value as a pedagogic concept is clear. Metacognition allows the learner to manage their learning more efficiently and to take an active rather than passive role in the learning process. The United Kingdom's Department for Education and Skills defined it as "the process of planning, assessing, and monitoring one's own thinking. Thinking about thinking in order to develop understanding or self-regulation" (DfES, 2007). Metacognitive strategies include planning ahead and preparing, self-monitoring through checking understanding, self-evaluation and review. Such activities are considered important as they create a more confident independent student aware of their own learning and able to apply the correct strategies in new learning settings.

It is possible to provide opportunities for reflection in both face-to-face and e-learning modes. Reflection can be achieved through reflective notebooks (Puntambekar, 2006) or blogs because such online journals (organised in chronological order) also allow students to review repeatedly the entries for revision purposes and to reflect on the progress manifested in the entries. Metacognition can be achieved online through computer mediated communication such as threaded discussion boards and emails. In each case, written dialogue allows the learner to re-read and reflect on the logged conversation. A study by Finegold & Cooke (2006) illustrated how students had positive attitudes towards this type of communication and in fact valued it specifically because the transcripts were recordable and could be reflected upon. Similarly, a study by Lightfoot (2006) demonstrated that when the students interacted with their lecturer and group peers they actually put significantly more thought into email communication compared to verbal face-to-face equivalents.

We conclude that a hybrid learning approach has a major role to play in 21st century higher education. It can produce a superior pedagogically-sound environment, combining the best features of face-to-face learning with those of e-learning. Our work and that of others reported here indicates that this is already happening in some institutions and fields of study. However, in order for the potential benefits of hybrid learning to be further realised, it is essential that teachers are provided with the support they need. As always, the teacher requires the qualities of a pedagogue; a teacher at heart equipped with enthusiasm and knowledge about learning (i.e. conventional pedagogy). Furthermore, in the context of a hybrid situation the teacher needs to extend these qualities to establish the role of an e-pedagogue, namely, an understanding of the new and emerging technology and knowledge of how to create and support online learning experiences. Probably the most important quality to have is enthusiasm and a readiness for the uptake of technology (Mehanna, 2004; Good, 2001).

CASE STUDY OF THE UTILISATION OF THE EDUCATIONAL CONSIDERATIONS AT BRUNEL UNIVERSITY

As part of a nationally funded e-learning project, the e-Learning Support Team at Brunel University investigated the development of hybrid learning within the context of the Schools at the University during 2007 / 2008. The Schools are relatively decentralised and independent from central administration at the University; it was essential that their unique characteristics and circumstances be taken into account during the investigation.

During the research phase of the project, the eight educational considerations discussed in this chapter were selected in terms of their relevance for hybrid learning (Stephenson, et al., 2008). The intention of the project was to identify sound and appropriate e-learning practices within the context of each School, using these educational considerations as the point of departure.

Table 1. Educational considerations and examples of their implementation

Educational considerations	Examples of e-learning practices within a hybrid learning approach at Brunel Schools
Outcomes-based learning	Announcement tool pop-up messages; provision of online study guide
Active learning	Range of Web links; online tasks linked to primary learning resources; online exercises
Collaborative learning	Online group work via blog / discussion / chat tools
Student-centred teaching	Online assignment submission; variety of online content resources; online glossary of terminology
Feedback to students	Summary postings on discussion tool; personal mail tool messages; online questions & 'model' answers; self-assessment quizzes; online assignment grade comments
Learner independence	Choice of online assignments, additional online learning resources
Learning styles	Use of video clips; links to YouTube / BBC (British Broadcasting Corporation) archives; links to online case studies and simulations
Reflection	Evaluation questions by means of the survey tool; personal blog postings

An Appreciative Inquiry (AI) methodology (Cooperrider, Whitney & Stavros, 2005) was used for the investigation, focussing on 'positive' e-learning practices that were effective in terms of the student learning experience. The AI methodology consists of a series of events which, taken as a whole, are designed to maximise the take-up of new or changed approaches in an organisation. In our case, the aim was to increase the use of the e-learning element of our blended learning approach in pedagogically-valid ways. The first stage of the method –"discovery" - was implemented through individual interviews with academic staff recognised as "early adopters" in each School. This was followed by the "development" stage in the form of focus groups of those same staff. In "discovery", the eight educational considerations were used as a means of eliciting examples of e-learning activities from staff who had not necessary explored the pedagogic rationale for the way they were using the University's VLE. In the "development" event, the same considerations were used to provide a common language in which to reflect back and share the outputs from the interviews in the focus group setting.

Evidence of the effectiveness of the identified e-learning practices was collected from students by means of a Personal Response System (PRS), as well as online student surveys. The collated findings validated the results of the two staff events for each School. In addition, the results were cross-validated by means of analysis of the daily student usage data of the virtual learning environment. Table 1 provides examples of the implementation of the educational considerations through the use of the e-learning tools available to the staff at our University.

The third stage of the AI methodology involved the reporting back of the findings to all the academic staff in each of the Schools. Again, the eight educational considerations were used in highly visual formats to structure the presentations and discussions. Detailed and specific examples of the way in which tools were used were provided. These "pre-summit" meetings indicated a high level of interest in the identified sound e-learning practices and an understanding of their relationship to the educational considerations. It was also evident that there was a willingness to build on the e-learning practices and to further develop hybrid learning strategies and plans for each School. Furthermore, it was evident to the project team that the framework provided by the making explicit of the educational considerations was useful and comprehensive.

The project was completed by final "summit" meetings in which a number of Schools shared their local practice with colleagues from other Schools. Again, very positive responses were forthcoming revealing that the process had proved very valuable in assisting staff to recognise the pedagogic validity of the designs they had incorporated, based on their implicit conceptions of how students learn. Staff welcomed the evidence of local and successful tool use which was explicitly related to the sound pedagogic principles expressed as educational considerations.

CONCLUSION

We have argued in relation to eight educational considerations that the e-learning elements of hybrid learning should be designed taking into account the same pedagogic principles as should underpin sound face-to-face teaching. Both face-to-face and online delivery modes lend themselves to the application of a common set of well-established pedagogic concepts. In some instances, application may be deemed to be more straightforward and/or provide more added-value in one mode rather than the other. In this regard neither is inferior to the other. However, we contend that this is not an issue. Where students are enrolled on campus-based programmes, they can benefit from the model which includes the strengths of both modes - the hybrid learning model. The full benefits of this will be achieved by a design strategy that incorporates both face-to-face and online delivery such that there is a discernable thread continuously linking elements of the two modes. Such a design would be in stark contrast to the "velcro approach" warned against by Clark (2003). We thus conclude by extending that of Shepherd (2005) who wrote that "a successful blended solution is like a balanced meal, combining a range of ingredients, each of which has a unique purpose". Our view is that the success of the blend depends not only on the ingredients, but also on how they are combined. The future pedagogic imperative for hybrid learning is that all elements (both face-to-face and online) are effectively integrated and seen to be so. In other words, we now need to work further on the recipes.

REFERENCES

Anderson, L. W., Krathwohl, D. R., Airasian, P. W., Cruikshank, K. A., Mayer, R. E., Pintrich, P. R., et al. (2001). *A taxonomy for learning, teaching and assessing: a revision of Bloom's taxonomy of educational objectives*. New York: Longman.

Badge, J. L., Cann, A. J., & Scott, J. (2005). e-Learning versus e-Teaching: Seeing the Pedagogic Wood for the Technological Trees. *Bioscience Education e-Journal, 5*. Retrieved January 10, 2007 from http://www.bioscience.heacademy.ac.uk/journal/vol5/beej-5-6.pdf

Badger, R., White, G., Sutherland, P., & Haggis, T. (2001). Note perfect: an investigation of how students view taking notes in lectures. *System, 29*, 405–417. doi:10.1016/S0346-251X(01)00028-8

Barfield, L. (2004). *Design for new media: Interaction design for multimedia and the web*. Harlow, UK: Pearson Addison Wesley.

Beard, R. M. (1969). *An outline of Piaget's Developmental Psychology*. London: Routledge & Kegan Paul.

Biggs, J. (2003). Teaching for Quality Learning at University (2nd ed.). Buckingham, UK: Open University Press.

Blass, E., & Davis, A. (2003). Building on Solid Foundations: establishing criteria for e-learning development. *Journal of Further and Higher Education, 27*(3), 227–245. doi:10.1080/0309877032000098662

Bligh, D. A. (2000). *What's the use of lectures?* San Francisco: Jossey-Bass.

Bloom, B. S. (Ed.). (1956). *Taxonomy of educational objectives. Book 1, Cognitive domain.* New York: Longman.

Boyle, T., Bradley, C., Chalk, P., Jones, R., & Pickard, P. (2003). Using blended learning to improve student success rates in learning to program. *Journal of Educational Media, 28*(2-3), 165–178. doi:10.1080/1358165032000153160

Bridge, P., & Appleyard, R. (2007). A comparison of electronic and paper-based assignment submission and feedback. *British Journal of Educational Technology*, (OnlineEarly article).

Bruner, J. S., Goodnow, J. J., & Austin, G. A. (1956). *A study of thinking.* New York: John Wiley & Sons, Inc.

Cai, Y., Lu, B., Fan, Z., Indhumathi, C., Lim, K. T., & Chan, C. W. (2006). Bioedutainment: Learning life science through X gaming. *Computers & Graphics, 30*(1), 3–9. doi:10.1016/j.cag.2005.10.003

Campbell, M., Gibson, W., Hall, A., Richards, D., & Callery, P. (2007). Online vs. face-to-face discussion in a web-based research methods course for postgraduate nursing students: A quasi-experimental study. *International Journal of Nursing Studies, 45*(5).

Cantoni, V., Cellario, M., & Porta, M. (2004). Perspectives and challenges in e-learning: towards natural interaction paradigms. *Journal of Visual Languages and Computing, 15*, 333–345. doi:10.1016/j.jvlc.2003.10.002

Chung, Q.B. (2005). Sage on the Stage in the Digital Age: The Role of Online Lecture in Distance Learning. *The Electronic Journal of e-Learning, 3*(1), 1-14.

Clark, D. (1999). *A Time Capsule of Training and Learning.* Retrieved March 1, 2007, from http://www.nwlink.com/~donclark/hrd/history/history2.html

Clark, D. (2003). *Blended Learning White Paper.* Retrieved January 16, 2007, from http://www.epic.co.uk/content/resources/white_papers/Epic_Whtp_blended.pdf

Clarke, A. (2004). *e-learning Skills.* Hampshire, UK: Palgrave Macmillan.

ComputerUser. (2004). *High-Tech Dictionary: Emoticons.* Retrieved March 20, 2007, from http://www.computeruser.com/resources/dictionary/emoticons.html

Cooperrider, D. L., Whitney, D., & Stavros, J. M. (2005). *Appreciative Inquiry Handbook: The first in a series of AI workbooks for leaders of change.* Brunswick, OH: Crown Custom Publishing, Inc.

Costa, M. L., Van Rensburg, L., & Rushton, N. (2007). Does teaching style matter? A randomized trial of group discussion versus lectures in orthopaedic undergraduate teaching. *Medical Education, 41*, 214–217. doi:10.1111/j.1365-2929.2006.02677.x

Cybinski, P., & Selvanathan, S. (2005). Learning Experience and Learning Effectiveness in Undergraduate Statistics: Modeling Performance in Traditional and Flexible Learning Environments. *Decision Sciences Journal of Innovative Education, 3*(2), 251–271. doi:10.1111/j.1540-4609.2005.00069.x

D'Alessandro, D. M., Kreiter, C. D., Erkonen, W. E., Winter, R. J., & Knapp, H. R. (1997). Longitudinal follow-up comparison of educational interventions: Multimedia textbook, traditional lecture, and printed textbook. *Academic Radiology*, *4*(11), 719–723. doi:10.1016/S1076-6332(97)80074-8

Daniels, H. (2005). *An introduction to Vygotsky* (2nd ed.). London: Routledge.

Darbyshire, P. (Ed.). (2005). *Instructional Technologies: Cognitive aspects of online programs*. Hershey, PA: IRM Press.

Denton, P., Madden, J., Roberts, M., & Rowe, P. (2007). Students' response to traditional and computer-assisted formative feedback: A comparative case study. *British Journal of Educational Technology*, (OnlineEarly article).

Derks, D., Bos, A. E. R., & von Grumbkow, J. (2007). Emoticons and social interaction on the Internet: the importance of social context. *Computers in Human Behavior*, *23*, 842–849. doi:10.1016/j.chb.2004.11.013

Dewhurst, D. G., & Norris, T. A. M. (2003). Helping teachers to embed e-learning materials into undergraduate pharmacology courses. *Bioscience Education e-Journal*, *1*(1). Retrieved January 10, 2007, from http://bio.ltsn.ac.uk/journal/vol1/beej-1-6.htm

DfES. (2007). *Thinking Skills: Glossary of Terms*. Retrieved March 7, 2007, from http://www.standards.dfes.gov.uk/thinkingskills/glossary/?view=get&index=^M

Drozd, M., & O'Donoghue, J. (2007). The use of a WebQuest to support undergraduate nurses. *Teaching and Learning in Nursing*, *2*, 63–67. doi:10.1016/j.teln.2007.03.001

Ellis, R. A., Goodyear, P., O'Hara, A., & Prosser, M. (2007). The university student experience of face-to-face and online discussions: coherence, reflection and meaning. *ALT-J*, *15*(1), 83–97. doi:10.1080/09687760601130057

Evans, C., & Edwards, M. (1999). Navigational interface design for multimedia courseware. *Journal of Educational Multimedia and Hypermedia*, *8*(2), 151–174.

Feldberg, R. S. (1999). Increasing student involvement in lectures: (very) low tech innovations in a biochemistry lecture class. *Biochemical Education*, *27*, 71–73. doi:10.1016/S0307-4412(98)00263-5

Finegold, A. R. D., & Cooke, L. (2006). Exploring the attitudes, experiences and dynamics of interaction in online groups. *The Internet and Higher Education*, *9*, 201–215. doi:10.1016/j.iheduc.2006.06.003

Flavell, J. H. (1977). *Cognitive development* (2nd ed.). Upper Saddle River, NJ, USA: Prentice-Hall International, Inc.

Gagné, R. M. (1985). *The conditions of learning and theory of instruction* (4th ed.). New York: Holt, Rinehart and Winston.

Gardner, H. (1983). *Frames of mind: The theory of multiple intelligences*. New York: Basic books.

Garrison, D. R., & Kanuka, H. (2004). Blended learning: Uncovering its transformative potential in higher education. *The Internet and Higher Education*, *7*, 95–105. doi:10.1016/j.iheduc.2004.02.001

Gillespie, H., Boulton, H., Hramiak, G., & Williamson, R. (2007). *Learning and teaching with virtual learning environments*. Exeter, UK: Learning Matters Ltd.

Good, M. (2001). On the way to online pedagogy. In J. Stephenson (Ed.), *Teaching and learning online: Pedagogies for new technologies*. London: Kogan Page Limited.

Grabe, M. (2005). Voluntary use of online lecture notes: correlates of note use and note use as an alternative to class attendance. *Computers & Education, 44*, 409–421. doi:10.1016/j.compedu.2004.04.005

Gredler, M. E. (2005). Learning and instruction: Theory into practice (5th ed.). Upper Saddle River, NJ: Pearson, Merrill Prentice Hall.

Griffin, D.K., & Stephenson, J.E. (2005). Interactive electronic lectures on genes and chromosomes. *CAL-aborate*, 8-9.

Kekkonen-Moneta, S., & Moneta, G. B. (2002). E-Learning in Hong Kong: comparing learning outcomes in online multimedia and lecture versions of an introductory computing course. *British Journal of Educational Technology, 33*(4), 423–433. doi:10.1111/1467-8535.00279

Kennedy, D. M. (2005). Standards for online teaching: lessons from the education, health and IT sectors. *Nurse Education Today, 25*, 23–30. doi:10.1016/j.nedt.2004.09.008

Knowles, M. (1990). *The Adult Learner: A Neglected Species* (4th ed.). Houston, TX: Gulf Publishing.

Kruse, K. (2005). *Gagne's nine levels of instruction: An introduction*. Retrieved January 23, 2007, from http://www.e-learningguru.com/articles/art3_3.htm

Laurillard, D. (1996). *The Changing University*. Retrieved January 26, 2007, from http://it.coe.uga.edu/itforum/paper13/paper13.html

Levy, Y. (2007). Comparing dropouts and persistence in e-learning courses. *Computers & Education, 48*(2), 185–204. doi:10.1016/j.compedu.2004.12.004

Liao, Y.-K. C. (2007). Effects of computer-assisted instruction on students' achievement in Taiwan: A meta-analysis. *Computers & Education, 48*, 216–233. doi:10.1016/j.compedu.2004.12.005

Lightfoot, J. M. (2006). A comparative analysis of e-mail and face-to-face communication in an educational environment. *The Internet and Higher Education, 9*, 217–227. doi:10.1016/j.iheduc.2006.06.002

Lu, E. Y., Ma, H., Turner, S., & Huang, W. (2007). Wireless Internet and Student-centered learning: A Partial Least-Squares model. *Computers & Education, 49*(2), 530–544. doi:10.1016/j.compedu.2005.10.009

Martínez, R. A., Mílans del Bosch, M., Henar Pérez Herrero, M., & Sampedro Nuño, A. (2007). Psychopedagogical components and processes in e-learning. Lessons from an unsuccessful on-line course. *Computers in Human Behavior, 23*(1), 146–161. doi:10.1016/j.chb.2004.04.002

Marton, F., & Saljo, R. (1976). On Qualitative Differences in Learning — 2: Outcome as a function of the learner's conception of the task. *The British Journal of Educational Psychology*, 46.

Mehanna, W. N. (2004). e-Pedagogy: the pedagogies of e-learning. *ALT-J, 12*(3), 279–293. doi:10.1080/0968776042000259582

Moreno, L., Gonzalez, C., Castilla, I., Gonzalez, E., & Sigut, J. (2007). Applying a constructivist and collaborative methodological approach in engineering education. *Computers & Education, 49*(3), 891–915. doi:10.1016/j.compedu.2005.12.004

Mullen, G. E., & Tallent-Runnels, M. K. (2006). Student outcomes and perceptions of instructors' demands and support in online and traditional classrooms. *The Internet and Higher Education, 9*, 257–266. doi:10.1016/j.iheduc.2006.08.005

Nielsen, J. (1998). *Jakob Nielsen's Alertbox - "Electronic Books – A Bad Idea"*. Retrieved from February 23, 2007, from http://www.useit.com/alertbox/980726.html

Olapiriyakul, K., & Scher, J. M. (2006). A guide to establishing hybrid learning courses: Employing information technology to create a new learning experience, and a case study. *The Internet and Higher Education*, *9*, 287–301. doi:10.1016/j.iheduc.2006.08.001

Oravec, J. A. (2003). Blending by blogging: weblogs in blended learning initiatives. *Journal of Educational Media*, *28*(2-3), 225–233. doi:10.1080/1358165032000165671

Perry, B. (2006). Using photographic images as an interactive online teaching strategy. *The Internet and Higher Education*, *9*, 229–240. doi:10.1016/j.iheduc.2006.06.008

Pilcher, E. S. (2001). Students' evaluation of online course materials in Fixed Prosthodontics: a case study. *European Journal of Dental Education*, *5*, 53–59. doi:10.1034/j.1600-0579.2001.005002053.x

Puntambekar, S. (2006). Analyzing collaborative interactions: divergence, shared understanding and construction of knowledge. *Computers & Education*, *47*, 332–351. doi:10.1016/j.compedu.2004.10.012

Race, P. (1994). *The open learning handbook: promoting quality in designing and delivering flexible learning*. London: Kogan Page Limited.

Ridgway, P. F., Sheikh, A., Sweeney, K. J., Evoy, D., McDermott, E., & Felle, P. (2007). Surgical e-learning: validation of multimedia web-based lectures. *Medical Education*, *41*, 168–172. doi:10.1111/j.1365-2929.2006.02669.x

Rosenkoetter, L. E. (2006). Moving toward online courses. *Radiography*, *13*(4), 271–275. doi:10.1016/j.radi.2006.04.005

Salmon, G. (2004). *e-moderating: the key to teaching and learning online* (2nd ed.). London: RoutledgeFalmer.

Salmons, J. (2007). *From working together to thinking together: Building collaborative advantage*. Retrieved March 26, 2007, from http://www.trainerspod.com/info/

Salter, G. (2003). Comparing online and traditional teaching – a different approach. *Campus-Wide Information Systems*, *20*(4), 137–145. doi:10.1108/10650740310491306

Sapp, D. A., & Simon, J. (2005). Comparing grades in online and face-to-face writing courses: Interpersonal accountability and institutional commitment. *Computers and Composition*, *22*, 471–489. doi:10.1016/j.compcom.2005.08.005

Sharpe, R., Benfield, G., Roberts, G., & Francis, R. (2006). *The undergraduate experience of blended learning: a review of the UK literature and practice*. Retrieved November 20, 2006, from http://www.heacademy.ac.uk/research/Sharpe_Benfield_Roberts_Francis.pdf

Shepherd, C. (2005). *The Blended Learning Cookbook*. United Kingdom: Saffron Interactive.

Stephenson, J. E., Brown, C., & Griffin, D. K. (2006). Electronic delivery of lectures in the university environment: An empirical comparison of delivery styles. *Computers & Education*, *50*(3), 640–651. doi:10.1016/j.compedu.2006.08.007

Stephenson, J.E., Murray, L.A., Alberts, P.P., Parnis, N.G., Sharma, A., Fraser, J.E., & Zammit, M.J. (2008). *Educational considerations for blended learning*. West London: Brunel University.

Stephenson, J. E., Rayne, R. C., & Griffin, D. K. (2007). Online assessment and feedback to facilitate higher order learning skills in classical and molecular genetics. In *Proceedings of the ECCE2007*.

Thorne, K. (2007). *Blended learning: how to integrate online and traditional learning*. London: Kogan Page.

Tomaska, L. (2000). Increasing student involvement in lectures by error-prone talks. *Biochemistry and Molecular Biology Education, 28*, 242–243.

Wong, S. L., Ab Jalil, H., Fauzi Mohd Ayub, A., Abu Baker, K., & Sai Hong, T. (2003). Teaching a discrete information technology course in a constructivist learning environment: is it effective for Malaysian pre-service teachers? *The Internet and Higher Education, 6*(2), 193–204. doi:10.1016/S1096-7516(03)00025-3

Woo, Y., & Reeves, T. C. (2007). Meaningful interaction in web-based learning: A social constructivist interpretation. *The Internet and Higher Education, 10*(1), 15–25. doi:10.1016/j.iheduc.2006.10.005

Young, A., & Norgard, C. (2006). Assessing the quality of online courses from the students' perspective. *The Internet and Higher Education, 9*, 107–115. doi:10.1016/j.iheduc.2006.03.001

KEY TERMS AND DEFINITIONS

Active Learning: Providing learning experiences which require input and involvement from the students.

Appreciative Inquiry (AI): AI is based on the assumption that every organisation has something that works well and these strengths can be the starting point for creating positive change (Cooperrider, Whitney & Stavros, 2005).

Collaborative Learning: Promoting communication and cooperation between students during their learning activities.

Feedback to Students: Providing information to learners on their progress in mastering learning outcomes.

Learner Independence: Encouraging learners to plan and undertake learning and accept responsibility for the outcomes.

Learning Styles: Making provision for learners to perceive and process information in different ways, for example visual, auditory, kinaesthetic and tactile.

Outcomes-Based Learning: Providing students with a clear statement of what is expected from them in their learning.

Personal Response System (PRS): Technology that offers a lecturer/tutor the opportunity to ask a group of students multiple-choice questions to which they reply individually by selecting a response on a hand-held wireless transmitter.

Reflection: Providing opportunity and encouragement for students to review and evaluate their learning.

Student-Centred Teaching: Providing a learning environment where the focus is on the activities of the learner rather than the activities of the lecturer.

Chapter 13
Hybrid Inquiry-Based Learning

Yuen-Yan Chan
The University of Hong Kong, Hong Kong

Hiu-Fung Lam
Sai Kung Sung Tsun Catholic School (Secondary Section), Hong Kong

Harrison H. Yang
State University of New York at Oswego, USA

Kai-Pan Mark
City University of Hong Kong, Hong Kong

Chi-Hong Leung
Hong Kong Polytechnic University, Hong Kong

ABSTRACT

This chapter proposes the hybrid inquiry-based learning (HIBL) model, a novel pedagogical model based on inquiry-based learning (IBL). In IBL, learning is achieved by questioning and learners are encouraged to invent new hypotheses instead of investigating questions posed by the instructor. This chapter first provides a holistic description of IBL. It begins with a brief history and survey on learning perspectives, pedagogical background of IBL is also provided. The IBL model, its implementations and variations, as well as the comparison of its pedagogical features against traditional teaching approaches are also given. This chapter further contributes the hybrid inquiry-based learning (HIBL) model, a new IBL model that integrates traditional and ICT-based implementations of IBL. By leveraging on the advantages of both classroom-based and web-based learning, the best sides of IBL can be elicited. A detailed example in Information Security education is also provided to illustrate the HIBL model.

INTRODUCTION

Advances in information and communication technology (ICT) bring much change in the way we teach and learn; they also nurture hybrid learning (Buzzetto-More & Sweat-Guy, 2006; Wang & Fong, 2008). Hybrid learning, which also referred to as blended learning (Garrison & Kanuka, 2004), is a novel pedagogical mode which combines the advantages of both traditional classroom environment and the cyberspace. The rapid development of ICT also greatly enhances knowledge sharing

DOI: 10.4018/978-1-60566-380-7.ch013

and building, and cultivates a pleasant supporting environment for inquiry-based learning (IBL). IBL is a constructivist pedagogy that emphasizes on the quest of truth, information, and knowledge through self-discoveries and peers collaborations. It can be achieved in traditional classroom environment, over the Internet, or a hybrid of the two.

This chapter centred on IBL. It first gives the definition of IBL, followed by a brief history and survey. Comparison of the pedagogical features between traditional and IBL teaching approaches is also given. An IBL model is provided to introduce its three essential steps, namely the initiation of inquiry, coaching of the inquiry process, and the assessment of the learning. Implementation examples of IBL in various environments, including those in traditional classroom-based instructions, as well as Web-based learning mode such as WebQuest, are also given. The chapter proposes the hybrid inquiry-based learning (HIBL) and provide its implementation details. It also contributes an HIBL exemplar to illustrate how IBL can be implemented in a hybrid learning mode.

The key objectives of this chapter are to introduce IBL as a whole and discuss how it can be implemented in hybrid learning environments. It aims at providing a foundational reference for future work in this area.

BACKGROUND

In this section, we provide the theoretical background for IBL and HIBL. We begin with a review on learning perspectives, namely Behaviorism, Cognitivism, and Constructivism. These perspectives contribute the theoretical background of IBL to various extends. In particular, IBL realizes most constructivist principles such as scaffolding and collaborative learning. We also provide literature review on learning theories related to IBL, and discuss their relationships with hybrid learning. We encourage readers to refer to other chapters of this handbook for literature review on hybrid learning.

A Review on Learning Perspectives

Psychologists began to study the nature of cognition and learning in late 1800s (Ormrod, 2006). Since then, the mainstream perspective of teaching and learning has been migrating. Starting from Behaviorism in the 50s, to Cognitivism in 70s and 80s, we are now in the era of Constructivist teaching and learning. In this section, we review the evolvement of the mainstream learning perspectives. We also introduce the related learning theories involved in subsequent sections.

1. Behaviorism

In early days of educational research, most researchers focused on response (learners' behavior) and stimuli (environmental events), which later evolved into Behaviorism in 1950s, a theoretical perspective in which learning and behaviors are described and explained in terms of stimulus-response relationships. Seminal behaviorist works include Pavlov's classical conditioning (Pavlov, 1927) and Skinner's operant conditioning (Skinner, 1954). The behaviorist principle being applied most frequently in teaching and learning is reinforcement: a response that is followed by a reinforcing stimulus is more likely to occur again. This principle is often applied in computer-assisted instruction (CAI) and early educational games.

2. Cognitivism

In around 1960s, researchers began to realize that the mechanism of how learning occurs could not be completely explained at the behavioral level. Instead, they proposed to consider thinking in additional to behavior. Gradually, their focus shifted from detail analysis of the stimuli-response relationship to the study of the processes involved in acquiring new knowledge and skills. Since then cognitive psychology emerged and such perspective is referred to as Cognitivism. Cognitive psychology studies how learning occurs and how knowledge is constructed within an individual. More specifically, it addresses mental phenomena such as memory, attention, concept learning, problem solving and reasoning (Neisser, 1967). Seminal cognitivist work include Piaget's Genetic epistemology (1970) and concept of equilibration (1985). Piaget (1970) suggests that human progress through a fixed four-stage sequence that included sensormotor, pre-operational, concrete operational and formal operational; and key cognitive tasks can not be taught if learners have not reached a particular stage of development. Piaget (1985) also suggests that learning is a dynamic, iterative process involving assimilation, accommodation, and equilibration. Cognitive psychology theories later led to information-processing model in 1970s which widely affects the development of information technology and computer systems. Contemporary instructional design and educational computer software also incorporate cognitivist principles such as taking steps to capture learners' attention, elicit learners' prior knowledge, and encourage long-term retention and transfer (R. M. Gagne, Briggs, & Wager, 1992; P. F. Merrill et al., 1996; Ormrod, 2006).

3. Constructivism

While cognitive psychologists focus on how learning occurs within an individual, constructivists suggest that knowledge cannot be delivered directly but to be constructed by the learners themselves. Also, knowledge is not absolute. Constructivists focus on how knowledge is constructed and propose a paradigm shift of learning from instructor-center to learner-center (Jonassen, 1991). Bruner (1986) proposes that learning is an active process in which new ideas are constructed from the current and past knowledge processed by the learners. According to the Social Development Theory (Vygotsky, 1978), learning process is further enhanced by interactions and collaborations with the others, especially when the others are more competent in the area being explored. Nowadays, constructivism become the mainstream perspective of teaching and learning and is widely evolved. Active developing areas include collaborative learning (Bruffee, 1984; Gokhale, 1995), project-based learning (Blumenfeld et al., 1991; Meyer, Turner & Spencer, 1997), as well as inquiry-based learning (Brown & Campione, 1996; Lim, 2001; Tsankova & Dobrynina, 2005; Chan, 2007; Tan & Chan, 2008).

Inquiry

Inquiry is a process to seek for information, knowledge, or truth through questioning. It is a quest for meaning and involves intellectual operations in order to comprehend the inquiring experience (Lim, 2001). Inquiry is a natural process in human development. Since the stage of infants, human beings begin to make sense of the world by inquiring. Such process begins with information and data gathering through applying the senses of seeing, hearing, touching, tasting, and smelling (Eggen & Kauchak, 1999: 553). Through the process of inquiry, individuals construct their perspectives of the natural and human-designed worlds (Martin-Hansen, 2002). Inquiry does not only target at a definite answer, rather, appropriate resolutions to the issues, as well as the development of inquiry skills and attitudes are also valued. Wells (1999) gives inquiry a charming description:

Inquiry is not a "method" of doing science, history, or any other subject in which the obligatory first stage in a fixed, linear sequence is that of students each formulating questions to investigate. Rather, it is an approach to the chosen themes and topics in which the posing of real questions is positively encouraged whenever they occur and by whomever they are asked. Equally important as the hallmark of an inquiry approach is that all tentative answers are taken seriously and are investigated as rigorously as the circumstances permit.

Inquiry should be guided and is not a context-free, undirected activity. The inquiry process and corresponding skills are also emphasized (Lim, 2002). According to Lim (2002), inquiry is driven by a specialized language, law and theories, methodologies of the disciplines and specific areas. For example, in scientific inquiry process, scientists formulate hypotheses, organize experiments, collect data, and analyze the findings in order to test the hypothesis (Martinello & Cook, 2000).

Traditional education does not favor inquiry. In conventional direct instruction, students are not encouraged to raise questions. They are learnt to listen and memorize standardized absolute answers. Fortunately this paradigm has been shifted in recent years. With the rise of constructivism, IBL also gains its importance in various education levels. The advancement of information and communication technology, which greatly facilitate the flow of information, further enhances the implementation of IBL.

Scaffolding

Scaffolding is a major constructivist concept evolved from Bruner's work (Bruner, 1986). It resembles how the scaffolds of a physical building are used to guide knowledge construction. In physical construction, scaffolds only serve as temporary support and will be removed when the building is completed. In learning theory, scaffolding refers to the process of providing learning supports so that learners can accomplish tasks that ordinarily cannot be performed on their own. In order to make scaffolding effective, the task should not be too simple that learners can quickly respond with ease (Roehler & Cantlon, 1997). Therefore, scaffolding is very suitable for IBL situations which involve non-trivial, open-ended problems. Instructional scaffolds can be provided both online and offline, including regular face-to-face meetings between the learners and the instructor, as well as relevant online reference materials prepared or collected by the instructor. Scaffoldings can also occur when students participate in online discussions. Therefore hybrid learning environments, which embrace both classroom face-to-face interaction and online communication, is very suitable for the implementation of instructional scaffoldings.

Knowledge Construction

One key focus of IBL is whether knowledge construction has occurred among the learners during the inquiry process. This involves two aspects: knowledge building and metacognition. Knowledge building is the creation of knowledge as social products (Scardamalia & Bereiter, 1994) or conceptual artifacts (Bereiter, 2002). Metacognition refers to learners' beliefs about their own cognitive processes, and their attempts to control the cognitive processes to optimize learning and memory (Ormrod, 2006). IBL can help promoting effective knowledge construction in many proven ways such as emphasizing the development of a conceptual understanding of academic subject matters (Anderson, 1993; White & Rumsey, 1994), promoting dialogues and interaction between instructor and learners (Hacker, 1998; Issacs, 1999), using authentic activities (Duffy & Jonassen, 1992), and establishing collaborative communities among learners (Scardamalia, & Bereiter, 1994; Tan & Chan, 2008). For effective implementation of IBL in hybrid learning mode, one should harness the above knowledge constructing features.

Learner Collaboration and Higher-Order Thinking

IBL features social cognition and the collaboration among learners. Therefore, learner collaboration is often encouraged in IBL activities. Collaborative learning (Rau & Heyl, 1990) is a learning model under social constructivism (Vygotsky, 1978; Dewey, 1933). In a collaborative learning environment, learners at different performance levels work together in small groups toward common academic goals. Collaborative learning also emphasizes the development and enhancement of higher-order thinking (Gokhale, 1995), a cognitive process in which learners go far beyond the specific information they have acquired, and be able to analyze, apply, and evaluate the acquired information. Many IBL practices also target at the advancement of learners' higher order thinking skills. One can see Alvarado & Herr (2003) and Audet & Jordan (2005) for collections of examples in various subject areas.

The Role of Information and Communication Technology in IBL

Alongside the evolvement of information and communication technology (ICT), the mainstream perspective in teaching and learning also evolves. Constructivist theories have been around since early twenty century (such as Dewey, 1933). Along the rapid advancement of technologies, constructivism gains a new level of importance that the current education paradigm is generally regarded as a constructivist paradigm (such as Jonassen, 1994): where learning is learner-centered with the teacher become a facilitator. IBL emphasizes on the inquiry process in which learners study the problem and its background information, work in group to discuss the problem solving strategies, and further explore and filter necessary information. Summarizing the findings of Blumenfeld et al. (1991) and Edelson, Gordin, and Pea (1999), the following contributions of ICT to IBL are identified:

1. Provides learning management and learning content management
2. Provides access to information
3. Serve as a channel for collaborative communication

1. Learning Management and Learning Contents Management

The basic properties of ICT offer benefits for IBL, which include the ability to store and manipulate huge amount of information and data, the ability to enable presentation of information in multimedia formats, the ability to perform complex computations, and the support of communication and expression (Edelson, Gordin, and Pea, 1999: 395). In particular, learning management systems (LMS) (Downes, 2000) can manage learners' learning interventions, provide administrative supports, and monitor learning progress, so that IBL can be conducted both online and offline. Learning content management systems (LCMS) can also work with LMS to deliver and manage the IBL learning objects (Downes, 2000; Chan, 2005) online.

2. WebQuest

ICT greatly facilitates distribution of information in the IBL environment. Dodge (1995) proposes WebQuest, a web-enabled inquiry-based pedagogical tool, which enables IBL activities to be easily designed and conducted with the help of the World Wide Web. WebQuest often exists in the form of a website that contains carefully designed instructional contents. In WebQuest, a portion or all of the information that learners interact with comes from the Web, thus provides a web-based environment for problem-solving, information processing, and collaboration. Furthermore, the World Wide Web also provides extensive sources of information necessary for the inquiry process.

3. Learner Collaboration and Knowledge Building

One characteristic of constructivist pedagogies is the emphasis of learner interactions and knowledge building. With their primary function of supporting information flow and data communication, ICT technologies greatly enhance collaboration between learners outside normal classrooms (Sawyer, 2006) and across countries (Media laboratory, 1999; Learning in Motion, 2003; Tan & Chan, 2008). For example, the 3I (Interdisciplinary, Inter-school, and International) Project Learning activities supported by the Knowledge Community knowledge building system (Tan & Chan, 2008) provide cross-cultural IBL experience to over 10,000 students and teachers globally.

INQUIRY-BASED LEARNING

IBL is elicited by Dewey's work on reflective thinking (Dewey, 1933). It is a constructivist student-centered pedagogy focuses on questioning, critical thinking, and problem solving (Bloom & White, 1993). IBL is based on the premise that inquiry is natural to and the most effective to human learning. The IBL instructional approach helps learner to seek for truth, information, or knowledge by questioning. Lim (2001) defines IBL as *an umbrella term covering various teaching models and instructional approaches using inquiry as a main vehicle for teaching and learning to promote higher-order thinking skills and self-directed learning.* Like many constructivist pedagogies, such as project-based learning and cooperative learning, IBL is often conducted in form of a project and targets at the enhancement of higher-order thinking skills. However, IBL distinguishes from general project-based learning as the later focuses on the development of the ultimate deliverables; while IBL emphasizes on the inquiry processes throughout the entire project.

The IBL Pedagogical Model

The pedagogical model of IBL can be generalized into three main parts: 1) initiating inquiry, 2) coaching during an inquiry, and 3) assessing inquiry-based learning (Lim, 2001; Tsankova & Dobrynina, 2005; Chan, 2007). It is illustrated in figure 1.

1. Initiating

Under the IBL model, the learning process, may it be a single lecture or a project that spans one semester, begins with a problem or a problem situation that involves multiple sub-problems. The problem should be non-trivial, which cannot be too simple that learners can quickly respond with ease. Prior to the inquiry process, a clearly described problem as well as the related information is released to the learners. The expected deliverables and the corresponding assessment scheme (which is often in the form of a rubric) are also released.

2. Coaching During an Inquiry

Right after the problem and the expected deliverables are clearly explained, the inquiry process can then begin. According to Tsankova and Dobrynina (2005), coaching is the delicate art of balancing the students' freedom to explore with the likelihood that the desired outcomes and direction taken by the investigation can be achieved successfully. Sufficient time should be given to the learners to conduct their inquiry, for

Figure 1. Components of IBL

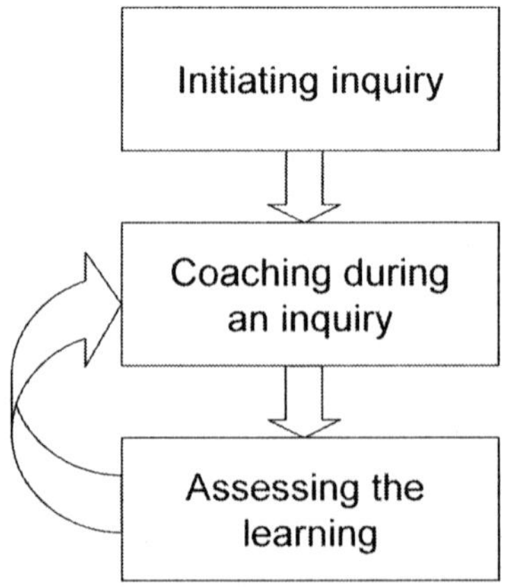

example, to fully analyze and comprehend the problem, plan how to investigate, and summarize and reflect on the results (Tsankova & Dobrynina, 2005: 94). Scaffolding, the process of providing learning supports so that learners can accomplish tasks that ordinarily cannot be performed on their own, is also critical in this step. When learners are asked to solve nontrivial problems, they often need greater support to reach the desired outcomes. With scaffolding helps, teachers can provide corresponding instructional aids to facilitate the learning process (Chan, 2007).

3. Assessing the Learning

Similar to many learner-centred learning approaches, in IBL, learners must be initially informed about how their learning will be assessed (Iannuzzi, 1999; Kulm, 1990; Lester & Lambdin-Kroll, 1990). Also, assessment of IBL should be driven by the inquiry process (Tsankova and Dobrynina, 2005). In the assessment process, feedbacks should be provided to the learners so as to help improving the quality of ongoing inquiry. Instead of evaluating the entire inquiry process as a whole in the end, milestones can be set up along the process so that the project is divided into stages (Chan, 2007). Learners can submit deliverables at different stages, while formative assessments are made upon receiving deliverables at intermediate stages, with the immediate feedbacks and comments provided. In this way, learners can proceed to subsequent project stages with references to the feedbacks obtained from intermediate deliverables, so that the quality of ongoing inquiry can be improved

Traditional Instruction and Inquiry-Based Learning: A Comparison

Traditional classroom teaching is one-way and instructor-centered, in which instructor delivers subject contents to learners in a single, monotonic direction. On the contrast, IBL is learner-centered and it emphasizes on the interactions between instructor and learners and among the learners. We summarize the comparison between traditional instruction and IBL in Table 1.

VARIATION OF IBL

IBL is a collective term covering teaching models that use inquiry as a main vehicle for teaching and learning (Lim, 2001). Here we introduce the variations of inquiry-based learning and give the areas

Table 1. Summary of comparison between traditional instruction and IBL

	Traditional Instruction	IBL
Instructional mode	Instructor-directed	Learner-centered
Instructional sequence	Inductive	Deductive
Learner engagement	One-way and passive	Two-way, active, and with a challenging mind
Instructor engagement	Deliver subject content, ask questions to check learners' progress	Guiding, exploring, conduct interactive dialogues to provide scaffolding
Instructor feedback	Corrective or negative feedback	Build on learners' response and facilitate further thinking
The use of learner input	For assessment	Assessment as well as for reference and decision making of further instructional activities
Instructor guidance	Directive	Organization and as a facilitator

of their applications. We first provide examples of classroom-based models, and will introduce the web-based and hybrid-mode implementation of IBL in subsequence subsections.

Non Web-Based Variations of IBL

Non web-based teaching and learning models refers to those activities that can be conducted without the use of ICT. The learning processes usually occur within classrooms or laboratories, but can also go beyond the normal classrooms. Examples include inquiry learning, guided discovery learning, project-based learning, problem-based learning, and case-based learning (Dai, 2007).

1. Inquiry Learning

In inquiry learning, a physical model or a phenomenon is presented to the students. The students are encouraged to ask questions and make educated guesses with reasoned arguments. Rapid discussions between teachers and students occur. By means of questioning and opened learning environments, teachers and students can interact based on the subject contexts and contents (Roth, 1998). Inquiry learning is often applied in the teaching of natural science and social studies.

2. Guided Discovery Learning

Guided discovery learning (Bruner, 1967) aims at finding out the underlying causes or structures of a phenomenon. It is based on the premise that learning is the most effective when learners discover facts and relationships for themselves. It is often conducted by engaging and guiding students in exploratory activities. The learning process can be student-initiated or teacher-initiated. Guided discovery learning is often applied in natural sciences education, such as in the occasions of experiments and systematic observations.

3. Project-Based Learning

Project-based learning consists of open-ended, extended research activities which are organized around a driving topic or question. It often results in tangible products such as physical models, documentaries, or project reports. Project based learning is usually multi-disciplinary and can be applied in real life projects, such as conducting survey with foreign visitors, and comparing the culture between two cities (Tan & Chan, 2008).

4. Problem-Based Learning

Problem-based learning (Schmidt, 1993) is similar to project-based learning, but it emphasizes on the development of students' problem solving skills. In problem-based learning, carefully designed problems or situated challenges are launched to facilitate students' self-directed learning activities. The process is usually coached by the teachers. The problems and challenges are non-trivial so that students cannot solve them quickly with ease. Problem-based learning is often applied in medicine, science, and engineering education. Its learning activities are often discipline-based.

5. Case-Based Learning

Case-based learning, or the case method, is started by Harvard Business School in 1920s (HBS, 2008). Under this model, real life cases are studied in order to find out patterns and regularities, lessons, or exemplary practices (Dai, 2007). It uses a case-based approach to engage students in the discussion of specific situations, which are typically real-world examples. This instructional method is learner-centered and involves intense interaction among the participants. Here the instructor's role becomes a facilitator of learner interactions. Case-based learning often applied in teaching and learning in business, medicine, law, social science, and education disciplines.

Web-Based and Computer Supported Variations of IBL

ICT and web technologies bring forth revolutionary changes to teaching and learning. Over last decade, ICT and web-supported IBL evolved as well. This subsection introduces simulation learning and WebQuest as examples. The latter, in particular, is much influential in the constructivist paradigm.

1. Simulation Learning

Simulation learning (Njoo, 1994) is a model based on discovery learning. With the help of computer simulation programs, students can undergo discovery learning by exploring in computer-created virtual environments. Simulation learning can encourage active engagements, promotes learner motivation, and develop creativity and problem solving skills. Learners can also learn and overcome obstacles, and make decisions in achieving ultimate goals (Dai, 2007). Applications of simulation learning include the learning of skills required in real world situations, such as those in urban planning, geography, communication, and sciences. For example, JASPER (JASPER, 2006), a Java-based simulation program, enables learners to simulate and study the performance of various communication protocols.

2. WebQuest

WebQuest is a web-enabled IBL model proposed by Dodge (1995). WebQuests often exist in the form of websites with contents designed according to the WebQuest model. Through a WebQuest, learners can directly explore to related information and resources in the World Wide Web; it thus provides a web-based environment for problem-solving, information processing, and collaboration. A number of research works prove that WebQuest is effective for inquiry-based learning (Peterson, Caverly & MacDonald, 2001; March, 2003; Chan, 2007).

The WebQuest framework (Dodge, 1995) specifies the following components:

- Introduction page: Sets the stage and provides some background information
- Task page: Specifies a duty or an assignment which is doable and interesting
- Resource page: Contains a collection (or the pointers) of information sources necessary to complete the task
- Process page: Gives a description of the procedures for the learners to accomplish the task. The process is usually broken down into clearly described steps
- Evaluation page: Includes an assessment rubric which describes how the learners will be evaluated
- An optional teacher page that includes information to help other teachers implement the WebQuest

After reviewing a number of classroom-based and ICT-based implementations of IBL, in the rest of this chapter, we specify Hybrid Inquiry-Based Learning (HIBL), a model for IBL implementation in a hybrid learning environment. The model combines features and advantages of both web-based and classroom-based IBL so as to elicit the best sides of inquiry-based learning.

HYBRID INQUIRY-BASED LEARNING

In this section, we define the model for Hybrid Inquiry-based Learning (HIBL). HIBL is a student-centered constructivist pedagogy which inherits three main steps in the conventional IBL model. In HIBL, a portion of the learning activities is migrated to the online platform; yet, traditional classroom-based interactions between teacher and students, as well as those among students are maintained. Integration between ICT-based and non ICT-based activities is also emphasized. We give HIBL the follow definition:

(Definition of HIBL) Hybrid Inquiry-Based Learning (HIBL) covers pedagogies and instructional approaches using inquiry as the main tool for teaching and learning and being implemented by a combination of ICT-based and non ICT-based methods, such as WebQuest, knowledge building communities, and conventional classroom teaching.

Based on the above definition, we further establish the HIBL model which will be introduced in detail in the following paragraph. We will also provide an exemplar in information security education to illustrate our proposal.

The HIBL Model

The HIBL model is depicted in the Figure 2. It is a three-step procedure with a feedback loop between step two and step three.

Step One: Initiating Inquiry

In this step, the problem, expected deliverables and corresponding assessment schemes are clearly presented to the learners. Related information is also provided. This step is delivered in two modes: traditional classroom-based mode and web-based learning mode. It is important to conduct face-to-face discussion and elaboration of the problem so as to clarify any misconceptions at the earliest stage, while the Web serves as a rich source for prerequisite references and resources. Prior to the classroom activity, the teacher prepares a WebQuest in accordance to the problem situation and collects related Web resources. The WebQuest is published before the lesson so that students can study it before the class. In the normal classroom setting, the teacher gives background and introduces the subject contexts, and describes the problem in detail. During the teaching, the teacher explains the learning outcomes, expected deliverables, and the evaluation criteria to the class with the help of the WebQuest.

Step Two: Coaching During an Inquiry

In this step, learners are provided with sufficient time to conduct the inquiry process. A Web-based discussion forum is established to facilitate the discussions between teacher and students and among students. Announcements related to learning can also be made through the forum. This step is highly learner-centered, while the teacher acts as a facilitator and provides scaffolding help when necessary. The learners interact among themselves actively and work towards the goals, such interactions can take place both online at the Web-based discussion forums and offline within classroom or in after-class meetings. Teachers can also post related questions to the discussion forum to elicit discussions. Teaching and scaffolding aids can be provided in both traditional classroom-based mode and web-based mode. During conventional classroom teaching, the teacher delivers subject contents to the students and encourages questions and discussions. Any issues observed from the Web-based discussions can also be discussed in a face-to-face manner. The teacher can also conduct peer-review of any intermediate deliverables submitted by the students.

Step Three: Assessing the Learning

Assessments enable the teacher to check the progress of learners and to identify any difficulties encountered by the learners. HIBL adopts both formative and summative assessments so that intermediate performance of the students can be fed back and referenced so as to fine tune the instruction and inquiry processes. In HIBL, classroom-based assessment activities can be taken in forms of student group presentations and in-class peer-assessments. These activities not

Figure 2. Depiction of IBL

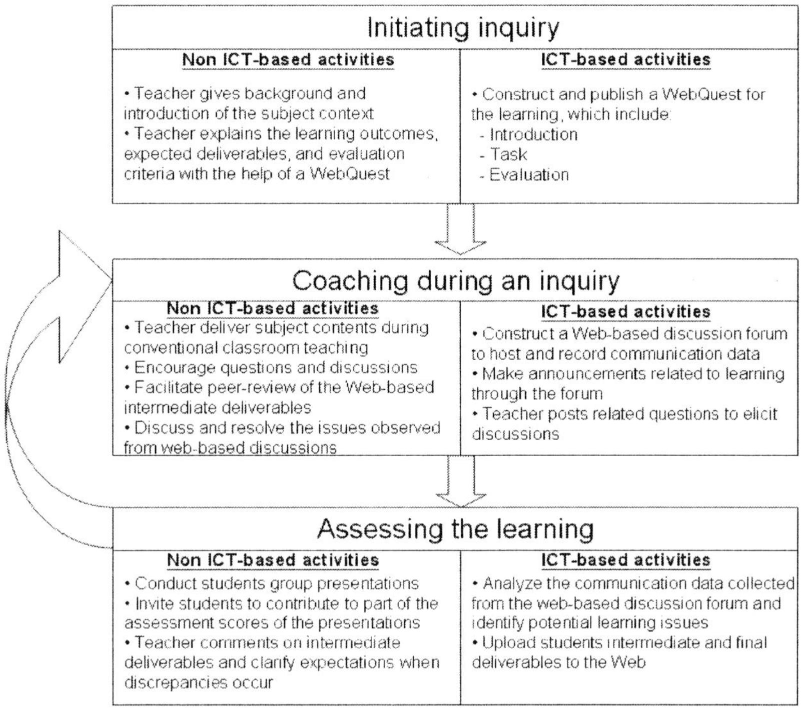

only enable the teacher to evaluate the learning progress of the students but also get the whole class involved and reflect upon their learning. Teacher can also comments on intermediate deliverables and clarify expectations when discrepancies occur. Communication data generated from the web-based forum discussions can also be analyzed to identify potential learning issues. Furthermore, students' intermediate and final deliverables can also be uploaded to the Web for peer-assessment purpose. Findings resulted in the formative assessments should serve as feedback to the second step so as to refine the coaching process.

AN HIBL EXEMPLAR IN INFORMATION SECURITY EDUCATION

In this section, an HIBL exemplar in information security education is provided. The exemplar delivers subject matters in Network Security via an HIBL pedagogical approach. IBL is recommended for teaching and learning in network security topics because it involves many forensics and investigating efforts. Also, there can be multiple security threats which make the situation non-trivial and open ended. IBL is also suitable for ICT education in general because ICT knowledge is highly practical and can be directly applied to real life situations. Therefore, it can also be taught effectively through authentic instruction strategies as IBL.

In the unit, a problem situation is launched in which an imaginary eBook company requests for consultancy services for strengthening the security of its online bookshop website after the occurrence of some security issues. Students forms into groups of 4 – 6 to act as consultants. The group should first propose how they plan to solve the problem (such as defining the sub-problems and how they will investigate and produce the solution). They then work out the project according to the proposals. The groups can interact with one another along the entire process via an online discussion forum. Finally, as a deliverable, students present the work in form of a website.

Overall Settings

1. Curriculum Background

Specifications related to the curriculum background are listed below.

a. Topic: Information Security Consultants
b. Unit: Network Security
c. Duration: 3 hours (Divided into 2 1.5 hours lectures)
d. Grade level: Second and third year Engineering undergraduates
e. Curriculum Connection: This unit is a part of the Computer Networks course. The 13-weeks course covers 7 main topics: (1) OSI reference model, week 1; (2) overview of TCP/IP, week 2; (3) physical layer, LAN, and WAN, week 3 – 5; (4) network layer and protocols, week 6 – 7; (5) transport layer and protocols, week 8 – 9; (6) application layer and protocols, weeks 10 – 11; (7) network security, weeks 12 – 13. The teaching detailed in this plan will be conducted in the last week where most concepts in networking and information security have already been covered
f. Key concepts being introduced include: (1) security of computer networks; (2) Secure Socket Layer (SSL); and (3) Public Key Infrastructure (PKI)

2. Instructional Goals

At the end of the unit, students are expected to achieve the following:

a. Get cognitively involved in issues related to security threats and their defense measures
b. Be able to identify security risks exist in a networked environment
c. Be able to make recommendation to secured computer networks
d. Be able to demonstrate IT consultancy skills, including those in problem investigation, problem solving, presentation, and documentation

3. Inquiry Questions

The inquiry questions include but not limited to the followings:

a. What are the security threats in computer networks?
b. What are the technologies to safeguard security in computer networks?
c. How to make recommendations to business managers and general computer users?

4. Assessment

At the end of the unit, students need to construct a Website to present their security consultancy report as deliverable. They are also required to submit project planning forms as intermediate deliverables. Assessment includes formative and summative elements and will be made based on two aspects: criteria and strategies. For assessing the criteria aspect, students should be able to apply their knowledge of information security to provide correct and sound solutions to the problem situation. Students should also be able to define sub-problems and methods to conduct an inquiry to solve the problem, and can critically reflect on the inquiry process. Here, the first requirement is related to the subject contents while the second requirement is related to the inquiry process. For assessing the strategies aspect, students are required to work in group as information security consultants to investigate into security of an imaginary online bookshop; they will provide advices and recommendation in information security. The groups are also required to develop a Website by consolidating the project plans, findings, and the proposed solution.

Pre-Instructional Preparation

Prior to the launching of the unit, a WebQuest is established according to the description in the previous section. The WebQuest details the problem situation and includes the hyperlinks to a collection of related Web resources. It should be published before the lesson so that students may study it before the class. An online discussion forum is also set up before the start of the inquiry process.

Instructional Procedures

Recommended schedule and detail instructional procedures are given in this subsection. The activities follow the three-step HIBL model as defined previously.

1. Step One: Initiating Inquiry

At the beginning of the lesson, the teacher asks the class to form into groups of 4 to 6 students, and make themselves teams of information security consultants. With reference to the WebQuest pre-established before the lesson, the teacher explains the inquiry task to the students in detail. Here, the teacher tells the class that they will receive an invitation to tender for consultancy from the client, eBook Company Limited, with the problem situation given in the Introduction page of the WebQuest, and their task is to produce the consultancy report as described in the Task page of the WebQuest. The assessment criteria are also specified in the Evaluation page. Contents that should be included in the Introduction page and Task page are specified in Figure 3 and 4, respectively. The problem described here is open-ended with more than one possible answer. For example, because

Figure 3. Problem situation to be included in the Introduction page

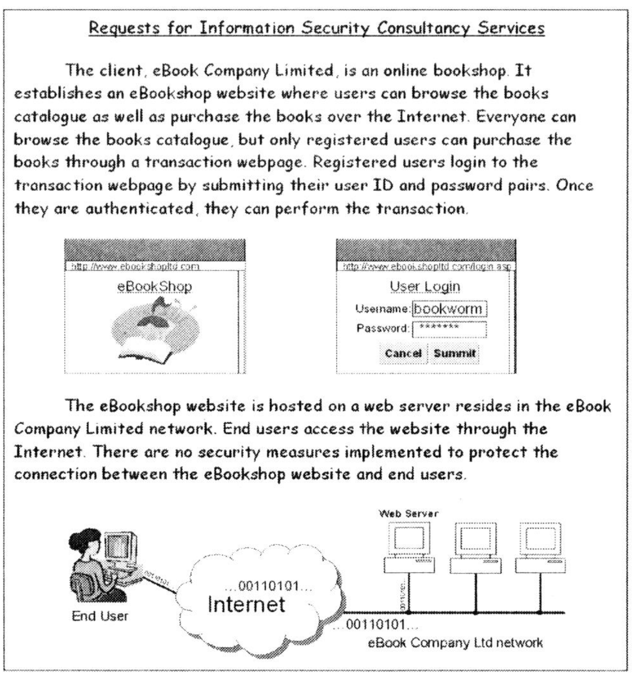

Figure 4. Inquiry tasks to be included in the Task page

Recently, a few users complain that some unsolicited transactions have been made through their accounts. A number of books orders are recorded but the corresponding users claim they have not made the actual purchases.

eBook Company Limited is seeking information security consultants to provide advices and recommendations to strengthen security of the eBookshop website. In particular, consultants should answer the following:

- Explain the possible reason(s) for the occurrence of incident above.
- Identify other potential security risks in the online bookshop website.
- Recommend solutions to strengthen security of the online bookshop.
- Besides username and password login, are there any other method to authenticate a user?
- Provide general information on security and privacy threats on the Internet and computer networks, and their corresponding defending measures.

The consultants should present their findings to the client in form of a Website that contains the following items:

- Overall problem statement
- Definition of sub-problems
- Descriptions of the problem solving process, including the tasks, schedule and milestones
- The solution
- URLs to useful resources and references; and
- (Optional) individual reflection of each of the group members

the connection is not SSL-protected, someone can eavesdrop on the network traffics and obtain the username and password information when a legitimate user logins; or the users repudiate having purchase the books. In next steps, teachers can guide students to look into the problem situation in terms of various security requirements such as authentication, confidentiality, non-repudiation, integrity, and availability; recommendations should also be made to address these aspects.

The Evaluation page includes an assessment rubric detailing the how the deliverable will be evaluated. A rubric is provided in figure 5 for reference.

2. Step Two: Coaching During an Inquiry

After the problem situation as well as the corresponding assessment criteria is explained to the students, the inquiry process can then begin. A suggested instructional schedule designed according to the HIBL model is given in Appendix A. In the schedule, two kinds of teacher activities are defined: in-class activities refer to those being conducted face-to-face in the class; while online activities refer to the actions to be taken by the teacher through the online discussion forum. The teacher can allocate amount of time on each item according to their teaching paces and instructional needs.

As scaffolding aids, the worksheets listed below are designed and can be released to students through the Resource page of the WebQuest. Group members can collaborate to produce a project website by consolidating these materials:

1. Project Planning Form (Appendix B)
2. Project Findings Form (Appendix C)
3. Individual Reflection Form (Appendix D)

Figure 5. Recommended assessment rubric to be included in the Evaluation page

	Scores			
Criteria	**1**	**2**	**3**	**4**
Organization	The materials are illy organized. Contents and information cannot be understood or very difficult to be understood.	Some effort in overall organization shown. The contents and information can be followed with little additional effort.	The contents and information are organised and easy to follow. Most of the materials are presented in structured sequence.	The contents and information are well organised in sound logical sequence. All materials are presented in well structured sequence.
Problem definition	The problem is wrongly defined; **or** the problem is mentioned without clear overall problem statement and no sub-problems are stated.	The problem is mentioned without clear overall problem statement. Related sub-problems are also stated but with insufficient elaboration.	The problem is well defined with a overall problem statement. Related sub-problems are also stated but with insufficient elaboration.	The problem is well defined with a overall problem statement. Related sub-problems are also indicated and elaborated.
Problem solving process	The problem solving process is barely mentioned.	The problem solving process is described but not in detail.	The problem solving process is described. Difficulties encountered in the projects are mentioned.	Detailed problem solving process is given. Steps are taken in well organized, logical sequence. Difficulties encountered in the projects and the corresponding resolutions are also given.
Conceptual knowledge	Cannot answer questions about subject.	Uncomfortable with the information and is able to address only rudimentary questions.	The solution is sound. Some understanding of subject knowledge is shown but fails to elaborate.	The solution is sound. Thorough understanding of subject knowledge demonstrated by explanations and elaboration.
Resources	No URL of resources are given.	One to two URLs of resources are given; **or** some irrelevant URLs are included.	About 10 URLs of relevant resources are given.	Relevant URLs are given and catergorized.

3. Step Three: Assessing the Learning

The summation assessment can base on the final website delivered by the students. Evaluation can be made according to the assessment rubric listed in the Evaluation page of the WebQuest (see table 2). In this particular exemplar, sound conceptual knowledge include identifying security risks in the eBookshop network and website, recommending solutions to strengthen security of the online bookshop, and providing general information on security threats in computer networks and their corresponding defending measures. The groups should also search for information about authentication methods alternate to username and password login.

Formation assessment can be made based on intermediate deliverables such as the project planning form (Appendix B), project findings form (Appendix C), and the individual reflection form (Appendix D). Discussion data collected from the online discussion forum can also be analyzed to assess the learning progress.

CONCLUSION

In this chapter, we review on various learning theories related to inquiry-based learning (IBL). We also provide detailed review on IBL, including its model, related theories, and various implementations. The IBL instructional approach helps learner to seek for truth, information, or knowledge by questioning; and is natural to and the most effective to human learning. Base on the pedagogical foundation of IBL, we further define the hybrid inquiry-based learning (HIBL), an extension of the IBL model which covers pedagogies and instructional approaches using inquiry as the main tool and being implemented by a combination of ICT-based and non ICT-based methods. We also contribute an HIBL exemplar in information security education. To conclude, hybrid learning is very suitable for IBL implementation, and HIBL can leverage on the best of both ICT-based and traditional classroom-based IBL activities. We have further illustrated its implementation by providing a detail exemplar.

Table 2. Detailed instructional schedule

	Teacher (In-class)	Teacher (Online)	Students
1. Laying background knowledge. **Objective:** Students begin to recognize the essential knowledge in the research area. Including general security and privacy threats on the Internet, Secure Sockets Layer (SSL), security services (authentication, confidentiality, non-repudiation, integrity, availability), and the measures for defense.			
a.	Recall prerequisite knowledge on networks and Internet basics such as LAN, IP, HTTP, URL and how network connections talk place. Ask students simple questions about networks and Internet basics.		Answer the questions raised by the teacher.
b.	Browse non-SSL enabled website and SSL-enabled website and compare their differences with the help of network analysis tools.		Have access to network connected computer to study the differences between SSL and non-SSL enabled websites and study their difference.
c.	With the help of crimes reports and news, brainstorm with students on possible security and privacy threats on the Internet.		Discuss in group about possible security and privacy threats on the Internet. Report the conclusion to teacher verbally.
d.	Introduce various security and privacy threats on the Internet. Such as eavesdropping, hacking, phishing, malware, spyware, and adware, spamming and junk mails, and violation of the confidentiality of data.	Response to students' questions about the topics through the online discussion forum.	Review the topics and raise related questions through the online discussion forum.
e.	Brainstorm with students on possible measures to defend the security and privacy threats. Use concept map to facilitate the brainstorming.		Discuss in group about possible measures to defend the security threats on computer networks. Report the conclusion to teacher in class verbally.
f.	Introduce the subject contents such as security services and the measures for defense.	Response to students' questions about the topics through the online discussion forum.	Review the topics and raise related questions through the online discussion forum.
2. Guide students to launch exploration and investigation. **Objective:** Students understand the problem situation, plan how they investigate into the problem situation and explore the possible solutions.			
a.	With reference to the WebQuest Introduction page, ask "With the help of the concepts introduced in pervious lessons, who would you explain the possible reason(s) for the occurrence of incident?", "With the help of the concepts introduced in pervious lessons, can you identify other potential security risks in the online bookshop website?", and "With the help of the concepts introduced in pervious lessons, can you recommend solutions to strengthen security of the online bookshop?"		
b.	Ask the students to propose how they would investigate into the problem situation and explore possible answers. Provide hints to the students with the help of the Resources page of the WebQuest.		
c.	Require students to complete the project planning form (Appendix A).	Post guiding questions to the online discussions forum. Analyze track records of student discussions.	Discuss in groups and complete the project planning form (Appendix A). Submit the form to teacher.

Table 2. continued

d.	Whole-class discussion of project planning forms.		Whole-class discussion of project planning form.
e.	Teacher approves the project planning forms.	Comment on the project planning form and assist students to revise the project planning forms.	Revise the project planning form when necessary. Submit the form to teacher.
3. Guide students to undergo the inquiry project. **Objective:** Students explore and investigate into the problem situation and produce findings.			
a.	Help students to analyze the situation of the eBookshop website. Guide the students to recall the security services and their functions, guide students to recall security and privacy threats on the Internet. Guide the students to consider the security risks and consequences due to the absence of security protection measures. Recall the security technologies (PKI, digital certificates, SSL). Guide the students to consider the functions of these technologies and how they provide security services.	Post guiding questions (that have discussed in the class) to the discussion forum.	
b.	Facilitates and coaches as students work in groups towards the project plans. Meet the small groups periodically to foster discussion according to the project plans the groups have submitted. Encourage students to record new findings and use the new information to make decision about further inquiries.	Provide supports to students through the online discussion forums. Answer questions in subject knowledge raised by students. Help ensuring the students work according to their project plans.	Work in collaborative groups according to the project plan to solve the problem. Record new findings and information. Meet in small groups to discuss the project regularly.
c.	Examine the student findings. Have further discussions with problematic groups.	Help examining the student findings.	Conclude the discussions and findings in point form.
4. Guide students to make connections among the investigation and findings, and critically reflect on the inquiry process. **Objective:** Students consolidate their findings into a short report and conduct critical reflection on their inquiry process.			
a.	Require students to complete the project findings form (Appendix C). (Student should work on their own in this part where teacher should give minimum assistance.)	(Student should work on their own in this part where teacher should give minimum assistance.)	Discuss in groups, fill in and submit the project findings form (Appendix C) to teacher.
b.	Whole-class discussion of project findings forms.		
c.	Guide the students to produce the presentation slides from the short project report.		Collaborate in groups to produce the presentation slides from the project planning form and the project findings form.
d.	Guide the students to critically reflect on the entire inquiry process. Including the knowledge gained within and beyond the subject, their feeling and comments towards the project, where they performed well and how to sustain, and where they did not perform well and how to improve. Collect the individual reflection forms from students (Appendix D)		Critically reflect the inquiry process. Complete the individual reflection forms (Appendix D) individually.

REFERENCES

Alvarado, A. E., & Herr, P. R. (2003). *Inquiry-based learning using everyday objects: Hands-on instructional strategies that promote active learning in grades 3-8.* Thousand Oaks, CA: Corwin Press.

Anderson, L. M. (1993). Auxiliary materials that accompany textbooks: Can they promote "higher-order" learning? In B. K. Britton, A. Woodward, & M. Blinkley (Eds.), *Learning from textbooks: Theory and practice.* Mahwah, NJ: Erlbaum.

Audet, R. H., & Jordan, L. K. (2005). *Integrating inquiry across the curriculum.* Thousand Oaks, CA: Corwin Press.

Bereiter, C. (2002). *Education and mind in the knowledge age*. Mahwah, NJ: Lawrence Erlbaum Associates.

Bloom, L. Z., & White, E. M. (1993). *Inquiry: a cross-curricular reader.* Englewood Cliffs, NJ: Prentice-Hall, Inc.

Blumenfeld, P. (1991). Motivating project-based learning: Sustaining the doing, supporting the learning. *Educational Psychologist, 26*(3&4), 369–398. doi:10.1207/s15326985ep2603&4_8

Brown, A. L., & Campione, J. C. (1996). Psychological theory and the design of innovative learning environments on procedures, principles, and systems. In L. Schauble & R. Glaser (Eds.), *Innovation in learning: New environments for* education (pp. 289-325). Hillsdale, NJ: Lawrence Erlbaum Associates.

Bruffee, K. A. (1984). Collaborative learning and the "conversation of mankind. *College English, 46*(7), 635–652. doi:10.2307/376924

Bruner, J. S. (1967). *On knowing: Essays for the left hand.* Cambridge, MA: Harvard University Press.

Bruner, J. S. (1986). *Actual minds, possible worlds.* Cambridge, MA: Harvard University Press.

Buzzetto-More, N., & Sweat-Guy, R. (2006). Incorporating the hybrid learning model into minority education at a historically black university. *Journal of Information Technology Education, 5*, 153–164.

Chan, Y.-Y. (2005). Creating reusable webquest objects with webquest authoring engine. In *Fifth IEEE International Conference on Advanced Learning Technologies* (pp. 282 – 284).

Chan, Y.-Y. (2007). Teaching queueing theory with an inquiry-based learning approach: A case for applying webquest in a course in simulation and statistical analysis. In *Proceedings of the 37th IEEE/ASEE Frontiers in Education conference* (pp. F3C-1-6).

Dai, Y. (2007, July 20). *Questions regarding Mary and Joan.* Lecture presented for the Advances in Educational Psychology Lectures in Faculty of Education, The Chinese University of Hong Kong, Hong Kong SAR.

Dewey, J. (1933). *How we think: a restatement of the relation of reflective thinking to the educative process.* Boston: Heath.

Dodge, B. (1995). WebQuests: A technique for internet-based learning. *Distance Education, 1*(2), 10–13.

Downes, S. (2000). *Stephen Downes – Learning objects.* Retrieved April 28, 2008, from http://www.downes.ca/files/Learning_Objects.htm

Duffy, T. M., & Jonassen, D. H. (1992). *Constructivism and the technology of instruction: A conversation.* Hillsdale, NJ: Lawrence Erlbaum Associates.

Edelson, D. C., Gordin, D. N., & Pea, R. D. (1999). Addressing the challenges of inquiry-based learning through technology and curriculum design. *Journal of the Learning Sciences, 8*(3), 391–450. doi:10.1207/s15327809jls0803&4_3

Eggen, P., & Kauchak, D. (1999). *Educational psychology.* Upper Saddle River, New Jersey: Prentice-Hall.

Gagne, R. M., Briggs, L. J., & Wager, W. W. (1992). *Principles of instructional design* (4th ed.). San Diego, CA: Harcourt Brace Jovanovich.

Garrison, D. R., & Kanuka, H. (2004). Blended learning: Uncovering its transformative potential in higher education. *The Internet and Higher Education, 7*(2), 95–105. doi:10.1016/j.iheduc.2004.02.001

Gokhale, A. A. (1995). Collaborative learning enhances critical thinking. *Journal of Technology Education, 7*(1), 22–30.

Hacker, D. J., & Tenent, A. (2002). Self-regulated comprehension during normal reading. In D. J. Hacker, J. Dunlosky, & A. C. Graesser (Eds.), *Metacognition in educational theory and practice* (pp. 165 – 191). Mahwah, NJ: Erlbaum.

Harvard Business School (HBS). (2008). *The case method*. Retrieved May 6, 2008, from http://www.hbs.edu/case/

Iannuzzi, P. (1999). We are teaching, but are they learning: Accountability, productivity, and assessment. *Journal of Academic Librarianship, 25*(4), 304–305. doi:10.1016/S0099-1333(99)80031-7

Issacs, W. (1999). *Dialogue: and the art of thinking together.* New York: Currency.

Jonassen, D. H. (1991). Objectivism vs. constructivism: Do we need a new philosophical paradigm? *Educational Technology Research and Development, 39*(3). doi:10.1007/BF02296434

Jonassen, D. H. (1994). Thinking technology: Toward a constructivist design model. In *Educational Technology* (pp. 34-37).

Kulm, G. (1990). New directions for mathematical assessment. In G. Kulm (Ed.), *Assessing higher order thinking in mathematics.* Washington, DC: American Association for the Advancement of Science.

Learning in Motion. (2003). *The knowledge forum.* Retrieved September 17, 2007 from http://www.knowledgeforum.com/

Lester, F. K. J., & Lambdin-Kroll, D. (1990). Assessing student growth in mathematical problem solving. In G. Kulm (Ed.), *Assessing higher order thinking in mathematics* (pp. 53-70). Washington, DC: American Association for the Advancement of Science.

Lim, B.-R. (2001). *Guidelines for designing inquiry-based learning on the web: online professional development of educators.* Unpublished doctoral dissertation, Indiana University at Bloomington.

Lim, B.-R. (2004). Challenges and issues in designing inquiry on the web. *British Journal of Educational Technology, 35*(5), 627–643. doi:10.1111/j.0007-1013.2004.00419.x

March, T. (2003). The learning power of WebQuests. *Educational Leadership, 61*(4), 42–47.

Martin-Hansen, L. (2002). Defining inquiry: Exploring the many types of inquiry in the science classroom. *Science Teacher (Normal, Ill.), 69*(2), 34–37.

Martinello, M., & Cook, G. (2000). *Interdisciplinary inquiry in teaching and learning (2nd ed.).* Pearson Education, NJ: Upper Saddle River.

Media Laboratory. (1999). *Future learning environment.* Retrieved September 17, 2007 from http://mlab.uiah.fi/fle/

Merrill, P. F., Hammons, K., & Vincent, B. R. (1996). *Computers in education.* Needham Heights, MA: Allyn & Bacon, Inc.

Meyer, D. K., Turner, J. C., & Spencer, C. A. (1997). Challenge in a mathematics classroom: Students' motivation and strategies in project-based learning. *The Elementary School Journal, 97*(5), 501–521. doi:10.1086/461878

Neisser, U. (1967). *Cognitive psychology.* New York: Appleton-Century-Crofts.

Njoo, M. K. H. (1994). *Exploratory learning with a computer simulation: Learning processes and instructional support*. Unpublished doctoral dissertation, Technische Universiteit Eindhoven, The Netherlands.

Ormrod, J. E. (2006). *Educational psychology: Developing learners (5th ed.)*. Upper Saddle River, NJ: Pearson Education.

Pavlov, I. P. (1927). *Conditioned reflexes* (G. V. Anrep, Trans.). London: Oxford University Press.

Peterson, C., Caverly, D. C., & MacDonald, L. (2001). Developing academic literacy through WebQuests. *Journal of Developmental Education, 26*(3), 38–39.

Piaget, J. (1970). *Genetic epistemology*. (E. Duckworth, Trans.). New York: Columbia University Press.

Piaget, J. (1985). *The equilibration of cognitive structures*. Chicago, IL: University of Chicago Press.

Rau, W., & Heyl, B. S. (1990). Humanizing the college classroom: Collaborative learning and social organization among students. *Teaching Sociology, 18*(2), 141–155. doi:10.2307/1318484

Roehler, L. R., & Cantlon, D. J. (1997). Scaffolding: A powerful tool in social constructivist classrooms. In *Scaffolding student learning: instructional approaches and issues* (pp. 6–42). Cambridge, MA: Brookline Books.

Roth, W.-M. (1998). Teacher questioning in an open-inquiry learning environment: Interactions of context, content, and student responses. *Journal of Research in Science Teaching, 33*(7), 709–736. doi:10.1002/(SICI)1098-2736(199609)33:7<709::AID-TEA2>3.0.CO;2-R

Sawyer, R. K. (2006). Analyzing collaborative discourse. In R. K. Sawyer (Ed.), *The Cambridge Handbook of The Learning Sciences* (pp. 187 – 204). New York: Cambridge University Press.

Scardamalia, M., & Bereiter, C. (1994). *Computer support for knowledge-building communities*. Hillsdale, NJ: Lawrence Erlbaum Associates.

Schmidt, H. G. (1993). Foundations of problem-based learning: some explanatory notes. *Medical Education, 27*(5), 422–432. doi:10.1111/j.1365-2923.1993.tb00296.x

Skinner, B. F. (1954). The science of learning and the art of teaching. *Harvard Educational Review, 24*, 86–97.

Tan, C., & Chan, Y.-Y. (in press). Knowledge community: A knowledge building system for global collaborative project learning. *Proceedings of the IEEE*.

Tsankova, J., & Dobrynina, G. (2005). Developing curious students. In R. H. Audet & L. K. Jordan (Eds.), *Integrating Inquiry Across the Curriculum* (pp. 85-89). Thousand Oaks, CA: Corwin Press.

Turner, K. (2006). JASPER (Java simulation of protocols for education and research). Retrieved May 8, 2008, from http://www.cs.stir.ac.uk/~kjt/software/comms/jasper.html

Vygotsky, L. S. (1978). *Mind in society: The development of higher psychological processes*. Cambridge, MA: Harvard University Press.

KEY TERMS AND DEFINITIONS

Collaborative Learning: A learning model in which learners at different performance levels work together in small groups toward common academic goals.

Higher Order Thinking: A cognitive process in which learners go far beyond the specific information they have acquired, and be able to analyze, apply, and evaluate the acquired information.

Hybrid Inquiry-Based Learning (HIBL): A pedagogical approach using inquiry as the main tool for teaching and learning and being implemented in hybrid learning mode with a combination of ICT-based and non ICT-based methods.

Inquiry: A process to seek for information, knowledge, or truth through questioning.

Inquiry-Based Learning (IBL): A constructivist student-centered pedagogy using inquiry as a main vehicle for teaching and learning. It focuses on questioning, critical thinking, and problem solving.

Scaffolding: The process of providing learning supports so that learners can accomplish tasks that ordinarily cannot be performed on their own.

WebQuest: A web-based implementation of inquiry-based learning which exists in the form of a website with essential contents including introduction page, task page, process page, evaluation page, and resource page.

APPENDIX A

APPENDIX B

Scaffolding Tool I: Project Planning Form

Project Planning Form

Group Number: ________________
Group Members: ______________________________________
____
____
____

Mission Definition State the problem that you are solving.
____
____
____
____
____
____

1. State any questions you would like to answer to help you solving the problem.

Question 1:
Question 2:
Question 3:

2. List at least 3 tasks and corresponding methods you plan to use to solve the problem.

Task 1:
Method for task 1:
Task 2:
Method for task 2:
Task 3:
Method for task 3:

3. Fill in the following table about the schedule and milestones of the project.

Table 3.

Task	Responsible members	Expected results / deliverables	Start Date	End Date
1				
2				
3				

Submit the form to the teacher by _____ (DD/MM/YYYY)________.

APPENDIX C

Scaffolding Tool II: Project Findings Form

Project Findings Form

Group Number: ________________
Group Members: ______________________________________
____
____
____

1. In a few sentences, summarize the problem situation of the online bookshop.

____
____
____
____
____
____

2. List out the methods you have used to help you solving the problem.

Method 1:
Method 2:
Method 3:
Other methods:

3. In spaces below, list any relevant findings you have made.
   i. Possible reason(s) for the occurrence of the incident.

a.
b.
c.

   ii. Other potential security risks in the online bookshop website.

a.
b.
c.

   iii. Solutions to strengthen security of the online bookshop.

a.
b.
c.

(Continue)

   iv. General information on security and privacy threats on the Internet and in computer networks, and their corresponding defending measures.
      a. ____

Defending measure: ____________________________________
   b. ____

Defending measure: ____________________________________
   c. ____

Defending measure: ___________________________________

d. Other security and privacy threats and their defending measures:

v. Alternate methods to authenticate users over the Internet.

a.

b.

c.

4. List out the references (e.g. books, websites, and newspaper cuttings) which involved in the project.

5. List out the useful web resources you encounter in the project.

i. URL 1

a. Title:

b. Short description:

c. URL:

ii. URL 2

a. Title:

b. Short description:

c. URL:

iii. URL 3

a. Title:

b. Short description:

c. URL:

iv. Other URLs

Submit the form to the teacher by _____ (DD/MM/YYYY)________.

APPENDIX D

Scaffolding Tool III: Reflection Form

Individual Reflection Form

Topic: Information Security Consultants

Group Number: __________________

Group Member: ____

Provide your feeling and comments towards the project in the spaces below:

1. Knowledge related to the subject that I have learnt from the project:
2. Knowledge not related to the subject that I have learnt from the project:
3. My feeling about the project (whether you like / dislike it and why):
4. I have done well in the following parts, and how I will sustain the effort:
5. I have not done well in the following parts, and how I will improve in the future:

Submit the form to the teacher by _____ (DD/MM/YYYY)________.

Chapter 14
Designing Blended Learning Communities

Liping Deng
University of Hong Kong, Hong Kong

Allan H. K. Yuen
University of Hong Kong, Hong Kong

ABSTRACT

This chapter seeks to highlight the unique characteristics of blended learning communities and the special design consideration they call for. The blended nature of a community is reflected through the interplay of the online and offline dimensions of a community and the mix of various media in support of community-wide interaction. The authors introduce the notion of blended learning community based on related literature on learning community and blended learning and put forward design guidelines for building such communities. Further, a pilot study was conducted to test out the proposed design principles in the context of pre-service teacher education with blogs as the main vehicle for online communication. The authors' work can contribute to a deepened understanding of learning communities situated in the blended media environment and provide a set of design principles for their development.

INTRODUCTION

Increasingly, the Internet has permeated every fiber of our daily lives and society at large. It has become a common practice for a co-located community to employ both online and offline media to maintain group connections and interaction. However, we still have relatively limited understanding as to the interplay between the online and offline dimensions of a community (Haythornthwaite & Nielsen, 2007).

DOI: 10.4018/978-1-60566-380-7.ch014

In this chapter, we seek to address this knowledge gap by focusing on the design issues for cultivating blended learning communities. Such an endeavor highlights the dynamic interplay of the online and physical dimensions of a community and brings to attention the challenges of creating synergies among various educational media.

In this chapter, the blended nature of a community is reflected and addressed in two ways: the first concerns the integration of the online and offline dimensions of a learning community. In particular, our research attention centers on blended communities stemming from physical ones. As such, the purpose of this chapter is to propose a number of design guidelines on how to extend offline communities to online space. The other aspect of blended communities deals with the mixture of multiple media in support of community-wide interaction. The proliferation of web-based technology poses a daunting challenge for educators to make appropriate selection and mix of different educational media. In this circumstance, a better understanding of the characteristics and values of new media becomes vital. Finally, we will chart out areas for attention when making sensible choice or mix of educational media in support of a blended learning community.

This chapter is structured as follows: first, we outline current research and practice in the area of learning community and blended learning to set a stage for the advent of the key concept - blended learning community. Then, drawing on general guidelines of building online communities proposed by Preece (2000), we delineate specific guidelines for building blended learning. Next, we report a pilot study conducted in the context of pre-service education where blogs were used to maintain social connections, promote reflection and peer support among student teachers. At last, the implications of our work and future trends in the field of blended learning communities are put into perspective.

THEORETICAL BACKGROUND

Learning Community

Rooted in social learning theories, learning community has become an increasingly popular notion in schools at all levels. It has been widely documented that learning communities have positive influence upon students' academic performance and school experiences (e.g. Zhao & Kuh, 2004). To begin with, one essential question that needs to be addressed is what constitutes a learning community? Deng and Yuen (2007) mapped out the structure of an online community and put interaction at the heart of community-based activities. Unlike casual and random online communications, interaction within a community is constant and continual (Conrad, 2005) with multiple members involved in two-way communications (Jones, 1997). On account that learning is social as well as intellectual (Dede, 1996), social interaction alone is not sufficient to ensure purposeful reflection and critical discourse vital for active learning (Garrison & Vaughan, 2008). Thus, at the heart of a learning community is an interactive process that engages students in social interaction and critical discourse.

A meaningful learning experience in a community context has two implications: "the first is to construct meaning from a personal perspective. The second is to refine and confirm this understanding collaboratively within a community of learners" (Garrison & Anderson, 2003, p. 13). As such, "the right balance and blend of collaborative and individual learning activities is the key ingredient" (Garrison & Anderson, 2003, p. 24) in a learning community. Therefore, the construction of a learning community calls for two sets of balance: 1) balance between individual and collaborative learning; and 2) balance between social interaction and critical discourse.

Blended Learning

In the educational context, technology is increasingly integrated into the infrastructure and daily practice of schools. The importance of technology in the educational realm has been widely accepted and E-learning has become a worldwide trend. Generally speaking, there are three modes of E-learning: technology-enhanced, blended and online mode (Garrison & Kanuka, 2004; Papastergiou, 2006). Blended learning that utilizes computer-mediated communication (CMC) tools to support face-to-face (F2F) instruction has become the most pervasive paradigm (Bonk, Kim

& Zeng, 2006; Harrington, Gordon, & Schibik, 2004). Blended learning holds the promise of improving pedagogy and cost-effectiveness as well as increasing access and flexibility (Graham, 2006). The students engaged in the blended mode were reported to have better academic performance and satisfaction level (Althaus, 1997) as well as stronger sense of community (Rovai & Jordan, 2004) than those in the sole face-to-face delivery mode. Often, *blended learning* and *hybrid learning* are used interchangeably in the literature although *blended learning* is much common (Mason & Rennie, 2006). We are in favor of *blended learning* over *hybrid learning* given that the word "blend" bears the connotation of mingling together in a well-balanced and harmonious way (Osguthorpe & Graham, 2003) which better reflects the essence of the mixed modes of learning. Likewise, the term - blended community - is also adopted for the sake of consistency.

Still, there is considerable ambiguity surrounding the definition of "blended learning" (Osguthorpe & Graham, 2003). For example, Garrison and Vaughan (2008) defined blended learning as the "thoughtful fusion of face-to-face and online learning experiences." (p. 5) Kerres and Witt (2003) interpreted blended learning as the mix of didactical methods and delivery formats. Mason and Rennie (2006) pointed out that although the original and still the most common meaning of blended learning referred to the combination of online and face-to-face teaching, the term had been used to accommodate wider and more complex combinations, for instance, the mixture of synchronous and asynchronous modes of communication, formal and informal ways of delivery. In our inquiry, we interpret the meaning of blended learning as two-fold: 1) the combination of F2F teaching and CMC; and 2) the combination of various media in support of teaching and learning. The upcoming discussion will outline the theoretical underpinnings of both aspects and highlight the critical issues at stake for designing blended learning.

When F2F Meets CMC

The uptake of blended learning in recent years represents the rejection of the 'either-or' view of learning online versus learning face-to-face (Mason & Rennie, 2006). The underlying premise for the combination of F2F and CMC is the supplementary relationship between these two (Osguthorpe & Graham, 2003). Web-based communications can extend and supplement co-located interaction (Koku, Nazer & Wellman, 2001). On the other hand, co-located interaction is often viewed crucial for building bonds and trust, especially at the initial stage of group formation (Conrad, 2002). The main promise of the blended mode lies in the combination of the advantages of both physical and online communications. However, such a synergy does not come easily and naturally. As Brush and colleagues (2002) noted that online and in-class discussions seemed to compete with each other and the smooth integration of the two was quite challenging. Hence the successful implementation of blended learning calls for thoughtful and meaningful integration of both online and offline experiences (Garrison & Kanuka, 2004). An important research agenda for future work is how to design online experiences compatible with face-to-face classes (Wallace, 2003).

Blending of Various Media

Besides, it is also advocated to employ various media – synchronous or asynchronous – to support diverse communication needs and learning styles (e.g. Haythornthwaite, Kazmer, & Robins, 2000). A mixed vehicle for discussions could maximize learning opportunities by accommodating the needs of students with different learning styles (Meyer, 2003). Underlying the mixture of various media is a conviction that each medium has its distinct affordances and constraints (Norman, 1993). Each medium facilitates or amplifies certain learning opportunities, while inhibits or

Figure 1. Dimensions of blended learning

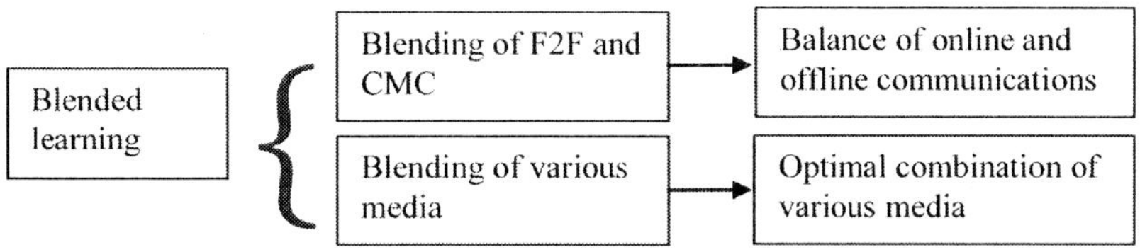

restricts others (Swan, 2005). Sensible selection and thoughtful integration of different media can provide richer and engaging learning experiences (Harrington, Gordon & Schibik, 2004). The rules of selection or the recipe for mixing, however, are by no means clear-and-cut given that our media landscape becomes increasingly complex with the new media co-existing with, instead of replacing, the old ones (Kerres & Witt, 2003). Further compounding the situation, the new communication tools can accommodate the needs of person-to-person, group, and mass communications as a contrast to traditional communication technology with usually single function, (Flanagin & Metzger, 2001). This poses great challenges for teachers and instructional designers to pick and blend various media for diverse learning objectives, contexts, and audiences.

One thing worth noting is that the aforementioned two dimensions of blended learning are not independent of each other but closely related and even overlapping. Within these two dimensions, two issues become essential to ensure a successful blended learning experience. The first is the balance between face-to-face and technology-mediated interaction (Osguthorpe & Graham, 2003). The use of the Internet media should center on those needs that are not supported adequately by the traditional media. In another word, the use of CMC tools should provide *added* values to classroom teaching. The second issue pertains to the optimal ways of blending various media for pedagogical purposes. There are, in a basic sense, two types of media in support of interaction within a community: one-to-one intrapersonal and many-to-many. Considering that community-wide interaction is at the heart of the community activities, as we mentioned earlier, it becomes critical to choose an appropriate media in support of many-to-many communications within the community.

Blended Learning Community

First, it is necessary to clarify what constitutes a blended learning community. Not all co-located communities that utilize certain type of Internet tools can be labelled as blended communities. For instance, simply putting lecture notes online for students to have an access at any time and anywhere should not be counted as a blended learning community. As we discussed earlier, a learning community entails a fusion of personal and collaborative, social and reflective acts. A blended learning community, therefore, should meet two criteria: first, Internet technology should be used to enable and facilitate intellectual and social interaction within the community. Second, online interaction should be multi-way involving a critical mass of community members (Jones, 1997). In this light, the sporadic use of person-to-person communication tools such as Instant Messenger among students does not amount to a blended community.

Central to our inquiry is a conviction that the overlapping of online and offline networks calls for special design consideration. Compared to the communities inhabiting solely in online or physical realm, blended communities have some unique characteristics. The pre-existing social connections can influence people's online engagement to a large degree. On the positive side, the existing social relationships can serve as a catalyst for online engagement due to a number of reasons (Kavanaugh, Carroll, Rosson, Zin & Reese, 2005). First, the existing social relationships and group cohesion might mitigate the problem of social presence online. Second, a high chance of physical encounters increases the likelihood of abiding by the norm of reciprocity and decreases the likelihood of lurking or "free-riding" online. On the downside, if the existing group cohesion is not strong enough, students might have little interest in extending community interaction to the online sphere (Deng & Yuen, 2007). The other side of the spectrum might be the same case. A densely knit community might make a parallel channel of online communication redundant (Ardichvili, Page & Wentling, 2003). That is to say, if face-to-face meetings can fulfill people's needs, extra online discussion seems neither necessary nor desirable. In short, the underlying social structure of an existing physical community – too dense or too loose – might undermine members' motivation for adopting CMC as an additional channel of interaction.

Other than social structure, the perceived affordances of various media can exert large effects on online engagements as well. As a well-established model, the technology acceptance model (TAM) advanced by Davis (1989) shows that users' perceived ease of use and perceived usefulness of certain technology directly affect its acceptance and adoption. In addition, there are several user-related factors associated with the level of online engagement. For example, Vonderwell and Zachariah (2005) remarked that learners' previous online experiences, learning style, content knowledge, and time issue were all determining factors for their online participation. The psychological maturity level and time management skills of the students were also reckoned significant for their adaptation to the blended mode of learning (Aycock, Garnham, & Kaleta, 2002). Besides, personal epistemology, that is, learners' perceptions of knowledge and learning process, was also found to influence their engagements with online discussion (Spatariu, Quinn, & Hartley, 2007).

Online Community Design

This section will first introduce a framework of building online communities by Preece (2000) as a foundation for the design principles to be discussed later. First and foremost, the design or development of an online community should start with getting to know members' needs (Preece, 2000). A balance should be struck between "designing the community and allowing it to emerge from the needs and agendas of its members" (Barab, MaKinster & Scheckler, 2004, p. 63). Preece (2000) delineated two associated processes at the heart of initial community-building efforts, that is, assessing community needs and analyzing users' tasks. In more concrete terms, community developers need to identify members' expectations, their notion of "what's in it for me", main purposes of the community, and meaningful group activities or tasks, be it information exchange, social interaction or mutual support.

On the basis of needs assessment, the online community building endeavors have two main focuses - usability and sociability (Preece, 2000). The usability aspect centers on the design of person-to-computer interaction that involves choosing or blending appropriate technologies in support of community interaction. The sociability aspect, on the other hand, deals with person-to-person interaction. In a general sense, there are three main issues associated with sociability in the online community construction – community goal, policy, and participants. Many researchers accentuated the importance of a thought-out and clearly articulated goal for community building. For instance, Kim (2000) contended that three fundamental questions had to be asked at the outset of community construction: 1) What type of community am I building? 2) Why am I building it? 3) Who am I building it for? Salmon (2000) remarked that the clarity of purpose was crucial from the beginning of community formation. In echo with this, Williams and Cothrel (2000) claimed that a clearly defined community focus and a solid structure of norms and guidelines were essential for the health of an online community. Like its offline counterpart, a vibrant online community necessitates clearly defined rules and guidelines. Members need to understand their rights and responsibilities and issues such as what are expected or appropriate online behaviors? How will new members be recruited? At last, the roles of various participants should be defined. Decisions should be made as to whether an online facilitator is necessary and who should take the role.

DESIGNING BLENDED LEARNING COMMUNITIES

At the heart of this chapter are critical design issues in building blended learning communities. Such an endeavor should take into consideration the physical context of learning communities and focus on creating a synergy among various media in support of their social and intellectual demands. Here, we will highlight design guidelines for building blended learning communities following the generic framework advanced by Preece (2000).

Assessing Community Needs

To begin with, the importance of the needs assessment is heightened when building a blended community. The critical question to be asked is not merely what members are needed, but what specific needs can be fulfilled through the added online communications. Community developers need to understand the social fabric of the existing physical communities and identify the possibilities for expanding community functions (Schwen & Hara, 2004). Emphasis should be put on identifying those needs media in use fail to or poorly accomplish (Hollan & Stornetta, 1992). Sensible questions to be asked include: to what extent do the media in current use fulfill the community's needs? How are users' satisfaction levels with the media in use? What will be the added values of having computer-mediated communications?

Informed by the studies reviewed earlier, we summarize the following factors that should be explored into during the process of needs assessment (Table 1). Factors at the community level encompass the underlying social structure of the existing communities, the media currently in use for community-wide interaction, and resources available. Meanwhile, various user-related characteristics should be probed into: members' comfort level with technology, habit, preferences and perceived affordances of various technologies, previous online experiences, perceived motivator or inhibitor for their online participation. This list, however, is not meant to be an exhaustive checklist, but a roadmap for the needs assessment with several major areas highlighted.

Usability Consideration

The usability dimension in the community development mainly concerns the selection of appropriate technology or technological platform. To appropriate technology in support of a blended learning community, one needs to take into consideration three main variables: 1) user and community characteristics, 2) learning tasks or objectives, and 3) affordances of specific technology. What we should strive for is an optimal alignment among these three variables. Needs assessment conducted earlier can serve as a vital step for a better understanding of the characteristics of the targeted communities and their members. Associated learning tasks or objectives should be in line with the essence of a learning community, that is, the combination of individual and collaborative learning processes involving social interaction

Table 1. Factors to be considered during needs assessment

Community-level	existing social connections media in current use resources available
User-level	comfort level with technology preference of media previous online experience perceived affordances of various media motivating and inhibiting factors for online participation

and critical discourse. With user characteristics and learning tasks clarified, it then comes down to the question of choosing appropriate technology and developing sensible blending formula. To achieve this, community developers need to be equipped with the knowledge of educational affordances of various technologies – old and new, online and offline. Efforts should be made to amplify unique benefits of CMC and to create synergy effects of various media.

Sociability Consideration

To build an online community among people with no previous connections, online socialization (Salmon, 2000) or social presence online (Wallace, 2003) plays a decisive role. For a blended community stemming from a physical one, the sociability consideration should focus on mobilizing the extant social connections and group cohesion. In case of unfavorable social conditions – be it too loose or too strong, efforts should be made to diminish the negative effects (Deng & Yuen, 2007). Social relationships in a loosely connected community can be cemented by more opportunities for face-to-face gatherings. For a densely knit community, it is suggested to cultivate the awareness of added values afforded by online communications.

Additionally, community goal, rules, and roles of participants should be addressed explicitly. The goal of the additional interaction via CMC should focus on the added benefits it might bring about to an offline community. A physical community will not naturally extend to online space given the availability of an online platform. A well-defined focus of online communications and guidelines for online participation are essential. The roles of various stakeholders should be negotiated with community members. Community developers can also look into the possibilities for migrating existing community rules, policies and leadership to online. Another area for consideration is the necessity for an online facilitator who can play an important role in initiating discussion and maintaining motivation (Youngblood, Trede, & Corpo, 2001). It is also advised to have community goal, guidelines, and roles of the participants clearly articulated, publicized, and made accessible in the online space. One thing worth noting is that all the sociability elements are not ironclad, but subject to constant negotiation as a community evolves. In a real sense, sociability can only be supported or cultivated within the community (Barab, MaKinster & Scheckler, 2004).

A PILOT STUDY: BUILDING A BLENDED LEARNING COMMUNITY WITH BLOGS

To test the proposed design principles and demonstrate how they can be put into practice, we conducted a pilot study with a group of student teachers at a local university in Hong Kong. Weblogs were used as the main tool to support online communications of this blended community of preservice teachers. The study focuses on a group of year four students from the Bachelor of Education program. During the 10-week teaching practice (TP), students were scattered in schools across Hong Kong. Regular face-to-face meetings with other peer students became difficult, if not impossible. We purposefully chose a class of year 4 students based on the assumption that this group might have stronger group cohesion and close social relationships after more than three years of studying together. We assumed this densely knit group might have more incentive to use CMC when it became geographically dispersed.

Needs Assessment

First, a paper-and-pencil questionnaire was employed as the needs assessment instrument before the students started their TP. Based on the aforementioned guidelines for building blended learning communities, survey questions were designed to gather information on the following aspects:

- User characteristics: their comfort level with technology, habit and preference of using various technologies
- Previous TP experiences in particular media used for peer interaction
- Perceptions of online community including their comfort level with and perceived usefulness of online communications
- Perceived motivating and inhibiting factors for their online participation

There were fifteen students in the class selected; thirteen of them (eight females and five males) participated in the study. The results of the questionnaire showed that the students were rather comfortable with technology. The majority of them (85%) had prior experiences with online discussion forums and instant messenger. 70 percent of them also had their personal blogs. When evaluating their comfort level with technology in general on a 4-point scale (1= very uncomfortable; 4= very comfortable), the mean value was 3.3. Face-to-face meetings were rated as the most popular means of peer interaction during their TP in the previous year. Other than that, phone and email also played an important role in connecting dispersed students. Instant messenger was rated the most favorable medium for peer interaction for the upcoming TP while about half of the students also opted to use email and blogs. Besides, informal interviews were conducted with the tutor and the student representative to gather more information of the class. They both confirmed our assumption that this group had close social connections. In the design process, the collaboration with the participating students and their tutor was regarded critical. The next section will delineate the process of usability and sociability design and major community-building decisions made.

Usability

The usability issue in this case is centered on choosing appropriate technology in support of a dispersed group of student teachers during their fieldwork. As we suggested in the earlier discussion, the selection of technology should strive for the alignment among three variables: user characteristics, meaningful learning tasks, and distinct affordances of technology. After gathering data on user characteristics through the questionnaire and informal interviews, the researchers worked with the tutor and the student representative on the issue of meaningful learning tasks. The goal was to make online activities a bonus, not a burden for students. Both the tutor and the student representative were reluctant to make the online activities required, and more in favor of a less formal online platform for students to document, share, and reflect on their teaching practice. We finally reached an agreement that the students' online participation would be voluntary and not counted as part of final assessment. Weblogs were chosen as the vehicle in support of online communication on account of their affordances

Figure 2. Major features of the community blog

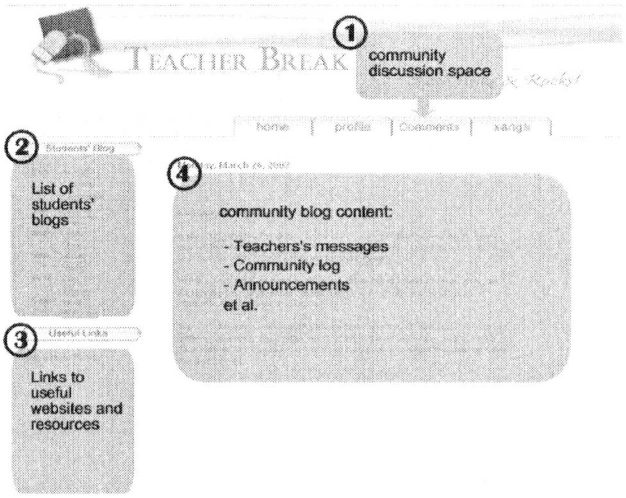

for both individual and community aspects of a learning community. As to be detailed in the later section, weblogs were considered potential in enhancing self-expression, self-reflection, social interaction and reflective dialogue in learning contexts. Reflection, in either individual or collective forms, was regarded the cognitive dimension of this learning community.

Meanwhile, since many of the students already had their personal blogs on Xanga (http://www.xanga.com), they were quite comfortable and familiar with this commercial platform. On this account, we finally decided to encourage students continue using this blogging platform and set up a community blog page there as well. The community blog was designed as the central node connecting individual blogs together given the interaction in blogosphere is distributed and fragmented (Efimova & de Moor, 2005). This community blog served multiple functions: first, it was the community bulletin board where the tutor can disseminate messages to students. Second, it served the function of an online reservoir of useful resources with links to other relevant websites or resources created. Third, community-wide discussion could be conducted on this shared online space as well. Students can voice out their suggestions or concerns at the discussion space. Figure 2 shows the screenshot of the community blog and its major features.

Sociability

To connect dispersed student teachers and promote peer support and reflection, blogs were used as the main tool for community-wide interaction. The guidelines of online participation, for example, whether the participation should be voluntary or compulsory, were made jointly by the researchers and the tutor. Students were encouraged to write one blog per week and they were expected to read and comment on each other's blogs. They were also encouraged to keep using other person-to-person channels (e.g. instant messenger, phone) to maintain communications. The tutor of this group of students also used the community blog as a channel for delivering messages. One of the researchers of the present study took the role of the online facilitator whose major responsibility were to monitor students' blogs, maintain the community blog, and provide technical assistance when needed. The goal, guidelines of the online community as well as the roles of various parties were clearly articulated and posted on the community blog.

Educational Affordances of Blogs

In simple terms, a weblog is a web application that contains periodic time-stamped posts usually organized in chronological order (Mason & Rennie, 2006). As a versatile and flexible medium, blogging is employed for a wide range of purposes from casual release of emotions to group collaboration (Nardi, Shiano, Gumbrecht, & Swartz, 2004). As one of the major players in the Web 2.0 trend, weblog, often shortened to blog, has evolved into a flexible and popular online publishing vehicle over the past decade. Concurrent with its uptake is a growing research interest in its educational affordances.

Related research work suggests that the educational values of weblogs include self-expression, self-reflection, social interaction, and reflective dialogue. Arguably, the greatest benefit of blogging was the opportunity it afforded for self-expression and self-reflection (Brescia & Miller, 2006). Blogs provide a convenient platform to document experiences, publish thoughts, and express feelings. Apart from text, bloggers can integrate pictures, audio or even video files into their blog space. In this way, blogs afford multi-modality ways of self-expression (Farmer, 2004). In addition, Stiler and Philleo (2003) explored into the application of blogs in the context of pre-service education and noted that they enhanced students' critical reflection. Ray and Coulter (2008) demonstrated that blogs could function as an effective reflective devises through their exploration into the role and function of blogs in language arts teachers' reflective practice.

Meanwhile, weblog is not just an online equivalent of personal journal. The embedded commenting and linking features transformed it into a different genre - social software. The combination of both self-expression and social interaction is regarded unique of weblogs (Richardson, 2006). As a network-based technology, blogs make it easy for learners to revisit, share, and seek feedback from peers, teachers or even outside experts. In the educational context, blogs can foster a sense of community and create a space for collaborative and cooperative learning (Ferdig, 2007). They could help bridge or prevent feelings of isolation among online learners by facilitating the expression of feelings, socialization, and the exchange of peer support (Dickey, 2004).

Preliminary Results

We registered another paper-based questionnaire after TP to investigate students' experiences and perceptions of blogging. The questionnaire consisted of both structured and open-ended questions. An informal interview was conducted with the tutor through which she shared her impressions of weblogs. The preliminary analysis indicated that the students perceived blogging as valuable for connecting a dispersed group, enabling self-expression and self-reflection. Blogs enabled student teachers to document their TP experiences, get in touch with each other and exchange ideas. They were also deemed valuable for facilitating the exchange of social and emotional support during their TP. Compared with their prior TP experiences, around 60 percent of the students felt more connected with peers owing to the added communications through blogs. The community blog was considered useful in strengthening the sense of community. In particular, students valued the messages the tutor posted, weekly summary of their blogs put together by the facilitator and the links to individual blogs from the central space.

Having said this, there were several problems among which participation might be a salient one. The average number of blogs produced by the students was only five and about half of the blog entries didn't get comments from fellow students. When we probed deeper into the barriers to students' engagement with blogs, we found time constraint as the biggest inhibiting factor. The students were indeed very busy serving the double roles as both teacher and student during TP. Besides time pressure, the use of other media also acted as interference in their blogging. As a manner of fact, about half of participants admitted that they preferred using other media to communicate with each other. After reading peers' blogs, some switched to other media to respond. Among the media they employed, phone and Instant Messenger were the most popular ones.

CONCLUSION AND IMPLICATIONS

In this chapter, we have sought to combine the concepts of learning community and blended learning and put forward the notion of blended learning community. Such an effort aims to draw attention to the relationships between the physical and virtual dimensions of a community. In addition, we have proposed a set of design guidelines on how to extend the communications and capacity of an offline community to the cyber space. We have introduced three key concepts of our study – learning community, blended learning, and blended learning community. At the core of a learning community were balancing acts between individual and collaborative learning, social and critical interaction. Blended learning in our inquiry has two-fold implications: combination of F2F and CMC experiences; and the mixture of various media in support of learning. Thus, the design of blended learning involves the balancing acts of employing diverse media - F2F and CMC, synchronous and asynchronous, old and new - in service of learning.

Meanwhile, we have highlighted special design consideration a blended learning community calls for in the dimensions of needs assessment, usability, and sociability planning. First, needs assessment for blended communities should center on the conditions of existing communities and the extra benefits of online communications. The notion of "blended community" also bring to attention the *physical* context of an online community which encompassed issues such as users' characteristics, the existing social as well as media contexts. Construction efforts on the usability aspect should strive for an optimal alignment among learning tasks, unique affordances of online technology, and characteristics of communities. The sociability work should seek to diminish the negative effects of the existing social relationships and amplify the positive ones.

We then shared our experience of applying the design principles in building a blended learning community among a group of student teachers during their teaching practice. Weblogs were used to support experience documentation, social interaction, and reflections. In general, the design principles we proposed for building blended learning communities were found constructive in several ways. First, they facilitated the all-important needs analysis process aiming at pinpointing the needs for a parallel online communication for an existing physical community. Meanwhile, they provided practical guidelines for choosing appropriate technology and using it sensibly and purposefully to support learning in a community setting. It is not our intention to provide a magic formula for community construction, but to highlight critical areas or designing and nurturing learning communities in blended fashion. As both descriptive as well as prescriptive principles, our guidelines can inform educators on how to design a vibrant learning community residing on the intersection of the online and offline realms.

Although blended learning has become a prevalent paradigm at schools at all levels, it has not been sufficiently attended to in the educational research (Kerres & Witt, 2003). The research attention paid to the communication dynamics of a community, online or offline, is far from enough (Haythornthwaite & Nielsen, 2007). How a community utilizes various communication tools to support online and offline interaction remains a fuzzy area. We still have quite limited knowledge regarding how to support a community with a wide spectrum of media based on their needs and contextual factors. Here we will present a research stance and related research areas that warrant more attention on the theme of blended learning community.

First, a holistic way is needed to study Internet media by contextualizing it in a broader social context and personal relationships (Boase & Wellman, 2005). Early research on the Internet tended to set the Internet in juxtaposition to and competition with the face-to-face communications (Baym, Zhang, & Lin, 2004). The past two decades have witnessed the increasing integration of computer-mediated communications in our everyday life (Haythornthwaite & Wellman, 2002). Accompanying this convergence trend is the growing recognition that studies on the cyberspace should not treat it as an isolated social phenomenon (Wellman & Gulia, 1999). Therefore, we advocate an integrative approach as a research stance when examining new Internet media. This integrative approach has two levels of implications: First, it embraces blended communities as an integral whole with both online and offline representations instead of as two separate entities. The online dimension is an extension, not a departure or an escape from the corresponding offline community. Such an integrative stance makes it imperative to examine the interplay among the online and offline dimensions of a community: how does the online extension affect the physical community? How does the existing physical context influence members' online interaction?

The second implication of the integrative approach is to situate new media within a fabric of various media in use. The proliferation of Internet-based media has opened up new opportunities for expressions and communications, yet at the same time, posed daunting challenges for teachers. To ensure an optimal blend of various media, teachers need to be equipped with knowledge of the strengths and drawbacks of CMC tools. In this respect, a comparative approach that puts new media alongside with other existing players in the media arena may be a promising avenue for future work. Only in this way can we distill the distinct affordances of emergent media and capture the dynamic patterns of interaction within a community. Nevertheless, the distinct attributes of certain technology is not fixed or predetermined. The successful utilization of technical tools will depend on how they correspond to learning tasks and learners' characteristics (Kozma, 1991). The question we should pose is not which technology will be the best solution, but what combination or blending will be the optimal package for specific contexts and learners. This calls for more experimental or exploratory studies on building blended learning communities in various settings in order to accumulate empirical evidence and practical knowledge in this area.

REFERENCES

Althaus, S. L. (1997). Computer-mediated communication in the university classroom: An experiment with on-line discussions. *Communication Education*, *46*, 158–174. doi:10.1080/03634529709379088

Ardichvili, A., Page, V., & Wentling, T. (2003). Motivation and barriers to participation in virtual knowledge-sharing communities of practice. *Journal of Knowledge Management*, *7*(1), 64–77. doi:10.1108/13673270310463626

Aycock, A., Garnham, C., & Kaleta, R. (2002). Lessons learned from the hybrid course project. *Teaching with Technology Today*, *8*(6), 9–21.

Barab, S. A. MaKinster, J. G., & Scheckler, R. (2004). Designing system dualities: Characterizing a web-supported professional development community. In S. A. Barab, R. Kling, & J. H. Gray (Eds.), *Designing for virtual communities in the service of learning* (pp. 53-90). Cambridge, UK: Cambridge University Press.

Baym, N. K., Zhang, Y. B., & Lin, M.-c. (2004). Social interaction across media. *New Media & Society*, *6*(3), 299–318. doi:10.1177/1461444804041438

Boase, J., & Wellman, B. (2005). Personal relationships: On and off the Internet. In A. L. Vangelisti & D. Perlman (Eds.), *The Cambridge Handbook of Personal Relationships* (pp. 709-723).

Bonk, C. J., Kim, K.-J., & Zeng, T. (2006). Future directions of blended larning in higher education and workplace learning settings. In C. J. Bonk & C. R. Graham (Eds.), *The handbook of blended learning: global perspectives, local designs* (pp. 550-567). San Francisco: Pfeiffer.

Brescia, W. F. J., & Miller, M. T. (2006). What's it worth? The perceived benefits of instructional blogging. *Electronic Journal for the Integration of Technology in Education, 5*, 44–52.

Brush, A. J. B., Bargeron, D., Grudin, J., Borning, A., & Gupta, A. (2002). *Supporting interaction outside of class: Anchored discussions vs. discussion boards*. Paper presented at the CSCL 2002, Mahweh, NJ.

Conrad, D. (2002). Deep in the hearts of learners: Insights into the nature of online community. *Journal of Distance Education, 17*(1), 1–19.

Conrad, D. (2005). Building and maintaining community in cohort-based online learning. *Journal of Distance Education, 20*(1), 1–20.

Davis, F. D. (1989). Perceived usefulness, perceived ease of use, and user acceptance of information technology. *MIS Quarterly, 13*(3), 319–340. doi:10.2307/249008

Dede, C. (1996). The evolution of distance education: Emerging technologies and distributed learning. *American Journal of Distance Education, 10*(2), 4–36. doi:10.1080/08923649609526919

Deng, L., & Yuen, A. H. K. (2007). Connecting adult learners with an online community: Challenges and opportunities. *Research and Practice in Technology Enhanced Learning, 2*(3), 1–18. doi:10.1142/S1793206807000385

Dickey, M. D. (2004). The impact of web-logs (blogs) on student perceptions of isolation and alienation in a web-based distance-learning environment. *Open Learning, 19*(3), 279–291. doi:10.1080/0268051042000280138

Efimova, L., & de Moor, A. (2005). *Beyond personal webpublishing: An exploratory study of conversational blogging practices.* Paper presented at the 38th Annual Hawaii International Conference on System Science (HICSS'05), Los Alamitos.

Farmer, J. (2004). Communication dynamics: Discussion boards, weblogs and the development of communities of inquiry in online learning environments. In R. Atkinson, C. McBeath, D. Jonas-Dwyer, & R. Phillips (Eds.), *Beyond the comfort zone: Proceedings of the 21st ascilite conference,* Perth (pp. 274-283). Retrieved October 27, 2007, from http://www.ascilite.org.au/conferences/perth04/procs/farmer.html.

Ferdig, R. E. (2007). Editorial: Examining social software in teacher education. *Journal of Technology and Teacher Education, 15*(1), 5–10.

Flanagin, A. J., & Metzger, M. J. (2001). Internet use in the contemporary media environment. *Human Communication Research, 27*(1), 153–181. doi:10.1093/hcr/27.1.153

Garrison, D. R., & Anderson, T. (2003). *E-learning in the 21st century: A framework for research and practice.* London: RoutledgeFalmer.

Garrison, D. R., & Kanuka, H. (2004). Blended learning: Uncovering its transformative potential in higher education. *The Internet and Higher Education, 7*(2), 95–105. doi:10.1016/j.iheduc.2004.02.001

Garrison, D. R., & Vaughan, N. D. (2008). *Blended learning in higher education: Framework, principles, and guidelines*. San Francisco: Jossey-Bass.

Graham, C. R. (2006). Blended learning systems. In C. J. Bonk & C. R. Graham (Eds.), *The handbook of blended learning: global perspectives, local designs* (pp. 3-21). San Francisco: Pfeiffer.

Harrington, C. F., Gordon, S. A., & Schibik, T. J. (2004). Course management system utilization and implications for practice: A national survey of department chairpersons. *Online Journal of Distance Learning Administration, 7*(4). Retrieved May 7, 2007, from http://distance.westga.edu/~distance/ojdla/winter74/harrington74.pdf.

Haythornthwaite, C., Kazmer, M. M., & Robins, J. (2000). Community development among distance learners: Temporal and technological dimensions [Electronic Version]. *Journal of Computer-mediated Communication, 6*. Retrieved May 18, 2006, from http://jcmc.indiana.edu/vol6/issue1/haythornthwaite.html

Haythornthwaite, C., & Nielsen, A. L. (2007). Revisiting computer-mediated communication for work, community, and learning. In *Psychology and the internet: Intrapersonal, interpersonal, and transpersonal implications* (2nd ed., pp. 167-186). Amsterdam: Elsevier.

Haythornthwaite, C., & Wellman, B. (2002). The Internet in everyday life: An introduction. In B. Wellman & C. Haythornthwaite (Eds.), *The Internet in everyday life* (pp. 3-44). Oxford, UK: Blackwell Pub.

Hollan, J., & Stornetta, S. (1992). *Beyond being there.* Paper presented at the ACM CHI'92 Conference on Computer-Human Interaction, Monterey, CA.

Jones, Q. (1997). Virtual-communities, virtual settlements & cyber-archaeology: A theoretical outline. *Journal of Computer Mediated Communication, 3*(3). Retrieved June 4, 2006, from http://jcmc.indiana.edu/vol3/issue3/jones.html

Kavanaugh, A., Carroll, J. M., Rosson, M. B., Zin, T. T., & Reese, D. D. (2005). Community networks: Where offline communities meet online [Electronic Version]. *Journal of Computer-Mediated Communication, 10*. Retrieved July 4, 2006, from http://jcmc.indiana.edu/vol10/issue4/kavanaugh.html

Kerres, M., & Witt, C. D. (2003). A didactical framework for the design of blended learning arrangements. *Journal of Educational Media, 28*(2), 101–113. doi:10.1080/1358165032000165653

Kim, A. J. (2000). *Community building on the Web*. Berkeley, CA: Peachpit Press.

Koku, E., Nazer, N., & Wellman, B. (2001). Netting scholars: Online and offline. *The American Behavioral Scientist, 44*(10), 1752–1774. doi:10.1177/00027640121958023

Kozma, R. B. (1991). Learning with Media. *Review of Educational Research, 61*(2), 179–211.

Mason, R., & Rennie, F. (2006). *Elearning: The key concepts*. London: Routledge.

Meyer, K. A. (2003). Face-to-face versus threaded discussions: The role of time and higher-order thinking. *Journal of Asynchronous Learning Networks, 7*(3), 55–65.

Nardi, B. A., Shiano, D. J., Gumbrecht, M., & Swartz, L. (2004). Why we blog. *Communications of the ACM, 47*(12), 41–46. doi:10.1145/1035134.1035163

Norman, D. A. (1993). *Things that make us smart: Defending human attributes in the age of the machine*. Reading, MA: Addison-Wesley.

Osguthorpe, R. T., & Graham, C. R. (2003). Blended learning environments: Definitions and directions. *The Quarterly Review of Distance Education, 4*(3), 227–233.

Papastergiou, M. (2006). Course management systems as tools for the creation of online learning environments: Evaluation from a social constructivist perspective and implications for their design. *International Journal on E-Learning, 5*(4), 593–622.

Preece, J. (2000). *Online communities: Designing usability, supporting sociability*. Chichester, UK: John Wiley & Sons.

Ray, B. B., & Coulter, G. A. (2008). Reflective practices among language arts teachers: The use of weblogs. *Contemporary Issues in Technology & Teacher Education, 8*(1), 6–26.

Richardson, W. (2006). *Blogs, wikis, podcasts, and other powerful web tools for classrooms*. Thousand Oaks, CA: Corwin Press.

Rovai, A. P., & Jordan, H. M. (2004). Blended learning and sense of community: A comparative analysis with traditional and fully online graduate courses. *International Review of Research in Open and Distance Learning, 5*(2). Retrieved October 10, 2007, from http://www.irrodl.org/index.php/irrodl/article/viewArticle/192/274

Salmon, G. (2000). *E-moderating: The key to teaching and learning online*. London: Kogan Page.

Schwen, T. M., & Hara, N. (2004). Community of practice: A metaphor for online design? In S. A. Barab, R. Kling, & J. H. Gray (Eds.), *Designing for virtual communities in the service of learning* (pp. 16-50). Cambridge, UK: Cambridge University Press.

Spatariu, A., Quinn, L. F., & Hartley, K. (2007). A review of research on factors that impact aspects of online discussions quality. *TechTrends, 51*(3), 44–48. doi:10.1007/s11528-007-0041-9

Stiler, G. M., & Philleo, T. (2003). Blogging and blogspots: An alternative format for encouraging reflective practice among preservice teachers. *Education, 123*(4), 789–798.

Swan, K., & Shea, P. (2005). The development of virtual learning communities. In S. R. Hiltz & R. Goldman (Eds.), *Learning together online: Research on asynchronous learning networks* (pp. 239-260). Mahwah, NJ: Lawrence Erlbaum Associates.

Vonderwell, S., & Zachariah, S. (2005). Factors that influence participation in online learning. *Journal of Research on Technology in Education, 38*(2), 213–230.

Wallace, R. M. (2003). Online learning in higher education: A review of research on interactions among teachers and students. *Education Communication and Information, 3*(2), 241–280. doi:10.1080/14636310303143

Wellman, B., & Gulia, M. (1999). Virtual communities as communities: Net surfers don't ride alone In M. Smith & P. Kollock (Eds.), *Communities in cyberspace* (pp. 167-194). London: Routledge.

Williams, R. L., & Cothrel, J. (2000). Four smart ways to run online communities. *Sloan Management Review, 41*(4), 81–91.

Youngblood, P., Trede, F., & Corpo, S. D. (2001). Facilitating online learning: a descriptive study. *Distance Education, 22*(2), 264–284. doi:10.1080/0158791010220206

Zhao, C. M., & Kuh, G. D. (2004). Adding value: Learning communities and student engagement. *Research in Higher Education, 45*(2), 115–138. doi:10.1023/B:RIHE.0000015692.88534.de

KEY TERMS AND DEFINITIONS

Blended Learning: The combination of face-to-face and computer-mediated communication tools or the mixture of various media in support of learning.

Learning Community: A group of people engaged in active and collaborative learning activities.

Blended Community: A community that is supported by both online and offline modes of communication.

Blended Learning Community: A community which utilizes various media – online or offline, synchronous or asynchronous – to support learning as individual and social act.

Community Design: Efforts or intervention made to cultivate social relationship or sense of belonging within a community.

Sociability: Person-to-personal interaction within a community that is crucial for community-building.

Computer-Mediated Communication (CMC): The communication mediated by computers. Generally speaking, there are two types of CMC: synchronous and asynchronous.

Chapter 15
Students Writing Their Own Lectures with a Wiki and the CSA

Cath Ellis
University of Huddersfield, UK

Sue Folley
University of Huddersfield, UK

ABSTRACT

This chapter examines why despite decades of research and overwhelming evidence questioning the pedagogical effectiveness of lecturing as a teaching and learning strategy, it remains the dominant pedagogical mode in most higher education institutions worldwide. The authors explore further why lectures are not the most appropriate teaching strategy in the current higher education climate for three main reasons: the way we now view 'knowledge'; the information society in which we are currently immersed; and the diverse background and experience of today's student population. The authors offer an alternative to the lecture which can achieve what a lecture aims to, but in a more student-centred way. Their alternative is informed by the contributing student approach, devised by Collis & Moonen (2001), whereby students collaboratively find, explore, share, and engage with the content which they would have otherwise received passively via a didactic lecture.

INTRODUCTION

For well over 50 years scholarly research has been questioning the effectiveness of lecturing. Despite this, it remains central to University teaching and learning practice. The resilience of lecturing to the ongoing criticism of it has left many scholars baffled and frustrated. As the rather exasperated title of Graham Gibbs' essay, 'Twenty Terrible Reasons for Lecturing,' makes plain, the arguments often put in its defence are rarely edifying, let alone erudite. In his conclusions he says 'I do believe there is far more lecturing going on than can reasonably be justified' (Gibbs, 1981, p. 12). In this paper we argue that deposing lecturing as the mainstay of teaching and learning in Higher Education is now more imperative than ever. We suggest, however, that to counter the resilience of lecturing requires a variety of strategic approaches and propose one such approach. This suggests replacing what lecturing

DOI: 10.4018/978-1-60566-380-7.ch015

should do through the use of a Contributing Student Approach (CSA): effectively having students write their own lectures. We start by examining the lecture itself, and then outline how in an industry characterised by widening participation, in a postmodern and information rich world, it is now obsolete. We then go on to explore why there is still so much lecturing going on and how it might be strategically replaced. We then examine the risks and benefits of using a CSA in combination with a wiki and argue how this compares favourably with lecturing. We end by outlining how the roles of students and academics change with this approach, concluding that it has the potential to bring about widespread institutional change and, ultimately, challenge the ubiquity of lecturing.

BACKGROUND

What are Lectures?

As many critics of lecturing have observed, it constitutes the mainstay of teaching and learning in Higher Education even though few cite any empirical research to support this assertion, and if they do cite a source it is often simply to someone else making the same assertion (Bligh, 1998; Gibbs, 1981; Irving & Young, 2004; Laing, 1996; Laurillard cited in Phillips, 2005; Stephenson, Brown, & Griffin, 2008).[1] This would suggest that it is such an obvious fact that there is little need to actually *prove* it.[2] Despite this, it would seem then that in many, if not most, university courses lectures form the 'bulk' of the student diet. Most are delivered through oration with the lecturer doing most if not all of the talking and the main student activity being taking notes and, hopefully, listening.[3] Recently the enthusiastic adoption of presentation software, such as PowerPoint and Keynote, has meant that students now often transcribe the lecturer's words directly from a screen, the absurdity of does not escape them! One student taking part in some recent research on the attitudes and expectations of the next generation of learners entering Higher Education emphasises this sentiment:

We have lectures where at the start you are given the slides, you are told that all the information is on Blackboard, and then you are sitting there for an hour while they read through the slides, and it is really frustrating. Why do I need to be here listening to somebody reading it when I can read it myself, and probably take it in a lot better? (Sheard & Ahmed, 2007, p. 57)

In a web-based world where things like banking, shopping and news can be accessed at any time or place, the lecture stands in stark contrast: taking place in a rigidly synchronous setting, timetabled in a regular pattern, to last a specified length of time and requiring everyone to be in the same place at the same time. Lectures often function as the 'spine' of subjects onto which other learning strategies, such as seminars and tutorials, are attached. Some scholars have argued (and I suspect many academics would agree) that the continued prevalence of lecturing as a pedagogical strategy would seem to suggest that there must be some value in them. The research would, however, advocate otherwise.

At this point it is useful to consider what it is that lecturers think that they achieve by delivering them. The lecture has been around for a long time and, as a consequence, a considerable amount of research has been conducted on them to evaluate their effectiveness as a pedagogical strategy. The most influential study into the effectiveness of lecturing was conducted by Donald Bligh in *What's the Use of Lectures?* First published in 1971, this much reprinted and highly influential work conducts an exhaustive literature review of decades of research into the effectiveness of lecturing. The most commonly cited reason for lecturing, and that which Bligh suggests it actually has the capacity to realise, is the imparting of information. He outlines other reasons commonly offered by lecturers which he groups under four headings: 1. The acquisition of information, 2. The promotion of thought, 3. Changes in attitudes, and 4. Behavioural skills (Bligh, 1998). He concludes that of the reasons academics frequently cite as to why they lecture that it is only effective in achieving one of these: helping students acquire information. Even then he finds that it is only *as* effective as other methods. He shows that lecturing is better than nothing (in other words students who attend a lecture learn more than students who sit in an empty room and stare at a blank wall), but that the other reasons often given do not have evidential support in any of the studies (Bligh, 1998). Beyond Bligh's comprehensive study into the pedagogical effectiveness of lecturing, there is an increasing body of scholarship which suggests that since lectures were first invented and put to use, the world, how it uses information and how it constructs and understands knowledge, has changed so substantially that the lecture is now, effectively, rendered obsolete. This is especially so in a postmodern, information rich world, where widening participation is becoming increasingly prioritised. It is useful to unpack these further one at a time.

Are They Effective?

Postmodernity

In recent decades postmodern theory has challenged long held assumptions about the nature of epistemology, and in particular the myth that there is such a thing as Truth – which is ultimately stable, knowable, explicable and therefore 'learnable'. Jean-François Lyotard (1984), in his short but influential work *The Postmodern Condition* offers a critique of established epistemological strategies, and famously announces the end of grand narratives (otherwise referred to as metanarratives or master narratives). These, he argues, are characteristic modernist strategies used to provide comprehensive explanations of knowledge and experience. In an often quoted passage he declares:

Simplifying to the extreme, I define postmodern as incredulity toward metanarratives. ...To the obsolescence of the metanarrative apparatus of legitimation corresponds, most notably, the crisis of metaphysical philosophy and of the university institution which in the past relied on it. The narrative function is losing its functors, its great hero, its great dangers, its great voyages, its great goal. (Lyotard, 1984, p. xxiv)

Here, and throughout *The Postmodern Condition,* Lyotard (1984) challenges the established understanding of the role and function of the University as a place for generating, authorising, legitimating and, ultimately, perpetuating 'knowledge'. In essence, he is arguing that in postmodernity, the academy, as a site of knowledge production, has changed fundamentally and forever. Writing a decade earlier, Michel Foucault pursued similar critiques of epistemology. In his highly influential 1969 publication *The Archaeology of Knowledge* he argues that knowledge, power and language are bound together discursively "as practices that systematically form the objects of which they speak" (Foucault, 1972, p. 49). Here Foucault challenges both the 'unitary' instincts of disciplinarity and also the means by which knowledge operates within them as 'discursive formations'.

This idea has been pursued in other branches of philosophy, particularly in what are sometimes referred to as the 'emancipatory discourses' such as postcolonial, feminist and Marxist theories. These theories challenge dominant or normative discourses (here colonial, patriarchal and capitalist respectively) whose discursive formations of power (which are often, if not always, generated within the academy) have justified and effected the subjection of colonised/indigenous peoples, women and working class people for centuries. It is, of course, the academy, through disciplines such as biology, anthropology, psychology, history and literature to name a few, which have discursively formed the Other as lesser- or sub-human and which have, in turn, been used to justify, defend and perpetuate acts of oppression and subjugation. This is often referred to as 'epistemic violence' and intervening in and overturning the ways and means by which it is generated and perpetuated is, of course, a central aim of emancipatory discourses.

Yet clearly if the authority of epistemology is to be challenged, the means by which it is 'transmitted' to future generations of scholars must also be challenged. After all, one of the key means by which epistemic violence has been maintained, protected and reinforced, sometimes over centuries, is by being legitimated through an unchallengeable process of 'transmission' from one generation of scholars to the next. Here, the lecture was, and remains, the most powerful weapon in the pedagogical arsenal of epistemic violence. In this way, and as Phillips points out, the lecture is "consistent with a modern view of knowledge" (Phillips, 2005, p. 4).[4] By presenting discursive formations as Truths to be learned and regurgitated, lectures give authority to the knowledge being presented and thereby operate as an important and powerful validating procedure. The very architecture of the lecture hall is a physical manifestation of this relationship with the focus and power vested with the 'sage on the stage' who is often also responsible for assessing the work of the students in the auditorium.

If the self-perpetuating cycles of epistemic violence are to be interrupted, both the nature of knowledge construction *and* the pedagogical strategies used to perpetuate them must be challenged and ideally changed. To put it simply, this requires removing the lecture from its pedestal and replacing it instead with an alternative strategy which prioritises the democratisation and sharing of knowledge. To be effective, this needs to be tackled on two fronts. First, academic staff need to take responsibility for *giving up* the authority and power with which lecturing provides them. Secondly, students need to be empowered and supported in generating and constructing their own knowledge, especially that which challenges established knowledge, rather than expecting and relying on being presented with it.

Information Rich World

In *The Postmodern Condition* Lyotard places considerable emphasis on the impact that computers have on our understanding of knowledge.

It is reasonable to suppose that the proliferation of information-processing machines is having, and will continue to have, as much of an effect on the circulation of learning as did advancements in human circulation (transportation systems) and later, in the circulation of sounds and visual images (the media). (Lyotard, 1984, p. 4).

Prescient as this was, writing in 1979 Lyotard could not have predicted the impact that the interconnection of computers and the invention of the World Wide Web would have on the world and the place of the academy within it.[5] Until fairly recently, information was stored permanently in hard copy: in books and journals. At the birth of the academy, these were both expensive and rare. As we have explained elsewhere (Ellis, 2008), in this context, lecturing provided a cheap and efficient transcription tool. As Brown and Race explain the early history of lecturing in European universities involved Masters reciting memorised tracts of text, which the students then transcribed (Brown & Race, 2002). The skill of lecturing rested in being able to recite the information accurately, clearly and slowly enough to allow students to write it down. In this context, the lecturer was one of the most if not the most important sources of information available to students. The value, for students, in having a 'good set of notes' was clearly apparent then, but its continued emphasis in current day study skills guides, in an e-world where the students' information cup is full to overflowing, is baffling. In this context, where students can access podcast lectures from experts in all fields working anywhere in the world, their local teachers cannot and really should not be their main source of information. Further, as Knight and Wood (2005) point out, while there is now more information to learn than ever before, "the increasingly easy accessibility of facts on the Internet is making long-term memorization of details less and less important. Students [...] will be required to apply conceptual knowledge to problem solving rather than simply to know many facts" (p. 298). Lyotard predicted that this shift would occur and suggests how the role of the University might change as a result:

knowledge will no longer be transmitted en bloc, once and for all, to young people before their entry into the work force: rather it is and will be served "a la carte" to adults who are either already working or expect to be, for the purpose of improving their skills and chance of promotion, but also to help them acquire information, languages, and language games allowing them both to widen their occupational horizons and to articulate their technical and ethical experience. (Lyotard, 1984, p. 49).

Alongside this shifting role of the University as an institution, the idea of knowledge 'half-life' is also important. Gonzalez defines the half-life of knowledge as: "the time span from when knowledge is gained to when it becomes obsolete" (Gonzalez, 2004, para 1). Different disciplines tend to experience different half-lives with some, such as languages, enjoying long 'half-lives' measured in decades and centuries, and others, such as computing, being measured in years and months (see P. Knight, 1997). There is in addition an overall 'shrinkage' in the length of time it takes for learning to become obsolete as George Siemens explains:

Learners as little as forty years ago would complete the required schooling and enter a career that would often last a lifetime. Information development was slow. The life of knowledge was measured in decades. Today, these foundational principles have been altered. Knowledge is growing exponentially. (Siemens, 2004, para 2).

In some disciplines where knowledge has a short 'half-life' academics are finding that by the time text books are written, edited, printed and distributed, a substantial amount of the knowledge contained within them is out of date or incorrect. This would seem to suggest that in many disciplines a significant proportion of material that a student learns within their undergraduate training will be obsolete certainly by the time they retire from their careers but also, possibly before they even enter their first graduate post. So surely instead of concentrating on pedagogies which are only effective in helping students acquire information, university teaching should focus instead on equipping students with the skills needed to turn information into knowledge both in terms of gathering, managing, filtering and evaluating information available to them and in terms of manipulating it and adding it to their existing knowledge so that it becomes their knowledge (see Brown & Race, 2002).

This strikes at the heart of a traditional core understanding of the role and purpose of the University: what is often referred to as the research-teaching nexus (see for instance Monash University, 2003). It is this nexus that ultimately distinguishes universities from other types of educational sectors (such as schools, further education colleges etc) in that at universities the teachers are research active and therefore teaching ideas that they take some part in generating. As outlined above, in modernity the traditional understanding of the research-teaching nexus was that academics, as scholars, produced knowledge and transmitted it to students primarily through lecturing. But the idea has recently been increasingly defined as a mutually supportive relationship whereby research informs teaching and whereby teaching inspires research *and* students to become researchers. In his influential 1990 publication *Scholarship Reconsidered,* Boyer offers a useful extension of the nexus in his explanation of one of his four scholarships: the scholarship of teaching. He argues that it should encourage: "students to be critical, creative thinkers, with the capacity to go on learning" (Boyer, 1990, pp. 23-24). In this sense, academics' expertise moves away from simply what they know, have discovered and can transmit to students, into their capacity to coach, guide and mentor students to develop the skills required to produce their own knowledge, now and in the future. If the only means by which a lecture can be pedagogically effective is in assisting students in the acquisition of information, then surely in this information rich world the purpose and role of lecturing is effectively redundant. As such, the investment made at the institutional level into the research-teaching nexus being facilitated through lecturing also needs to be rethought.

Widening Participation

Developed nations are becoming increasingly post-industrial and as Knight (1997) explains "knowledge is being recognized as the single most important economic resource", (para 1).[6] In 1999 the British Labour Government announced an ambitious target of having 50% of the adult population participate in Higher Education by 2010. In what has come to be known as the 'widening participation' strategy, universities have been rewarded for welcoming an increasing proportion of students who were previously excluded from Higher Education because of their class, 'race', gender, physical ability etc. The range of their skills and abilities (in terms of such things as computer literacy, oral and written communication, awareness of scholarly practices etc) and of their prior knowledge is much wider than any previous cohort of students. Significantly, and as Laurillard points out, lecturing can only ever work as an effective teaching methodology if lecturers know very well the "capabilities of the students, and on the students having very similar capabilities and prior knowledge" (Laurillard, 1993, p. 108). She goes on to suggest that in a world where "students were selected through standardised entrance examinations" (p. 108) for admission to university, this was something about which a lecturer could be fairly certain. They could be confident that students would share and understand their idiolect, cultural references, social aspirations and, until relatively recently, their religious convictions and gender. Lecturers could also be confident that their prior knowledge and training in things such as essay writing and the use of standard written English was almost uniform, that their learning needs and that their potential employer expectations were fairly similar. Laurillard suggests that "open access and module courses make it most unlikely that a class of students will be sufficiently similar in background and capabilities to make lectures workable as a principal teaching method" (Laurillard, 1993, p. 108). Now more than ever, it is ridiculous to assume that the needs of all students can be met in a learning environment dominated by or lecturing.

So Why are We Still Doing So Many of Them?

As we have argued elsewhere "the lecture's ubiquity is matched only by its obduracy" (Ellis, 2008, p. 2). So while it makes up the bulk of the student diet regardless of its limited efficacy, it has proven stubbornly resistant to any attempts to undermine it. There are lots of reasons offered as to why this is so, and these issues are well explored in the literature but they are worth covering briefly here. First and foremost, lecturers and students alike are strongly wedded to them. Apart from anything else, lectures are fantastically self-indulgent and a significant boost to the ego. After all, they give academics an opportunity to talk, uninterrupted, in front of a captive audience for a prolonged period of time about ideas with which they are fascinated(Gibbs, 1981). Secondly, there is a strong weight of expectation that lecturing is what academics 'do'. After all, for many of us, the word 'lecturer' is part of our job title. Academics were students once themselves, and then, as now, the lecture formed the bulk of their learning diet, so many continue to teach in the same way they were taught(Gibbs, 1981). This is exacerbated, as Phillips points out, by a lack of requirements for formal teaching qualifications in Higher Education (Phillips, 2005). Further, the very infrastructure and administrative systems of Higher Education institutions, such as architecture, workloads, timetabling, part-time hourly paid rates, peer observation systems and module validation procedures, all reinforce the understanding that academics are expected to lecture (Gibbs, 1981; Phillips, 2005).

Another pressure which encourages the use of lectures is student expectation. As the research of Sander et al shows, for students entering Higher Education, the most frequently expected teaching and learning methods is formal lectures even though this ranked very highly in terms of the teaching and learning methods that students did not want (Sander, Stevenson, King, & Coates, 2000). This would seem to suggest that many students are embarking on a University education despite the fact that they will experience lectures not because of it. This begs the question, how many students are choosing not to embark on Higher Education at all precisely because of lectures?

As Knight & Wood have shown confounding this expectation can have a negative effect on student evaluations: "because students at present are used to having most large courses taught in the lecture format, the unfamiliar demands of an active-engagement course may take them out of their comfort zone, resulting in lower student ratings for the instructor" (J. K. Knight & Wood, 2005, p. 306) (see also Stefani, 2001). It is possible that some students may prefer the lecture experience precisely because it is a passive learning experience that does not require much effort on their part. Knight & Wood (2005) report how students complained about a more interactive teaching and learning format because academics "were not teaching them very much, but rather making them learn the material on their own" (p. 303). While rather gratifying for the teachers, this emphasises how entrenched and normative the passive lecture experience has become for students. To put it simply, attending lectures becomes a learning habit for students that becomes hard to break and is therefore easy for them to articulate as an expectation. This expectation can be difficult for academics to refuse to meet. Tormey and Henchy offer a useful reflection on this point:

If we were motivated to change, however, we were not sure our students were. We recognised that, although they were in their first year in university, our students had already developed their learning strategies in relation to a didactic post-primary education system. [...] Most of our students were among those that had been most successful within that system. At the very least this might lead one to expect that many of them would be more comfortable with a didactic lecturing style than with the more engaged, relational style which we sought to develop. (Tormey & Henchy, 2008, p. 305)

It is hardly surprising then that lecturing has proved so difficult to shift and indeed why there is so much literature encouraging better lecturing practice.

The other big problem that lecturing presents is that in its most basic form it is primarily instructional. As research into peer-assisted learning has demonstrated, (see for instance Bhalerao & Ward, 2001; Falchikov & Blythman, 2001), one of the most effective ways of learning something is to explain it to someone else. As such, some of the more mischievous critics of lecturing have suggested that the only person who really learns anything in a lecture is the lecturer. Given the discussion above about empowering students to construct their own knowledge, it surely makes more sense for students to do this rather than the lecturer. It is this which is at the basis of our strategic approach to replacing it.

A STRATEGY FOR CHANGE: REPLACING LECTURES WITH THE CONTRIBUTING STUDENT APPROACH

For all of the reasons outlined above, it would seem imperative that, if not abolished altogether, that at least a significant proportion of lectures should be replaced with alternative teaching and learning strategies. However, the above mentioned obduracy of lecturing in Higher Education indicates that this is no easy feat, and even replacing some lecturing would constitute a big step forward for any institution in terms of achieving substantive change. The field of institutional change is, of course, an important and growing area of research and the various strategies proposed for achieving it have had mixed success. Inevitably, 'top down' approaches, such as institutional directives outlawing lecturing or limiting the amount of contact hours consumed with lecturing, will inevitably crash against the rocks of academic autonomy which, while valuable and to be defended, is too often used as a defence against change and is thus, at least in part, responsible for the perpetuation of lecturing.

What we are suggesting here is that a strategic approach needs to be taken if the primacy and prevalence of lecturing is to be effectively challenged. To effectively challenge the ubiquity of lecturing, it is important that several strategies are used to replace it. In other words, there is little point replacing it with something equally ubiquitous. Elsewhere we have suggested another strategic approach, using screencast lectures to 'wean' lecturers off lecturing (Ellis, 2008). What we propose here is a means by which it may be *partially* achieved and that is by having students write their own lectures. Importantly, we are not suggesting here that students write lectures or, worse still, that they lecture each other. As such, we are not concentrating our attention on having students replace what lectures currently achieve for them in their learning, but rather, we are proposing that students work together to build things which replicated what lectures *should* achieve. Our proposal is to use a strategy where students are primarily working together to produce their own learning materials.

The Contributing Student Approach

The theoretical principles behind this approach to student learning have been developed by Collis & Moonen in their influential book *Flexible Learning in a Digital World* (Collis & Moonen, 2001). Their emphasis on the 'U turn' in pedagogy has come to be known as the 'Contributing Student Approach' (CSA). The foundation for their work is in line with that outlined above with reference to there being a shift from an industrial to an information age (Reigeluth cited in Collis & Moonen, 2001). The key element of their work is that student learning should move from one of primarily acquisition to one of primarily participation and contribution (see also Barr & Tagg, 1995). They argue that:

The emphasis on contribution means that new learning materials will become available for all students, based on participant contributions. The learner gradually takes on a role of co-responsibility for the learning experience of the group as a whole. The emphasis of the course shifts from the content to be studied, towards the activities that will be experienced in order to integrate the content into one's larger professional identity. (Collis & Moonen, 2001, p. 95).

This, they argue (drawing on the work of Reigeluth) is part of a larger paradigmatic shift in pedagogy, which aligns itself with the second approaches in the following pairings: "Adversarial vs cooperative, Bureaucratic vs team organization, Autocratic vs shared leadership, One-way communications vs networking and Division of labour vs integration of tasks" (Reigeluth cited in Collis & Moonen, 2001, p. 23).

The opportunity to put a contributing student approach into practice has really only been feasible since the advent of flexible, accessible and user-friendly tools such as wikis. This is, in the end, something that would be very difficult to achieve in the rigidly time limited and synchronous learning environment which is a traditional classroom. A wiki (the name derives from WikiWiki a Hawai'ian word which means 'fast') is defined as: "a collection of Web pages that are linked to each other, and reflect the collaborative works of many authors" (Beldarrain, 2006, p. 142). The use of a wiki, along with other Web 2.0 tools, brings particular advantages, many of which have been identified by Collis & Moonen already (Collis & Moonen, 2008). First, and most obviously, the wiki is a shared space which is always available equally to all students. The fact that it easily accommodates a work in progress means that teachers and peers can correct and retarget student work easily and, perhaps most importantly, early so it is a useful and powerful tool for diagnostic and formative feedback. Because it records who has contributed, a wiki makes it very easy to see who has done what, when and where, and this makes it particularly useful for assessing group work, a notoriously problematic issue in Higher Education (see for instance Booth & Hyland, 2000; Bourner, Hughes, & Bourner, 2001; Frost, 2001). It also keeps a history of contributions which can be easily re-established, which safeguards against both innocent errors and malicious sabotage. A wiki is particularly powerful in its capacity to develop reciprocity and to allow students to develop and exploit their own particular talents, learning styles and learning objectives (all things that Chickering and Gamson identify as a key principle of effective course design (Chickering & Gamson citied in Collis & Moonen, 2006).

There are a growing number of successful examples of using wikis and a CSA in the literature. Hamer (2006) reports on using a wiki and the CSA in a computing course to replace traditional 'lecture based' teaching with class meetings. In another example Watson had his students construct their own text book again using a wiki and had subsequent groups of students edit and update it (Evans, 2006, p. 30). Until relatively recently, wiki tools were beset with problems which had the potential to limit their effectiveness for a Contributing Student Approach. Even the most simple wiki tools required at least some web-authoring knowledge which made them inaccessible to the less-computer literate. They also required cumbersome registration administration to allow students access and some were not able to be restricted and, thereby, protected from external access. Hamer (2006) outlines some of these problems. Recently more accessible SCORM compliant wikis have been constructed as building blocks for use within proprietary and open source VLEs and the wiki tool created by Learning Objects is a good example. It requires similar skills to those required to edit a word document so even students with low levels of computer-literacy can engage with it with relative ease. By being embedded in the VLE, the tool has the specific advantages of having students automatically registered and identified, of it being a safe and familiar space for them to access and work within and of being 'safe' from external scrutiny.

The Benefits

The CSA has very real and significant benefits to students over their learning experiences with lecturing. The most obvious comes is that, rather than being given the information from a lecturer, the students take ownership of the material that they construct, the structure they build it into, and ultimately of the knowledge that they produce and share. Through this process, students take responsibility for their own learning outcomes and of the skills that they develop in the process of working together and constructing their materials. The skills they develop, none of which are usually achieved in a lecture experience, are as follows:

- Filtering information
- Collaboration
- Working alone
- Decision making
- Reading/research
- Negotiation
- Evaluation
- Team work
- Writing as process: drafting, editing, referencing, proof reading

Obviously knowledge acquisition is an important component of this process. As Brown & Race point out, it is only by first understanding the information, then by being manipulated by the student and ultimately added to their existing knowledge that information becomes *their* knowledge (Brown & Race, 2002) again, something that is difficult to accomplish in a lecture. As opposed to the inherently passive learning that takes place in a lecture hall, the contributing student approach by its very nature involves active learning. This results in both a deeper understanding which arises from learning something for oneself and from teaching something to someone else. Students having opportunities to discover and pursue their own interests, a crucial element of constructivist pedagogical theory, is of course vital here and again something for which students have limited opportunity in lecture-dominated learning. In addition, this approach has the capacity to instil broader understanding by covering more of the curriculum than may have been possible through a standard lecture format and the student understanding of that material can be checked more easily and more consistently than if it is delivered in a lecture.

All in all, this approach fosters more meaningful learning than a lecture can possibly achieve. As Wilson explains, this approach is:

- Active
- Constructive
- Intentional
- Authentic
- Cooperative (Wilson, cited in Collis and Moonen 2006)

One of the key benefits, available to both students and staff, is the reusability and cumulative nature of the work conducted. If it is designed for this purpose, and if appropriate ethical clearance and release is facilitated, the work generated and contributed by students can be reused, added to and updated year by year. This allows the peer learning to happen from one cohort to the next as well as from one student to another within that cohort. This puts a kind of cumulative potential and value into the student work for future years which is a marked change from other kinds of student activity in traditional teaching and assessment processes. As Watson (cited in Evans, 2006) points out, usually most, if not all, of the work students produce for their degree courses is read only by the person marking it and rarely is any further use made of it. In any other context this would be considered a monumental waste of effort and material.

The Risks

As with any significant pedagogical change, the use of the Contributing Student Approach to replace lectures brings potential risks which generate anxieties. Collis & Moonen have addressed a considerable number of the risks associated with the CSA in general in their various publications (Collis, 2005; Collis, de Boer, & van der Veen, 2001; Collis & Moonen, 2008). There are, however, several which are worth addressing which are specific to the issue of using the CSA to replace lectures

'What if They Get it Wrong?'

Perhaps the most obvious concern about having students constructing their own course materials is to do with Quality Control (see Hamer, 2006), what if they do not get it 'right'? This, of course, starts from an assumption that there is a 'right' for students to get which, as outlined above, is problematic in a postmodern world and in disciplines with a short knowledge half-life. Further to this, the way that lectures are currently delivered, we currently cannot be certain that their understanding of all of the material is 'right'. Their understanding of material is only checked through assessment which is necessarily partial. In practice, it is likely that in a CSA only few students will get things *horribly* wrong, and the process of checking and correcting understanding becomes an important part of the learning process.

'How Can I Cover All the Content?'

Covering the content is often cited as a justification for lecturing. But as Bligh points out: "What is important is what the students learn, not how much the lecturer covers" (Bligh, 1998, p. 7; Gibbs, 1981). Brown & Race agree pointing out that "the amount of information available on a given topic is now so enormous, that it's impossible for students to write down everything you want to get across to them on a topic, especially within the timescale of a normal one-hour lecture period" (Brown & Race, 2002, pp. 50-51). A CSA has the potential to cover much more 'content' than would ever be possible via lecturing, especially if it used cumulatively year after year, with students editing, correcting, updating and adding to the work of previous cohorts. Instead of providing students with *what* they do not know, the CSA shifts the emphasis to an awareness *that* they do not know, thereby inspiring life-long learning.

'Will it Increase My Workload?'

Any decision to shift away from lecturing potentially creates a workload imposition which in itself can be used as a justification to avoid change(see Gibbs, 1981). The question, however, fails to recognise that lecturing constitutes a considerable workload imposition in terms of the time it takes to research, prepare, deliver and update them every year. Workload is, however, something about which Collis and Moonen are, justifiably, concerned and they give it considerable time and emphasis in their work (Collis & Moonen, 2001). The CSA need not be a considerable workload imposition if the tasks the students undertake are well designed and carefully managed. After all, in having the students build their own materials, students are taking on a lot of the work themselves. The academic's workload need not grow, but rather shift from doing the work themselves to managing, supporting, guiding, checking and rewarding students as they do it instead.

'What if My Colleagues and Institution Don't Approve?'

Academics may feel reluctant to make the move away from lecturing and towards the Contributing Student Approach because of concerns that their colleagues, line-manager or even their institution as a whole will not 'approve' of their doing so. As we have outlined above, change in Higher Education generally tends to happen bottom-up rather than top-down. As Gilly Salmon claims most, if not all, executive management teams in Higher Education Institutions are keen for this kind of innovation and change to take place, although the mechanisms they put in place to support such change may at times appear to suggest otherwise (Salmon, 2005). In theory, at least, institutions and middle managers in Higher Education are generally supportive of innovation so this should provide no genuine barrier.

'What if the Students Don't Do the Work?'

Anxieties that students simply will not contribute are also very real, but are similar to those found in other kinds of innovative steps towards more active learning approaches. Arguably, students are not doing a great deal, apart from writing notes, in a standard lecture anyway. The usual, and perhaps quite clichéd, response to this concern is that if the activity offers genuine rewards, in terms of benefits to student learning, is well designed and managed, with clear expectations and guidelines, if good practice is modelled, and if appropriate technical support is offered, then students will do what is asked of them. The concern, however, is part of a larger issue relating to student expectations. As outlined above, what students *expect* and what they *want* are not always closely aligned. Similarly, what they *want* is not necessarily the same as what they *need* to learn effectively. It is also possible that student expectations come to reflect that which is offered to them. So, if students are offered passive, instructional and instrumental learning experiences when they first enter the academy then it is possible that that is what they will come to expect and, thereby, feel entitled to. As Phillips explains, students can be resistant to student-centred approaches because of "commonly-accepted paradigms about the nature of study", (Phillips, 2005, p. 9). He suggests: "The view that 'I'm paying to be taught, so teach me!' is increasingly apparent in modern universities, despite evidence (Marginson 1993; A C Nielsen Research Services 1999) that employers want generic, lifelong skills from graduates", (Phillips, 2005, p. 9). The whole issue of managing student expectations and entitlements is a core component of managing any kind of institutional strategic change of this kind and warrants further investigation than is possible within the scope of this paper.

PUTTING IT INTO PRACTICE

The strategy of using the CSA to replace lectures in a course will obviously not be uniformly applicable or effective. There are several options available. The option of replacing all of the lectures with a CSA is the most radical option, but is likely to be the most risky. Replacing some or just one of the lectures, choosing those whose content is most obviously suited to adaptation to a CSA, offers a less risky first step.

In the literature there are many suggestions and examples offered by Collis and Moonen, and by other scholars, about how the contributing student approach can be applied in practice. Examples include the 'sandwich approach', the 'before, during and after' approach (Collis & Moonen, 2001, p. 92) and the jigsaw method (Aronson cited in Collis & Moonen, 2001, p. 102) could all be used to replace lecturing. When compared to the roles usually taken in a lecture situation, the contributing student approach represents a marked shift and one that is importantly moving in the direction of student-centred and active learning. Now the sorts of roles students take on including:

- Resource gathering
- Writing
- Editing and checking
- Layout and illustration
- Composing an executive summary
- Designing follow-up activities

In each instance, the roles and responsibilities can be organised so that everyone does a little bit of each role on each topic, or that people do different roles on different topics or even the same role on each topic. Similarly, the roles of the teacher change. These can include:

- Commissioning editor
- Guiding and supporting
- Communicating expectations
- Overseeing editor

- Chairing
- Moderating

If, as Bligh (1998) suggests, the dominant student experience and expectation of lecturing is of 'information inputting' rather than 'information processing' then the contributing student approach offers a marked change in the roles of both student and teacher. As Hamer (2006) found, the student becomes co-creator of learning materials, and takes responsibility for selecting form a variety of real-world resources. They take on the role of extending the work of others, and can become responsible for both self- and peer-evaluation. They also become designers and builders of a learning resource that has a use within the course and the potential for use outside it. The lecturer's role also changes in significant ways (Evans, 2006). Instead of being the authority and the provider of information and knowledge, they are instead the chairperson or coordinator. Their input reduces, which also sees a reduction in preparation time, allowing them to use the time instead to lead, guide and/or design materials. The role of synchronous classroom based sessions also changes to being a meeting, with the potential for students to take on administrative roles in terms of taking minutes and apportioning responsibilities and actions.

CONCLUSION

It is becoming increasingly clear that the lecture needs to be deposed as the mainstay of teaching and learning in Higher Education. As Tormey and Hency remark:

The need for us to continue to re-think the traditional lecture is clear. Our data show that even those students whose learning styles cause them to value the traditional lecture are far from comfortable with it. Many other students have moved further, and identify that they learn best in contexts other than the traditional lecture. (Tormey & Henchy, 2008, p. 313)

Identifying the need for change and effecting it are, however, two very different things. Rather than focussing on how the format might be improved by adopting different strategies, as so many texts on the pedagogy of lecturing endorse, achieves little more than moving from what lectures currently achieve to what they might achieve. Our strategy here, instead, is to focus on what lectures *should* achieve and then find a more effective and student-centred means of achieving this than a rigidly synchronous, face-to-face session. This is particularly important. Through this strategic approach it is possible that lecturers, students and institutions in an industry concentrating on widening participation, in a postmodern and information rich world, will be more likely to give up their investment and reliance on lecturing and start exploring other more innovative teaching and learning possibilities.

REFERENCES

Barr, R. B., & Tagg, J. (1995). From Teaching to Learning. In D. DeZure (Ed.), *Learning from Change*. London: Kogan Page.

Beldarrain, Y. (2006). Distance Education Trends: Integrating new technologies to foster student interaction and collaboration. *Distance Education, 27*(2), 139–153. doi:10.1080/01587910600789498

Bhalerao, A., & Ward, A. (2001). Towards electronically assisted peer assessment: a case study. *ALT-J, 9*(1), 26–37. doi:10.1080/0968776010865677З

Bligh, D. (1998). *What's the Use of Lectures?* Exeter, UK: intellect.

Booth, A., & Hyland, P. (2000). *The Practice of University History Teaching*. Manchester, UK: Manchester University Press.

Bourner, J., Hughes, M., & Bourner, T. (2001). First-year Undergraduate Experiences of Group Project Work. *Assessment & Evaluation in Higher Education*, *26*(1), 19–39. doi:10.1080/02602930020022264

Boyer, E. L. (1990). *Scholarship Reconsidered: Priorities of the Professoriate*. Princeton, NJ: The Carnegie Foundation for the Advancement of Teaching.

Brown, S., & Race, P. (2002). *Lecturing, a practical guide*. London: Kogan Page.

Collis, B. (2005). *The Contributing Student: A Blend of Pedagogy and Technology*. Paper presented at the Educause Australasia.

Collis, B., de Boer, W., & van der Veen, J. (2001). Building on Learner Contributions: A Web-Supported Pedagogic Strategy. *Educational Media International*, *38*(4), 229–240. doi:10.1080/09523980110105169

Collis, B., & Moonen, J. (2001). *Flexible Learning in a digital world*. London: Kogan Page Ltd.

Collis, B., & Moonen, J. (2006). The Contributing Student: Learners as Co-developers of Learning Resources for Reuse in Web Environments. In D. Hung & M. S. Khine (Eds.), *Engaged Learning with Emerging Technologies*. Dordrecht, The Netherlands: Springer.

Collis, B., & Moonen, J. (2008). Web 2.0 tools and processes in higher education: quality perspectives. *Educational Media International*, *45*(2), 93–106. doi:10.1080/09523980802107179

Ellis, C. (2008). 'You Can't Do That in a Classroom!': How Distributed Learning Can Assist in the Widespread Adoption of Hybrid Learning Strategies In J. Fong, R. Kwan, & F. L. Wang (Eds.), *Hybrid Learning and Education First International Conference, ICHL 2008 Hong Kong, China, Proceedings* (pp. 1-16). Berlin, Germany: Springer.

Evans, P. (2006). The Wiki Factor. *Biz Ed*, 28-33.

Falchikov, N., & Blythman, M. (2001). *Learning Together: Peer Tutoring in Higher Education*. London: RoutledgeFalmer.

Foucault, M. (1972). *The Archaelogy of Knowledge* (A. M. Sheridan Smith, Trans.). London: Tavistock.

Frost, C. (2001). The Reporter: assessing vocational group journalism projects. *Journalism Studies*, *2*(3), 423–432. doi:10.1080/14616700120062257

Gibbs, G. (1981). *Twenty terrible reasons for lecturing*. Paper presented at the SCED.

Gonzalez, C. (2004). The Role of Blended Learning in the World of Technology [Electronic Version]. *Benchmarks Online*. Retrieved November 20, 2008, from http://www.unt.edu/benchmarks/archives/2004/september04/eis.htm

Hamer, J. (2006). Some experiences with the "contributing student approach". [ACM Digital Library]. *ACM SIGCSE Bulletin*, *38*(3), 68–72. doi:10.1145/1140123.1140145

Irving, Z., & Young, P. (2004). Enabling Robert to learn like Susan: the use of lectures in undergraduate teaching of Social Policy. *LATISS: Learning and Teaching in the Social Sciences*, *1*(2), 121–137. doi:10.1386/ltss.1.2.121/0

Knight, J. K., & Wood, W. B. (2005). Teaching More by Lecturing Less. *Cell Biology Education, 4*, 298–310. doi:10.1187/05-06-0082

Knight, P. (1997). *The Half-Life of Knowledge and Structural Reform of the Education Sector for the Global Knowledge-Based Economy* [Electronic Version]. Retrieved November 20, 2008, from http://www.knight-moore.com/pubs/half-life.html

Laing, G. K. (1996). The Lecture A Teaching Strategy For Large Groups: A Reprise [Electronic Version]. *Faculty of Commerce - Accounting & Finance Working Papers*. Retrieved November 24, 2008, from http://ro.uow.edu.au/accfinwp/66/

Lammers, W. J., & Murphy, J. J. (2002). A Profile of Teaching Techniques Used in the University Classroom: A Descriptive Profile of a US Public University. *Active Learning in Higher Education, 3*(1), 54–67. doi:10.1177/1469787402003001005

Laurillard, D. (1993). *Rethinking University Teaching*. London: RoutledgeFalmer.

Lyotard, J.-F. (1984). *The Postmodern Condition: A Report of Knowledge* (G. Bennington & B. Massumi, Trans.). Manchester, UK: Manchester University Press.

Monash University. (2003). *The Teaching-Research Nexus: A Discussion Paper*. Monash University, Centre for Higher Education Quality.

Phillips, R. (2005). Challenging The Primacy Of Lectures: The Dissonance Between Theory And Practice In University Teaching. *Journal of University Teaching & Learning Practice, 2*(1).

Salmon, G. (2005). Flying not flapping: a strategic framework for e-learning and pedagogical innovation in higher education institutions. *ALT-J, 13*(3), 201–218. doi:10.1080/09687760500376439

Sander, P., Stevenson, K., King, M., & Coates, D. (2000). University Students' Expectations of Teaching. *Studies in Higher Education, 25*(3), 309–323. doi:10.1080/03075070050193433

Sheard, M., & Ahmed, J. (2007). *Engaging the 'Xbox Generation of Learners' in Higher Education* [Electronic Version]. Retrieved November 26, 2008, from http://www2.hud.ac.uk/edu/research/docs/xbox_research_report.pdf

Siemens, G. (2004). Connectivism: A Learning Theory for the Digital Age [Electronic Version]. *elearnspace*. Retrieved November 20, 2008, from http://www.elearnspace.org/Articles/connectivism.htm

Stefani, L. (2001). We Might Have to Learn it but we Shouldn't have to think about it. In H. Edwards, B. Smith, & G. Webb (Eds.), *Lecturing Case Studies, Experience and Practice*. London: Kogan Page.

Stephenson, J. E., Brown, C. B., & Griffin, D. K. (2008). Electronic delivery of lectures in the university environment: An empirical comparison of three delivery styles. *Computers & Education, 50*(3), 640–651. doi:10.1016/j.compedu.2006.08.007

Tormey, R., & Henchy, D. (2008). Re-imagining the traditional lecture: an action research approach to teaching student teachers to 'do' philosophy. *Teaching in Higher Education, 13*(3), 303–314. doi:10.1080/13562510802045337

KEY TERMS AND DEFINITIONS

Collaborative Learning: To work together, in a joint intellectual effort.

Contributing Student Approach: An approach to learning developed by Collis & Moonen (2001)

Lecture: An exposition of a given subject delivered before an audience or a class, as for the purpose of instruction.

Pedagogy: The principles, practice, or profession of teaching

Teaching Strategy: The methods used to facilitate student learning

Web 2.0: Collaborative web tools e.g. wiki, blogs, podcasting

Wiki: A collaboratively authored, linked, set of web pages

ENDNOTES

1 Lammers and Murphy, in their 2002 article, review some literature of empirical research that has been done into the proportion of teaching and learning time taken up with lecturing, and they report on the findings of their own research. (Lammers & Murphy, 2002, p. 56)

2 In any case, proving or disproving this could prove difficult, as the term lecture could be used used by an academic to describe anything on the spectrum from the teacher orating for the full session, to a much more discussion- or activity-based teaching session.

3 The quip that "a lecture is a process in which information passes from the notes of the lecturer to the notes of the student without passing through the minds of either" is perhaps pertinent here (attributed to RK Rathbun by Gilstrap & Martin cited in Stephenson et al., 2008, p. 640)

4 Phillips (2005) helpfully takes this point even further arguing that 'Lectures and lecturing are consistent with a pre-modern view of controlling knowledge' (p4) an idea which is also pertinent to anxieties about other examples of the democratisation of knowledge in the postmodern era over which lecturers have little if any control. A good example is anxieties many lecturers voice about students' use of Wikipedia as a scholarly resource. Tormey and Henchy make an important related point: "We also felt our content matter clash with our methods in that we found ourselves asking our students to critically reflect on the educational writings of Rousseau, Dewey, Mary Wollsonecraft, and Paulo Freire, while we (in Freire's terms) 'lectured [them] into sleepy silence'." (Shor cited in Tormey & Henchy, 2008, p. 305).

5 His predictions that 'A professor is no more competent than memory bank networks in transmitting established knowledge' (p.53) and that students would only need to be taught 'how to use the terminals' (p. 51) are perhaps a little wider of the mark (Lyotard, 1984) .

6 Again, this is something Lyotard (1984) observed saying: "It is widely accepted that knowledge has become the principle force of production over the last few decades; this has already had a noticeable effect on the composition of the work force of the most highly developed countries and constitutes the major bottleneck for the developing countries. In the postindustrial and postmodern age, science will maintain and no doubt strengthen its preeminence in the arsenal of productive capacities of the nation-states. Indeed, this situation is one of the reasons leading to the conclusion that the gap between developed and developing countries will grow even wider in the future" (Lyotard, 1984, p. 5).

Chapter 16
A Mixed Reality Approach to Hybrid Learning in Mixed Culture Environments

Victor Callaghan
University of Essex, UK

Liping Shen
Shanghai Jiao Tong University, China

Michael Gardner
University of Essex, UK

Ruimin Shen
Shanghai Jiao Tong University, China

Minjuan Wang
San Diego State University, USA

ABSTRACT

This chapter describes a conceptual framework that aims to augment existing eLearning systems with a 3D virtual classroom environment to provide geographically dispersed online learners with a sense of being together and part of a natural class. The virtual classroom model the authors present is based on a combination a 'massively multi-user' games technology system from Sun Microsystems Research Labs, a distance learning platform based at Shanghai Jiaotong University and a mixed reality environment developed at Essex University. Learning is, to some extent, a social activity as it involves relationships between people (between students, between students and teachers). Networked technology has a global reach bringing not just new opportunities but also complex multi-cultural and pedagogical issues. Thus, in this chapter the authors discuss both the technology and the socio-educational aspects of designing online Mixed Reality Hybrid Learning systems

DOI: 10.4018/978-1-60566-380-7.ch016

INTRODUCTION

The Internet has opened the possibility for "anyone, anytime, anywhere" communication, accelerating the pace of globalisation, as network services become affordable international commodities consumed by an increasingly multicultural market. For example, banking services are available via the Internet 24/7 to account holders as they roam the globe.

Education has the potential to be such a global service. Ron Perkinson, the Principal Education Specialist for the International Finance Corporation (part of the World Bank Group) estimated that the value of the global education market in 2005 was worth a little over US$2.5 trillion with the private higher education market being valued at over $400 billion worldwide (about 17% of the overall education market). In 2005 the international student population worldwide was 115 million, growing at a rate of approximately 15% per annum, with about half of this increase being due to China (Perkinson, 2006). Education is becoming increasingly important in modern knowledge-based economies (Clarke, Callaghan, 2007) where learning is rapidly becoming a life long process, as borne out by figures such as, 40% of undergraduates in US and 65% of students enrolled in Singapore's private higher education establishments are over 25. Such facts speak for themselves and form a driver to find effective new ways of meeting the growing demand for learning services.

In a parallel trend, online games are growing massively in popularity. According to a survey by comScore, a market analyst company, there are 217 million online gamers worldwide (double the number of students), growing at a rate of 17% per annum[1]. The market analysis firm DFC Intelligence, has estimated that the worldwide online game market is worth around $4 billion now and will grow to $13 billion by 2012 with about 50% of the market being the Far East, 25% in the USA and 18% in Europe. Major markets such as South Korea, China, Japan and the US all gross over $100 million per annum. For example the Chinese online gaming market value in 2007 was some $1.2 billion (9.36 billion Yuan) with the number of online gamers in China estimated at around 59 million in 2008[2]. Males continue to dominate the online gaming market although the gender gap is narrowing in countries such as Malaysia, Singapore and Korea where the female gaming population stands at 48 percent, 47 percent and 36.5 percent, respectively. The networked nature of the technology gives it a global, location-independent reach, creating massive commercial opportunities. For example a single game, *World of Warcraft*, from Blizzard Entertainment, grossed over $100 million in several different countries in its first year. We share the view that network education and Massively Multi-User Games (MMUG) technology share a common computational framework and that the massive investment in games technology could be synergistically exploited to provide cost effective forms of educational services to a diverse multicultural audience (Winston, Moore, Pearson, Hall, Shadbolt, Weston, 2008).

This chapter seeks to show how traditional eLearning systems can be augmented with games technology to provide an increased sense of realism for multi-cultural online learners (our aim is to provide as natural a feel to online lectures, as possible). We approach this by first describing our existing eLearning system based at Shanghai Jiao Tong University and secondly by describing our mixed-reality environment (Mirtle) based at Essex University. We then present our work on Socio-Educational aspects of learning, such as multi-cultural issues from San-Diego State University, before concluding with a discussion on how these approaches might be integrated into a single framework.

Background

Online Learning Systems

The rapid evolution of information technology has led to new ways of learning and education. Many education institutions and corporations promote eLearning to provide better learning and teaching environments. Products such as WebCT[3] and Blackboard[4] have been in use for the past few years. Many online colleges such as the UK Open University[5], the Hong Kong Open University[6] and the Network Education College of Shanghai Jiao Tong University[7] have developed and deployed their own eLearning platform and infrastructure to provide adaptive and efficient eLearning services. Today, eLearning has become heavily learner-centred, emphasizing pervasive and personalized learning technologies (Thomas, 2008). As both the traditional classroom learning and web-based learning offer strengths and suffer from limitations, it is now a trend for eLearning systems to combine the best aspects of the two into blended learning (Kim 2007). Blended learning (BL) integrates seemingly opposite approaches, such as formal and informal learning, face-to-face and online experiences, directed paths and reliance on self-direction, and digital references and collegial connections (Rossett, Frazee, 2006). In our approach we blend natural class derived lectures, packaged in a classroom setting using both live video and simulated rooms, together with archived and offline activities afforded by the system and wider infrastructure.

Online Games

We contend that online education can benefit from developments in the computer games industry, which enjoys massive industrial investment. Thus, whilst this paper is not advocating the use of games as an instrument of learning (although we recognise this is a strong area of research in itself), we are arguing that there is potential synergy in the underlying technology platforms that can support both games and education. In particular, we have identified a commonality with virtual environments. As part of supporting this hypothesis, we review the relevant aspects of the games industry.

Originally computer games were designed to be used by a single person or a small group via a local network. However, with the advancement of the Internet, new categories of games emerged specially designed to exploit global connectivity. Online games, such as the *World of Warcraft* MMPORPG, (Massively Multiplayer Online Role-Playing Game) series by Blizzard Entertainment[8], brought simulator modelling to new levels by offering vast, highly detailed worlds to be simultaneously used by large numbers of online users. Broadband technology has allowed this medium to extend further, with higher data-transfer speeds making it possible for detailed worlds, normally found in offline games, to be brought online. The latest generations of computer games consoles have been designed for broadband Internet connectivity, allowing traditional offline game genres (such as racing) to be updated so players can challenge opponents online from anywhere in the world. The success of computer games that were designed to be played online has led to a new genre of online social communities (for example, Linden Labs, Second Life) where people can log-in to the virtual world "seeing" and "interacting" with other users, without any of the mission-based objectives or tournaments found in traditional online computer games. Second Life[9] has expanded to the point where businesses have been established in the virtual environment, with real-world money being exchanged for products and services traded within the virtualised space. Several real-world multinational companies and "high street brands" have opened their own Second Life virtual outlets[10], and some real countries, such as the Maldives and Sweden, have even created their own Second Life embassy[11]. Traditional universities are also beginning to offer services in

Figure 1. Sun's Wonderland Environment

online virtual worlds; for example, Harvard Law School set up a simulated courtroom in Second Life where students can practise their advocacy skills whereas Edinburgh University uses it to deliver an MSc course on eLearning (Shepherd 2007). Currently (2008), over one hundred higher education institutions are listed on the Second Life site with many enthusiastically pursuing the vision for a globally networked virtual classroom environment[12]. Another notable example is the Sun Microsystems' MPK20; a virtual meeting environment for supporting Sun's business activities[13].

In our work we are using such online social community game environments to host our virtual classroom environment, in particular, we have chosen Wonderland as our development platform (see figure 1). In the following paragraph we will discuss Second-Life and Wonderland in a little more detail, with a view of understanding the key issues, which affect the choice of platform.

The development of the Wonderland platform by Sun Microsystems was originally conceived as a tool to support collaborative working by the workforce within Sun. As such it had a number of clear design goals, which were to:

- Focus on social interaction, formal and informal
- To be emotionally salient
- Have a strong sense of social presence, allowing for discussion of sensitive topics
- Have spontaneous, unplanned interactions, particularly socializing before and after planned events to build trust
- Enhance communication during formal interactions
- Be designed for collaboration
- Have a seamless document sharing with no need to switch contexts
- Have extreme extensibility
- Allow developers to add any sort of new behaviour

As such the key strengths of Wonderland can be characterised as:

- Support for live application sharing
- Ability to integrate with business data
- Internal or external deployment options
- Highly scalable
- Support for very large to very small groups
- Open and extensible (open source, open art path)
- 100% Java
- Spatial audio as a core feature
- Extensive telephony integration

Figure 2. Milgram's Reality-Virtuality Continuum

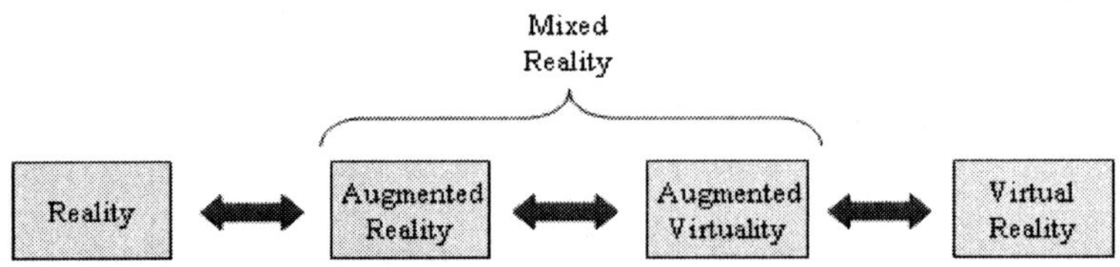

Wonderland is therefore very different to the commonly used SecondLife platform. The Wonderland platform is primarily intended to be tailored and integrated by organisations within their own infrastructures whereas Second Life is a publicly accessible online[14] service with very large numbers of users who can make use of a virtual economy to organise their lives. However, SecondLife has been used extensively by teaching institutions to carry out online teaching[15]. There is no doubt that SecondLife has been used very successfully to support online teaching and learning. However, there are several issues around its use, particularly concerned with the privacy and security for participants taking part in online sessions, and whether there are sufficient controls in place for organisations to use it as part of their formal teaching infrastructure.

At its core, SecondLife is a commercial operation which has its own set of imperatives. However, it does service a very large community (comScore reported nearly 1.3 million people logged in during March 2007), and particularly has key strengths in a number of areas, such as the ability to add behaviours to worlds using a rich scripting language (LindenScript) and the relative ease of creating 3D objects and adding them to the world.

As an alternative to SecondLife, there is the open source Opensim platform[16] which can be used to create a SecondLife-like environment, "able to run in a standalone mode or connected to other OpenSimulator instances through built in grid technology". The providers claim "it can also easily be extended to produce more specialized 3D interactive applications".

This is, in effect, a Second Life compatible server (Second Life has already open sourced their client), which can be installed and modified as needed by organisations. The OpenSim Grid capability is particularly interesting as it allows different worlds to be linked and promises to provide an easy mechanism for users to move between different worlds. However, it is not as platform-agnostic as Wonderland as it relies on the Mono and .Net software frameworks.

More advanced approaches are exploring connecting the real-world with a virtual environment. Collectively known as Mixed-Reality, this term can be broken down further using the Reality-Virtuality Continuum (see figure 2) (Milgram, Kishino, 1994) into: a) Augmented Reality, where the system consists of virtual components being added to a real-world environment (Hughes, Stapleton, Hughes, Smith, 2005); and b) Augmented Virtuality, where real-world features are added to a virtual environment (Davies, Callaghan, Shen, 2007) (Davies, Callaghan, Gardner, 2008). Such technological advances underpin our vision to bring innovative mixed-reality solutions to remote education environments.

Cultural Models for Designing Culturally Sensitive Instruction or Games

Teaching is a profoundly cultural act raising important socio-educational issues. Challenges associated with any cross-cultural interaction, such as the misunderstandings that arise from our unknown assumptions, also influence teaching and learning (Hall 76). As Pai and Adler argued, culture and education are inextricably related; and they "define" each other. "The processes of teaching and learning are influenced by the core values, beliefs, and attitudes, as well as the predominant cognitive and communication styles and linguistic patterns, of a culture" (Rogers, Wang, 2008).

With the increasing global outreach of online programs and courses, there is a great need to design and deliver online learning that can be engaging to a culturally diverse audience. Several models have been suggested for creating online instruction, each illuminating important considerations. Researchers have suggested adding a cultural dimension to the widely used instructional design model--ADDIE (Analyze, Design, Develop, Implement, and Evaluate) (Thomas, Mitchell, Joseph, 2002). This cultural dimension consists of intention, interaction, and introspection. The intentional attribute of learning would encourage the designer to consider and make their cultural bias explicit. The interaction parameter would involve the collaboration of designer, subject-matter expert, and end-user throughout the model phases to facilitate the melding of culture into the end product. Finally, introspection on the part of designer ensures that he or she is considering his or her own thoughts, beliefs, attitudes, desires, and feelings toward the cultures represented in the instruction. A Cultural Adaptation Process model has been proposed that helps to categorize culturally adapt materials for particular learner groups based on the type of content, instructional methods, and media used (Edmundson 2007). A "multiple cultures model" emphasizes the importance for sustainable learning outcomes to include elements from both the learner's own culture and those from the emerging global academic or training culture (from industry, government, or higher educational institutions) (Henderson 1996).

Because of the instant nature of the interaction, virtual learning environments (including online games) pose greater need for cultural considerations. In addition, a game itself is a cultural activity and it thrives on being interesting and engaging to players around the world. Players need to be able to communicate, share understandings, follow the same rules and be part of an international team to carry out the tasks as designed. However, the aforementioned models address cultural issues in designing or conducting formal instruction. Social and cultural aspects of online games are becoming a popular research topic. In this chapter, we attempt to address some of the cultural challenges when adopting learning and games technology in virtual or hybrid environments. It is worth noting that whilst this project is operating as an international collaboration, our initial deployment plans are to provide the service within a single country (looking at the consequences to the technology for differing cultural settings). In later work we plan to extend this to address cross cultural operation (eg supporting students in multiple cultures). In the following we first introduce the host eLearning environment (the Shanghai Jiao Tong NEC); we then describe the virtual reality environment that will be added to it (the Essex MiRTLE system).

THE SHANGHAI E-LEARNING PLATFORM

The e-Learning system developed at the SJTU Network Education College (NEC) acts as the host platform for the virtual reality-learning environment (MiRTLE). As such the NEC platform provides the essential infrastructure to manage and deliver lectures to students in a real classroom, at home or even outdoors. Currently, the SJTU NEC delivers varied education to some 17,000 China based students. The philosophy underpinning the SJTU NEC is that natural classrooms and traditional teaching are the best means to deliver high quality education to students. Thus, the researchers and developers have made great effort to leverage existing and emerging ICTs to augment the function of a traditional classroom and to digitalize the content, so as to deliver lessons to geographically distributed students. At the same time much effort has been made to give the online students a feeling of being in a real class wherever they may reside.

The Shanghai e-Learning platform provides "always on" hybrid learning services which are accomplished through extending the real classrooms and also supporting web-based adaptive learning. The core of the platform are distributed Standard Natural Classrooms (SNC), which are high-tech spaces to provide natural human-machine interaction and context-aware services for teachers and students (see figure 3). They are equipped with numerous smart devices/sensors and specially developed software. The fully interactive lectures are then delivered to PCs, laptops, PDA, IPTV and mobile phones in real-time by using large-scale media streaming to multi-mode terminals through heterogeneous networks. Enabling this real-time (live) connection between the teacher and students is a considerable challenge, but this is a distinguishing feature of the Shanghai approach. Later, we will explain how the virtual classroom seeks to promote further the natural classroom model, by providing a simulated online classroom that aids dispersed online learners to feel part of a real class.

The Standard Natural Classrooms (SNC)

As was explained earlier, the motivation underpinning the work at Shanghai Jiao Tong e-Learning Lab is to create teaching and learning environments that are as natural as the technology allows. This contrasts to most other approaches that are akin to television studios or videoconference systems. In many of these systems teachers are required to remain at a computer, using the keyboard and mouse to manage the lecture that, in addition to limiting interaction, scalability, mobility and maintenance also loses much of the effectiveness of traditional classroom education. This weakness is widely recognised and much effort has been made to bridge the gap between real-time remote classroom and traditional classroom activities in

Figure 3. A typical SNC in use at the online college

projects such as the Tsinghua University Smart Classroom (Shi, Xie, Xu, 2003].

By supplementing real classrooms with pervasive computing technologies we have created numerous SNCs across China. These classrooms are equipped with high-tech devices, tools and software infrastructure that are configured in a unified *standard* way. In these classrooms, teachers can move freely, use multiple *natural* modalities to give the lecture and interact with remote students as they would in traditional classrooms. The classrooms are interconnected through broadband IP network or through two-way satellite links. Depending on the student's circumstance they can select to attend the class in person (where the lecturer is), visit a remote centre (with an interactive video feed of the lecture) or view the lectures in their own home or on a mobile phone. Figure 4 shows the classroom setup of a typical SNC in use at NEC. The touch screen display and interactive whiteboard and presentations (e.g. PowerPoint) allow the lectures to be delivered whilst capturing spontaneous interaction such as handwriting. A special 'Laser e-pen' gives the lecturer the freedom to write from any position in the classroom. To optimize the video scene, a pan-camera automatically tracks the instructor when he/she moves about in the classroom. An additional camera faces the students to measure their attention, which provides useful feedback to the teacher when optimising the pace of the lecture. A feedback screen, facing the lecturer, displays the questions and poll results, which the teachers can use to fine-tune their lecturing. Other devices are provided to collect contextual information and to control the classroom equipment. For example, RFID (Radio Frequency IDentifier) tags are used to identify and track students and occupancy sensors manage the lighting. Using this hi-tech environment, the teacher can move freely, demonstrate his body language, and interact with learners as naturally and easily as in a traditional face-to-face classroom.

Technologies are leveraged to support multimodal interactions in our SNCs. The students-teachers interactive communication is dealt with in a natural way through handwriting, audio command and laser pen, thus eliminating the limit of desktop based interaction in traditional tele-education systems. In previous studies this has been found to help change students from passive learners, frequently observed in traditional eLearning, to engaged learners who are behaviourally, intellectually, and emotionally involved in their learning tasks (Wang 2007). During lectures, the live classroom scenes are transmitted to remote SNCs and displayed on wall-mounted large screens. Simultaneously, video from the remote SNC are transmitted back to the lecturer. For learners using PC at home or mobile devices, the live teacher's video is delivered together with the audio and lecture notes (but without any backwards transmission of video from the student's to the lecturer's environment). When a teacher talks to a specific student, this student's video is transmitted to all the SNCs. The teacher can use voice-commands to perform some common actions such as "next slide" or "previous slide". Students can send text messages to the instructor through their cell phone using an SMS (Short Message Service) or the text window of the SNC system. Students' messages will be displayed on the instructor's feedback screen, to inform the instructor of their learning progress, questions, or any other feedback, that the instructor could respond to.

In a similar way to writing on chalkboards or whiteboards in a traditional classroom, teachers may write on the touch screen with an electronic pen. Such electronic pen writing has the advantage for students of allowing greater focus on the lecture (without the distraction of writing)

Figure 4. The typical SNC setup

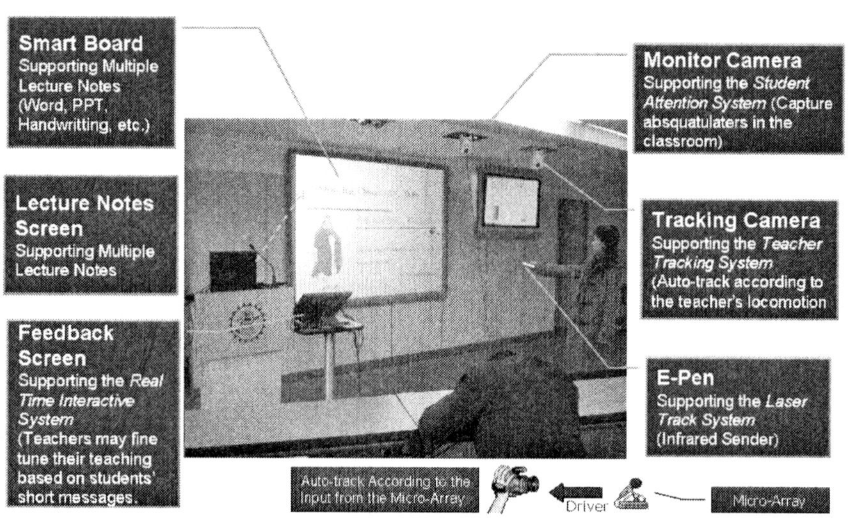

and sharing a common writing medium between remote environments (including remote students using PCs or mobile devices). For instance, a student might write the solution to a question that the teacher has just posed. The teacher's freedom is further enhanced as the laser pointer allows them to write on the projected screen. Emotion aware technology is also employed and is described in the MiRTLE section.

Large Scale Media Streaming

The aim of pervasive learning is to enable learners to access education resources using any available network devices anytime, anywhere. The SJTU NEC platform supports three types of multimedia access:

- Live lecture broadcast
- Lecture-on-demand (LOD)
- Downloading archived lectures

The challenges here range from the adaptation of educational content based on the current context (eg device computing capacity, screen size and network bandwidth etc) to considerations of efficient and reliable media transmission for large-scale concurrent user access.

Typical media streaming e-Learning systems are one-to-many (eg one lecture delivered to many locations) or, less frequently, many-to-many (eg tutorial or project discussions). One-to-many multicasting can dramatically improve the network bandwidth efficiency. Multicast can be either performed in Internet Protocol (IP) layer or application layer. IP multicast has the advantage of efficiency, but the critical requirements of routers, scalable inter-domain routing protocols and robust congestion control mechanisms make it difficult to implement on heterogeneous inter-networks such as CERNET (Chinese Education and Research NETwork), telecom ADSL, dial-up network or mobile networks. Application layer multicast is based on a high-level virtual network leveraging unicast to perform multicast by data replication. As there is no need for support from routers, flexible congestion control mechanisms could be exploited to ensure the quality of data transmission. In recent years, application layer multicast (ALM) has gained more attention amongst researchers. In pervasive learning environments, users are either based in remote classrooms, at home or mobile with users being distributed as a sparse mix of heterogeneous technologies. Therefore, our implementation takes the form of a hybrid multicast model that combines ALM and IP multicast running on a tree-like network topology. Data is distributed in two ways, either in the form of tunnel distribution (based on UDP unicast at the application layer across different multicast domains) or IP multicast within a multicast domain.

We also provide content adaption for different user devices, especially for mobile users. When participating in live class, students presently have four media configuration options:

1. Active presentation (eg PowerPoint), audio, and a small video of the real-time classroom,
2. Video and audio of the instructor only,
3. Enlarged display of the active presentation with audio
4. Close-up display of the instructor's facial expressions and their body language with audio.

A recent survey at SJTU NEC revealed that 85% of the students prefer option 1 (Wang, Shen, Novak, Pan, 2008**).** The students generally held the opinion that the presentation, audio, and video mode provided a better context for learning. One factor was that this configuration gave a better feeling of being in a real classroom with the instructor and many other students nearby. Catering to this need we have provided three types of media streams for mobile users:

1. An instructor's presentation screen from his desktop
2. The instructor's facial expressions from a video camera, and
3. An audio stream of an instructor's voices from a microphone.

Mobile phones need a GPRS (General Packet Radio Service) or CDMA (Code Division Multiple Access) capability to work with the eLearning platform. However, GPRS bandwidth is relatively small, being approximately 28.8kbps for downloading and 10kbps for uploading. Thus each of the three streams is reduced to 8kbps, so that it can fit to the available bandwidth of GPRS. Figure 5 shows a typical display on the mobile phone (Nokia 6600).

Adaptive and Personalized Web-Based Learning Services

The web-based learning system provides services which students can use to conduct asynchronous self-paced learning anytime anywhere. It comprises the following components:

1. Content based retrieval search engine - enables the students to find their desired materials conveniently and quickly
2. Answer machine - responds to students' questions automatically,
3. Data analysis centre and self-organized learning community - analyses students learning patterns and provides personalized services
4. Miscellaneous tools - assignment system and examination system.

We now, by way of an example, introduce the data analysis centre. E-Learning classes can be an order of magnitude larger than traditional classrooms. This raises several challenges such as a much-increased diversity in student ability and progress. E-Learning students come from different backgrounds, bear highly diverse knowledge structures and work in every walk of life. Thus, a challenge is, given such diversity, how do we provide personalized services based on the learner profiles and learning behaviours? Furthermore, how do we provide feedback on learning states to teachers? In order to answer these questions, we have developed a component we refer to as the Data Analysis Centre, to monitor the whole process of teaching and learning, to analysis the student study behaviour, and to provide personalized learning services (see figure 6). As is well known, learning behaviour is very complex. During the learning process, learners may browse

Figure 5. Live lecture on a mobile phone Nokia 6600

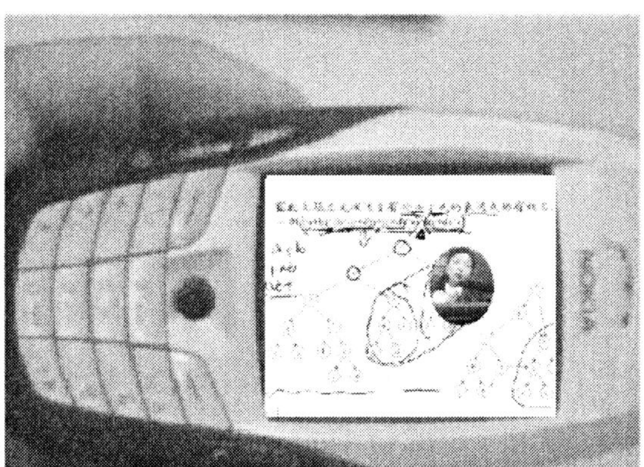

online courses, query the course materials, submit questions, perform examinations, and so on. All of these behaviours represent the learning interest and intent of the learners. We collect all these activities in log-files for further analysis.

Both traditional and online learners experience deficiencies rooted in their isolation, sometimes described as 'lonely learning'. To address this issue we employ collaborative learning methodologies where we group learners into communities of similar educational state and introduce learning that requires group interaction. Every learner, in a learning community, is either the consumer or the provider of knowledge and the learning goals are fulfilled through students helping each other. We implemented a prototype of self-organizing learning community to cluster learners automatically, which helps learners share their learning experiences and exchange learning materials during the learning process (Yang, Han, Shen, Kraemer, Fan, 2003).

As we explained at the outset, our philosophy is to mirror the natural teaching environment as closely as the available technology allows. One particular issue we have encountered is that geographically dispersed learners (eg on a PC in their home) can have a feeling of isolation. In a natural classroom, learners can see and talk to each other. They get both a social and academically supportive presence. In a bid to try to recreate some of the elements of a natural classroom, we have embarked on work of creating g a virtual classroom, where representations of students, in the form of avatars (from games), can inhabit a shared space, either socialising or providing mutual support. Our work towards these aims is described in the following sections.

MIRTLE

The objective of the MiRTLE (Mixed Reality Teaching & Learning Environment) is to provide an online virtual classroom to augment the Shanghai Jiao Tong e-Learning platform described earlier. It is intended to provide a mixed reality environment for a combination of local and remote students (both dispersed and local students are able to see and talk with each other, in addition to the teacher). The environment is intended to augment existing teaching practice with the ability to foster a sense of community amongst remote students, and between remote and co-located locations. In this sense, the mixed reality environment links the physical and virtual worlds.

The Mixed Reality Teaching Environment

Our longer-term vision is to create an entire mixed-reality campus but in this paper we describe the core component: a mixed-reality classroom. In the physical classroom the lecturer is able to deliver the lecture in their normal way but they will have a large display screen mounted at the back of the room that shows avatars of the remote students

Figure 6. Data analysis centre

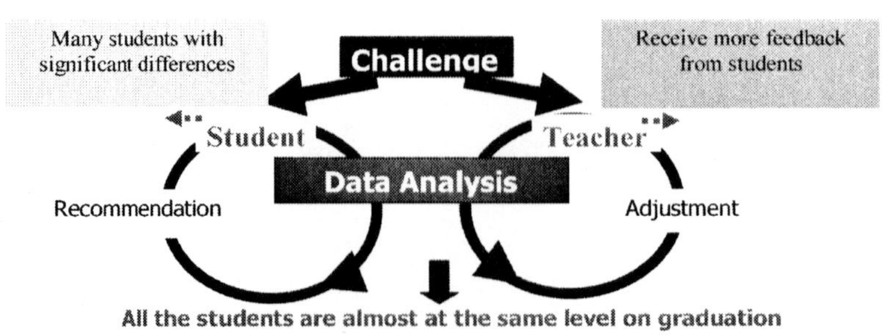

who are logged into the virtual counterpart of the classroom.

Thus the lecturer will be able to see and interact with a mix of students who are present in both the real and virtual world (see figure 7). Audio communication between the lecturer and the remote students is made possible via a voice bridge. A camera is placed on the rear wall of the room to deliver a live audio and video stream of the lecture into the virtual world.

From the remote students' perspective, they will log into the MiRTLE virtual world and enter the classroom where the lecture is taking place. Here they will see a live video of the lecture as well as any slides that are being presented, or an application that the lecturer is using (see figure 8). Spatial audio is employed to enhance their experience such that it is closer to the real world. They have the opportunity to ask questions just as they would in the physical world via audio communication. Additionally a messaging window is provided that allows written questions or discussion to take place.

In addition to the virtual-classroom, the MiRTLE virtual world offers a common room where students can meet socially. A demonstration room is provided which is populated with a whiteboard, slideshows and NPCs that, for example, provide an audio commentary to describe the MiRTLE project itself. We intend that this will provide an environment for vicarious learning to take place.

The Mixed Reality Technology

MiRTLE is built using open source tools, in particular the Sun Microsystems' Darkstar Project and Wonderland platforms. Sun's Project Darkstar[17] is a computational infrastructure to support online gaming (Burns, 2007). Project Wonderland[18] is a client-server architecture and set of technologies to support the development of immersive online simulations, virtual and mixed reality environments. A noteworthy example of this is Sun's MPK20 application; a virtual building designed for online real-time meetings between geographically distributed Sun employees.

Wonderland

In more detail, Project Wonderland[19] is based on several technologies including Project Looking Glass to generate a scene and jVoiceBridge[20] for

Figure 7. Lecturer view of remotely located students

adding high fidelity immersive audio. The graphical content that creates the visible world as well as the screen buffers controlling the scene currently uses Java3D. Additional objects/components to Wonderland (such as a camera device to record audio and video, as seen from a client), make use of other technologies such as the Java Media Framework[21]. Graphical content can be added to a Wonderland world by creating objects using a graphics package such as Blender or Maya. Project Wonderland, including Sun's exemplar MPK20 environment, is being developed as an open source project that is open to all members of the software development community. However, users of Project Wonderland are not restricted to developers; the project also provides binaries that can be downloaded and extended with user-developed content and worlds.

Project Wonderland provides a rich set of objects for creating environments, such as building structures (eg walls) and furniture (eg desks). An additional feature of Wonderland is its provision of shared applications: standard software applications, such as word processors, web browsers and document presentation tools, can be used and shared by all participants. Thus, for example, a virtual whiteboard can be drawn on by one or several users and PDF documents and the presentations can be viewed. Blender has been used to create the objects that populate the world. These objects are then exported to the X3D open standards file format for use in the world. To aid ease of use, and to ensure that users receive the current version of the client, Java Web Start Technology[22] has been employed.

A distinguishing feature of Project Wonderland is its support of spatially realistic audio, enabling participants to converse and experience a sense of audio direction and intensity of those they are talking to, or hearing in the distance.

A user is represented as an avatar. There are currently two types of avatar featured in the Wonderland environment. First are NPCs (Non-player characters), which are static in the virtual world, often forming background characters, providing audio explanations over the voice-bridge, or otherwise just simply adding to the general ambience of the environment via private conversations

Figure 8. Student view of lecture

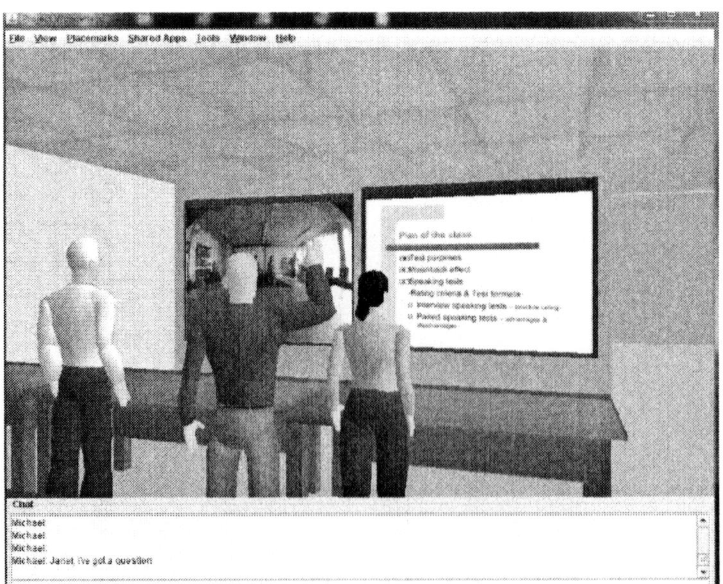

between two people. The other type of avatar is the PC (Player Character), which individually represents a single user. Each PC is capable of walking around the virtual world (displayed via an animation). Eventually it is intended that a PC would have an appearance similar to that of its real-world (human) controller, however at the moment, unless coded with a specific template, a simple avatar is automatically generated upon login. To aid identification, each PC avatar is augmented with the login name of its controller. A controller can speak through their avatar to others in the world via the voice-bridge and a microphone and speaker, or use a dedicated chat window for text-based messages. The scene generated by Wonderland can be viewed from first-person or several third-person perspectives. We have used this technology to develop a virtual classroom.

Emotion Aware Technology

In a traditional class, the flow of leaning material between teacher and student is mediated by both verbal (eg questions) and non-verbal (eg a perplexed look) communication. Most teachers recognise that emotion plays a crucial role in motivation, interest, and attention but, in most current online learning systems, there has been a bias towards the cognitive and relative neglect of the affective needs of a student (Picard, Papert, Bender, Blumberg, Breazeal, Cavallo 2004). It has been shown that the human brain is not just purely a cognitive information processing system, but also a system in which both affective functions and cognitive functions are inextricably integrated with each other (Isen 2000). Whilst most online virtual worlds support language communication (eg text, verbal), apart from emoticons in text messaging, there is little non-language based communication support in online environments. In virtual worlds, this problem becomes more acute as avatar representations are used in place of video views of people. Given the importance of none verbal communication in teaching (eg being able to observe the emotional state of a recipient of learning material), supporting this is important if virtual worlds are to be successful for online learning. However, providing such technology presents a formidable challenge. The most widely used techniques in affect recognition involve facial expressions and body gestures (Chen, Huang 2000) (De Silva, Miyasato, Nakatsu, 1997), speech (Amir, Ron, 1998) (Dellaert, Polzin, Waibel, 1996), physiology (Leon, Clarke, Callaghan, Sepulveda 2007) (Lisetti, Nasov, 2004) or a combination of multiple modalities.

In the MiRTLE project we have addressed this issue by developing an emotion sensing system based on interpreting physiological signals from a small 'skin contact' sensor connected to a Sun Small Programmable Object Technology (SPOT)[23] wearable wireless computer (see figure

Figure 9. The physiological emotion sensing hardware

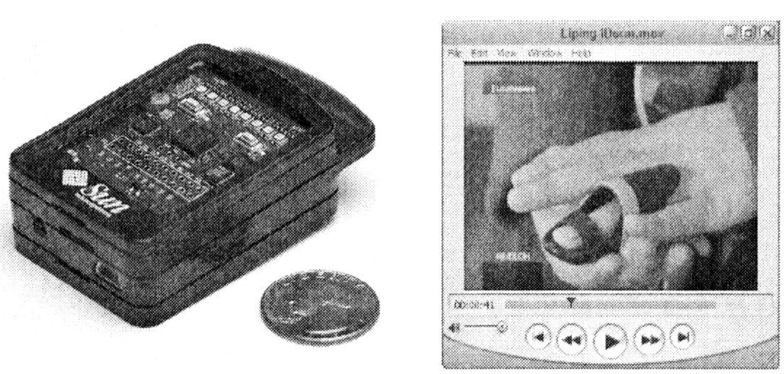

9) as a means of interfacing between physical and virtual worlds.

Emotion recognition methods based on physiological signals have been widely researched and offer some advantages when compared to alternative techniques. They are well suited for real-time use (Leon, 2007) and can recognise a plethora of distinct emotions. The only requirement is the use of a biophysical sensor which is usually small and non intrusive. The MiRTLE sensor takes the form of a finger clip, shown in figure 9. It has been shown that emotions can be described in terms of arousal (degree of excitement) and valence (negative/ positive emotion) (Lang, 1995). A model of emotion, as a function or arousal and valance, was proposed by Russel (figure 10) (Russel, 1980). Skin resistance has been shown to be a useful way of sensing arousal (Picard 2001] and heart-rate provides a method of obtaining valence (Hanjalic, 2006).

We have conducted a preliminary study on an affective model for eLearning that uses the system shown in figure 9 to detect emotions from physiological signals (Shen 2007) (Kalkanis 2008) (Shen 2008). In more detail, the physiological data for emotion detection used by our prototype is derived from two bio-sensors measuring skin conductance (SC) sensor measuring electrodermal activity and a photoplethysmograph measuring blood volume pressure (BVP) and heart rate. Using this prototype we have achieved a best-case accuracy (86.5%) for four types of learning emotions (Shen 08). Emotions are shown on avatars as colours, which are then interpreted by other occupants of the shared virtual space (both students and teachers).

In addition we are investigating the use of this technology on the core SJTU e-Learning platform to act as a context sensor, which would automatically mediate the flow of educational content to learners using, for example, mobile phones. We are also using the emotional data to provide a class 'emotion meter' to provide composite feedback to lectures, so they can adjust their delivery accordingly (Shen 07).

MiRTLE Deployment Issues

Figure 11 illustrates the deployment of MiRTLE within a basic institutional infrastructure. The key components for MiRTLE are the Wonderland server which hosts the virtual world and manages

Figure 10. Russell's Circumplex Model of Affect

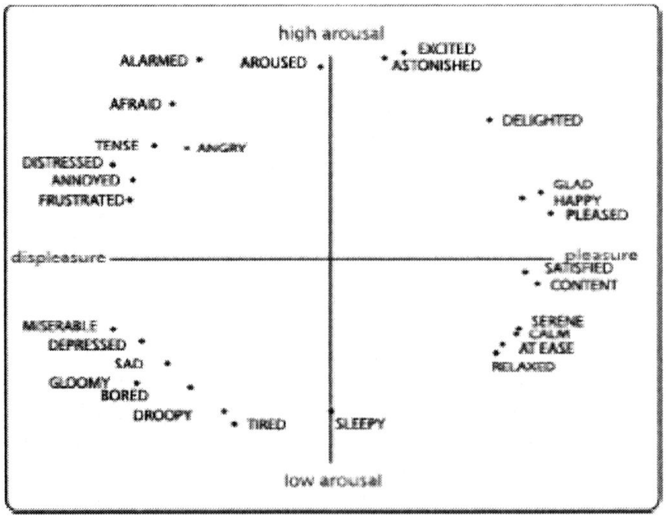

Figure 11. MiRTLE installation

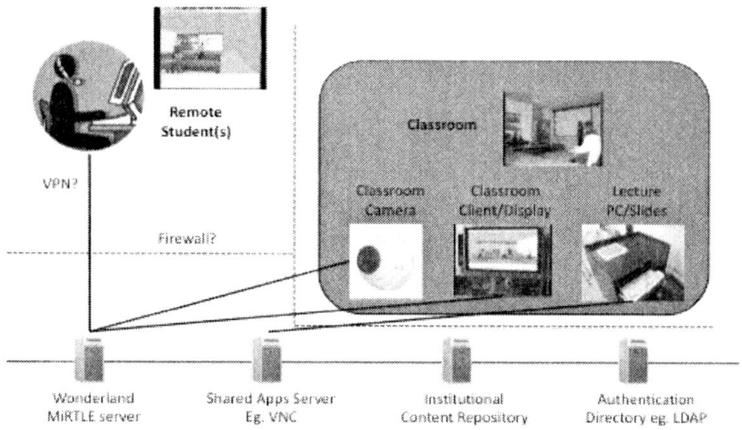

the interaction with the client machines, and a shared applications server that uses VNC (Virtual Network Computing) to host shared applications that are used within the MiRTLE world (e.g. shared office applications, web-browsers, desktops, etc). This shared application server is particularly important, as it is used by a real-time class to host the display of the lecturers presentation, which is synchronised with the main display in the real lecture room and the in-world display to the online students. This ensures that the students in the real classroom see the same slides as the students in the virtual classroom. At the time of writing (2008) the cost of such a minimal entry-level system is of the order $25,000.

Mirtle has been designed to be used by non-technical people. From the lecturers point of view working in Mirtle should be no different to their normal routine of using the class audio/visual podium to control their slides. This is however, just the minimal set of components required to host MiRTLE. Most institutions would also make use of content repositories and learning management systems (such as Moodle) to manage their content and lecture materials. Also, there is an authentication system that controls access to university resources, which can make use of a user directory (such as LDAP) and identity management controls. Thus, the implementation requires a number of key components to be integrated together.

Further complications may arise depending on the intended use of the system. For example, if the MiRTLE system is only intended for internal use within a university, it is likely that most of the system components will reside behind the universities firewall. However, given the system is designed to support remote students this may then require a VPN (Virtual Private Network) to be setup to allow remote users (e.g. students at home) to log into the system and make use of these university resources. Alternatively it is possible to consider a hybrid solution where certain components (such as the main MiRTLE server, classroom camera, etc) are publicly accessible, and other components (such as the institutional content repository) remain behind the universities firewall. This is further complicated when more advanced scenarios are considered, such as having multiple MiRTLE teaching rooms located in different institutions, and with remote students also participating from different locations. This would require the use of a federated access management system (such as Shibboleth) to control and manage access to all of the shared system resources within a given federation, allowing Darkstar-based students access to the full range of educational media available in the SNC.

As in the existing Shanghai platform, to access the system students need to use the Internet (broadband or GPRS) to log onto the Sun Darkstar server in Shanghai that, in turn, will create an avatar representation of them (which they will have previously selected as part of customising their account). We are planning to use such customisation as one of the vehicles to explore the effects of cultural diversity by providing a rich set of operational modes that will reflect social preferences. For example, students will be able to create environments in which they are isolated or highly social avatars. Likewise the amount of personalised information available to other online students will be under their control, as will some of the options for interaction with lecturers and other students. In the following section we will discus some of these issues.

SOCIO-EDUCATIONAL ISSUES

Cultural Effects in Student Engagement

With the increasing global outreach of online programs and courses, designing and delivering online learning that can be engaging to a global audience is an area that is in need of more systematic research. Recent studies have revealed that learning outcomes improve when learners are better engaged in learning, such as by establishing their own goals, exploring appropriate resources, and working with others in groups (Picciano, 2002) (Wang, 20004) (Wang, 2006). In an online setting, students may present themselves cognitive, socially, and emotively (Wang, 2007). Social presence is about presenting oneself as a "real person" in a virtual learning environment. Cognitive presence is about sharing information and resources, and constructing new knowledge. Emotive presence is about learner's expression about their feelings of self, the community, the learning atmosphere, and the learning process. Research into online pedagogies (Cybergogy) of engaged learning through information and communication technologies shows that students learn better when they are socially, cognitively, and emotively immersed in the learning process (Wang,2006).

Cultural attributes, however, can affect online presence and learner perceptions. Learners' cultural attributes affects how they perceive an online learning setting and how they present themselves online, cognitively, socially, and emotively (Wang, 2006) (Wang C, 2007). Therefore, it is essential that cross-cultural issues in online learning be examined more critically (Rogers, 2008). With the increasing global outreach of online programs and courses, there is a great need to design and deliver online learning that can be engaging to a culturally diverse audience. In the following section we will discuss some of the issues concerned with integrating these approaches on the Shanghai e-Learning platform that will guide our research agenda for our next phase of work.

Privacy Issues and Control of Virtual Environments

Privacy is a sensitive issue in pervasive computing systems, one that critically affects the acceptance of networked services by consumers (Callaghan, 2008) (Shadbolt, 2008). A key concern for the use of online services like Second Life is the potential lack of control of the online space, and the privacy of participants taking part, especially given this is an open access commercial platform. Privacy and security is addressed by the Wonderland platform, which aims to solve the problem through the use of its own dedicated open client-server architecture, which can be fully integrated with whatever access and control mechanisms are required. This increasing need to protect data and resources available within virtual worlds is considered by Timothy Wright from the University of Notre Dame in the WonderDAC project[24]. In this project, access in virtual worlds is broadly classified into the following 3 types:

- spatial access (who can move their avatar where)
- media access (who can view which images or hear what sounds)
- object use/mutability (who can use and change which VR objects)

Most commercial online systems only consider rudimentary spatial access control and ignore more detailed control requirements. WonderDAC (Wonderland with discretionary access control) has developed a simple prototype, to add basic discretionary access controls to the Project Wonderland platform. Further plans are in place to evolve WonderDAC along several lines: spatial object access, non-spatial object access, audio chat access, avatar cloaking, and access to WonderDAC information through a user interface. This is illustrated in figure 12, where the avatar 'twright' is able to see more content than the avatar 'bench-40' based on the access control settings.

Pedagogical Implications for the Use of Virtual Environments

Previous research has reported on the need to consider pedagogical principles in the design of new e-learning services (Gardner, 2003). Much of our previous work has been based on adapting the Mayes conceptual framework as a tool to aid in the design and evaluation of e-learning services (Mayes, 95). There is a need for conceptual frameworks that bridge theory and design. Mayes offers such a framework which describes three broad modes of learning which are mapped onto appropriate design principles. The modes or stages of learning are:

- Conceptualisation - the coming into contact with other people's concepts.
- Construction - the building and testing of one's knowledge through the performance of meaningful tasks.
- Dialogue - the debate and discussion that results in the creation of new concepts.

It is important to note that 'conceptualisation' is about other people's concepts, 'construction' is about building knowledge from combining one's own and other people's concepts into something meaningful. 'Dialogue' refers to the creation of new concepts (rather than knowledge) that triggers another cycle of the re-conceptualisation process.

Figure 12. Discretionary access control in WonderDAC

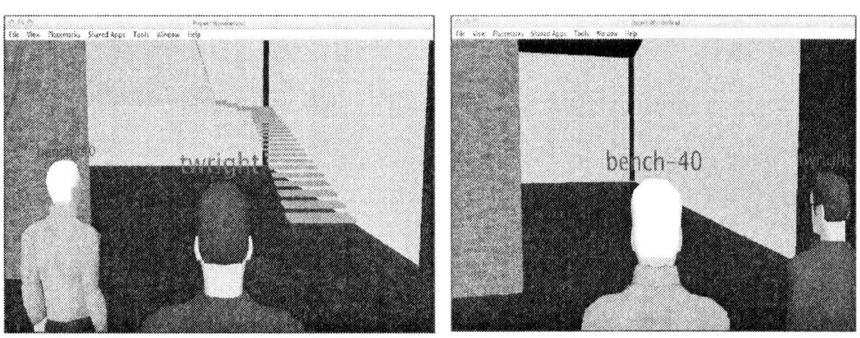

Much of our earlier work was based on the use of so-called Web 1.0 technologies, and mapping these to appropriate stages of the Mayes conceptual framework. In MiRTLE we are considering how this can now be extended to include immersive environments. Some useful progress has been achieved by considering this in terms of social networking theories, including the notion of different types of learning relationships (Fowler, 99). However, in terms of virtual environments such as MiRTLE, we need to consider how guidance can be provided to fully exploit the characteristics of these environments. In particular, we need to go beyond just purely emulating current practise (which in effect is what MiRTLE is doing in terms of using a virtual environment to support online lectures), to exploring new innovative ways of exploiting this technology, which build on the key affordances of virtual reality.

Once characteristic of virtual environments that seems to offer the most opportunity for innovation is that of 'immersion'. In that it is possible to immerse students in different ways according to their educational need. This has been mapped back to the Mayes framework and is illustrated in figure 13. In this figure, we have identified characteristics of immersion, which are relevant to each of the three stages of the Mayes framework. So for the conceptualization stage, the main emphasis should be on the psychological immersion of the student in the abstract space of the learning domain. For example, this could be achieved graphically by representing the key concepts and relationships of the subject matter, and allowing the student to explore these concepts within the 3D space. For the construction stage, the main emphasis is on the physical immersion of the student within the context of the learning domain. Here we could simulate a particular problem-based learning scenario, allowing the student to experiment with the course of their actions, through this scenario. Finally for the dialogue stage, the main emphasis is on the social immersion of the student with a given social network. Here we consider how the virtual world can facilitate social interaction and collaboration around different domains.

Clearly there remains some way to go in fully developing these approaches. However, if we are to truly offer new and innovative teaching and learning within virtual reality then it is vital that the development of these systems is grounded within an appreciation of the pedagogy and proper design guidelines.

INTEGRATED SYSTEM

Figure 14 provides a view of the combined Mirtle and NEC system architecture. In this, SNCs are equipped with numerous cameras and media

Figure 13. Mayes and virtual reality

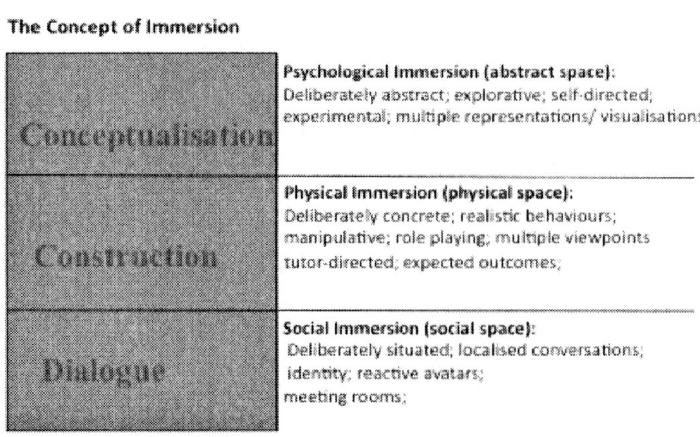

devices that are offered to the network via a set of powerful media servers. Concurrently another server runs a copy of Sun's Darkstar that maintains an instance of a simulated SNC.

Video and audio feeds from the NEC media servers are coupled to the Darkstart server that merges the live and simulated feeds and offers them to the wider network. Students using the system use the network to connect either directly to the NEC server, or indirectly via the Darkstar server, which encapsulates the media streams within a virtualised classroom environment. By connecting to either server the remote students can either get direct media feeds or versions wrapped within virtualised classroom delivered to a range of devices such as PCs, laptops, PDAs, IPTVs and mobile phones. Network connections are effected through various networks such as Shanghai Telecom ADSL, GPRS, IPTV, two-way satellite and the Internet. Cultural aspects are encoded as rules and policies as part of the personalisation system, The backend systems consist of the existing e-Learning services described earlier. From figure 14, the system can be seen to be composed of the following main parts:

a) Standard natural Classrooms: Interconnected classrooms fitted with technology to provide natural human-machine interaction and context-aware services for teachers and students
b) Virtual Classroom server: A Sun Darkstar server that maintains an instance of the virtual classroom and all the user avatars
c) NEC Media Servers: Large-scale media streaming (for multi-mode terminals) delivering fully interactive lectures to PCs, laptops, PDA, IPTV and mobile phones through heterogeneous networks
d) Personalised Services: Providing multiple services for learning management and quality control, such as dynamic learning services, collaborative learning communities and personalized recommendations. These personalisation services are where the cultural rules and policies are contained
e) Courseware Centre: A searchable repository for recorded lectures and supporting learning material

Our work to-date has focused on the technology design, which has been the principal focus of the discussion in this chapter. However, we recognize that as our work progresses the user behaviour, in respect to configuration choices, offers a rich source of research data. For example, choices of virtual versus video environments, use of archived versus live and media preferences can all be instructive for both the underlying technology design and understanding cultural preferences. Likewise, in addition to its role in learning, the emotional feedback intrinsic to the system could provide a useful insight into user issues. Clearly, this is an ambitious vision, with much work remaining to be completed and we look forward to reporting out findings at the various stages of our ongoing research.

SUMMARY

This paper describes a conceptual framework aimed at the creation of a pervasive eLearning platform, sensitive to socio-educational issues, that has the potential to harness emerging technology to support the new globalised digital economy by providing anytime, anywhere, anyone learning.

We have built and tested the Standard Natural Classroom (SNC), the Virtual Classroom (Mirtle) and the affective learning system but, at the time of writing, whilst these have been used and evaluated independently, we have not integrated them nor evaluated them as an integrated whole. Thus, for now, and until we complete this work, this remains a conceptual framework. However, whilst still at an early stage, these are real working

Figure 14. The integrated system

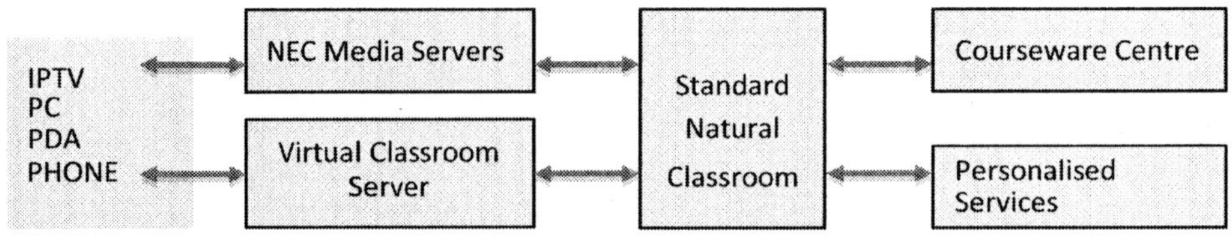

systems and we hope that sharing the knowledge we have gained so far will prove useful to others who may be considering such systems.

A fundamental axiom of the Shanghai work is that the learning environment should be as natural (close to the traditional classroom) as the technology will allow. This is facilitated on the Shanghai platform by employing real-time interactive media feeds direct from an actual classroom connecting real students and teachers. Mirtle extends this principle by seeking to provide a means to counter the isolation of remote students who, in traditional eLearning settings, are unable to benefit from the social or collaborative attributes of a natural classroom,

In this work we have explored the feasibility of employing technology that is more commonly used for games which, in addition to increasing the natural ambience of online learning, brings considerable cost and technology synergies by adopting the massive online-games market technology for online-education.

We have discussed various socio-educational issues including culture, privacy and pedagogy. We have recognized the role that social and collaborative learning groups have in learning and we have identified that one of the drawbacks of existing eLearning enterprises is that they are generally devoid of such support. Our principal addition to the e-Learning system was a mechanism to provide such a social sense. Likewise, in order to realise this vision for a globalised pervasive learning environment, we need to understand and cater for the effects of differing cultures. To those ends we are including considerations of the needs of culture in our technological design. For example, the amount and type of interactivity is configurable and avatar appearance will have a multicultural dimension. Finally, we recognise that other human qualities can play an important factor in learning performance and, as part of the social-educational space, we have devised an emotion monitoring and mediation system, as part of this experimental framework.

ACKNOWLEDGMENT

We are very pleased to acknowledge John Scott and Marc Davies whose work has contributed to this chapter. We are grateful to Sun Microsystems for financial support of the MiRTLE project and gratefully acknowledge the key role that Bernard Horan and Kevin Roebuck have played in making the MiRTLE project more than a virtual reality.

REFERENCES

Amir, N., & Ron, S. (1998). Toward automatic classification of emotions in speech. In *Proceedings of ICSLP* (pp. 555–558).

Callaghan, V., Clarke, G., & Chin, J., (2008). Some socio-technical aspects of intelligent buildings and pervasive computing research. *Intelligent Buildings International Journal*, 1(1).

Chen, L., & Huang, T. (2000). Emotional expressions in audiovisual human computer interaction. In *Proceedings of ICME* (pp. 423–426).

Clarke, G., & Callaghan, V. (2007). Ubiquitous computing, informatization, urban structures and density. *Built Environment Journal, 33*(2). Burns, B. (2007). *Darkstar: The Java game server*. Sebastopol, CA: O'Reilly.

Davies, M., Callaghan, V., & Gardner, M. (2008). Towards a mixed reality intelligent campus. In *Proceedings of IET International Conference on Intelligent Environments 2008*, Seattle (pp. 21-22).

Davies, M., Callaghan, V., & Shen, L. (2007). Modelling pervasive environments using bespoke & commercial game-based simulators. In *2nd International Conference on Life System Modelling and Simulation (LSMS'07),* Shanghai, China.

De Silva, L., Miyasato, T., & Nakatsu, R. (1997). Facial emotion recognition using multimodal information. In *Proceedings of ICSP* (pp. 397–401).

Dellaert, F., Polzin, T., & Waibel, A. (1996). Recognizing emotion in speech. In *Proceedings of ICSLP* (pp. 1970–1973).

Edmundson, A. (2007). Globalized e-learning cultural challenges. Arlington, VA: Information Resources Press.

Fowler, C. J. H., & Mayes, J. T. (1999). Learning relationships: From theory to design. *ALT-J, 7*, 6–16. doi:10.1080/0968776990070302

Gardner, M., Fowler, C., & Scott, J. (2003). A process to support the design of new e-learning services. In *Proceedings of Technology Enhanced learning conference* (*TEL*),Turin, 2003

Hall, E. (1976). *Beyond culture*. New York, NY: Doubleday.

Hanjalic, A. (2006). Extracting moods from pictures and sounds: towards truly personalized TV. *IEEE Signal Processing Magazine, 23*(2), 90–100. doi:10.1109/MSP.2006.1621452

Henderson, L. (1996). Instructional design of interactive multimedia: A cultural critique. *Educational Technology Research and Development, 44*(4), 85–104. doi:10.1007/BF02299823

Henderson, L. (2007). Theorizing a multiple cultures instructional design model for e-learning and e-teaching. In A. Edmundson (Ed.), *Globalizing e-learning cultural challenges* (pp. 130-153). Hershey, PA: Information Science.

Hughes, C. E., Stapleton, C. B., Hughes, D. E., & Smith, E. M. (2005). Mixed reality in education, entertainment, and training. *IEEE Computer Graphics and Applications, 25*(6), 24–30. doi:10.1109/MCG.2005.139

Isen, A. M. (2000). Positive affect & decision making. In M. Lewis & J. Haviland (Eds.), *Handbook of emotions* (pp. 720). Guilford, NY: The Guilford Press.

Kalkanis, X., Callaghan, V., & Gardner, M. (2008). Towards end-user physiological profiling for video recommendation. In *4th IET International Conference on Intelligent Environments (IE08)*, University of Washington, Seattle, USA.

Kim, W. (2007). Towards a definition and methodology for blended learning. In *International Workshop on Blended Learning 2007 (WBL 07),* University of Edinburgh, Scotland.

Lang, P. J. (1995). The emotion probe: Studies of motivation and attention. *The American Psychologist, 50*(5), 372–385. doi:10.1037/0003-066X.50.5.372

Leon, E., Clarke, G., Callaghan, V., & Sepulveda, F. (2007). A user-independent real-time emotion recognition system for software agents in domestic environments. *Engineering Applications of Artificial Intelligence, 20*(3), 337–345. doi:10.1016/j.engappai.2006.06.001

Lisetti, C. L., & Nasoz, F. (2004). Using noninvasive wearable computers to recognize human emotions from physiological signals. *EURASIP Journal on Applied Signal Processing*, (11): 1672–1687. doi:10.1155/S1110865704406192

Mayes, J. T. (1995). Learning technologies and groundhog day. In W. Strang, V.B. Simpson, & D. Slater (Eds.), *Hypermedia at work: Practice and theory in Higher Education*. Canterbury, UK: University of Kent Press.

Milgram, P., & Kishino, A. F. (1994). Taxonomy of mixed reality visual displays. *IEICE Transactions on Information and Systems . E (Norwalk, Conn.)*, *77-D*(12), 1321–1329.

Perkinson, R. (2006). International higher education plenary address. *The UK's International Education Conference*, Edinburgh, UK.

Picard, R., Papert, S., Bender, W., Blumberg, B., Breazeal, C., & Cavallo, D. (2004). Affective learning - a manifesto. *BT Technology Journal*, *22*(4), 253–269. doi:10.1023/B:BTTJ.0000047603.37042.33

Picard, R. W., & Scheirer, J. (2001). The Galvactivator: a glove that senses and communicates skin conductivity. In *9th International Conference on Human-Computer Interaction*, New Orleans, LA.

Rogers, P. C., & Wang, M. J. (2008). Cross-cultural issues in online learning. In P. Rogers & G. Berg (Eds.), *Encyclopedia of Distance and Online Learning*. PA: IGI Publishing.

Rossett, A., & Frazee, R. V. (2006). Blended learning opportunities. *American Management Association White Paper*. Retrieved from http://www.amanet.org/blended/

Russel, J. A. (1980). A circumplex model of affect. *Journal of Personality and Social Psychology*, *39*(6), 1161–1178. doi:10.1037/h0077714

Shadbolt, N., & O' Hara, K. (2008). *The spy in the coffee machine - The end of privacy as we know it*. Oxford, UK: Oneworld Publications.

Shen, L., Callaghan, V., & Shen, R. (2008). Affective e-learning in residential and pervasive computing environments. *Journal of Information Systems Frontiers (special issue on "Adoption and Use of Information & Communication Technologies in the Residential/Household Context"), 10*(3).

Shen, L., Leon, E., Callaghan, V., & Shen, R. (2007). Exploratory research on an affective e-learning model. In *International Workshop on Blended Learning 2007 (WBL 07)*, University of Edinburgh, Scotland.

Shepherd, J. (2007, May 8). It's a world of possibilities. *The Guardian*.

Shi Y.C., Xie W.K, Xu G.Y., (2003). The smart classroom: Merging technologies for seamless tele-education. *IEEE Pervasive Computing, 1536-1268(3)*, 47-55.

Thomas, M., Mitchell, M., & Joseph, R. (2002). The third dimension of ADDIE: A cultural embrace. *TechTrends*, *46*(2), 40–45. doi:10.1007/BF02772075

Thomas, S. (2008). Pervasive scale: A model of pervasive, ubiquitous, and ambient learning. *IEEE Pervasive Computing / IEEE Computer Society [and] IEEE Communications Society*, *7*(1), 85–88. doi:10.1109/MPRV.2008.20

Wang, C.-M., & Reeves, T. C. (2007). The Meaning of Culture in Online Education: Implications for teaching, learning, and design. In A. Edmundson (Ed.) *Globalizing e-learning cultural challenges* (pp. 2-17). Hershey, PA: Information Science.

Wang, M. J. (2004). Correlational analysis of student visibility and learning outcomes in an online setting. *Journal of Asynchronous Learning Networks*, *8*(4), 71–82.

Wang, M. J. (2007). Designing online courses that effectively engage learners from diverse cultural backgrounds. *British Journal of Educational Technology, 38*(2), 294–311. doi:10.1111/j.1467-8535.2006.00626.x

Wang, M. J., & Kang, J. (2006). Cybergogy of engaged learning through information and communication technology: A framework for creating learner engagement. In D. Hung & M. Khine (Eds.), *Engaged learning with emerging technologies*. New York: Springer Publishing.

Wang, M. J., Shen, R. M., Novak, D., & Pan, X. Y. (2008). The impact of mobile learning on learning behaviors and performance: report from a large blended classroom. *British Journal of Educational Technology, 38*(2), 294–311. doi:10.1111/j.1467-8535.2006.00626.x

Winston, R., Moore, R., Pearson, I., Hall, W., Shadbolt, N., & Weston, J. (2008). *Skills evolution report 2008: A vision: the future of workplace skills*. Sheffield, UK: Ufi Limited.

Yang, F., Han, P., Shen, R. M., Kraemer, B. J., & Fan, X. W. (2003). Cooperative learning in self-organizing e-learner communities based on a multi-agents mechanism. In *Proceedings of AI2003,* Perth, Australia (pp. 490-500).

KEY TERMS AND DEFINITIONS

Cultural Engagement: Making technology useful for different races

eLearning: Network delivered computer based instruction,

Hybrid Learning: Mixed natural classroom and online style teaching

Learning Technology: Technology used by students

Mixed Reality: Simultaneous use of both real and virtual environments

Online Teaching: Network delivered computer based instruction

Smart Environments: Technology supported environments

ENDNOTES

1 www.comscore.com/press/release.asp?press=1521
2 http://news.xinhuanet.com/english/2008-01/21/content_7467275.htm
3 www.WebCT.com
4 www.Blackboard.com
5 www.open.ac.uk
6 www.ouhk.edu.hk
7 www.nec.sjtu.edu.cn
8 www.wow-europe.com
9 secondlife.com
10 news.bbc.co.uk/1/hi/technology/6054352.stm
11 news.bbc.co.uk/1/hi/world/europe/6310915.stm
12 secondlifegrid.net/how/education_and_training
13 research.sun.com/projects/mc/mpk20.html
14 Since writing the first version of this chapter, in November 2009, Linden Labs announced an enterprise version of Second Life that can be located on a company's server and intranet, closed off from the public internet
15 http://blogs.sun.com/wonderland
16 opensimulator.org
17 www.projectdarkstar.com
18 g3d-wonderland.dev.java.net
19 Since writing this paper in 2008, Sun have released a new version of Wonderland (v0.5), which includes many improvements such as support for jME (Java Monkey Engine), a high performance scene graph based graphics API.
20 jvoicebridge.dev.java.net
21 java.sun.com/products/java-media/jmf
22 java.sun.com/products/javawebstart
23 www.sunspotworld.com
24 http://blogs.sun.com/wonderland

Chapter 17
Discourse Analysis on Hybrid Learning and Teaching and the Changing Roles of Teachers and Students in Hong Kong

Xu Zhichang
The Hong Kong Institute of Education, Hong Kong

Wang Lixun
The Hong Kong Institute of Education, Hong Kong

ABSTRACT

This chapter is based on a research project on hybrid teaching and learning. This emerging hybrid mode is gaining popularity in tertiary institutions because the new technologies have integrated the classroom and online teaching and learning into an organic productive environment. The research project adopts a discourse analysis approach and intends to investigate issues arising regarding the hybrid mode in a higher education institute in Hong Kong. These issues include 1) the discourse features of teaching and learning in the classroom face-to-face (FTF) and online computer-mediated communication (CMC); 2) the changing roles of teachers and students in the emerging hybrid environment; and 3) the implications of the hybrid mode on the effectiveness of teaching and learning. In addition, this research project also adopts questionnaire surveys among the teaching staff of a language education faculty and students of three courses offered in the hybrid mode to discover their attitudes towards the hybrid teaching and learning mode. The research findings suggest that in the hybrid environments, the traditional roles of the teachers as information providers, knowledge transmitters, supervisors and assessors, and the students as learners, participants, and respondents are still dominant. However, the teachers are also increasingly putting on new 'hats' as expert learners, facilitators, course designers and organizers. Apart from being learners, the students are also taking on new roles as topic contributors, meaning negotiators, information providers, strategic communicators and monitors.

DOI: 10.4018/978-1-60566-380-7.ch017

Figure 1. Blackboard online CMC discussion board

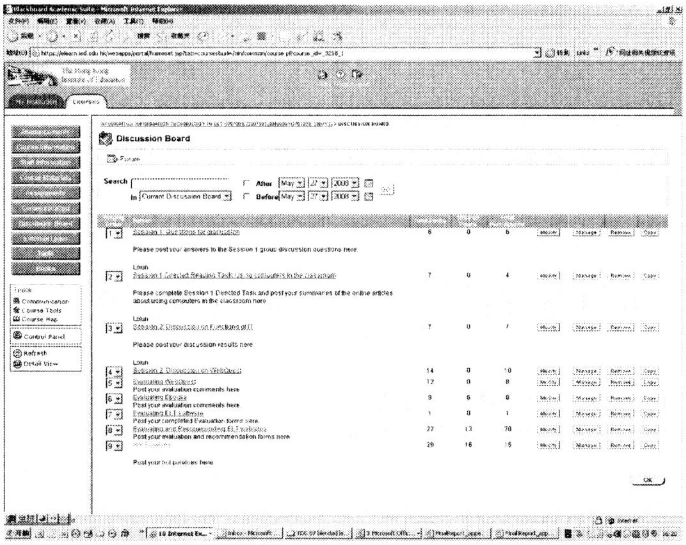

INTRODUCTION

The hybrid teaching and learning mode has been gaining popularity worldwide. This mode, consisting of classroom face-to-face (FTF) interaction and computer-medicated communication (CMC), reflects the hybrid nature of our current higher education institutions and "the natural process of how people really learn" (Masie, 2006, p. 26).

The three courses that are under investigation in this research project, namely "Vocabulary Studies", "Language and Societal Modernization" and "Introduction to Language Studies", have involved different hybrid teaching and learning modes. The first two courses were taught and delivered through 80% classroom FTF and 20% online CMC by means of synchronous 'Blackboard' discussion forums (c.f. Figure 1). The third course was taught and delivered by means of lectures, seminars, online quizzes and wiki-book collaborative academic writing projects (c.f. Figure 2). The online component of the third course involves around 20% to 30% of the teaching and learning time.

Since 2002, the language education faculty involved in this research project has been promoting the use of Blackboard in course teaching, i.e., the hybrid mode of teaching and learning. Online discussion has become a very important supplement to face-to-face interaction in the emerging hybrid mode. In addition to the use of Blackboard as an medium for instruction, the research project team have also explored other options on CMC, including online quizzes, and wiki-book collaborative academic writing group projects.

This chapter adopts both qualitative and quantitative research methodologies to investigate 1) the discourse features of teaching and learning in the classroom face-to-face (FTF) and online computer-mediated communication (CMC); 2) the changing roles of teachers and students in the emerging hybrid teaching and learning environment; and 3) the implications of the hybrid mode on the effectiveness of teaching and learning. Firstly, the research project is to describe and analyze both classroom FTF and online CMC interactions among teacher-student, student-student, and teacher-student-(re)sources and to discover certain discourse patterns. A discourse analysis (DA) approach is adopted including theories on classroom discourse hierarchy and the IRF/E (Initiation-Response-Feedback/Evalu-

Figure 2. Online wiki-book discussion forum

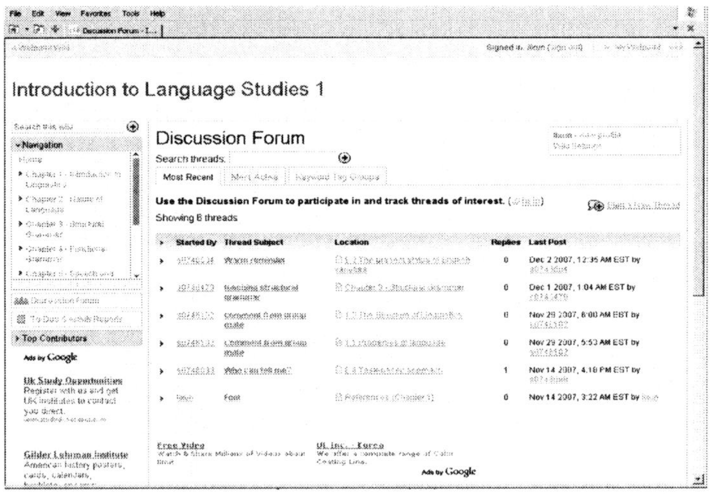

ation) patterning (McCarthy, 2002, pp. 14-17). The discourse "act" (Stenström, 1994, p. 30) analysis is conducted using both classroom FTF and online CMC discourse data. Secondly, the research project is to make use of the discourse analysis to discover the changing roles of teachers and students in the emerging hybrid teaching and learning environment. It can be noted that teachers and students worldwide take up new roles as new technologies are being introduced into education. The hybrid mode has re-configured the traditional constructs on learning, teaching, classroom dynamics, online discourse, and the roles and responsibilities of the teachers and the students. Thirdly, the research project is to address the issues arising in the hybrid teaching and learning mode, and to discuss the implications of the hybrid mode on the effectiveness of teaching and learning in higher education institutions.

LITERATURE REVIEW

This research project involves a discourse analysis approach. Discourse analysis is "the study of the relationship between language and the contexts in which it is used" (McCarthy, 2002, pp. 5-7). This project mainly investigates language and content-based teaching and learning through the analysis of classroom FTF and online CMC interaction. As far as the classroom FTF discourse and the online CMC discourse are concerned, the data for the project has been analyzed based on the theories of the "hierarchy of classroom interaction" (Coulthard, 1977, pp. 99-100), i.e. lesson, transaction, exchange, turn, move and act. A discourse "act" signals what the speaker intends to communicate. According to Stenström (1994, p. 30), an "act" is the "smallest interactive unit", and it can be identified and categorized into 28 "primary acts", including "accept", "acknowledge", "agree", "alert", "answer", "apology", "call-off", "check", "closer", "confirm", "disagree", "evaluate", "greeting", "inform", "invite", "object", "offer", "opine", "query", "question", "react", "reject", "reply", "request", "smoother", "statement", "suggest", and "thanks". The "written" texts in the CMC context, in contrast with the transcribed texts of classroom FTF interactions, are unique in that they contain not only features of hypertext but also features of both written and spoken discourse. This type of written texts can be located on a continuum of spoken-written discourse proposed by Leech, Deuchar & Hoogenraad (2006, p. 151), where "conversation", "e-mail message", "lecture", "newspaper", and "a serious printed book" are placed between typical speech and typical writing.

People have widely accepted that technology transforms knowledge, and that new technologies make "new things" possible "in a new way" (Noss & Pachler, 1999, p. 195). Recent publications on online education, e.g., Warschauer & Kern (2000), Kwan & Fong (2005), Juwah (2006), and Fong, Kwan & Wang (2008) have focused on e-learning pedagogy and the various technical and practical features of interaction and interactivity in the new hybrid teaching and learning environments. While this project takes "online education" as part of its research paradigm, its focus is on the synchronic online "Blackboard" discussion forum, online quizzes and wiki-book collaborative projects as supplementary tools for the classroom FTF teaching and learning. In this regard, this project draws on, as its theoretical and analytical framework, the research and publications by Davis & Brewer (1997) on the "context and contact in electronic discourse" and by Laurillard (2002) on her classification of five different media types for learning and teaching, i.e., "narrative", "interactive", "adaptive", "communicative", and "productive" media (pp. 81-174). In addition, this project also draws on the literature on the hybrid combination of online CMC and classroom FTF interactions, including Topper (1997), Skill & Young (2002), Larson & Keiper (2002), Ellis, Calvo, Levy, & Tan (2004), Pearson (2006), Jones, Garralda, Li & Lock (2006), Ng, Yeung & Hon (2006), Xie, DeBacker, & Ferguson (2006), Condie & Livingston (2007), Reisetter, Lapointe, & Korcuska (2007), Smith & Kurthen (2007), and Fong, Kwan & Wang (2008).

As far as classroom-based research is concerned, according to van Lier (2001, p. 90), "most current views of language education are based on the assumption that social interaction plays a central role in learning processes, as a quick glance at the dominant terminology shows. Communication, negotiation of meaning, co-construction, cooperative learning, responsive teaching, and many other terms like them testify to a fundamental shift from conditioning, association, and other laboratory-based notions of learning to human learning as it is situated in the everyday social world of the learner".

The traditional classroom environments have undertaken considerable transformations due to the development in teaching and learning theories and the introduction of new technologies. Nunan (1992) has investigated "collaborative" classroom teaching and learning. Lowerison, Sclater, Schmid and Abrami (2006) have investigated the student perceived effectiveness of computer technology use in post-secondary classrooms. Hill (2006) has compared the similarities and differences in traditional learning and technology-enhanced classroom, including online flexible learning environments. The purpose of investigating classroom-based teaching and learning is to find out the extent to which new technologies change the nature of the classroom discourse.

As far as the roles and responsibilities of teachers and students in the Hong Kong context are concerned, Chan (2003, p. 34) summaries that "schools in Hong Kong, in Western standards, are traditional, rule-bound institutions, where independence, individuality and creativity are far less valued than obedience, conformity, discipline and diligence, which are actively encouraged", therefore, "teachers generally regarded themselves as mainly/more responsible for the majority of the language-related decisions" and "they preferred the responsibilities for these activities to be taken mainly by themselves, rather than handed over to the students" (Chan, 2003, p. 49).

However, over the last few decades, there has been a major paradigm shift in Hong Kong from teacher-centred to learner-centred teaching and learning. According to Ng, Murphy, & Jenkins (2002, p. 463), "in a learner-centred mode, the focus is shifted to the constructive role of the learner, which differentiates it from a teacher-centred model in which knowledge is transmitted from teacher to learner". The paradigm shift and the introduction of new technologies into education have inevitably resulted in the multiple and changing roles of both teachers and students in Hong Kong. Kwan & Lopez-Real (2005, p. 284) have identified three distinct clusters arising from the teachers/mentors' perceptions of their roles, namely "the pragmatic (such as provider of feedback, observer, instructor and role model), the inter-personal (such as counselor, equal partner and critical friend) and the managerial (such as assessor, quality controller and manager).

The discourse analysis of the "acts" of the participants (including teachers and students) in both classroom FTF and online CMC interactions can reflect the changing roles of teachers and students in the hybrid teaching and learning environments.

HYBRID DISCOURSE ANALYTICAL FRAMEWORK

The analytical framework for the research project is primarily developed from differing stages for computer-mediated discourse analysis proposed by Job-Sluder & Barab (2004, p. 384). There are three guiding principles for establishing the current analytical framework for the hybrid teaching and learning discourse analysis. Firstly, the analysis draws on insights from traditional or conventional discourse analysis, including spoken discourse, written discourse, and classroom discourse, and it is grounded in empirical, textual observations of online CMC and classroom FTF interactions for teaching and learning purposes. Secondly, the analysis accounts for certain unique features of the technology-enhanced classroom FTF discourse and the online CMC discourse in relation to hypermedia or hypertext, (a)synchronicity, netiquette and the use of Netlish/Weblish (as in chatgroup, BBS, Instant Messaging, MSN or Blackboard discussion forums and in Weblogs or blogs). Thirdly, the analysis characterizes language use that is above or beyond the level of sentence or utterance in both online CMC and classroom FTF discourse, with a focus on the emerging patterns of language use, interaction, participation, and the changing roles of teachers and students in the hybrid teaching and learning environment (Xu, 2008).

The hybrid discourse analytical framework consists of *context* analysis and *content* analysis. Content analysis includes *structural* analysis, *semantic* analysis, *interaction* analysis, and *participation* analysis. The major components for each of these analyses are illustrated as follows:

1. **Context analysis:** Including course information (course titles, objectives, major content, modes of teaching or delivery), participant demographics (age, gender, educational background), medium variables (language, the degree of technology-enhancement, temporality, synchronicity, and classroom or online discourse conventions, i.e. the netiquette), and social context (identities and power relationships of participants)
2. **Content analysis:** Including *structural* analysis (classroom FTF and online CMC discourse hierarchy, i.e. lesson-transaction-exchange-turn-move-act versus forum-thread-exchange-posing-move-act; teacher-talk/posting versus student talk/posting; text versus hypertext), *semantic* analysis (discourse move and act identification and categorization, functions of the utterances/postings, i.e. recreational or educational, and topic development), *interaction* analysis (interaction as a means of knowledge construction, i.e., sharing, negotiating, and applying newly constructed knowledge, and teacher-student-content interactions), and *participation* analysis (the contribution and engagement of the teachers and the students, the changing roles of the teachers and the students)

Table 1. The discourse "acts" of the teacher and the students in a classroom FTF lecture/tutorial

Teacher's acts	Students' acts
Inform (174), Statement (118), Acknowledge (47), Question (33), Evaluate (27), Opine (24), Request (21), Alert (19), Suggest (16), Check (9), Thanks (8), Reply (5), Invite (3), Agree (2), Apology (1), Call-off (1), Confirm (1), Greeting (1), Offer (1).	Statement (39), Inform (38), Answer (17), Confirm (8), Greeting (7), Opine (3), Apology (2), React (2), Reply (2), Check (1), Thanks (1).

CLASSROOM FTF AND ONLINE CMC DISCOURSE DATA ANALYSIS

The three courses that are involved in this research project are offered in the hybrid teaching and learning environment. They include "Vocabulary Studies", "Language and Societal Modernization" and "Introduction to Language Studies". The first two courses comprise 80% classroom FTF component and 20% online CMC component. The third course comprises lectures, seminars, online quizzes and wiki-book collaborative academic writing projects.

In terms of the *content* analysis, a number of lectures were recorded and transcribed, and a number of "Blackboard" discussion forums were downloaded. Due to the limited space for this chapter and the selective nature of discourse analysis, the data of one lecture and one "Blackboard" discussion forum are selected and analyzed in terms of discourse hierarchy, and discourse "act" identification and categorization.

In the 150-minute FTF lecture/tutorial, 631 discourse "acts" have been identified and categorized. The teacher performs a total of 511 acts while the students 120. The distribution of the different types of the teacher's and the students' acts in the sequence of frequency is shown in Table 1 (with the number of acts in brackets).

In contrast with the classroom FTF discourse, in the three-hour online CMC discussion forum, 999 discourse "acts" have been identified and categorized. The teacher performs a total of 277 acts while the students 722. The distribution of the different types of the teacher's and the students' acts in the sequence of frequency is shown in Table 2 (with the number of acts in brackets).

Table 1 shows that in the classroom FTF discourse, the teacher performs predominantly the acts of "inform", "statement", "acknowledge", "question" and "evaluate", while the students perform the acts of "statement" and "answer". The students also "inform", but the number of their "inform" acts is significantly smaller than that by the teacher. In contrast, Table 2 shows that in the online CMC discourse, the students perform the major acts of "inform", "statement", "opine", "question", "evaluate" and "suggest", while the teacher also performs the acts of "statement", "inform" and "evaluate", however, the number of these acts is much smaller than that by the students. The following are examples of the students performing the acts of "inform" (Table 3), "statement" (Table 4), "opine" (Table 5), "ques-

Table 2. The discourse "acts" of the teacher and the students in an online CMC discussion forum

Teacher's acts	Students' acts
Statement (55), inform (54), evaluate (43), thanks (32), opine (17), agree (12), request (11), suggest (9), greeting 7), answer (5), alert (5), closer (4), question (4), offer (3), react (3), reply (3), confirm (3), call-off (2), check (2), accept (1), invite (1) and apology (1)	Inform (150), statement (135), opine (80), question (70), greeting (51), agree (43), evaluate (39), alert (34), suggest (23), react (19), thanks (17), answer (13), reply (13), invite (8), object (8), apology (7), check (6), query (4), acknowledge (4), offer (3), closer (2), confirm (2), request (1), and call-off (1).

Table 3. The "inform" act

Author: S1 **Creation date:** Tuesday, January 29, 2008 2:48:47 PM CST **Date last modified:** Tuesday, January 29, 2008 2:48:47 PM CST **Total views:** 22 **Your views:** 4
The policy of "biliteracy and trilingualism" on language education has applied to Primary 1 to Secondary 6 students since 2003, when a new three-year senior secondary education structure was introduced to Hong Kong.

Table 4. The "statement" act

Author: S2 **Creation date:** Tuesday, January 29, 2008 4:05:31 PM CST **Date last modified:** Tuesday, January 29, 2008 4:05:31 PM CST **Total views:** 5 **Your views:** 1
Actually, my mother tone is totally different from Cantonese, althoush i come from Guangdong. As a matter of fact, I come from Shantou, where people speak Chaoshannese. But I learn to speak Cantonese from TVB or fashion HK movise. As my cousin and relatives live in HK, sometimes, I need to use my Cantonese to communicate with them, so, like this, as a result, I pick up Cantonese.

Table 5. The "opine" act

Author: S3 **Creation date:** Tuesday, January 29, 2008 2:24:51 PM CST **Date last modified:** Tuesday, January 29, 2008 2:24:51 PM CST **Total views:** 17 **Your views:** 5
From my point of view, HK people will treasure Mandarin ability the same as English ability. The reason is that English is the main advantage for HK people to make more profit than other Asian peoples. And Mandarin is due to the rising international demand of Mandarin speakers, which would be beneficial to us because of the high language similarity between Cantonese and Mandarin (compared to the similarities between Mandarin and foreign languages like English and French).

Table 6. The "question" act

Author: S4 **Creation date:** Tuesday, January 29, 2008 1:55:08 PM CST **Date last modified:** Tuesday, January 29, 2008 1:55:08 PM CST **Total views:** 21 **Your views:** 5
Oh. I see. But are there any distinct boundaries between every 'language changing' period? And how can people know or realize it when the society has already step into a brand-new period?

tion" (Table 6), "evaluate" (Table 7) and "suggest" (Table 8) in the online CMC discourse.

In addition to the classroom FTF discourse and online CMC discourse analysis, a number of questionnaire surveys have also been conducted. These include surveys among the students and the faculty teaching staff on their attitudes towards hybrid teaching and learning, and surveys among teachers and students on the changing roles of themselves in the emerging hybrid classroom FTF and online CMC environments.

The questionnaire survey on the students' attitudes towards hybrid teaching and learning shows that 83.3% of the participants agree or strongly agree that "it is good to have a combination of FTF and online tutorials"; 97.2% of the participants agree or strongly agree that "FTF tutorials form an integral part of the module learning";

Table 7. The "evaluate" act

Author: S5 **Creation date:** Tuesday, January 29, 2008 3:57:27 PM CST **Date last modified:** Tuesday, January 29, 2008 3:57:27 PM CST **Total views:** 13 **Your views:** 1
frankly, until now i and xiaodi don't understand what you've talked about the simple and traditional character. i think it's no big deal, whatever we learn, simple or traditional.

Table 8. The "suggest" act

Author: S6 **Creation date:** Tuesday, January 29, 2008 1:34:57 PM CST **Date last modified:** Tuesday, January 29, 2008 1:34:57 PM CST **Total views:** 20 **Your views:** 4
I assume we will be doing our own research based on the various topics and posting them up here. And when someone post other information, we can lead a discussion? Thanks.

94.5% of the participants agree or strongly agree that "online tutorials give us a sense of freedom, leisure and autonomy in terms of our involvement and participation in the discussion forums"; and 80.6% of the participants agree or strongly agree that "the current ratio of FTF and Online tutorials (8:2) is appropriate"

The questionnaire survey on the teachers' attitudes towards hybrid teaching and learning shows that 91% of the staff have used Blackboard as an integral part of the hybrid teaching and learning mode; 52% of the staff have used Discussion Board in the Blackboard system in their teaching; and 39% of the staff regard Discussion Board as being most useful for reasons including 1) to supplement FTF interaction, 2) to create a channel for students to express and share ideas; and 3) to increase flexibility in teaching and learning. In general, over half of the staff comment that they will use Discussion Board more in the future. The reasons include: 1) students may be more willing to discuss issues online. Students who would not express during class time can express freely; 2) it will be much more useful if the students can initiate the discussion or interaction themselves; 3) it is useful to get feedback; 4) it supplements FTF discussion or interaction; 5) it encourages students to continue discussion after class (since sometimes the discussion can not be completed during lectures; 6) it promotes sharing of knowledge in terms of looking at others' points of view; 7) it enables teachers to have more interaction with their students, and 8) it helps create a peer evaluation and collaborative teaching and learning culture.

The other two questionnaire surveys among a group of 28 primary and secondary school teachers in Hong Kong and a group of 24 students from a higher education institution in Hong Kong are concerned with the teachers' and students' self-reflections on their multiple and changing roles in the hybrid teaching and learning environments. The surveys involve a brainstorming session with the teachers and the students regarding the existing and emerging roles of the teachers and the students in the hybrid teaching and learning environments in Hong Kong. The roles are then listed in a table, and the teachers and the students are invited to rank the extent to which they perceive themselves as taking up the listed roles. Table 9 shows the extent to which the teachers perceive themselves as the roles they take up.

Table 10 shows the extent to which the students perceive themselves as the roles they take up.

Table 9. The roles of Hong Kong teachers

Role ranking	Roles	Percentage	Notes
1	information provider; knowledge transmitter; guide; assessor;	100%	
2	course designer; facilitator; advisor;	96%	
3	mentor; organizer; carer	93%	'Carer' is ranked relatively high, probably due to the fact that the majority of the respondents are primary school teachers.
4	monitor; social worker	89%	
5	decision maker; team-leader;	86%	
6	participant (team-member); friend	82%	
7	manager	75%	
8	expert learner; entertainer	68%	
9	actor/actress/star	64%	
10	researcher	57%	

DISCUSSION

The introduction of new technologies into education has changed and challenged the traditional notions and practices on teaching and learning. Interaction and discussion play a crucial role in the teaching and learning processes. Ellis & Calvo argue that "learning through discussions is a key aspect of the student learning experience in higher education" (2004, p. 263). Smith & Kurthen suggest that "interaction, between instructor-student and between students, is at the heart of education, whether FTF, fully online, or blended-hybrid" (2007, p. 458). The analyses of classroom FTF and online CMC data and the results of the questionnaire surveys show that the hybrid teaching and learning environment can enhance discussion and interaction between the teacher and the students, among students themselves, and between the teacher, students and the course content materials.

The discourse "act" analyses and comparisons of the classroom FTF and online CMC data show that there has been a shift from knowledge transmission to knowledge construction in the hybrid teaching and learning environment. In the classroom FTF discourse, the teacher still plays a dominant role in terms of disseminating knowledge or leading the classroom discussion and interaction. Among the total discourse "acts" in a typical lecture, the acts of "statement", "inform", "opine" and "suggest" come almost exclusively from the teacher, while the students only perform the discourse "acts" of "accept" and "answer". In the online CMC discourse, the students play a leading role as far as the "act" variety and distribution are concerned. The "inform" and "statement" and "opine" acts by the students outnumber those by the teacher significantly. In addition, the total acts by the students in an online discussion forum far exceed those by the teacher. The implications of these findings indicate that

Table 10. The roles of Hong Kong students

Role ranking	Roles	Percentage	Note
1	learners; participants; respondents; team-builders	100%	
2	teacher helpers; listeners	96%	
3	topic contributors; strategic communicators	92%	
4	meaning negotiators	88%	
5	meaning makers; peer competitors	79%	
6	information providers;	75%	
7	monitors	63%	The role of 'monitors' in the online CMC context refers to the fact that the students monitor the teacher's online presence (TOP) and other students' online presence (SOP)

the hybrid teaching and learning environment facilitates the shift from knowledge transmission to knowledge construction. The hybrid environment helps create rich zones of development "in which all participants learn by jointly participating in activities in which they share material, socio-cultural, linguistic, and cognitive resources" (Gutiérrez, Baquedano-López, Alvarez, & Chiu, 1999, p. 88). In addition, these hybrid zones also provide a model for "understanding how meaningful collaboration can be created and sustained and how difference and diversity can serve as resources for learning" (Gutiérrez, Baquedano-López, Alvarez, & Chiu, 1999, p. 92). According to Holec (1981), autonomous learners hold the responsibilities of determining the objectives, defining the contents and progressions, selecting methods and techniques to be used, monitoring the procedures of acquisition, and evaluating what has been acquired. The variety and number of "acts" that the students have performed in the hybrid environment, including "inform", "statement", "opine", "question", "evaluate", "suggest", "object", and "query" indicate that the students are not only taking more responsibilities in their own learning, but also taking up newer roles in their learning process.

In the hybrid teaching and learning environment, the traditional IRF/E (Initiation, Response, Feedback/Evaluation) pattern of classroom discourse pattern has been challenged. As a result, new patterns are emerging. In the classroom FTF discourse, there is an increasing deviation from the traditional IRF/E pattern. The introduction of new teaching technologies, such as PowerPoint and multimedia presentation equipment in the classroom and Blackboard discussion platform, have given rise to complex and dynamic patterns of educational discourse. In the emerging hybrid teaching and learning environment, a new dimension is added in the form of participants interacting with the course content materials through a variety of media in text, graphics and hypertext. In addition, the traditional concepts of participation and interaction can also be interpreted differently in the hybrid teaching and learning environment, in which "students' participation is based on authentic competence, rather than on traditional school criteria such as age, language background, education, or ability" (Gutiérrez, Baquedano-López,

Alvarez, & Chiu, 1999, p. 89). The interaction in the hybrid teaching and learning environment has increasingly included the interaction among the students themselves and a learning community largely due to the changing roles of the students. In the meantime, interaction also involves the course content materials in the form of multimedia text, graphics and hypertext.

The hybrid teaching and learning environment enhances the sustainable relationship between the teachers and the students. The traditional IRF/E classroom discourse pattern has evolved in that the teacher is perceived as more of a "participant" on the same interaction platform with the students. This helps sustain the teacher-student relationship as the teacher is no longer regarded as the sage on the stage but a guide on the side, while the students take more active roles in the learning process. In the hybrid environment, the teaching and learning are perceived as a journey or a process rather than a product-oriented outcome. In terms of a sustainable relationship, the teachers and the students are expected to take up multiple and complementary roles. The students take more responsibility for their learning, and have more control over the relevance of the subject matter, the level of involvement and participation, and the contribution of the knowledge construction. In the meantime, the teachers take a bigger variety of roles as facilitators, organizers, monitors, managers and researchers during the teaching and learning processes. As a result, the effectiveness of teaching and learning can be largely enhanced.

In addition, the hybrid teaching and learning environment reinforces the multiple and changing roles of the teachers and the students. The questionnaire surveys in this research project show that the traditional roles of the teachers and the students have shifted and have become increasingly dynamic. According to Gutiérrez, Baquedano-López, Alvarez, & Chiu (1999, p. 88), teaching and learning in the hybrid environment requires participants to constantly "negotiate their roles and understandings as they co-participate in various problem-solving activities". In this sense, the hybrid teaching and learning environment has a "democratization effect" (Smith & Kurthen, 2007, p. 472). Although the traditional roles of the teachers as "information providers", "knowledge transmitters", "guides", "assessors", "course designers", "facilitators", "advisors" are still dominant, new roles of teachers, as they perceive themselves as "mentors", "organizers", "carers", "monitors", "social workers", "decision makers", "team-leaders", "participants", "friends", "managers", "expert learners", "entertainers", "actor/actress/stars" and "researchers", are evolving. These roles serve a variety of functions including "pragmatic" (such as mentors, expert learners), "inter-personal" (such as team-leaders, friends), and "managerial" (such as organizers, monitors, and managers). In the meantime, while the students are still perceiving themselves as "learners", "participants", "respondents", "team-builders", "teacher helpers" and "listeners", they are also increasingly regarding themselves as "topic contributors", "strategic communicators", "meaning negotiators and makers", "peer competitors", "information providers" and "monitors" in the hybrid teaching and learning environment.

CONCLUSION

This chapter is concerned with the discourse analysis of hybrid teaching and learning combining classroom FTF and online CMC interactions in the context of a Hong Kong higher education institution. It has adopted a discourse analysis approach in terms of identifying, categorizing and analyzing the discourse "acts" of the teachers and the students in both classroom FTF and online CMC interactions. The research data have shown that the hybrid teaching and learning environment not only facilitates the paradigm shift from teacher-centredness to student-centredness, but also enhances the sustainable relationship between the teachers and the students, and reinforces the multiple and changing roles of the teachers and the students in Hong Kong.

The research findings indicate that in the hybrid teaching and learning environment, while the traditional roles of the teachers as information providers, knowledge transmitters, and assessors, and the students as learners and participants are still dominant, the teachers are increasingly putting on new "hats" as facilitators, expert learners, monitors, entertainers and researchers, and the students as topic contributors, meaning makers and negotiators, information providers and strategic communicators. The multiple and changing roles of the teachers and the students imply that a paradigm shift has been taking place and the teachers and the students are expected to be aware of the shift and make adjustments in their teaching and learning accordingly.

According to Skill and Young (2002, p. 24) "the likely future will be neither solely online learning nor solely instructor-led classroom learning". They propose that "for many of us who have been working with various learning models, it appears that hybrid or blended models most frequently emerge as the most effective learning strategy. This likelihood suggests that the creation of new learning environments should embrace both virtual and real spaces. Understanding how best to integrate these two modes of learning is and will continue to be a significant challenge for educators" (Skill and Young, 2002, p. 24). In the future, more research needs to be done in terms of how the hybrid environment creates a dynamic space for teaching and learning and how the traditional classroom discourse evolves into newer patterns, which in turn, may lead to increased effectiveness in teaching and learning.

ACKNOWLEDGMENT

This paper is based on an IRG funded research project (RG27/2006-2007) of the Hong Kong Institute of Education. The authors wish to acknowledge the editors and the two anonymous reviewers from Editorial Advisory Board of the "Handbook of Research on Hybrid Learning Models: Advanced Tools, Technologies, and Application". The authors also wish to acknowledge their research assistants Scarlett Zhou and Winnie Au-Yeung for data collection and chapter formatting.

REFERENCES

Chan, V. (2003). Autonomous Language Learning: the teachers' perspectives. *Teaching in Higher Education*, *8*(1), 33–54. doi:10.1080/1356251032000052311

Condie, R., & Livingston, K. (2007). Blending online learning with traditional approaches: changing practices. *British Journal of Educational Technology*, *38*(2), 337–348. doi:10.1111/j.1467-8535.2006.00630.x

Coulthard, M. (1977). *An introduction to discourse analysis*. London: Longman Group Limited.

Davis, B. H., & Brewer, J. P. (1997). *Electronic Discourse: Linguistic Individuals in Virtual Space*. New York: State University of New York Press.

Ellis, R. A., Calvo, R., Levy, D., & Tan, K. (2004). Learning through discussions. *Higher Education Research & Development*, *23*(1), 73–93. doi:10.1080/0729436032000168504

Ellis, R. A., & Calvo, R. A. (2004). Learning Through Discussions in Blended Environments. *Educational Media International*, *41*(3), 263–274. doi:10.1080/09523980410001680879

Fong, J., Kwan, R., & Wang, F. L. (2008). *Hybrid Learning and Education.* Berlin, Germany: Springer.

Gutiérrez, K. D., Baquedano-López, P., Alvarez, H. H., & Chiu, M. M. (1999). Building a Culture of Collaboration Through Hybrid Language Practices. *Theory into Practice*, *38*(2), 87–93. doi:10.1080/00405849909543837

Hill, J. R. (2006). Flexible Learning Environments: Leveraging the Affordances of Flexible Delivery and Flexible Learning. *Innovative Higher Education*, *31*, 187–197. doi:10.1007/s10755-006-9016-6

Holec, H. (1981). *Autonomy and Foreign Language Learning*. Oxford, UK: Pergamon.

Job-Sluder, K., & Barab, S. A. (2004). Shared "We" and Shared "They" Indicators of Group Identity in Online Teacher Professional Development. In S. A. Barab, R. Kling, & J. H. Gray (Eds.), *Designing virtual communities in the service of learning* (pp. 377-403). Cambridge, UK: Cambridge University Press.

Jones, R. H., Garralda, A., Li, D. C. S., & Lock, G. (2006). Interactional dynamics in on-line and face-to-face peer-tutoring sessions for second language writers. *Journal of Second Language Writing*, *15*, 1–23. doi:10.1016/j.jslw.2005.12.001

Juwah, C. (2006). *Interactions in Online Education: Implications for theory and practice*. London: Routledge.

Kwan, R., & Fong, J. (2005). *Web-based Learning: Technology and Pedagogy*. Hong Kong: World Scientific.

Kwan, T., & Lopez-Real, F. (2005). Mentors' perceptions of their roles in mentoring student teachers. *Asia-Pacific Journal of Teacher Education*, *33*(3), 275–287. doi:10.1080/13598660500286267

Larson, B., & Keiper, T. A. (2002). Classroom Discussion and Threaded Electronic Discussion: Learning in Two Arenas. *Contemporary Issues in Technology & Teacher Education*, *2*(1), 45–62.

Laurillard, D. (2002). *Rethinking University Teaching: A Conversational Framework for the Effective Use of Learning Technologies* (2nd ed.). London: RoutledgeFalmer.

Leech, G., Deuchar, M., & Hoogenraad, R. (2006). *English Grammar for Today: A New Introduction* (2nd ed.). London: Palgrave MacMillan.

Lowerison, G., Sclater, J., Schmid, R. F., & Abrami, P. C. (2006). Student perceived effectiveness of computer technology use in post-secondary classroom. *Computers & Education*, *47*, 465–489. doi:10.1016/j.compedu.2004.10.014

Masie, E. (2006). Chapter Two: The Blended Learning Imperative. In C. J. Bonk & C. R. Graham (Eds.), *The handbook of blended learning: Global Perspectives, Local Designs* (pp. 22-26). San Francisco: John Wiley & Sons, Inc.

McCarthy, M. (2002). *Discourse Analysis for Language Teachers*. Cambridge, UK: Cambridge University Press.

Ng, C., Yeung, A. S., & Hon, R. Y. H. (2006). Does online language learning diminish interaction between student and teacher? *Educational Media International*, *43*(3), 219–232. doi:10.1080/09523980600641429

Ng, K. C., Murphy, D., & Jenkins, W. (2002). The teacher's role in supporting a learner-centred learning environment: voices from a group of part-time postgraduate students in Hong Kong. *International Journal of Lifelong Education*, *21*(5), 462–473. doi:10.1080/02601370210156754

Noss, R., & Pachler, N. (1999). The challenge of new technologies: doing old things in a new way, or doing new things? In P. Mortimore (Ed.), *Understanding Pedagogy and its Impact on Learning* (pp. 195-211). London: Paul Chapman Publishing Ltd.

Nunan, D. (1992). *Collaborative language learning and teaching.* New York: Cambridge University Press.

Pearson, J. (2006). Investigating ICT using problem-based learning in face-to-face and online learning environments. *Computers & Education, 47*, 56–73. doi:10.1016/j.compedu.2004.09.001

Reisetter, M., Lapointe, L., & Korcuska, J. (2007). The Impact of Altered Realties: Implications of Online Delivery for Learners' Interactions, Expectations, and Learning Skills. *International Journal on E-Learning, 6*(1), 55–80.

Skill, T. D., & Young, B. A. (2002). Embracing the Hybrid Model: Working at the Intersections of Virtual and Physical Learning Spaces. *New Directions for Teaching and Learning, 92*, 23–32. doi:10.1002/tl.76

Smith, G. G., & Kurthen, H. (2007). Front-Stage and Back-Stage in Hybrid E-Learning Face-to-Face Courses. *International Journal on E-Learning, 6*(3), 455–474.

Stenstrom, A.-B. (1994). *An introduction to spoken interaction.* New York: Longman.

Topper, A. (1997). *Comparing Face-to-Face and Electronic Discourse: Issues and Questions Raised in a Research Study.* Paper presented at the Annual Meeting of the American Educational Research Association, Chicago, IL.

van Lier, L. (2001). Constraints and resources in classroom talk: Issues of equality and symmetry. In C. N. Candlin & N. Mercer (Eds.), *English language teaching in its social context: a reader* (pp. 90-107). London: Routledge.

Warschauer, M., & Kern, R. (2000). *Network-based Language Teaching: Concepts and Practice.* Cambridge, UK: Cambridge University Press.

Xie, K., DeBacker, T. K., & Ferguson, C. (2006). Extending the traditional classroom through online discussion: The role of student motivation. *Journal of Educational Computing Research, 34*(1), 67–89. doi:10.2190/7BAK-EGAH-3MH1-K7C6

Xu, Z. (2008). When Hybrid Learning Meets Blended Teaching: Online Computer-Mediated Communication (CMC) Discourse and Classroom Face-to-Face (FTF) Discourse Analysis. In J. Fong, R. Kwan, & F. L. Wang (Eds), *Hybrid Learning and Education* (pp. 157-167). Berlin, Germany: Springer.

KEY TERMS AND DEFINITIONS

Changing Roles of Teachers and Students: As a result of the introduction of information technology into the education contexts, new roles of the teachers and students emerge and evolve. The blended mode of teaching and learning has a democratization effect on the teachers and students, which gives rise to the changing roles of teachers and students.

Classroom Face-to-Face (FTF) Interaction: Classroom face-to-face (FTF) interaction refers to the interaction between the teacher and the students, and among the students themselves in the traditional classroom setting. The term face-to-face (FTF) is used to stand in contrast with computer-mediated communication (CMC) interaction through online channels.

Discourse Analysis: Discourse analysis is used in this chapter as a research approach, studying the relationship between language use in the form of FTF and CMC interactions and the teaching and learning contexts.

Hybrid Teaching and Learning: The hybrid mode in education is a result of the introduction of information technology into teaching and learning. It essentially consists of classroom face-to-face (FTF) interaction and computer-medicated communication (CMC) for overall teaching and learning purposes.

Online Computer-Mediated Communication (CMC): Online computer-mediated communication (CMC) stands in contrast with classroom face-to-face (FTF) interaction. It refers to the communication in the education contexts between the teacher and the students and among the students themselves in the form of synchronous or asynchronous discussion forums.

Chapter 18
Pedagogy Reconsidered in a Multimodal Blended Environment

Barbara O'Byrne
Marshall University Graduate College, USA

ABSTRACT

Blended course delivery has wide applications across diverse educational settings. By definition, it is multimodal and involves multiple delivery formats. However, scant research has examined the impact of multimodal, blended delivery on university pedagogy. This chapter makes the case for close examination of the theoretical and pedagogical foundation of blended learning and proposes that research is needed to establish and validate the constructivist principles associated with blended learning. A longitudinal analysis of surveys and in-depth interviews with instructors from a distance education graduate school in the United States identified and contextualized features of learner-centered pedagogy linked to blended learning.

INTRODUCTION

Blended learning, an outgrowth of e-delivery, is central to the current discourse on technology and learning because of its connections to multimedia and its applications to a wide range of educational settings. For some, blended learning is, "any instruction where content is delivered both online and in onsite facilities" (Mossavar-Rahmani & Larson-Daugherty, 2007, p. 67). Defined in this way, blended or hybrid learning is a delivery model distinct from face-to-face delivery and from e-learning that takes place entirely in an asynchronous context. However, advances in electronic delivery, including CD-ROM, podcasting and video conferencing, are bending and broadening this definition (El-Gayar & Dennis, 2005; Sankey & Smith, 2004). The virtual classroom can now have the immediacy of a face-to-face learning environment. This investigation defines blended learning as a portion of learning done in real time, whether in a face-to-face or a virtualized meeting, and a portion conducted asynchronous, typically on a learning platform such as Blackboard.

DOI: 10.4018/978-1-60566-380-7.ch018

Multimodal is a core concept within any understanding of blended delivery, and links the latter with multiplying and morphing tools associated with Internet technologies that rely upon audio, visual, and interactive tools to engage participants (Brusilovsky, 2001; Console, 2004). These tools have expanded the range of learning styles and diversified the learning experiences supported by online learning environments. For this reason, any understanding of blended learning must take into account not only multiple delivery formats but also a wide range of electronic tools designed to actualize instructional goals.

As advances in technology propel the ongoing morphing of tools and delivery models, fundamental questions arise about the nature of learning, pedagogy and instructional design within blended learning environments. Educators caught up in the transformation of delivery models must embrace and address these challenges. How have education courses changed as formats of delivery have have multiplied and diversified? How do instructors make decisions about the delivery medium and the nature of learning activities within a medium? These questions link decisions about tool use and delivery options to the broader context of learning assumptions, theories and methodologies associated with different delivery models. The goal of this investigation is to capture some of the shifts in the instructional topography of education courses resulting from multimodal, blended delivery models and to situate these changes "within a pedagogic cultural agenda where knowledge and reflection are still important" (Watson, 2001, p.261).

The heart of this investigation is the impact of human computer interaction on teaching and learning in blended graduate distance education courses. The multimodal, blended delivery model presents a unique lens through which to view the topic because it includes synchronous, face-to-face, and asynchronous elements. Developers of blended courses must directly address questions of whether content should be delivered face-to-face or electronically, and which multimodal tool best suits a particular learning goal.

This need to consider both live and electronic delivery within the framework of a single course enlarges a debate previously centered on the polarities of electronic or live teaching and learning. The discussion brought to the foreground important questions about learning and teaching with computers. How does teaching in an electronic environment compare to teaching face-to-face? How does the role of the instructor change in blended learning environments? How is learning influenced when mediated through electronic tools? These pedagogical concerns, in the background of electronic delivery since its inception, became more visible with the advent of blended learning. Larger questions about learning theory and the nature of knowledge lie beneath the surface of delivery choices.

Mapping the impact of these changes in methods will require systematic research with different learning populations, distinct disciplines, and from a multitude of perspectives, including instructors, learners, programs, and institutions. This investigation will focus on these questions from the perspective of graduate educators developing distance education courses for educational professionals. It will show how adopting a longitudinal view uncovers the ways blended learning is re-shaping the instructional practices and assumptions of university educators working with professional learners in graduate distance educations programs.

BACKGROUND

In order to consider the question of the relationships between educational technology and instructional methods, three areas must be addressed. First, advances in multimedia tools must be contextualized within the parameters of a blended learning environment. Secondly, underlying theoretical assumptions that are embedded in human computer interaction must be acknowledged and evaluated. Finally, since research validates theory, it is essential to take stock of significant research trends in instructional practice related to educational technology, and in particular, studies related to blended learning environments.

Multimodal Tools

First generation online tools such as discussion boards enabled the learning community to extend beyond the boundaries of face-to-face meetings and shifted the locus of class interactions from instructor-to-student to student-to-student (Crook, 1994; Ravencroft, 2001). Over the last ten years, a proliferation of multimedia tools such as webcams, online videoconferencing, podcasts and collaborative web tools such as blogs and wikis have expanded the range of learning experiences and preferences supported by online learning (Zang, 2005). When added to the online component of blended learning environments, these tools became powerful catalysts in the development of interactive learning communities beyond the classroom (Mossavar-Rahmani & Larson Daugherty, 2007; Sankey & St. Hill, 2005). These tools have opened up online learning to a wide range of learners. Any discussion of blended learning would be impossible without noting the centrality of these multimedia tools.

Theoretical Framework

Certain epistemological premises inform and anchor this investigation. Constructivist theory posits that knowledge is inseparable from the knowing subject and as such, always retains a subjective or context-bound identity. Individuals actively construct all knowledge. Conceptualizing knowledge as a verb contrasts with the positivist, rational view that situated knowledge as an objective reality located outside the individual and validated by deductive reasoning and empirical theory. This paradigm shift about the nature of knowing has immediate consequences for theories of thinking, learning, and teaching.

Two main branches have emerged in constructivist epistemologies. One places the locus of knowledge-making within the individual. Piaget's cognitive theory emphasized knowledge construction as a mental activity essentially taking place within the head of an individual. The second branch, identified with Vygotsky, posits that all knowledge is constructed through internalized language. As such, thought is inseparable form its social or cultural context. The preeminence of language in knowledge construction separated social constructivism from theories that prioritized cognition. Crook (1994) drew attention to the more subtle meaning Vygotsky attached to social interactions. Social did not necessarily mean an interpersonal exchange but could be encoded into semiotics, into sign systems that "are present even when no one is in the room" (Crook, 1994, p. 27). This broader understanding of social interactions has powerful implications for technology-enhanced learning. Computers make use of these sign systems as intrapersonal tools that transform mental functions and extend the social dimension of computer-assisted instruction far beyond interpersonal dimension of chats, discussion, and even collaborative projects (Ravencroft, 2001).

An unresolved tension between Piaget's belief in the individual discovery process and Vygotsky's insistence on the social nature of all knowledge is acknowledged in this investigation. Even the refined understanding of social as mediated in signs and tools (Crook, 1994; 2001) does not bridge the gap between Piaget's cogitating child and Vygotsky's socialized child who develops knowledge within the context of language in all its mediated forms. This tension is more pronounced in disciplines such as mathematics and engineering, whose practitioners have questioned the efficacy of Piaget's discovery-based practices, especially where novices lack background knowledge of the subject (Mayer, 2004). On the other hand, disciplines such as literacy acquisition and linguistics support the social model of knowledge development. This investigation cannot resolve this tension, nor ignore its implications for research. It can disclose that it is focused on educational professionals who have considerable knowledge of pedagogy. The study operates within a social constructivist framework. This theoretical lens informs its design.

While the shift to a constructivist paradigm of knowledge is acknowledged in virtually every field of inquiry, the field of education has had a paradoxical relationship with the practice of its principles. Pockets of research have developed around specific applications of constructivism, including constructionism, anchored instruction, and problem-based learning. Each of these has enjoyed limited success as applications of the principles of constructivism in educational settings. While embraced at the epistemological level for more that forty years, constructivist principles have been slow to inform instructional practice.

Nowhere is this more apparent than in higher education where traditional modes of lecture and seminar continue to dominate the topography of teaching even though the principles of learner-centered instruction have been available and endorsed by university educators for decades. While there have been pockets of change at the instructor and, in some cases, the school level, the prevailing model of university instruction through the 1990s supported a transmission, content-centered model of learning and teaching more associated with objective, positivist epistemologies. Students were told to think for themselves but were taught from a framework that did the thinking for them or misrepresented knowledge as remembering and reproducing facts on tests and assignments. Dalsgaard and Godsk (2007) summarized the organizational features of face-to-face classroom instruction such as the need for a pre-determined, sequenced curriculum that impeded authentic knowledge construction associated with a constructivist epistemology.

Research on Electronic Learning

Research on electronic learning parallels, overlaps and informs the topic of blended learning. One strand of early research focused on student learning and satisfaction with electronic forms of delivery. E-learning is associated with modest gains in learning (Sankey & St. Hill, 2005; Zang, 2005). Some evidence suggests that these gains are extended when learners have the benefit of a mixed delivery model that blends live and electronic learning (El-Gayar& Dennis, 2005). Greater participant satisfaction results once learner norms are clarified (McCrory, Putnam & Jansen, 2008). Recent research has attempted to match learning styles with online activities (Brinkerhaff & Koroghlanian, 2007; Mossavar-Rahmani & Larson-Daugherty, 2007; Yang & Cornelius, 2005).

While earlier research noted the affinity of independent or 'isolated' learners for electronic learning, Leu, Kinzer, Corio and Cammack (2004) claimed that learning associated with the new technologies is more successfully and more frequently socially constructed. Some research supports this view. Ghislandi and Job (2005) and Su (2005) established that online learning is equally effective with different learning styles, as measured by academic achievement, further discounting the view that e-learning more suited to independent, 'solo' learners.

A second strand of early research focused on the impact of different delivery models on programs. These investigations described and evaluated online delivery models for individual courses and programs. Bell and Lefoe (1998) demonstrated the value of experimentation and identified an 'outcome-based integration model' as essential in refining online delivery. Other research focused on the development of online degree programs, and generally described the effectiveness of modular design in scaffolding learning (Carter-Wells, Ivers, & Lee, 2003). Similarly, Wade, Riordan and Power (1997) observed the importance of interactive approaches to course design to meet the learning needs of participants.

A limitation of these early studies on instructional design is the absence of systematic, sustained research in multiple disciplines. Both the newness of the field and the rapid pace of change in technology make such studies difficult to construct, and hence the dearth of broad generalizations associated with robust theory-making. A consensus is emerging in the literature of the need for systematic research into the impact of the new technologies on teaching, as well as on learning. Console (2004) drew attention to a lack of understanding about how e-learning is transforming both pedagogy and institutions and identified three main research themes: pedagogy of e-learning, the technology of e-learning, and strategies for integrating online courses within existing systems. Cook (2002), echoing Console's call for the creation of theory, advocated 'evolutionary approaches' in establishing a theoretical basis for e-pedagogy, consistent with the newness and diversity of the field. There is a particular need for research that "helps us understand the culture and context of different learning situations and their impact on students' learning." (Issroff & Scanlon, 2002, p. 10).

Recent research on blended learning in universities with adult learners reflects an emerging trend to ground research within specific cultural contexts. Donnelly (2006) conducted a significant case study on the group processes of teacher educators in a blended problem-based learning environment. The principal goal was to describe the process of constructing problem-based learning modules and integrating these into the online component of a blended learning environment and to document the ways in which learners understood and made sense of the change in pedagogy. Ausburn (2002) identified three design features important to adult learners: course announcements and reminders from the instructor, course documents such as syllabi and grading procedures, and information on specific assignments, including instructions on how to proceed with learning tasks. The study also identified the five most important instructional goals an instructor should address in an online course: options for individual/ customization, an environment that supported self-directed learning, an array of authentic learning experiences, and opportunities to communicate with peers and with the instructor. Studies such as these are beginning the work on establishing the characteristics of blended learning as it interfaces with distinct learning populations. This investigation will add to the knowledge base by focusing the particular context of a blended learning environment supporting professional learners in a distance education program.

Where others have focused on the features or designs indigenous to online environments, this research will explore the dynamic relationships between 'humans and machines' as these relate to instructional design and delivery decisions. Understanding the contours of these transactions is an essential first step in constructing pedagogies of multimodal, blended delivery. Scant research has directly addressed the question of how and why instructors reach decisions to deliver learning activities live or electronically, or the impact of digital resources and online delivery on the construction of course learning activities. Addressing these questions is an essential epistemological task for blended or multimodal learning.

Drawing upon the suggestions of Console (2004), this investigation will enlarge the understanding of the impact of blended learning on pedagogy by conducting research on instructional methods and assumptions associated with the shift to multimodal delivery among instructors who work with professional learners. The approach will draw upon a specific need in e-learning, derived both from its newness and from the rapid pace of technological change, to develop and articulate "evolutionary theory" rather than starting with an established theory. This investigation will demonstrate and evaluate changes over time in instructor design and delivery decisions associated with a shift to multimodal, blended courses.

The last fifteen years have seen a quickening of the pace of change in the direction of more student-centered learning among universities experimenting with online education. The goal of this investigation is to provide a framework to document and begin to make sense of the relationship between education technology and university teaching and learning. It is essential to develop a unique and precise research lens through which to make sense of these changes in teaching and learning and this presupposes a review of relevant research.

FOCUS OF THE CHAPTER

How to capture change in pedagogy? How to convey change in empirical and descriptive terms? These were the challenges of this investigation. Two insights guided the process. Change in institutions is more visible over time and when observed from different perspectives. The task is complicated because this longitudinal perspective is only beginning to emerge in blended learning. Further, the ongoing and rapid transformation of educational technology gives the field a mercurial character that eschews categorization and quantification. Mindful of these limitations, the study proposes that snapshots of data taken at different points in time and from different points of view can be compared, and this analysis may provide a starting point to illuminate how multimodal delivery is changing pedagogical assumptions and instructional methods distance graduate education. For this reason, this research will adapt a longitudinal methodology to uncover salient changes in pedagogy associated with a shift to a blended delivery at a university serving a population of adult learners.

The decision to focus on instructors as the subject of research reflects an awareness that change is not simply measured by shifts in learner outputs, quantified as plus or minuses on test scores, final grades, or student surveys. It also reflects the position that educators are by nature self-reflective, and that their perspectives needed to be included in conversations about pedagogy, learning and technology (Watson, 2001). The goal of this investigation is to uncover key factors and processes associated with the shift to blended learning. Four questions guided the current investigation:

1. Did the option of online blended delivery have an impact on instructors' choice of delivery method?
2. Were there any significant changes in instructors' knowledge and use of technology tools associated with blended delivery?
3. What were the long-term changes in instructional methods associated with blended delivery?
4. What was the impact of blended delivery on interactions with students?

Establishing and determining the meaning of changes in these four areas would begin to map some of the markers of pedagogies of blended delivery.

Methodology

Research Setting

A detailed description of the research setting explains how these questions could be realistically addressed in this investigation. The Graduate School of Education and Professional Development of Marshall University in West Virginia began to deliver electronic course delivery in 1997 as an option to assist with its mission in graduate distance education. Instructors from different program areas, including this researcher, were encouraged to experiment with different formats of online delivery within the WebCT, and later Blackboard, platforms. Instructors were free to select delivery options, ranging from use of electronic tools to support face-to-face classes to 100% electronic delivery. However, the majority of electronic graduate classes between 1998 and 2008 were taught as blended courses, defined as

80% electronic and 20% live (two to five live meetings). Since 2004, instructors and programs have experimented with 100% online delivery. It was within the context of a learning community with considerable experience and expertise with electronic delivery and having the freedom to make course delivery decisions that the current research emerged.

Participants

Thirty-seven full-time instructors in 2001 and 43 full-time instructors in 2008 were the principal subjects of this study. These include representatives from several graduate programs including, special education, literacy education, curriculum and instruction, counseling, leadership studies and school psychology. Of the 37 original instructors, 27 remained in 2008. In 2001, participants' range of experience with teaching online ranged from zero (0) to five (5) years, and averaged 1.9 years of experience. By 2008, 37% had been involved with different forms of electronic delivery for more than 8 years, 26% for both 6-8 and 3-5 years, and 11% for 2 years and less.

Research Design

A qualitative research design made sense in a field that is unmapped and where the researcher is interested in the experiences of the participants. The study employed a mixed-methods approach to gain understanding of how faculty perceptions and use of blended, multimodal delivery changed between 2001 and 2008. This first component of the study adopted a longitudinal approach to identify changes in instructor use, understanding, and attitudes connected with electronic delivery. The 2008 survey consisted of ten questions, seven of which asked respondents to select a response from four options. The remaining three questions asked respondents to select all relevant responses from a list of ten items. Data from a survey administered in 2001 were compared to data from the 2008 survey, using descriptive statistics. Twenty–four (63%) faculty completed the original survey in 2001. Twenty–eight (65%) faculty completed the follow-up survey in 2008.

The second phase of the research involved thematic analysis of nine interviews with instructors from a cross-section of graduate education program areas who had been involved in blended learning from 2001-2008. The interviews were structured around common questions but were sufficiently open-ended to allow participants to elaborate and interpret themes as they wished. The goal of the interviews was to expand on the meaning of factors identified by the survey data as indicators of change. The 'emergent theory' methods of Glaser and Strauss (1967) guided the analysis of interview materials.

ANALYSIS OF DATA

Surveys

A positive shift towards blended delivery was evident in changes in the delivery choices of instructors. In 2001, there were 53 blended courses, all of which had some live meetings. By 2008, course offerings reflected blends of live and Internet delivery and total online asynchronous delivery. There were 54 blended courses and 41 e-courses, delivered totally online. These shifts demonstrate the flux in electronic delivery. In 2001, instructors, on average, had developed 3-4 courses utilizing online delivery, with 46% of faculty developing 0-2 courses, 25% developing 3-5 online courses, another 25% developing 6-8 online courses, and the remaining 4% developing more than 8 online courses. By 2008, 26% had constructed more than 8 courses and 15% had developed 6-8 courses. Another 26% had developed 3-5 courses. Thirty-three percent of respondents had developed between 0 and 2 courses. This number included both 16 instructors hired between 2001 and 2007 and instructors who elected not to

Table 1. Percentages of tool use in 2001 and 2008

Tool	2001	2008
Mail	100%	93%
Discussions	96%	85%
Dropbox	17%	85%
Paths/Links	46%	52%
Calendar	58%	82%
Quizzes	38%	44%
Video	13%	19%
Audio	8%	19%
Survey	NA	37%

teach online. The preliminary finding supports the contention that instructors shifted more of their courses to a blended delivery model between 2001 and 2008.

In 2001, the majority of instructors (58%) rated their technological skill level for using electronic delivery as "intermediate" and an equal percentage (21%) indicated "novice and "advanced."

In 2008, users of electronic delivery rated themselves as advanced (44%), intermediate (44%), and novice (4%). Two respondents (7%) indicated they did not use electronic delivery and had limited observer knowledge of this form of delivery. The upward shift in perceived skill level establishes that instructors were becoming more comfortable and proficient in the technology indigenous to blended delivery. When juxtaposed with earlier findings of an increase in the number of blended courses constructed, these data support the contention that instructors were actively involved in shifting their courses to blended delivery as opposed to relying on university technological support to make the transition. The perceived growth in technological knowledge came at least in part from practice and experimentation involved with the construction of online components of blended courses.

It might be expected that instructors' growing technology expertise would be evident in different patterns of use of the tools within WebCT, and later Blackboard, learning platforms. Table 1 summarizes data on tool use from 2001 and 2008.

In 2001, use of communication tools, including mail (100%) and discussions (96%) was universal. This remained true in 2008, with some counter-indication of less generalized use of the discussion tool. Use of the quiz tool was slightly higher in 2008 (44%), as were the use video (from 13% to 19%) and audio (from 8% to 19%) links and clips. Use of embedded links went up slightly (+6%). Use of surveys, not mentioned in 2001, appeared on 37% of responses in 2008. The use of the assignment dropbox (+68%), used for assignment submission and instructor feedback, and of the calendar tool (+24%), principally used to indicate due dates for learning activities, showed significant increases in use. The dramatic shifts in use of tools found on the WebCT and Blackboard learning platforms are significant because both of these tools are connected with course learning activities.

Instructors were asked about changes in instructional methods and learning activities connected with online instruction. In 2001, virtually all respondents (96%) indicated that blended learning had led to changes in courses, with 50% of respondents citing planning and organization as the chief impact of online delivery on their teaching. Table 2 summarizes the data on the

Table 2. Impact of online delivery on teaching

Impact on...	2008
planning and organization	36%
accommodating different learning styles	32%
changes in course construction	24%
% of respondents not teaching online	8%

impact of the online component on blended course construction.

A significant shift evident in the data from 2008 was the refinement in identifying specific ways in which online delivery was influencing teaching. First, instructors had an enlarged awareness of how online delivery was affecting their teaching. Thirty-six percent cited planning and organization as the central way in which online delivery was changing their teaching, while 32% indicated the importance of accommodating different learning styles. Twenty-four percent of faculty indicated that online delivery caused them to re-conceptualize the way their course was constructed.

The relationship between learning activities linked to use of electronic tools is crucial to any pedagogy of blended delivery. In 2001, 79% of instructors indicated that online delivery had changed "the type of assignments" they made, but few referred to the role of the tools in relation to the assignments. Changes in assignments were characterized by more writing, more reading, and more emphasis on independent learning. While 96% of instructors used the discussion tool, few were utilizing the discussion board for group projects or saw its potential for work done in stages or drafts. In fact, 42% in 2001 believed online learning resulted in less group work and discussion. Few courses or programs had figured any way to accommodate practicum experiences in the online medium.

By 2008, there was a tremendous expansion in the range of learning activities shifted to the online components of blended courses as seen in Table 3.

The data on learning activities illuminate the diversification of learning activities shifted to online delivery. Additionally, the data reflect the expansion of user technical knowledge, as indicated by 39% of respondents who indicated

Table 3. Learning activities shifted to online delivery

Learning Activities	2008
No difference	4%
Collaborative projects	65%
Drafts or stages	50%
Assignments w/ multimedia features	35%
Peer feedback	61%
Digital demos	23%
Video segments	19%
Projects w/ web authoring tools	39%
Materials w/ multimedia	39%
% of respondents not teaching online	8%

Table 4. Impact of online delivery on student interactions

Descriptions of Interactions	2008
Same as in live class	5.3%
More individual interactions with students	56%
More frequent interactions with students	63.2%
Students initiate more interactions	57.9%
Different forms of interaction	63.2%
More immediate feedback on assignments	52%
Students interact more with each other as much or more than with instructor	36%
Students more into groups that operate autonomously	10.5%
Students regularly share information with instructor and peers	52%
N/A (Do not teach online)	8%

they created learning activities involving web-authoring and multimedia tools. Other responses captured the realization that learning online could be as social as that in a live class. Sixty-five percent (65%) of respondents were now using the electronic platform for collaborative projects and 61% were using online tools for peer feedback. These results demonstrated a growing realization that online learning involved knowledge that was socially constructed, confirming the hypothesis of Leu, Kinzer, Coiro, and Cammack (2004) that "the socially skilled learners will be advantaged over 'monastic learners' children who rely solely on independent learning strategies" (p. 1598). These results confirm new uses for the tools built into the learning platforms. Instructors adapted and refined tool use to re-construct learning activities, informed by the tools of the learning platform and multimedia applications.

Frequency and forms of interactions with students are essential components of pedagogy, and it is important to establish any impact of a shift to blended delivery. In 2001, 92% of instructors perceived that online delivery had changed their interactions with students but limited their descriptions to an increase in the number of interactions with students via mail and the discussion board. Results from the 2008 survey showed a sea change in that instructors acknowledged both increased and diversified communications with students associated with the online components of blended delivery. Table 4 summarizes instructors' perceptions of changes in interactions with students.

Instructors characterized the effects on online delivery as resulting in more individual contacts with students (56%), more immediate feedback on assignments (52%) and students sharing information with instructor and peers (52%). In addition and perhaps more significant were the mutations in patterns of communication indigenous to blended delivery. It is highly significant that in 2008, 36% of respondents report that students interacted with each other as much or more than with the instructor.

A longitudinal study of survey data captured changes in pedagogy related to the use of blended, multimodal delivery. Analysis of survey data from 2001 and 2008 from the same population illuminated key factors that contribute to an emerging pedagogy of blended, multimodal learning. While there was evidence that instructors shifted more of their course to the blended delivery model, there was no consensus about what this model entailed. There were significant variations in the proportions of the course conducted live and electronically, and even wider variations in the use of tools to support the learning. A defining feature of blended delivery was it fluidity. Additional research will need to identify what is included under the blended umbrella, particularly addressing the possibilities extended by podcasting and video conferencing.

Secondly, instructors expressed growing confidence in their technological expertise. This expressed itself in tool use in the WebCT and later Blackboard shells. Some tools, such as the assignment dropbox and the calendar, increased dramatically, but several showed consistent use in 2001 and 2008. The most significant findings about tool use were the tremendous increases in the use of the dropbox and calendar. At the very least, this fact meant that instructors had learned to use these tools to organize learning use of the basic tools within the learning environment.

When juxtaposed with changes in learning activities, it becomes clear that changes in the use of these tools related to changes in assumptions and practices of learning activities. It was evident that instructors emphasized planning and organizing in ways that were different from traditional courses. Moreover, instructors both re-constructed assignments to accommodate different learning styles and took advantage of multimodal tools to construct diversified learning experiences, appealing to a wider range of learning styles. The shift to assignments featuring socially constructed knowledge is a solid indication of the adaptability of the blended model to authentic learning experiences.

Interviews

The finding of survey data from 2001 and 2008, however, are suggestive rather than definitive. To say that a significant proportion of instructors shifted more courses to blended and to e-course delivery formats does not provide much insight into the thinking behind the shifts. Similarly, statistics on the impact of the online environment on teaching do not provide fine enough details on the nature of changes in course construction. The detailed statistics similarly confirm changes in tool use but require more elaboration to provide a framework through which to understand these decisions. How did collaborative learning experiences develop in online environments? What changed in learning experiences? What factors influenced decisions about what would be accomplished in the online environment and what would be done at the face-to-face meetings? Addressing these questions extends understanding of the impact of blended learning on pedagogy. The interviews with instructors probed these areas.

Metaphors of Course Design

Metaphors used to describe course design captured deeper shifts in thinking about the online component of blended learning. 'Uploading', 'Idiosyncratic', 'personalized', 'random' and 'technology for technology's sake' were common descriptors developers used to describe design principles in 2001. Design informed by these metaphors appeared as dancing icons, catchy tunes and a startling array of fonts, colors, and formats heralding an era of experimentation and a fascination with the possibilities of electronic learning. Materials and assignments were placed on the shell and students were expected to construct their own 'random' paths and sequence through the materials and activities.

Behind these metaphors were understandings of teaching and learning that reflected a tension between the thinking of traditional face-to-face course design and nascent online design principles. Instructors reported, "We had no directions"; "we tried lots of different ways to manage the course," and "copied from one another." Instructors referred to 'uploading' to describe online courses in 2001. They spoke of uploading files and PowerPoint presentations used in live classes. There was a clear expectation that these components would be the basis of the electronic course content. Said one more experienced respondent, "faculty arrived with suitcases of materials and requested assistance in loading it into a shell" while another worried, "that the content of the online course could never duplicate what he could do in face-to-face meetings." Assignments were added as the course went on, as were content files and tools; changes were often made to files, either to correct errors or to clarify information. In these ways, instructors showed the hold of face-to-face ways of operating and the difficulty of constructing courses in the unmapped electronic terrain.

On the other hand, there was an embracing of self-directed learning reflected in the practice of allowing students to work their way through the materials at their own pace, in ways that respected their autonomy and different learning styles. The 'random' concept emerged because instructors associated the electronic environment with a non-linear, student-centered approach to learning. The influence of Piaget's discovery learning principles could be seen in these attempts to use the new technology to break free of pedagogical restraints imposed by the bureaucratization and to create a learning space informed by constructivist thinking.

The descriptions of course design in the first years of blended learning reflected a tension between holding onto past practices and embracing the possibilities of the new technologies. As instructors became more familiar with the tools and operation of the online learning platform, metaphors to explain course construction in 2008 shifted to images of 'road maps,' 'modules' and 'user-friendly' designs, reflective of growing knowledge about how to construct the electronic components of blended courses. When asked to describe differences in most recently developed blended courses, respondents referred of the availability of design guides that assisted both faculty and students in navigating online learning. Secondly, instructors noted that courses had become more compressed. Whereas the typical course in 1999 was ten to fifteen folders, each corresponding to a course topic usually derived from the face-to-face delivery model, the same courses in 2008 was organized into six-eight learning modules, each of which dealt with significant learning outcomes expected in the course.

Course shells were less cluttered and more uniform in font and design. Common processes and approaches led to more effective learning, a finding confirmed by the research of Manton, Fernandez, Balch, and Meredith (2004). This uniformity, in turn, made space for the unique features of the online environment to emerge. Instructors came to the realization that some topics needed to be addressed before others, and many spoke of the need to build up 'a knowledge base' before tackling advanced problem-solving within a discipline. Instead of randomized learning experiences, or transferring content, successive iterations of online courses in 2008 reflected greater concern constructing online components that served the teaching and learning goals.

From Assignments to Learning Experiences

The interviews uncovered an evolving pattern in thinking about course assignments, as designated in most face-to-face environments or learning experiences, as more commonly referenced in online environments. The first significant factor emerged from recognition of the value of the features on online tools in assisting with learning experiences, as reflected in the 2008 data showing dramatic increases in use of the assignment tools. Having an electronic place to house and access assignments, rubrics, feedback, and exemplars solved a common complaint of educators in face-to-face environment where assignments often became detached from the course experience. In the electronic environment, the assignment always remained part of the course. It became a point of reference in future student-instructor dialogues. The integration of assignments into the fabric of the course emerged clearly in the interviews as a positive feature of online learning.

The transparency and accessibility of assignments and assessments in electronic environments was a distinct feature of electronic learning. Blended delivery accelerated the practice of systematically sharing learning goals with students through use of exemplars and rubrics. Many instructors noted that it was more common for students to revisit an assignment simply because the tools facilitated the transmission of timely feedback and encouraged resubmission as part of the learning activity. Again, while all of this was possible in face-to-face learning, it simply did not take place on the scale actualized with blended learning.

Framed in this way, assignments took on a more prominent role as learning activities integrated into the course learning processes, rather than discrete ends in themselves. In addition, as instructors gained understanding of the capabilities of the electronic tools, assignments were recast as broader and more authentic learning experiences that became the 'work' and focus of the course. One instructor noted:

My earlier idea was that my course would be the same and that I was just delivering it in a different way; however, as I got more involved with electronic learning, feedback from students made me realize that the assignments and the discussion around them were course content.

In this way, instructors shifted from the transmission model supported by the traditions and structures of face-to-face delivery and focused more on authentic learning experiences that emphasized the student as an active knower. Other responses captured the need for clear and specific performance expectations in the online component of blended learning. Several respondents reported that a shift in mindset was required to view the online course from the perspective of the student who had only the information and tools in the shell as a guide.

Social Dimensions of Learning

While survey data had demonstrated that the use of the discussion tool was as frequent in 2001 as in 2008, the interviews showed changes in the purpose and structure of online discussions. As instructors acquired the skills to group and re-group students according to different learning needs, discussions became more focused. The open-ended participant discussions that dominated the early years of electronic delivery gave way to discussions organized by groups and topics. Here the role of the instructor as orchestrator is clearly evident. Instructors commented, "In the past I just let the discussion direct itself and I found myself reading through reams of material, a lot of which was more affirmations of what others had written." There was a clear understanding that the instructor needed to structure the groups to maximize learning. "If the instructor does not have a good reason for the discussion, don't have one. Discussion just to use the tool is a waste of time." Gains from well-managed online discussions were noted as well: "I have had deeper online discussions about course topics than I have ever had in face-to-face meetings" and "Online discussions can extend over several days so people are not just writing the first thing that comes into their minds." The conclusion that online discussions were deeper and more engaged than face-to-face dialogues extended a finding of McCrory, Putnam and Jansen (2008).

In 2001, the prevailing view was that online learning was for the self-directed autonomous learner while in 2008, 65% of respondents reported using the online shells for collaborative projects. One factor in this shift was the maturation of increasingly sophisticated web authoring tools that allow a range of collaborative projects. The proliferation of blogs, wikis and webquests provide instructors tools that supported a range of collaborative projects impractical in face-to-face learning environments. The tools did not create the collaborative learning activities but they did create the conditions that made them feasible. "I saw ways to create projects that I never could attempt in face-to-face learning; "My projects grew more involved with each version of my course; what started as an isolated discussion topic became the most important project in the course." These observations support the research of Ausburn (2004) and Donnelly (2006) that concluded that the new technologies were especially powerful for collaborative projects. There was a growing recognition among instructors that in the electronic medium, group work or collaborative work was course content (Cook, 2002; Crook, 2001). In turn, this transformation from assignments that reflected learned content to learning experiences as course content shifted a larger shift to student-centered learning.

Changes in Face-to-Face Meetings

Changes in blended course design influenced decisions about face-to-face meetings as much as online components. These changes can be organized around the purpose, number and duration of live meetings in blended courses. Initially, most instructors used the live meetings to cover topics that could not be easily done online and to coordinate upcoming learning activities. The presentations featured the traditional format of lecture/discussion and a PowerPoint. It was common for instructors and students to arrive at live meetings with the entire course run off. Said one respondent, "I was always afraid of students' misunderstanding what was online or not looking at it; the paper version was the real course." Some reported using the time for demonstrations and collaborative projects that required extensive interaction. The number of live meetings in the early years fluctuated between three and six. Most instructors mentioned that a portion of the live meeting was devoted to discussing upcoming projects and assignments.

By 2008, the live meetings had undergone a reorganization and transformation, reflective of a shift in emphasis from content to learning. Live meetings became more focused on learner objectives, and these centered on learning activities that could not be easily done online: role playing in counseling, individualized 'in the moment' reading lessons in literacy, group activities in elementary education, and simulations in education leadership, requiring immediate feedback and interaction between and among participants. In 2001, the live meetings were three hours, as were typical in traditional face-to-face classes. Faculty interviewed in 2008 reported a shift towards differentiated class times, as determined by the learning needs of participants. A session might be longer or shorter than the usual three hours; it might involve an individual meeting, small groups of students, or the whole class. It was evident that the shift to blended delivery transformed the format and the content of live sessions as much as it reshaped the content of electronic course components.

New Roles for Instructors

The interviews identified distinct shifts in the role of instructors as delivery options diversified. Face-to-face delivery tended to lock instructors into a week-to-week preparation model that emphasized content and weekly topics. The bureaucratization of education implicitly promoted a transmission model of knowledge in which the instructor assumed the principal role as disseminator of information. The shift to a blended learning environment provided a viable context in which instructors could see themselves as facilitators, guiding student-centered learning as distinct from conveyers of information. Comments from instructors reflected an awareness of a role change: "I had to get used to not having this live bunch in front of me each week"; "A lot of my work now has to get done before the class starts."; "I spend much more time setting things up and making sure the technology is working on the class shell." These comments reveal an awareness of a change in role already documented in research (Ravencroft, 2001; Yang & Cornelious, 2005).

The construction and organization of learning experiences in electronic environments further refined the role of facilitator. As instructors experimented with online delivery, several began to reconstruct their learning experiences into active learning experiences, and this in turn shifted their perception of their role as instructor from facilitator to orchestrator. "If one thing is different for me, it is that I have to plan everything carefully." "What I know about my discipline comes out in how I set up the course." Instructors found they could use their expertise in a given discipline to construct learning experiences that engaged students in authentic situations. Whereas this possibility was always available in face-to-face classrooms, the particular features of the electronic environment provided the medium and the tools to re-conceptualize learning from the learner's perspective. Whereas face-to-face classes emphasized the role of the instructor as organizer and presenter of course topics, the electronic environment set up the instructor's role as developer and organizer of authentic learning experiences.

CONCLUSIONS AND FUTURE TRENDS

The longitudinal approach of this investigation provided a window on the impact of blended, multimodal delivery on university instructors' thinking and professional practice. When applied to the challenge of capturing changes in instruction related to the blended environment, it illuminated dimensions of the interactions between humans and machines that shifted the typography of graduate pedagogy from processes and structures that supported a transmission model to those that supported student-centered learning and active knowledge construction.

Survey data provided a broad outline of the ways in which instructors structured the online components of blended courses. Analysis of data from 2001 and 2008 from the same population illuminated key factors that contribute to an emerging pedagogy of electronic learning. The first is that there is no single delivery model synonymous with blended delivery. There were significant variations in the proportions of the course conducted live and electronically, and even wider variations in the use of tools to support the learning. A defining feature of blended delivery seems to be its fluidity. Secondly, while over time instructors ranked their technological expertise as higher and more expert, they used the same basic tools present in 2001 on the WEB-Ct and later Blackboard shells. Some tools, such as the assignment dropbox and the calendar, increased dramatically but several showed consistent use in 2001 and 2008. In and of itself, this fact means little more than instructors had learned to use these tools to organize learning use of the basic tools within the learning environment. Dramatic changes were evident, however, in the ways in which the online tools were used to construct learning activities. Collaborative projects, those involving peer feedback, and assignments done in drafts or stages were normative in blended learning classes.

While the descriptive statistics illuminated changes associated with multimodal online delivery, in-depth interviews with course developers clarified evolving ideas and practices about blended delivery. Instructors re-thought basic premises of learning and teaching while they experimented with online delivery. This led to a re-framing of courses as learning experiences rather than as a series of content topics. The focus of the course shifted from content to learning, actualizing the epistemological intent of social constructivism, as envisioned by Vygotsky. The nature of the learning experiences emerged as process-based, authentic and richly collaborative. Further, the maturation of multimodal, web-authoring tools made it possible for instructors to construct collaborative learning projects that supported a variety of learning styles and most important, dispelled the perception that online learning was a solitary venture. Collaborative learning and online discussions, together with offline interactions provided the instructor with an environment that made a place for socially constructed knowledge; their knowledge of pedagogy created authentic learning experiences within this environment.

The goal of this investigation was to make sense of how blended learning environments, combining both face-to-face and online elements, is shaping teaching and learning for professional learners in a distance graduate education program. The longitudinal perspective provided a method to identify and document changes in instructional practice. It demonstrated that instructors both experimented and reflected as they shifted from face-to-face courses to blended designs. The centrality of pedagogy in their design processes, a central finding of this study, identified the impact of educational technology on teaching and learning. An intriguing pattern in the data supported the premise that the shift to blended learning provided many university instructors with the opportunity and the tools to move from a content-based curriculum, based on a transmission model, to a learning-centered pedagogy that realized constructivist principles. The electronic classroom did what forty years of traditional university pedagogy could not accomplish. It actualized the shift in emphasis from the teacher to the learner, and set in motion a conversation about the theoretical principles that explain teaching and learning with educational technology. This finding can easily be overstated; it will take studies with different populations to verify if this finding has validity beyond the boundaries of the graduate educators involved in distance education.

This inquiry focused on the importance of grounding the theory of blended learning in research and in particular, longitudinal research. It demonstrated how such an approach can provide a clearer understanding of the relationship between pedagogy and blended learning environments. The longitudinal investigation made sense of change in a rapidly transforming technological environment. A wider research angle and a firmer theoretical base will only be possible if data are gathered and stored, and if those involved with all forms of blended delivery of learning recognize the value of both capturing data and reflecting on its meaning. Parallel studies with different learning communities are necessary to confirm, extend, refute and refine the main findings of the current investigation. Such investigations will gradually extend the theoretical base of blended pedagogy through 'cross- disciplinary triangulation' (Cook, 2002; Watson, 2001).

More refined analyses of online and offline learning experiences are needed. Secondly, more detailed studies on the nature and processes of learning communities in blended learning environments must be undertaken. While problem-based learning has received some attention (Donnelly, 2006), other learning theories identified with constructivist, collaborative learning need to investigated. The dramatic shifts in thinking about assignments, and assessment suggest that extended research is needed on the ways in which online environments support learner-centered, authentic assessment. Examples are electronic portfolios and assessment linked and diagnostic assessments that guide and inform student learning.

This investigation leaves to others the task of providing blueprints for developing successful blended learning environments; similarity it eschews the temptation of providing advice on best practices. It validates the importance of asking questions about pedagogy and learning, and of conducting research to address those questions. It charges professional educators and researchers with the task of recognizing, challenging, and documenting the shifting typography of teaching and learning in 're-mediated' (Cook, 1994) electronic environments in which human and computers interact.

REFERENCES

Ausburn, L. (2004). Course design elements most valued by adult learners in blended online education: An American perspective. *Educational Media International, 41*(4), 327–337. doi:10.1080/0952398042000314820

Bell, M., & Lafoe, G. (1998). Curriculum design for flexible delivery-massaging the model. In *Proceedings ASCITE 98 Conference* (pp. 65-73).

Brinkerhaff, J., & Koroghlanian, C. M. (2007). Online students' expectations: Enhancing the fit between online students and course design. *Journal of Educational Computing Research, 36*(4), 383–393. doi:10.2190/R728-28W1-332K-U115

Brusilovsky, P. (2001). Adaptive hypermedia. *User Modeling and User Adapted Interaction, 11*(1/2), 87-110. Retrieved from http://www.sis.pitt.edu/~peterb/papers/brusilovsky-umuai-2001.pdf

Carter-Wells, J., Ivers, J., & Lee, J. (2003). Developing an online degree program: Design, delivery, unique features. In *Proceedings of the TECH ED Conference Presentation*, Ontario, CA.

Console, G. (2004). E-learning: The hype and the reality. *Journal of Interactive Media in Education, 12*, 1-18. Retrieved April 15, 2008, from http://www.jme.open.ac.uk/2004/12

Cook, J. (2002). The role of dialogue in computer-based learning: an evolutionary approach to theory. *Journal of Interactive Media in Education, 5*, 1–28.

Cooner, T. S. (2005). Dialectical constructivism: Reflections on creating a web-mediated enquiry-based learning environment. *Social Work Education, 24*(4), 375–390. doi:10.1080/02615470500096902

Crook, C. (1994). *Computers and the collaborative experience of learning.* London: Routledge.

Crook, C. (2001). The social character of knowing and learning: implications of cultural psychology for educational technology. *Journal of Information Technology for Teacher Education, 10*(1&2), 19–36.

Dalsgaard, C., & Godsk, M. (2007). Transforming traditional lectures into problem-based blended learning: challenges and experiences. *Open Learning, 22*(1), 29–42. doi:10.1080/02680510601100143

Donnelly, R. (2006). Blended problem-based learning for teacher education: lessons learnt. *Learning, Media and Technology, 31*(2), 93–116. doi:10.1080/17439880600756621

El-Gayar, O., & Dennis, T. (2005). Effectiveness of hybrid learning environments. *Issues in Information Systems, 6*(1), 176–182.

Ghislandi, P., & Job, R. (2005). Collaborative learning for an online higher education course: a case study. In *Proceedings of the Fifth IEEE International Conference on Advanced Learning Technologies, (ICAL'05).*

Issroff, K., & Scanlon, E. (2002). Educational technology: The influence of theory. *Journal of Interactive Media in Education, 6*, 1–13.

Leu, D. L., Kinzer, C. K., Coiro, J. L., & Cammack, D. (2004). Towards a theory of new literacies from the Internet and other information and communication technologies. In R. B. Ruddell & N. J. Unrau (Eds.), *Theoretical Models and Processes of Reading* (5th ed.) (pp. 1570-1613). Newark, DE: International Reading Association.

Manton, M., Fernandez, B., Balch, D., & Meredith, M. (2004). Forced to conform? Using common processes and standards to create effective e-Learning. *Journal of Interactive Media in Education, 14*, 1–15.

Mayer, R. (2004). Should there be a three-strikes rule against pure discovery learning? The case for guided methods of instruction. *The American Psychologist*, *59*(1), 14–19. doi:10.1037/0003-066X.59.1.14

McCrory, R., Putnam, R., & Jansen, A. (2008). Interaction in online courses for teacher education: Subject matter and pedagogy. *Journal of Technology and Teacher Education*, *16*(2), 155–180.

Mossavar-Rahmani, F., & Larson-Daugherty, C. (2007). Supporting the hybrid learning model: A new proposition. *MERLOT Journal of Online Learning and Teaching*, *3*(1), 67–78.

Ravenscroft, A. (2001). Designing E-learning interactions in the 21st century: revisiting and rethinking the role of theory. *European Journal of Education*, *36*(2), 133–156. doi:10.1111/1467-3435.00056

Sankey, M., & Smith, A. (2004). Multimodal Design and Hybrid Course Materials: Developing a New Paradigm for Course Delivery at USQ. In *Proceedings of the Common Ground Publishing Pty Ltd and RMIT University, International Conference on Computers in Education 2004*, Melbourne, Australia.

Sankey, M., & St. Hill, R. (2005). Multimodal design for hybrid learning materials in a second-level economics course. In *Proceedings of the 11th Australasian Teaching Economics Conference* (pp. 98-106).

Stockley, D. (2006). Building a successful e-learning strategy. *Enterprise Information*, *2*(7).

Su, D. (2005). A comparative evaluation and correlation between learning styles and academic achievement on e-learning. In R. Kwan & J. Fong (Eds.), *Web-based Learning: Technology and Pedagogy, Proceedings of the 4th International Conference* (pp. 193-202). Singapore: World Scientific Publishing Co. Pte. Ltd.

Watson, D. (2001). Pedagogy before technology: Re-thinking the relationship between ICT and teaching. *Education and Information Technologies*, *6*(4), 251–266. doi:10.1023/A:1012976702296

Yang, Y., & Cornelious, L. (2005). Preparing instructors for quality online instruction. *Online Journal of Distance Learning Administration*, *8*(Spring). Retrieved February 26, 2008 from http://www.westga.edu/~distance/spring81/yang.htm

Zang, D. (2005). Interactive multimedia-based e-learning: A study of effectiveness. *American Journal of Distance Education*, *19*(3), 149–162. doi:10.1207/s15389286ajde1903_3

KEY TERMS AND DEFINITIONS

Blended Learning: An environment in which learning is done in real time whether in a face-to-face meeting or a virtualized meeting and asynchronously, typically on a learning platform, as indicated by the learning experience.

Constructivism: An epistemological theory that maintains that all knowledge is actively constructed by humans and as such has no independent objective reality.

Content-Centered: An emphasis in pedagogy that places transmission of content at the center of instructional processes and goals.

Hybrid Learning: Another name for blended learning that emphasizes the combination of features of electronic and face-to-face delivery.

Learner-Centered: An emphasis in pedagogy that places the learning experience at the center of instructional processes and goals.

Multimodal: Tools associated with Internet technologies that rely upon different media.

Social Constructivism: Associated with Lev Vygotsky, the theory that all knowledge was mediated through its social or cultural context.

Chapter 19
Knowledge Acquisition in a Hybrid Graduate Teacher Training Program

Thanh T. Nguyen
Bridgewater State College, USA

ABSTRACT

How can one leverage the technological benefits of an online classroom without losing both the interpersonal advantages of face-to-face contact and pedagogically sound classroom management techniques? A blended learning environment, combining both traditional face-to-face and online interaction, is a valid higher-education solution that many instructors are adopting in place of 100% online teaching environments. Like total online courses, blended courses offer students the convenience of online access to both lecture/course materials and asynchronous classroom discussions. However, the key feature of a blended learning environment is the ability to use traditional face-to-face sessions to foster and stimulate an online social culture that facilitates knowledge acquisition through interpersonal and group discussion and disclosure. This study examines pedagogical, social and demographic factors that contribute to students' knowledge acquisition in an 80-20 (80% online and 20% in-class) blended learning environment.

KNOWLEDGE ACQUISITION THROUGH ONGOING DISCOURSE

Knowledge acquisition is not a stand-alone entity but, rather, is constructed over time through social engagements and ongoing discourses within cultural contexts and value systems. Based on assumptions of the social constructivism theory, an individual acquires knowledge only through his or her engaged social activities. When members of a community get together and interpret a world as their shared world, they form a set of beliefs and culture, and, over time, knowledge about their world. In this social negotiation process or a "zone of proximal development (ZPD)," students contribute to and learn from each other's pragmatic knowledge while adjusting to a group consensus on a topic (Kim, B., 2001, Vygotsky, 1978).

DOI: 10.4018/978-1-60566-380-7.ch019

In a traditional, face-to-face, classroom, communication and human connections are great assets for knowledge acquisition and the construction of the learning community. Exchanges between teachers and students and among students happen spontaneously. Teachers can recognize non-verbal cues and are able to motivate each student on an individual basis. These connections are necessary for students and teachers to share values, ideas, and goals. When a course moves online, communication dynamics are altered. Non-verbal communication cues disappear and, since students converse asynchronously, spontaneous interaction is impossible. However, taking into consideration that online education allows students opportunities to learn independently – from anywhere at any time – and to construct and acquire learning at their own pace, online education provides many advantages for students beyond the classroom walls (Coates & Humphreys, 2001).

In designing an oline instruction, educators relied on brain research looking at how complex and interconnected the brain is and how the mind constructs meaning. Because the brain seeks meaning through different patterns, instructions should be designed with the process of reflective inquiry that allows students to connect problems directly to their lives (Gibson & McKay, 1999). Since learning is influenced not only by new information but also by emotions and personal biases, "the need for social interaction… is somewhat like the weather. (It is) ongoing and the emotional impact of any lesson or life experience may continue to reverberate long after the specific event." (Caine and Canine, 1991, p. 82)

In teacher training programs, it is particularly crucial for teacher candidates to understand and be able to share their personal emotions and biases in group discussions. Candidates must be able to justify their thoughts through spontaneous interactions and feedback in a traditional face-to-face classroom. Over a period of time, candidates are hoped to alter or form their new sets of values in responding to diverse learners. This traditional model has worked for full time students who can form their own study groups beyond class time. Unfortunately, in graduate teacher education programs in the United States, many teacher candidates are already teaching in schools but required to take courses for teaching certification. Taking into consideration of their limited time, can a blended learning environment still provide candidates a place where they can share their personal emotion, values and believes?

THE 80-20 BLENDED LEARNING ENVIRONMENT

The 80-20 Blended Learning Environment Model was developed in the early 1990s by Rensselaer Polytechnic Institute's Anderson Center for Innovation in Undergraduate Education in response to the lack of interaction in distance learning for corporate training courses. This model allows students to spend 80 percent of their time to engage with online materials at their pace and 20 percent to interact synchronously with the instructor and other students (Lister, et. al, 1999). The 80-20 model attempted to build its format on social activities that would capture all the benefits of interactive online tools for students to construct their own knowledge through discourses that would mimic hands-on activities in a face-to-face classroom (Wilson and Mosher, 1994). In examining student perceptions, Black (2001) found that students preferred and were more satisfied with hybrid courses than either online-only or classroom-only courses, especially when the students' level of computer expertise increased. When an online classroom is blended into a face-to-face classroom, a higher achievement rate is realized in comparison with similar face-to-face or fully online courses (Dziuban and Moskal, 2001).

In designing a blended learning environment, instructors assumingly must plan their courses differently than for either a traditional or 100%

online classroom. They should contemplate questions such as:

- What percentage of course time do students need to meet face-to-face and online?
- How long do students need to know each other offline before building an online community?
- How much and what type of support do students need for using the Internet and the courseware platform?
- How do demographic factors such as gender, age, number of teaching years, and type of teaching license seeking influence individual online participation?
- What type of course assignments and instructions allow students to gain greater subject-matter knowledge?
- What reading and writing levels are needed for moving course assignments online?
- How much interaction is needed for discussion?

For this paper, the research questions are:

- Is a 20% face-to-face/online meeting ratio sufficient for teacher candidates to make significant interpersonal connections with classmates and the instructor and to feel comfortable enough to actively participate in the online community?
- Would an 80% online/face-to-face meeting ratio be enough for candidates to scaffold their knowledge through connecting and reflecting on their assigned readings, and to contribute to and learn from each other's pragmatic knowledge?
- How do gender, age, and years of teaching experience relate to candidate willingness to participate online and ability to master course materials?

FINDINGS

Forty questionnaires were administered to and collected from graduate candidates in a masters-level education program. Using open-ended questions together with a Likert scale (1 to 5 for strongly disagree to strongly agree), candidates were able to reflect on their 20% face-to-face meeting class time and how the 80% online learning environment scaffold their knowledge.

Regardless of their limited time while working and studying, candidates stated how important it is for them to be physically connected with their classmates in the 20% face-to-face meeting time. The online learning setting, on the other hand, provided them ongoing discussion forums in which they had more time to reflect on their own while seeking to understand different sets of values and beliefs presented by their classmates. When asked how much candidates understand the course outcomes before and after the semester, candidates reported different average scores, 2.867 for pre-test and 4.227 for post-test. Using the t-test statistic to determine a p-value, the result indicates a statistically significant difference between the two groups.

Building a Learning Community through 20% Face-to-Face Meetings

In building an online learning community, an icebreaker exercise at the first face-to-face meeting played an important role for candidates to connect with their classmates. This connection allowed candidates to connect their "real" to their virtual classmates when the course moved online. Candidates were paired with other candidates who they had never met before. Based on the "Ws list", or the basic questions "Who, What, Where, Why, When and How", each pair was asked to interview each other, then went in front of the class to introduce the interviewee to their classmates. Candidates then posted their interviewed information onto the first meeting discussion online forum on

Table 1. Significant differences found in gender, age, years of teaching and level of seeking license

Gender	t(40)	4.176 (Female)	p< 0.026
Age	t(40)	4.217 (22 to 32 years)	p<0.010
Number Years of Teaching	t(40)	4.311 (0 to 3)	p<0.019
Level of Seeking License**	t(40)	4.467 (Initial)	p<0.020

* p: statistically significant difference

** Level of Massachusetts Teaching License: Initial (first teaching license), and Professional (advanced teaching license)

BlackBoard®. This activity helped candidates recognize their classmates, not only in a face-to-face meeting but also in online discussions. Some students stated,

I liked the first face-to-face meeting because we could discuss people's jobs, careers, [and] aspirations. I found this exercise extremely interesting. (Survey # IT201)

I listened to people's stories and wrote briefly their physical descriptions so that I would remember who they are online. (Survey # ED201)

The second face-to-face meeting refreshed candidates' memories after a couple online classes. Candidates were able to reconnect their classmates' online writing with classmates in person. This reconnection in building their relationship played an important role for candidates to move online again in the next many online meetings. Another acknowledged,

In all four courses I have taken, the second face-to-face meeting was the most helpful in connecting with classmates. (Survey # IT408)

The final meeting face-to-face provided opportunities for candidates to present, discuss, and learn how other classmates were either designing their teaching units or solving problems that K-12 candidates and teachers face daily.

The final face-to-face meeting helped because I saw the progression of the projects online and the culminating presentation in person. (Survey # IT208).

Case study presentations were an outstanding vehicle to swap ideas. (Survey # ED 234)

T-test statistic was used to determine a p-value of different variables such as Gender, Age, Number of Years Teaching, and Level of Seeking License (See Table 1). Females reported 4.176 on average, 3.865 for males. Candidates from 22 to 32 years of age reported 3.755 on average, 2.863 for the group from 33 to 54 years of age. Candidates with first-three-year teaching experience reported 4.311 on average, 3.530 for three years plus. Candidates seeking initial license reported 4.467 on average, 4.122 for those who sought their professional license.

The result indicates a statistically significant difference between males and females, younger and older candidates, less and more than three years teaching experiences, and seeking initial or professional license. Over all, female, young teachers, teachers with less than three years of teaching experiences, and those seeking initial license were more satisfied in these four face-to-face meetings

Reflections on an 80% Online Learning Experiences

Activities for the 80% online classroom included: read assigned readings, answer weekly questions not only based on reading materials but also incorporated both personal and professional experiences on discussion forum. Candidates were required to read their classmates' answers then provided feedback. Once they received feedback, they had to respond to feedback in order to build in an online discourse. These online activities helped scaffold candidates' new knowledge. Following are the results of measurements for the 80% online classroom activities as well as features of social constructivism curriculum design.

More Reading Time

When candidates were asked to reflect on their online learn experiences, candidates reported that online learning allowed them to have more time for comprehending assigned readings before posting answers. Overall, candidates rated these questions at 4.338 on average. Using the t-test statistic to determine a p-value, the result showed no statistically significant difference for gender, years of teaching, level of seeking license or matriculated candidates. Significant difference was found between younger (4.625 on average) and older (4.139 on average) candidates. The result indicated that more reading time played a significant difference for younger candidates because they needed more time to connect assigned reading materials with their personal and professional experiences.

Importance of Selecting Assigned Reading Materials

Selection for reading online played an important role in designing an online curriculum. Candidates agreed that selection for assigned reading materials should be relevant to a candidate's professional and personal life. Overall, candidates rated this question at 3.796 on average. Using the t-test statistic to determine a p-value, the result showed no statistically significant difference for gender, years of teaching experiences, level of seeking license, or matriculated candidates. Significant difference was found between younger (4.000 on average) and older (3.570 on average) candidates. The result indicated that selecting relevant reading materials played a significant difference for younger candidates.

Online Discussion and Feedback

Online discussion forums provided an import environment for candidates to acquire new knowledge through social discourse. When candidates posted their answers and provided feedback to each other with their views and experiences based on the same set of reading materials, they in due course would share a set of beliefs and culture, and, over time, knowledge about their world. When candidates were asked to reflect on their weekly online discourse, they reported that these activities allowed them opportunities to reflect and connect to their own knowledge and built their empathy toward others, gaining new knowledge or opening up to different views from reading classmate's posting and feedback. Overall, candidates rated this question at 4.042 on average. Using the t-test statistic to determine a p-value, the result showed no statistically significant difference for age, years of teaching experiences, or matriculated candidates. Significant difference was found between females (4.140 on average) and males (3.878 on average), and initial license candidates (4.556 on average) and professional license (3.800 on average). The result indicated that online discourse played a significant difference for female and for candidates seeking initial teaching license (See Table 2).

In measuring online learning experiences, the surveyed candidates were asked if their online learning experience was positive, enjoyable, offering a sense of ownership of the course, or empowering. Overall, candidates responded to these questions at 4.194 on average. Using the t-test statistic to determine a p-value, the result showed no statistically significant difference for matriculation and level of seeking license. Significant difference was found between females (4.280

Table 2. Significant differences found in age and years of teaching for online discussion and feedback

Gender	t(40)	4.140 (Female)	p< 0.032
Level of Seeking License	t(40)	4.556 (Initial)	p<0.019

* p: statistically significant difference
Positive Learning Online Experiences

on average) and males (3.867 on average), younger (4.391 on average) and older (4.000 on average) candidates, and less than three years (4.404 on average) and more than three years (3.900 on average) experiences. The results indicated that female and young candidates and candidates with less than three years of teaching experience had a positive and enjoyable experience as well as a sense of ownership and a feeling of taking control of their learning in an online discourse design (See Table 3).

Changing Opinions on Issues

Candidates were asked if they changed opinions on issues through this 80-20 Blended Learning Environment Model. Overall, candidates rated this question at 3.300 on average. Using the t-test statistic to determine a p-value, the result showed no statistically significant difference for all variables. However, candidates reported in individual journal entries:

While I did not reverse any opinions, I did receive good suggestions that I will use. (Survey # ED102)

When I was feeling strongly about a particular topic, occasional comments from others helped soften my opinion. (Survey # ED205)

Different experiences and backgrounds of classmates give them perspectives I hadn't considered. (Survey # ED204)

One of the key components for online learning is to require candidates to keep track of their learning growth through weekly reflection in a journal. In reflecting this requirement, candidates were asked if journal entries helped them keep track of their learning growth in an online classroom. Overall, candidates responded to this question at 4.235 on average. Using the t-test statistic to determine a p-value, the result showed no statistically significant difference for matriculation and teaching experiences. Significant difference was found between female (3.795 on average) and males (3.467 on average), younger ((3.806 on average) and older ((3.528 on average) candidates, and seeking Initial license (3.768 on average) and Professional (3.320 on average) candidates. The results indicated that females, young teachers and candidates who seek initial license agreed that keeping their weekly journal helps their online learning experiences (See Table 4).

Summary for the 80-20 Blended Learning Environment Model

This study shows that females, young candidates, and candidates with less than three years of teach-

Table 3. Significant differences found for positive learning online experiences

Gender	t(40)	4.280 (Female)	p< 0.017
Age	t(40)	4.391 (22 to 32 years)	p<0.010
Number Years of Teaching	t(40)	4.404 (0 to 3)	p<0.029

* p: statistically significant difference

Table 4. Significant differences found for journal entries

Gender	t(40)	3.795 (Female)	p< 0.012
Age	t(40)	3.806 (22 to 32 years)	p<0.025
Level of Seeking License	t(40)	3.768 (Initial)	p<0.036

* p: statistically significant difference

ing experience, and those seeking initial license are more appreciative of the 20% face-to-face meeting times in a hybrid classroom (See Table 5) than males, older teachers, and candidates with more than three years of teaching experience or seeking professional teaching license. When asking for a candidate's attitudes towards the online component, young candidates were likely to think that having more time to read assigned readings plays an important role for their learning. They also pointed out that these assigned reading materials should be relevant to their personal and professional experiences. Although candidate did not change their views on issues, females and candidates seeking initial license indicated that the online discussions and providing as well as receiving feedback enhance their learning. When asked about learning experiences with online components, female, younger, and those with less than three years of teaching candidates reported their significantly positive learning experiences as well as having their sense of ownership and a feeling of empowering of their learning. Keeping weekly journal entries also played an important role for females, young teachers and candidates who seek initial license to keep track of their learning growth.

CONCLUSION

This study is to examine attitudes of graduate candidates in a teacher education program toward 80-20 blended learning environment model. The findings indicated that this model worked well for young and female teacher candidates and for those who seek training for their first teaching license. Evidently, when a question of which model - a traditional face-to-face classroom, an e-learning classroom, 100% online, or a hybrid model with a combination of face-to-face and online - is best fit for a teacher graduate training program, one must ponder on the question, "What is it that the instructor want to achieve?"

If a course is designed based on assumptions of a social constructivism theory in which an

Table 5. Summary for the model

	Gender	Age	Number Years of Teaching	Matriculation	License
20% face-to-face meeting	Female	Young	0-3 years	n/s*	Initial
More Reading Time	n/s*	Young	n/s*	n/s*	n/s*
Selection for reading		Young	n/s*	n/s*	n/s*
Online Discussion and Feedback	Female	n/s*	n/s*	n/s*	Initial
Positive Learning Online Experiences	Female	Young	0-3 years	n/s*	n/s*
Changing Opinions on Issues	n/s*	n/s*	n/s*	n/s*	n/s*
Journal Entries	Female	Young	n/s*	n/s*	Initial

* p: statistically significant difference

individual acquires knowledge only through his or her engaged social activities, then the focal question should be on how to engage learners. In a traditional face-to-face classroom, teachers can lecture and engage students in a spontaneously discussing mode. Teachers can recognize non-verbal communication cues and are able to motivate each student on an individual basis. These human connections are important for knowledge acquisition. While the advantage of spontaneous exchanges combined with non-verbal communication cues play significant roles in a teacher training program, this setting would eliminate those who have other commitments, such as a family, and cannot come to classes every week.

On the other hand, if a course is designed to accommodate busy adult learners, then the e-learning with 100% online model is best fit. The question of how to engage learners online still needs to be addressed. Even if these adult learners fully participate, the feeling of missing the connection between written words and real human beings is still hard to prevail over.

Ultimately, a hybrid model with a combination of face-to-face and online would provide an online classroom without losing both the interpersonal advantages of face-to-face contact. In a blended learning environment, which combines both traditional face-to-face and online interaction, students can take advantage of the convenience of online access to both lecture/course materials and asynchronous classroom discussions, while the face-to-face sessions can foster and stimulate an online social culture that facilitates knowledge acquisition through interpersonal and group discussion and disclosure.

As this study indicates, utilizing the social constructivism by means of online discussion boards appears to benefit learners at the graduate level for teacher education programs. Further studies are needed in addressing the following questions: Can this model be used in an undergraduate program for math or chemistry courses? Can ongoing discourse of social constructivism develop an understanding for knowledge acquisition in a biology lab? Since gender seems to play a significant result in this survey research, can this hybrid model bridge the difference in other undergraduate programs?

Moving a course online is not simply taking your syllabus and your face-to-face classroom activities online. It calls for a paradigm shift in your pedagogy. Would you prefer to have a physician who watches a video of an operation by the best surgeons, learns how to operate with hands-on guidance from those surgeons, engage in a question-and-answer discussion in class, then takes a test? Or would you would prefer a physician who has all of the above but before he takes the test, shares and discusses, with classmates, his interpretation of the video as well as his learning and experiences online instead of in class only? Human beings are diverse in many ways, from personal learning styles to their methods of interpreting information presented to them. The online component of hybrid classes allows learners to sort out their differences and to collaboratively learn from interpretation, experiences, and lessons among themselves at anytime and anywhere that an expert cannot offer.

As more and more colleges have moved their courses online, the questions of reserving the quality of education have been ongoing discussions for many faculty members and administrators. It is not the question of which one: online, hybrid or face-to-face model is better. It's the question of how to design a curriculum that will deliver the most effective method for a quality education, and yet respond to the need of the population. Variables such as age, gender, social economic or ethnic are important when examining how content of a course is designed into an online course.

ACKNOWLEDGMENT

Thank you Arthur Lizie, Ph.D. for providing some feedback and Titania Nguyen for editing this manuscript.

REFERENCES

Black, G. (2001). A Comparison of Traditional, Online and Hybrid Methods of Course Delivery. In *Proceedings of the International Conference on Teaching Online in Higher Education: "Synthesizing Online Teaching Strategies*

Caine, R. N., & Caine, G. (1991). *Making connections: Teaching and the human brain.* Alexandria, VA: Association for Supervision and Curriculum Development.

Coates, D. & Humphreys, B. (2001). Evaluation of Computer-Assisted Instruction in Principles of Economics. *Educational Technology & Society, 4*(2).

Dziuban, C., & Moskal, P. (2001). Evaluating distributed learning at metropolitan universities. *Educause Quarterly, 24*(4), 60-61. Retrieved April 15, 2006, from http://www.educause.edu/ir/library/pdf/eqm01412.pdf

Gibson, S., & McKay, R. (1999). Application of brain research and constructivist theory. In *Proceedings of the 8th International Conference on Thinking*, Edmonton, AB.

Kim, B. (2001). Social Constructivism. In M. Orey (Ed.), *Emerging perspectives on learning, teaching, and technology.* Retrieved April 15, 2006, from http://www.coe.uga.edu/epltt/SocialConstructivism.htm

Lister, B., Danchak, M., Scalzo, K., Jennings, W., & Wilson, J. (1999). The Rensselaer 80:20 Model for Interactive Distance Learning. In *Proceedings of the EDUCAUSE 1999 conference presentation.* Retrieved February 8, 2006, from http://www.educause.edu/ir/library/html/edu9907/edu9907.html

Spanier, G. B. (2001). *Higher Education's Biggest Unrecognized Opportunities.* Penn State College President's Speech. Retrieved February 14, 2006, from http://www.psu.edu/ur/GSpanier/speeches/FSU_opportunities_011402.html

Vygotsky, L. (1978). *Mind and Society: The Development of Higher Psychological Processes.* Cambridge, MA: Harvard University Press.

Wilson, J., & Mosher, D. (1994). The prototype of the virtual studio classroom. *Journal of Instruction Delivery Systems, 8*(3).

Young, J. (2002). *'Hybrid' Teaching Seeks to End the Divide Between Traditional and Online Instruction: By Blending Approaches, Colleges Hope To Save Money And Meet Students' Needs.* Retrieved February 8, 2006, from http://chronicle.com/free/v48/i28/28a03301.htm

KEY TERMS AND DEFINITIONS

Asynchronous Discussion: Participants do not all have to be present at the same time for discussions; therefore, having clear expectations and clear-cut due dates helps participants plan their schedule ahead of time for the entire course.

Blended Learning Environment: A combination of a traditional face-to-face classroom and online interaction.

Hybrid Course: A course is designed with both online and face-to-face classroom activities.

Ice-Breaker Exercise: An effective way of starting a team-building effort before moving a course online. This interactive and enjoyable session help participants get to know each other. They would be more contented in exchanging their ideas online since they can connect written words with classmates whom they met.

Initial License: The first certified teaching license level in Massachusetts, USA.

Learning Community: Participants are actively engaged in learning together and from each other. Even if they do not always share common values and beliefs, they still can share and discuss theirs in a safe environment and learn among themselves.

Non-Verbal Communication: A way to communicate through facial expression, eye contact, gesture, body language or posture, paralanguage, humor, etc.

Online Curriculum: Course is designed for online classroom, and must be different with a traditional face-to-face classroom.

Online Discussion or Interaction: Discussions via chat room, discussion board, webcam, or email.

Paradigm Shift: A change from one way of thinking to another. It's a revolution or a transformation that is driven by agents of change.

Professional License: Advanced certified teaching license level in Massachusetts, USA.

Social Constructivism: A theory in which an individual acquires new knowledge through social engagements.

Synchronous Interaction: Participants and the instructor interact in real time.

Chapter 20
A Hybrid Learning Model Using an XML-Based Multimedia Podcasting System

Joseph Fong
City University of Hong Kong, Hong Kong

ABSTRACT

Due to heavy workload and tight working schedule, it is difficult for part-time students at City University of Hong Kong to 'digest' course materials and to understand the content of the course. Therefore, it will be convenient if a lecture presentation with course materials is recorded and posted into the Internet. Then, students can easily attend the lecture on-line in anywhere or watch back the video archive of the presentation through the Web. This chapter aims to provide a solution to achieve a hybrid learning model (HLM) including e-learning and traditional teaching platform by synchronizing video, audio and image files which are used in a presentation. In addition, this is targeted to record and to retrieve by using an on-line podcasting system and an XML SMIL technology respectively.

INTRODUCTION

The most important concept of the project is the application of Podcasting (http://en.wikipedia.org/wiki/Podcast) which is a digital media file, or a series of such files, distributed over the Internet using syndication feeds for playback on portable media players and personal computers. A podcast is a specific type of webcast which, like 'radio', can mean either the content itself or the method by which it is syndicated; the latter is also termed podcasting. Another similar term is Video Podcast (http://en.wikipedia.org/wike/Video_podcast) which refers to a term used for the on-line delivery of video on demand video clip content. The term is an evolution specialized for video, coming from the generally audio-based podcast and referring to the distribution of video to which users can subscribe using a PC, TV, set-top box, media center or mobile multimedia device. The following is the definition of Podcasting in this project: 'A podcast is a web-based technology to synchronize multimedia elements including video, audio, and any graphic files. It also refers to the distribution of the mentioned

DOI: 10.4018/978-1-60566-380-7.ch020

elements which users can retrieve them by using a podcast player.' (http://en.wikipedia.org/wike/Video_podcast)

Besides, this project introduces SMIL 2.0 (Bulterman and Rutledge, 2004) (Kennedy and Slowinski, 2002) which stands for Synchronized Multimedia Integration Language, and which is a text-based, XML standardized format. It is a language to combine animation, picture, and media objects into single coherent presentation to standardize all the documents for Podcasting through the Web. The reason for choosing this language for Podcasting purpose is because SMIL provides a time element insides its library. We can simply control the multimedia elements in and out or play and stop in the screen at any moment of time by a few codes of programme. Another web technology used is AJAX. AJAX (http://www-128.ibm.com/developerworks/xml/library/x-ajaxslideshow/?ca=dgr-lnxw01AjaxSlid) (McEvoy, 2003) stands for "Asynchronous JavaScript and XML". The architecture of AJAX can be explained in the following diagram. They can be shown in Figure 1.

When a Web browser, or client, makes a GET or POST request to the Web server, the server formats an HTML response with some JavaScript code on it. That code calls back the server for more information as needed. Those requests can be made as simple GET or POST requests. The JavaScript code then parses the response, often encoded as XML, and updates the HTML on the page dynamically to reflect the new data. In addition to XML, engineers are returning data encoded in the JavaScript Serialized Object Notation (JSON) format. This data is easier for a browser to understand but not for other client types.

AJAX helps the project in displaying the multimedia elements, especially for graphic files. It supports a quicker communication between the server and client machine. Therefore, it helps in displaying documents (i.e. Power-Point files) in graphic format (i.e. jpeg files) and also in support drawing (i.e. writing explanatory notes) by a hand-writing pad. Furthermore, the main programming language for the project is C# which is a simple, type-safe, object-oriented, general-purpose programming language. It provides code-focused developers with powerful tools and language support to build rich, connected Web and client applications on the ASP.NET Framework. The reason to choose this language is because it has a variety of libraries and APIs which helps the development of the system.

Podcasting is the automatic distribution of mp3s via XML file. Listeners of podcasts use a wide variety of podcast software to download their favorite lectures automatically. What podcasters do is to create an pd3 with their own voice, content, music, whatever, and then release it to the students. One can also create an XML file in minutes using a Text Editor or Microsoft Word for editing the podcasting file.

There is not yet a software tool that captures hand-written notes in recording a lecture. The major contribution of this paper is that it can put video, hand-written notes, and presentation document, for example, PowerPoint, into a screen layout for the lecturer to record the lecture whiling writing notes on a tablet and for the students to review the lecture and download the hand-written notes afterward.

1.1 The Framework of the System

The development of the Hybrid Learning Module were divided into two phases: (1) Developing an On-line Tutorial System and (2) Developing a Podcasting System. In the first phrase, the system UI and the functionality of On-line Tutorial System will be developed. There are three systems that are the main development goal for this phrase.

- On-line Document Display System
- Visual/ Voice System
- Hand-writing System

The On-line Document Display System provides an interface for lecturers to upload documents prepared for a presentation such as power-point files and to display them. whenever they want. Again, AJAX will be used for the main development language. In addition, before uploading documents to a database, it has a function to convert from power-point files to jpeg files that are used when starting a presentation.

The Visual/ Voice System can be treated as the same function of running traditional lectures in a classroom. There is no class written for .Net on video conferencing. Therefore, there is a need to use H.323 protocol and TAPI 3 Telephony for the development. With the API of WaveIn/ WaveOut in C#, it can be achieved. The goal for this system is to create a kind of video conferencing system so that the image and voice of lectures can be displayed through camera to the Web. Sample for displaying the video conference system is shown in Figure 2.

AJAX technology will be used to develop a hand-writing system as well. The explanation of AJAX can be found from previous section. With regard to the system, it can be used to write explanatory notes using a hand-writing pad by lecturers during a presentation. In order to write notes freely, the whole system will be developed for presentation using a tablet PC. Presenters can write their notes in a defined pad shown on an interface as shown in Figure 3.

Figure 1. Sample of SMIL and AJAX interaction

Sample code for SMIL

```
--><!DOCTYPE smil PUBLIC "-//W3C//DTD SMIL 2.0//EN"
"http://www.w3.org/2001/SMIL20/SMIL20.dtd"><smil
xmlns="http://www.w3.org/2001/SMIL20/Language">
  <head>
    <meta name="title" content="Empty SMIL2 Slideshow"/>
    <meta name="generator" content="GRiNS Pro for SMIL 2.0, v2.0 alpha win32 build 71"/>
    <meta name="project_html_page" content="external_player.html"/>
    <layout>
        <root-layout id="PC_Window" backgroundColor="navy" width="640" height="480" />
        <region id="audioRegion_1_P" />
        <region id="bkgd_imageRegion_P" left="0" width="640" top="2" height="480" z-index="1"
/>
        <region id="MainView_P" left="364" width="220" top="115" height="180" z-index="2" />
        <region id="Controls_P" left="420" width="120" top="405" height="31" z-index="2" />
        <region id="Captions_P" left="366" width="225" top="323" height="48" z-index="2" />
        <region id="MS_P" left="1" width="342" top="282" height="90" z-index="2" />
        <region id="Local_P" left="1" width="342" top="185" height="90" z-index="2" />
        <region id="MS_P" left="66" width="237" top="87" height="93" z-index="2" />
        <region id="Ad_P" left="24" width="322" top="418" height="58" z-index="2" />
        <region id="Titles_P" left="0" width="342" top="0" height="368" z-index="3" />
        <region id="Branding" regionName="Branding_P" left="381" width="259" top="462"
height="15" z-index="2"/>
    </layout>
```

Time element for SMIL

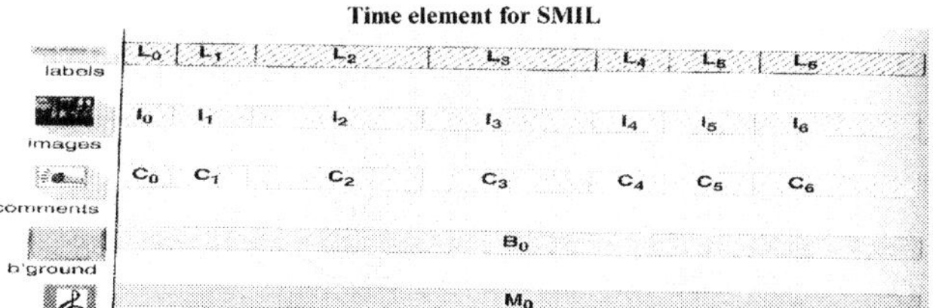

The Ajax model of Client-Server interaction

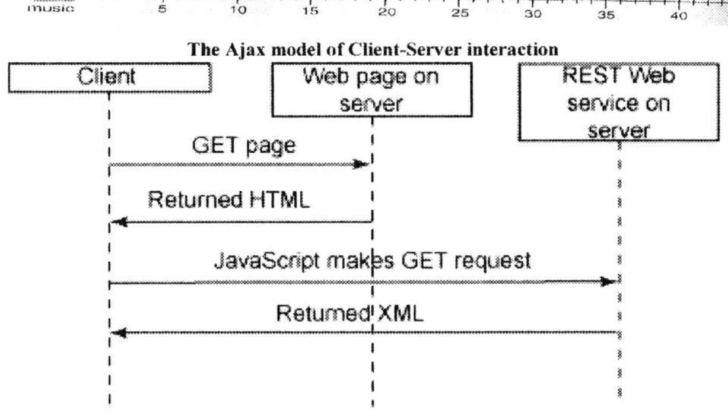

Figure 2. Video conference sample

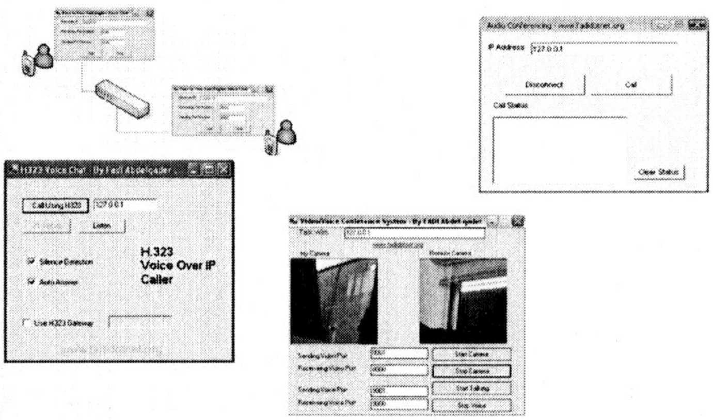

After that, the Podcasting System will finally be developed in the second phase. There are two systems that are the main development goal for this phase.

- SMIL Conversion System
- Podcasting System

The SMIL conversion system will convert the existing multimedia files (video, audio, pictures, etc) into a single SMIL file. Then all of these elements will be organized in a web server for users' streaming through our system. As for the Podcasting System, it will be used to run all elements as a movie according to the structure of the SMIL file constructed by the SMIL Conversion System. It will embed a SMIL player (like Real Player, Windows Media Player, or any player supporting SMIL). The following shows how the system will look like. The system will be divided into several regions. Different regions are responsible for displaying different multimedia elements. Sample for running a SMIL file is shown in Figure 4.

2 METHODOLOGY

The whole project can be split into five systems named (1) On-line Document Display System, (2) Video/ Audio System, (3) Hand Writing Display

Figure 3. Sample for hand written notes computerization

Figure 4. Sample screen for a running SMIL

System, (4) SMIL Conversion System, and (5) Podcasting System. The architecture of the Module is illustrated in Figure 5.

The basic structure of the software can be divided into two phases. Phase I captures video recording, hand-written notes writing and PowerPoint presentation document in three files, that is, one file for each item (Figure 6). Phase II synchronizes the display timing of these three files into one file and board casting the file on a screen (Figure 7).

2.1 Phase I Step 1: On-Line Document Display System

This system helps to convert document(s) used for presentation to JPEG files. Another function is to display the JPEG files to screen. It is divided into several modules: Document Convert Module, Document Display Module, and AJAX Listener. Firstly, a document file will be passed to Document Convert Module. The module will be used to convert the file into several JPGE files and to store them into database. Secondly, On-line Document Display Module will be assisted by calling AJAX Listener. The AJAX Listener will get the JPEG files from the Database and send it back into the Document Display Module. Finally, The On-line Document Display Module will also be used to display the JPEG files on screen.

2.2 Phase I Step 2: Video/ Audio System

For an illustration, see Figure 7.

2.3 Phase I Step 3: Hand-Writing System

This system helps to display hand-written notes used for presentation. Another function is to record the notes into several JPEG files. It is divided into several modules: Hand-writing Configuration Module helps to configure the hand-writing pad in a good condition (Figure 8). Hand-writing Display Module helps to display the hand-written note on screen. Record Module helps to record the screen displayed the hand-written note into JPGE file, and AJAX Listener is used to update the screen capture to the database. We expect that 10 pages will be reserved for each presentation.

Figure 5. Architecture of the module

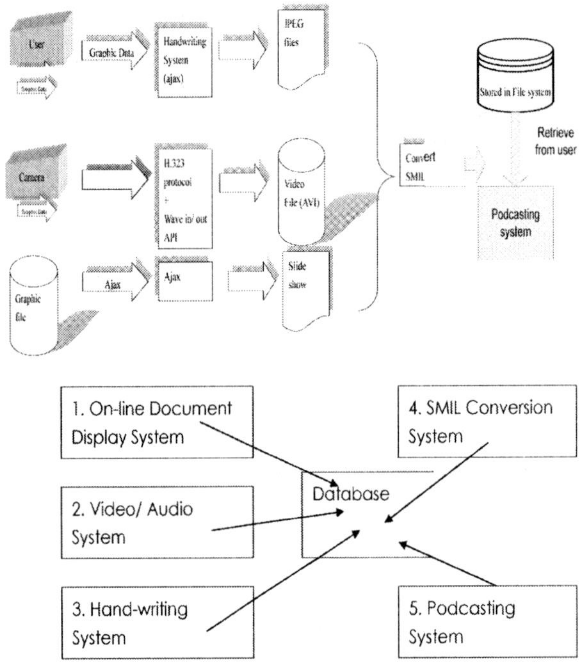

Figure 6. Algorithm for handling Power Point file

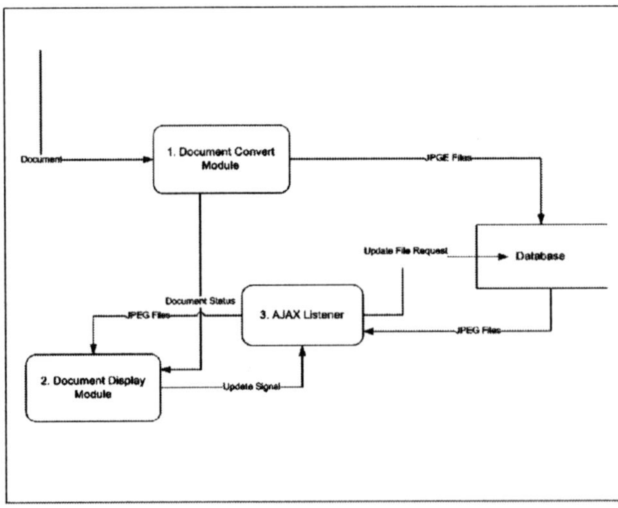


```
Begin
Input file name of
source ppt
Input file name of target
jpeg
Call document convert
module with source ppt
Store jpeg files to
database after
converting by the
module
If presentation start
Display jpeg files
  Store time frame
  Endif
End
```

2.4 Phase II Step 4: SMIL Conversion System

This system helps to convert multimedia elements stored in the database to SMIL format (Figure 9). A SMIL file designed for podcasting is needed to be defined a lot of requirements so that we use Time Status and SMIL Conversion Models to build up this file. Data Retrieve Module aims to retrieve all the data from the database. Time Status Module helps to add time element to a SMIL format file. SMIL Conversion Module helps to combine data

Figure 7. Algorithm for handling video file

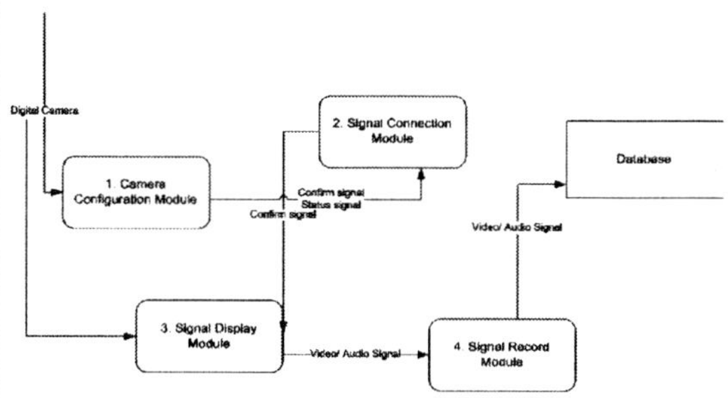

Begin
Input camera configuration
Check network and video signals
If signals correct and presentation start
Start to record and to display
Store time frame to database
Store video and audio to database
Endif
End

Figure 8. Algorithm for handling handwriting file

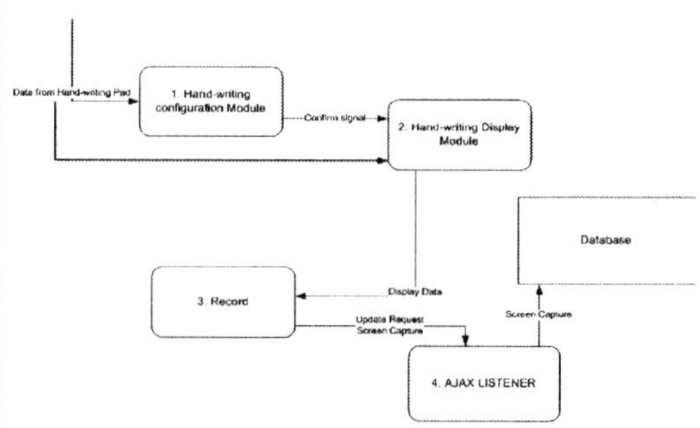

Begin
Check handwriting configuration
If signal correct and presentation start
Input handwriting note on pad
Record note to jpeg via Listener
Store time frame to database
Store jpeg files to database
Endif
End

Figure 9. Algorithm for storing PPT, video and handwriting files into SMIL

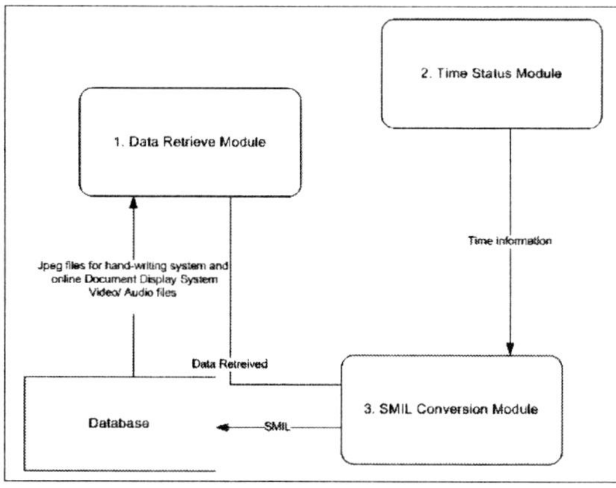

Begin
Open ppt jpeg files and time frame
Open handwriting jpeg files and time frame
Start to convert ppt & handwriting files according to time frame records
Store SMIL file to database
End

from two modules to the SMIL file and to store it into the database.

2.5 Phase II Step 5: Podcasting System

This is the simplest system of the whole project and contains one module called Display Module (Figure 10). SMIL files are generated through the SMIL Conversion System. The module will listen to user requests and get the appropriate SMIL file from the database and play it by using SMIL player.

There are four modules in this system. Camera Configuration Modules helps to configure the camera in order to display on screen. Signal Connection Module aims to establish a network connection between the camera and the system. Signal Record Module helps to record the camera signal and Signal Display Module helps to display images.

3 PROTOTYPE WITH A CASE STUDY

Dr. Fong, an Associate Professor of the City University of Hong Kong, teaches several computer courses. During these courses, he needs to deliver a PowerPoint presentation and demonstration. Sometimes, he also needs to write down explanatory notes in order to enhance participants' understanding of the course materials. In his experience, he discovered that the participants might not get a full understanding of the course materials. Therefore, he wants to take the advantage of using the on-line tutorial system to record the whole course and let his student view on-line or retrieve it later.

The operation steps for using the software are: (1) Capture the lecture by using a tablet with a stored PowerPoint file and a video camera pointing to the lecturer. (2) Execute the Podcasting software CALS[9](Computer Assist Lecturing Software) by entering the name of the PowerPoint file, and the directory for storing the to-be-generated three files of video, hand-written and PowerPoint document. (3) Convert the generated three files into executable files for Podcasting and install it into a web site ready for students and lecturer to browse and download.

3.1 Preparing to Generate a SMIL File

The presenter needs to operate several systems such as On-line Document, Video/Audio, Hand Writing, and SMIL Conversion during his presen-

Figure 10. Algorithm for display SMIL File

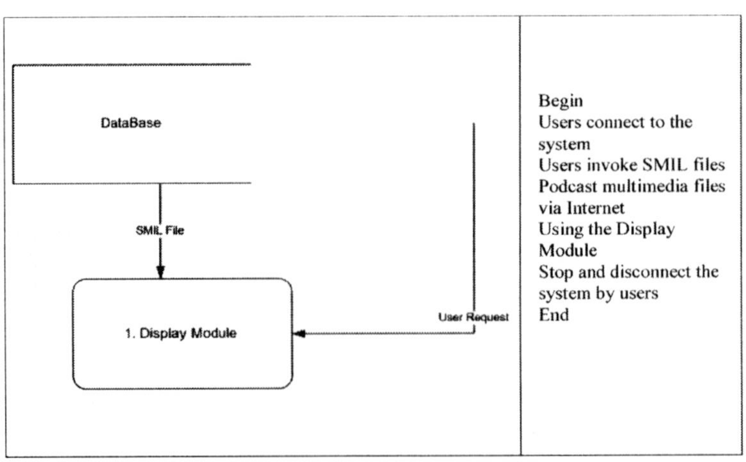

Figure 11. Screen dumps for case study

1.	Before starting the course, Dr Fong needs to login to the system by his own account. Then, he needs to input the path and file name of the source as well as the path and file name of the target in the first part of the On-line Document Display System in order to convert from a ppt file to several jpeg files that can be displayed by the Podcasting System.	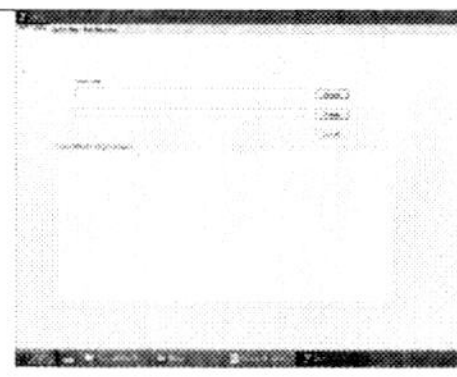
2.	Sometimes, if a presenter does not need to show a power-point file, the conversion process cannot be invoked In this case, a power-point file is needed for the presentation; the system will display an interface to Dr. Fong to convert power-point slides to JEPG files. He also needs to implicitly indicate a path for storing the JEPG files. And then, he needs to pass the "Convert" button	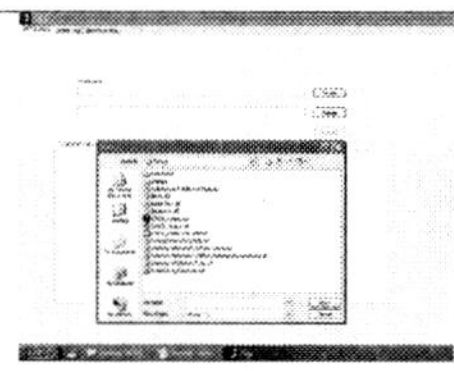
3.	After converting the power-point file, he also needs to indicate the path and file name for storing videos as well as the path and name file for storing hand-writing notes. Actually, these two parts are in connection with the Video/ Audio and the Hand-writing Systems respectively	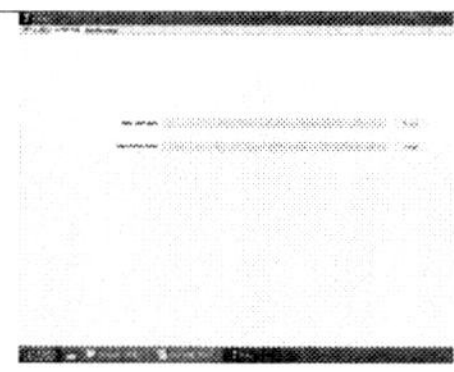
4.	The slides will be converted to JEPG files and it will be listed controlled by the presenter into the screen when the presentation starts. Before recording, Dr. Fong needs to configure the video camera and to make sure the camera that is connected to computer. We use a high standard webcam that has been installed into a tablet PC in advance. Dr. Fong will control the webcam by himself. In other words, we have no extra man-powers during the presentation.	
5.	As a hand-writing option is selected, the Hard-writing System will detect whether or not the hand-writing pad is connected to the computer.	Hand-Writing Pad is detected
6	Finally, the recording of video, slide, and hand-writing note will be started or stopped synchronously when 'Record All' button or 'Stop Record All' button is pressed. The SMIL Conversion	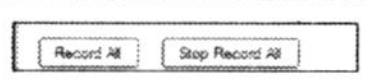

tation in each lecture (Figure 11). The following explain how Dr. Fong operates the system to achieve the purpose. He is going to lecture a course named Data Warehouse and Data Mining. In this lecture, he needs to prepare materials such as (1) Self presentation in mpeg format, (2) Power-Point in jpeg format, and (3) Hand-written explanatory notes in jpeg format. In order to facilitate this case study, the presentation is assumed to last for 5 minutes.

3.2 On-line Podcasting a SMIL File

Students can use RealPlayer to run and to view SMIL files. They can access our Podcasting system through the Internet and select an appropriate course code as shown in Figure 12. And then, the course information and each lecture will be displayed is shown in Figure 13 and can be selected by students. After that, a screen layout of a podcasting presentation will be run as shown in Figure 14. It has been consisted of video mpeg file, power-point jpeg file, and handwriting note jpeg file that have been constructed according to Section 3.1 - Preparing to Generate a SMIL File. Therefore, we assume that the system will have a delay. Students want to retrieve all the contents

Figure 12. Open page of the podcasting web

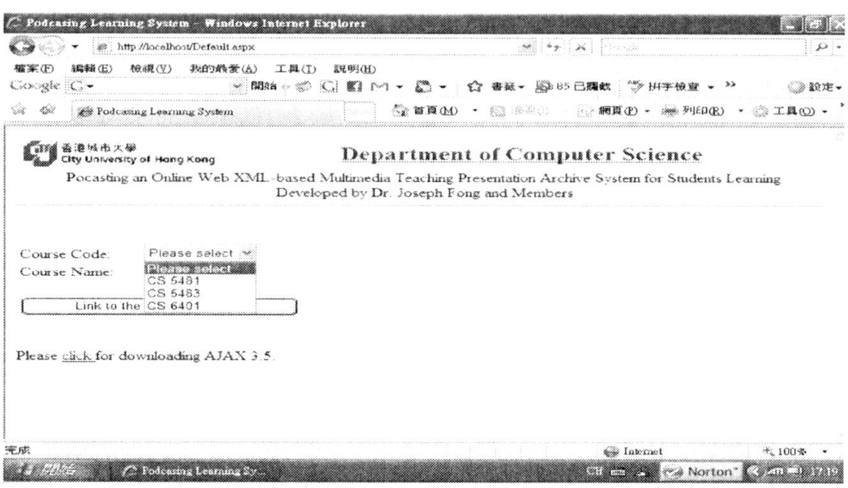

Figure 13. Selecting a podcasting lecture

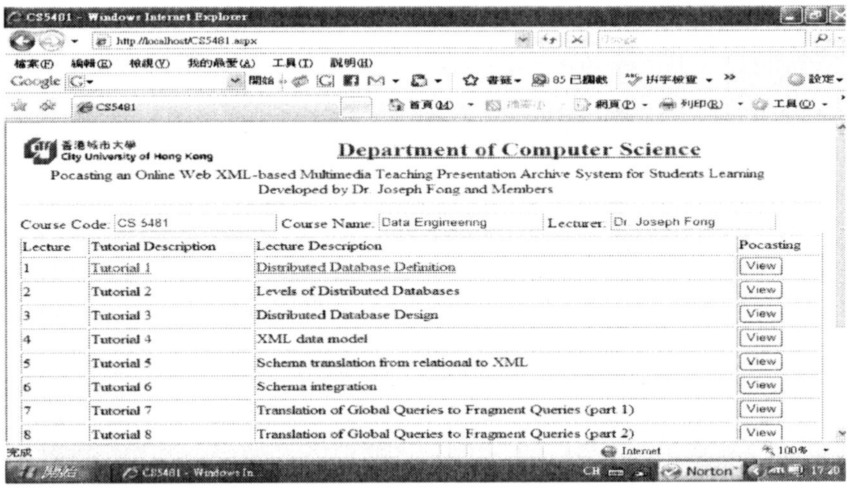

Figure 14. Screen layout of a podcasting presentation

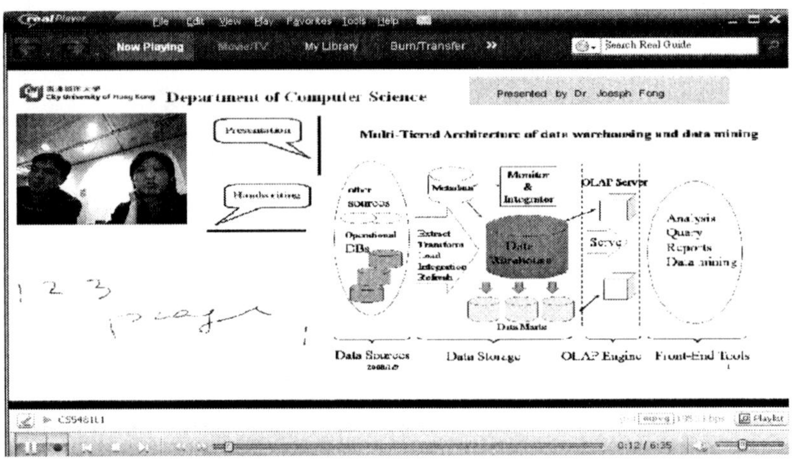

of the presentation. They should connect to the web server and pass some authentication procedures before viewing the presentation. And then, the Podcasting System will be invoked. After finishing the presentation, if students want to see more about the presenter, they can click on the top right-hand corner named "Presented by Dr. Joseph Fong". Then, another presentation will be invoked as shown in Figure 15 for displaying presenter information.

4 CONCLUSION

Dr Fong has been using the CALS for his lecturing and students are also using the podcasting record to review the lecture. The benefit is for students listening to the lecture without copying hand-written notes from the lecturer because they can always download the hand-written notes later on the course web site. Such benefit can save them much time which can be used to concentrate on the lecture itself. The browse of the lecture record-

Figure 15. Presenter information

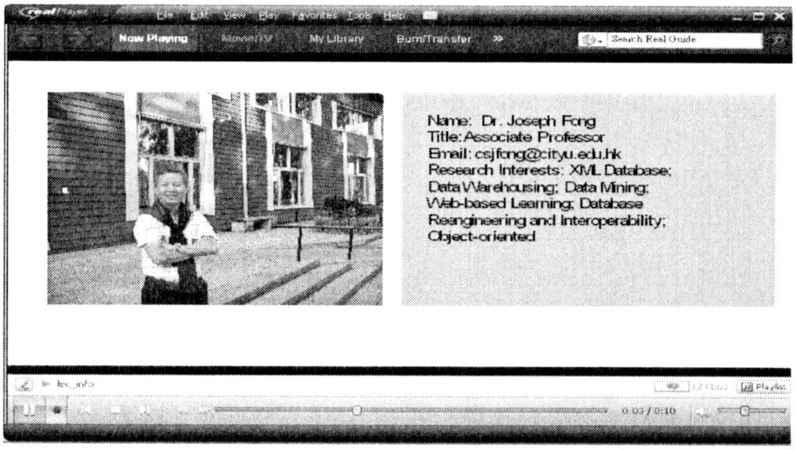

ing can be move forward and backward, which is very handy for student to use.

The prototype of the on-line tutorial system is designed to demonstrate the feasibility of applying SMIL to implement a podcasting system consisting of power-point presentation, hand written notes computerization, and video conference recording. Students can facilitate to learn in any places or review their lectures as a supplement classroom learning by using the system. The success of this system depends on the utilization of the system by students and their learning productivity, which can be recorded on the course web site (http://jfong/cs.cityu.edu.hk). The contribution of this paper is to enable students to combine classroom learning with eLearning (learning on the web) for classroom materials review on-line. It encourages students to learn anywhere and at any time by using the Internet. Future enhancement will be focused on how to improve the quality and performance of the system.

REFERENCES

Bulterman, D. C. A., & Rutledge, L. (2004). *SMIL 2.0 Interactive Multimedia for Web and Mobile Device*. Berlin, Germany: Springer.

Ewington, S. (2007). *CodeProject: Web Ink/Drawing Control*. Retrieved from http://www.codeproject.com/mobilepc/webinkctrl.asp

Fong, J. (n.d.). *Welcome to Dr. Fong's education application projects*. Retrieved from http://jfong.cs.cityu.edu.hk

Herrington, J. (2007). *Rich AJAX slide shows with DHTML and XML*. Retrieved from http://www-128.ibm.com/developerworks/xml/library/x-ajaxslideshow/?ca=dgr-lnxw01AjaxSlid

Kennedy, T., & Slowinski, M. (2002). *SMIL Adding Multimedia to the Web*. SAMS.

McEvoy, S. (2003). *Fundamentals of Programming the Microsoft Windows Media Platform*. Redmond, WA: Microsoft Press. *Podcast*. (n.d.). Retrieved from http://en.wikipedia.org/wiki/Podcast

The Ambulent Player demos page. (2008). Retrieved from http://www.cwi.nl/projects/Ambulant/Demos.shtml

Video podcast. (n.d.). Retrieved from http://en.wikipeda.org/wiki/Video_podcast

Section 4
Hybrid Learning Systems

Chapter 21
Blended Learning Systems:
New Directions in Graduate Management Education

Owen P. Hall Jr.
Pepperdine University, USA

ABSTRACT

Distance learning has come a long way since Sir Isaac Pitman initiated the first correspondence course in the early 1840s. Today the growing role of globalization calls for new and innovative learning systems for management education. To meet these challenges the traditional classroom model for delivering executive business education is giving way to a more holistic learning paradigm in which both the pedagogical and andragogical focus are on knowledge acquisition and management decision-making. The one-size-fits-all educational approach of the past is being supplanted by customized, web-based learning systems. The purpose of this chapter is to introduce a blended learning system that combines the best of both web-based learning and time-honed classroom practices for delivering cost-effective graduate management education.

INTRODUCTION

The demand for graduate management education is once again on the rise. Presently applications are up across most of the MBA programs as reported by the Graduate Management Admission Council. This renewed surge in interest can be attributed, in part, to globalization, technology, and changing demographics. Developing a world-class MBA program in today's dynamic educational and business environment calls for the increased use of learning support technologies (Li, 2007; Shih, 2003; Thomas, 2007). Blended learning systems (BLS), in particular, offer both a customized and an integrated learning experience through the use of traditional classroom learning experiences combined with the power of the Internet (Bonk, 2006). Blended learning environments, often characterized as hybrid learning, usually embrace many options for presenting content and interacting with students in both individual and collaborative contexts including a substantial e-learning aspect (Shroff, 2007).

DOI: 10.4018/978-1-60566-380-7.ch021

Figure 1. E-learning success model

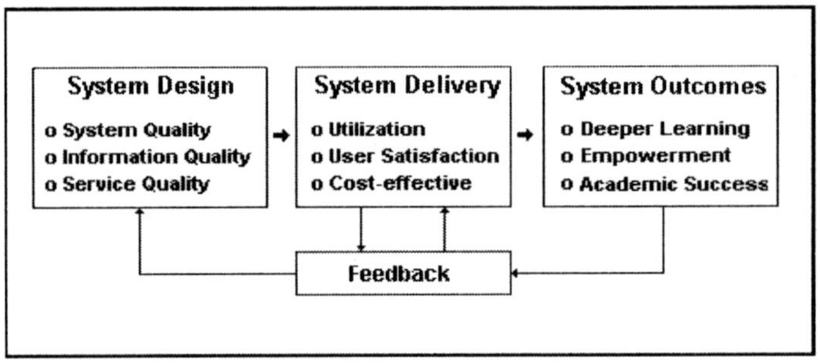

In this regard, BLS are well-suited to meet the challenges associated with graduate management education since they provide instructional content at a time, location and pace convenient to the student (Jorgensen, 2002).

The complexities and interrelated nature of modern business practice call for an integrated learning approach to graduate management education (Fry, 2007). One learning strategy that recognizes the need for an integrated yet flexible learning experience is the Instructional Management System (IMS) cooperative initiative (Graves, 1999). This initiative is designed to promote systematic thinking regarding the delivery of higher education, to improve learning outcomes, and to increase return on instructional investments. Specific principles of the IMS initiative are: 1) Education involves more than a single course; 2) A course is more than content; 3) Content is more important than lecture notes; 4) Convenience is important, and 5) Quality assurance requires an integrated learning approach. The IMS initiative calls for the increased use of Internet resources to promote integrated learning and to improve outcomes. Blended learning systems are designed to support the IMS initiative.

A second initiative that supports blended learning is the E-Learning Success Model (Delone, 2003). This model design suggests that the overall effectiveness of blended learning depends on the attainment of success at each of three stages: system design, system delivery, and system outcomes. The efficacious use of this paradigm will require the integration of all three stages. Figure 1 presents an overview of the e-learning success model.

This paradigm consists of three distinct, but interconnected, phases: system design, system delivery and system outcomes. Each phase consists of a number of specific performance metrics. For example, service quality can be measured using availability, reliability and response time. Assessment rubrics can be used for evaluating each performance metric. The model's architecture suggests that the overall effectiveness of e-learning depends on the attainment of success at each of three stages as well as in the aggregate.

The chapter is organized as follows 1) a review of the current slants and trends in worldwide MBA programs; 2) an overview of blended systems and technology; and 3) an assessment of empirical results associated with blended learning technologies.

MBA PROGRAM TRENDS

MBA programs come in a variety of shapes and sizes which are designed to take into account the diverse student backgrounds. Table 1 provides an overview of the basic characteristics associated with three of the most common types of the MBA programs: executive, professional, and residential. The primary difference between these programs is

Table 1. MBA program types overview

Characteristic	Executive	Professional	Residential
Lock-Step	√√		√
Lecture		√	√√
Andragogical	√√	√	
Schedule	Weekends	Weeknights	Weekdays
Timeframe	20 months	30 months	12-18 months
Electives		√	√√
Focus	Strategic	Technical	Technical

√ = level of intensity

the level of student work experience. The cohort group in most residential programs consists of students in their mid-twenties with nominal work experience. Students in the professional program are generally in their early to mid-thirties with at least ten years of experience. For executive type programs, the students are in their mid-forties with extensive managerial know-how. Typically, an executive MBA (EMBA) program involves a lock-step process in which the entire student cohort remains together throughout the course of study. The primary focus of most EMBA programs is on strategic leadership which is in contrast with the more technically oriented focus (e.g., finance spreadsheets) associated with professional and residential programs. Another feature common to EMBA programs is the andragogical bent. The term andragogy was coined by Malcolm Knowles in the 1970s to emphasize that the learning process for adults is different from that for children (Davenport, 1985). Knowles viewed the teacher as a facilitator who aids adults in becoming self-directed learners. This characteristic of self-learning and learning from other students is a particular characteristic of working adult MBA programs. In this regard, executive and professional curricula tend to have less emphasis on the traditional lecture and more emphasis on experiential learning venues (e.g., business simulations).

Table 1 clearly underscores the fact that one size does not fit all when it comes to MBA programs. In fact, the rapidly changing global landscape is causing many business schools (b-schools) to continually realign MBA curricula with evolving business practices (Schmotter, 2004). Some current directions include:

- Expanded opportunities for international studies including travel abroad
- Increased potential for education-to-business (E2B) experiences
- Greater focus on ethics and valued-centered leadership
- Increased use of Internet and related learning technologies
- More emphasis on experiential learning

MBA program designers recognize the need for content integration. The focus of an integrated business learning environment is on how core management functions such as operations, finance and marketing are linked. Accordingly, the educational direction is moving away from "course silos" and towards "content and theme integration" (Cotner, 2003; Steiner, 2000). To meet these challenges the MBA curriculum needs to serve as a gateway connecting the various business disciplines to the specific learning theme constructs. For example, EMBA type programs have taken the lead in utilizing a thematic approach to curriculum design as illustrated by the following:

- **Leadership:** To inspire and work with others to achieve common goals
- **Change management:** To improve critical thinking and decision-making skills and to formulate cost-effective plans with specific performance metrics
- **Innovation:** To foster an appreciation of the growing reliance on technology and how it can be used to enhance competitive advantage
- **Globalization:** To develop an international mindset including an awareness of different belief structures and cultural sensitivities
- **Strategic perspectives:** To integrate economic, social, technological and political trends into a holistic approach to business management

This EMBA thematic template can be used in the other types of MBA programs (Latham, 2004). In this regard, the debate continues on the appropriate level of technical emphasis in graduate management education. Interestingly, many "new" MBA curriculums have reduced the number of credit hours for quantitative type courses in favor of the themes listed above as well as electives (Kleiman, 2007; Richards-Wilson, 2006; Bennis, 2005). The compelling argument is that management is inherently qualitative. That being said, the pedagogical issue is how to keep the curriculum focused on these major themes, while at the same time developing the detailed skills required for daily operations. This is particularly the case for students enrolled in a residential MBA program who are interested in obtaining employment after graduation. This challenge is where blended learning can help. The Internet can deliver technical content as well as support thematic perspectives consistent with the nature and characteristics of the student cohort group (e.g., business simulation).

For example, virtual internships are finding wide spread application throughout higher education (Brookshire, 2007; Kerfoot, 2007; Hopkins, 2005). Web-based internships (WBI) provide students at remote or smaller institutions with the capability to obtain work experience with firms that are operating on a worldwide basis. Additionally, with the growth of electives and emphases in most residential MBA programs WBIs provide students with the opportunity to match directly their business interest with an appropriate firm. Furthermore, WBIs offer both the firm and the student more flexibility in addressing specific work assignments. WBIs also are an effective recruiting vehicle for both the employer and student. An important variation on WBIs and growing trend are virtual tours. The Web offers a wide range of virtual sites that can be easily integrated into the lesson plan. These tours provide students with direct insight into the integrative nature of business management. In the near future learners will be able to experience real-time guided facility tours that feature the ability to interact directly with onsite management and staff (Pettijohn, 2002).

In contrast to the need for residential students to acquire relevant work experience, there is the increasing demand for senior managers trained in making decisions involving supply chain management (SCM) and information systems (IS). This learning requirement is based on the growing role of SCM and IS throughout business and government. SCM information planning systems are being used to help improve the flow and efficiency of the supply chain and reduce inventory. These systems are intended to automate the different steps of the supply chain into a single seamless application. Connecting the supply chain of a business with its suppliers and customers into a single integrated network both optimizes costs and opportunities for finding additional competitive advantages. This development has been a major driver for the business-to-business explosion. The basic issue is to identify the most effective approach for introducing SCM and IS into the EMBA curriculum. Again, this is where the web can help. Internet-based supply chain simulations provide a context for managers to explore the dynamics of supply operations, which would not be possible in the traditional classroom setting. Business simulations have long been found particularly effective in developing both individual and team management skills (Aguino, 2005). For example, one business simulation designed for graduate management education is the "Global Supply Chain Game." This simulation operates on a continuous timeframe with ongoing events and interactive outcomes. Results show that students have been consistent in appreciating the value of the game as a tool in simulating the complexities of a global supply chain and facilitating learning about how to successfully manage this environment (Corsi, 2006). SCM simulations are not limited to large scale enterprises but are also available for learning about small-to-medium size businesses (SMB). The advent of new cost-effective information technologies including virtual networking and the allure of expanding markets provide ample opportunities for SMB managers to more fully align their business models with the overall global supply network through network-based simulators (Wadhwa, 2006).

BLENDED LEARNING SYSTEMS

Blended learning systems (BLSs) are educational constructs that combine the best practices of both traditional classroom and Internet-based educational platforms. Specific characteristics of the blended learning model include:

- A balanced approach between traditional and Internet learning formats
- Archival student performance data gathered throughout the entire program
- Possibility for students to engage in extensive virtual collaboration
- Proactive learning diagnostics
- Remedial instructional support for students

This last characteristic is of particular importance since many students enrolled in MBA programs do not have an undergraduate degree in business. Therefore, specific topics such as statistical reasoning and accounting basics can be presented via a web-based "bootcamp" on a customized basis. A blended learning approach enhances the learning experience for students with a variety of backgrounds by providing self-paced customized content (Mortera-Gutierrez, 2006).

System Design

One of the main attributes of blended learning is providing course content in an integrated format via one convenient portal. Figure 2 illustrates the structural concept of a blended learning system for MBA programs. In this setting, the learning net serves as a conduit that connects students with the course content, peers, instructors and the external business environment.

This learning support system is geared towards supporting the student throughout the MBA program. A major learning objective in graduate management education is enhancing decision-making skills, including the ability to develop cognitive competencies. These competencies involve problem solving, critical thinking, searching for relevant information, making informed judgments, using information efficiently, conducting observations, and creating new ideas. Invariably, busi-

Figure 2. MBA blended learning paradigm overview

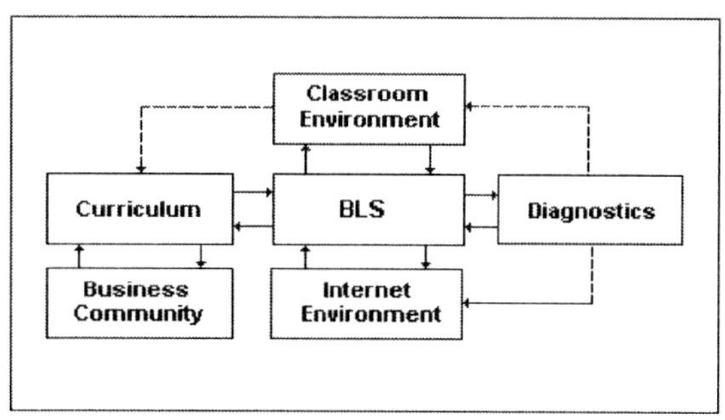

ness decisions are outcomes of multi-discipline discussions featuring extensive interactions. A blended learning environment provides an ideal vehicle for enhancing students' experiences in understanding how to capture inputs from a distributed group. This process tends to mirror the work environment that many working managers experience. Another learning focus for managers is to develop a comprehensive understanding of sources of business information. The continuing enhancement of search engines and digital libraries provides an opportunity for students to "drill down" on topics, such as industry analysis, technology and globalization.

Learning Support Systems

Figure 3 illustrates the variety of learning support systems associated with the blended model.

This graphic underscores ways in which traditional and web based learning methods can be used in combination to optimize knowledge and content delivery. For example, the BLS environment supports group analysis via linear and threaded chatrooms. This learning system provides a vehicle for stimulating "common interest groups" by allowing individuals to link across classes to other students working on similar projects. On the one hand, the traditional classroom setting (Synchronous, Personal) tends to be effective for team presentations that require a great deal of face-to-face interaction. On the other hand, the threaded chatroom environment (Asynchronous, Internet) supports the working manager's requirement for flexibility. Developing a sense of community (SOC) is an essential ingredient for a lock-step degree program such as an EMBA. Blogs provide an approach for maintaining SOC in a virtual environment and for facilitating team assignments (Flatley, 2005). Blogging can be used to provide individual or group views on a particular subject or topic, current events or a personal journal (Clyde, 2005). Blogging provides the student with the capability to maintain an electronic log of learning challenges and insights which can be helpful to other members of the class (Oravec, 2003).

Customized Learning with Artificial Agents

A fundamental tenet of the BLS design is that one size does *not* fit all. That is, students do not learn at the same pace and they are impacted dif-

Figure 3. Learning dimensions

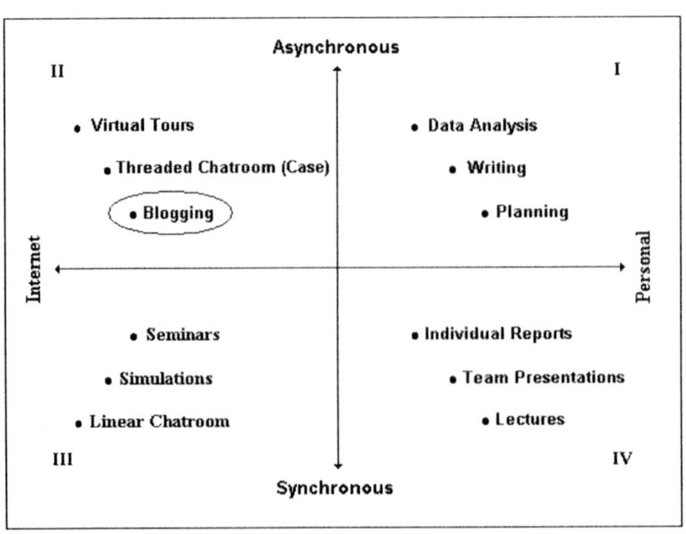

ferently by the learning environment. One key to effective learning via BLS is a customized lesson plan wherein the specific strengths and weaknesses of each student are identified and measured and appropriate feedback is provided. This is where artificial intelligence (AI) systems can play a helpful role. AI can be used to design lesson plans and learning experiences based on student performance and background. The use of AI to assist in the learning process is receiving increased attention (Lin, 2005). More specifically, synthetic agents, a major branch of AI, can generate customized learning plans derived from student accomplishments, backgrounds, and expectations using a set of conditional rules. For example, if a student is having difficulty mastering a particular subject or theme as detected by testing, simulation or self-assessment, then the synthetic agent would prescribe specific additional learning content to be provided to the student via the BLS. This content can take the form of videos, computing tutorials or simulations.

Typically, synthetic learning agents should possess the following four basic characteristics: autonomy, proactivity, adaptability and sociability. A well-designed synthetic tutorial agent should be able to assess the student's current knowledge state and to modify both the lesson plan and content level. One approach, albeit not the only one, for evaluating a learner's knowledge state is via real time simulation. Additionally, the "social" interface between the agent and the learner should be highly visual. It is within this type of design context that the specific learning objectives can be achieved and maintained (Matsatsinis, 2003). This capability of providing customized content based on specific factors is particularly useful for students whose job assignments often mirror the specifics found in the identified content. Used in this way a student can directly apply the lesson plan material to the workplace.

Table 2 shows more specifically how intelligent agents could be used to support a lesson plan involving, for example, net present value (NVP). The first column lists some basic learning plan objectives. The second column identifies the primary resources used by a student in connection with each session objective. The third column shows additional material identified by the instructor that is designed to support each lesson objective. For example, after developing a forecast using a virtual applet a student may wish to better understand the mechanics behind NPV analysis. At this point an interactive simulation can provide the student with an in-depth review of NPV analysis. This type of capability is sufficiently general to evoke a wide range of interest among students. The fourth column highlights some examples of customized content presented to the student based on both student performance and characteristics.

Table 2. Net present value (NPV) example

Session Learning Objectives	Primary Resource	Support Resources	Customized Resources
Appreciate the role of NPV in business operations	Introductory lecture notes	Streaming video	Industry specific NPV applications
Understand the different NPV inputs	e-chapter	Articles that illustrate NPV	Expert system consultation
Compare NPV and IRR	Linear chatroom	Slideshow	Blog
Develop NPV analysis using computer models	NPV applet	Interactive simulation	Threaded chatroom
How to interpret the results	Business case	Application articles	Industry-specific testimonials

For example, after reviewing and discussing a case on capital budgeting a student can choose to view specific applications.

This level of detail and specificity helps reinforce the basic ideas introduced in the NPV case. Again the specific applications are "captured" by the agent in real time. Figure 4 shows a sample customized resource case and consultation for a net present value learning application. The student is guided through a series of prompts regarding the case and explanations are provided for each prompt. The consultation can be taken more than once since, among other things, some of the prompts are randomized. The use of this expert system is not limited to entering students requiring preparatory work but can also be used as a refresher by continuing students. For example, a student in a finance course that is struggling with the notion of net present value (NPV) would be directed to a consultative system that outlines the basic NPV process.

This type of learning construct has been used successfully in a variety of business disciplines including the field of accounting (McDuffie, 2006). Specifically, an auditing expert system was constructed to assist students to better understand and apply GAAP (Generally Accepted Accounting Principles). The reported results show that students who used this system performed better on course examinations. Expert Systems have also been employed to assist students in mastering database design (Post, 2005). Specifically, the system provides the student with the capability to create database designs and receive feedback in real time. Another agent, called AutoTutor, engages in a conversation with the student using three-dimensional interactive simulations (Graesser, 2005). This system has demonstrated a nearly one letter grade improvement in the learning process.

Empirical Evidence

A number of surveys have been conducted on student performance and perceptions of blended learning (Kim, 2006; Web, 2005; Condone, 2004; Wang, 2003). The general consensus of these investigations is summarized below:

- BLSs offer a high degree of interaction and collaboration that can be more effective than traditional classroom methods.
- BLSs represent a long-sought solution to the ongoing challenges associated with graduate management education by providing students with a dynamic, personal and scalable experience for continuous learning in a flexible environment.

Figure 4. NPV expert system consultation

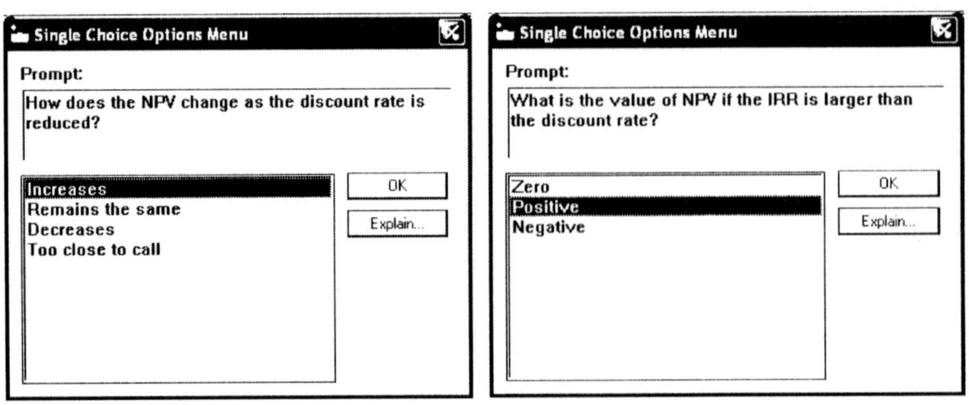

- BLSs provide the learner with a purposeful entry to the Internet and to online learning resources.
- BLSs connect learners and instructors on a 24/7 basis. They also underpin the development of new patterns of relationships between education and business through virtual learning arrangements.

Additionally, students report that web-based learning support systems allow them to remain current with assignments and in contact with their study teams even while on extended travel status.

In a recent study of BLS used in a graduate management course, the overall student response as measured by a number of survey dimensions was positive (Hall, 2006). The results of the survey revealed that:

- 69 percent reported that the course fully met their expectations (only five percent indicated that the course did not). More specifically, the survey results indicated that the presentation of course content and assignments via the Internet were found to be more effective than traditional classroom methods.
- 80 percent of the respondents indicate that this was their first blended based course and that they spent an average of 4.83 hours/week reviewing the course materials online
- 67 percent of the students found the blended course design more effective than traditional instructional methods. Furthermore, student usage of digital library assets increased.
- 93 percent of those responding to the survey indicated that they found this course design supported of their work schedule. This positive response can be attributed to the fact that nearly 75 percent of the students missed one or more classes due to business activities yet they were able to remain engaged in the course.

These results are consistent with the notion that BLS fosters new and robust learning patterns (Miller, 2003). BLS provides a vehicle for moving from a teaching-centric towards a learning-centric educational paradigm, which is particularly attractive for working adults pursuing graduate management education. The evidence suggests that subject mastery is not eroded as a result of Internet-based learning as long as students remain persistent (Mclaren, 2004). The results from a similar study show a statistically significant positive correlation between self-directed learning (SDL) ability and information systems competency in students with above average SDL ability (Shinkareva, 2007). The study data also indicate that motivation is an important factor for learning technology in an online course, regardless of the students' SDL ability. Additionally, students with a higher level of SDL ability are likely to exhibit higher level of self-efficacy for learning and performance, and higher levels of effort regulation. Improving retention and identifying "at risk" learners is another challenge that can be addressed in a blended learning environment (Hughes, 2007). Another course level study, this one in business communications, found that students in a blended course environment demonstrated a higher rate of active learning practices and yielded similar levels of measurable improvement in writing as did those students in a traditional classroom setting (Sauers, 2004).

In terms of future trends and directions, a recent comprehensive survey on the extent and promise of blended education found the following general patterns (Allen, 2007):

- Blended courses are not more prevalent than fully online courses. The proportion of schools offering blended and online courses is nearly identical.
- Academic leaders do not regard blended courses as holding more promise than fully

online courses. This view appears to be true regardless of size and type of school with the only exception being the small number of schools which offer blended courses but not online courses.

- Blended courses are *not* just a stepping stone to offering online courses or programs. There are far more blended courses and programs being offered than would be present if institutions were using them only as a transition to fully online courses.
- The market for online/blended delivery has a lot of room for growth. Consumer preference for online and blended delivery far exceeds reported experience, and consumer openness to these delivery modes far exceeds preference.

Further research is needed at the course, curriculum and delivery levels to continue to assess both the effectiveness and direction of blended learning compared with traditional and online delivery modes (Brannon, 2005; Changchit 2003; Palmer, 2002).

IMPLEMENTATION

The use of blended systems throughout graduate management education is growing rapidly albeit unevenly (Kim, 2007; Blass, 2003). Developing a comprehensive implementation plan is a necessary condition for ensuring a successful system deployment. Implementing a blended design for graduate management education is not a simple task. A number of specific steps must be taken to ensure a successful system deployment. These steps include:

- **Thinking Long Term:** Link the BLS design to the mission statement of the institution. Look ahead five years in terms of development direction and tempo.
- **Developing Content:** The development and acquisition of web-based content can account for upwards of 50 percent of the overall budget
- **Comparison Shopping:** Carefully evaluate the portal providers. There are over 100 potential vendors. Any disruption in providing 24/7 learning will court disaster.
- **Implementing a Phased Approach:** Consider prototyping the BLS in a specific EMBA section for gaining experience and confidence

To reap the full potential of the blended model, the design must involve more than simply "attaching" a series of websites to the standard classroom format (Skill, 2002). Generally, the course structure must be redesigned to provide a seamless transition between face-to-face learning and asynchronous learning (Conway, 2005).

Student "buy-in" represents a key factor to the successful implementation of the BLS paradigm. Students must be convinced that the convenience and richness of Internet resources offsets the perceived notion that they can only learn in a classroom. One way to accomplish this is to have students serve as co-producers, thus giving the class additional ownership (Brown, 2003). Other keys to success include that the system is operational on a 24/7 basis and is easy to use (Biass, 2003). Another "buy-in" modality involves organizing students into self-sustaining support teams. This helps ensure that no one is left behind. In this regard, students tend to participate to a greater extent in learning systems that are content-rich and that feature extensive variety (Kathawala, 2002).

Arguably, the single most important element of the blended model is faculty "buy-in" and orientation. Some faculty have been reluctant to embrace a blended course structure. This is due to technology phobia, a lack of motivation and no additional compensation (Crooks, 2003). While some institutions do provide some incremental resources for course development, the general perspective is that it is up to faculty to make the transition as part of the modernization of academia. One approach to help ameliorate some faculty concerns is through the use of web-based training modules. These systems not only introduce the faculty to the "power" of the Internet but also show them how to design and implement a blended-based course.

The deployment of BLS on a wide-scale basis will result in significant direct and indirect costs for schools of business. Often, these costs are both difficult to estimate and measure. Institutions need to develop a cost structure that recognizes the local context and cultural conditions as these will influence outcomes and analyses (Bates, 2005). The total cost associated with infrastructure development is often underestimated. Furthermore, faculty and staff development costs are not fully understood, particularly the extra time required for faculty to learn how to use the technology and develop appropriate content (Normand, 2008). One cost structure paradigm that has been designed to address these challenges is called INSIGHT (Nicol, 2003). The structure consists of three basic cost considerations: 1) infrastructure, 2) value added, and 3) academic support. This system allows program designers to evaluate competitive priorities within the context of the overall institution, e.g., student expectations versus faculty expectations.

In addition to cost considerations, some additional administrative challenges in implementing the BLS paradigm include the following:

- Training faculty for successful system deployment and usage
- Providing high quality and consistent system access
- Setting specific performance goals and metrics
- Preparing students for entry and ongoing use
- Sustaining system operation and flexibility
- Establishing the overall culture

Developing the internal capability to deploy the BLS is complex and expensive. Furthermore, an internalized approach may not take advantage of ongoing developments in delivery technology, e.g., search engine technology. One implementation strategy that helps overcome these issues consists of developing institutional partners with both content and application service providers (Sorel, 2001). This approach draws on the basic ideas behind supply chain management and is consistent with the increased use of suppliers in large volume operations, such as those found in most business programs. Measuring ongoing effectiveness and performance is key to the successful sustainability of a blended system, such as the one outlined in this chapter (Weippl, 2007; Bersin, 2002).

Designers of graduation management programs need both learning theories and best practice models to formulate effective curriculum formats in the ever changing business and academic environments. Furthermore, feedback is needed on how specific efforts to date have matched the preferred learning environment of students. One system for collecting such feedback is the Online Learning Environment Survey (OLES). This data collection system provides a practical approach for collecting student perception, expectation and performance feedback (Pearson, 2005). Design tools like INSIGHT and OLES provide a comprehensive "community of inquiry" framework which can lead to cost-effective strategies for redesigning courses and curricula into blended learning experiences (Garrison, 2008). Any "community of inquiry" framework needs to be forward-looking since many new learning technologies and delivery modes are either still on the drawing boards or have yet to be conceptualized. A good example of the former is artificial agents designed to support the student throughout the entire course of study.

CONCLUSION

Interest in graduate management education is growing, due in part, to the impact of globalization, technology, demographics, and corporate operations. Furthermore, the use of web-based learning systems in business education is also on the rise (Vaughan, 2007; Wall, 2007). These learning systems hold out considerable promise for enhancing graduate management education in a changing global environment. As a result of these developments, many MBA programs are increasingly focused on customization, experiential learning, and results assessment. The purpose of this chapter has been to illustrate how blended learning systems (BLSs) can address these trends and challenges. BLSs, often known as hybrid learning systems, optimize the use of the Internet to deliver learning content for business courses and programs, while simultaneously enhancing faculty and peer group interactions. BLSs provide an opportunity for collaborative learning that can have a positive impact on the educational experience (Graham, 2001). Another feature of the BLS is real-time feedback. This capability can be provided in a variety of ways, including business simulations and related experiential learning assignments. Real-time feedback presents both the instructor and student with insights into subject areas that require more in-depth attention. Providing the broadest range of tutorial instruction optimizes students' opportunities for effective learning. Asynchronous real-time feedback is particularly attractive for working managers engaged in extensive travel and other work-related assignments. The BLS strategy outlined herein is designed to significantly alter the three pillars of traditional MBA instruction - fixed time, fixed location, and fixed learning pace - with a more flexible and customized learning process. The blended learning net also can be used to improve the delivery and effectiveness of traditional MBA programs (Latham, 2004). Specific benefits of the BLS paradigm for MBA type programs include the following:

- Affords an integrated perspective on the course/program
- Presents instructional-rich content including real-time feedback
- Offers courses designed for specific learning applications with real-time feedback
- Increases student team participation and interaction
- Improves quality control through content integration
- Supports quality assurance through rubric measurements
- Provides direct linkage with Internet and library resources

A number of additional developmental tasks need to be addressed to further improve the effectiveness of blended learning in graduate management education. These efforts include enhanced interactive simulations, real-time videos, virtual experiential exercises, and improving the sense of community through, for example, the use of blogs. Furthermore, the introduction of artificial intelligence models for student assessment and mentoring will greatly improve the capability of the BLS to deliver effective customized content. In terms of an implementation strategy, consideration should be given to developing a strategic partnership with both content and application service providers. Specifically, using an "outsourcing" implementation strategy should ensure both a reliable learning resource as well as timely technological updates.

Higher education, in general, and management education, in particular, is undergoing a fundamental shift from a teacher-centric process to a learning-centric environment that focuses on customized learning (Hitz, 2005). In graduate management education, this transformation is being fueled by the need to produce educated managers that can compete on a global basis. The vehicle for facilitating this reformation is the Internet. Blended learning nets, which combine the best in classical learning with web-based support systems, provide both the rigor and flexibility to meet the challenges and requirements of today's managers.

REFERENCES

Allen, I., Seaman, J., & Garrett, R. (2007). Blending In: The extent and promise of blending learning in the United States. In *Proceedings of the The Sloan Consortium*.

Aquino, K., & Serva, M. (2005). Using a dual role assessment to improve group dynamics and performance. *Journal of Management Education, 29*(1), 17. doi:10.1177/1052562903262482

Bates, A. (2005). *Technology, e-learning and distance education* (2nd ed.). Abingdon, UK: RoutledgeFalmer.

Bennis, W., & O'Toole, J. (2005). How business schools lost their way. *Harvard Business Review, 83*(5), 96.

Bersin, J. (2002). Measuring e-learning effectiveness. *e-learning, 3*(3), 36.

Biass, E., & Davis, A. (2003). Building on solid foundations: Establishing criteria for e-learning developments. *Journal of Further & Higher Learning, 27*(3), 227. doi:10.1080/0309877032000098662

Bonk, C., & Graham, C. (2006). *The Hand Book of Blended Learning*. New York: John Wiley & Sons.

Brannon, T. (2005). Learner Interactivity in Higher Education: comparing face-to-face, hybrid and on-line instruction. *Distance Learning, 2*(2), 1.

Brookshire, R. (2007). An end-user information systems curriculum for the 21st century. *Journal of Computer Information Systems, 47*(3), 81.

Brown, R., & Murti, G. (2003). Student partners in Instruction: third level student participation in advanced business courses. *Journal of Education for Business, 79*(2), 85.

Changchit, C. (2003). An investigation into the feasibility of using an internet-based intelligent system to facilitate knowledge transfer. *Journal of Computer Information Systems, 43*(4), 91.

Clyde, L. (2005). Educational blogging. *Teacher Librarian, 32*(3), 43.

Condone, S. (2004). Reducing the distance: A study of course websites as a means to create a total learning space in traditional courses. *IEEE Transactions on Professional Communication, 47*(3), 190. doi:10.1109/TPC.2004.833692

Conway, R., & Easton, S. (2005). Strategies for Enhancing Student Interaction and Immediacy in Online Courses. *Business Communication Quarterly, 68*(1), 23. doi:10.1177/1080569904273300

Corsi, T. (2006). The real-time global supply chain game: New educational tool for developing supply chain management professionals. *Transportation Journal, 45*(3), 61.

Cotner, J., Jones, R., & Kashlak, R. (2003). Effectively Integrating an International Field Study into the EMBA Curriculum. *Journal of Teaching in International Business, 15*(1), 5. doi:10.1300/J066v15n01_02

Crooks, S., Yang, Y., & Duemer, L. (2003). Faculty perceptions of web-based resources in higher education. *Journal of Educational Technology Systems, 31*(2), 103. doi:10.2190/E68Q-KW1G-JK5B-TTRM

Davenport, J., & Davenport, J. A. (1985). A chronology and analysis of the andragogy debate. *Adult Education Quarterly, 35*(3), 152. doi:10.1177/0001848185035003004

Delone, W., & Mclean, E. (2003). The Delone and Mclean model of information systems success: A ten year update. *Journal of Management Information Systems*, *19*(4), 9.

Flatley, M. (2005). Blogging for enhanced teaching and learning. *Business Communication Quarterly*, *68*(1), 77. doi:10.1177/108056990506800111

Fry, H., Pearce, R., & Bright, H. (2007). Reworking resource based learning: A case study from a masters programme. *Innovations in Education and Teaching International*, *44*(1), 79. doi:10.1080/14703290601081373

Garrison, R., & Vaughan, N. (2007). *Blended Learning in Higher Education: Framework, Principles, and Guidelines*. San Francisco: Jossey-Bass Publishers.

Graesser, A. (2005). Auto Tutor: An intelligent tutoring system with mixed-initiative dialogue. *IEEE Transactions on Education*, *48*(4), 612. doi:10.1109/TE.2005.856149

Graham, M., & Scarborough, H. (2001). Enhancing the learning environment for distance education students. *Distance Education*, *22*(2), 232. doi:10.1080/0158791010220204

Graves, W. (1999). The instructional management system cooperative: converting random acts of progress into global progress. *Educational Review*, *34*(6), 32.

Hall, O. (2006). Enhancing management education using hybrid learning nets: A perspective from working adults. *Journal of Business Management*, *12*(1), 2006.

Hitz, S., & Turnoff, M. (2005). Education goes digital; the evolution of online learning and the revolution in higher education. *Communications of the ACM*, *48*(10), 59. doi:10.1145/1089107.1089139

Hopkins, S. (2005, February 8). Keeping tech jobs in the country. *ECU News Bureau*.

Hughes, G. (2007). Using blended learning to increase learner support and improve retention. *Teaching in Higher Education*, *12*(3), 15. doi:10.1080/13562510701278690

Jorgensen, D. (2002). The challenges and benefits of asynchronous learning networks. *The Reference Librarian*, *77*, 3.

Kathawala, Y., Abdou, K., & Elmuti, D. (2002). The global MBA: a comparative assessment for its future. *Journal of European Industrial Training*, *26*(1), 14. doi:10.1108/03090590210415867

Kerfoot, B., Conlin, P., Travison, T., & McMahon, G. (2007). Web-based education in systems-based practice. *Archives of Internal Medicine*, *167*(4), 361. doi:10.1001/archinte.167.4.361

Kim, K., & Bonk, C. (2006). The future of online teaching and learning in higher education. *Educasue Quarterly, 4*.

Kleiman, L., & Kass, D. (2007). Giving MBA programs the third degree. *Journal of Management Education*, *31*(1), 81. doi:10.1177/1052562906286874

Latham, G., Latham, S., & Whyte, G. (2004). Fostering integrative thinking: adapting the executive education model to the MBA program. *Journal of Management Education*, *28*(1), 3. doi:10.1177/1052562903252647

Li, F., Lau, R., & Liu, W. (2007). Emerging E-Learning Technologies. *International Journal of Distance Education Technologies*, *5*(2), 2.

Lin, F. (2005). *Designing Distributed Learning Environments with Intelligent Software Agents*. Hershey, PA: Information Science Publishing.

Matsatsinis, N., Moraitis, P., Psomatakis, V., & Spanoudakism, N. (2003). An agent-based system for products penetration strategy selection. *Applied Artificial Intelligence*, *17*(10), 901. doi:10.1080/714858317

McDuffie, R., Smith, S., & Murphy, L. (2006). Impact of an audit reporting expert system on learning performance: a teaching note. *Accounting Education*, *15*(1), 189. doi:10.1080/06939280600551585

Mclaren, C. (2004). A comparison of student persistence and performance in online and classroom business statistics experiences. *Journal of Innovative Education*, *2*(1), 1. doi:10.1111/j.0011-7315.2004.00015.x

Mortera-Gutierrez, F. (2006). Faculty best practices using blended learning in e-learning and face-to-face instruction. *International Journal on E-Learning*, *5*(3), 313.

Nicol, C., & Coen, M. (2003). A model for evaluating the institutional costs and benefits of ICT initiatives in teaching and learning in higher education. *Association of Learning Technology Journal*, *11*(2), 46.

Normand, C., Littlejohn, A., & Falconer, I. (2008). A model for effective implementation of flexible program delivery. *Innovations in Teaching and Education International*, *45*(1), 25. doi:10.1080/14703290701757351

Oravec, J. (2003). Blending by Blogging: weblogs in blended learning initiatives. *Journal of Educational Media*, *28*(2), 225. doi:10.1080/1358165032000165671

Palmer, J. (2002). Web site usability, design and performance metrics. *Information Systems Research*, *13*(2), 151. doi:10.1287/isre.13.2.151.88

Pearson, J., & Trinidad, S. (2005). OLES: An instrument for refining the design e-learning environments. *Journal of Computer Assisted Learning*, *21*, 396. doi:10.1111/j.1365-2729.2005.00146.x

Pettijohn, J. (2002). Virtual Tours – A tool for enhancing and enlivening the international business class. *Journal of Business education, 75*(5), 291.

Richards-Wilson, S. (2006). What every business school needs to know about its master of business administration. *Journal of Education for Business*, *82*(2), 95. doi:10.3200/JOEB.82.2.95-100

Sauers, D., & Walker, R. (2004). A comparison of traditional and technology-assisted instructional methods in the business communication classroom. *Business Communication Quarterly*, *67*(4), 430. doi:10.1177/1080569904271030

Schmotter, J. (2004). On two-plus decades: A world of difference. *Selections*, *4*(1), 3.

Shih, Y. (2003). A survey of distance education challenges and technologies. *International Journal of Distance Learning Technologies*, *1*(1), 1.

Shinkareva, O. (2007). The Relationship between Adult Students' Instructional Technology Competency and Self-Directed Learning Ability in an Online Course. *Human Resource Development International*, *10*(4), 417. doi:10.1080/13678860701723737

Skill, T., & Young, B. (2002). Embracing the blended model: Working at the intersection of virtual and physical learning spaces. *New Directions for Teaching and Learning*, *2002*(92). doi:10.1002/tl.76

Sorel, R., Dear, R., & Edge, D. (2001). Evolution of web-based distance learning strategies. *International Journal of Educational Management*, *15*(4/5), 245.

Thomas, K. (2007). Methods to Enhance Student Learning: A Student Appraisal of the 2007 Annual Learning Technologies Showcase. *Library Hi Tech News*, *24*(8), 4. doi:10.1108/07419050710835938

Vaughan, N. (2007). Perspectives on blended learning in higher education. *International Journal in e-learning, 6*(1), 81.

Wadhwa, S., Saxena, A., & Kumar, A. (2005). A KM motivated web-based supply chain simulator: facilitating e-learning for SMEs. *International Journal of Business Performance Management, 8*(2), 2007.

Wall, J., & Ahmad, V. (2008). Lessons learned from a case study in deploying blended learning continuing professional development. *Engineering, Construction, and Architectural Management, 15*(2), 185.

Wang, Y. (2002). Assessment of learner satisfaction with asynchronous electronic learning systems. *Information & Management, 41*(1), 75. doi:10.1016/S0378-7206(03)00028-4

Webb, H. (2005). Teaching with the case method online: Pure versus blended approaches. *Decision Sciences Journal of Innovative Education, 3*(2), 223. doi:10.1111/j.1540-4609.2005.00068.x

Weippl, E. (2007). Dependability in e-assessment. *International Journal in e-learning, 6*(2), 293.

KEY TERMS AND DEFINITIONS

Blended Learning: Combining both classroom and web-based instruction.

Business Teaching Strategy: A process for providing management know-how.

Distance Learning: Knowledge acquisition over the Internet.

Graduate Management Education: MBA type programs.

Hybrid Delivery: Using the Internet to support the overall learning strategy.

Integrated Learning: Combining the core management functions.

Chapter 22
Medical Hybrid Learning Tools

Liana Stanescu
University of Craiova, Romania

Dumitru Dan Burdescu
University of Craiova, Romania

ABSTRACT

This chapter describes original modalities of combining traditional methods and technologies in medical learning with good results. The electronic tool is TESYS, a non-commercial e-learning platform designed for completing and improving traditional medical learning by using new methods. Traditional learning is thus blended together with e-learning, offering the students and teachers the possibility to permanently evaluate the learning and teaching process. Besides the usual functions of an e-learning platform, TESYS includes elements of originality. The first one is a database with medical images collected during the process of diagnosing patients, which also include other useful information (diagnostic, treatment, evolution) in order to complete the currently limited number of images found in university courses and medical books. The second element of originality is the content-based visual query module designed for this multimedia medical database, which uses features that are automatically extracted from images (color, texture, regions). The content-based visual query used both in the e-learning and e-testing process stimulates learning by comparing similar cases along with their particularities, or by comparing cases that are visually similar but with different diagnosis.

INTRODUCTION

Medical teaching is probably one of the most important areas where the application of the hybrid solutions for students training can prove very useful. Engineering teaching is another area where hybrid learning offers a lot of advantages. If we consider specialties like economics or exact sciences, they can be entirely and successfully based on electronic learning. This is not applicable to medical teaching. In this case it cannot be obtained the direct transfer of knowledge, teacher's experience, especially for the practice classes made in hospitals, where the teacher presents the medical case, the investiga-

DOI: 10.4018/978-1-60566-380-7.ch022

tions, the diagnosis, the treatment, an overview of the patient evolution or comparative studies with other cases from his medical practice. In these cases, the student can directly follow the teacher's logic, the way he analyzes the medical case and the evolution of the patient. Each of these cases is practically unique because the disease and the patient are unique.

Taking into account technological development and advantages of the electronic learning, we consider that it is a good idea to introduce the hybrid learning in the medical domain, because (Masie, 2002):

- Web-based learning activities are introduced to complement face-to-face work
- "Seat time" is reduced, though not eliminated altogether
- The web-based and face-to-face components of the course are designed to interact pedagogically to take advantage of the best features of each
- Students can learn via the Internet while in different places and at various moments of time

As a result, it was designed and implemented an e-learning platform that enhances the traditional learning methods, allowing students to access modern methods to pass information and test their knowledge.

This chapter presents the non-commercial e-learning software tool, TESYS, designed for medical education. The software platform is intended to complete and improve any traditional learning methods, offering teachers and students modern of learning and assessing methods. The TESYS platform also contains a series of modules for evaluating the activity and involvement of both teacher and student in the e-learning process, while the analysis made conducts to the elaboration of a recommendation to each of them regarding the improvement of the quality of training. The platform is already used together with the traditional method at the University of Medicine and Pharmacy from Craiova, for teaching the disciplines of gastroenterology and urology. Of course, other faculties of the University of Craiova use also the TESYS platform for normal and distance learning (Stanescu et al, 2007; Burdescu and Mihaescu, 2006; Burdescu and Mihaescu, 2008). The chapter also presents a number of scenarios for medical hybrid learning.

For example, the student can attend the course in the classroom and then he can use the software tool from anywhere and anytime in order to download the course files, to follow the bibliographic references to other additional materials proposed by teacher. Also, the users can use the platform for communicating with other students, teachers, secretaries and administrator.

Unlike other similar platforms, which are used on a large scale in different domains including the medical one, TESYS offers several elements of originality, which allow students to benefit from an increased volume of knowledge and a better modality of checking and assessing their professional training.

The first original element brought by the TESYS platform in the hybrid learning is a multimedia medical database, updated by specialists with images acquired from different patients during the diagnosis and treatment processes. Each image can include a series of alphanumerical information: diagnosis, treatment, and patient evolution. It means that along with the electronic teaching documentation for the classic teaching methods, there is a database with medical images.

In the medical learning process, the courses in traditional or electronic format are accompanied in many cases by a series of images. For example, at a gastroenterology course, for the presentation of the ulcer diagnosis, the teacher shows students images that are relevant for this diagnosis, highlighting the changes in color, texture or shape of the sick tissue, in comparison to a healthy one. In general, the number of images that are presented is minimal. Accordingly, the existence of a digital library with medical images collected by the teacher in the process of patients' diagnosis and investigation raises considerably the variety of knowledge being communicated during the face-to-face work.

This medical image database can be used both for completing and improving the learning and testing process. It uses a modern query method, namely content-based visual query, which represents the second element of originality rendered by TESYS. Medical e-learning is the most important direction for using content-based visual query, besides diagnostic aid and medical research, as presented in the specialty literature (Muller at al, 2004).

Students can use the medical image database for completing the traditional training process. They can query the database in two different ways:

- Traditionally, by the text-based method; for example, the diagnostic is written and all the images associated to it are searched in the database.
- By content-based query; in this case keywords or other texts are not used. The query uses the characteristics extracted from images (for example color or texture). This type of query is implemented taking into account the whole image, or only parts of it (regions). In the first case the name of the query is content-based image query. It will find in the database all the images that are significantly similar to the query image. In the second case, the name of the query is content-based region query. It needs to be selected one or several regions used as query regions and it searches in the database all the images that contain the selected regions. In this case it is necessary to have an automated region extraction algorithm for images, using certain characteristics, for example color (Smith, 1997; Del Bimbo, 2001).

The above-presented scenarios allow students to see a big number of images and their associated information in a simple and direct manner. They only have to select a query image and find similar ones. This method stimulates learning, by comparing similar cases or by comparing cases that are visually similar, but with different diagnostics (Muller at al, 2004), things that are difficult to achieve in traditional learning mode.

For testing students' knowledge, we also propose an original solution that use the multimedia medical database and content-based visual query and complete a traditional mode for medical knowledge testing: the teacher presents to the student a medical image, he has to study it, establish a diagnosis and make observations. Moreover, the electronic solution challenges the student to recognize similar images that are included in the same diagnosis class, or visually similar images, but of different diagnosis. Such complex testing allows the teacher to evaluate student's knowledge more efficiently and thoroughly so that he can take the right decisions. The role of proficient testing methods is very important in the medical domain, where establishing a wrong diagnosis based on the imagistic investigations can have serious consequences on a patient.

By its functions and its original elements this platform can be used both by students of medical higher education and by specialized interns, family doctors and young specialists in the process of continuous medical learning.

The objectives of this chapter, organized by sections, are the following:

- Section 2 will develop upon concepts which form the base of hybrid learning, as well upon the most important international achievements in the field;
- Section 3 will present the functions of TESYS platform in detail, the structure of the database with images and medical information, the algorithms used for processing these information in order to collect

characteristics such as the color, texture and regions, as well as the original method in which the content-based image query and content-based region query in medical e-learning and e-testing is used;

- Section 4 will introduce a few ideas for further development of the TESYS platform in order to bring new benefices in hybrid learning ;
- Section 5 consists of conclusions.

The Problems Overview and Related Work

The concept of e-learning refers to the use of Internet technologies for providing a multitude of solutions which can improve the level of knowledge and performance (Rosenberg, 2001; Wentling at al, 2005). The term e-learning can have a series of synonyms: web-based learning, online learning, distributed learning, computer-assisted instruction or internet-based learning (Ruiz at al, 2006). From the historical point of view we can speak about two types of e-learning (Ward at al, 2001):

- Distance learning – implies the use of technology for training students who are in remote locations from the central point
- Computer-assisted learning – implies the use of computer in the process of learning and teaching

These two modalities were united under the concept of e-learning because the Internet has become the integrating technology.

E-learning consists of many components:

- Creating and developing training materials, which form the learning content. We are referring here to learning objects in the form of distinct and independent units of training material with a view to reaching the learning objectives (Littlejohn, 2003)
- Content management; it includes all the administrative functions (storing, indexing, cataloging) of the learning objects (Ruiz at al, 2006)
- Content delivery that can be synchronous (real-time instructor-led delivery where all the learners receive information simultaneously) or asynchronous (Wentling et al, 2005)
- Content standardization; the most well-known set of standards is the Advanced distributed Learning: Sharable Content Object reference Model (SCORM) (Fallon and Brown, 2003)

A concept which is very close to e-learning and which even precedes the Internet is multimedia learning. Multimedia e-learning uses more media (text, graphics, animation, video, audio) in the learning content which is accessed by students through the computer. The value of multimedia in learning is demonstrated in many papers. Researches show how multimedia can extend and augment learning. For example, in (Shank, 2007; Hede and Hede, 2002; Mayer, 2003) the authors describe the benefits of multimedia in learning:

- Alternative perspectives
- Active participation
- Accelerated learning
- Retention and application of knowledge
- Problem-solving and decision-making skills
- System understanding
- Higher-order thinking
- Autonomy and focus
- Control over pacing and sequencing information
- Access to support information

Due to all the advantages (increased accessibility to information, better updating solutions, personalized training, better distribution, standardization of content, better efficiency in achieving knowledge and aptitudes) e-learning has become more important and more frequently used in the last decade (Ruiz et al, 2006). Among the domains in which it is used there is the also the medical field, but in this case it is adopted a hybrid process that combines the traditional learning methods with the electronic ones (Moberg and Whitcomb, 1999; Ward et al, 2001). The accomplished studies, including those focusing on medical domain, indicated that the students substantially appreciate the e-learning method, but they do not consider it as a replacement of the traditional learning which has other advantages. Also, studies have shown that e-learning can lead to a significant 50% decrease of costs in the process of learning (Ruiz et al, 2006).

The blended or hybrid learning, though a relatively new term, represents an approach, which is well-known by trainers. These modern learning techniques are achieved by combining virtual and physical resources. For example the teacher can hold a course, but for this he has to provide an online tutorial, or other possibilities to access the database (Masie, 2002).

A hybrid course is designed to integrate face-to-face and online activities so that they reinforce, complement, and elaborate one another, instead of treating the online component as an add-on or duplicate of what is taught in the classroom.

It should also be distinguished the flexibility of the hybrid model, from the teaching point of view. The teacher will decide what kind of activities will be made in the class or on-line, taking into account the learning goals, course objectives, content, and available resources.

The powerful technological development and the large utilization of the Internet contributed to the development of medical e-learning resources to support the traditional training: MedEdPortal from Association of American Medical Colleges (http://www.aacm.org/mededportal), End of Life/Palliative Resource Center (http://www.eperc.mcw.edu), The Health Education Assets Library (HEAL http://www.healcentral.org), Multimedia Educational Resource for Learning and Online Teaching (MERLOT http://www.merlot.org) or International Virtual Medical School (IVIMEDS http://www.ivimeds.org).

Accessing these digital libraries we observed that they offer to students very useful functions of the highest quality that meet the needs of today's health sciences educators and learners. These functions are too less or not accessible in traditional learning style. Some of them are:

- Search, either with a simple keyword search or with an advanced search
- Browse by Medical Subject Heading (MeSH) or by collection
- All digital content types
- View or play resources
- View detailed cataloging information (metadata) about the resource
- Download chosen files as a packaged archive (zip file)
- Submit resources for peer review and publication

It is important to emphasize the fact that these digital libraries contain many types of data: text, images, sound, video, graphics and animation for the improvement of the learning content.

Most of these digital libraries provide also an imagistic component but which has more limited possibilities than the TESYS platform, i.e. a multimedia database with medical images, which can be queried according to content or even traditionally and which can be used both in the electronic training process and in the process of electronic testing. This solution is provided only by two systems which are currently used in the medical education: **ASSERT** – developed by the Purdue University in collaboration with the Department of Radiology of the Indiana University and the School of Medicine from the University of Wisconsin (Shyu et al, 1999) and **MedGIFT**, developed at the University Hospital Geneva. MedGift is used together with Casimage (http://

www.casimage.com/), which contains a database with radiological images which has been in use for several years already. There are over 60.000 images collected from more than 10.000 medical cases. The database can be queried from the internal network of the hospital and a part of it is made public on the Internet (Muller et al, 2005).

The Functions of the Medical Virtual Platform

The main goal of the application is to give students the possibility to download course materials, take tests or sustain final examinations and communicate with all parties involved. To accomplish this, four different roles were defined for the platform: sysadmin, secretary, professor and student.

Roles

The main task of sysadmin users is to manage secretaries and all activity on the platform. A sysadmin user may add or delete secretaries, or change their password. He may also view the actions performed by all other users of the platform. All actions performed by users are logged. This way the sysadmin may check the activity that takes place on the application. The logging facility has some benefits: an audit may be performed for the application with the logs as witness; security breaches may also be discovered.

A sysadmin user may block an IP so that no user will be able to access the application from that IP. Finally, the overall activity of users represents valuable data. This data may be off-line analyzed using machine learning or even data mining techniques so that important conclusions may be obtained regarding the quality of service for the application. The quality of service may have two indicators: the learning proficiency of students and the capability of the application to classify students according to their accumulated knowledge. A statistics page is also available. It displays the number of users that entered the application, the total number of students, and the number of students with and without activity, as well as other information that gives an overall view on the activity on the application.

Secretary users manage sections, professors, disciplines and students with actions like add, delete or update. The secretaries have also the task to set up the structure of study years for all sections and the possibility of searching students using different criteria like name, section, year of study or residence. The secretaries have a large set of available reports regarding the student's status. Among them there is a list of students who took all the exams, a list of students who requested grants for taking an exam one more time and many other reports specific to secretary work.

The main task of a professor is to manage the assigned disciplines while the discipline is made up of chapters. The professor sets up chapters by specifying the name and the course documentation (figure 1). Only students enrolled in a section in which a discipline is studied may download the course's document and take tests or examinations. Besides setting up the course's document for each chapter, the professor manages test and exam questions. For each chapter the professor has to define two pools of questions, one used for testing and one used for exams. He specifies the number of questions that will be randomly extracted to create a test or an exam. Let us suppose that for a chapter the professor created 50 test questions and 60 exam questions and he has set to 5 the number of test questions and to 10 the number of exam questions that are to be randomly withdrawn. It means that, when a student takes a test from this chapter, 5 questions from the pool of test questions are randomly withdrawn. When the student takes the final examination at the discipline from which the chapter is part, 15 questions are randomly withdrawn: 5 from the pool of test questions and 10 from the pool of exam questions. This way of generating tests and exams is intended to be flexible enough for the professor. The teacher

Figure 1. Professor's view over a discipline

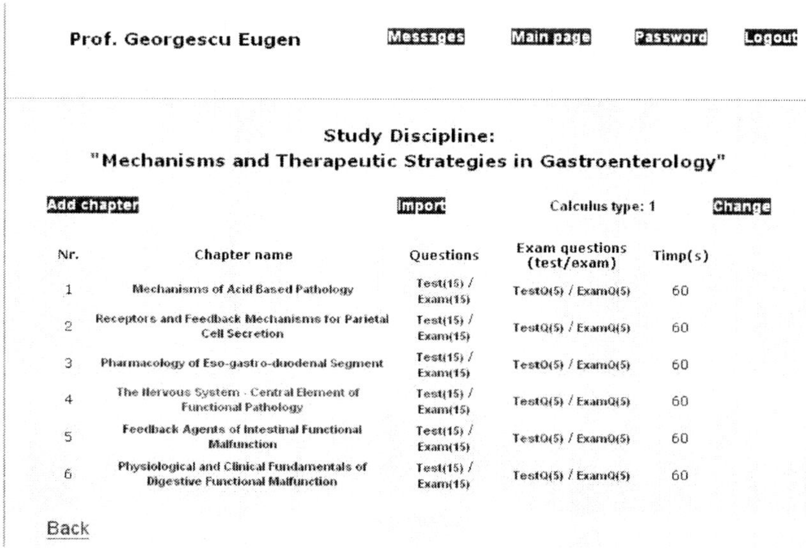

can offer the students diverse examinations or testing variants.

All tests and exams are taken under time constraints. For each chapter the professor sets up a number of seconds necessary to answer questions of that chapter. When a test or exam is taken all the seconds are summed up thus obtaining a maximal interval of time in which the student has to finish the test. The elapsed and remaining time are managed by the server and presented to the student after each answered question.

The professor has also flexibility for creating and editing questions. A question may contain pictures, and thus equations, images, formulas or other graphics may be imbedded in it. For each question the professor sets up the visible answers and the correct answers. For example, if a question has four possible answers he will have to check the checkboxes called A, B, C and D stating that the student will have four choices. Error checking is enforced such that when a question has three visible answers and the correct answer is D an error is shown to professor and the question cannot be saved.

There are two implemented formulas that may be used for calculating grades. For each discipline the professor chooses and sets any of the formulas such that it will be used for all tests and exams taken at that discipline.

Professors have also the possibility of searching students using different criteria and a large set of available reports that help them in working with students.

The sysadmin and professor, they can monitor the activity of every student for each discipline and this is another function very useful in the hybrid learning. The monitoring facility provides a good view over the activity of the student. The system keeps tracking when the student logged in, how much time he spent until logging out, which courses were downloaded, how many tests were taken and from which chapters.

The application offers students the possibility to download course materials, take tests and exams and communicate with other parties involved, as professors and secretaries.

Students may download only course materials for the disciplines that belong to sections where they are enrolled. They can take tests and exams with constraints that were set up by the secretary through the year structure function (figure 2).

Figure 2. Student's template for answering test questions

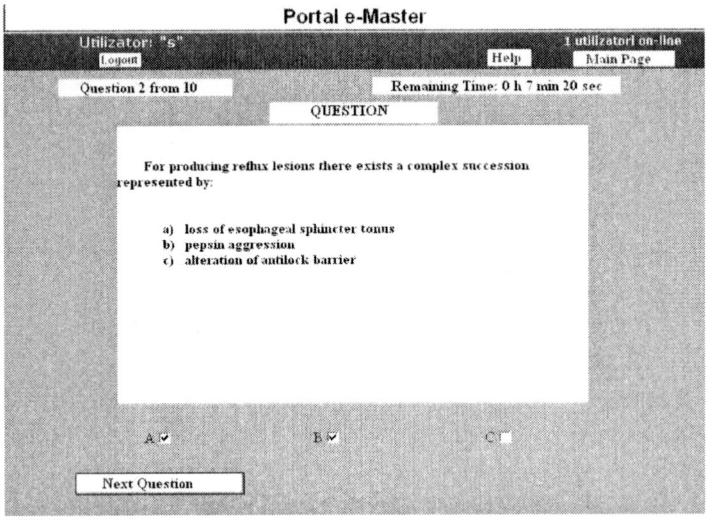

Students have access to personal data and can modify them as needed. A feedback form is also available. It is composed of questions that check aspects regarding the usability, efficiency and productivity of the application with respect to the student's needs.

All users must authenticate through username and password and their identity is periodically verified. If the username and password are valid the role of the user is determined and the appropriate interface is presented. The platform assigns a set of actions that the user may perform. Each time a user initiates an action the system checks if that action is allowed. This approach ensures security at user's level and makes sure that a student may not perform actions that are assigned to professor, secretary or sysadmin users.

A record of sustained tests is kept for all students. In fact, the taken test or exams are saved in full for later use (for example, the teachers need different reports). That is why a student or a professor may view a previously taken test or exam if needed. For each question is presented what the student checked, which was the correct answer, which was the maximum score that could be obtained from that question and how many points did the student obtain. At the end it is presented the final formula used to compute the mark and the grade itself.

Besides these core functions for the on-line testing some other are implemented or currently under development. A message board is available for professors, secretaries and students to ensure peer-to-peer communication. This facility is implemented within the platform such that no other service (e.g. email server) may be necessary.

In order to enforce the year structure function that is set up by the secretary a grant/revoke system is implemented for students, secretaries and professors. A student may request to the professor and secretary a grant to take an exam. This situation occurs when the student fails the exam or wants to increase the grade and taking the examination for a second time is preconditioned by other actions like taking more tests, paying fees, etc. If a professor and/or a secretary revoke an exam the student cannot sustain that exam until the requirements of the professor and/or the secretary are fulfilled.

The logging facility that is mainly used by sysadmin is transparently implemented for all users (secretaries, professors and students). Whenever one of them performs an action (e.g. a student starts or finishes an exam) that action is recorded for later use.

This division of activities according to their role insures security in the development of processes on the platform, as well as the recording of information referring to activities developed during a period of time. This way the activities performed by users with the help of the platform can be easily restored.

Medical Image Database

Further on, the chapter briefly presents the way in which the medical image database is managed for educational purposes. This implies the insertion of images and the launch into execution of some pre-processing algorithms for extracting information related to color and texture, as well as the significant color regions. Thus the images are prepared for the next stage, which is that of content-based query by color and texture.

Database Structure and Management

The professors have the possibility to insert new images in the multimedia database, together with their relevant information, namely: path and name of the image file, the diagnosis, as well as supplementary information that include specialists' observation regarding the disease and the way in which it is illustrated by image, treatment and evolution.

For realizing the content-based visual query, all the images loaded in the database are automatically processed, in three steps:

1. The extraction of color feature
2. The extraction of texture feature
3. The extraction of significant color regions

For extracting the color feature, the images are pre-processed, namely they are transformed from the RGB color space to HSV color space and quantized to 166 colors, being thus prepared for a future query. The HSV color space is preferred, for its properties (compactness, completeness, naturalness and uniformity) which allow it to be proper for usage in the content-based visual retrieval (Smith, 1997; Del Bimbo, 2001).

For the quantization of the HSV color space, the solution with 166 colors was chosen. Because the hue represents the most important color feature, it needs the finest quantization. In the circle that represents the colors, the primary colors red, green and blue are separated by 120 degrees. A circular quantization with 20 degree step separates sufficiently the colors. The saturation and the value are each quantized to three levels. The quantization produces 18 hues, 3 saturations, 3 values and 4 greys, that means 166 distinct colors in the HSV color space. The color information from the image is represented by means of the color histogram and by the binary color set. The color information is stored in the database as a vector with 166 values and it is used furthermore in the content-based image query and content-based region query (Smith, 1997). The similarity between the query and target image is computed using the histogram intersection (Smith, 1997).

Together with color, texture is a powerful characteristic of an image, which is present in nature and in medical images also. Thus a disease can be indicated by changes in the color and texture of a tissue (Muller et al, 2004).

There are many techniques used for texture extraction, but there is not any certain method that can be considered the most appropriate, this depending on the application and the type of images taken into account. The effectuated studies on medical images indicated that among the most representative methods of texture detection are the Gabor filters, reason for which it was chosen for extracting the color texture feature from medical images in the database (Muller et al, 2004).

The Gabor characteristics vector is computed for 3 scales and 4 orientations (Stanescu et al, 2007), so the texture feature is represented for each image as a 12-dimension vector stored in the database.

For detecting image color regions, it was chosen the color set back-projection algorithm, introduced initially by Swain and Ballard and then developed in the research projects at Columbia University, in the content-based visual retrieval domain (Smith, 1997). This technique provides the automatic extraction of regions and the representation of their color content. The extraction system for color regions has four steps (Smith, 1997).

1. The image transformation, quantization and filtering (the transformation from the RGB color space to HSV color space and the quantization of the HSV color space at 166 colors)
2. Back-projection of binary color sets
3. The labeling of regions
4. The extraction of the region features

The color regions detected by applying this algorithm on each medical image are stored in the database with the following characteristics: the color set, the area (the number of pixels) and the minimum- bounding rectangle that bounds the region. All this information is used later in the e-learning and e-testing process that uses content-based region query.

Medical Image Database Query for Learning Purpose

The medical image database can be visualized by browsing the images and their attached information, or can be simply queried by text. For example, the student introduces a diagnosis and the images included in the specified diagnosis will be returned from database.

A more modern solution is that of an image database query based on content. This supposes that there are not keywords or other textual information, but only an image is chosen from database, and the system will return a number of images similar with the query image taking into consideration the following characteristics: color, texture or shape automatically extracted. This process is called content-based image query (Smith, 1997; Del Bimbo, 2001).

In TESYS we use the content-based image query based on color and texture features that requires the selection of an image as a query image and retrieval of all those images from database which best resemble it, taking into consideration the color and texture features, each in equal parts. Also, for every image, detailed information is displayed.

Content-based visual query is a searching method based on similarity and not on the equality. It will return images visually similar with the query image, with the same diagnosis or different diagnosis. For computing the similarity between a query and a target image from database, the color characteristic (represented by a 166 values vector) and the texture characteristic (represented by a 12 values vector), in equal weights were considered. The images are displayed to the student in the descending order of the similarity computed with the histogram intersection distance.

In content-based region query it is necessary to select an image and to display the image color regions detected with the color set back-projection algorithm (figure 3). Next, the user must tick one or more color regions (this are relevant regions that indicate the existence of a disease) for content-based region query. The result is a set of images from the database that contain the query region(s), based on ascending order of the computed distance. Taking into account that the color information of each region is stored as a color binary set, the color similarity between two regions is computed with the quadratic distance between color sets (Smith, 1997).

With the help of this method, the student can analyze a lot of images from the same diagnosis, he can see the changes in color, texture or shape of the seek tissue reflected in the image. The content-based visual query offers to the student

Figure 3. The detected color regions with color set back-projection algorithm

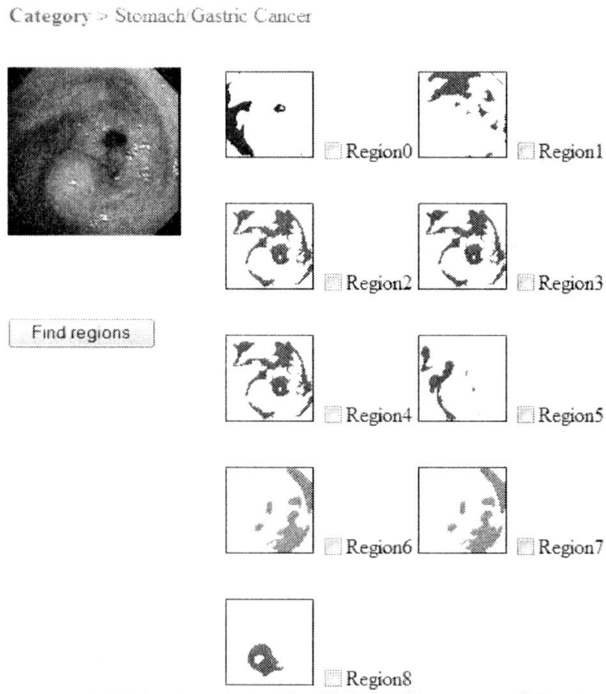

a variety of options, raises his curiosity, because the student can select any image from the database and the query response can be different because the database is permanently updated.

E-Testing Solutions Based on the Medical Image Database

The medical image database and content-based visual query can be used in e-testing also. The original e-testing solution proposed in the TESYS platform, can be done in two different ways:

- Using content-based image retrieval
- Using content-based region retrieval

In the first case, the testing process is the following: an image from the multimedia database that represents the query image is displayed. The student is asked to establish the diagnosis and to give details that will be added in text type controls. The "Content-based Image Query" option should be activated next. The content-based image query system will return a number of images from the multimedia database that can be relevant or non-relevant for the query.

For each image retrieved by the system, the student has to establish if this is relevant or non-relevant for the query image, meaning the image is or not included in the same diagnosis. The number of similar images retrieved automatically by the system can be established by the teacher before the testing (for example between 5 or 10 similar images). Also, the teacher has the possibility to establish the number of images on which the testing is done and to what diagnosis they belong.

The utilization of this e-testing system for medical hybrid learning shows that such testing environment is recommended to contain 3 query images and for each of them to be retrieved 5 similar images. This modality keeps students interested and offers the teacher a good idea about their capacity to accumulate knowledge necessary to establish a correct diagnosis for certain patology.

At the end of the test, the student will be automatically marked. He will receive the corresponding mark for each relevant image retrieved (the relevance is automatically established based on diagnosis). Also, the student can visualize the correct solution of the test, the correct diagnosis from the database and other information introduced by teacher will be displayed. This way, he can observe his errors and understand why images similar by color and texture are included in different diagnosis.

The electronic testing that uses the content-based region query comes to complete the first modality of testing. This is considered more complex, because a fine granularity approach to image retrieval is adopted. The student's testing takes into consideration the relevant color/texture regions automatically detected from medical images. The student has to select the option 'Regions Detection' and the relevant regions will be detected automatically by the system. In general, in an image there are many normal regions (healthy tissue) and a single relevant region for the diagnosis, which presents changes in color and texture in comparison to the normal one; the student has to recognize the abnormal region in the image. After that, the student has to mark the corresponding region and select the option "Content-based region query", which will retrieve a number of images from database (5 up to 10), that contain regions similar to the query region.

The student has to establish which images from the images automatically retrieved by the system are relevant for the query region (figure 4). Also, in this case, the student is automatically marked, getting the points for each relevant region recognized, relevance established based on the image diagnosis from the database. Also, at the end of the test, the student can visualize the correct results.

FUTURE WORK

For improving and extending the functions offered by the TESYS e-learning platform a first direction of development we intend to follow is the utilization in an original manner of a modern concept - topic map – in medical e-learning. Few existent papers report on the successful utilization of this concept in e-learning, especially through the visualization in a very intuitive manner of the information provided to students.

Regarding the use of the topic map in the TESYS platform will be followed two completely new directions, which were not found in any other software products with application in medical e-learning:

1. The topic map will be used mainly to to see the MeSH thesaurus containing medical terms.

For this purpose, the topic map will be built and populated in an original manner, mapping an xml file, that can be downloaded free to a xtm file that contains the structure of topic map. In the first stage only a part of the MeSH thesaurus will be used, namely the part that includes the medical diagnosis's names, due to the fact that the most important information attached to medical images is the diagnosis. It is important to be mentioned that the extension of the topic map with other information from the medical thesaurus can be done easily.

The student can navigate through the topic map depending on the subject of interest, which brings significant advantages. The student does not have to be familiar with the logic of the database, he will learn about the semantic context, in which a collection and its single items are embedded and he may find useful items he would not have expected to find at the beginning. The hierarchical structure of the descriptors from MeSH thesaurus, that has also multiple relationships between the medical terms, and each term may have a series of

Figure 4. An example of e-testing using the content-based region query on medical image database

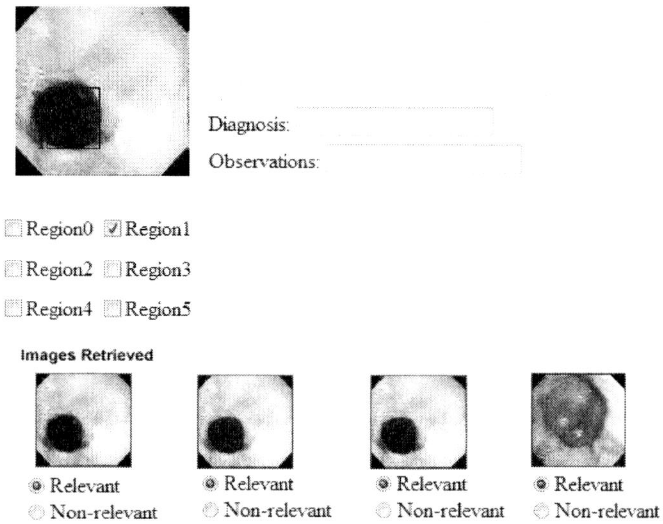

synonyms, can not be properly visualized only by means of a topic map that offers to the student the opportunity to understand exactly these things.

2. The second direction refers to the utilization of the topic map in order to make a semantic query on the multimedia database containing medical information and images.

In the topic map, since the occurrences are stored in the database, every topic will be defined as a database query. This query may be simple: the topic "peptic ulcer", for example, will initiate a query for "peptic ulcer" in the diagnosis field of the table Images in the database. Consequently, every relevant image of "peptic ulcer" will be retrieved. The database search can be done in two ways:

- Using a single topic
- Using the topic and all the synonyms, if there are

The second query modality is very useful in the learning process, because the images are introduced in the database by different specialists, and for diagnosis they can use synonyms, very known in the medical language, but less known by students.

This access path can be combined for retrieving the information of interest with the content-based visual query on the multimedia medical database.

The second direction followed in our approach refers to the estimation of the way in which the platform can evaluate learners. In this respect we shall develop separate software modules with the following functions:

1. The evaluation modules that will evaluate the students' activities and the teaching process. This way it is possible to supervise the student's activity to all disciplines (the time spent studying the platform, courses he had downloaded, the tests), the learning method in time and the efficiency of this process.
2. The analyzing module that will use a machine-learning algorithm for obtaining knowledge regarding learners. The e-assessment tool will produce data about the activity of learners and will pass this data to the analysis module. Whenever a

learner performs specific actions he is classified by the decision tree and conclusions are obtained. These conclusions may be regarded by recommendations for learners having as final goal helping them in reaching educational objectives.

3. The final module is the one referring to quality. The input of this module will be represented by learner's activity (data used for creating learner's model) and by goals (the criteria that need to be optimized to obtain better evaluation environment). Conclusions obtained by the quality module regard the level of fulfilling the proposed goals. The recommendations represent advice for course managers and learners. The aim of these recommendations is to increase the quality of the evaluation environment.

CONCLUSION

This chapter presents in detail the functions of an original platform for medical e-learning that completes with good results the traditional way of performing this activity and a number of scenarios to follow in the medical hybrid learning. The implemented platform creates an environment in which students can download course materials and take tests or exams in different disciplines. Sysadmin, secretary and professors manage the entire infrastructure of the application. The task of the secretary is to manage the general infrastructure consisting of sections, professors, disciplines and students. Professors have to manage their assigned disciplines, which means editing courses and questions for testing or examination purposes.

The chapter also presents the original way of using a multimedia database with color medical images and alphanumeric information in the medical hybrid learning process. The teachers manage the database by inserting images collected with different medical devices, in the process of patients' investigation. These images are automatically processed in three steps:

1. The extraction of color feature, by transforming the image from RGB color space to HSV color space quantized to 166 colors
2. The extraction of texture feature using Gabor filters
3. The extraction of color regions using the color-set back projection algorithm

Within the learning process, the multimedia database can be consulted in a modern way, image or region-based manner. The chapter also presents an e-testing modality of students from medical domain that uses the same database and the two modern query methods.

The medical image database and content-based visual retrieval used in the training and testing processes help to increase students' ability to find the correct diagnosis and to choose between very similar images as color and texture, which are included in different diagnosis, reducing the probability for the future physician to establish a wrong diagnosis which may have serious consequences on patient's health. The e-testing system doesn't only test students' knowledge, but based on answers, the student can learn from the errors he has made. For each kind of pathology, the teacher can determine the student's level of knowledge and also, at general level, the student's capacity to establish a correct diagnosis based on the imagistic investigations, frequently used nowadays.

The solution of e-learning and e-testing using content-based visual query on a database with medical images is used in parallel with traditional techniques at the University of Medicine and Pharmacy from Craiova for disciplines such as urology and gastroenterology.

During the year 2007, 60 students used the e-training module based on image database and content-based visual query in the study of the gastroenterology discipline. Each of them accessed the database approximately 9 times, spending on this an average of 200 minutes.

The 60 students participated also in the electronic testing, using the image database and content-based visual query at the same discipline. It was recorded an improvement in the number of correctly established diagnosis based on medical images. In 2006, when this multimedia component was not used, the average number of images correctly analyzed and diagnosed was 5 out of 10, and in 2007, using the multimedia database, an average of 7 was obtained. This improvement, in such relatively short time (one year) clearly indicates that this modality can bring important benefits in raising the level of students' education. Of course, this development can be influenced by other factors (the intellectual capacity of the students, for example), so the system's efficiency must be observed for a longer period of time.

The students who were tested by this method found it attractive, innovative, and with big advantages in testing the level of knowledge achieved. Also, the teachers consider that text and images used together to present medical information can have a positive impact on traditional medical learning.

REFERENCES

Burdescu, D. D., & Mihaescu, C. (2006). TESYS: E-learning application built on a Web platform. In *International Conference on E-Business,* Setubal, Portugal (pp. 315-319).

Burdescu, D. D., & Mihaescu, C. (2008). Blending e-learning and knowledge management for optimizing learning paths. In *Advances on Artificial Intelligence, Knowledge Engineering and Databases (AIKED08)*, Cambridge, U.K. (pp. 396-402).

Del Bimbo, A. (2001). *Visual information retrieval.* San Francisco, CA: Morgan Kaufmann Publishers.

Fallon, C., & Brown, S. (2003). *E-learning standards: A guide to purchasing and deploying standards-conform e-leraning.* Boca Raton, FL: St. Lucie Press.

Hede, T., & Hede, A. (2002). Multimedia effects on learning: Design implications of an integrated model. In *ASET Conference,* Melbourne, Australia.

Littlejohn, A. (2003). *Issues in reusing online resources. Reusing online resources: A sustainable approach to e-learning.* London: Creative Print and Design.

Masie, E. (2002). *Blended learning: the magic is in the mix.* In A. Rossett (Ed.), *The ASTD E-Learning Handbook.* New York: Mcgraw Hill.

Mayer, R. (2003). The promise of multimedia learning: Using the same instructional design methods across different media. *Learning and Instruction*, 125–139. doi:10.1016/S0959-4752(02)00016-6

Moberg, T., & Whitcomb, M. (1999). Educational technology to facilitate medical students' learning: background paper 2 of the medical school objectives project. *Academic Medicine, 74*, 1146–1150. doi:10.1097/00001888-199910000-00020

Muller, H., Michoux, N., Bandon, D., & Geissbuhler, A. (2004). A review of content-based image retrieval systems in medical application – clinical benefits and future directions. *International Journal of Medical Informatics, 73*(1), 1–23. doi:10.1016/j.ijmedinf.2003.11.024

Muller, H., Rosset, A., Garcia, A., Vallee, J., & Geissbuhler, A. (2005). Benefits of content-based visual data access in radiology. *Radiographics, 25*, 849–858. doi:10.1148/rg.253045071

Rosenberg, M. (2001). *E-Learning: Strategies for delivering knowledge in the digital age.* New York: McGraw-Hill.

Ruiz, J., Mintze, M., & Leipzig, R. (2006). The impact of e-learning in medical education. *Academic Medicine, 81*(3). doi:10.1097/00001888-200603000-00002

Shank, P. (2007). *The value of multimedia in learning.* Preluat de pe http://www.adobe.com/designcenter/thinktank/valuemedia/The_Value_of_Multimedia.pdf

Shyu, C., Brodley, C., Kak, A., & Kosaka, A. (1999). ASSERT: A physician-in-the-loop content-based retrieval system for HRCT image databases. *Computer Vision and Image Understanding, 75*, 111–132. doi:10.1006/cviu.1999.0768

Smith, J. (1997). *Integrated spatial and feature image systems: Retrieval, Compression and analysis.* Ph.D. thesis, Columbia University, Graduate School of Arts and Sciences, New York.

Stanescu, L., Mihaescu, C., Burdescu, D. D., Georgescu, E., & Florea, L. (2007). An improved platform for medical e-learning. In *Advances in Web-Learning-ICWL* (pp. 392-403).

Ward, J., Gordon, J., Field, M., & Lehmann, H. (2001). Communication and information technology in medical education. *Lancet, 357*, 792–796. doi:10.1016/S0140-6736(00)04173-8

Wentling, T., Waight, C., Gallaher, J., La Fleur, J., Wang, C., & Kanfer, A. (2005). E-Learning: A review of literature. *University of Illinois National Center for Supercomputer Applications.* Retrieved November 22, 2005, from http://learning.ncsa.uiuc.edu/ papers/elearnlit.pdf

KEY TERMS AND DEFINITIONS

Binary Color Set: Equivalent with a limited histogram, that contains 1 for color presence or 0 otherwise

Color Histogram: A representation of the distribution of colors in an image, derived by counting the number of pixels of each of given set of color ranges in a typically two-dimensional (2D) or three-dimensional (3D) color space

Content-Based Visual Query: The application of computer vision to the image retrieval problem, that is, the problem of searching for digital images in large databases. The search analyzes the actual contents of the image, represented by colors, shapes, textures, or any other information that can be derived from the image itself

Image Segmentation: The first stage in image analysis, which seeks to simplify the data into its basic component elements or objects within the scene.

Image Similarity Measure: Quantifies the degree of correspondence between features in query and target images

Low-Level Image Features: Primitive features characterizing image content, such as color, texture, and shape that are automated extracted from images and used in content-based visual query

Multimedia Database: A database that hosts one or more primary media types such as documents, images, videos or audio.

Multimedia Learning: The use of two or more media (text, graphics, animation, audio or video) to produce content that learners access via Internet

Chapter 23
Applying Web 2.0 Tools in Hybrid Learning Designs

Mark J. W. Lee
Charles Sturt University, Australia

Catherine McLoughlin
Australian Catholic University, Australia

ABSTRACT

This chapter explores how educators can harness the potential of a new wave of social software to respond to the challenges of tertiary education in the new millennium, by combining the interactivity and immediacy of face-to-face instruction with the openness, connectivity, and flexibility afforded by the new tools and technologies. It also argues for a new conceptualization of "hybrid" or "blended" learning in the Web 2.0 era, and presents a number of exemplars of Web 2.0-based hybrid learning that typify the emergence of a new pedagogy for the digital age. Finally, it concludes with a discussion of the issues, barriers, and dilemmas that exist in implementing an effective hybrid approach to learning within a formal education setting.

INTRODUCTION: TOWARDS A NEW DEFINITION OF HYBRID LEARNING IN THE WEB 2.0 ERA

Hybrid course delivery, sometimes called "blended learning," has no single definition, nor is it a new concept. The idea of fusing or combining different approaches or modes of teaching and learning, with the hope of achieving the benefits of each of the constituent approaches and enabling a range of experiences for learners, has been part of pedagogical theory for quite some time (Williams, 2003).

The terms "hybrid learning" and "blended learning" have been found to represent many levels of meaning and may encompass multiple different perspectives (Sharpe, Benfield, Roberts, & Francis, 2006). Since the advent of e-learning, however, the focus in the literature has appeared to be predominantly focused on the combination of delivery modes, i.e. face-to-face (F2F) and online. Education practitioners and researchers need to consider the possibility that such distinctions may become

DOI: 10.4018/978-1-60566-380-7.ch023

decreasingly significant or even irrelevant in a networked society (Hargreaves, 2004; Castells, 2004a, 2004b; Rudd, Sutch, & Facer, 2006) where information and communication technology (ICT) tools, including Web 2.0 and mobile technologies, are becoming increasingly pervasive, and where we are witnessing wider, societal shifts such as the merging of formal and informal learning. The new wave of ubiquitous computing and social software tools makes possible a fresh repertoire of learner–teacher interaction, distributed collaboration, and communication, and their transformative effects on society, learning, and networking are becoming increasingly visible.

In this chapter, the authors argue that a broader definition or conceptualization of hybrid learning is needed that incorporates innovative technologies, pedagogies, and learning designs, and that respects the need for student choice, self-direction, and autonomy. The chapter highlights the affordances of Web 2.0-based social software tools and how they can be leveraged for learning, in addition to proposing a framework, "Pedagogy 2.0," which demonstrates the potential of networked learning and an extended conceptualization of hybrid learning that capitalizes on these affordances and tools.

DIMENSIONS OF HYBRID LEARNING

Hybrid learning sometimes refers to approaches to teaching that require students to meet for face-to face-classes while much of the course content and interaction is provided online. Some authors distinguish between "supplemented" e-learning, in which online supplementary materials are provided to augment traditional face-to-face delivery, and truly "blended" e-learning, in which a significant proportion of learning activities are carried out on the Internet. In other cases, hybrid or blended programs refer to programs of study that provide students with an option of taking some courses fully online and some in face-to-face classes (known at some institutions as "mixed mode") (Williams, 2002). This technology-driven approach is not accepted by Bleed (2001), who argues that simply bolting on technology is not a sufficient condition for effective blended learning. Instead, he and other researchers would argue that effective hybrid learning design brings together sound classroom and online methodologies and is based on student-centered instruction (i.e. follows a learner-centered approach), effective and timely teacher intervention, peer-to-peer interaction, and the provision of multiple learning resources in a highly interactive learning context (Garrison, Kanuka, & Hawes, 2002).

Sharpe et al. (2006) maintain that blended learning may refer to transformative practices and course reengineering that entail changing forms of interaction, pedagogy, and learning. In some rare instances it may refer to a learner-centered holistic paradigm in which students take greater initiative and control. When the term "flexible learning" became popular, it, too, was intended as a mix of face-to-face and online learning, usually in response to student demands for variety, access, recognition of varied learning styles, and student control over the learning experience. With an increasingly diverse student base, larger student cohorts, and the need for practical, skills-based approaches to prepare graduates for their future vocations, higher education institutions have tried to maintain quality by adopting e-learning solutions that provide choice in terms of the time and place of learning (Matheos, Daniel, & McCalla, 2005).

Many hybrid models call for student and teacher participation and an instructional design approach that intentionally supports both specific learning outcomes and flexible delivery by blending modes of instruction, technologies, and learning activities. Such an approach, based on the concept of hybridization, brings together two dissimilar forms of learning (online and face-to-face) to create a third. McCray (2000) argues that when both face-to-face and online learning are effectively combined, the result is an educational experience highly conducive to student learning. However, as the term hybrid learning is interpreted in many different ways and appears to be ill-defined, there is no guarantee that a "hybrid learning" experience will provide quality learning outcomes. Other authors have commented that because of this lack of a precise definition, the term has potential as it enables institutions to adopt their own particular style of blended learning and assume ownership of it (Driscoll, 2002).

Clearly, even the most cursory review of the literature shows that, from all the stakeholder perspectives (institutional, organizational, student, teacher, etc.), learning experiences have evolved and are continuing to evolve to exploit combinations of pedagogical approaches that combine both traditional and technology-enriched learning tasks and interactions. For instance, Singh and Reed (2001) identify a number of dimensions of blended learning that include: online and offline learning; structured and instructed learning; customized content and off-the shelf-content; and finally, experiential work-based learning and traditional learning. Other researchers offer a diverse range of ingredients and approaches to create a blended learning approach, using a raft of tools, technologies, and modes of instruction (see for example, Gribbins, Hadidi, Urbaczewski, & Vician, 2007; Sharpe et al., 2006). Pedagogies include but are not limited to peer-to-peer learning, individual learning, problem-based learning, collaborative learning, and independent study. Most recent models of hybrid or blended learning draw on ICTs and networked technology in an attempt to serve students who need flexibility, asynchronous learning, collaborative, social experiences, choice, and interactivity.

Figure 1 (adapted from Cross, 2005) provides an overview of selected dimensions of blended learning, and shows that the "blend" can be assembled from a variety of learning tasks, pedagogies, environments, technologies, and media that form continua. The list of possibilities is endless, and the ultimate decision on which dimensions to include or exclude is influenced by learner needs as well as by institutional priorities.

Hybrid Learning, Flexible Learning, and Course Management Systems

Like blended learning, flexible learning is a set of educational approaches and systems concerned with providing learners with increased choice, convenience, and personalization to suit their needs. In particular, flexible learning provides learners with choices about where, when, and how learning occurs, by using a range of technologies to support the teaching and learning process.

Flexible learning approaches are often designed using a full range of teaching and learning theories, pedagogies, and forms of interaction to provide students with opportunities to access information and expertise, contribute ideas and opinions, and correspond with other learners and mentors. These activities may occur through the use of Web-based platforms such as course management systems (CMS's) containing collaborative learning tools that are asynchronous (e.g. discussion boards) and/or synchronous (e.g. chat rooms), and are thus designed as a "blended" approach, with content available electronically and remotely as well as incorporating face-to-face classroom tutorials and lectures. The inclusion of a variety of instructional techniques helps ensure that learning is not merely dependent on traditional forms of didactic instruction, but incorporates learner activity and engagement in a range of independent learning tasks. As a result, improved learning outcomes are often reported (Dziuban, Hartman, Juge, Moskal, & Sorg, 2005; Dziuban, Hartman, & Moskal, 2004; Twigg, 2003).

The rationale for the uptake of CMS's has often been to ensure that institutions can implement cost-effective strategies in the face of decreased government funding and ever-growing enroll-

Figure 1. Dimensions of hybrid / blended learning (Adapted from Cross, 2005)

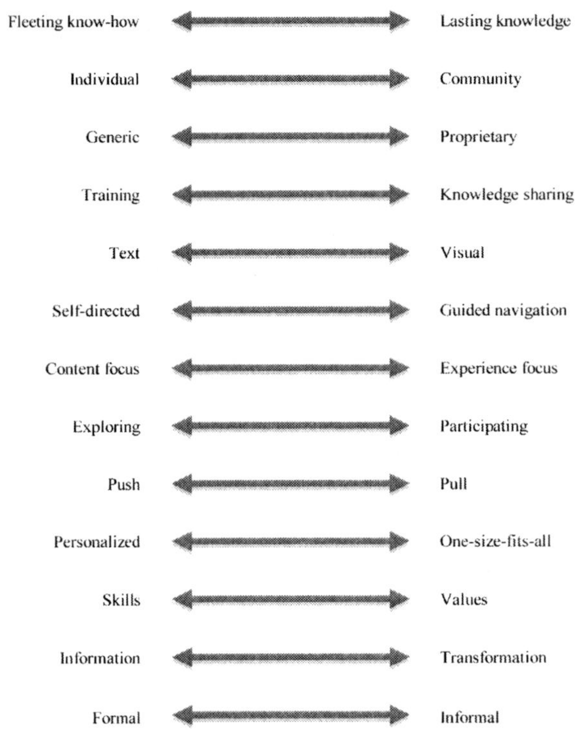

ments. By using CMS's such as WebCT, Blackboard, and Moodle institutions in the UK, USA, and Australia have been able to expand access to educational courses, increase enrollments, and provide flexibility by offering "hybrid" learning experiences that combine an online component within a CMS, and an on-campus component. Commercial off-the-shelf software and content have been purchased by many universities to provide users with easy to use, pre-packaged study modules, a "toolbox" of learning objects, bulletin boards, and assignments, and to facilitate teaching and learning in the "e"-mode for novice teachers. Integrated systems are now used worldwide for online, on-campus, and hybrid courses, giving a narrower and more limited definition to the term "blended learning." The limitations of such approaches are now increasingly evident, and as we move towards the latest generation of dynamic, user-centered collaborative applications such as Web logs (blogs), wikis, and social networking, there is clearly a need for new conceptualizations of the term "hybrid learning." The main issue is that CMS's can limit pedagogy and in fact often impose their own approach to learning, which is to provide access to a limited range of content, de-contextualize learning, and place constraints on learners by creating a lock-step approach. This is evidenced in the fact that the main purpose is to manage resources, content, enrollments, and assessment, and to provide administrative and managerial support to teachers in the e-environment. Teachers simply "plug in" their content to predefined spaces instead of adopting individual pedagogies to match learner needs. One author, Lane (2008), has commented that "This orientation is very different from the development of knowledge through a constructivist, learner-centered, or inquiry-based approach... In constructivist pedagogy, the instructor's role is to provide a rich learning environment, which often includes rich social interaction, self-assessment, and independent projects. These techniques are better supported by Web 2.0 applications… The more a CMS promotes traditional pedagogy, the more it will limit faculty productivity" (p. 5).

Despite these limitations, voiced by a number of researchers across the globe, institutions have been adopting hybrid learning practices to meet student demands for flexibility, choice, control, and access. E-learning solutions built on CMS's do offer a range of tools to students, which are often combined with on-campus experiences, and such delivery models have begun to characterize higher education institutions over the past two decades. While modes of communication and interaction continue to evolve and change with the growth of mobile technologies, there is an expectation that students will have anywhere, anytime interactivity and connectivity. In the words of Sharpe et al. (2006): "There is an increasing recognition that students are making use of their own technology as well as those provided for them and that they are doing this in ways that are not planned for, difficult to predict and may not be immediately visible to their teachers and researchers" (p. 4). The impact of such changes on the quality of learning depends on the degree to which pedagogies and course delivery can be engineered to ensure high-quality learning experiences. Masie (2002, p. 59) comments: "blended learning adds significantly greater opportunity for the learner to master the material and move towards transfer and performance." Clearly, offering students a variety of delivery modes, a blend of learning experiences, and a mix of technologies would serve a broader spectrum of learning styles than a mono-instructional approach. The successful growth and expansion of blended or hybrid learning depends on the capacity to transform content and interaction modes as new technologies emerge, and to ensure a quality learning experience. But what does this mean in the context of the new generation of learners and the rise of social software?

Hybrid Learning and the Digital Learning Landscape: New Learners, New Needs, New Expectations

Beyond the convenience factor and financial benefits accruing from blended learning, advances in ICTs have an impact on the acquisition and management of knowledge and skills, and it is critical that institutions understand and respond to the changing expectations and capabilities of their students and staff. Today's students demand a high degree of freedom and autonomy in personalizing their learning, combined with ample opportunities for peer-to-peer collaboration, interactivity, and socio-experiential learning. It is essential that the appropriate mix between on-campus experiences and online learning be planned in order to facilitate efficient and effective learning (Cobcroft, Towers, Smith, & Bruns, 2006). The main issue is not one of terminology but of assuring that pedagogies and learning environments cater to the needs of students. Oliver and Trigwell (2005, p. 2) observe: "… there is little merit in keeping the term 'blended learning' as it is currently understood. It is either inconsistent (and so useless as a way of understanding practice) or redundant, because it attributes to learning something that we already know only applies to teaching or instruction." In an era when there is rapid technological development and change, the authors believe that the term "hybrid learning," if it is to have meaning, should reflect learner-centered pedagogies and dialogic practices that include a range of technologies.

Hilton (2006) discusses how a number of "disruptive forces" are shaping current practices in tertiary education. These include: the unbundling of content; the shift from "provider push" to "demand pull;" the arrival of ubiquitous access to information and services; and the rise of the "pure property" view of ideas that is a departure from the spirit of collaboration and sharing that forms the basis of the open source and open content movements. Along with these changes institutions are facing increased pressure to adopt improved, innovative, and cost-efficient modes of teaching.

This current education landscape sits against the backdrop of broader societal changes. The globally-connected world of the new millennium is characterized by constant social mobility and diversification of life trajectories, where individuals are expected to have multiple career paths and engage in re-skilling at various stages. Mobile and broadband connectivity, lifelong learning, and flexible working hours are drivers of learning on-demand (Punie & Cabrera, 2006). In light of these factors, there is a need to rethink models for teaching and learning in order to meet the needs and expectations of millennial learners, and to equip them with the literacies, digital competencies, and skills needed to participate fully in today's networked society. The term "hybrid learning" has the flexibility to include these elements, but it currently lacks theoretical rigor and is applied inconsistently.

In this digital landscape, our students are changing. Tertiary student profiles indicate that most students juggle work and study and are technology-savvy, and that for many, social networking tools are central to both their academic and social lives (Windham, 2005). These students have high expectations of how they should learn, demand "24x7," "always-on" Internet connectivity, and want to select the technologies and learning environments that best meet their needs and preferences (Conole & Creanor, 2006; Windham, 2005). As savvy and informed consumers, "Most undergraduates now expect the same level of service from university administrations that they receive from their ISP [Internet Service Provider] or mobile phone provider. If they are not happy with a provider, they switch" (Barnes & Tynan, 2007, p. 177). Tertiary education institutions and their leaders must therefore ensure that they are responsive to student needs and demands, failing which they run the risk of being left behind, or worse still, suffering the consequences of increased attrition rates and decreasing funding.

Researchers have addressed the possibilities of employing emerging technologies and adding them to the raft of hybrid learning designs now in operation in higher education across the world (Ellis, Steed, & Applebee, 2006; Vaughan, 2007). Dede (2000) points out that "well-designed learning experiences using several instructional media with differing characteristics... enable all students to utilize their most effective ways of learning" (p. 15). While the classic model of blended learning (face-to-face plus an online component) continues to thrive, new technologies are beginning to make an impression on teaching and learning practices. For example, podcasting of recorded lectures enables students to hear the lectures without attending in person, thus potentially diminishing the need to come on campus. Web 2.0 and its accompanying suite of social software applications are already having an impact on students' modes of participation and interaction. How will the term "hybrid learning" change in the new era? The authors maintain that to remain a useful construct, it must become infused with a learner-centered pedagogical approach that includes emerging forms of learning based on networking, participation, peer production of knowledge artifacts, distributed learning, and strategic use of social software tools.

Web 2.0: New Possibilities, Applications, and Practices

"Web 2.0" refers to an apparent second generation or improved form of the World Wide Web that emphasizes collaboration and sharing of knowledge and content among users. Characteristic of Web 2.0 are the socially-based tools and systems referred to collectively as social software, which includes but is not limited to blogs, wikis, Really Simple Syndication (RSS) and podcasting feeds, peer-to-peer (P2P) media sharing applications, social networking sites, and social bookmarking utilities. These new tools make possible a new wave of online behavior, distributed collaboration, and social interaction, and are already having a transformative effect on society, triggering changes in how we communicate and learn. A few examples will illustrate the new forms of communication and participation enabled by Web 2.0-based social software tools. Users are now engaged in creative authorship by being able to produce and manipulate digital images and video clips, tag them with chosen keywords, and make this content available to their friends and peers worldwide through Flickr, MySpace, and YouTube. Other individuals write blogs and create wiki spaces where like-minded individuals comment on, share, and augment these sources, thereby engaging in a new genre of dynamic "personal publishing" (Downes, 2004).

While Web 2.0 does not entail radical changes in the technical specifications of the Internet or of the World Wide Web, most proponents of the concept describe it in terms of new possibilities and applications. O'Reilly (2005a, 2005b) believes that these new applications have emerged due to a changing socio-cultural context, giving rise to the perception of revolutionary new uses for the same technologies. In reviewing definitions of Web 2.0, Atkinson (2007) notes that many regard Web 2.0 as indefinable and amorphous as it refers to not one, but many developments, some emerging from familiar technologies and others from more nascent innovations. Others say that debate about the term is irrelevant, as what is more important are the concepts, practices, and key ideas underpinning it (Alexander, 2006). For example, for many Web 2.0 advocates, the terms "co-creation" and "users add value" encapsulate the practices of those who participate in and use social software, showing that it is not just an assembly of tools, but a set of concepts, practices, and attitudes that define its scope. This can be exemplified by contrasting two sites, *Encyclopædia Britannica Online* (2008) and *Wikipedia* (2008), the former maintained by a commercial organization and the latter by an open community. In Wikipedia, users can participate and create content, and in doing so become "prosumers" (both consumers and producers). They mix, amend, and recombine content, collaboratively and open to a global audience, inviting revision and commentary. Moreover, the added dimension of scale means that the more people using the tools, the greater the network effect. The combined efforts and collective intelligence of hundreds of individuals can result in the co-production of resources such as Wikipedia entries, illustrating the power of the "wisdom of crowds" (Surowiecki, 2004)—a concept that acknowledges that when working cooperatively and sharing ideas, communities can be significantly more productive than individuals working in isolation. It is this "architecture of participation" (Barsky & Purdon, 2006, p. 65) that ensures that Web 2.0 is continually responsive to users.

IMPLICATIONS OF WEB 2.0 FOR HYBRID LEARNING DESIGN AND PEDAGOGY

The advent of the new wave of tools and technologies provokes us to consider the implications for and potential applications to current hybrid learning patterns in colleges and universities (Berg, Berquam, & Christoph, 2007). Anderson (2004) observes that "The greatest affordance of the Web for educational use is the profound and multifaceted increase in communication and interaction capability" (p. 42), which is even more evident in Web 2.0 when compared to the set of linked information sources that characterized "Web 1.0." In other words, the new social software applications can also be viewed as pedagogical tools that stem from their affordances of information discovery and sharing.

With the rich and varied functionality of social computing in mind, together with its "always on" culture and participatory attributes, it is useful to consider the affordances and potential value adding of these new and emerging tools and technologies for millennial learners. The new affordances of Web 2.0 are now making learner-centered education a reality, with tools that enable collaborative writing (wikis, Google Docs & Spreadsheets), media sharing applications (Flickr, YouTube, TeacherTube), and social networking sites (MySpace, Facebook, Friendster, Ning) capable of supporting multiple communities of learning. These tools enable and encourage informal conversation, dialogue, collaborative content generation, and the sharing of information, giving learners access to a wide raft of ideas and representations of knowledge. It is important to remember that these tools can also be used in combination and to engage people through communication, co-production, and sharing. Through these activities, social and cognitive benefits accrue, both to individuals and to the community of users who support and take part in them (Boyd, 2007; Barsky & Purdon, 2006). Higher education institutions are already beginning to customize their course offerings and styles of delivery to incorporate these innovations (See Table 2 later in the chapter, which contains a number of examples that typify innovative hybrid learning practices assisted by Web 2.0 tools and affordances.)

In addition to the expansion and growth in popularity of Web 2.0 services and tools, the increased prevalence of user-generated content has implications for learning environments in higher education, and is already influencing pedagogical choices and approaches (Williams & Jacobs, 2004). In what can be described as a user-driven revolution, there is a shift away from the production of Web content by traditional, "authoritative" sources, towards content is that is generated by the users themselves. In the case of higher education, these users are students, and they now have the tools, spaces, and skills to contribute ideas and publish their views, research, and interpretations online. Content can now come from many sources, partly as a result of the ease with which social software can be used to create, share, augment, tag, and upload content. In what has been called a "rip, mix, and burn culture" and a "digital democracy," all participants can become active creators of content; for academia, responding to this partly means moving beyond the confines of CMS's and tapping into a wider pool of expertise to include community-generated and maintained learning resources. Table 1 depicts some of these key elements and their implications.

Mejias (2005, p. 1) observed that "... social software can positively impact pedagogy by inculcating a desire to reconnect to the world as whole, not just the social part that exists online," referring to the isolating and de-contextualized experience of much text-based traditional education. Many social software applications straddle virtual and real social worlds, as they entail both online and offline interactions and visual/verbal connectivity. For example, Flickr and YouTube facilitate the sharing of photos and videos with both "real world" and "virtual" friends; social networking sites like MySpace, Facebook, Ning, and Friendster allow users to build an online identity by customizing their personal profiles with a range of multimedia elements, as well as interacting with existing contacts and establishing new relationships. These new practices are in many ways congruent with the move towards a hybrid approach to learning delivery, in which face-to-face learning is combined with online activities (Veronikas & Shaughnessy, 2004).

PEDAGOGY 2.0 AS A NEW MODEL FOR HYBRID LEARNING

The authors propose what they call *Pedagogy 2.0* as the basis for a hybrid learning framework that aims to focus on desired learning outcomes in order to exploit more fully the affordances and potential for connectivity enabled by social software tools. In a networked society enabled by a range of high-speed technologies, learners have access to ideas, resources, and communities to support their learning, driven by personal needs and choice (*personalization*), and they need to

Table 1. Core ideas and values underpinning Web 2.0 and corresponding educational implications

Core idea	Educational implications
User-generated content	Content is no longer pre-packaged and delivered as a static/fixed bundle, but is made available in dynamic digital form with options for editing and re-use. Student-created content is adding to the pools of learning resources available, while creativity, co-production, teamwork, and peer review are seen as desirable skills.
Collective intelligence	Collaborative production, editing, and review of media and content that transcends classroom and institutional walls; drawing on ideas and expertise from outside the formal learning environment; folksonomic tagging to add explicit meanings to ideas, e.g. social bookmarking as a form of collaborative information discovery and management.
Architecture of participation	Connectivity and networking effects add value, as students are able to go beyond the limits of course management systems and the "walled gardens" they impose to connect with peers and a global community and actively contribute to the development and advancement of the community.
Open access, open source	Easy-to-use, customizable, and extensible tools, emerging from an open source development community, allow learners to create, publish, and share files, ideas, and content. A spirit of openness, rather than containment of information within closed communities, institutions, or organizations, gives learners access to a vast repertoire of knowledge sources.
Mashups (through APIs that enable [re-]mixing)	The mixing of any number of digital media resources enables the creation of new interpretations and representations of ideas through a number of modalities (text, graphics, video, audio).

develop self-regulatory skills and techniques to support both their formal and lifelong learning endeavors. Pedagogies need to engage learners in the social processes of knowledge creation rather than the mere consumption of instructor-supplied information (*productivity*), and also scaffold linkages, dialogue, and connections with global distributed networks and communities (*participation*) for the purposes of idea sharing, inquiry, and problem solving. Personalization, productivity, and participation form the three Ps of Pedagogy 2.0, and these overlapping elements are depicted in Figure 2.

The interdependence between ideas, individuals, communities, and information networks, supported by technology, underpin the principles of Pedagogy 2.0, and the processes depicted in Figure 2 are desired learning outcomes, while also providing principles for the design of learning environments. For example, while student-generated content is a worthwhile outcome of learning as it is evidence of knowledge construction, the principle of active learner contribution must inform the learning task design, and educators must provide opportunities for learners to become producers of resources and ideas so that they move beyond mere assimilation of inert information. This approach stands in stark contrast to the transmissive pedagogies that characterize the ways in which many CMS's have been used, such as the tendency to emphasize the uploading of pre-packaged content, syllabi, and teacher-designed tasks.

Although not dependent on the technology, Pedagogy 2.0 capitalizes on the core energies and affordances of Web 2.0—a raft of tools that support learner autonomy, increased levels of socialization and interactivity, access to learning communities, and peer-to-peer networking—while facilitating personal choice, collaboration, participation, and creative production. Pedagogy 2.0 is envisioned as an overarching concept for an emerging cluster of practices that advocates learner choice and self-direction, and engagement in a hybrid mix of flexible, relevant learning tasks and strategies. While it is not intended a prescriptive framework, it distills a number of guidelines characterizing effective hybrid learning environments, such as choice of resources, tasks, learning supports, and communication modalities:

- *Content:* Should consist of micro units of content (micro-content) that augment

Figure 2. Key elements of Pedagogy 2.0

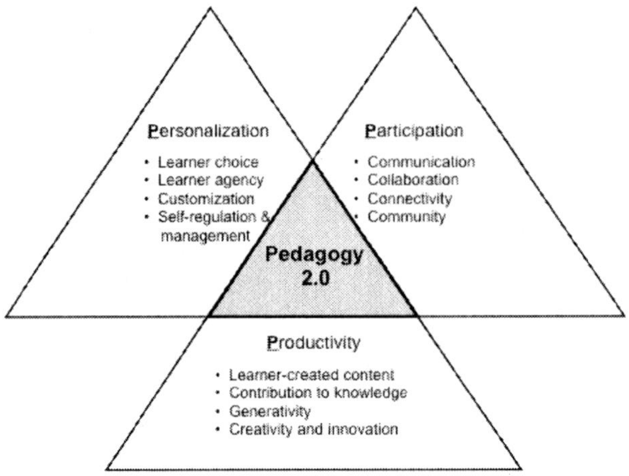

thinking and cognition; may include a wide variety of learner-generated resources accruing from students creating, sharing, and revising ideas;

- *Curriculum:* Curricula should not be fixed but dynamic, open to negotiation and learner input, consisting of "bite-sized" modules, inter-disciplinary in focus, and blending formal and informal learning;
- *Communication:* Students should be offered multiple opportunities for open, social, peer-to-peer, and multi-faceted forms of visual, verbal, and auditory communication, using multiple media types to achieve relevance, clarity, and immediacy;
- *Learning processes:* Learner-centered, contextualized, reflective learning processes should be designed and integrated with thinking processes to provide iterative, dynamic, performance-based, and inquiry-oriented experiences;
- *Resources:* Learning resources should include multiple informal and formal sources that are media rich, interdisciplinary, and global in reach;
- *Scaffolds:* Support for students should come from a network of peers, teachers, experts, and communities;
- *Learning tasks:* Authentic, personalized, experiential, learner-driven tasks should be designed that enable the creation of content and ideas by learners.

These principles are derived from the exemplary practices of a growing number of teachers in tertiary education who have begun to demonstrate how social software tools offer rich possibilities for students to create and share ideas, connect, and participate in broader learning communities that are not confined to the classrooms in which formal teaching and learning activities take place. Some of these Web 2.0-based hybrid learning exemplars are illustrated in Table 2. Through these pedagogical strategies, learners take on active roles such as creators of content, peer mentors, researchers, innovators, and entrepreneurs.

THE NEXT WAVE OF HYBRID LEARNING: ISSUES AND CHALLENGES

Hybrid learning designs are many and wide-ranging, bringing together a range of pedagogies, media forms, learning environments, technologies, and learners, globally, across a wide range of in-

Table 2. Exemplars of Web 2.0-based hybrid learning, illustrating the principles of Pedagogy 2.0

Institution and country	Reference(s)/ author(s)	Description of learner and teacher tasks	Hybrid / blended learning dimensions	Web 2.0 technologies used
University of Connecticut, USA	Miller (2006, 2007)	Students studying a General Psychology course participate in informal discussions about the course material following each week's lectures. These discussions are recorded and distributed to the rest of the class as part of a podcast series entitled iCube (Issues In Intro). The students also download and listen to two additional types of instructor-created podcasts, namely *precasts*, which are short enhanced podcasts previewing material prior to each lecture, and *postcasts*, which are short post-lecture podcasts containing re-explanations of selected concepts.	Blends teacher-guided instruction with learner-centered approaches; uses a mix of media and includes learner- generated content in addition to teacher-produced resources	• Podcasting
Bentley College, USA	Frydenberg (2006)	Students in an introductory information technology class work in pairs or groups and produce vodcasts to teach topics based on the course lecture materials to their peers. The instructor supplies the course topics, which the students choose from and negotiate/adapt. He also provides basic instruction on video recording and editing techniques, and sets up the RSS feed for sharing the vodcasts.	Blends synchronous individual and group work, peer collaboration and asynchronous resources	• Vodcasting
University of North Carolina at Pembroke, USA	Sener (2007)	Students use a wiki to create a Web-based encyclopedia containing entries on a variety of subjects related to law, criminal justice, sociology, and criminology. In addition to generating and entering initial content, students also edit, revise, and organize the content. The instructor supplies the technology framework and assesses the students' work, providing constructive feedback about their encyclopedia entries and the content therein.	Blends media for learning, synchronous and asynchronous modes, formal and informal learning	• Wikis
Macomb Independent School District, Michigan, USA	Wenzloff (2005); Richardson (2006)	Student teachers use the social bookmarking site Furl to bookmark and tag Web sites and share them with their instructor and peers. The instructor uses the export feature of Furl to quickly and easily generate online as well as paper handouts of the resources he has bookmarked for the class. He also subscribes to the RSS feeds of his students' Furl sites, to examine the sites they are reading as well as the comments they have written about the sites.	Blends student-generated content and peer resources with syllabus content; synchronous and asynchronous communication	• Social bookmarking / tagging • RSS
Open University, UK	Kukulska-Hulme (2005)	Students attending German and Spanish summer schools use digital voice recorders and mini-camcorders to record interviews with other students and with native speakers, as well as to create audio-visual tours for sharing with their peers via the Web. The instructors supply the recording equipment and provide guidance to the students in completing the various activities, for example, by providing sample topics/questions for the student-led interviews.	Blends face-to-face and online learning; different media types (text, audio, video)	• Media/file sharing

continued on the following page

Table 2. continued

Institution and country	Reference(s)/ author(s)	Description of learner and teacher tasks	Hybrid / blended learning dimensions	Web 2.0 technologies used
Fashion Institute of Technology, USA	Harris (2007a, 2007b)	Students studying an art history class visit the Metropolitan Museum of Art, where they take photos of exhibits using their mobile phones, upload them to Flickr, and use the site's tools to tag, annotate, and write descriptions and comments about the photos. They participate in a "Scavenger Hunt" in which the objective is to locate and photograph works of art that pertain to a number of vocabulary words and terms they have studied in class (to be used as tags for their uploaded photos). The instructor organizes the field trip to the museum and provides scaffolding for the activity by establishing the technology infrastructure (Flickr group) and supplying the keywords for the Scavenger Hunt. She also evaluates the students' work as part of their mid-term assessment.	Blends experiential learning with traditional pedagogy, field trips, and authentic assessment; also blends a number of media forms for learning	• Media sharing (photographs—Flickr) • Social tagging
Mt. San Jacinto College, USA	Helms (2007); D. Helms, personal communication	Health Sciences students use the social networking site Ning to create Web 2.0-based Web pages to teach others about the dangers associated with drug use and abuse. Working in groups, they each take on one of four roles: Web Designer, Multimedia Designer, Researcher, and Copyrighter. The instructor assigns each group with a specific drug to research and provides "job descriptions" for each of the four roles. Ning allows the students to integrate various forms of multimedia by drawing on the vast resources already published on the Web, for example in image libraries and on media sharing sites such as YouTube, without the need to learn complex Web authoring and programming techniques. The students also use the blogging and threaded discussion features of Ning to engage in constructive and reflective discourse about the content they have produced.	Blends online and offline activities, role-playing, and inquiry-based learning, plus a range of media types	• Social networking sites (Ning) • Blogs • Media sharing
University of Michigan, USA	Yew, Gibson, & Teasley (2006)	Students in a database and information class use blogs and RSS as a means by which to converse, interact, and share knowledge with one another and with their instructor. The posts on their individual blogs are aggregated on a central "Class Remix" site, where they are encouraged to improve upon, change, and/or integrate the group's knowledge contributions. Students tag their posts openly and in a collaborative manner to facilitate the organization, sharing, and coordination of the group's knowledge artifacts. The instructor teaches regular face-to-face classes and encourages students to share relevant questions, answers, and observations pertaining to the material taught in the classes via the individual and class blogs.	Blends modes of interaction and communication; formal and informal learning	• Blogs • RSS • Social tagging

continued on the following page

Table 2. continued

Institution and country	Reference(s)/ author(s)	Description of learner and teacher tasks	Hybrid / blended learning dimensions	Web 2.0 technologies used
University of Leicester, UK	Edirisingha, Salmon, & Forthergill (2006, 2007)	"Profcasts" are used to enrich blended learning in a second- and third-year undergraduate engineering module entitled Optical Fibre Communication Systems. The profcasts contain material designed to support learning distinct from that which is facilitated through structured on-campus or e-learning processes alone. The professor releases weekly profcasts to supplement online teaching through updated information and guidance on the weekly activities, and to motivate his students by incorporating relevant news items, anecdotes, and jokes. He also makes use of a framework based on Salmon's e-tivities (2002) model to facilitate active learning in the hybrid environment.	Blends learning activities, media, and temporality	• Podcasting
Open University of Hong Kong Hong Kong, China	Lui, Choy, Cheung, & Li (2006)	Students studying a year-long Software Engineering and Project Management course are required to write reflective blog entries in response to stimulus questions / topical issues posed by the instructor on a monthly basis. The students are encouraged to use the blogs as information sharing spaces by accessing one another's sites and providing peer feedback, as well as to develop their blogs into a form of logbook or e-portfolio as evidence of their learning journeys and outcomes.	Blends face-to-face and online learning; traditional and new social media	• Blogs
Edith Cowan University, Australia	Luca & McLoughlin (2005a, 2005b)	Final-year undergraduate multimedia students work in teams in which they take on the roles of programmers, graphic designers, and project managers. Each team negotiates a topic aimed at meeting industry needs with their tutor, then works with clients to create solutions to design problems and develop a project brief based on elicited requirements. Blogs are used as a project management tool to promote clear and transparent communication between team members for the purpose of sharing given tasks, as well as a learning journal and reflective writing tool in which students document their learning processes, assessment processes, and team dynamics.	Blends face-to-face and online learning; teacher-directed and student-directed learning; classroom-based instruction and authentic, industry-based learning; asynchronous, blog-based communication and real-time interaction	• Blogs

stitutional and workplace settings. The published work on hybrid or blended learning is extensive and varied (see, for example, Bonk & Graham, 2005; Vaughan, 2007; Garrison & Vaughan, 2008; Garrison & Kanuka, 2004; Garrrison, Kanuka, & Hawes, 2002; Twigg, 2003). Many hybrid learning designs have arisen from institutional needs to cater for diverse students while reducing costs and enabling teachers to manage large classes and associated resources (content, enrollment, and assessment). The limitations of CMS's are becoming increasingly evident, as such systems tend to be based on a managerial pedagogy of downloading content, responding to instructor questions, and uploading assignments. Inquiry-based and independent learning are more likely to foster enhanced, higher-order thinking outcomes, and are better supported by Web 2.0

technologies, which allow user control, access to diverse and rich resources, and aggregation and sharing of information and resources. In addition, the social and communicative tools of the Web 2.0 era allow users to creatively adapt new tools to produce knowledge, leverage collective intelligence, and build social capital (Lee, McLoughlin, & Chan, 2008). With this having been said, the next wave of hybrid learning designs should not be seen as technology-driven but socially-oriented, capable of being learner-centered and affording learner choice, and integrated with pedagogies that are capable of engendering the creation of knowledge and the building of community. New hybrid designs will also be flexible, interactive, and communicative, drawing on the power of "mash-ups" of individually-proven applications and tools and using these to facilitate innovative, connected, and collaborative learning tasks. The terms "hybrid learning" and "blended learning" are likely to remain, but as broader, umbrella terms for a cluster of student-centered designs that bring together formal and informal learning spaces as well as local and global communities, so that the learner experience combines the three Ps of personalization, participation, and productivity (Figure 2).

Today, tertiary education institutions are confronted by significant change driven by multiple external factors. Among these are the shifts in the characteristics and needs of learners, the tensions between the relative costs and benefits of physical versus virtual environments, and the need to consider hybrid learning environments that not only incorporate the physical and virtual, but also take into account the blending of other dimensions to achieve a high degree of learner choice and autonomy. All of these factors present critical challenges that impact upon the institutional planning of tertiary education providers. Moreover, it must be noted that designing effective hybrid learning environments not only requires commitment to integrating ICTs, but also entails going beyond "bolt-on" information provision to facilitate engagement, collaboration, connection, and the creation of a communities of scholarly inquiry and practice in which learners can participate flexibly. Online methods for learning and teaching need to be "viewed as a new context for learning, not just as a tool" (Salmon, 2004, p. 17), and this is a reminder that hybrid learning strategies driven solely by technology are unlikely to optimize learning outcomes for students. Instead, as noted by Singh and Reed (2001), it is crucially important to work with learners to select the "right" technologies to align with their preferred learning styles and to achieve learning outcomes that are "just-in-time" for their dynamic and ever-changing needs and situations. Putting these principles into practice necessitates advance planning, sound strategy, and a thorough understanding of the range of options, pedagogies, and tools currently available to support learning.

A further challenge is that educators and instructional designers may not be fully aware of the potential and range of social software tools, and may need opportunities for professional development to reveal how Web 2.0 applications can support teaching, learning, and assessment. There is a need to make time for collaboration, exploration, and discussion of what pedagogic models best achieve the desired learning outcomes. For the principles of Pedagogy 2.0 to be realized, institutional change is needed to equip educators with the skills and facilities that make it easier to engage learners in social networking while encouraging them to become active partners in the creation of educational pathways that will give them the competencies they need for work and life in the networked age.

Last but not least, the deployment of educational technologies—including those of Web 2.0 and beyond—must be underpinned by an explicit learning paradigm and informed by pedagogical and instructional design theories that support learner self-direction and agency, while taking into account the social aspects of effective learning. The centrality of these factors to the success of learning is irrespective and independent of the mode of delivery.

CONCLUSION

In this chapter, the authors presented a broader conceptualization of hybrid learning, and argued for approaches that prioritize the need for student choice, self-direction, and autonomy by exploiting and leveraging the affordances of Web 2.0-based social software tools. In line with the philosophy and ethos of the Web 2.0 movement as well as the broader societal shifts against the backdrop of which it has emerged, a framework, Pedagogy 2.0, was proposed that demonstrates the potential of networked learning that engages and addresses the needs of millennial learners. The framework has the potential to achieve transformative pedagogical approaches by advocating the centrality of the principles of personalization of content and activities, productive engagement of students in creative, active learning tasks and knowledge building, and participatory activities that link students to communities, resources, and networks in which they have opportunities to share ideas, collaborate, and communicate.

With the advent of ICTs and e-learning, we have managed to overcome the confines of the traditional classroom in a physical sense, but remnants of instructor-centered pedagogies remain, even in virtual learning environments. Even today, hybrid or blended learning designs often operate as an extension of face-to-face learning environments. While "learner-centered," "constructivist" instruction has become somewhat of a mantra in tertiary education, there continue to be significant gaps between the espoused and enacted pedagogies of teachers, both in face-to-face and online settings. Hybrid learning approaches combining multiple delivery modalities, supported by the capabilities and affordances of Web 2.0 and social software technologies, present us with promising ways in which to fulfill the pedagogic promise of student-centered learning.

The emergence and uptake of social computing tools has brought about awareness that learning need not be confined to a single space or a single source. Multiple designs for hybrid learning models are possible, as resources and content multiply and new environments for learning, both real and virtual, become available. It has been said that "technology has given us a communications toolkit that allows anyone to become a journalist at little cost and, in theory, with global reach. Nothing like this has ever been remotely possible before..." (Gillmor, 2004, p. xii). However, obstacles and barriers remain. Can teachers, whose traditional frame of reference is formality, understand, value, and take advantage of the ways in which informal learning can occur through online social networking and beyond the formal spaces of classrooms, libraries, and laboratories? Can we extend our classrooms to link with open communities that are constantly sharing, revising, and creating new ideas? Can academia, with its established legacy of transmissive pedagogy, rise to the challenge and affect the kinds of changes that are both necessary and inevitable in the new age? The challenge is to foster the creation of blended learning environments driven by learner-centered pedagogies that capitalize on social software tools and participatory media, while nurturing innovation and creativity. This can be achieved by employing a hybrid model whereby social software tools and other resources are used strategically to create opportunities to leverage what our students do naturally: socialize, network, and collaborate.

REFERENCES

Alexander, B. (2006). Web 2.0: A new wave of innovation for teaching and learning? *EDUCAUSE Review*, *41*(2), 33–44.

Anderson, T. (2004). Toward a theory of online learning. In T. Anderson & F. Elloumi (Eds.), *Theory and practice of online learning* (pp. 33-60). Athabasca, AB: Athabasca University.

Atkinson, R. (2007). Web 2.0: Next-g, a sequel, or more of the same? *HERDSA News, 29*(2), 20–22.

Barnes, C., & Tynan, B. (2007). The adventures of Miranda in the brave new world: Learning in a Web 2.0 millennium. *ALT-J . Research in Learning Technology, 15*(9), 189–200.

Barsky, E., & Purdon, M. (2006). Introducing Web 2.0: Social networking and social bookmarking for health librarians. *Journal of the Canadian Health Libraries Association, 27*(3), 65–67.

Berg, J. E., Berquam, L., & Christoph, K. (2007). Social networking technologies: A "poke" for campus services. *EDUCAUSE Review, 42*(2), 32–44.

Bleed, R. (2001). A hybrid campus for the new millennium. *EDUCAUSE Review, 36*(1), 16–24.

Bonk, C. J., & Graham, C. R. (Eds.). (2005). *Handbook of blended learning: Global perspectives, local designs*. San Francisco: Pfeiffer.

Boyd, D. (2007). The significance of social software. In T. N. Burg & J. Schmidt (Eds.), *BlogTalks reloaded: Social software research & cases* (pp. 15-30). Norderstedt, Germany: Books on Demand.

Castells, M. (2004a). Afterword: Why networks matter. In H. McCarthy, P. Miller, & P. Skidmore (Eds.), *Network logic: Who governs in an interconnected world?* (pp. 221-225). London: Demos.

Castells, M. (2004b). *The network society: A cross-cultural perspective*. Northamption, MA: Edward Elgar.

Cobcroft, R., Towers, S., Smith, J., & Bruns, A. (2006). *Mobile learning in review: Opportunities and challenges for learners, teachers, and institutions*. Paper presented at the Online Learning and Teaching Conference 2006, Brisbane, QLD.

Conole, G., & Creanor, L. (2007). *In their own words: Exploring the learner's perspective on e-learning*. London: JISC.

Cross, J. (2005). Foreword. In C. J. Bonk & C. R. Graham (Eds.), *Handbook of blended learning: Global perspectives, local designs* (pp. xvii-xxiii). San Francisco: Pfeiffer.

Dede, C. (2000). *The role of emerging technologies for knowledge mobilization, dissemination, and use in education*. [Commissioned report]. Washington, DC: U.S. Department of Education.

Downes, S. (2004). Educational blogging. *EDUCAUSE Review, 39*(5), 14–26.

Driscoll, M. (2002). Blended learning: Let's get beyond the hype. *E-learning, 3*(3), 54.

Dziuban, C. D., Hartman, J., Juge, F., Moskal, P. D., & Sorg, S. (2005). Blended learning: Online learning enters the mainstream. In C. J. Bonk & C. R. Graham (Eds.), *Handbook of blended learning: Global perspectives, local designs* (pp. 195-208). San Francisco: Pfeiffer.

Dziuban, C. D., Hartman, J. L., & Moskal, P. D. (2004). Blended learning. *EDUCAUSE Center for Applied Research Research Bulletin, 2004*(7). Retrieved January 10, 2007, from http://www.educause.edu/ir/library/pdf/ERB0407.pdf

Edirisingha, P., Salmon, G., & Fothergill, J. (2006). *Enriching a blended learning environment with podcasts and e-tivities: A case study*. Paper presented at the First International Blended Learning conference: Promoting dialogue in innovation and practice, Hertfordshire, England.

Edirisingha, P., Salmon, G., & Fothergill, J. (2007). Profcasting—a pilot study and guidelines for integrating podcasts in a blended learning environment. In U. Bernath & A. Sangrà (Eds.), *Research on competence development in online distance education and e-learning: Selected papers from the 4th EDEN Research Workshop in Castelldefels/Spain* (pp. 127-137). Oldenberg, Germany: BIS-Verlag der Carl von Ossietzky Universität Oldenburg.

Ellis, R. A., Steed, A. F., & Applebee, A. C. (2006). Teacher conceptions of blended learning, blended teaching and associations with approaches to design. *Australasian Journal of Educational Technology, 22*(3), 312–335.

Encyclopædia Britannica Online. (2008). Retrieved May 12, 2008, from http://www.britannica.com/

Frydenberg, M. (2006). Principles and pedagogy: The two P's of podcasting in the information technology classroom. In D. Colton, W. J. Tastle, M. Hensel, & A. A. Abdullat (Eds.), *Proceedings of ISECON 2006* (§3354). Chicago: AITP.

Garrison, D. R., & Kanuka, H. (2004). Blended learning: Uncovering its transformative potential in higher education. *The Internet and Higher Education, 7*(2), 95–105. doi:10.1016/j.iheduc.2004.02.001

Garrison, D. R., Kanuka, H., & Hawes, D. (2002). *Blended learning: Archetypes for more effective undergraduate learning experiences*. Calgary, AB: University of Calgary.

Garrison, D. R., & Vaughan, N. D. (2008). *Blended learning in higher education*. San Francisco: Jossey-Bass.

Gillmor, D. (2004). *We the media: Grassroots journalism by the people, for the people*. Sebastopol, CA: O'Reilly Media.

Gribbins, M. L., Hadidi, R., Urbaczewski, A., & Vician, C. (2007). Technology-enhanced learning in blended learning environments: A report on standard practices. *Communications of the Association for Information Systems, 20*, 741–759.

Hargreaves, D. H. (2004). Networks, knowledge and innovation. In H. McCarthy, P. Miller, & P. Skidmore (Eds.), *Network logic: Who governs in an interconnected world?* (pp. 79-88). London: Demos.

Harris, B. (2007a, October 25). Flickr in art history class. *smARThistory* [Web log]. Retrieved November 3, 2007, from http://smarthistory.org/blog/88/flickr-in-art-history-class-how-fun/

Harris, B. (2007b). Midterm. *Art Survey: HA 112 at FIT*. Retrieved November 3, 2007, from http://smarthistory.org/artsurvey/?page_id=13

Helms, D. (2007). *Group project*. Retrieved November 2, 2007, from http://www.msjc.edu/hs/hs123_group_project.html

Hilton, J. (2006). The future for higher education: Sunrise or perfect storm? *EDUCAUSE Review, 41*(2), 58–71.

Kukulska-Hulme, A. (2005). *The mobile language learner—now and in the future* [Webcast]. Plenary session delivered at the Fran Vision till Praktik (From Vision to Practice) Language Learning Symposium, Umeå, Sweden. Retrieved February 3, 2006, from http://www2.humlab.umu.se/video/Praktikvision/agnes.ram

Lane, L. M. (2008). Toolbox or trap? Course management systems and pedagogy. *EDUCAUSE Quarterly, 31*(2), 4–6.

Lee, M. J. W., McLoughlin, C., & Chan, A. (2008). Talk the talk: Learner-generated podcasts as catalysts for knowledge creation. *British Journal of Educational Technology, 39*(3), 501–521. doi:10.1111/j.1467-8535.2007.00746.x

Luca, J., & McLoughlin, C. (2005a). Can blogs promote fair and equitable teamwork? In H. Goss (Ed.), *Balance, fidelity, mobility: Maintaining the momentum? Proceedings of the 22nd ASCILITE Conference* (pp. 379-386). Brisbane, Australia: Queensland University of Technology.

Luca, J., & McLoughlin, C. (2005b). Supporting collaborative learning with blogs. In P. Kommers & G. Richards (Eds.), *Proceedings of World Conference on Educational Multimedia, Hypermedia & Telecommunications 2005* (pp. 3711-3715). Chesapeake, VA: AACE.

Lui, A. K., Choy, S., Cheung, Y. H. Y., & Li, S. C. (2006). A study on the perception of students towards educational weblogs. *Informatics in Education*, *5*(2), 233–254.

Masie, E. (2002). Blended learning: The magic is in the mix. In A. Rossett (Ed.), *The ASTD e-learning handbook: Best practices, strategies, and case studies for an emerging field* (pp. 58-63). New York: McGraw-Hill.

Matheos, K., Daniel, K., & McCalla, G. I. (2005). Dimensions for blended learning technology: Learners' perspectives. *Journal of Learning Design*, *1*(1), 56–76.

McCray, G. E. (2000). The hybrid class: Merging online instruction and the traditional classroom. *Information Technology and Management*, *1*(4), 307–327. doi:10.1023/A:1019189412115

Mejias, U. (2005). A nomad's guide to learning and social software. *The Knowledge Tree: An E-Journal of Learning Innovation, 7*. Retrieved December 10, 2006, from http://knowledgetree.flexiblelearning.net.au/edition07/download/la_mejias.pdf

Miller, D. B. (2006, October 18). Podcasting at the University of Connecticut: Enhancing the educational experience. *Campus Technology*. Retrieved April 10, 2007, from http://campustechnology.com/news_article.asp?id=19424&typeid=156

Miller, D. B. (2007). *iCube*. Retrieved April 10, 2007, from http://icube.uconn.edu/

O'Reilly, T. (2005a). *Web 2.0: Compact definition?* Retrieved November 28, 2006, from http://radar.oreilly.com/archives/2005/10/web_20_compact_definition.html

O'Reilly, T. (2005b). *What is Web 2.0: Design patterns and business models for the next generation of software*. Retrieved December 15, 2006, from http://www.oreillynet.com/pub/a/oreilly/tim/news/2005/09/30/what-is-web-20.html

Oliver, M., & Trigwell, K. (2005). Can "blended learning" be redeemed? *E-Learning*, *2*(1), 17–26.

Punie, Y., & Cabrera, M. (2006). *The future of ICT and learning in the knowledge society*. Luxembourg: European Communities.

Richardson, W. (2006). *Blogs, wikis, podcasts, and other powerful tools for classrooms*. Thousand Oaks, CA: Sage.

Rudd, T., Sutch, D., & Facer, K. (2006). *Towards new learning networks*. Bristol, UK: Futurelab.

Salmon, G. (2002). *E-tivities: The key to active online learning*. London: Kogan Page.

Salmon, G. (2004). *E-moderating: The key to teaching & learning online* (2nd ed.). London: RoutledgeFalmer.

Sener, J. (2007). *University of North Carolina at Pembroke—cjencyclopedia.com: Online encyclopedia of Criminal Justice*. Retrieved March 10, 2007, from http://www.sloan-c-wiki.org/wiki/index.php?title=University_of_North_Carolina_at_Pembroke_--_cjencyclopedia.com:_Online_Encyclopedia_of_Criminal_Justice

Sharpe, R., Benfield, G., Roberts, G., & Francis, R. (2006). *The undergraduate experience of blended e-learning: A review of UK literature and practice*. York, UK: The Higher Education Academy.

Singh, H., & Reed, C. (2001). *Achieving success with blended learning* [white paper]. Lexington, MA: Centra Software.

Surowiecki, K. (2004). *The wisdom of crowds*. New York: Doubleday.

Twigg, C. A. (2003). Improving learning and reducing costs: New models for online learning. *EDUCAUSE Review*, *38*(5), 29–38.

Vaughan, N. D. (2007). Perspectives on blended learning in higher education. *International Journal on E-Learning*, *6*(1), 81–94.

Veronikas, S. W., & Shaughnessy, M. F. (2004). Teaching and learning in a hybrid world: An interview with Carol Twigg. *EDUCAUSE Review*, *39*(4), 50–62.

Wagner, E. (2006). On designing interaction experiences for the next generation of blended learning. In C. J. Bonk & C. R. Graham (Eds.), *Handbook of blended learning: Global perspectives, local designs* (pp. 41-54). San Francisco: Pfeiffer.

Wenzloff, J. (2005). *Furl, furled, furling: Social on-line bookmarking for the masses*. Retrieved July 10, 2007, from http://www.classroomhelp.com/workshop/Furl_Guide.pdf

Wikipedia. (2008). Retrieved May 12, 2008, from http://www.wikipedia.org/

Williams, C. (2002). Learning online: A review of recent literature in a rapidly expanding field. *Journal of Further and Higher Education*, *26*(3), 263–272. doi:10.1080/03098770220149620

Williams, J. (2003, June). Blending into the background. *E-Learning Age Magazine*, 1.

Williams, J. B., & Jacobs, J. (2004). Exploring the use of blogs as learning spaces in the higher education sector. *Australasian Journal of Educational Technology*, *20*(2), 232–247.

Windham, C. (2005). The student's perspective. In D. G. Oblinger & J. L. Oblinger (Eds.). *Educating the Net Generation* (pp. 5.1-5.16). Washington, DC: EDUCAUSE.

Yew, J., Gibson, F. P., & Teasley, S. D. (2006). Learning by tagging: The role of social tagging in group knowledge formation. *Journal of Online Learning and Teaching*, *2*(4), 275–285.

KEY TERMS AND DEFINITIONS

Architecture of Participation: A term used to describe the nature of innovation in the open source movement, whereby individuals can share, create, and amend software, thereby participating in the creation of improved forms of software. This can help turn a good idea or piece of software into a best-quality product as many users and developers can adapt, change, and improve it.

Authentic Learning: Learning that encourages learners to engage in real-world problems and projects that are meaningful and interesting to them, and that have relevance beyond the classroom.

Blended E-Learning: A learning delivery approach in which core learning activities are undertaken both via the Internet as well as in traditional, face-to-face settings, as distinct from the practice of simply supplementing face-to-face instruction with online resources and materials, e.g. through a course Web site. *See also* supplemented e-learning.

Blog: *See* Web log.

CMS (Course Management System): An integrated suite of software tools designed to manage courses or other learning interventions. Commercial examples are Blackboard and WebCT, although many open source alternatives, such as Moodle and Sakai, exist. In addition to the provision of online learning content and activities and the facilitation of online assessment, CMS's typically support a range of administrative functions including learner enrollment, workflow, records management, and resource management.

Collaborative Learning: An umbrella term for a variety of teaching and learning approaches that involve joint intellectual effort by learners, or by learners and teachers. Learners engage in a common task in which each individual depends on and is accountable to each other. Groups of learners work together in searching for understanding, meaning, or solutions, or in creating an artifact of their learning such as a particular product.

Collective Intelligence: A form of intelligence that results from the cooperation, collaboration, and/or competition of a large number of individuals. *See also* wisdom of crowds.

Flexible Learning: A broad term used to describe the design and delivery of programs, courses, and learning interventions in such a way as to cater for student demands for variety, access, recognition of diverse learning styles, and student control over and customizability of the learning experience. It is often incorrectly used in an interchangeable manner with other terms such as "open learning," "distance learning," "work-based learning," as well as "e-learning," which are all instances or forms of flexible learning in that they provide flexibility to the student in terms of time/pace, place, access, content, and/or delivery mode.

Informal Learning: Refers to learning that does not take place in formal education and training environments, but instead occurs as a result of everyday life and professional practice, e.g., at home, work, and throughout society. It has no defined curriculum and is not planned or pedagogically conscious. Many researchers and theorists have suggested that informal learning accounts for up to 75% of our learning. *See also* lifelong learning.

Inquiry-Based Learning: A term used to describe a range of instructional strategies based on premises that are centered around the need for learners to ask questions, then actively seek out answers to those questions. It is commonly used in the teaching of science. The teacher takes on the role of a "facilitator" who supports learners rather than simply giving them the answers, encouraging them to take responsibility for their learning through active exploration, discovery, and reflection.

Lifelong Learning: A term that recognizes that learning is not confined to childhood and/or the classroom, but instead takes place continuously throughout life and in a range of contexts and situations, including formal, non-formal, and informal situations. *See also* informal learning.

Mash-Up: Content or material that is collected from several Web-based sources, then modified, re-mixed, and/or re-combined to create a new formulation of the material. A mash-up is typically a digital media file including one or more the following: text, graphics, audio, video, and animation. Mash-ups are commonly seen in "Web 2.0" services and social software tools such as blogs, wikis, RSS and podcast feeds, media sharing sites (e.g. YouTube) and social networking sites (e.g. MySpace, Facebook). *See also* micro-content, Web 2.0, social software.

Micro-Content: Very small, basic units of digital content or media that can be consumed in unbundled micro-chunks, and aggregated and reconstructed in various ways. Micro-content often forms the basis of micro-learning. *See also* mash-up.

Pedagogy 2.0: Digital tools and affordances, especially those emanating from the Web 2.0 movement, call for a new conceptualization of teaching and learning that is focused on participation in communities and networks for learning, personalization of learning tasks, and production of ideas and knowledge. Pedagogy 2.0 is a response to this call. It represents a set of approaches and strategies that differs from teaching as a didactic practice of passing on information; instead, it advocates a model of learning in which students are empowered to participate, communicate, and create knowledge, exercising a high level of agency and control over the entire learning process. *See also* Web 2.0.

Personal Publishing: A process in which an individual actively produces his/her own content and information and publishes it on the World Wide Web for others to see and/or use. For example, the maintenance of a personal Web log (blog) as an online diary is an instance of personal publishing. *See also* user-generated content, Web log, Web 2.0.

Podcast: A portmanteau that combines the words "iPod" (the name of Apple's popular music player) and "broadcast." Refers to the distribution of digital audio files, typically in MPEG Layer 3 (MP3) format, through a syndication protocol such as RSS. The user subscribes to one or more feeds or channels of his/her choice using a podcast aggregation program, which periodically polls the feeds for new audio files and downloads them automatically to the user's hard disk as they become available. *See also* RSS.

Problem-Based Learning: A form of authentic, inquiry-based learning in which students learn by working collaboratively in groups to solve problems, and reflecting on their experiences. The problems are typically challenging and open-ended, mirroring problems in the real world in that they are often ill-structured and do not result in neat, convergent outcomes. *See also* inquiry-based learning.

Prosumer: A portmanteau formed by contracting word "producer" with the word "consumer," signifying the blurring of the distinction between the two roles in today's knowledge economy.

RSS (Really Simple Syndication): A technology originally designed to facilitate the publication of text summaries of additions to frequently-updated Web sites, such as news sites and Web logs. The user subscribes to the feed(s) of one or more RSS-enabled Web sites by configuring a news reader or aggregator program installed on his/her computer with the URL(s) of the eXtensible Markup Language (XML) file(s) that comprise the feed. The program periodically checks the feed for new content and downloads it as it becomes available. RSS 2.0 feeds permit the inclusion of enclosures, which permit multimedia files (such as MP3 files in the case of podcasting) to be referenced in the feed.

Social Networking: A social network is a social structure comprising various nodes, which generally represent individuals or organizations, that are tied together by one or more specific types of interdependency, e.g. common values, shared visions, exchange of ideas, mutual financial benefit, trade, friendship/kinship, or even dislike and conflict. In the context of the Web 2.0 movement, the term is commonly used to refer to Web sites like MySpace, Facebook, Ning, Friendster, and LinkedIn, which attract and support networks of people and facilitate connections between them for social and professional purposes. The "blogosphere" (a term used to describe the cultural and social milieu surrounding Web logging and its users) may also be viewed as an example of an online social network. *See also* Web 2.0, social software.

Social Software: The most common modern usage of this term is to refer to the software tools and applications of the Web 2.0 movement that support group interaction, communication, and collaboration, including but not limited to Web logs (blogs), wikis, Really Simple Syndication (RSS) and podcasting feeds, peer-to-peer (P2P) media sharing applications, and social bookmarking utilities. However, some argue that the Internet has in fact always comprised a network of individuals connected through social technologies like e-mail, chat rooms, and discussion boards (now referred to as the "Web 1.0" technologies). *See also* Web 2.0, social networking.

Student-Generated Content: Content that is produced by students, often for sharing with peers and/or a wider audience on the Internet, as distinct from instructor-supplied content such as course notes and textbooks. It is arguable that the main benefits to be gained from student-generated content lie in the processes of content creation and knowledge construction, as opposed to the end products themselves. *See also* user-generated content.

Supplemented E-Learning: A term used to describe an approach whereby supplementary materials are provided via a Web site to augment traditional, face-to-face delivery, but in which the learning activities themselves are largely not carried out online. *See also* blended e-learning.

User-Generated Content: A term that refers to Web-based content created by ordinary users or members of the general public, e.g. pictures posted on Flickr, videos uploaded to YouTube, or encyclopedia entries written in Wikipedia. Such "Read-Write" applications are a key characteristic of the Web 2.0 movement, which encourages the publishing of one's own content and commenting on or augmenting other people's. It differs from the "Read Only" model of Web 1.0, in which Web sites were created and maintained by an elite few. *See also* personal publishing.

Web 2.0: A term used to describe an apparent second generation or improved form of the World Wide Web that emphasizes collaboration and sharing of knowledge and content among users. Characteristic of Web 2.0 are the socially-based tools and systems referred to collectively as social software. *See also* social software.

Web Log: Blogs (short for "Web logs") are Web sites that were originally intended to allow individuals to maintain their own personal journals or diaries and make them available for public viewing on the Internet. Blogs are typically easy to use and adopt an informal, journal-entry style, making them much more convenient to update and add to than traditional Web sites. They are an example of a social software application that typifies Web 2.0, including the rise of user-generated content and personal publishing. Blogging can also be an intensely social activity, as most blog platforms allow for contributions to be made by multiple users; furthermore, bloggers with similar interests often engage in dialogue on one another's sites and create connections among themselves to form worldwide social networks. *See also* Web 2.0, social software, social networking, personal publishing, user-generated content.

Wiki: A Web site whose pages and content can be easily created and edited by users, within their Web browsers. An example of user-generated content that epitomizes the Web 2.0 movement and capitalizes on the "wisdom of crowds," wikis operate on the principle of collaborative trust, as visitors are free not only to create new content as on a discussion board, but also to edit one another's contributions. The name "wiki" is of Hawaiian origin, "wiki wiki" meaning "quick" or "informal," a reference to the speed and ease with which wikis can be accessed and their content modified through any standard Web browser. The best-known wiki example is Wikipedia, a free content encyclopedia written collaboratively by volunteers that has grown to become one of the most popular sites on the Internet. *See also* Web 2.0, social software, user-generated content, wisdom of crowds, collective intelligence.

Wisdom of Crowds: A concept that relates to the aggregation of information in groups and communities of individuals. It recognizes that the innovation, problem-solving, and decision-making capabilities of the group are often superior to that of any single member of the group. The term was used as the title of a book written by James Surowiecki, published in 2004. *See also* collective intelligence.

Chapter 24
Deployment of a Web Based Critiquing System for Essay Writing in Hybrid Learning Environment

Fion S.L. Lee
Hong Kong Baptist University, Hong Kong

Kelvin C.K. Wong
Hong Kong Baptist University, Hong Kong

William K.W. Cheung
Hong Kong Baptist University, Hong Kong

Cynthia F.K. Lee
Hong Kong Baptist University, Hong Kong

ABSTRACT

This chapter describes the use of a Web-based essay critiquing system and its integration into in a series of composition workshops for a group of secondary school students in Hong Kong. It begins with a review and application of the hybrid learning approach, followed by a description of latent semantic analysis, a methodology for corpus preparation. Then, the distribution computing architecture for essay critiquing system is described. It explicates the way in which the system is integrated with a writing pedagogy implemented in the workshop and the feasibility evaluation result is derived. The positive result confirms the benefits of hybrid learning.

INTRODUCTION

English is taught as a second language for students in Hong Kong. Among the four language skills, writing seems to be difficult to many second language students and they feel stressful in composition lessons. They have either difficulty in generating ideas to have a good coverage of the composition topic or insufficient time to well-organize their ideas and thoughts within the lessons. Although process writing has been practiced for some time

DOI: 10.4018/978-1-60566-380-7.ch024

and teachers are encouraged to give feedback to students' writing drafts, they also find it stressful to provide immediate individual formative feedback within a lesson, especially when the class size is large. To alleviate this learning and teaching barrier, a web-based system called Essay Critiquing System (ECS) is developed. ECS makes use of an automatic text analysis technique known as Latent Semantic Analysis (LSA) to give students just-in-time feedback for reflecting on the essay content and organization of ideas. Based on the feedback, students can further revise their drafts independently and repeatedly until they find their essays good enough to be submitted to teachers for grading. It is believed that it is an effective way to challenge and encourage students to revise their essays' contents and organization. This teaching mode is related to hybrid learning as it is integrated with both the online composition learning process using ECS and face-to-face meetings in which the teacher reviews the submitted drafts, provides written and/or verbal feedback to the students, and grades the final drafts.

In this paper, a review of hybrid learning and LSA in learning will first be provided. Following a brief overview of ECS, the methodology for preparing the corpus to be used by the critiquing system will be presented in detail. Apart from it, a three-tiered architecture that makes the system scale well to meet the analysis need will then be shown. Finally, the integration of ECS into a process approach to teaching composition and the preliminary results of the feasibility evaluation will be described.

A BRIEF REVIEW OF HYBRID LEARNING

Definition, Objective, Functions and Effectiveness of Hybrid Learning

Learning in contemporary education relies on various media and channels for achieving a rewarding result. More and more courses are designed with a hybrid learning environment that facilitates interactive learning. Hybrid learning refers to the learning that blends online and face-to-face delivery in which substantial proportion of the content or activity is delivered or carried out online (Picciano & Searman, 2007). The main objective of hybrid learning is to provide an opportunity to allow students to be more engaging in the learning process. It can also facilitate students to drive the learning process directly and make learning become more autonomous. The Internet is used to deliver and mediate the learning process. It is expected that the combination of this online experience and face-to-face contact between students and with instructors can lead to a meaningful and valuable outcome to all involving parties (Reynard, 2007). Sife et al. (Sife et al., 2007) also suggested other benefits of adopting information communication technologies in education. They include more convenient information access, synchronous and asynchronous learning, more effective communication, improved collaboration and cooperation, etc. In addition, many research projects have demonstrated that the adoption of online or virtual learning practice for facilitating face-to-face learning can result in an enriched education environment (Long et al., 2007, Poysa et al., 2005).

The online activities in hybrid learning are conducted in various forms. They include dissemination of course materials by teachers, course document access by students, assignment submission, online discussion and sharing, project coordination, online examination and so forth (Buzzetto & Sweat, 2006). With the advanced development of media technology and Web 2.0, the online activities in the blended learning mode has been enriched: audio, music, motion graphics, simulation, real time demonstration, and interactive mechanism can now be easily adopted as parts of the learning experience (Kim, 2008).

Given the variety of technologies and activities, educators can choose the most appropriate one to serve their teaching and learning purposes for different groups of students. For example, in the redesign process for a security course in Boise Sate University, computerized voting, online discussion, and lab analysis tool were adopted in conjunction with the face-to-face class for the module of application threats and systems development. For the module of business problem and security management, online reading materials were used to support the in-class meeting (Tabor, 2007).

Hybrid learning, however, generates mixed results. The adoption of hybrid learning is regarded as a cost- and learning-effective measure to operate learning programmes. For instance, the blended learning model provides a self-paced and customized environment to enhance the experience of working adults who may not be able to attend the face-to-face lecture class due to their business activities. A hybrid learning net optimizes the learning experience of students, who received executive management education in an internet-oriented MBA programme, by using E-books as the central element of the learning net structure, supplemented with other online tools such as e-library, online cases, business simulator, online test, industry tours and on forth (Hall, 2006, Hall & Dudley, 2006). The network includes functions to support faculty-to-student and student-to-student interactions. In Picciano and Searman's study (Picciano & Searman, 2007), hybrid learning which was applied to K-12 schools promoted the trend of using electronic technologies to support the students. As reported in the study, potential challenges could be shortage of teachers with sufficient experience in adopting online tools in K-12 schools, especially those located in rural regions. Although the adoption of hybrid learning may reduce the chance of face-to-face meeting between students and instructors, it is well accepted by students. Previous study on a hybrid college course at Appalachian State University showed that a class taught via both face-to-face and online channels (using WebCT) had almost the same pass and drop-out rates as those of a class taught solely face to face (Hensley, 2005). It implies students taking the courses in blended learning model feel indifferent with taking the traditional face-to-face courses.

Technical Support for Hybrid Learning

To support the adoption of hybrid learning, systems such as AutoTutor, Intelligent Essay Assessor, or Willow can be chosen. AutoTutor is an online tutoring system that allows learners contribute answers to questions (Graesser et al., 2008). The AutoTutor is shown on the screen as an animated agent who has facial expression, gesture, and gaze. At the same time, dialogue appears with synthesized speech that includes inflection and intonation. AutoTutor can assess the progress of learners by comparing their contribution to the discussion topic of the good aspects, i.e. a set of key concepts of the ideal answer. It is assessed based on whether every good aspect is covered by learner's response. If a good aspect is mentioned by the learner, AutoTutor would move on to another good aspect until all good aspects of that particular topic are covered. Then, a summary would be generated by AutoTutor to show the assessment results (Craig et al., 2004). Intelligent Essay Assessor is a tool to assess the quality of essay content. It provides immediate evaluation on essays together with feedback on errors of grammar and spelling ("Pearson Education," 2008). The technique used by Intelligent Essay Assessor to assess essay is by comparing the essays with the previous graded ones. The score of an essay is based on the grading of pervious essays that are similar. This technique offers a "holistic" scoring showing the overall content similarity. The score reflects how well an essay's meaning matches that of the previous graded ones. This idea is similar to having a human grader who assesses each essay as a whole instead of consider individual component of an essay (Foltz et al., 1999). Apart from these two systems, Willow is another option. Willow is a free-text Computer Assisted Assessment (CAA) system (Perez et al., 2006). CAA is defined as the effective use of computers to assess student learning (Perez et al., 2005). Teachers using Willow are not required to go through training. The system just requires having several different correct answers in plain text for each question. When using the system, a teacher can choose to use a course from the system, i.e. a collection of questions that focuses on a topic. He can also create a new question or modify an existing one. Answer for each question can be input by teacher or based on the previous correct answers of students as reference. The system can support the allocation of questions by referring students' past performance to determine the suitable questions for them.

APPLICATIONS OF LATENT SEMANTIC ANALYSIS IN LEARNING

Latent Semantic Analysis (LSA) is a text analysis technique usually adopted for hybrid learning. For example, AutoTutor system mentioned in the last section uses LSA to measure the quality of learner contribution (Graesser et al., 2008).

LSA is a mathematical technique for computing the semantic similarity between pieces of textual information (for example, sentences, paragraphs or essays) with the help of a large corpus (Landauer et al., 1998, Landauer & Psotka, 2000), and is commonly used to support learning. It works out a matrix showing the co-occurrence of terms and texts. In LSA, a 'term' means any word that appears in more than one text. The matrix takes into consideration of the occurrence frequency for a term in a single text and the occurrence frequency across texts.

LSA is commonly used to support the tutoring aspect in education (Lemaire, 1999, Wiemer-Hastings et al., 1999). It is adopted by Summary Street, an educational software system for assisting writing and revision activities (Foltz et al., 2000). A main function of this system is to provide feedback on a student summary to see whether the summary covers important source content. Trials were conducted with the system and the results showed that the system is useful especially when students work with a summary for a harder text.

LSA has also been adopted in the development of an automated essay grader (Foltz et al., 2000) and critic, and was found to be able to score as accurately as human in the study. They implemented the tool for an undergraduate course and found that there was improvement in writing as students could write and revise the essays online. Apex is yet another system that adopts LSA to help assess a student essay based on its content. Their experiments showed that there was a significant correlation between the human grades and the Apex grades. That is, using Apex for essay evaluation could generate similar outcomes as graded by human (Lemaire & Dessus, 2001).

A CRITIQUING SYSTEM FOR ESSAY WRITING

In view of integrating online means into English writing courses for obtaining more fruitful results, a web-based essay critiquing system that uses LSA has been proposed in (Cheung et al., 2007, Wong et al., 2007) with some promising results reported. For the reason of completeness, the ECS is briefly presented in this section. More details can be referred back to (Cheung et al., 2007).

ECS contains teacher input, student input, database that stores student answers and reference materials from external sources, text segmentation and preprocessing engine, LSA engine, semantic matcher and critic feedback to students. Generally speaking, the teacher decides on an essay topic for students, and collects some relevant background materials of the topic such as articles from the Internet resources or textbooks to build a corpus. Then, the teacher identifies a list of possible sub-themes of the topic and extracts related paragraphs from good student essays of past years or model essays from some books. Before feeding the training data (including the articles and the sample essays) into the LSA engine, all articles are first broken down into sentences and preprocessed, e.g. stop-word removal and stemming.

The LSA engine, after training, is ready to receive new essays from students. Upon receiving a new essay, the semantic similarity between each sentence of the new essay and each of the sub-themes can be computed in real time. When the computation step is completed, the sub-themes that are found missing in the students' essays can be identified and reported to students for their consideration to further revise their essays. Also, the texts in the student essays that match against one of the sub-themes are highlighted in color along with a short phrase describing the sub-theme. This can encourage students to take a new look at the organization of their essays.

CORPUS PREPARATION METHODOLOGY

Since ECS adopts LSA which is a statistical method, its performance depends very much on the size and the quality of the corpus prepared for the semantic analysis. According to previous experience, the corpus preparation step is one of the most crucial ones for the critiquing system to provide accurate feedback to the student.

As described in (Cheung et al., 2007), ECS needs (1) a set of sub-themes which are related to the essay topic, (2) good essay samples with sentences matched with those sub-themes marked, and (3) relevant but unmarked articles. Both (1) and (2) can be completed with teacher's assistance whereas (3) is obtained from the Web.

The detailed steps for preparing the corpus of the critiquing system are shown in the following.

1. Prepare a stop list which includes a number of common or meaningless words like articles, pronouns, numbers, etc.
2. Collect a set of good essay samples (say written by some previous students), where careful spell-check is normally needed.
3. Create a list of sub-themes by carefully scanning the essay samples. For example, for a topic "*More and more married couples in Hong Kong choose not to have their own children nowadays. Do you support their choice? Use specific reasons and examples to support your opinion.*", the titles of the sub-themes could be:
    a. Women's independence
    b. Career consideration
    c. Economic consideration
    d. Change of lifestyle
4. Go through each sentence of the essay samples and mark the phases that are related to different sub-themes manually. For instance, based on the aforementioned example, some of the phases marked to be under different sub-themes are shown as follows: (the indices shown at the end of each phrase indicate the source documents.)
    a. Women's independence
        - Women's independence [c1.doc]
        - Can find a job [c1.doc]
        - Better education [c1.doc]
        - women don't want to marry just for a baby [c1.doc]
    b. Career consideration
        - Love working instead of taking care of a baby [c1.doc]
        - Discourage mothers from returning to work [c1.doc]
        - Career opportunities [c11.doc]
        - Do not want their staff to be pregnant [c11.doc]
    c. Economic consideration
        - Child care is expensive [c1.doc]
        - Expense [c10.doc]

- Spend a lot of money [c11.doc]
- Economic development [c12.doc]

d. Change of lifestyle

- Have a peaceful life [c1.doc]
- Peaceful life style [c1.doc]
- Childlessness becomes a new lifestyle [c1.doc]
- Enjoy current lifestyle [c10.doc]

5. Collect relevant texts from the Web where the marking as described in Step 4 is not needed. According to the previous experiments, the total number of words of a corpus to be good enough for the application usually falls between 20,000 to 40,000.
6. Treat each sub-theme and each sentence of the texts collected from the Web as a 'document'. Apply the stop list for stop word removal. Use WordNet ("The MIT Press," 2008) as a dictionary for stemming and perform the semantic analysis using LSA[1] as described in (Cheung et al., 2007). Then, for each sub-theme, remove the terms with the highest scores because these words are less discriminative in general. Also, remove the words that appear in more than 80% of the sub-themes. Regarding the size of the corpus we have collected, this step takes around 30 minutes. In many cases, it is found that some parameter tuning for those thresholds and the dimension of LSA can help further improve the system accuracy.

In principle, one can follow the six steps to have a corpus prepared for an essay topic to be released to the students. The methodology has been tested for more than five different topics. It was found that Steps 3 and 4 are not mechanical and one may need to iterate the two steps before a satisfactory performance of the critiquing system can be obtained. The main causes include (1) insufficient sub-theme coverage of the essay samples, and (2) indistinguishable sub-themes initially created by the teacher. For the former, some additional phrases need to be created and associate them with the sub-themes that lack a sufficient number of related sample phrases. For the latter, the phrases matched to the sub-themes should be reviewed to see if some merges or splits are needed. Currently, study is being carried out to investigate if some automatic phrase clustering scheme can be derived so as to further reduce the time and effort required for carrying out Steps 3 and 4.

A SCALABLE SYSTEM ARCHITECTURE FOR PROVIDING JUST-IN-TIME FEEDBACK

With the corpus carefully prepared and tested, the teacher can release the topic to the students to work on in class. Students write essays using Microsoft Word and submit their drafts to ECS to get feedback in a just-in-time manner. As previously mentioned, ECS needs to first extract terms from the student submitted essay in Word file[2], and then perform stop word removal and stemming steps. A cosine value between each sentence of the essay and each sub-theme is computed. Results higher than a threshold value will cause the corresponding sentences to be highlighted as relevant to that sub-theme. As the possible number of terms for a topic is typically large and pre-processing steps are rather costly, it is found that a typical PC server is not powerful and stable enough to manage a high volume of requests for the essay critiquing services coming all at a time. And, such peaked requesting period is not unusual, especially when it is near the end of the lessons where a number of students would like to have the final check.

To address the scalability requirement, a three-tier computing architecture is adopted. The web-based module is installed for interaction with the students in the front-end server (presentation layer) and the LSA computation module in a set

Figure 1. A three-tiered system architecture for essay critiquing system

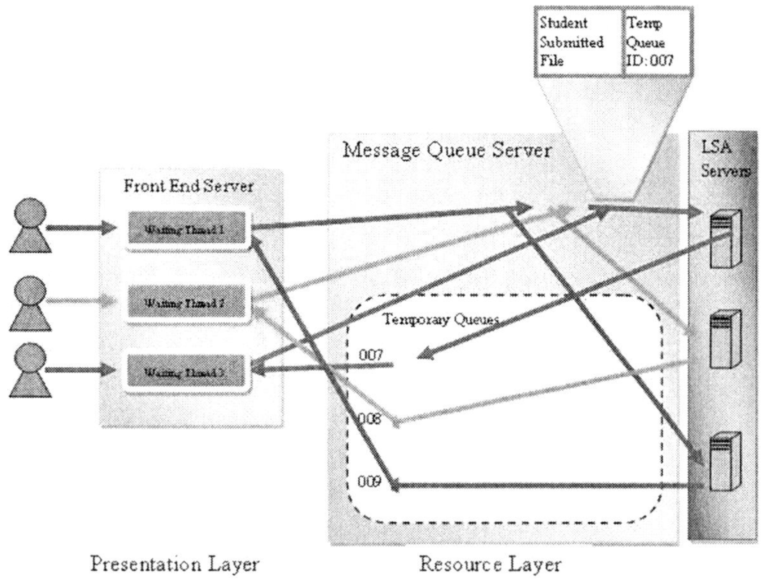

of backend servers (resource layer), as shown in Figure 1, in particular. By such a separation and together with the recent message queuing technologies[3], it is tried to make the front-end server very responsive regarding essay submission and very stable regarding submission status updating. The use of the message queue is to support a reliable asynchronous communication between the presentation layer and the backend layer. Technically speaking, if a student submits an essay, the front end server (presentation layer) will create a thread for the message queue to call back. After the LSA-based analysis of the submitted essay, the call back method will be invoked and the result will be stored into the database in the front end server. With this design, additional LSA backend servers can be easily added and the front end server can automatically make use of them for balancing the load without the need to modify any code. This is very important as it is hard to predict ahead of time how many students will make use of the system. The proposed architecture makes the extension very viable for even a secondary school setting. The system with four LSA backend servers have been rigorously tested in a real school setting and the performance was found to be very satisfactory.

SYSTEM INTEGRATION WITH WRITING PEDAGOGY

It is believed that the critiquing system developed in this study, even though with reasonable accuracy and scalable, will not be able to reach its full potential unless a proper writing pedagogy is adopted. Referring to the literature, there was a major change in approaches to teaching writing and composition in the 1970s and 1980s (Applebee, 1986). The pedagogies began to move away from a focus on the final written product to the writing process. The shift gives a reduced emphasis on rhetorical structure, vocabulary, and grammar (Hinkel, 2004). It emphasizes the importance and contribution of multi-drafts in the writing process. In the new approach, teachers take the role of a facilitator providing formative feedback on content and organization to each student draft. This feedback is important for students to revise their writing, especially on preliminary drafts (Ferris,

1995, Hedgcock & Lefkowitz, 1994). Therefore, Myers (Myers, 1986) suggested keeping a portfolio for each student in which all writing drafts are dated and stored. The important changes on each draft from the last draft should be indicated. This information allows the teacher to make a rough estimate about the frequency and influence of pre-writing. However, this teacher-student interactive process presents serious problems for secondary school teachers who have large-sized classes such as in the Hong Kong teaching environment. As responding to student drafts is indeed a very time-consuming job, it is impossible for the teachers to read every student draft and provide feedback during the composition class. If the student drafts are collected and returned with teacher feedback on the next day, it will take at least a few days to complete a composition.

To alleviate teachers' workload in providing feedback in the writing process, the ECS developed in this project can provide just-in-time formative feedback to students. The feedback takes two forms: (1) new sub-themes suggested to include, and (2) the visualization of the existing sub-themes' organization. Whenever a student is running out of ideas to continue writing his/her essay, he/she can submit his/her essay to the system. The system will suggest some sub-themes related to the essay topic for his/her consideration to be included in his/her essay. Figure 2 is a screenshot of the system with suggested sub-themes shown on the left while the student draft is on the right. When a student wants to read the organization of the sub-themes he/she has made for further revision, he/she can select a sub-theme from a list of covered sub-themes detected by the system. The distribution of that sub-theme in the essay will be highlighted with three typefaces, representing varied degrees of relevance. This can help the student take a new look at the essay organization. Figure 3 is a screenshot of the system with covered sub-themes and their detected locations shown with the correspondence sentence highlighted. With these feedbacks, students can further revise their essays accordingly. Also, as the feedback is immediate, there is no need to wait for the teacher's hints/comments before students can further revise their essays. This can speed up the writing process. Besides, the system that is web-based allows learning to take place anywhere as long as there is Internet connection. This feature enables students to practice writing outside the classroom.

As suggested by Myers (Myers, 1986), students should have a portfolio to store all their writing drafts. ECS can record all the writing draft submissions with date and time automatically. Both the teachers and students can retrieve any submitted

Figure 2. A screenshot of ECS with suggested sub-themes shown on the left hand side of the essay

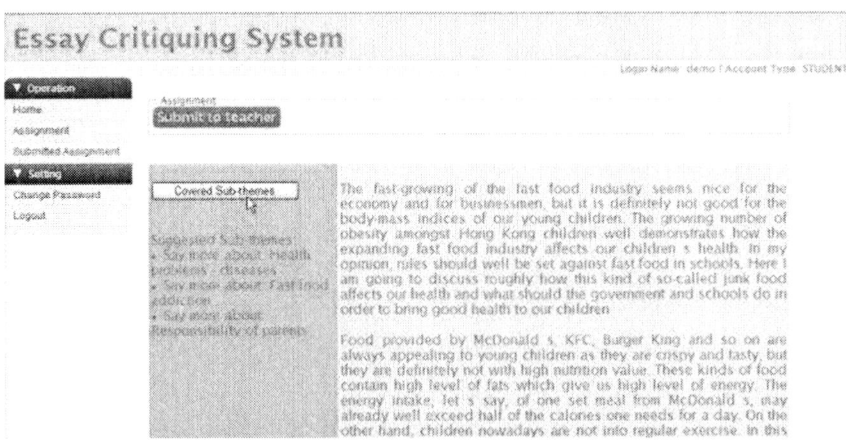

drafts for reference. This relieves students from handling the portfolios manually and allows them to concentrate on their writing.

Although the use of ECS can reduce teachers' workload in providing feedback during the student writing process, there is no less work, if not more, left to teachers. Since students can get feedback from ECS, teachers are left with more time and energy to collect corpus and good essay samples, and prepare sub-themes with appropriate corpus for the new essay titles.

FEASIBILITY EVALUATION

In order to evaluate the feasibility of integrating ECS into the process approach, an experimental study was conducted. A series of five writing workshops was conducted in a secondary school. The subjects were the Secondary 4 and 5 (equivalent to GCSE level) students. In each workshop, they were asked to write a 300-word composition on an argumentative topic with ECS. They are encouraged to use ECS, but on a voluntary basis. There was no limit on the number of submissions and revisions for system feedback. After each workshop, the final essay was marked by the teacher who can access all the student drafts. He also gave face-to-face feedback to students at the beginning of the subsequent workshop, ranging from language problems, organization of ideas within and between paragraphs to their use of the system, based on his reading of students' multiple drafts. An anonymous questionnaire was administrated at the end of the last workshop. Twenty-seven subjects returned the questionnaires.

The results of the questionnaire indicated that an average score of 4.04 on a 5-point scale (5 for very great, 3 for moderate and 1 for very least) was given by the subjects for the extent to which they thought ECS could improve their essay content in terms of number of ideas and arguments. The average score for the assistance in essay organization improvement was 3.78.

Figure 3. A screenshot of ECS with covered sub-themes and their detected locations shown with the corresponding sentences highlighted

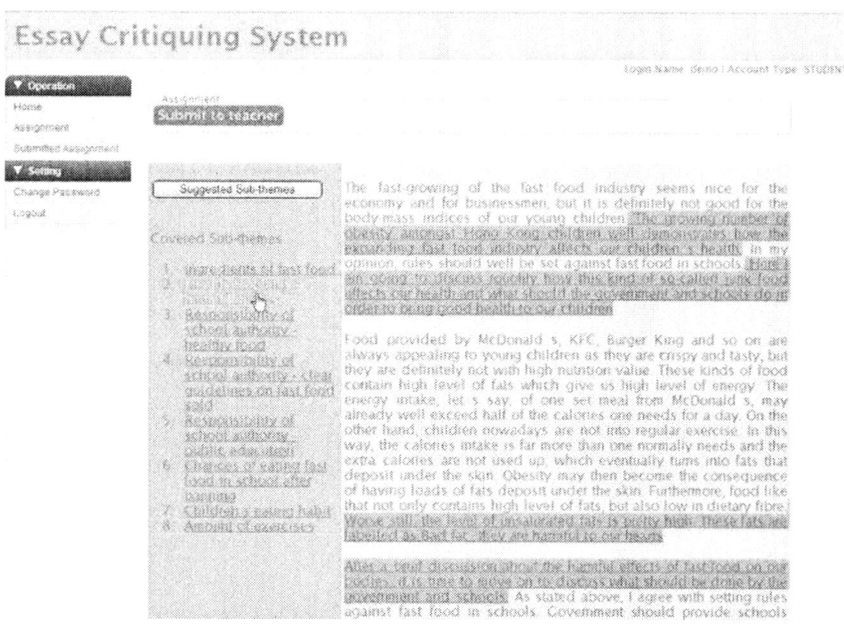

Twenty-five out of 27 respondents agreed that the teacher should continue to adopt this system for their essay writing in the future.

Although the ECS was well-received by the subjects, some difficulties were encountered if it is to be integrated into the normal composition writing class. A typical secondary school may require students to write a composition every two weeks. This will give teachers a great concern on the use of this system as corpus preparation is a very time-consuming task. In this regard, two ways are suggested. One way is to form a project team to prepare corpus for a list of commonly adopted composition titles and make them available to all the school teachers. Another way is to study the possibility of automating the corpus preparation process with some sentence clustering techniques in order to reduce the time and efforts in this process. The availability of computer rooms is another difficulty. As each student requires a computer with the Internet connection for writing, it will be very difficult for a typical secondary school in Hong Kong to schedule a computer room for every composition class. Due to this difficulty, the workshops carried out in this experiment were scheduled during weekends. However, the penetration of WiFi technology will soon reach each and every classroom for the years to come. Students by then can easily get connected to computer tools/ services like ECS in ordinary classrooms. It is believed a variety of hybrid learning approaches would emerge and be adopted to help the next-generation to learn more effectively.

CONCLUSION

To conclude, the paper has described the Web-based Essay Critiquing System (ESC) and reported the way in which it is integrated into a face-to-face teaching context. During the class, teachers are expected to teach both the essay development technique and the instruction of using the system. When students understand how to use ESC, they may choose to receive immediate feedback from the system instead of queuing up for the comments of teachers. In such a way, teachers can be free up for students who need more attention and assistance. After the traditional lessons, teachers may use the system to give more self-practice essay writing exercises to students to enhance their writing ability. Besides, when teachers receive more training on how to perform analysis based on the system, they can understand students' writing processes and essay development. This is especially useful for teachers to identify students who are less capable but cannot be identified during the time constrained face-to-face lessons.

The positive feasibility evaluation result in this study has increased the confidence in pursuing the hybrid learning approach, and the proposed learning mode is one of the feasible methods only. Given some teaching constraints (e.g. availability of a computer room for each lesson) described in the paper, it is felt that installing WiFi network on the school campus can release part of the problems. Finally, it is expected that a blend of Web-based and face-to-face classroom learning is a more interactive and dynamic approach than the traditional static pen-and-paper and face-to-face classroom learning, and it is a trend of pedagogy development.

ACKNOWLEDGMENT

We would like to thank Mr. Man-Kam Chan and Ms. Patricia Wong for their assistance throughout the project, and to the principal, teachers and students of Munsang College for their contributions to this study. This project is supported by the Quality Education Fund of the Hong Kong Government of Special Administration Region, China.

REFERENCES

Applebee, A. N. (1986). Problems in Process Approaches: Toward a Reconceptualization of Process Instruction. In A. P. Petrosky & D. Bartholomae (Eds.), *The Teaching of Writing* (pp. 95-113). National Society for the Study of Education.

Buzzetto, N. A., & Sweat, R. (2006). Incorporating the Hybrid Learning Model into Minority Education at a Historically Black University. *Journal of Information Technology Education, 5*, 153–164.

Cheung, W., Mørch, A., Wong, K., Lee, C., Liu, J., & Lam, M. (2007). Grounding Collaborative Learning in Semantics-Based Critiquing. *International Journal of Distance Education Technologies, 5*(2), 40–55.

Craig, S. D., Driscoll, D. M., & Gholson, B. (2004). Constructing Knowledge from Dialog in an Intelligent Tutoring System: Interactive Learning, Vicarious Learning, and Pedagogical Agents. *Journal of Educational Multimedia and Hypermedia, 13*(2), 163–183.

Ferris, D. R. (1995). Student Reactions to Teacher Response in Multi-draft Composition Classroom. *TESOL Quarterly, 29*(1), 33–53. doi:10.2307/3587804

Foltz, P. W., Gilliam, S., & Kendall, S. (2000). Supporting Content-Based Feedback in On-Line Writing Evaluation with LSA. *Interactive Learning Environments, 8*(2), 111–127. doi:10.1076/1049-4820(200008)8:2;1-B;FT111

Foltz, P. W., Laham, D., & Landauer, T. K. (1999). The Intelligent Essay Assessor: Applications to Educational Technology. *Interactive Multimedia Electronic Journal of Computer-Enhanced Learning*. Retrieved November 21, 2008, from http://imej.wfu.edu/articles/1999/2/04/

Graesser, A. C., D'Mello, S. K., Craig, S. D., Witherspoon, A., Sullins, J., McDaniel, B., & Gholson, B. (2008). The Relationship between Affective States and Dialog Patterns During Interactions with AutoTutor. *Journal of Interactive Learning Research, 19*(2), 293–312.

Hall, O. P. (2006). Enhancing Management Education Using Hybrid Learning Nets: A Perspective from Working Adults. *Journal of Business and Management, 12*(1), 45–58.

Hall, O. P., & Dudley, T. L. (2006). The Role of Hybrid Learning Nets in Executive Management Education. *Information Systems Education Journal, 4*(26).

Hedgcock, J., & Lefkowitz, N. (1994). Feeback on Feekback: Assessing Learner Respective to Teacher Response in L2 Composing. *Journal of Second Language Writing, 3*(2), 141–163. doi:10.1016/1060-3743(94)90012-4

Hensley, G. (2005). Creating A Hybrid College Course: A Case Study and Recommendations for Beginners. *Journal of Online Learning and Teaching*. Retrieved February 22, 2008, from http://jolt.merlot.org/vol1_no2_hensley.htm

Hinkel, E. (2004). *Teaching Academic ESL Writing: Practical Techniques in Vocabulary and Grammar*. Mahwah, NJ: Lawrence Erlbaum Associates, Inc.

Kim, W. (2008). Using Technologies to Improve E-learning. *Journal of Object Technology, 7*(8), 51–56.

Landauer, T., Foltz, P., & Laham, D. (1998). An Introduction to Latent Semantic Analysis. *Discourse Processes, 25*, 259–284. doi:10.1080/01638539809545028

Landauer, T., & Psotka, J. (2000). Simulating Text Understanding for Educational Applications with Latent Semantic Analysis: Introduction to LSA. *Interactive Learning Environments*, *25*(2), 73–86. doi:10.1076/1049-4820(200008)8:2;1-B;FT073

Lemaire, B. (1999). Tutoring Systems based on Latent Semantic Analysis. In S. P. Lajoie, & M. Vivet (Eds.), *Artificial Intelligence Education*. Amsterdam: IOS Press.

Lemaire, B., & Dessus, P. (2001). A System to Assess the Semantic Content of Student Essays. *Journal of Educational Computing Research*, *24*(3), 305–320. doi:10.2190/G649-0R9C-C021-P6X3

Long, G. L., Vignare, K., Rappold, R. P., & Mallory, J. (2007). Access to Communication for Deaf, Hard-of-Hearing and ESL Students in Blended Learning Courses. *International Review of Research in Open and Distance Learning, 8*(3). Retrieved November 21, 2008, from http://www.irrodl.org/index.php/irrodl/article/view/423/933

Myers, M. (1986). The Teaching of Writing in Secondary Schools. In A. P. Petrosky & D. Bartholomae (Eds.), *The Teaching of Writing* (pp. 148-169). National Society for the Study of Education.

Pearson Education. (2008). *Intelligent Essay Assessor*. Retrieved November 21, 2008, from http://www.knowledge-technologies.com/prodIEA.shtml

Perez, D., Alfonseca, E., Rodríguez, P., & Pascual, I. (2006). Willow: Automatic and Adaptive Assessment of Students' Free-Text Answers. In *Proceedings of the 22nd International Conference of the Spanish Natural Language Proceeding Society*.

Perez, D., Gliozzo, A., Alfonseca, E., Strapparava, C., Magnini, B., & Rodríguez, P. (2005). About the effects of combining Latent Semantic Analysis with other Natural Language Processing techniques for free-text assessment. *International Journal Signos*, *38*(59), 325–343.

Picciano, A. G., & Searman, J. (2007). K-12 Online Learning: A Survey of U.S. School District Administrators. *Journal of Asynchronous Learning Networks, 11*(3). Retrieved November 21, 2008, from http://www.sloan-c.org/publications/survey/pdf/K-12_Online_Learning.pdf

Poysa, J., Lowyck, J., & Hakkinen, P. (2005). Learning Together "Three"-Hybrid "Place" as a Conceptual Vantage Point for Understanding Virtual Learning Communities in Higher Education Context. *PsychNology Journal*, *3*(2), 162–180.

Reynard, R. (2007). *Hybrid Learning: Maximizing Student Engagement Campus Technology*. Retrieved February 22, 2008, from http://www.campustechnology.com/article.aspx?aid=48204

Sife, A. S., Lwoga, E. T., & Sanga, C. (2007). New Technologies for Teaching and Learning: Challenges for Higher Learning Institutions in Developing Countries. *International Journal of Education and Development Using ICT*, *3*(2), 57–67.

Tabor, S. W. (2007). Narrowing the Distance: Implementing a Hybrid Learning Model for Information Security Education. *Quarterly Review of Distance Education*, *8*(1), 47–57.

The, M. I. T. Press. (2008). *WordNet: An Electronic Lexical Database*. Retrieved November 21, 2008, from http://mitpress.mit.edu/catalog/item/default.asp?ttype=2&tid=8106

Wiemer-Hastings, P., Wiemer-Hastings, K., & Graesser, A. C. (1999). Improving an intelligent tutor's comprehension of students with Latent Semantic Analysis. In S. P. Lajoie & M/ Vivet (Eds.), *Artificial Intelligence Education*. Amsterdam: IOS Press.

Wong, C. K., Lee, S. L., Lee, F. K., Cheung, K. W., Mørch, A. I., & Liu, J. (2007). A Pilot Study on the Impact of the Web-based Essay Critiquing System on Writing at the Tertiary Level. In *Proceedings of the 2007 International Joint Conference on e-Commerce, e-Administration, e-Society, and e-Education.*

KEY TERMS AND DEFINITIONS

Corpus: A collection of writings of a particular kind or on a particular subject.

Essay Critiquing System: A system examines critically on essay writing.

Hybrid Learning: Learning that blends online and face-to-face delivery in which substantial proportion of the content or activity is delivered or carried out online.

Latent Semantic Analysis: A mathematical technique for computing the semantic similarity between pieces of textual information (for example, sentences, paragraphs or essays) with the help of a large corpus.

Pedagogy: The art of professional of teaching.

Sub-Theme: A part of a topic of discussion.

ENDNOTES

1. In the implementation of ECS, the singular value decomposition (SVD) step needed by LSA is performed using the Matrix Toolkits for Java (MTJ) which support structured sparse matrix computation.
2. The Apache POI (API to access Microsoft format files) module is used for the term extraction.
3. Apache ActiveMQ 5.0.0 Release http://activemq.apache.org/

Chapter 25
Ramping up to Hybrid Teaching and Learning

Raj Boora
University of Alberta, Canada

John Church
University of Alberta, Canada

Helen Madill
University of Alberta, Canada

Wade Brown
University of Alberta, Canada

Myles Chykerda
University of Alberta, Canada

ABSTRACT

Hybrid learning models attempt to create an environment that can harness the best parts of both face-to-face and online modes of content delivery. The creation of these environments can be achieved in a very straightforward manner. However, the challenge is to develop these environments so that they fit the needs of the students, the abilities of the instructors, and also the nature of the content, all of which are numerous and varied. Deciding what elements to put online and what elements to deliver face-to-face presents a significant challenge, as the number of tools available to instructional staff will increase significantly over the next decade. Once the means of delivery are understood, it is possible to take the idea of hybrid teaching and learning environments one step further by first making the most of online and face-to-face delivery separately and then using them together when the need arises.

INTRODUCTION

Technology has been changing classrooms for many years. From the printing press, to the advent of radios to bring live events from around the world closer, technology has allowed students and their instructors to connect with the world in a way that was not possible a generation before. While this observation is often suggested as part of the reason that the adoption of new technology is infuriatingly

DOI: 10.4018/978-1-60566-380-7.ch025

slow in education, there are always pioneers who are willing to try something new.

For many instructors at the post secondary level, the new technology is the Internet, which is a source of information that was not available to senior instructional staff when they were undergraduates. The Internet is not a single technology; it is a collection of technologies that enable and enhance communication as many of the technologies that came before it. The environments created by the integration of Internet technologies with traditional teaching methods are often referred to as "blended" or "hybrid". These two terms are used interchangeably in both the literature and in conversation, leading to some confusion (Riffell and Sibley, 2005; Garrison & Kanuka, 2004) as to why both continue to exist. Through this chapter, the term hybrid will be used as a general descriptor for two types of course designs, multimodal and parallel.

Commonly, hybrid or blended learning courses (and their related classrooms or environments) are described as having some element of traditional face-to-face interaction as well as some element of online support or interaction as part of the course delivery (Riffell and Sibley, 2005; Garrison & Kanuka, 2004). In these environments, the choice of content delivery may be dictated by the instructor, or it may be up to the student depending on the instructor's own willingness to adapt their course material to alternative delivery formats. As there can be great variation of this mix, hybrid learning as a term may best be used to describe a range of environments that incorporate differing amounts of face-to-face and computer mediated interaction. In combining the two modes, perhaps a better descriptor than the currently used terms of blended or hybrid, would be "multimodal". Looking at course designs ranging from completely off line (face-to-face) to completely online (virtualized), multimodal course designs would be those that sit in the middle.

In multimodal environments, the use of the secondary mode of interaction is often limited to predefined experiences, and there is often little consideration given to student initiated interaction either face-to-face or online. In addition to asynchronous technologies provided by Course Management Systems (CMS) such as Blackboard's WebCT, these courses are now able to make use of Virtual Classroom Technologies (VCT) such as Elluminate. Keegan *et.al.* (2005) concluded that virtual classrooms have great potential as they are able to leverage the respective advantages of all available classroom systems. These virtual learning environments provide an opportunity for more interaction between students and instructors than asynchronous technologies alone. It should be noted that these benefits will only be seen if the pedagogy is the driving principle not the technology.

Nascent to the multimodal course designs that have interaction modes dictated by the instructor is the "parallel learning environment". These environments generally have all, or at least the majority, of their content online. They also provide a venue for face-to-face time between the instructor and other students in addition to an online environment. A parallel learning environment is a truly unique course design, which allows students to choose how they access their course materials and interact with each other. Students could choose to attend class in person or through the virtual classroom system. Some students could choose to discuss ideas over chat, while others may use in-class discussion, with both groups of students being able to carry on the exchange of ideas using a threaded discussion board within their CMS. If the technology is available, students who prefer the online format may also be able to access the face-to-face classroom through synchronous technologies. This configuration could also allow the instructor to be online with students meeting face to face. This is of course a significant step forward for the instructor. Table 1 depicts the differentiation of hybrid course designs and how the multimodal and parallel course designs relate to each other.

Table 1. A continuum of hybrid course designs/learning environments

<table>
<tr><td>Face-to-Face</td><td>Multimodal</td><td>Virtualized</td></tr>
<tr><td colspan="3">Instructor defined interactions</td></tr>
<tr><td colspan="3">Participant defined interactions</td></tr>
<tr><td>Face-to-Face</td><td>Parallel</td><td>Virtualized</td></tr>
</table>

Students are among the main drivers of technology adoption on many campuses (Garrison & Vaughan, 2008). Though the final decision to adopt any given technology rests with the instructor, department, or faculty, student demand is one of the main determining factors (Tetiwat & Huff, 2002). Bonk *et.al.* (2005) found that students prefer course delivery models that allow them to determine to a great degree the composition of their learning environment. Goldberg (2004) and others have noted that students will choose courses based on convenience: including the time classes are offered and the mode in which they are offered.

Increasingly, students appear to prefer courses that have an online component. This is not to say that all students choose their courses based on the availability of online material, as many students still have some preference for face-to-face methods. Traditional environments are familiar, and students feel that they can connect with the instructor, give and receive feedback, or influence the direction of a class. Despite trepidations surrounding not being able to connect with the instructor or other students, technology integration through the use of asynchronous tools that are a part of CMS are still viewed in a positive manner by students (Jennings, 2005).

Ideally, regardless of how much technology is integrated into a course, the technology should never become the focus. As technology fades to the background and as the delivery of course material becomes independent of time, location, and eventually even device, hybrid learning environments will start to become far more common. Location free and time independent learning that leverages available technologies in a seamless manner is the holy grail of the teaching and learning enterprise, not only eLearning. Hybrid teaching/learning models attempt to bring the content of a course to the student in as meaningful and convenient a manner as possible. In so doing, allowing both the instructor and student to focus on content, rather than the many other factors that are a reality in education today (Goldberg, 2004, Bonk 2005, Jennings 2005).

This chapter features a number of case studies and concludes with a parallel course design that was implemented as a pilot at the University of Alberta. The Center for Health Promotion Studies in co-operation with the Faculty of Education and with the support of the Office of the Vice Provost of Information Technology collaborated on an ambitious project. The goal of this project was to create a time and location agnostic, well supported, and ultimately relevant course for students while minimizing the learning curve for the instructor and technology support staff. This successful pilot of a parallel learning environment provided some valuable insights for moving beyond the pilot and into regular production.

This chapter also provides background and examples for those wishing to move courses, or parts of courses online. We begin with ways to describe course content as well as goals and suggestions for creating hybrid teaching/learning environments. Bonk *et.al.* (2005) correctly noted,

...the forms and functions of blended learning are simultaneously mind boggling and inspiring .... The promises (and, hopefully, the benefits) of blended learning are extensive. For instance, some

promote increased learning, others point to the reduction in the need for brick and mortar, and still others allude to engagement, collaboration, success, ownership, and higher quality learning. Further research and innovation in the blended learning arena will help sort out the key contributions, benefits, and impact areas. (p. 552)

BACKGROUND

In determining how to arrive at a hybrid design, instructors must first be able to identify the type of instructional design that they are starting with. Traditional environments have classically made use of simple communication and representation tools to deliver content. Classic examples of these methods include: didactic delivery in a large lecture hall, hands-on-experience in a lab, print materials or textbooks in distance education. These learning environments can be categorized into three basic groupings: High Think, High Touch and High Tech.

- High Think courses are typified by lectures and often make use of thought experiments, descriptive examples and some multimedia.
- High Touch courses involve a lab environment where students manipulate equipment and materials as part of their learning process.
- High Tech courses, while seemingly representing the hybrid environments are actually updated distance or correspondence based learning environments from the past that focus on student directed learning through the use of online applications, VCT, and content that has been specifically adapted for use online.

Types of Traditional Environments

High Think

Best represented by the lecture hall, High Think involves a teacher lecturing to a group of students on a particular topic who may or may not be paying attention, taking notes, or following the arguments that the instructor is making. These classes follow a time tested and very cost effective model (at least in terms of total instructor time vs. number of students) that can be extended as far as a voice can be made to reach. One lecturer piped into several halls may reach several hundred students simultaneously. There is no limit to the type of content that can be delivered in this manner so long as it can be described using language that is understood by the group. High Think course designs depend largely on the skill of the instructor to communicate the content, so more skilled orators may be able to move through content faster than those who are not as skilled. High Think may not be the most effective for all types of content, but it will not completely fail any content either (Fyreniu *et.al.*, 2005).

High Touch

High Touch refers to hands-on, lab or workshop based experiences. It allows students to learn from an expert or qualified resource how to perform a task using specific equipment or techniques. High Touch learning environments often leverage multiple resources to provide students with concrete experiences (Haury & Rillero, 1994). Students tend to have a reasonable amount of control in these learning environments as they are often able to move through the content at their own pace.

Lab-based environments are however notoriously costly and not every field of study lends itself to hands-on exploration in a lab. Large scale phenomena and those experiments that involve ethical consideration are possible, but not in the typical space, time, or budget allotted to single term course. High Touch environments provide enormous benefits in terms of experience, but are limited in scope compared to lecture-based learning.

Evaluating the learning resulting from High Touch environments is more difficult than the learning from traditional High Think environments. Simply being able to complete a lab procedure will not always reveal whether learning objectives have been achieved. Haury & Rillero (1995) discussed assessment techniques for these environments, and they continue to improve. Collaborative projects, learning portfolios, reflective journals, and peer review are but a few options when it comes to assessing performance-based learning objectives that are typical in High Touch environments (Conway *et.al.*, 1993; Goldfinch, 1994; Garrison & Vaughan, 2008).

High Tech

Distance or correspondence based education models were among the first to take advantage of new communication technologies. The development of the Internet has been a boon to these course designs where the terms "distance" and "correspondence" have largely been replaced by eLearning. High Tech course designs typically use self guided, modular instruction that can be delivered to students with minimal instructor involvement. This model is attractive to many administrators as supposedly a single instructor can handle a large number of students with minimal time investment after course materials are prepared. Students however often find these High Tech environments isolating and many fail to complete these courses for that very reason. Some students however, thrive on the independence and have an incredibly positive experience, as they are able to fit the demands of the course in and around their other life roles (working, home/family, leisure). Typically, instructors who are highly involved with these course designs find that they require a significant time investment, contrary to the impression that many administrators may have.

Types of Hybridization

Courses and delivery methods are not readily interchangeable. It is best to identify the type of course that is being adapted before selecting the type of hybridization. Traditional courses may fall into one of three general categories: "High Think", "High Touch" and "High Tech". Once identified, each of the traditional categories have unique ways to move along the hybridization pathway.

A High Think course would be similar to the traditional "chalk and talk" approach where the instructor is the leader and the students are largely passive, unless polled by the instructor by some means (e.g., Q & A, discussion in pairs or small groups, clickers). Such courses are good candidates for multimodal delivery, with supplementary materials being delivered online. If however, the instructor would like to have more interaction with the students these are ideal types of courses to be delivered in parallel or to be virtualized. Once hybridized, these courses resemble many of the modern distance education course offerings around the world.

High Touch courses are best categorized as lab-based courses that require the use of specialized equipment. These courses can make great use of simulations that can recreate some laboratory experiences and are ideal candidates for multimodal delivery. Because of a need to manipulate actual equipment in other types of labs these courses are not ideal candidates for wholly online or parallel delivery.

High Tech courses are characterized as those that are student directed, following instructional designs that originated in distance education. Increasingly these courses are making use of virtual classroom technologies to augment the other synchronous or asynchronous tools that are often part of the CMS that is used to house these courses. Offering a multimodal or parallel delivery option can in a seemingly "backward" step, advance these courses that are already online. These delivery models can help those students who feel isolated or need additional structure in their learning environment. Once a starting course design has been categorized, a hybridization type can be selected, followed by training the instructor and potential support staff to ramp up to hybrid learning.

Typical Hybridization Pathways

Often instructors struggle with finding time to deliver content in a different way or increasing amounts of content within a limited amount of time. Students will struggle with how to fit new methods of course delivery around their other responsibilities. Administrators struggle with limited resources: availability of capable instructors, sufficient space, and increasing enrollments to name but a few. While hybrid course designs will not be the solution to all these concerns, the best elements of traditional and modern environments can be integrated in hybrid courses to create very satisfactory solutions.

High Think environments might face enrollment issues with either too many or too few students or too much content to deliver. These environments are ideal candidates for being hybridized to any of the three hybrid environments – multimodal, parallel or virtual. These courses can make use of multimodal environments to increase contact time with students and to provide additional resources in an attempt to move through additional material modes. Multimodal environments can increase instructor/student and student/student contact time, provide additional resources, and increase the amount of material that can be covered. If the number of instructors is an issue, High Think environments can be virtualized to allow those students who are able to move through material on their own to do so and to provide those students who require more assistance with synchronous support through VCT. Parallel environments may also work for High Think courses where off campus students may want or need to attend classes with those who are able to attend the class in the traditional manner. Parallel delivery may also be a viable option if both traditional and distance/online sections of the same course are being offered and instructors would like to combine the students into one class.

High Touch classes are ideal candidates for multimodal course designs as they require some element of face-to-face instruction. If resources exist aspects of the course can be simulated, allowing some High Touch courses to be completely virtualized. Complete virtualization using simulations must be integrated with traditional High Touch classes. This hybridization pathway is not dissimilar to the way that pilots are trained in motion simulators before they enter a real cockpit. This way, precious resources are not consumed as the student works through the introductory stages of their learning.

High Tech courses can also be hybridized, even though this may seem counter intuitive. These courses can, if the resources exist, be delivered in parallel with face-to-face courses similar to hybridized High Think courses. This may be a solution where there are low or unpredictable enrollment patterns, or low completion rates as there may be something missing in the learning experience that can be regained by introducing regular, scheduled contact with both students and the instructor using VCT.

Benefits and Challenges of Hybrid Teaching Learning Environments

Published descriptions of creating hybrid environments provide many useful insights into the motivation, advantages, and challenges faced in the development and delivery of these environments. The challenges are worth confronting as students have described hybrid environments as the most effective approach in addressing their needs (Jennings (2005).

Tsang *et.al.* (1999) noted that virtual classrooms offer a solution for those individuals who are unable to attend regular classes. They also correctly predicted, as did Goldberg (2004), that hybrid learning environments would become popular within a decade. Both Tsang *et.al.* (1999) and Goldberg (2004) pointed out that the use of collaboration tools such as video conferencing, shared whiteboard, and chat rooms are key to the success of online delivery.

Bonk et.al. (2002) provided a unique look at various types of hybrid course design by studying the same cohort of students as they moved through asynchronous, synchronous online environments, and finally a traditional face-to-face environment. These authors noted that substantial changes are required of everyone involved. However, issues with the use of computer mediated communication declined with the addition of face-to-face sessions that provided the human reference point for later interactions. Subsequently Boora *et.al.* (2005) included a face-to-face component within a graduate level course partially to address these concerns (Master of Educational Studies FAQ, 2008).

Students in Bonk *et.al.*'s (2002) study appreciated the flexibility of the (asynchronous) first phase and some commented that they were able to transfer skills from the synchronous phase to the face-to-face phase with ease. Students, who may not have gained as much from the synchronous phase, felt that they learned the most from the face-to-face phase. Instructors felt that the ability to give specific online feedback was a great bonus. They also appreciated the standardization of content and flexibility in the facilities afforded for problem solving, knowledge application, and student communications.

Continuing from these findings, Bonk *et.al.* (2002) arrived at set considerations for course design, these included: communications with students, design of content and working with technology. With respect to communicating with students, Bonk *et.al.* (2002) suggested providing direct feedback over email was most effective. Content should be targeted to the students and in a constructivist manner, building on the student's prior knowledge and experience, selected to match what the students can apply directly. Managing the content in this manner also ensures that students are not overwhelmed with material that is not relevant to their learning. Students should also have opportunities to demonstrate their learning in a meaningful context, i.e. a lab setting with similar equipment and materials that is familiar to them, or that was used during their education. Finally, the course should be designed to use technology that is available and tested within the context where it will be deployed.

Bonk *et.al.* (2002) noted that blending technologies in the classroom can have an impact on students' social identity and social relationships, team-building, and decision-making, as well as the mentoring, scaffolding, and overall role of the instructor. As a result, blended courses are learner centric with project-based learning and other active learning strategies employed to provide choices and opportunities for students to demonstrate their knowledge. However, courses in which content is mostly or entirely delivered online are often negatively affected by motivation and retention issues.Students may find that real life concerns such as jobs, families, or other occupations start to take precedence over what was originally to be class work or study time.

Bonk's work underlines the need to ensure an understanding of the technologies to be used in the delivery of each course. This work also helps to enhance our understanding of the types of hybridization course designs that could be employed along with some of the benefits and challenges that face both students and instructors.

Considerations Regarding Communications

Nain-Shing *et.al.*'s (2004) findings were similar to those identified by Bonk (2002). These included logistical, instructional, and economical advantages for the student and conveniences for the instructor. For example, the flexibility of being able to use and reuse recorded material within a single course, or potentially through a range of courses. Recorded materials are almost always used in asynchronous delivery, but as Nain-Shing *et.al.* (2004) pointed out, an increasing number of online courses are using synchronous technologies as well.

Combining synchronous and asynchronous elements in a multimodal course design provides, according to Nain-Shing *et.al.* (2004), one more benefit for the classroom environment. Synchronous tools act as a means to help mitigate feelings of isolation among the student population and can also help reduce the negative impact online delivery can have on students' attention. (Krogstie, 2005).

Keegan *et.al.* (2005) provided some insight as to why students may feel less isolated with the addition of synchronous technologies. One of the benefits of using synchronous tools within multimodal course design is that it creates a learning environment similar to the traditional classroom. In a traditional classroom, there is real-time feedback to students as the instructor interacts both verbally and non-verbally. Moving online, into the multimodal environment, using both voice and text, students are able to participate through several communication channels simultaneously. With these channels in place, students are able to feel comfortable in environments that may be new to them in an academic context. Once comfortable, students are able to participate meaningfully within a course, hopefully remaining engaged and motivated within the learning environment.

Keegan *et.al.* (2005) raised a number of points about successful transitions from face-to-face to a hybrid environment. Beyond the basic need for testing and support of hardware and software, there should also be a shared understanding of the capabilities and limitations of the technology by everyone involved. Particular attention should be paid to sound as the principle means of interactivity and ensuring adequate support is available so that all participants can focus on their particular roles. While directly transitioning a traditional lecture to a virtual lecture is possible, the development of interactive or graphical elements that can help with pacing and maintaining students' attention should be considered. This will help those learners who generally have shorter attention spans online than with face-to-face delivery.

Shorter attention spans in the online environment may be due to the loss of certain cues that are present in the traditional classroom. So even though students describe blended environments (Jennings (2005) as the most effective in addressing their needs, these environments lack non-verbal cues such as hand gestures, poses, smiles, and classroom positioning that could potentially be captured using a video conference tool. However, such cues are lost when using audio tools - a common part of virtual classroom environments. Even if there is video support, the video may only be a "talking head" as the instructor sits at a desk and talks to a screen rather than being broadcast from their traditional place within the classroom as in front of a whiteboard. Students receive their cues from instructors as they track them around the room, laugh at jokes, or enthusiastically raise their hands in response to questions. As valuable as these cues are, they are often overlooked when moving to multimodal instruction. These cues, though seemingly trivial, provide important feedback to those involved in the class and care should be taken to retain them. One strategy to replicate these signals is through the use of emoticons in asynchronous discussions as well as in synchronous chats that can occur "out of channel" in many virtual classroom systems. Replication of these cues does however rely on a conscious design decision to include, as part of instructors' activities during the delivery of the course, a way to monitor and incorporate non-verbal cues as they pass among students and between the students and instructors (Benbunan-

Fich 2002: 94, Fjuk 1998 as quoted in Keegan *et.al.*, 2005, Jennings 2005).

CASE STUDIES

High Think Case Study: United Kingdom

The Salters Chemistry program, which originated in 1983 at the University of York (Bennett & Luben, 2006), created a decidedly High Think approach to chemistry instruction. At the high school level, traditional chemistry courses are delivered through a mix of in-class, home and lab work, a High Touch design. The Salters program removes the lab work from the mix in favour of class discussions, case studies, context-based problems, and other more student-centered activities. In 2005, Bennett et.al. published a study describing the preferences of 222 chemistry teachers with regards to their teaching styles and attitudes towards Salters Advanced Chemistry in terms of: student and teacher motivation, chemical knowledge and development of concepts, learning activities, assessment, challenge to students and teachers, and teacher support. Overall, teachers agreed that the Salters based course was more motivating both for students and teachers, that it would lead to more students being interested in chemistry and going on to study chemistry at the post-secondary level, and that it would encourage students to become more independent.

One of the major issues teachers had with Salters was that it takes a greater time investment on the part of teachers and students. Planning lessons and learning exercises that are contextually relevant to the students is a corner stone of the Salters curriculum and the student context changes from year to year. Also, because so many of the assessments are not traditional workbooks and quizzes, teachers must employ newer, more varied, and more time consuming methods of student evaluation (Bennett *et.al.*, 2005).

The course described in this case study would be an ideal candidate for being hybridized into a multimodal environment. Additional material and conversations could take place outside the classroom, and new material could be incorporated rather quickly. Depending on the students and the needs of a particular class, this course could also be run virtually or in parallel.

High Tech/High Touch Hybridization Case Study: China

East China University of Science and Technology changed the delivery of their demanding Biochemistry program to include online materials in addition to the textbook that had been created in-house and was already in use. Animations, still images, and multimedia presentations were created to supplement the textbook and made available to the students online. In addition to the resource materials, the online section of the course provided students with a discussion board. The time required to develop these online resources was considerable, but the feedback from the students was extremely positive (Ouyang *et.al.*, 2007).

The adaptation to a multimodal environment in this situation proved to be positive as the students gained the ability to access additional materials outside of a face-to-face classroom environment.

High Tech/High Touch Hybridization Case Study: USA

Parallel environments are significantly different from multimodal environments because they combine parts of traditional face-to-face teaching methods and parts of online methods using synchronous and asynchronous technologies. If students choose to attend a face-to-face lecture they are in a traditional environment with the exception of some additional technology employed within that classroom, Students wanting an online experience are able to make use of synchronous and asynchronous technologies as they move through the course content. These parallel environments, despite the benefits they present in theory, are only recently being created and are facing a number of unresolved issues. Triantafillou *et.al.* (2006) created parallel learning environments using multipoint control units and streaming technology. Though this provided some advantages in terms of structure and flexibility of delivery there were issues with cost, collaboration, and complexity. McFarlin (2008) also created a parallel environment and reported that grades increased in his undergraduate physiology course. McFarlin's class time was split equally for all students between face to face and WebCT. The major difference for the students was the availability of self-paced learning modules based on lectures. Preparing the content took between 16 and 20 hours per lecture.

McFarlin was motivated to create a parallel course environment based on student feedback. Students expressed concerns that the original course was not making use of modern instructional technologies which would give them access to certain course materials outside of class time. Instructional staff responded by delivering half the lectures for the course via the institutional CMS, WebCT. The resources provided in the online lessons included multimedia slideshows that were enhanced through the use of quizzes and audio. Students were only able to progress through the online content if they completed quizzes found inside WebCT and in the PowerPoint presentations, the latter added by using Articulate (McFarlin 2008).

The CMS environment was also enhanced through the use of an avatar to deliver class announcements in a more personal manner to the students. Students were also able to feel more connected with their instructor during face-to-face instruction through the use of student response systems (SRS). By using SRS the instructor was able to gage student comprehension quickly and easily.

McFarlin found that the students who received the hybrid course scored 9.9% higher than those who received the traditional lecture format. As marks were given for different elements within each course a direct comparison cannot be made on the basis of grades. Fortunately, the first and second mid term examinations were the same in both the traditional and the hybrid environments. Students in the hybrid environment scored 10.5% and 17.6% higher than those in the traditional learning environment. It should be noted that the two lecture types were taught during different semesters over the three year analysis with the hybrid course being taught in the latter half.

One of the major drawbacks that McFarlin noted was the time to create the online lectures. A conservative estimate was between 16 and 20 hours of development time per online lecture. However, now that this time has been invested, McFarlin noted that updating these materials should require far less time.

Featured Case Study: Canada

The experiences of Triantafillou *et.al.* (2006) and McFarlin (2008) were similar to what the authors of this chapter experienced with HPS 507 (Public Policy and Health Promotion). From the outset, it was understood that technology was not the most important feature of the course and that as Gašević *et.al.* (2008) eloquently stated, "The complexity of student environments must be managed and students will define 'the best way' to learn". It was understood that this classroom would be a challenging environment and while the intent was to recreate an online experience that was as similar as possible to the face-to-face environment, accommodations were made to ensure the strengths of the respective environments were maximized.

HPS 507 Background

In the spring of 2006, Dr. John Church responded to an internal University of Alberta funding RFP for the Teaching with Technologies Initiative (TTI). The Teaching with Technology Initiative was a new source of support for instructors being pilot-funded through the Office of the Vice-Provost (Information Technology). The goal of the TTI was to assist instructors exploring instructional approaches that are enhanced through the use of leading-edge information and communications technologies, and to provide the instructors with evaluative feedback to improve their teaching practice.

TTI was intended to:

- Facilitate Faculties investigating alternative space designs, teaching methods, and educational technologies.
- Examine the benefits, costs, opportunities, and risks associated with using innovative educational methods and technologies.
- Disseminate teaching strategies, implementation considerations, and findings of the TTI projects to the campus community to promote a greater understanding of the opportunities afforded by information and communications technologies.

Instructors selected to participate in TTI were allocated teaching space in the Telus Building, University of Alberta, and up to twelve hours a week of support from Graduate Assistants (GAs) for the duration of the Fall Term. GAs were intended to set-up classroom technologies, provide technical support during class, and assist in the development of instructional resources. The Telus Building was designed to facilitate multimedia synchronous instruction to both campus-based and distance students, although visual communication with distance students was only possible through video-conferencing at a limited number of fixed sites.

For the Winter 2006 Term, technologies available within the designated TTI classroom in the Telus Building included wireless access, a student response system, dual digital projection, a digital whiteboard, and laptop computers. TTI GAs and instructors worked closely with staff from Academic Information & Communication Technologies (AICT) E-Learning and Classroom Technologies to obtain the tools and training necessary for success.

Health Policy and Health Promotion (HPS 507)

Prior to the TTI initiative, HPS 507 had been offered exclusively to campus-based graduate students for several years and had been taught in one form or another for over ten years. The course was designed to ground the student in the structures and processes associated with public policy, and to facilitate the critical multi-disciplinary evaluation of selected health-related incidents and issues, with a specific emphasis on health promotion. While emphasis was placed on the Canadian context, case examples and general readings come from a variety of international jurisdictions. The course is a core requirement of the Master of Public Health – Health Promotion degree offered through the Centre for Health Promotion Studies, School of Public Health, at the University of Alberta.

Through the content and structure format of this course, the students are expected to learn:

1. To define public policy
2. To identify the components of the public policy process
3. To assess the strengths and weaknesses inherent in the public policy process
4. To critically evaluate the contribution of the public policy process to selected health policy-related incidents
5. To understand how multi-disciplinary frameworks might be applied to assess health policy-related incidents and issues

6. To explore the impact of public policy on health promotion
7. To explore new conceptual ground by extending and extrapolating from the information, ideas, and paradigms.

This course was designed to allow the participants to develop critical thinking skills that are fundamental to assessing the context, process, and the expected and unexpected outcomes associated with health policy. Accordingly, the first half of the course was devoted to establishing a foundational knowledge of public policy through exploration of the structures, processes, and determinants of health policy. This was achieved through a guided-discovery, discussion format supported by weekly readings and guiding questions posted on WebCT. Distance students participated through parallel weekly, web-forum discussions. The second half of the course involved the exploration of health policy issues through guest presentations from practitioner guided discussion, and including a facilitated, interactive simulation exercise and case examples from health promotion practitioners.

The intention of offering this course through the TTI was to create a virtual classroom version of the course to allow distance- and campus-based students to interact simultaneously in either asynchronous or synchronous environments with a single instructor. A total of five campus-based students and six distance students participated in the course. The student furthest away from the University of Alberta was based in Belgium. Both campus-based and distance students were required to interact in both synchronous and asynchronous environments for a certain percentage of the course through the use of WebCT and Elluminate. The objectives of offering HPS 507 in a virtual classroom format were:

- to enhance the linkage between e-learning and campus-based students
- to foster collaborative learning through the delivery of a single graduate course
- to develop a preliminary model for the use of complementary technologies to enhance the overall learning experience of CHPS graduate students.

With the exception of the introductory and concluding classes, and the simulation exercise, students were free to choose which weekly sessions to attend in the alternate delivery mode (asynchronous/synchronous). In addition, many sessions were audio recorded and posted on WebCT for review.

During the simulation exercise, all elements of the virtual classroom were brought into play. Students were divided into two groups, regional health managers and board members, with relatively equal representation from distance and campus-based students in both groups. Because students had to meet outside of regularly scheduled classroom times to prepare for in-class sessions, arriving at a time when everyone could meet on-line and coordinating the facility and support personnel was challenging. One group defaulted to teleconferencing because it was more flexible to coordinate. During the in-class simulation sessions, students were equipped with individual computers so that they could text message with each other during the simulation. Break-out rooms were also used so that each group could run separate WebCT sessions to strategize. The combination of WebCT with voice and text, PowerPoint, and web camera allowed participants to be fully engaged in a real time interaction during the full group aspects of the class.

Students were evaluated on overall participation (5%), simulation exercise participation (15%), simulation exercise written assignment (15%), a mid-term assignment (20%), and a term assignment (45%). Having described the supportive infrastructure and course process, we now turn to outlining the benefits and challenges identified by the students, the main instructor, guest instructors and the technology support person assigned to the course.

Student Perceptions

In general, students found the use of WebCT and Elluminate to be a positive experience with two-thirds of those responding to an exit survey indicating that they would be interested in taking another virtual classroom course. Facilitators identified by students included: the combination of WebCT, Elluminate and Web camera, especially for distance students. For distance students, this was their first experience with a course in which they could see the instructor and other students interacting in a classroom setting. While the quality of the video feed remained somewhat choppy, distance students appreciated being able to have text, voice and visual simultaneously. They recognized that the ability to offer this in a smoother format would likely improve in the future.

Students also identified several disadvantages related to the virtual classroom. For example, coordinating schedules to allow distance students to attend more synchronous sessions than normal and for campus-based students to interact with distance students in the asynchronous environment was challenging. Schedule coordination proved particularly challenging for the two-class simulation exercise. For distance students, participating in the synchronous environment required more time commitment than normal. For campus-based students, participating in the asynchronous environment added to the overall course workload. As one student described it, "when you have to put your thoughts in writing in an interactive on-line forum, you really have to think about what you are going to say". In the synchronous learning setting, verbal responses are more spontaneous. Although unrelated to the technology specifically, students would have appreciated a clearer understanding of the time commitment required prior to the beginning of the course.

Presenters' Perceptions

Dr. Helen Madill, the Graduate Programs Coordinator, conducted interviews with the presenters and analyzed the transcripts. Of the five presenters who used Elluminate, two had also used PowerPoint, two had also used web cameras, and one had used a lap top computer. All guest presenters had previous experience with teleconference and videoconference technology. Four of the five guest presenters had done face-to-face presentations previously in the course.

For presenters, the major facilitators to the blended learning approach included: ability to engage distance students as part of the in-class experience; the overall reliability of the technology and technical support; TTI funding support; no travel costs for distance participants; and instructor leadership during question and answer sessions.

Potential barriers included: lack of efficiency in signing on distance students; lack of ability to read body language and other visual cues normally associated with face-to-face interaction; periodic glitches with the technology (i.e., individual loss of connectivity); classroom design was not well suited to the number of people or course pedagogy – room was to large, audio and lighting not appropriate; general time lag when compared to face-to-face interaction; and better briefing for presenters on the technology and its impact on presentations (i.e., need to distribute hand-outs electronically in advance).

For the course instructor, the amount of time and preparation required to interact with students on-line, including participation and assessment of weekly on-line postings, proved daunting when added onto the preparation for and delivery of in-class sessions. Having more time in advance to prepare and to work with the technology support person on process and uploading of course materials would have improved delivery. The short preparation timelines meant that the instructor was not able to adequately communicate with students in advance of the course about what the weekly process would look like. Although he had taken a WebCT training course prior to the start of the course, the instructor was largely unfamiliar with teaching in the Internet environment. Having said this, the instructor was impressed by how well the various technologies worked together and the possibilities presented by the virtual classroom. From his point of view the virtual classroom provided students with a richer, although more intense, learning environment.

Many presenters found the Elluminate process distracting, particularly the texting and question and answer procedures. Those with the greatest amount of experience with university level teaching/learning situations were the most positive about the technologies that were employed. With the exception of the instructor, presenters did not see using Elluminate for other purposes as they already had access to excellent teleconference and videoconferencing systems in their own work environments, were used to using these systems, and considered that their agencies were fortunate to have ready access to these technologies.

Main Technical Issues

During the course, the technical support person kept a log of all reported issues and solutions. The log is summarized below:

1. Connectivity: Several distance students would frequently lose connection to the Elluminate meeting. All students were asked what kind of connection they used and the GA determined that the students having difficulty staying in the meeting were using a computer connected via a home wireless network. Although Elluminate is typically not network intensive, wireless connections can have a wide range of problems associated with their signal quality. Any of these factors may have caused disconnects and students were advised to use a wired connection for increased stability.
2. Inability to reconnect if a meeting was lost past the boundary time: When a meeting was created, the user can designate a 'boundary time,' which signifies how many minutes before and after the meeting's timeframe a user can connect to the meeting. In one instance, class continued later than the official end time and a student lost their connection. Due to the time being past the 15 minute boundary, they were not able to reconnect to the meeting. Either staying to designated class times, or informing the meeting administrator if class is likely to continue later than officially planned can solve this problem.
3. Elluminate text messaging: Elluminate's text messaging feature was often used by distance students to chat before class began. However, these messages do not fade away over time nor does Elluminate post a time stamp along with the message. Several guest presenters commented that it seemed rude for people to be chatting during class using text when in fact the messages were conversations that had occurred before class began. At this time, there is nothing in particular that can be done about this other than being aware that messages may have been present in the window for some time even if a person did not initially notice them.
4. Feedback/echoing: This often occurred if a distance learner's microphone was open and they were not using a headset. If another person spoke, their voice was transmitted through all speakers and then was picked up by any open microphones, thus being retransmitted throughout the audio circuit. There are several possible solutions to this problem. The easiest solution is to ensure all distance learners have a headset with a microphone and earpiece. This ensures that only the speaker's voice will be transmitted. Another option is to select "must mute speakers when talking" in the audio menu. This setting will mute a user's speakers whenever their microphone is released. This option may be problematic if anyone else tries to speak or interrupt the participant as they will be unable to hear anything until they stop transmitting.

5. Room setup: Figuring out the best equipment situation for different meetings and room setups can be very challenging. In this class situation the tabletop conference microphones worked very well. However, students had to be careful in several ways: they could not drop items on the desk such as books, water bottles, etc, and had to remain mindful to speak loudly and clearly so that learners at a distance could understand what was being said. Due to the open mic situation of the room, feedback could easily occur, which meant that at all times someone had to be monitoring the computer to which the microphones fed. This proved to be less of an issue as both the assistant and instructor became more familiar with the technology over the course of the term. However, the Telus facilities were designed for a specific purpose that did not match the requirements for delivering the course. The large room was not well-suited to a smaller, group-discussion format. The microphone system was not ideal for group discussion. The lighting was not ideal for a small group of students.
6. On-line grading system: The instructor was unable to use the on-line grading system in a fashion that would permit feedback to students while ensuring individual confidentiality.

FUTURE TRENDS AND CONCLUSIONS

By identifying the strengths of an existing course, and understanding the weaknesses of the various technologies involved within the three forms of hybrid course designs, instructors and designers can work together to create a course that meets most of the needs of those involved. This premise, while simple, should form the basis for any decision to move a course to the hybrid environment. Though parallel learning environments may be attractive solutions, evidence from the case studies suggests that parallel environments require a significant resource investment that cannot be ignored before the course is offered and throughout the delivery. Multimodal courses require significant investment to develop resources before they are deployed, but then require annual review and updating. Virtualized courses are resource dependant the technology used can be a significant cost in terms of technical and student support personnel.

After identifying the weaknesses that one would want to avoid in the design of a new course, the advantages of each of the three environments can be leveraged. Multimodal designs have advantages related to students and instructors familiarity with the main mode of instruction and allow for additional support modes to be added. Multimodal courses would include face-to-face courses with significant online resources or online courses where participants meet occasionally over the course of the term. Parallel courses are able to incorporate the best of face-to-face and online instruction. While complicated to manage, the parallel learning environment might be ideal for situations where students or instructors are unable to be at a specific location at the same time, but are able to co-ordinate schedules. Virtual environments offer students complete control of time and some freedom for instructors.

The move toward hybridization of course delivery also suggests a move toward another type of hybridization. Interdisciplinary courses are gaining popularity particularly in higher education as the differentiation between nascent disciplines starts to erode. Even between disciplines that are not related on the surface, some options for interdisciplinary work are starting to emerge. For example, in increased use of the Scientific Method in Arts to design courses to properly explore and deliver the content of these collaborations, hybrid learning environments might be the ideal means of delivery. Likely, these interdisciplinary courses will benefit most from multimodal designs, but they might also be well suited for parallel or virtual designs.

The trend toward globalization and interdisciplinary studies is increasing. Not offering students courses that are reflective of this reality is irresponsible on the part of those institutions that are tasked with preparing future leaders. Wieman and Perkins (2005) suggested that not connecting students with the "real world" is a disservice as it will lead to lack of student engagement and content that is irrelevant to their world. The extensive use of communication technologies in all hybrid environments goes a long way to making these "real world" connections, as it allows students an opportunity to communicate their needs and their world views to instructors who are then able to create materials and learning opportunities that have "real world" applications. In creating these learning opportunities, instructors should take care not to simply add one mode onto another as an "extra" (Garrison & Vaughan, 2008).

Thomas's (2007) idea of transliteracy will become increasingly important as instructors begin to connect content with "real world" issues facing students. The use of Web2.0 tools like blogs and wikis in addition to services like YouTube and social networks like Facebook can and should be integrated into hybrid courses. Instructors and students who are able to become transliterate are able to communicate their ideas in a host of new ways beyond text and the spoken word.

Trends in hybridization of course designs will certainly continue as the needs of learners, instructors and administrators change. When moving toward hybrid teaching/learning, it is best to consider the following:

- To hybridize any course element, a large investment of time will be required
- To instruct a hybrid course, a large amount of instructor and (potentially) course support time will be required
- Appropriate investment of time will result in great benefits for students, who ultimately will bring in additional resources for instructors and administrators
- Technology alone is not the answer, the pedagogical needs of courses, students, and instructors must be considered in any new course design. Technology must then be selected chosen based on those needs

REFERENCES

Bennett, J., Gräsel, C., Parchmann, I., & Waddington, D. (2005). Context-based and conventional approaches to teaching chemistry: comparing teachers' views. *International Journal of Science Education, 27*(13), 1521–1547. doi:10.1080/09500690500153808

Bonk, C. J., Kim, K., & Zeng, T. (2005). In C. J. Bonk & C. R. Graham (Eds.), *Handbook of blended learning: Global perspectives, local designs* (pp. 550-568). New York: Pfeiffer Publishing.

Bonk, C. J., Olson, T. M., Wisher, R. A., & Orvis, K. L. (2002). Learning from focus groups: An examination of blended learning. *Journal of Distance Education, 17*(3), 97–118.

Boora, R., Peacock, K., Davies, J., Carbonaro, M., Bainbridge, J., & Snart, F. (2005). Implementing a synchronous learning system in distance programs: Impressions from within a faculty of education. In G. Richards (Ed.), *Proceedings of the World Conference on E-Learning in Corporate, Government, Healthcare, and Higher Education 2005* (pp. 546-559). Chesapeake, VA: AACE.

Conway, R., Kember, D., Sivan, A., & Wu, M. (1993). Peer assessment of an individual's contribution to a group project. *Assessment & Evaluation in Higher Education, 18*(1), 45–56. doi:10.1080/0260293930180104

Fyrenius, A., Bergdahl, B., & Silen, C. (2005). Lectures in problem-based learning–why, when and how? An example of interactive lecturing that stimulates meaningful learning. *Medical Teacher, 27*, 61–65. doi:10.1080/01421590400016365

Garrison, D., & Kanuka, H. (2004). Blended learning: Uncovering its transformative potential in higher education. *The Internet and Higher Education*, 7(2), 95–105. doi:10.1016/j.iheduc.2004.02.001

Garrison, D. R., & Vaughan, N. D. (2008). *Blended learning in higher education.* Jossey-Bass: San Francisco, CA.

Gašević, D., Jovanović, J., Knight, C., & Richards, G. (n.d.) *Ontologies for effective use of context in e-learning settings*. Retrieved February 22, 2008, from http://elluminate.athabascau.ca/play/cidersession-080118.jnlp

Goldberg, M. (2004). Learning technologies, past, present and future. In *Tenth Australian World Wide Web Conference*. Retrieved February 22, 2008, from http://ausweb.scu.edu.au/aw04/papers/edited/goldberg/Ausweb.ppt

Goldfinch, J. (1994). Further developments in peer assessment of group projects. *Assessment & Evaluation in Higher Education, 19*(1), 29–35. doi:10.1080/0260293940190103

Haury, D. L., & Rillero, P. (1994). *Perspectives of hands-on science teaching*. Retrieved February 1, 2008 from http://www.ncrel.org/sdrs/areas/issues/content/cntareas/science/eric/eric-toc.htm

Hybrid Learning. (2008). *Hybrid Learning*. Retrieved April 10, 2008, from http://www4.uwm.edu/ltc/hybrid/about_hybrid/index.cfm

Jennings, A. (2005). *Implementing an Integrated Web-Based Synchronous eLearning Collaboration Platform at Tertiary Level for Part-Time Mature Evening Students*. Retrieved February 25, 2008 from https://www.cs.tcd.ie/publications/tech-reports/reports.05/TCD-CS-2005-67.pdf

Judith, B., & Lubben, F. (2006). Context-based chemistry: The salters approach. *International Journal of Science Education, 28*(9), 999–1015. doi:10.1080/09500690600702496

Keegan, D., Schwenke, E., Fritsch, H., Kenny, G., Kismihók, G., Bíró, M., & Gábor, A. Ó'Suilleabháin, G., & Nix, J. (2005). Virtual classrooms in educational provision: synchronous elearning systems for European institutions. *ZIFF Papiere, 126*. Retrieved February 23, 2008, from http://www.fernuni-hagen.de/ZIFF/synchronous.pdf

Krogstie, B., & Bygstad, B. (2005). Introducing a virtual classroom in a master course: Lessons learned. In *Proceedings of the Third International Conference on Education and Information Systems: Technologies and Applications (EISTA)*, Orlando, Florida.

Master of Educational Studies FAQ. (2008). University of Alberta. Retrieved April 9, 2008, from http://www.mes.ualberta.ca/general/frequentlyaskedquestions.html#residencies

McFarlin, B. K. (2008). Hybrid lecture-online format increases student grades in an undergraduate exercise physiology course at a large urban university. *Advances in Physiology Education, 32*, 86–91. doi:10.1152/advan.00066.2007

Nian-Shing, C. Kinshuk, Hsiu-Chia, K., & Taiyu L. (2004). Synchronous learning model over the Internet. *Proceedings of IEEE International Conference on Advanced Learning Technologies* (pp. 505-509). Retrieved February 25, 2008 from http://ieeexplore.ieee.org/xpls/abs_all.jsp?arnumber=1357466

Ouyang, L., Ou, L., & Zhang, Y. (2007). An integrated strategy for teaching biochemistry to biotechnology specialty students. *Biochemistry and Molecular Biology Education, 35*(4), 267–271. doi:10.1002/bmb.67

Riffell, S., & Sibley, D. (2005). Using web-based instruction to improve large undergraduate biology courses: an evaluation of a hybrid course format. *Computers & Education, 44*(3), 217–235. doi:10.1016/j.compedu.2004.01.005

Tetiwat, O., & Huff, S. (2002). Determinants of the adoption of web-based educational technology: A preliminary data analysis of New Zealand tertiary educators. In *Proceedings of the International Conference on Computers in Education (ICCE)*. Washington, DC: IEEE Computer Society.

Thomas, S., Joseph, C., Laccetti, J., Mason, B., Mills, S., Perril, S., & Pullinger, K. (2007). Transliteracy: Crossing divides. *First Monday.* Retrieved March28, 2008 from http://www.uic.edu/htbin/cgiwrap/bin/ojs/index.php/fm/article/view/2060/1908

Triantafillou, V., Markopoulos, P., Villios, K., & Ilaridis, P. (2006). Synchronous e-learning room: Scenarios, tools and usage. *Fourth International Conference on Multimedia and Information and Communication Technologies in Education, 2*, 983-987. Retrieved February 25, 2008, from http://www.formatex.org/micte2006/pdf/983-987.pdf

Tsang, H. W., Hung, L. M., & Ng, S. C. (1999). A multimedia distance learning system on the Internet. In *1999 IEEE International Conference on Systems, Man, and Cybernetics* (pp. 243-246). Retrieved February 19, 2008, from http://ieeexplore.ieee.org/xpls/abs_all.jsp?arnumber=825265

KEY TERMS AND DEFINITIONS

High Tech: A student centred learning approach that is primarily self-directed, self-paced and technology mediated.

High Think: A teacher centred didactic means of educating students. It requires only a teacher to speak and students to listen. It may include other educational aids such as slides or writing as on a whiteboard, but these things aren't required.

High Touch: A student centred teaching method that involves students doing hands on exercises to gain knowledge in a specific domain. It is typically overseen by a subject matter expert and makes learning a multi modal experience.

Multimodal Learning Environment: A course that is primarily delivered in one mode, with a secondary mode being used to deliver enrichment, also referred to as Blended or Hybrid Learning. Examples of this include a traditional lecture with resources available to students through a CMS.

Parallel Learning Environment: A course designed to have students move through either face to face or online only content at the same time, interacting with each other using VCT or in person as allowed for by social or spatial constraints.

Student Response Systems (SRS): AKA "clickers", are RF or IR based remotes that are used in a classroom by students to answer questions posed by the instructor.

Transliteracy: The ability to use multiple platforms, such as the Internet, television, instructors, textbooks, etc, to assimilate and integrate information into a coherent understanding of a topic.

Virtual Classroom Technology (VCT): Synchronous technologies that create an environment that allows individuals within a class to share audio, video and text. These environments attempt to recreate as many facets of the face-to-face classroom as possible on a screen.

Chapter 26
Knowledge Management for Hybrid Learning

Stefanie Sieber
University of Bamberg, Germany

Andreas Henrich
University of Bamberg, Germany

ABSTRACT

The merging of knowledge management and hybrid learning has gained more and more attraction and has been put in the focus of interests lately, for the simple reason that both areas can benefit from each other. As a result, this chapter deals with knowledge management for hybrid learning. This chapter begins with a short introduction, followed by a brief clarification showing our understanding of hybrid learning. Afterwards, knowledge and associated attributes are defined precisely – definitions are derived and taxonomies for knowledge are described. This section closes with a first reflection on knowledge in the context of hybrid learning. Subsequently, the authors take a closer look at knowledge management by introducing different schools of thought and models for knowledge management. Opportunities to delve deeper into the subject individually are offered passim. The main part of the chapter provides a comprehensive view of knowledge management for hybrid learning. The described features range from general conclusions to theoretical aspects, exemplary projects, and finally practical aspects – previous deliberations are brought together, current insights concerning the research perspective are described and tools as well as techniques which foster knowledge management for hybrid learning are presented. Finally, a critical reflection as well as an outlook and some thoughts concerning future issues conclude this chapter.

INTRODUCTION

Knowledge management as well as learning in general or e-learning and hybrid learning in particular are two areas that have developed independently in the past. Lately these fields are starting to converge, and theories, methods, and findings are being combined. These joint considerations benefit both areas with new insights and enhancements but also increase the complexity and number of obstacles for

DOI: 10.4018/978-1-60566-380-7.ch026

Figure 1. Shift in learning paradigms reflected by number of existing systems (Graham, 2005, p. 6)

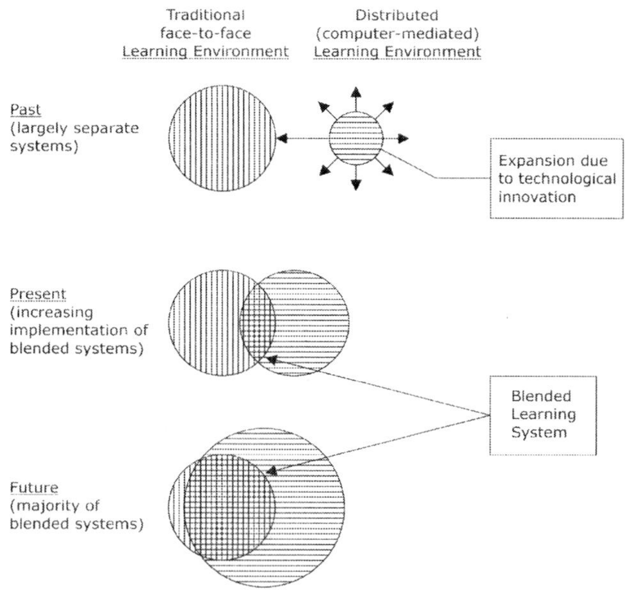

those interested in these topics and those in charge of setting up a proper solution for a specific setting. Individually, the area of hybrid learning already brings with it a vast number of settings. The virtual parts of learning can range from a minimum support up to a broadly considered, pedagogically sophisticated offer. Of course traditional learning can be scaled the same way.

Figure 1 shows the shift of learning paradigms by summing up the resulting number of systems assigned to each paradigm, and it gives an impression of the consequential increasing importance of blended and hybrid systems, respectively.

Knowledge management, on the other hand, can be strictly formalized and strategically grounded in a learning institution, or can be more informal, dynamic and self-paced. If an attempt is made to combine these two already complex and partially opposing areas, it is just a simple matter of mathematics to realize that complexity increases and the number of possibilities is overwhelming.

The main objective of this chapter is therefore not to describe one way of setting up knowledge management for hybrid learning, but instead to build a continuum of possibilities and opportunities that knowledge management offers for hybrid learning – and the other way round – considering a variety of important aspects that differ from one setting to another. Depending on the particular instance, one setting can turn out to be extremely helpful while it is hardly of use for a different problem or field of application.

HYBRID LEARNING

Real learning gets to the heart of what it means to be human.

Through learning we re-create ourselves.

Through learning we become able to do something we never were able to do.

Through learning we re-perceive the world and our relationship to it.

Through learning we extend our capacity to create, to be part of the generative process of life.

Figure 2. Blended learning continuum(**Jones, 2006)**

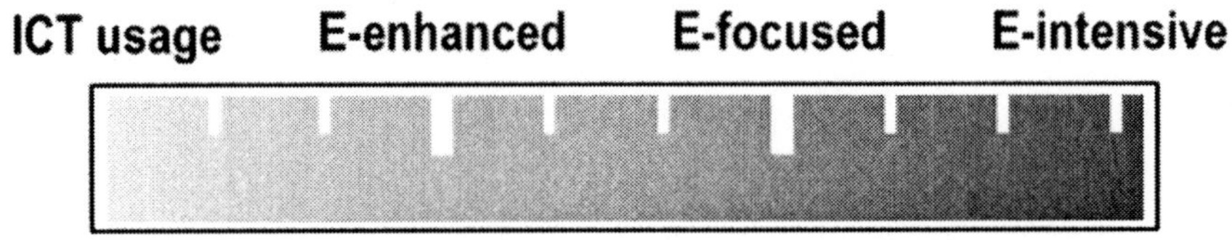

There is within each of us a deep hunger for this type of learning. (Senge, 2006, pp. 13-14)

Since this whole book is dedicated to the area of hybrid learning, definitions have been given in previous chapters. In addition, there are already good definitions and descriptions as for instance in Bonk, Graham, Cross, & Moore (2005). Therefore, the intention behind this part of the chapter lies in clarifying our understanding of hybrid learning rather than giving a broad literature review and discussion on possible definitions, understanding, and views of hybrid learning.

There is a variety of approaches to defining hybrid learning. For our concerns, we adopt the perspective that defines hybrid learning as a mix of two general approaches to learning – the traditional classroom learning on the one hand, and the technology enhanced e-learning on the other hand. "The hybrid instructional model is a blend of conventional face-to-face instruction and Web-based distance learning. In other words, a hybrid instructional model consists of both classroom face-to-face meetings and distance learning" (Koohang & Durante, 2003, p. 106), where distance learning or distance education "is any form of teaching and learning in which teacher and learner are not in the same place at the same time, with information technology their likely connector" (Gilbert, 1995). Briefly stated "Blended learning is the integration of classroom learning with elearning" (Siemens, 2005).

We also adopt the term "blended learning" since – in our opinion – the terms "hybrid learning" and "blended learning" are interchangeable and can be used synonymously. "Blended" therefore also refers to the mix of traditional classroom learning and technology enhanced distance learning, as defined above.

In order to visualize our understanding of hybrid learning we use the continuum of blended learning introduced in Jones (2006) that is shown in Figure 2.

This chapter is meant to serve as guideline for anyone in charge of a particular instance of learning that takes place in a hybrid environment consisting of face-to-face as well as virtual parts. This may be as teacher at a university, school, or in a unit of an enterprise responsible for further education of employees. Hence, we explicitly include university as well as enterprise settings on a general stage in order to be of use for a variety of specific settings.

KNOWLEDGE

Knowledge is the only resource that increases with use. (Probst, Raub, & Romhardt, 1999, p. 1)

To be able to talk about knowledge management, it is important to agree about what is to be managed. Therefore, this section gives a broad but considerate definition of knowledge. The general definition will then be followed by a distinction of different knowledge types according to varying differentiations. Finally, this part concludes with some reflections about the definition and the – as assumed – special kind of knowledge concerning hybrid learning.

General Definition

The term itself derives its origin from philosophy as an elementary problem from the early stage of this science. Debates in this area typically start with Plato's formulation of knowledge as "justified, true, and believed". Perception is, according to Plato, only achieved because of prenatal knowledge. In contrast, Aristotle, Plato's student, already disagreed and argued that knowledge is abstraction gained by experience and reflection. These two Greek philosophers are the first known representatives of two contrary approaches to epistemology, the branch of philosophy concerned with the nature and scope of knowledge, – Plato and rationalism on the one hand, and Aristotle and empiricism on the other hand. These early roots were later continued and strengthened by the two mainstreams of modern epistemology: Continental rationalism and its representative René Descartes and British empiricism with its advocate John Locke. A third mixed approach was founded by Emmanuel Kant by trying to combine the two contrary approaches.

Since nature and scope of a subject are commonly initially expressed in a profound definition, definitions of knowledge are available in abundant supply. To start at a general and neutral point, the Oxford English Dictionary[1] provides a very broad definition: knowledge, noun (i) information and skills acquired through experience or education (ii) the sum of what is known in a particular field or in total (iii) awareness or familiarity gained by experience of a fact or situation.

Proceeding in trying to get a suitable definition for the concerns of hybrid learning, we employ the differentiation of the well-known chain data, information, knowledge, and wisdom, which serves as an important aid in defining the term knowledge and delimiting its boundaries. In the field of information technology, at least two different branches concerned with an appropriate definition of knowledge can be found – information science and knowledge management. Roots of today's common definitions can therefore be found in both of these branches (Sharma) and will briefly be described below.

Nevertheless, one of the first definitions unexpectedly comes from a completely different field at a quite early stage; art of poetry and one of its famous representatives T.S. Eliot. At the beginning of his play "The Rock", published in 1934, the questions "Where is the life we have lost in living? Where is the wisdom we have lost in knowledge? Where is the knowledge we have lost in information?" (Eliot, 1934, p. 7) are part of the first scene. Hence Eliot is supposed to be the first to have promoted this hierarchy.

Looking closer at the branch of information science, roots can be found in a publication by Harlan Cleveland. The article "Information as Resource", published in the journal "The Futurist" in 1982 (Cleveland, 1982), picks up Eliot's suggestions and provides the three-level hierarchy of information, knowledge, and wisdom. Cleveland's focus is on depicting information as a special intangible resource that is expandable, compressible, substitutable, transportable, diffusive, and shareable all at once. In the following, knowledge is distinguished in a bottom-up differentiation to information.

The branch of knowledge management and its early roots for defining knowledge are represented by two authors – Milan Zeleny and Russell L. Ackhoff. Zeleny (1987) supplies a four-level hierarchy that explicitly includes data as its first syntactic layer. This layer is followed, bottom-up, by information, knowledge, and wisdom. The important shift, according to Zeleny, happens between the layers of information and knowledge, since data and information are always just partial or atomic by nature and knowledge and wisdom are, in contrast, holistic, integrative, and most importantly expressed through systemic network patterns. To signify his definition, Zeleny remarks that "knowledge is not 'processing of information' but a coordination of action" (Zeleny, 1987, p. 59). The state of management and metaphors

Table 1. Association of management description and metaphors with data, information, knowledge, and wisdom (Zeleny, 1987, p. 60)

	Management	Metaphor
Data	Muddling through	KNOW-NOTHING
Information	Efficiency (measurement + search)	KNOW-HOW
Knowledge	Effectiveness (decision making)	KNOW-WHAT
Wisdom	Explicability (judgement)	KNOW-WHY

describing the state of knowledge at a particular level, as shown in Table 1, facilitates a deeper understanding.

In contrast, Ackhoff's insights (1989) classify the content of the human mind in five categories: data, information, knowledge, understanding, and wisdom. His definition of data and information is quite simple; data are symbols and products of observation, while information is contained in descriptions and inferred from data. The final differentiation of all categories is accomplished by employing the different lifetimes of those categories: "Information, like news, ages relatively rapidly. Knowledge has a longer life-span, although inevitably it too becomes obsolete. Understanding has an aura of permanence about it. Wisdom, unless lost, is permanent; it becomes a permanent endowment of the race." (Ackhoff, 1989, p. 9) The finding that information, knowledge, and understanding focus on efficiency, while wisdom adds value by requiring judgement and can therefore, in contrast to previous stages, not be automated, concludes his deliberations.

Figure 3 summarizes the different definitions and shows the most common hierarchies.

Numerous variations and extensions of these basic models exist and have been summarized, broadly described, and carefully examined by various authors. For further literature review, two of them should be mentioned: Rowley (2007) offers a sophisticated literature overview of definitions as well as the origins of the structure in the beginning, and he finally revises the hierarchy by outlining several findings and including a well-considered discussion, while Hey (2004) first provides broad definitions, and then takes a closer look at the links between two particular levels.

To summarize, nowadays common understanding of the main hierarchy data, information, knowledge, and wisdom is briefly defined according to Ahsan & Shah (2006): "Data is seen as simple facts that can be structured to become information. Information, in turn, becomes knowledge if it is interpreted, put into context, or when meaning is added to it. (...) Finally, when values and commitment guide intelligent behavior, behavior may be said to be based on wisdom. " (Ahsan & Shah, 2006, p. 272)

Of course there are different approaches that attempt to get a suitable definition. Nonaka & Takeuchi (1995, p. 58) address the definition problem by defining knowledge according to its differences and communalities to and with information. Their definition of knowledge after all is coined by three observations. "Knowledge is about beliefs and commitment" and "Knowledge is about actions" express differences between knowledge and information, while "Knowledge is about meaning" describes common features. These observations finally conclude in the predication that "information is a necessary medium or material for eliciting and constructing knowledge".

Figure 3. (Sub-)models of the hierarchy data, information, knowledge, understanding, and wisdom

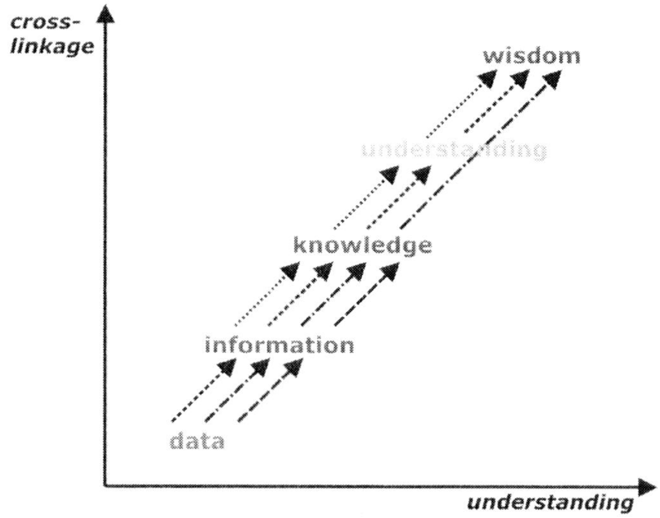

Taxonomies of Knowledge

A scientific paper dealing with definition and types of knowledge has almost no alternative but to start with the distinction of tacit and explicit knowledge that was first made public by Michael Polanyi (Polanyi, 1967). His famous expression "We can know more than we can tell" (Polanyi, 1967, p. 4) constitutes this distinction. Polanyi shows that human beings actually "know" certain aspects and issues without actually being aware of knowing, even if explicitly questioned.

Tacit knowledge, according to Polanyi's definition, always requires two things: the two terms of tacit knowing that need to be logically connected in order to become tacit knowledge. Moreover, tacit knowledge consists of three constituting aspects: the phenomenal, the semantic, and the ontological aspects, each of them expressing a particular connection between the two terms of tacit knowing. The functional structure of tacit knowing expresses the fact that "(...) in an act of tacit knowing we attend from something for attending to something else" (Polanyi, 1967, p. 10).

In a final step, Polanyi reasons that the attempt to explicitly formalize all tacit knowing is condemned to failure; identifying problems for instance – mathematical or other nature – requires tacit knowledge that often cannot be explicified.

These thoughts about the distinction of different knowledge types were later taken up and extended by the work of Ikujiro Nonaka and Hirotaka Takeuchi (Nonaka & Takeuchi, 1995). The core foundation of this knowledge and knowledge creation are classified by two dimensions: the epistemological dimension and the ontological dimension. The two dimensions and their features are shown in Figure 4.

The epistemological dimension has two values: explicit and tacit knowledge as defined by Polanyi. Tacit knowledge herein includes cognitive as well as technical elements and is created "here and now", while explicit knowledge is more about past events or objects, or the "there and then". Linking to Bateson (1973), these two types of knowing are also attributed with "analog", referring to tacit knowing, and "digital" concerning explicit knowledge.

The ontological dimension symbolizes the different levels of knowledge which create entities such as individuals, groups, organizations and inter-organizational entities. Strictly, knowledge can only be created by individuals. In order to

Figure 4. The two dimensions of knowledge and knowledge creation (Nonaka & Takeuchi, 1995, p. 57)

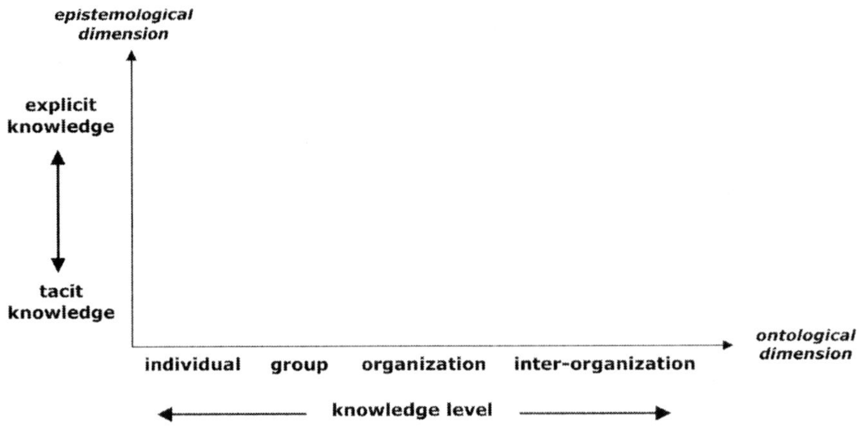

enable organizational or even inter-organizational knowledge creation, it has to be understood that organizational knowledge creation amplifies the knowledge created by individuals (Nonaka & Takeuchi, 1995, p. 59).

Other contributors to this area, like Beckman (1999), also start with the work of Polanyi but add a third kind of knowledge – implicit knowledge. The accessibility of knowledge is used as criterion for this distinction. Tacit knowledge is therefore only indirectly accessible and always involves "(…) difficulty through knowledge elicitation and observation of behaviour" (Beckman, 1999, pp. 1-4). In contrast, implicit knowledge is accessible more easily through discussions or the querying of the knowledge carrier; however, this kind of knowledge has to be located before it can be communicated. Obviously, explicit knowledge is characterized by its direct accessibility.

Of course, tacit and explicit knowing are not the only origins for distinguishing different kinds of knowledge. Hence, the overview given in this section cannot be all-embracing. Nonetheless, a few selected and miscellaneous distinctions should be mentioned in order to provide further interesting aspects.

One further classical distinction that is often chosen is the differentiation of declarative and procedural knowledge. Concisely stated, declarative knowledge is the knowledge of facts about the world. In contrast, procedural knowledge is knowledge concerning how to do something (Anderson, 1976, p. 78).

Other criteria that can be employed are the degree of formalization (Beckman, 1999) or the stage where knowledge is needed and accessed – before, during, or after knowledge-related activities. Various authors like Davenport & Glaser (2002) or El Sawy & Majchrzak (2004) are working on the accessibility of knowledge at certain desired stages.

Knowledge in the Context of Hybrid Learning

The general definition, and especially the data, information, knowledge, wisdom chain, is certainly also applicable for hybrid learning, but of course the context of hybrid learning provides several special aspects and attributes that need to be considered.

If we apply the findings presented above to this context, the ontological dimension of knowledge and knowledge creation consists of four different perspectives: the perspective of a single user, the perspectives of groups of users, the organizational, and the inter-organizational perspective.

Moreover, the context of hybrid learning presents at least two kinds of users that need to be considered: learners on the one hand, and teachers or tutors on the other hand. Even additional complexity increases due to each learner's and teacher's choice to adopt different perspectives. Taking into account the structures usually applied for learning, a learner can adopt an intra-course perspective, a broader view including all courses of a particular semester, or, more generally, a particular time unit, and finally an all-embracing perspective involving all courses constituting a particular course of study or training. Similarly, a teacher can adopt the following perspectives: starting bottom up, a teacher also can adopt an intra-course perspective and a semester-wide view including all courses the teacher is in charge of for a particular semester or time unit, as well as the all-embracing perspective.

Of course these deliberations also apply to the organizational perspective. Herein, the structural organization of the institution in charge of providing the knowledge has to be considered; different granularities depending on the specific structure are possible. In the instance of universities, perspectives can be the view of a single chair or the perspective of a whole faculty. Naturally, equal deliberations can be made for enterprises of all sizes.

Further – more informal – questions arising from dealing with knowledge in the context of hybrid learning are various: What exactly is knowledge in the context of hybrid learning? How does knowledge differ from information and data or content in this context? In which manner is knowledge in learning? Who actually creates content and knowledge? How can knowledge belonging to the non-digital part of hybrid learning be digitalized? Are there special types of content? How is the content used? Which part of the content can be used to which extent?

Some of these questions can already be answered by applying the definitions given above. The imprecise definition of knowledge prevents the limitation of knowledge to certain aspects of hybrid learning. What became obvious is the indispensability of paying particular attention to tacit knowing. Especially in hybrid learning where a certain factor of distance separates teachers and students at a given time, tacit knowledge seems even harder to caption, convert, and communicate than it already is. The question of whether this endeavour is possible at all will be discussed in section 5 of this chapter.

Therefore, general questions concerning the creation, maintenance, and conversion of knowledge need to be discussed initially and will be answered in the next section by presenting models for knowledge management. Specific questions which take into account the kind of content and special features of hybrid learning will be answered in section 5 of this chapter.

This section concludes with an assertion of Thomas H. Davenport and Laurence Prusak published in "Working Knowledge" in order to, in conclusion, express the multiplicity of knowledge.

Knowledge is a fluid mix of framed experience, values, contextual information, and expert insight that provides a framework for evaluating and incorporating new experiences and information. It originates and is applied in the minds of knowers. In organizations, it often becomes embedded not only in documents or repositories but also in organizational routines, processes, practices, and norms. (Davenport & Prusak, 1998, p. 5)

KNOWLEDGE MANAGEMENT

The key to success is to bake specialized knowledge into the jobs of highly skilled workers – to make the knowledge so readily accessible that it can't be avoided. (Davenport & Glaser, 2002, p. 108)

Since the last section described our understanding of knowledge – knowledge in general as well as peculiarities of knowledge in the context of hybrid learning – the literal next step is now to think about ways of how to manage knowledge. Since knowledge is considered to be the most important resource of today's economy, it should be appropriately managed.

(...) the real, controlling resource and the absolutely decisive 'factor of production' is now neither capital nor land nor labor. It is knowledge. (Drucker, 1993, p. 6)

The field of knowledge management arose as part of general management theories in the 1990s, and therefore most of the classical literature deals with organizational knowledge management. Since we explicitly do not exclude organizational settings, and most of the publications include a general consideration of knowledge management, most of these deliberations can be considered useful or can even be substituted for knowledge management in hybrid learning. The overall assumption upon which this section is based, is the conviction that knowledge management in general has the objective to ensure the delivery of the right information to the right person at the right time. This assumption seems tenable and applies to knowledge management for organizational concerns as well as for the concerns of hybrid learning.

In particular, there is a variety of different schools of thought for knowledge management that will be briefly described below. The practical aspect of knowledge management, basically referring to knowledge management tools, will be directly integrated into the next part of this chapter and will concentrate solely on knowledge management for hybrid learning, since there are a huge number of tools available in general.

Knowledge Management According to Nonaki and Takeuchi (Nonaka & Takeuchi, 1995)

Ikujiro Nonaka and Hirotaka Takeuchi are often seen as cofounders of knowledge management. Their book "The Knowledge-Creating Company", published in 1995, is still one of the foundations of many publications and entrepreneurial decisions. Although their thoughts were originally meant to be relevant just for knowledge management in organizations, their work concerning knowledge creation has become an international standard throughout the entire domain of knowledge management.

Based on Michael Polanyi's definition and distinction of tacit and explicit knowledge, Nonaka and Takeuchi develop a theory of organizational knowledge creation which is considered to be the most important asset for successfully managing knowledge, and therefore serves as the core part of their theory. The important part that constitutes most of knowledge creation is "the mobilization and conversion of tacit knowledge" (Nonaka & Takeuchi, 1995, p. 56). According to this model, knowledge is created by a continuous transformation between tacit and explicit knowledge that takes place between individuals.

The central part of this theory is therefore a model describing the different modes of knowledge conversion – the SECI-model. The four existing transformations – socialization, externalization, combination, and internalization – are shown in Figure 5.

The first mode is the conversion from tacit to tacit knowledge – socialization. An individual acquires tacit knowledge during the process of experience-sharing with others. The most common way of gathering tacit knowledge takes place by observation, imitation, and practice and is an important part of programs like training-on-the-job. Knowledge gathered by socialization is called "sympathized knowledge".

Figure 5. The four modes of knowledge conversion (Nonaka & Takeuchi, 1995)

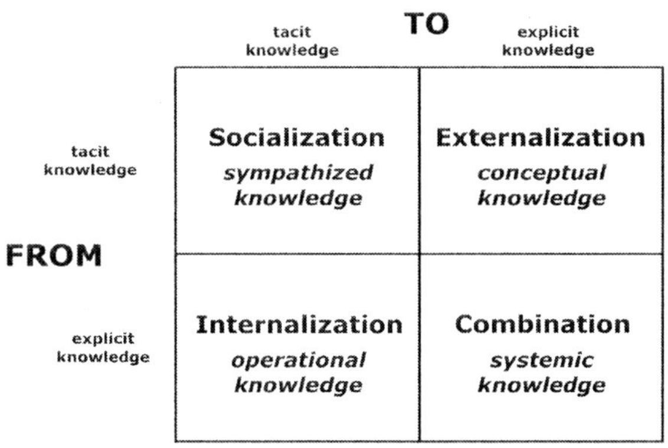

The transformation from tacit to explicit knowledge – called externalization – serves as the second part of this model. The mode is "(...) typically seen in the process of concept creation and is triggered by dialogue or reflection" (Nonaka & Takeuchi, 1995, p. 64). Even simple writing can be an act of converting tacit knowledge into explicit knowledge. The knowledge resulting is usually called "conceptual knowledge".

Thirdly, explicit knowledge is transferred to explicit knowledge. This mode is the combination that happens when concepts are systemized and different parts of explicit knowledge are combined in order to create new knowledge. Existing information is sorted, added, combined, and categorized and therefore gains new value. The output of this mode is referred to as "systemic knowledge".

Finally, the process of converting explicit knowledge to tacit knowledge, internalization, takes place. All experiences gained by socialization, externalization, and combination are adapted and integrated into an individual's knowledge base by being converted to tacit knowing. Experiences of others, personal experiences, or information gathered become part of "what an individual knows". This process is often referred to as "learning by doing" and produces "operational knowledge".

Obviously, the process of transforming knowledge is supposed to take place several times. The continuous and dynamic interaction of these modes results in a knowledge spiral that is shown in Figure 6. Recalling the different dimensions of knowledge, it is important to be aware that this process does not take place within a single individual but requires interaction with others in order to shift between the different modes.

At a later stage the SECI-model was completed by the concept "Ba" that "offers an integrating conceptual metaphor for the SECI model of dynamic knowledge conversions" (Nonaka & Konno, 1998, S. 45). "Ba" can be thought of as a shared space where knowledge can be exchanged. Hence, "if knowledge is separated from ba, it turns into information, which can then be communicated independently from ba" (Nonaka & Konno, 1998, S. 41).

Knowledge Management According to Davenport and Prusak

Another popular school of thought is knowledge management according to Thomas H. Davenport and Laurence Prusak. The basis for the whole theory is established by ten general principles of knowledge management (Davenport, 1996).

1. Knowledge management is expensive (but so is stupidity!)

Figure 6. The knowledge spiral (Nonaka & Takeuchi, 1995)

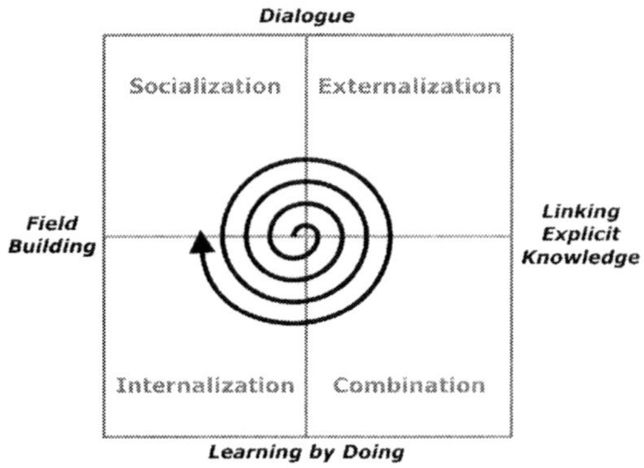

2. Effective management of knowledge requires hybrid solutions involving both people and technology
3. Knowledge management is highly political
4. Knowledge management requires knowledge managers
5. Knowledge management benefits more from maps than models, more from markets than hierarchies
6. Sharing and using knowledge are often unnatural acts
7. Knowledge management means improving knowledge work processes
8. Access to knowledge is only the beginning
9. Knowledge management never ends
10. Knowledge management requires a knowledge contract

Getting more specific, the process of knowledge management is divided into three subprocesses: knowledge generation, knowledge codification and coordination, and knowledge transfer (Davenport & Prusak, 1998). These sub-processes have been carefully examined in a detailed study of over 25 international enterprises. Concerning the sub-process of knowledge generation, this process is divided into five modes: acquisition, dedicated resources, fusion, adaption, and knowledge networking. For the sub-process of codifying knowledge, the authors emphasize the importance of basic principles and the consideration of different knowledge types. The sub-process of knowledge transfer however should be coined by priorities like the indispensability of a common language in order to share knowledge – not just everybody being capable of speaking a certain language, but also having a common background like "mechanical engineer" in order to understand each other.

In order to further clarify the whole process of knowledge management, attention also has to be paid to the different roles of knowledge workers. Therefore in "Thinking for a Living" (Davenport, 2005) a classification system to segment knowledge workers is developed. Transaction, integration, expert, and collaborative are the four categories of segmentation that should be applied.

These theories emphasize the significance and importance of knowledge workers concerning the organizational success. Since the knowledge workers are the center of these theories, they can be considered useful for the concerns of knowledge management for hybrid learning where, obviously, the learner should be the focus of efforts most of the time.

Knowledge Management According to Probst, Raub, and Romhardt (Probst, Raub, & Romhardt, 1999)

The theory of knowledge management according to Gilbert Probst, Steffen Raub, and Kai Romhardt seems most prevalent in the German-speaking world. The resulting model is a best-practice model that was developed in collaboration with many well-known, not only German but international, companies.

The theoretical groundwork is constituted by the following general understanding of knowledge and knowledge management. Knowledge and the creation of knowledge result in a continuum that exists between data and knowledge. Concerning knowledge management, Probst, Raub, and Romhardt state that "knowledge management can be applied to individuals, groups, or organizational structures" (Probst, Raub, & Romhardt, 1999, p. 37). Since this theory and model arose in the organizational environment, they aim at the improvement and increase of the organizational knowledge base. The organizational knowledge base though consists of individual and collective knowledge assets. Improvement of this base therefore enhances individual and collective knowledge which is why this model is described here.

The best-practice model pinpoints six core processes of knowledge management, describing and addressing the main operational problems: knowledge identification, knowledge acquisition, knowledge development, knowledge sharing and distribution, knowledge utilization, and knowledge retention. However, difficulties may not only occur due to direct operational problems, but due to the fact that knowledge management is not embedded within an overall strategy. Therefore, the two additional building blocks – knowledge goals and knowledge assessment – are added in order to turn the model into a management system with knowledge itself "(…) in the centre, as the sole structuring principle" (Probst, Raub, & Romhardt, 1999, p. 35). Figure 7 shows all assets, and the resulting logical interrelationships between the single assets.

Other Schools of Thought and Contributors

There are, of course, many others that have also contributed and are still benefiting the area of knowledge management who cannot all be named and specified in appropriate depth. In order to nonetheless encourage a broad view of different directions that can and have been taken, a select few are characterized.

Peter Senge's vision, theories, and work about learning organizations has for instance significantly influenced the area of knowledge management. According to Senge a learning organization is "an organization that is continually expanding its capacity to create its future" (Senge, 2006, p. 14). His book "The fifth discipline" (Senge, 2006), first published in 1990, identifies four disciplines – personal mastery, mental models, shared visions, and team learning – as central aspects of learning organizations. Since the four disciplines themselves are indeed distinctive but it is nonetheless vital that they are developed as an ensemble, Senge places systems thinking as fifth and most important discipline for successfully bringing a learning organization into existence. The four core disciplines, and the fifth discipline in particular, are described in Senge (2006), while Senge (1995) is meant to serve as a guideline for practitioners.

Another approach is defined by looking at knowledge management from an even more pragmatic side. The so-called "communities of practice" arose in the 1990s and their importance was – among others – already emphasized and approved by early publications by John Seely Brown, Paul Duguid, and Estee Solomon Gray. Brown & Duguid (1991) deduce the opportunities of communities of practice and how companies should envision themselves – as "(…) a community-of-communities, acknowledging in

Figure 7. Building blocks of knowledge management (Probst, Raub, & Romhardt, 1999, p. 34)

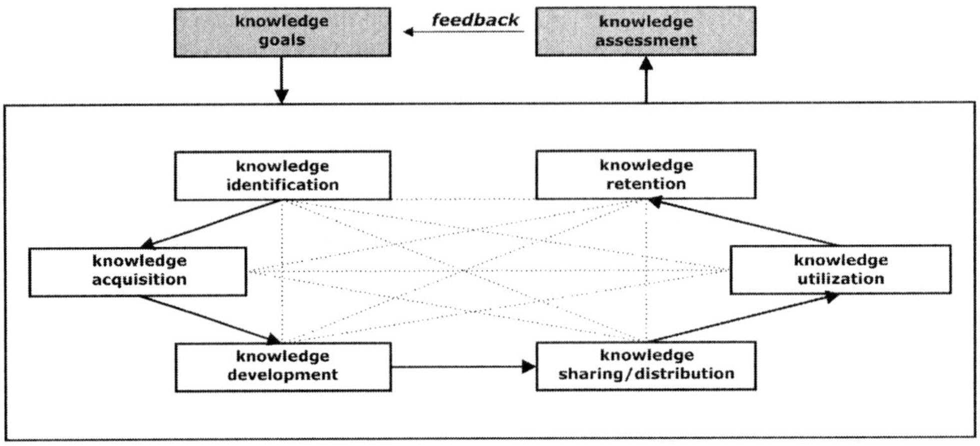

the process the many noncanoncial communities in its midst" – while Brown & Gray (1995) describe how companies such as Xerox and National Semiconductor are learning to foster and support communities of practice in order to facilitate the sharing of knowledge.

At a slightly later stage, communities of practice were significantly influenced by Etienne Wenger and his work. Wenger proposes "...a framework that considers learning in social terms" (Wenger, 1998, p. 9) in his book "Communities of Practice". Meaning, practice, community, and identity are the components that need to be integrated in order to apply a social theory of learning. The discussion of these components and implications of their connectedness set the seminal concept of communities of practice. Subsequently, the book "Cultivating Communities of Practice" (Wenger, McDermott, & Snyder, 2002) describes how to successfully develop and facilitate different kinds of communities.

A management strategy implemented in knowledge is business-process-oriented knowledge management which has, to a great extent, been examined by Peter Heisig. According to his observations and theories, the key success factor is minimizing barriers for efficient knowledge management, and therefore the integration of knowledge management tasks directly into daily work tasks and the daily business process (Heisig, 2001). A model specifically designed for business-process-oriented knowledge management – the GPO-WM® – is the consequent result of his studies. The model includes a reference model as well as a procedure model and tools supporting analysis and finally the creation of solutions (Heisig, 2005).

As mentioned before, this section is meant to serve as a brief summary. There are different papers, like Alavi & Leidner (2001), providing a good overview and a broad literature review that can be used to delve into the subject.

KNOWLEDGE MANAGEMENT FOR HYBRID LEARNING

What e-learning has done is set a context for KM. (Barron, 2000)

The implications of knowledge management for e-learning are huge. Rather than simply relying on instruction, we can use well-structured information as well as productivity enhancing tools to help people learn and improve their performance. (Rosenberg, 2001, p. 109)

In contrast to other sections, this one starts with two quotations describing different views on knowledge management and learning.

First of all, these two brief quotations already reveal a minor problem concerning the area of knowledge management for hybrid learning. Publications dealing specifically with the integration of hybrid learning and knowledge management are hard to find. Most of the previous and current research issues concerning knowledge management and learning address e-learning in general and not hybrid learning in particular. Since our definition of hybrid learning was intentionally widespread, most of the findings can be considered useful for the particular area of hybrid learning as well. We therefore also use the term "e-learning", depending on the origin and original subject of the work referred to. While selecting theories and results, we carefully analyzed the usefulness for and transferability to the area of hybrid learning. Additionally, we were trying to add thoughts and features referring to the special character of hybrid learning in contrast to pure e-learning.

Secondly, these two quotations serve as a first distinction of how knowledge management and hybrid learning can be integrated and combined. The first quotation by Clark Aldrich, the former research director of the Gartner Group responsible for creating and building the company's e-learning practice, refers to learning in the context of knowledge management. It illustrates one direction of the relationship between the fields of knowledge management and e-learning or hybrid learning. Starting from the area of knowledge management, the main objective lies in delivering information and knowledge to people, as well as connecting people to each other. This goal is obviously accomplished when either self-paced or collaborative e-learning takes place (ITtoolbox, 2004). Hence e-learning can foster knowledge management and its objectives.

The second quotation looks at this relationship the other way round. The quotation cites Marc Rosenberg who is a management consultant, writer, educator, and leading figure in the world of training, organizational learning, e-learning, knowledge management, and performance improvement. It describes a way of looking at knowledge management from the perspective of learning. The field of e-learning or hybrid learning also, by definition, involves information and knowledge. Obviously, every area dealing with information or knowledge workers can benefit from theories and findings in the area of knowledge management, especially if achieving the increase of information and knowledge of individuals or groups is the main objective, as it is for learning. Therefore, knowledge management can help to improve the experience and success of e-learning or hybrid learning for every concerned party. Since this whole book is concerned with hybrid learning, we adopt this view of initiating knowledge management from hybrid learning.

If we now rely on the definition and distinctions of knowledge presented earlier, the differentiation of tacit and explicit knowing becomes an important aspect, since similarities to informal and formal learning can be drawn immediately. Formal learning and explicit knowledge obviously seem to be connected, as well as tacit knowledge and informal learning. As soon as parts of the learning experience are self-paced and not formally defined, like in face-to-face parts of hybrid learning, informal learning becomes more and more important. The following quotation ought to convey the impression of these thoughts and their importance for hybrid learning.

I usually ask audiences at my keynote speeches about their experiences with e-Learning or On-Line Learning? When I ask how many people in the audience have recently taken an On-Line Course, the response is often between 20 and 30 percent. One day, my tongue got a bit tied and I asked the question with a few changes.

'How many of you have learned things on-line recently?'

Suddenly, almost 98% of the hands in the audience went up. I was shocked until I realized how I had fundamentally changed the question. (Masie, 2002)

Since the process of knowledge generation is one crucial factor for knowledge management in any case, the presented findings employ an even greater importance of knowledge generation for the area of hybrid learning. First of all, knowledge generation is split by definition. On the one hand, information is transferred and hence knowledge is supposed to be created in the face-to-face parts of learning; on the other hand, the self-paced learning complements the face-to-face part and contributes additional information and knowledge. For one thing, this separation determines a variety of points of knowledge generation that need to be considered, and for another thing, the informal part of learning increases and the capturing of information and knowledge gets harder, since, in order to manage knowledge successfully by using tools or techniques, it has to be explicitly expressed in digitalized form. Special attention must therefore be paid to the generation of knowledge or more precisely the digitalization, formalization and revealing of existing information and knowledge.

In order to show possible solutions for these problems, the application of the knowledge management models presented in the previous section concerning the area of learning are examined and presented in the following part. This first part also takes into account more specific approaches to integrating knowledge management and hybrid learning.

The second part takes a closer look at the more practical and pragmatic aspects of this integration by introducing different techniques and tools already offering possibilities for actually implementing this integration, or at least parts of it.

Research Perspective

One way of trying to employ knowledge management for hybrid learning is to transfer existing knowledge management models into the context of hybrid learning. Hence the knowledge management models presented above will now be carefully examined and tested for their applicability and usefulness in the area of hybrid learning.

Woelk & Agarwal (2002), as well as Nübel (2005) transferred the SECI-model to a learning context. Woelk & Agarwal first enhance the SECI-model by a fifth phase – cognition – which is supposed to represent the application of knowledge that has been exchanged in previous phases to a specific problem and a sixth phase – feedback – embodying the evaluation of learners' progress. Figure 8 shows the results of these extensions plus the combination of knowledge management and e-learning.

The original phases of the SECI-model are assigned as follow: Socialization takes place when tacit knowledge is transferred from the knowledge holder to the knowledge seeker, since direct interaction is necessary in order to successfully transfer the knowledge from one person to another. Concerning hybrid learning, socialization happens in face-to-face-meetings on the one hand, or, on the other hand, in any section of the virtual part where questions are answered and different issues are discussed with two or more persons participating. Most important of all, socialization does not necessarily require a teacher, but can also take place between two or more students. Since socialization is one of the most important aspects to consider if tacit knowledge is examined, it is crucial for the success of hybrid learning to foster socialization, especially in the virtual parts of the hybrid learning concept, by providing a range of tools that allows a comfortable and intensive exchange of all participants and therefore represent at least parts of informal learning.

In contrast, externalization occurs if a knowledge holder formalizes knowledge that is stored

Figure 8. Phases of the SECI-model with e-learning enhancements (Woelk & Agarwal, 2002, p. 2)

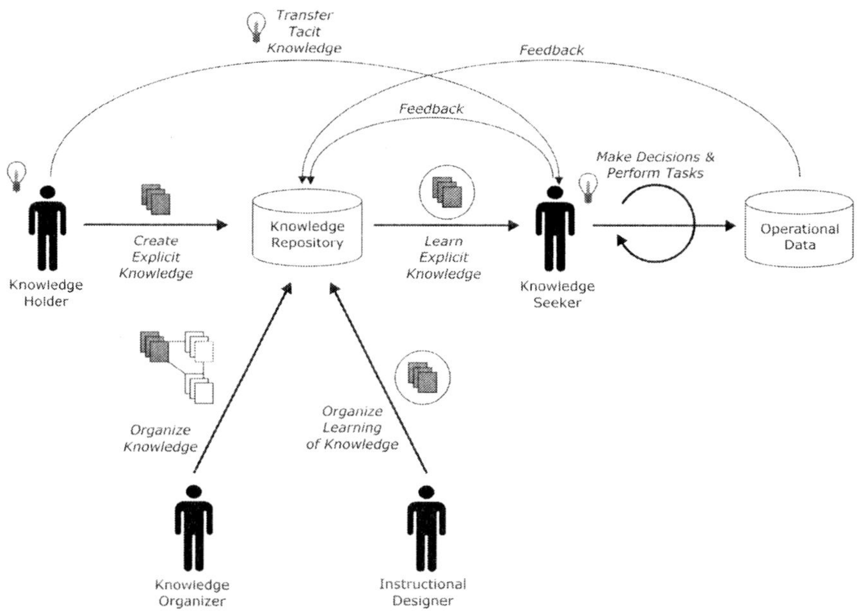

in a knowledge repository. Speaking in terms of hybrid learning, knowledge can be explicitly formalized by creating lecture notes or by providing information of different kinds in the learning environment. Additionally, knowledge can also be represented or created by a participant that shares her/his insights by posting in a public forum or contributing in a collaborative task.

Combination in this model is supported by knowledge organizers and instructional designers. Existing knowledge can be structured according to superior aspects, or new aspects of knowledge can be abstracted from different single assets. In the context of hybrid learning, combination can again be performed by a single user or by a group of users – i.e. self-paced or collaborative. A group of users can, for example, rework the results of a face-to-face meeting and connect these results to previous parts of other sessions. Specialists can also process existing material with pedagogical techniques and take into account aspects of self-paced learning.

To complete a first circulation of the four phases, internalization finally takes place when a knowledge seeker learns the knowledge existing in the knowledge base and hence extends his personal knowledge. For hybrid learning, this phase can be associated with traditional learning as well as self-reflection. The number of participants necessary to perform this task varies – generally the learner is the only participant needed, but nevertheless, she/he can be supported by a teacher or a group of other learners while performing this task.

It is obvious, that the boundaries of the different phases are smooth and that some activities can be assigned to one as well as another phase. This finding merely emphasizes the interdisciplinary and cross-linking of hybrid learning.

These results and considerations are confirmed in Nübel (2005). Nübel presents an application of the SECI-model as result of an intensive study including ten different companies. This application is shown in Table 2.

Obviously, communities turn out to be a core feature for successful application. This finding already combines two different models of knowledge management – the SECI-model, as presented above, and communities of practice as a second model.

Table 2. Phases of the SECI-model and corresponding possibilities for knowledge transformation (Nübel, 2005, p. 235)

Phase of SECI-model	Possibilities for knowledge creation and conversion
Socialization	Communities, face-to-face-meetings
Externalization	Exchange in communities by using forums, chats etc.
Combination	Exchange in communities by using forums, chats etc.
Internalization	Application of what has been learned to a specific context

An approach dealing especially with communities of practice is presented in Leblanc & Abel (2008). The environment introduced is called E-MEMORAe2.0 and is one of the successors of the initial project MEMORAe, a system fostering the capitalization of knowledge in the context of organizations. E-MEMORAe2.0 is especially designed to support e-learning; particularly "E-MEMORAe2.0 is an environment which enables learners to access, share, and capitalize knowledge" (Leblanc & Abel, 2008, p. 112).

The overall objective of this environment is to foster the access and exchange of information at any time. Hence the capitalization of knowledge on the three different levels of knowledge creation as provided by Nonaka & Takeuchi (1995) – individual, group-wise, and organizational – is the focus. Each level is provided with a memory and facilitated by the use of a shared ontology. The ontology can be used for navigation. Additionally, a vertical navigation employing topic maps is offered. Information exchange is fostered by offering the possibility to switch between the different levels of memories, of course the possibility to add resources and information on everyone of the different levels of memory, and finally by employing a special forum "(...) structured according to the knowledge to learn, allowing the students to communicate in a more contextual way: the learning activity that is carried out" (Leblanc & Abel, 2008, p. 111).

First evaluations have already shown that the transfer of different levels of knowledge creation to an environment has positive effects and increase the usability for students. Nevertheless, the authors are still working on improvements for a better integration of the forum, since students tend to not use the forum, probably because of the extensive face-to-face parts.

In contrast, Pettenati & Ranieri (2006) propose a reference model that employs communities of practice with an emphasis on informal learning. The presented model is framed by a social networking layer that is supposed to foster informal learning and collaboration. Moreover, this layer helps "(...) to create a social climate and a shared social grounding" (Pettenati & Ranieri, 2006, p. 349) that cultivates motivation and a group culture which both have been found to be indispensable for a high level of participation. The importance and usefulness of social awareness have also been examined by other authors such as Braun & Schmidt (2006). The inner layers organization and collaboration management are more specifically designed to support the activities of collaborative groups such as management of user, content, and communication. Figure 9 shows the reference model and its individual layers.

Similar deliberations concerning the use of communities of practice as a core concept of modern knowledge management for e-learning and hybrid learning are employed by various authors in different levels of depth. Varlamis & Apostolakis (2006) are developing a framework for building virtual communities supporting lifelong learning. As a special feature, they explicitly add a knowledge base that serves as memory of these communities.

Figure 9. Reference model for collaboration in distributed communities of practice (Pettenati & Ranieri, 2006, p. 351)

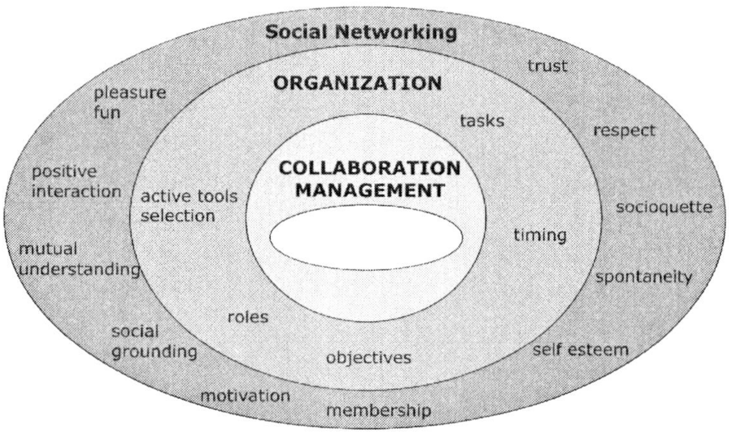

Although the SECI-model and communities of practice are indisputably the most dominant models when it comes to integrate knowledge management and learning, other models also offer opportunities that have to be kept in mind. The technique described by Davenport & Prusak (1998) especially takes into account informal knowledge and its formalization by dividing the general process of knowledge management into the three sub-processes of knowledge generation, knowledge codification, and knowledge transfer. In contrast, the Probst, Raub & Romhardt (1999) model can be employed to add an overall strategy to hybrid learning and connect this strategy with a clearly defined circle of knowledge integrated into the hybrid learning strategy.

As the combination of the SECI-model and communities of practice have already proven, a combination of different models seems to be the most sufficient way to integrate knowledge management and hybrid learning in order to meet the specific needs that every particular environment brings with it. The previous remarks have shown that there are models and techniques that integrate knowledge management and hybrid learning without explicitly naming it. Hence, the application of knowledge management models to the particular environment of hybrid learning is of course not the only way to integrate knowledge management and hybrid learning.

In order to think about possible combinations or the integration of two different areas, a first step can, for example, comprise the outline of some important differences. Rosenberg (2001) compared training and knowledge management according to different viewpoints. Since training in this case is defined as classroom or online learning or a combination of both, the results can be applied to e-learning as well as hybrid learning. The specific results are shown in Table 3.

Adapted from his findings, instruction vs. information as the core essence seems to be the most crucial difference between training and knowledge management. So the enrichment of hybrid learning with opportunities to inform the user without strictly interrupting can also provide a useful integration.

The project "learning in process" (lip)[2] aims at this objective by adding context awareness (Schmidt, 2005). According to the project findings, the separation of e-learning and knowledge occurs due to "(...) their respective limited and isolated consideration of context" (Schmidt, 2005, p. 204). Hence the project aimed at "(...) integration of working and learning on a process level and learning management, knowledge management,

Table 3. Comparison of training and knowledge management (Rosenberg, 2001, p. 77)a

Training	Knowledge Management
Purpose is to instruct.	Purpose is to inform.
Requires the interruption of work to participate (even online).	Normally requires less work interruption than training.
Program dictates how the user will learn.	User determines how s/he will learn.
Goal is to transfer skill and knowledge to user.	Goal is to be a resource to the user.

human capital management and collaboration solutions on a technical level" (Schmidt, 2005, p. 205). Briefly stated a matching procedure is employed to present context-specific information to the user. The complete process is shown in Figure 10.

Since this process takes into account the user's context, information can be presented based on the competency and missing assets of the individual user. The entire approach is described in depth and summarized in Schmidt (2008). These thoughts have been continued with "APOSDLE"[3], the advanced process-oriented self-directed learning environment. APOSDLE is based on "re-using a wide variety of knowledge artifacts within an organization (…) for learning" (Bonestroo, Ley, Kump, & Lindstaedt, 2007, p. 9).

Besides, there are also other authors dealing with context awareness related to e-learning and knowledge management, like Pedroni (2007), who is working on the development of special tools for context management as an additional axis for learning environments. In addition to those project-specific and more pragmatic approaches, there are also contributions dealing with identifying barriers of this integration in general, as for instance Ras, Memmel, & Weibelzahl (2005). These authors identified eight different integration problems and provide possible solutions as well as future issues. The problems are problems on a conceptual level, problems on a technical level, problems of neglecting learning process, problems of the amount of guidance provided, problems of context neglect, problems of structuring and annotating content, problems of lack of interactivity, and problems of dynamic adaption, whereby some of them have already been addressed above and approaches to solutions have been provided. Further attempts to solutions can be found in Ras, Memmel, & Weibelzahl (2005).

Figure 10. LIP Matching process (Schmidt, 2005, p. 209)

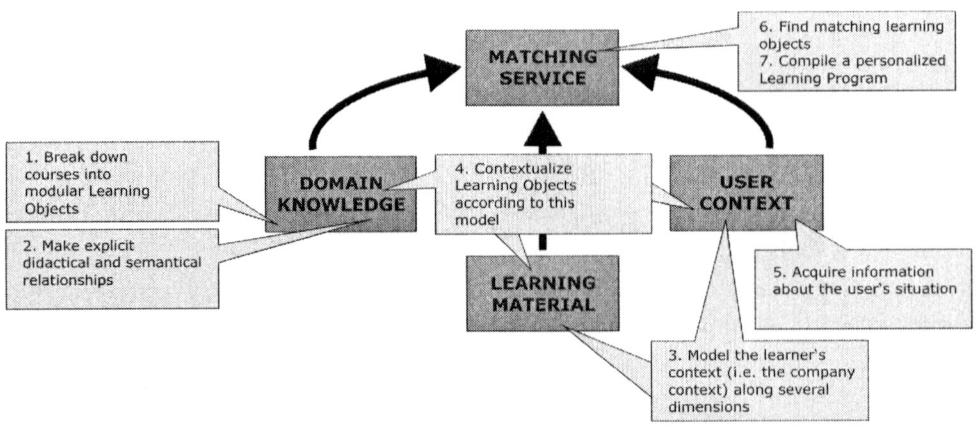

Knowledge Management Tools and Techniques: State of the Art

As previously stated, we are now going on an excursion to the area of knowledge management tools and techniques suitable for the context of hybrid learning. Table 4 shows a general overview – tools for learning and knowledge management are presented on the one hand, and, on the other hand, tools supporting and fostering communication and cooperation that can be used for learning as well as for knowledge management.

Since these tools for communication and cooperation are considered in a separate chapter of this handbook, a further exploration of details is not provided here. General tools for learning and knowledge management are also skipped due to the fact that the named methods are rather general and have already been examined by various other authors and contributions such as Hoffmann (2001).

Hence, our strategy is to present different continuative approaches that can also be used for knowledge management. In addition, these approaches can be considered useful, especially in the context of hybrid learning, since most of them are related to the area of learning in some case. The presented approaches are assigned to two different categories – structured approaches and more or less unstructured approaches.

Representatives that can be assigned to this category are metadata models like the Resource Description Framework (RDF)[4] and the Dublin Core Standard (DC)[5], which are often connected to the Semantic Web. On the one hand, annotations offer help detecting existing knowledge; on the other hand, these possibilities can be used to model and describe knowledge that was not explicitly formalized before. Techniques that can be used for similar purposes are Topic Maps[6] and ontologies. Ontologies are used to define a semantic context for digital content. In order to set up ontology, a specific language like OWL[7] is needed. Ontologies define relationships between different concepts, for example by using techniques like RDF or DC. Obviously – recalling the previous deliberations – representing context is one of the key concepts for integrating knowledge management and hybrid learning. Furthermore, ontologies are common throughout the domain of knowledge management as well as in the area of e-learning. The use of ontologies can therefore be very helpful. Ontologies are, for instance, used in (Leblanc & Abel, 2008) fostering the integration as described above. Another approach using ontology in web based learning is described in Sridharan, Tretiakov, & Kinshuk (2004). The framework, shown in Figure 11, using ontologies, represents the core of this approach.

The role of ontology is to support the effective knowledge acquisition and creation processes in the learning environment. Ontology plays the role of a binding factor that brings various knowledge

Table 4. Overview on common tools for learning and knowledge management (Nübel, 2005)

Learning	Tools	Knowledge Management
Online training material	Forums	Knowledge databases
Online courses	Chats	Expert databases
Web-based trainings	Bill-Boards	Yellow Pages
Glossaries	Virtual classrooms	Best Practices
	Groupware	Project reports
	Whiteboards	
	Application Sharing	

items and processes together to provide a richer and integrated view of the knowledge domain to the learners. It allows for interrelating, combining, and thus reusing standalone knowledge units. (Sridharan, Tretiakov, & Kinshuk, 2004, p. 664)

Topic Maps are, in contrast, an ISO-standard for the representation and exchange of knowledge that can also be used in combination with ontology. A Topic Map consists of different topics that are connected by a specified relationship and can therefore also be used to reason new knowledge. An approach showing the use of Topic Maps – a tool currently mainly assigned to the area of knowledge management – is presented in Dicheva, Dichev, & Wang (2005). The toolkit TM4L[8] was developed as an "ontology-based environment to complement existing TM editors and visualization tools for the area of e-learning" (Dicheva, Dichev, & Wang, 2005, p. 1).

Figure 11. Framework for knowledge management in web based learning (Sridharan, Tretiakov, & Kinshuk, 2004, p. 664)

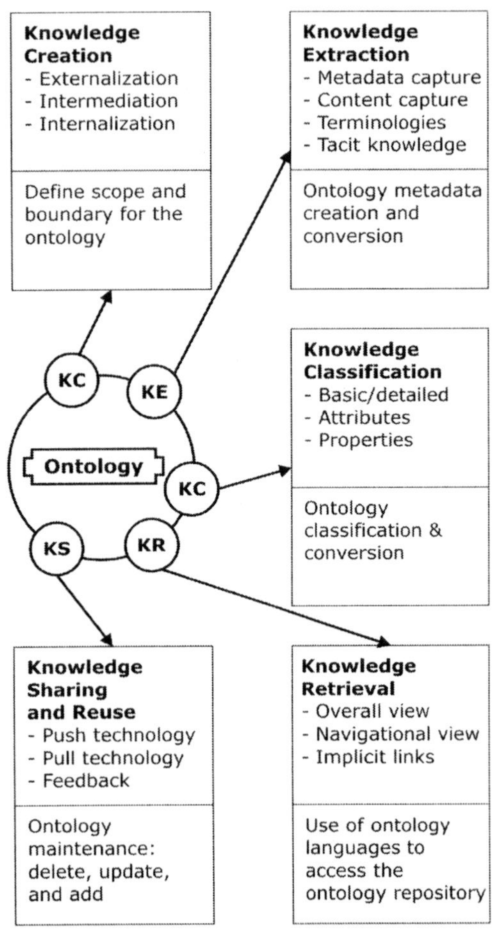

Proceeding with the category of unstructured approaches, delegates of this section are methods like Mind Maps or technologies like blogging and tagging. All these methods are highly suitable to formulate knowledge that was gained by informal learning or in non-digital parts of hybrid learning classes.

Mind Maps are a semantic organization tool that has been used to foster learning and support visualization and structuring. In contrast to Topic Maps, Mind Maps do not require the representation of any semantic meaning symbolized by connections. A particular use case is described in Willis & Miertschin (2006). In contrast, Chacón (2003) shows a quite different approach of how to use Mind Maps for web based learning – Mind Maps are used to develop learning templates.

More recently, issues of social computing have been gaining interest in the area of knowledge management and learning. Collaboration tools like blogs and wikis are integrated into the learning environment in order to offer a more informal method of communication. Also, the technology of tagging can be used to structure existing knowledge. However, since all of these are text-based, they are mainly of use for supporting explicit knowledge transfer. The usability for covering more informal aspects of learning roughly depends on underlying models of usage.

There are various contributions analyzing the use of social software for the concerns of hybrid learning. An example of how to integrate social aspects has already been described above and was originally presented in (Pettenati & Ranieri, 2006).

FUTURE TRENDS & CONCLUSION

Since possibilities for integrating knowledge management and hybrid learning have now been outlined, this chapter must take a look at critical issues of this integration.

Firstly, there are critical voices concerning the externalization of implicit knowledge. The question of whether the nature of tacit knowledge has been understood at all is discussed and reasoned in detail by Tsoukas (2003). According to Tsoukas, Nonaka's & Takeuchi's interpretation of tacit knowledge is erroneous since "it ignores the essential ineffability of tacit knowledge, thus reducing it to what can be articulated" (Tsoukas, 2003, p. 425) and "(...) tacit knowledge cannot be 'captured', 'translated', or 'converted', but only displayed, manifested, in what we do". The main critique is that knowledge creation is not an organizational process but a process of socialization. Exactly that point is referred to in models adopting the SECI-model for the purpose of hybrid learning presented above.

Main progress and future development will have to focus on the improvement and spreading of technologies like ontologies or RDF employed for knowledge management in the area of hybrid learning. The concepts and existing work of those possibilities sound promising, but there are numerous technical problems and issues that need to be worked on.

This chapter has given a broad overview of the foundations of knowledge and knowledge management in order to allow a profound estimation of presented approaches for knowledge management in the context of hybrid learning.

It is obvious that the process of bringing knowledge management for hybrid learning into existence has only just started and that there are a lot of obstacles and problems that have to be cleared and solved. But what should also have become obvious is that the process has already begun and that there are a lot of benefits that this integration can and will bring to both areas of knowledge management and hybrid learning.

At this stage of the process, critical issues and voices are easy to find but – to repeat Rosenberg's (2001) summary – there are at least some implications that knowledge management already delivers for e-learning.

Rather than simply relying on instruction, we can use well-structured information as well as productivity enhancing tools to help people learn and improve their skills. (Rosenberg, 2001, p. 109)

REFERENCES

Ackhoff, R. L. (1989). From data to wisdom. *Journal of Applied Systems Analysis*, *16*, 3–9.

Ahsan, S., & Shah, A. (2006). Data, information, knowledge, wisdom: A doubly linked chain? In *Proceedings of the 2006 International Conference on Information & Knowledge Engineering* (pp. 270-278). Las Vegas, Nevada: CSREA Press.

Alavi, M., & Leidner, D. E. (2001, March). Review: Knowledge management and knowledge management systems: Conceptual foundations and research issues. *MIS Quarterly*, *25*(1), 107–136. doi:10.2307/3250961

Anderson, J. R. (1976). *Language, memory, and thoughts.* Hillsdale, NJ: Lawrence Erlbaum Associates.

Barron, T. (2000, August). *A smarter frankenstein: The merging of e-learning and knowledge management.* Retrieved March 03, 2008, from http://www.learningcircuits.org/2000/aug2000/barron1.htm

Bateson, G. (1973). *Steps to an ecology of mind.* London: Granada Publishing.

Beckman, T. J. (1999). The Current State of Knowledge Management. In J. Liebowitz (Ed.), *Knowledge Management Handbook* (pp. 1-22). Boca Raton, FL: CRC Press.

Bonestroo, W., Ley, T., Kump, B., & Lindstaedt, S. (2007). Learn@Work: Competency advancement with learning templates. In *Proceedings of the 3rd Workshop on Learner-Oriented Knowledge Management & KM-Oriented E-Learning* (pp. 9-16).

Bonk, C. J., Graham, C. R., Cross, J., & Moore, M. G. (2005). *Handbook of blended learning.* San Francisco, CA: Pfeiffer.

Braun, S., & Schmidt, A. (2006). Socially-aware informal learning support: potentials and challenges of the social dimension. In *Innovative Approaches for Learning and Knowledge Sharing, EC-TEL 2006 Workshop Proceedings* (pp. 126-131).

Brown, J. S., & Duguid, P. (1991). Organizational learning and communites-of-practice: Toward a unified view of working, learning, and innovation. *Organization Science, 2*(1), 40–57. doi:10.1287/orsc.2.1.40

Brown, J. S., & Gray, E. S. (1995, January). *The people are the company*. Retrieved February 11, 2008, from http://www.fastcompany.com/magazine/01/people.html

Chacón, F. (2003). Mind-mapping for web instruction and learning. *The Convergence of Learning and Technology - Windows on the Future 2003.*

Cleveland, H. (1982, December). Information as resource. *The Futurist*, 34–39.

Davenport, T. H. (1996). *Some principles of knowledge management*. Retrieved February 21, 2008, from http://www.strategy-business.com/press/16635507/8776

Davenport, T. H. (2005). *Thinking for a living.* Boston, Massachusetts: Harvard Business School Press.

Davenport, T. H., & Glaser, J. (2002, July). Just-in-time delivery comes to knowledge management. *Harvard Business Review*, 107–111.

Davenport, T. H., & Prusak, L. (1998). *Working knowledge.* Boston, Massachusetts: Harvard Business School Press.

Dicheva, D., Dichev, C., & Wang, D. (2005). Visualizing topic maps for e-Learning. In *Proceedings of the Fifth IEEE International Conference on Advanced Learning Technologies.* Washington, DC: IEEE Computer Society.

Drucker, P. F. (1993). *Post-capitalist society.* New York: HarperBusiness.

El Sawy, O. A., & Majchrzak, A. (2004). Critical issues in research on real-time knowledge management in enterprises. *Journal of Knowledge Management, 8*, 21–37. doi:10.1108/13673270410548469

Eliot, T. S. (1934). *The Rock.* London: Faber & Faber Limited.

Gilbert, S. W. (1995). Why distance education? A special bulletin. *American Association for Higher Education.*

Graham, C. R. (2005). Blended learning systems - definition, current trends, and future directions. In C. J. Bonk, C. R. Graham, J. Cross, & M. G. Moore (Eds.), *Handbook of Blended Learning* (pp. 3-21). San Francisco, CA: Pfeiffer.

Heisig, P. (2001). Business process oriented knowledge management. In K. Mertins, P. Heisig, & J. Vorbeck (Eds.), *Knowledge Managment - Best Practices in Europe* (pp. 13 - 36). Berlin: Springer-Verlag.

Heisig, P. (2005). *Integration von Wissensmanagement in Geschäftsprozesse.* Berlin, Germany: Kai Mertins.

Hey, J. (2004). *The data, information, knowledge, wisdom chain: The metaphorical link.* (I. O. Commission, Ed.). Retrieved 02 05, 2008, from http://ioc.unesco.org/Oceanteacher/OceanTeacher2/02_InfTchSciCmm/DIKWchain.pdf

Hoffmann, I. (2001). Knowledge management tools. In K. Mertins, P. Heisig, & J. Vorbeck, *Knowledge Management - Best Practices in Europe* (pp. 74-94). Heidelberg, Germany: Springer-Verlag.

ITtoolbox. (2004, September 30). *Knowledge Management Knowledge Base*. Retrieved March 26, 2008, from http://knowledgemanagement.ittoolbox.com/documents/popular-q-and-a/knowledge-management-and-elearning-integration-2846#

Jones, N. (2006). *CELT - About Blended Learning*. Retrieved May 20, 2008, from http://celt.glam.ac.uk/Blended-Learning-at-Glamorgan/?c=about_BL

Jones, N. (2006). E-College Wales, a Case Study of Blended Learning. In C. J. Bonk, C. R. Graham, J. Cross, & M. G. Moore, *Handbook of Blended Learning*. San Francisco, CA: Pfeiffer.

Koohang, A., & Durante, A. (2003). Learners' perceptions toward the Web-based Distance learning activities/assignments portion of an undergraduate hybrid instructional model. *Journal of Information Technology Education*, (2): 105–113.

Leblanc, A., & Abel, M.-H. (2008). E-MEMORAe2.0: an e-learning environment as learners community support. *International Journal of Computer Science & Applications*, *5*(1), 108–123.

Masie, E. (2002, July 23). *Elliott Masie's Learning Trends*. Retrieved March 27, 2008, from http://trends.masie.com/archives/2002/7/23/238-learning-on-line-vs-e-learning-a-season-of-deals-starts.html

Nonaka, I., & Konno, N. (1998). The concept of "Ba": Building a foundation for knowledge creation. *California Management Review*, *40*(3), 40–54.

Nonaka, I., & Takeuchi, H. (1995). *The knowledge-creating company.* New York: Oxford University Press.

Nübel, I. (2005). *Integration von E-Learning und Wissensmanagement.* Aachen, Germany: Shaker Verlag.

Pedroni, M. (2007). E-learning and knowledge management: Context structuration. *Proceedings of the 2007 Informing Science and IT Education Joint Conference* (pp. 99-106).

Pettenati, M. C., & Ranieri, M. (2006). Informal learning theories and tools to support knowledge management in distributed CoPs. In *Innovative Approaches for Learning and Knowledge Sharing EC-TEL 2006 Workshops Proceedings* (pp. 345-355).

Polanyi, M. (1967). *The Tacit Dimension.* New York: Anchor Books.

Probst, G., Raub, S., & Romhardt, K. (1999). *Managing knowledge.* Chichester, UK: John Wiley & Sons Ltd.

Ras, E., Memmel, M., & Weibelzahl, S. (2005). Integration of e-learning and knowledge management - barriers, solutions and future issues. In *WM 2005* (S. 155-164). Heidelberg, Germany: Springer-Verlag.

Rosenberg, M. J. (2001). *E-Learning: Strategies for delivering knowledge in the digital age.* New York: McGraw-Hill.

Rowley, J. (2007). The wisdom hierarchy: representations of the DIKW hierarchy. *Journal of Information Science*, 163–180. doi:10.1177/0165551506070706

Schmidt, A. (2005). Bridging the gap between knowledge managment and e-learning with context-aware corporate learning. In *WM 2005* (pp. 203-213). Heidelberg, Germany: Springer-Verlag.

Schmidt, A. (2008). Enabling learning on demand in semantic work environments: The learning in process approach. In J. Rech, B. Decker, & E. Ras, *Emerging Technologies for Semantic Work Environments: Techniques, Methods, and Applications.* Hershey, PA: IGI Publishing.

Senge, P. M. (1995). *The fifth discipline fieldbook.* London: Nicolas Brealey Publishing. Sharma, N. (n.d.). *The origin of the "data information knowledge wisdom" hierarchy.* Retrieved February 11, 2008, from http://www-personal.si.umich.edu/~nsharma/dikw_origin.htm

Senge, P. M. (2006). *The fifth discipline.* London: Random House Business Books.

Siemens, G. (2005, June). *Elearnspace.* Retrieved March 25, 2008, from http://elearnspace.org/doing/blended.htm

Sridharan, B., Tretiakov, A., & Kinshuk. (2004). Application of Ontology to Knowledge Management in Web Based Learning. *Proceedings of the Fourth IEEE International Conference on Advanced Learning Technologies* (pp. 663-665).

Tsoukas, H. (2003). Do We Really Understand Tacit Knowledge? In M. Easterby-Smith, & M. A. Lyles, *The Blackwell Handbook of Organizational Learning and Knowledge Management* (pp. 410 - 427). Malden, MA: Blackwell Publishing.

Varlamis, I., & Apostolakis, I. (2006). A Framework for Building Virtual Communities for Education. *Innovative Approaches for Learning and Knowledge Sharing, EC-TEL 2006 Workshop Proceedings*, (pp. 165-172).

Wenger, E. (1998). *Communities of practice.* New York: Cambridge University Press.

Wenger, E., McDermott, R., & Snyder, W. M. (2002). *Cultivating communities of practice.* Boston: Harvard Business School Press.

Willis, C. L., & Miertschin, S. L. (2006, April). Mind maps as active learning tool. *Journal of Computing Sciences in Colleges, 21*(4), 266–272.

Woelk, D., & Agarwal, S. (2002). Integration of e-Learning and Knowledge Management. In M. Driscoll & T. C. Reeves, *Proceedings of the E-Learn 2002 World Conference on E-Learning in Corporate, Government, Healthcare & Higher Education* (pp. 1035-1042). Norfolk, Virginia: Association for the Advancement of Computing in Education (AACE).

Zeleny, M. (1987). Management support systems: Towards integrated knowledge management. *Human Systems Management, 7*, 59–70.

KEY TERMS AND DEFINITIONS

Hybrid Learning: Hybrid Learning is located in the continuum of blended learning and therefore a mix of different forms of information and knowledge transfer.

Knowledge: Knowledge is information enriched with context and interpretation. Various distinctions for different kinds of knowledge exist and are used according to the associated purpose.

Knowledge Management: Knowledge Management in general is the process of gathering, maintaining, processing, and providing knowledge. There are specific models for knowledge management – of a formal as well as a more informal character – that integrate knowledge management into complex settings.

Knowledge Management for Hybrid Learning: Knowledge management for hybrid learning is the integration of two separately developed branches that brings benefits to both branches and offers opportunities for an actually already existing connection – knowledge & learning.

ENDNOTES

1 AskOxford. (n.d.). *Knowledge*. Retrieved November 24, 2008, from http://www.askoxford.com/concise_oed/knowledge?view=uk

2 *Lip*. (n.d.). Retrieved November 24, 2008, from http://www.fzi.de/ipe/projekte.php?id=226

3 *APOSDLE*. (n.d.). Retrieved November 24, 2008, from http://www.aposdle.tugraz.at/

4 *Resource Description Framework*. (n.d.). Retrieved November 24, 2008, from http://www.w3.org/RDF/

5 *Dublin Core*. (n.d.). Retrieved November 24, 2008, from http://dublincore.org/

6 *Topic Maps*. (n.d.). Retrieved November 24, 2008, from http://www.topicmaps.org/

7 *OWL Web Ontology Language*. (n.d.). Retrieved November 24, 2008, from http://www.w3.org/TR/owl-guide/

8 *TM4L*. (n.d.). Retrieved November 24, 2008, from http://compsci.wssu.edu/iis/nsdl/download.html

Chapter 27
Model for an Interaction Assessment Strategy in Hybrid Learning Including Web 2.0 Resources

Raquel Hijón-Neira
Universidad Rey Juan Carlos, Spain

Angel Velázquez-Iturbide
Universidad Rey Juan Carlos, Spain

Jonay Rodríguez-Martín
Universidad Rey Juan Carlos, Spain

ABSTRACT

Who being a Hybrid Learning teacher in the Web 2.0 era has not made him/herself ask this question: "Are students working effectively while they are not in face to face class?" Sometimes the questions are asked but he/she does not have the knowledge to create an Interaction Assessment Strategy that could provide this information. The authors present in this chapter a Model that provides the steps and data that should result in a much better teaching/learning process. Thus, the Model presents the questions that should be made, the data model that should be worked on, the visualizations that should better fit each type of data and the process of analysis teachers could make to improve different features, such as: the way of presenting information to the students through the year, prevent students' dropping outs and failures, and generally improve the pace of teaching.

INTRODUCTION

Nowadays, the movement from the traditional classroom towards the online one is already an issue. All of us agree the university courses are now under the group of Hybrid or fully online courses. Due to this rapid development of online or blended courses, new ways of keeping track of the amount and quality of work done by students is necessary, since the face to face classes are no longer available or are substituted, in a way, by the online ones. Therefore, new ways of keeping and

DOI: 10.4018/978-1-60566-380-7.ch027

eye on the student while working out of sight of the educator is necessary.

One of the more disturbing features for instructors of online education is their lack of knowledge of the activities students perform in the course website. Actually, instructors know of students' participation by means of different electronic tools. They also have available statistics about students' accesses and downloads. These statistics are typically shown as dimensional tables, or statistical charts (e.g. bar, lines or pie charts). Web mining techniques and tools provide a different approach to obtain information about students' activities. However, they are often too sophisticated for the mean instructor. In summary, instructors lack tools to track students' activity that offer sophisticated analysis of students' activities and are easy to use.

The more accurate and varied information the e-learning system can provide, the better feedback teachers can work on. This information can be used for several purposes. Firstly, it can give information about the web site usage, so its structure can be improved. Secondly, information about patterns of usage by students can be extracted as in Srivastava, Cooley, Deshpande, & Tan (2000). These patterns can be used as a basis to analyze and enhance students' performance.

To set up the problem to analyze, firstly there is a brief description of how other Learning Management Systems (LMS) do this analysis of interactions; following to that, there is an explanation of the previous work done in this analysis of interactions, and finally there is an explanation of the analysis of interactions system developed at our department.

How Other LMS Analyze Interactions

In previous studies such as in "E-Learning Platforms Analysis and Development of Students Tracking Functionality" Hijón & Velázquez (2006a) there have been made a comprehensive assessment of these LMS. In particular, it was taken into account the student tracking functionality they presented for analysis of interactions. Among the wide range of systems the market offers, either open source or property code ones, the study considered some of the most relevant ones, such as: Moodle, Claroline, Dokeos, Nicenet, DotLRN, Sakai, OpenUSS, Mindflash, Blackboard and WebCT.

None of these LMS offered good analysis of interactions that usefully help teachers foresee what the students behavior is going to be, neither had a good interface to filter this analysis. Therefore, the result is that the interactions analysis they offer is not used by teachers, thus this may mean this type of analysis of interactions functionality in LMS needs to be improved and publicized. The general way to show the information in these systems is by tabular representation of the information, which results in many cases in the necessity of downloads of the data to other systems for further information processing and graphical visualization that is not always done.

Previous Work in Analysis of Interaction

Teachers need more and more an aid from the e-learning system that provides information about how students interact with it. Thus, some applications that try to resolve the problem of keeping an eye on the student while working out of sight of the educator have already been developed in different areas of e-Learning. *In Distance learning management systems*, Ramani & Rocha (2000) describe tools for letting instructors easily view student participation in a Web-based class using charts and graphs to display student participation. Reffay & Chanier (2002) identify clusters and cliques within the online class. These tools focus not on the individual student, but rather on class activity as a whole. Although both sets of tools are interesting and potentially useful in aiding the understanding of web based discussion forums, they are not built on an analysis of the discussion evaluator's workflow, which is a critical requirement for improving online teaching effectiveness. In Mazza & Dimitrova (2005) Ricardo Mazza and his colleagues had developed an Application named CourseVis that visualized interactions of students with an e-learning site, and then they moved towards moodle and offered what they have called GISMO which is an application that can be installed into Moodle. In University of Edinburgh, Hardy, Bates, Hill, & Antonioletti (2007) have also made tracking and visualization of student use of online learning materials. *In forums,* Integrated Participation Evaluation Tool (iPET) by Saltz, Hiltz, Turoff, & Passerini, (2007) that is a web-based application combining social network analysis and visualization to enable distance learning instructors and students to improve their participation in online discourse and so improve their overall learning experience. *In e-testing,*Costagliola, Fuccela, Giordano, & Polese (2007) presented a system for the logging and visualization of the learners' behavior during the execution of structured test based on Multiple Choice question type. In *Social Network analysis* by Martinez, Dimitriadis, Rubia, Gómez, Garrachón, & Marcos (2002), Researchers have used SNA to understand participation within online communities. For example, researchers have used traditional SNA data-gathering techniques, such as student surveys, to analyze the network created in a distance learning environment. From the student side, in Amelung, Piotrowski, & Rösner (2006) and in Rösner, Amelung, & Piotrowski, (2006) it is presented *eduComponents*, new modules to be integrated into a LMS that provide specialized content types offering functions for managing hybrid learning, such as possibilities to answer tests or send assignments, and they give some reporting and statistics to students, that help them track their learning progress that they value very positively.

Considering the discovery of access patterns, in the article "Towards Evaluating Learners' Behaviour in a Web-Based Distance Learning Environment" Zaïane and Luo (2001) have designed and implemented a prototype as a tool for educators to apply association rules to discover relationships between learning activities that learners perform, sequential analysis to discover interesting patterns in the sequences of on-line activities, and clustering to group similar access behaviours. For example, an analysis of student use of a courseware website by Peled and Rashty (1999) found that the most popular online activities were passive and involved getting information rather than contributing. Their conclusion is that the students were very goal oriented in their use of the web site. Further information can be gained from knowing when students access resources such as in "ViSION: Visualization Student Interactions Online" by Sheard, Albrecht, & Butbul (2005). This can help educators understand student's preferred learning patterns. A study carried out by McIsaac, Blocher, Mahes, & Vrasidas, (1999) explored interactions of doctoral students with an online environment and they concluded that student interactions were goal focussed. For instance, in a study of student use of a first year geology website by Hellwege, Gleadow, & McNaught (1996), the log file analysis showed that students accessed the most recent lecture notes first, picking up a couple of key slides, before returning to a previous lecture. As a result, it was shown that students were accessing resources according to immediate need. In this way, another study by Hijón and Velázquez (2006b) of this characteristics showed that the average connections to the CMS was over thirty minutes, in the midday and late hours and on week days rather than on the weekends.

So it can be observed that to obtain further and completer analysis of students interactions, firstly, it is necessary to have tools and systems that collect and present these information to teachers, secondly, it is necessary, either to download these tracking information towards systems that provide with a more complete statistical and visual analysis or to enhance these previous tracking systems with functionality that provides teachers with the complete analysis of interactions from easy to reach and use interfaces. Therefore, the steps followed in our university are going to be explained.

How We Have Filled the Gap in Our University: Tracking System Developed

We have addressed this problem in an *in house* Learning Management Tracking System called Merlin and used by our Department. The architecture of the tracking, visualization and analytic tools developed of Merlin has four different layers. The bottom layer contains the Learning Management System. The second one contains four different tools for tracking and recording students' activity. They use different approaches to gather this information: logs (Log Tracking Tool, LTT) as has been shown (Hijón and Velázquez 2005), cookies (Cookies Tracking Tool, CTT) as in Hijón-Neira, Urquiza-Fuentes, Domínguez-Mateos, & Velázquez-Iturbide (2007a) is detailed, an ad-hoc user information gathered using the student's login name (Ad-Hoc Tracking Tool, ATT) explained in Hijón-Neira, Velázquez-Iturbide, & Herrera-Cabanillas (2007b), and e-surveys also in Hijón, et al. (2006). The third layer contains the visualization and statistics tools (Hijón and Velazquez 2008a) such as Prefuse, Spotfire and Yale a data mining tool. On top of it, there is a presentation layer that unifies all the applications into what is called the Merlin system, which also provides an adaptive tutorial to guide the user (teacher) through the system.

With the data collected we carried out a study in 6 different computer science degree courses in two different universities, Rey Juan Carlos University of Madrid, Spain, and Thames Valley University of London, UK. The period of study was from October 2006 to July 2007, with about 400 students interacting with the e-learning system, which was our Merlin in the university of Madrid, and Blackboard in London.

We have presented in Hijón, Velazquez, Barn, & Oussena (2008b) how by the analysis of students interactions with e-learning systems, teachers can modify students outcomes by looking at and interpreting the interaction data; and how by addressing some policies to prevent failures or drop outs in an early stage, there may be a need to modify the established pace of teaching. Some conclusions of this cross universities analysis were: considering their access patterns by morning or evening sessions, that students in morning sessions work harder, possibly because they have more spare time, but fail also more, probably because they do not make the most of their time. Furthermore, the ones in the evening sessions get better grades, probably they are more brilliant students, or with better skills, hence most of them also have jobs outside university. Considering their access patterns by exam performance, students that pass are more constant in keeping up with their work as the year goes by than those that do not pass; moreover, students that pass work harder over the year, increasing the amount of work done towards the final exam than the rest; Finally, the higher percentage of absenteeism in the morning probably explains that they are less motivated and do not have a job or a family to maintain as those in the evenings. Considering the evolution of their access pattern through the year, pass and good students make a much bigger effort at the beginning of the course and it clearly increases towards the midterm/final exam in subjects that run throughout the year and the final exam for the one semester ones; they are more consistent in keeping up with their work over the year, the later consult more their final grade in June; also, students that failed and were absent in the February exam tend to start to work again on the subject towards June and May respectively; all in all, there is a clear tendency to work harder towards the exams dates, and in average more in the second half of the year.

We are in the position now of stating a model to define this type of tracking systems for e-Learning that would lead to the analysis of students' interactions; where the information that have to be store, the queries that should be made over it and the way of representing different types of data as well as the process to analyze students access patterns is explained. Consequently, any person, group of persons or institution could look at it when trying to develop and effective tracking system.

The rest of the chapter is structured as follows; in section 2 we describe the Hybrid Learning Model for web 2.0; following to that, in section 3 there is the explanation of the structure the previous Model proposes, with its four phases: the questions, data and representation model, as well as the pattern discovery phase are detailed explained; following to that, section 4 explains with an example the functionality of the Model. Section 5 describes an example of application for the hybrid Learning model into a LMS. Finally, the conclusions are explained.

E-LEARNING MODEL FOR WEB 2.0

An e-learning Model for web 2.0 includes much more resources the web 1.0 offered. We are going to see first, the main differences between web 1.0 and web 2.0, secondly, differences between traditional or face to face teaching and the hybrid learning teaching, and finally, the e-learning system for web 2.0 we have developed the model on.

Web 1.0 vs. Web 2.0

The web has definitely changed, web 1.0 was only readable, few people created content in it; furthermore, to create content it was necessary to be and expert (or geek). Thus, the contents where static, all that could be seen where documents, and the only way of surfing the web was by using a browser. Therefore, the movement towards web 2.0, allowed the content to be also writeable, without having to be an expert to be able to do it, users can create content. The dynamic content is based on any user creating it, allowing also pictures, videos, links and sites to be place, letting not only browsers, but also, RSS readers, PDAs, mobile phones, etc into it.

Hybrid Learning in Web 2.0

As shown in Figure 1 the traditional or face to face teaching has many differences from the hybrid learning one. The former, is teacher centered, magisterial classes thought in class and students passively receiving the knowledge, which form their individual knowledge. The latter, also has a teacher creating the curricular material, which students receive, but those can also communicate with the teacher using the students work spaces, such as blogs, wikis, forums and email, that would be asynchronous communications, therefore not dependable on a fix schedule. Also, tutoring session can be individual, group and also virtual if using applications such as chat, videoconference or messenger, that would be synchronous or schedule dependable. Both, teachers and students could organize debates that encourage participation and therefore the collective knowledge. Therefore, teaching does not have to be coordinated by time and place as in face to face, in hybrid learning there are some resources that have to be coordinated, and some others that allowed a different students pace.

Web 2.0 Hybrid Learning Components Studied

The proposed Hybrid learning model studied, using web 2.0 resources, has been made regarding the following components: course material, this is to say, the curricular material teachers present to the students (course modules); and a set of components related with the former, which are chats, questionnaires, forums, resources (such as documents, presentations, video, pictures, etc.),

Figure 1. Traditional face to face vs. hybrid learning

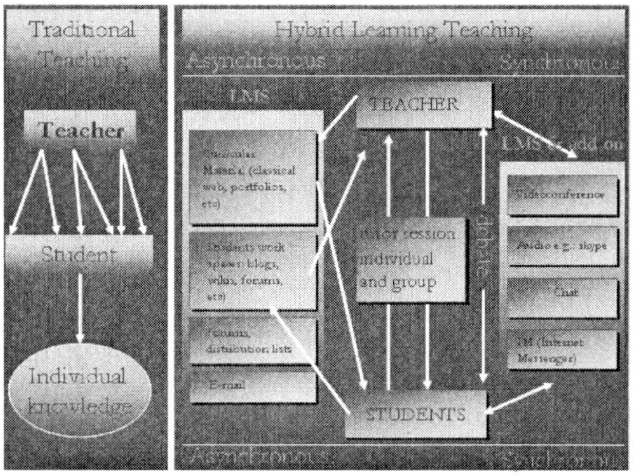

surveys, wikis and a log that records every interaction the students do into the system.

STRUCTURE THE MODEL PROPOSES

As it can be seen in Figure 2 the model has four different phases, each one tries to fulfill the objective set on the top box, and after their respective processes, each phase final product is obtained, and would help in the making of the consecutive phase.

The first phase of the model takes into consideration "What do we need to know about students' interactions?" Then a comprehensive set of questions have to be place; finally, the organization and correlation among them would result in the Question Model.

The second phase of the model allows the creation of a structured data base, once the information that needs to be gathered is clear, this phase would

Figure 2. Structure of the hybrid learning model

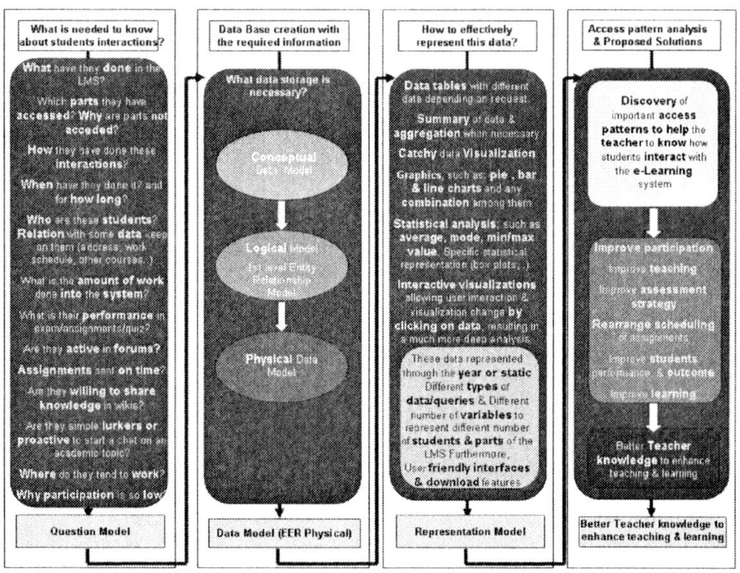

obtain the Entity relationship Model that would result in a Data base with all the required data to do the analysis of students' interactions.

The third phase of the model is the representation phase, where the best way to represent each type of data and a method to determine should be taken.

Finally, the forth phase is the pattern analysis of students interactions, identifying important patterns to help the teacher to know how students work. This analysis should have the general objectives of improve learning and teaching. The outcome of this phase is the Analysis Model, where for each problem, lack or dysfunction, there should be a proposed solution.

Question Model

The question Model proposes a structure that allows the creation of "any questions presented to the teacher that would help him/her to analyze students' interactions". So the structure of it is shown in Figure 3, it has six columns, the first one correspond to the assessment question (AQ); the second one to the action to analyze, naturally, those are specific of the module they belong to. The third is the part of the LMS, each part of the hybrid learning model we have based the study on. Naturally, each part can be subdivided into the category course, this is to say, there may be 1, 0 or n occurrences of each part in a module. The forth part is who the question is doing assessment

Figure 3. Question model, representation model and pattern discovery phase

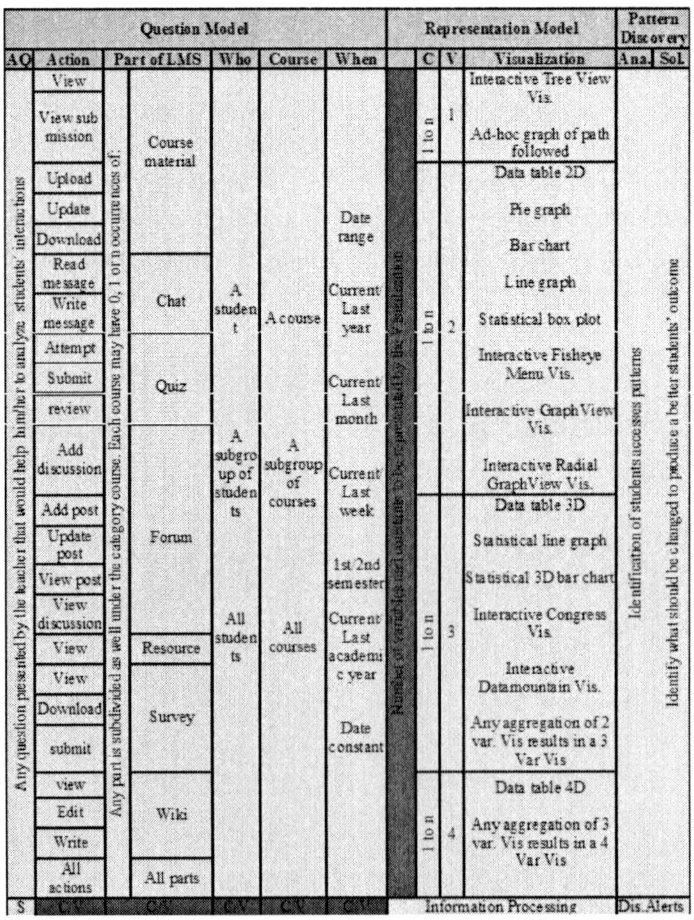

of learning and performance. The last part, is the fifth, and stands for when, or what period of time is the question being placed.

The model works as follows: The question has to be asked, and based on its functionality the variables and constants (marked with V and C) have to be found among the parts the Question Model proposes; by looking at the model its easy the determination of variables and constants. Notice that, in some questions the variable is marked below the question, which means that it appears an additional variable that should go into the next phase, such as the grades (to include performance). All in all, the variables and constants are all included in the Data Model.

The set of variables and constants are the entries to the Representation Model, that propose different visualizations to the set of variables, and then subjective opinion about the visualizations should lead to choose one or the other.

The visualization is the entry to the Pattern discovery phase, when teachers identify access patterns and propose a solution.

Data Model

The Data Model presented offers the EER Diagram of the necessary data base to do the analysis based on the results of the previous phase, the Question Model. In the Figure 4 the second level is shown, with the tables each part of the proposed web 2.0 Hybrid learning Model studied may have, as well as the compulsory fields and main relationships.

As it can be observed the Data Model has the required entities to store the data the hybrid learning system needs to keep all the data for further assessment of students' interactions.

For easier understanding, references of entities and modules in the next figure are done by an associated number in brackets.

The Data Model *core* (1) contains the entities *course, module* and *user*, which are related with almost every other entity in the system. This is to say, every part the web 2.0 hybrid learning LMS has is related to them.

For instance, the *chat* entity (2) is associated to the *course* entity, a *course* may have none or many chats; a chat can have none or many *chat_messages*; and a *chat message* is written by a *chat user*; the chat user is related, 1 to 1, to the main entity *users*. Almost the same thing happens with the entities that form the part forum (3).

The entities that maintain the data for *questionnaires* (4) are related with the main entities of the *Core* (1) and also with the entities in the *grades module* (9) and the *questions* module (8) that maintains a categorized data base of questions to create the questionnaires.

A *wiki* is associated to a *course* and the entity *wiki_entries* (5) has one occurrence for each entry in the *wikis* entity; each *wiki_entry* belongs only to a *user*, it is a 1 to 1 relationship.

The *log* module (6) keeps a temporal track with the sequence of actions that has happened to the entities into the core module as well as many other related entities. Thus, in the *time* field, it is kept a temporal record of what and when has anything occurred, maintaining a record with anything between courses and users.

The *resources* module (7) only contains an entity that keeps a record for any resource associated with a course.

The survey module (10) contains the entities to storage surveys made that are related to a course and it corresponding notes associated to a user.

Representation Model

The representation model pretends to offer the visualization, graph, chart or table that best fits the data to be shown; therefore, a previous analysis of them has been made. The different types of visualizations are: data tables, simple graphs,

Figure 4. Second level – logical model (EER diagram)

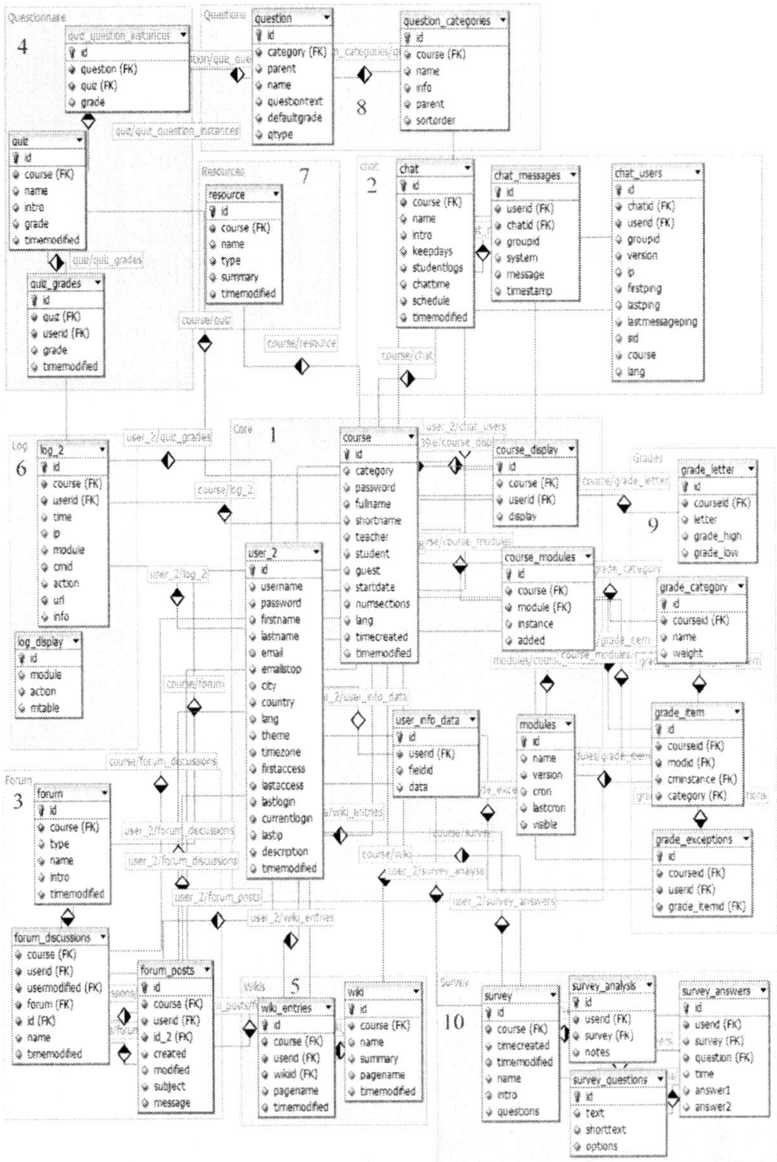

such as pie charts, bar charts and line graphs, *ad-hoc* graphs, such as most followed path and summary of accesses.

Interactive Visualizations, which allow, just by clicking, zooming or scrolling, find more information about data, or a third "hidden" variable, this is the case of the *Congress* visualization, when by clicking in the visualization more information about the data shown is offered; or a *Fish Eye Menu* that allows scrolling back and forth to see the variables; or a *Graph View*, an interactive social graph that nicely represents clusters of information and also highlights the node selected and allows zooming; or a *Data Mountain* visualization, that by clicking on data more information about the marked dot appears on the top label; or a *Tree View* visualization, where grouped conceptual information appears when clicking on a branch of data, allowing the displaying of information only by clicking.

Statistical Visualizations, that offer more information about the data displayed, such as media, mode and minimum/maximum value. Usually this type of visualizations allows more data variables to be displayed on them. One of them is a *Boxplot* visualization that represents different groups of data independently drawn on a Cartesian Diagram; another type is a *3 variables Bar Chart* that allows a third variable to be displayed on a bar chart; and the last one is *Line Graph* visualization that also permits 3 variables to be displayed on the same graph.

The Representation Model (see previous Figure 3) works as it follows: the entries to the model are the number of variables or constants the previous phase produces, and depending on the number of each kind the query to be represented has, a type of graph can be selected. Thus, the visualizations that offer the same number of variables are grouped together, the number of constants is not important for the determination of the graphs, since there can be from 1 to n.

Pattern Discovery Phase

Or the phase where teachers have to discover students access patterns. Entries to this phase are the visualization of the interactions data in the Hybrid Learning System; and it is in this phase, once the student access pattern is discovered when the solution have to be taken. The model also proposes that when a type of access is discovered, the system alerts the teacher or the students, depending on the case; of what is probably going to happened is this behavior is maintained. For instance, there are here a couple of examples of this phase, if we wish to know:

Example 1

Question Phase

- Do students have different access pattern in the morning courses from the evening ones?
- If there is any difference, is it extensible to all the morning or evening courses?

Representation Phase

It has been chosen a Statistical Boxplot comparison of grades and Bar Chart Visualization of accesses through the year representing two different courses, on the left "Software Engineering" and on the right "Language Processors".

Analysis / Solution Phase

Analysis: first of all, if it is considered that a higher number of hits on the module pages results in a bigger amount of work done on them, then it was found that students in the morning classes worked harder than those in the evening, this can be observed by looking at the bottom part of the visualizations where a bar chart represented the total amount of hits. Secondly, by looking at the upper part of the graphs, where a box plots represent each group of students for both courses; it could be observed than the average of students failing were higher in the morning session. Finally, also for both courses, the averages of students that manage to get more than a "pass" grade were higher in the evening sessions.

As a result, students in morning sessions work harder, possibly because they have more spare time, but fail also more, probably because they do not make the most of their time. Furthermore, the ones in the evening sessions get better grades, probably because they are more brilliant students, or with better skills, hence most of them also have jobs outside university.

Solution: Teachers and educators should set out policies to prevent the morning class from absenteeism in the final exam, and both booster motivation and enhance attitudes towards the course; by handing out more assignments and practical exercises during term time, and periodic refreshers to keep them up to date with class.

Example 2

Question Phase

- Do students that get a similar exam performance have similar access patterns?
- Is it possible to find a difference among them?
- Is there any difference among courses that last one semester or that run all over the year?
- If they belong to the first group, between the first and second semester?

Representation Phase
In this case the selected "Language Processors" course is represented on the left in the morning shift and on the right in the evening one. And both shifts offer two different visualizations a Boxplot Comparison of the grades on the top and a Bar Chart of the accesses on the bottom.

Analysis/Solution Phase
Analysis: On the other hand, in courses that run throughout the year, students *failing* start at work later in the year (May and June in the morning session, and April and May in the evening one), therefore is already too late even if they seem to work hard; *absent* students work less from the beginning of the course. In subjects that last one semester, students *failing* and *absent* in the February exam tend to start working again on the subject towards June and May respectively.

Solution: to prevent failures and abandoners, teachers and educators should encourage students to start working sooner on the course and to maintain the amount of work done constantly.

By looking at the access data from the first stages of the course, different groups of students can be identified; therefore teachers can put in place measures to prevent *absent* students from not taking the final exam and potential failing students not doing as much work as is required to pass.

EXAMPLE OF THE MODEL FUNCTIONALITY

In the next Figure 5 there are a set of examples of use of the Hybrid Learning Model for an Interaction Assessment Strategy.

For instance, in the first question, "Student group by exam performance (grades)" The model has identified two variables: one is the students, and the other one the grades (which are marked below the question), and two constants: a selected course and a selected date. Then the Representation Model has two variables and two constants as entries to it, which means any graph that represents two variables can be chosen; *Interactive Graph View* has been proved very efficient when talking about identifying social groups of students. Finally in the pattern discovery phase, teachers should identify different groups of students rapidly, and identify measures to improve the bad performers' ones.

Another example we want to point out of the table, is the last one, What are the most proactive students?" clearly to identify them is necessary to select the actions of each part that imply participation, such as downloading, add discussion, write messages, etc.

AN EXAMPLE OF APPLICATION FOR THE HYBRID LEARNING MODEL

The model can be implemented in many different ways and in all different LMS systems. We have created a new module for the Moodle LMS that can be automatically installed into any running Moodle system; the Figure 6 on the top shows one of the interfaces named AIAS (Ad-Hoc Interactions System) where user selects the type of

Figure 5. Example of use of the model with a set of questions

Question Model						Representation Model			Pattern Discovery	
Assessment Question	Action	Part of LMS	Who	Course	When	V	C	Visualization	Analysis	Solution
What has a student done in a selected course?	All actions	All parts	A selected	A course	1st & 2nd semester	[illegible]	[illegible]	Pie graph with percentages of each part	Identification of parts/modules less acceded in the course	Propose activities to make them participate, extra assignments, email them with directions
	[illegible]	V	C	C	C					
Who had acceded to a selected part and how many times?		All parts	A selected	A course	Date range	2	2	Interactive Fisheye Menu Vis.	Identification of lurkers or passive students	Propose a minimum of participation by fix date
		V	V	C	C					
Comparison of amount of work done in all courses by a student	All actions	All parts	A selected	All courses	Current academic year	3	2	Statistical line graph, with a line representing each course	If patterns are not similar, it may mean, he/she is not as encouraged in one of the subjects	Adapt resources, timing and know how to enhance the worse courses
	V		C	V	V					
What has a student done through the year in a course	All actions	All parts	A selected	A course	Current academic year	[illegible]	[illegible]	Statistical 3D bar chart by month	Identify patterns of use separately by month of the year. Identify months of inactivity in some parts	Develop policies to increase students work hours these periods
	V	V	C	C	V					
Comparison of work & performance achieved in 2 courses (e.g. Two shifts)	All actions	All parts	All students	A selected group	Last academic year	4	1	Statistical 3D bar chart (2)	Do students that make good grades follow a certain path? Is possible to identify possible dropping outs or failures in early stage?	Identity possible droppers or failing students in an early stage, then, adjust teaching policies.
V	V		C	V	V					
What is the most popular part of the course	All actions	All parts	All students	A course	1st semester	[illegible]	2	Interactive Congress Vis. summarized by part	Offers different curves for each part and by clicking on them, the student's name	Identify parts not acceded as much as expected & who are the students on each part of the curve
	[illegible]	V	V	C	C					
Students group by exam performance (grades)			All students	A course	Date constant	[illegible]	[illegible]	Interactive GraphView Vis.	Identify social groups of students; testify if friends make similar grades. Rapidly identify them in a group.	Obtain a clear picture of the results of students. Clearly identify them.
V			V	C	C					
What is the most followed part in a course?	All	All parts	All	A course	2nd semester	[illegible]	[illegible]	Ad-hoc graph of path followed	Clearly identify what students tend to do more when entering a course	Get the knowledge, depending on results, remake a teaching strategy
V				C						
Who has sent the assessment on time?	upload	Course material	All students	A course	Date constant	[illegible]	[illegible]	Data table	Identify students that follow the rules	Probably create policies to try to encourage all students to send things on time (if they are many)
	C	C	V	C	C					
In which time-frame students are more active to interact with different course material?	All actions	Course material	All students	A course	Current month	[illegible]	[illegible]	Bar chart of partial totals, representing: in the y-axis the hours, in the x-axis the days of the week	Identify hours that are most likely to get the students connected during the week and weekends.	Offer them new material in the more active hours, so the attitude is more proactive.
V	C	C	C	C	C					
What is the students' geographical location when connecting to the system?	All actions	All parts	All students	All courses	Current month	2	2	Interactive Radial GraphView Vis.	Identify their geographical location may be really important with fully online courses, or Erasmus students	Consider geographical zone times in order to ask for assigments or plan a chat for instant.
V			V	C	C					
What are the most proactive students?	Download; Upload/Update; Write message; Submit review; Add Discussion add/update post; download/submit; Edit/write	Co. Material; Chat; Quiz; Forum; Survey; Wiki	All students	A course	Current year			Data table ranking with the students names totalizing each part and offering also a general total by students	Identify the amount of students that do not make the average of required participation in the different parts the course have (material, chat, quiz, forum, survey) By selecting the actions that require a more participative attitude.	Plan actions to make them work: send them an email requiring their presence for instant may be a thing
		V	V	C	C					

values he/she wants to study for each dimension (that, as can be observed are the ones the Question Model has identified); and then, thanks to the *ajax* technology the following interface is generated ad-hoc depending on the previously selected data (see bottom part).

The module developed following the model has much more functionality that has been generated following the proposed model resulting in very easy to use interfaces providing a very useful tool for teachers needing to obtain information about how are their students working into the system. Therefore, many other implementations can be developed following the model, but the more accurately developers follow it, the better the final result is.

CONCLUSION

It is very important for a teacher in the web 2.0 era to be able to "see" and evaluate the kind of work students do while working beyond their eyesight; so teachers procedures can be readjust to what the class demands, and they also may have other ways of evaluation of the amount and quality of the work students have performed during the course. Almost all LMS in the market offer some kind of analysis of students' interactions, but it has been found insufficient for the complex task of analyzing interactions. Thus, as seen in the previous works in this field, authors have had to develop new systems for tracking interactions or at least, have had to download this tracking data onto other systems that should provide this further assessment so much needed. Such is the case in our university, where enhanced tools for analysis and visualization have been developed and used to improve the teaching-learning process.

A review of the movement from the traditional face to face class towards the online one has also been made. With the wide development of web technology new ways of communication and participation within a class have appeared,

Figure 6. Top, main interface of AIAS, bottom, second interface generated based on the variables selected

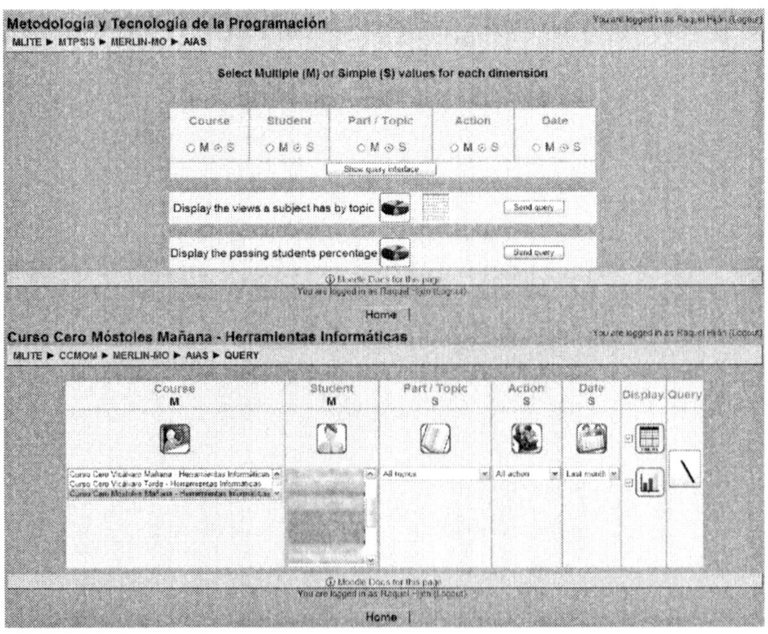

namely: forum, chats, wikis and so on, that are part of what are called "the web 2.0 resources" that have made possible the movement from the traditional teaching towards a much more student participative teaching learning process.

Once the importance of the analysis of students' interactions has been explained and the e-learning or hybrid learning background that is valid nowadays has also been centered, there is the explanation of the hybrid learning model for analysis of students' interactions including web 2.0 resources. First, it is explained the structure the model proposes, which consists on four phases; the first one proposes a Question Model, that defines a comprehensive set of data these systems should provide; the second one proposes a Data Model, that details what data should the system storage for the analysis, the detailed modules, entities and relationships among them; the third phase offered a Representation Model that consisted on the definition and classification of different types of visualizations for the data, depending on the questions being placed into the system; the last phase proposes a Better teacher knowledge to enhance the Teaching-Learning Process by the discovery and analysis of students access patterns and the measures that can be applied to improve teaching, participation, the assessment strategy, learning and the students outcome.

Following to the explanation of the Model, there is an example of the functionality of the model that has proved that any developed system that would implement the four phases should obtain all that is needed to improve the teaching learning process in the web 2.0 eras.

Finally, in our university we have applied the model to develop a new module for the widespread Moodle LMS that has resulted in a very good tool for the complete analysis of the students' interactions, therefore it can also help other institutions and developers.

All in all, in one hand, we have effectively developed a Hybrid Learning Model for Analysis of Students interactions using Web 2.0 resources, that would help teachers with the difficult task of improve learning and teaching by getting the important information about students' accesses. On the other hand, we have also taken special care in the phase of the model that implies visualization of access and performance data, due to the importance that it has to pursue user understanding. Furthermore, the question model combined with the Data Model makes easy to get to know all the information the system should provide, and may also help developers to do the software analysis of an application/module that gets this functionality. Finally, teachers that follow the structure the model proposes, in any type of LMS should get important information that may lead them to improve their teaching and their students' learning pace in an Hybrid Learning Strategy.

REFERENCES

Amelung, M., Piotrowski, M., & Rösner, D. (2006). EduComponents: Experiences in e-assessment in computer science education. In *ITiCSE '06: Proceedings of the 11th annual conference on Innovation and technology in computer science education* (pp. 88–92). New York: ACM Press.

Costagliola, G., Fuccela, V., Giordano, M., & Polese, G. (2007). Logging and visualization of learner behaviour in Web-based e-testing. In *ICWL, International Conference on Web Based Learning,* Edinburgh, United Kingdom.

Hardy, J., Bates, S., Hill, J., & Antonioletti, M. (2007). Tracking and visualization of student use of online learning materials in a large undergraduate course. In *ICWL 2007,* Edinburgh, UK (pp. 280-287).

Hellwege, J., Gleadow, A., & McNaught, C. (1996). Paperless lectures on the Web: An evaluation of the educational outcomes of teaching geology using the Web. In *Proceedings of 13th Annual Conference of the Australian Society for Computers in Learning in Tertiary education (ASCILITE '96)*, Adelaide, Australia.

Hijón, R., & Velázquez, A. (2005). Steps towards the analysis of students' activity in e-learning platforms. E-Learn 2005. Association for the Advancement in Computing in Education. ISBN: 1-880094-57-6.

Hijón, R., & Velázquez, A. (2006a). E-Learning Platforms analysis and development of students tracking functionality. In *ED-MEDIA 2006 -- World Conference on Educational Multimedia, Hypermedia and Telecommunications (AACE)* (pp.2823- 2828).

Hijón, R., & Velázquez, A. (2006b). Web, log analysis and surveys for tracking university students. In *Proceedings of IADIS International Conference on Applied Computing* (pp. 561-564).

Hijón, R., & Velazquez, A. (2008a). How to improve assessment of learning and performance through interactive visualization. In *The 8th IEEE International Conference on Advance Learning Technologies (ICALT'08)* (pp. 472-476).

Hijón, R., Velazquez, A., Barn, B., & Oussena, S. (2008b). A comparative study on the analysis of students' interactions in e-Learning. In *The 8th IEEE International Conference on Advance Learning Technologies (ICALT'08)* (pp. 20-22).

Hijón-Neira, R., Urquiza-Fuentes, J., Domínguez-Mateos, F., & Velázquez-Iturbide, A. (2007a). Assessing the usability of a cookies-based access monitoring tool for a CMS. In *ICALT 2007* (pp.262-264).

Hijón-Neira, R., Velázquez-Iturbide, A., & Herrera-Cabanillas, V. (2007b). Blended learning tools for assessing students interactions. *CEDI 2007 – II Congreso Español de informática, VIII Simposio Nacional de Tecnologías de la Información y las Comunicaciones en la Educación – SINTICE 2007*, Zaragoza, Spain.

Martinez, A. Dimitriadis, Y., Rubia, B., Gómez, E., Garrachón, I., Marcos, J.A. (2002). Studying social aspects of computer-supported collaboration with a mixed evaluation approach. In *Proc. Conf. Computer Support for Collaborative Learning (CSCL)* (pp. 631-632). Philadelphia, PA: Lawrence Erlbaum Associates.

Mazza, R., & Dimitrova, V. (2005). Generation of graphical representations of student tracking data in course management systems. In *Ninth International Conference on Information Visualisation (IV'05)* (pp. 253-258).

McIsaac, M. S., Blocher, J. M., Mahes, V., & Vrasidas, C. (1999). Student and teacher perceptions of interaction in online computer-mediated communication. *Educational Media International, 36*(2), 121–131. doi:10.1080/0952398990360206

Peled, A., & Rashty, D. (1999). Logging for success: Advancing the use of WWW logs to improve computer mediated distance learning. *Journal of Educational Computing Research, 21*, 413–431.

Ramani, L., & Rocha, H. (2000). *Interaction map: Information visualization techniques in web-based distance education environments* (Tech. report IC-00-17). Universidade Estatual de Campinas, Brazil.

Reffay, C., & Chanier, T. (2002) Social network analysis used for modelling collaboration in distance learning groups. In *Proc. Intelligent Tutoring System Conference* (pp. 31-40). Berlin, Germany: Springer-Verlag.

Rösner, D., Amelung, M., & Piotrowski, M. (2006): E-Learning-Komponenten zur Intensivierung der Übungen in der Informatik-Lehre – ein Erfahrungsbericht. In P. Forbrig, G. Siegel,& M. Schneider (Eds.), *GI-Fachtagung Hochschuldidaktik der Informatik*. Bonn, Germany: GI-Verlag.

Saltz, J. S., Hiltz, S. R., Turoff, M., & Passerini, K. (2007). Increasing participation in distance learning courses. *IEEE Internet Computing, 11*(3), 36–44. doi:10.1109/MIC.2007.64

Sheard, J., Albrecht, D., & Butbul, W. (2005). ViSION: Visualization student interactions online. In A. Treloar & A. Ellis (Eds.), *Proceedings of the Eleventh Australasian World Wide Web Conference* (pp. 48-58).

Srivastava, J., Cooley, R., Deshpande, & Tan, P. (2000). Web usage mining: Discovery and applications of usage patterns from Web data. *SIGKDD Explorations, 1*(2).

Zaïane, O., & Luo, J. (2001). Towards evaluating learners' behaviour in a Web-based distance learning environment. In *Second IEEE International Conference on Advanced Learning Technologies (ICALT'01)*.

KEY TERMS AND DEFINITIONS

Hybrid Learning: The combination of multiple approaches to learning. Blended learning can be accomplished through the use of 'blended' virtual and physical resources. A typical example of this would be a combination of technology-based materials and face-to-face sessions used together to deliver instruction.

LMS (Learning Management System): A set of software tools designed to manage user learning interventions Interaction: A kind of action that occurs as two or more objects have an effect upon one another.

Visualization (Information Graphics): Visual representations of information, data, or knowledge.

Web 2.0: A term describing the trend in the use of World Wide Web technology and web design that aims to enhance creativity, information sharing, and, most notably, collaboration among users.

Chapter 28
The Polyphonic Model of Hybrid and Collaborative Learning

Stefan Trausan-Matu
Politehnica University of Bucharest, Romania

ABSTRACT

This chapter presents a model for hybrid and collaborative learning based on an analogy with musical polyphony, starting from Bakhtin's ideas of dialogism. The model considers different voices (participants) inter-animating and jointly constructing a coherent tune (a solution, in problem solving), enabling other voices to adopt differential positions and to identify dissonances (unsound approaches). This chapter introduces also software tools, which visualize the discussion threads in a chat and the influences that an utterance has on the subsequent ones. Such tools help both teachers and learners to evaluate and enhance the learning process. The model helps to understand how learners inter-animate when they participate to collaborative chats for problem solving or other learning activities, including Hybrid Learning.

INTRODUCTION

In recent years, collaborative tools on the web, like message forums, instant messengers (chats, for example, Yahoo messenger with two or more participants), wikis, blogs and folksonomies became very popular, adding a new dimension to the web and bringing a new generation, Web2.0. It is very important that this new generation appeared before the generation expected by many: the semantic web. This fact is very significant because it emphasizes also theoretical issues important for learning theory and practice: The socio-cultural paradigm ("knowledge is built socially") of Web2.0 is now much more successful in the competition with the cognitive paradigm ("knowledge is acquired individually"), which fundaments the semantic web and Artificial Intelligence (AI).

These different two paradigms have direct correspondence also in the way we see and support learning with computers. Instead Computer-Based Learning or Intelligent Tutoring Systems (ITS), two leading paradigms of the last decades, we discuss now about Hybrid Learning and Computer-

DOI: 10.4018/978-1-60566-380-7.ch028

Supported Collaborative Learning (CSCL, see also Koshmann, 1999). Moreover, even the appearance of the idea of Hybrid Learning may be explained also by the failure of the ideas that learning is only a knowledge transfer process that may be achieved individually, solely with the use of totally online learning. Meanwhile, the difficulties of achieving artificial intelligence in the strong sense (totally imitating humans) leave far away the ideal of totally replacing professors by artificially intelligent assistants (as, for example, ITS supporters hoped).

The analysis of the problems in achieving strong AI has an important significance for this chapter because it emphasizes the role and specific features of dialog. The famous Turing test of AI (Turing, 1950), which was not passed yet, is in fact verifying if a computer program may enter into a dialog with a human exactly like a human. The difficulty of developing computer programs that enter into a dialog with humans suggests us to leave humans to dialog themselves, inclusively for learning purposes. This chapter is focusing exactly on this kind of communication, and it has as a main goal to analyze what happens in human dialogs for learning and to see how dialog may be used by small groups of students for learning collaboratively in chat conversations.

The last years showed that the use of chat conversations in Computer-Supported Collaborative Learning proved to be an effective way of complementing traditional classroom teaching (Stahl, 2006), being well suited also for Hybrid Learning. The polyphony theory and the associated model of inter-animating voices are empowering the achievement of these aims, encompassing both written (be it in chat or in manuals or web documents) and spoken human language (e.g. in classroom learning). Consequently, even a theory of Hybrid Learning may be developed in this idea: The voices of professors enter in polyphony with those of the students both in classrooms and collaborating using online tools.

It is a consensus that CSCL belongs to a socio-cultural approach, based on the ideas of Vygotsky (1978). However, these theories do not capture the peculiarities of the conversational, dialogical nature of collaboration in CSCL. Consequently, several researchers (Koshmann, 1999; Stahl, 2006; Trausan-Matu & all, 2006; Trausan-Matu & all, 2007b) proposed dialogism as a basic model of CSCL. Dialogism is Bakhtin's theory that everything, spoken or written, is a dialog (1973, 1981). Starting from dialogism, more elaborated theories and models may be developed, based also on the polyphony idea introduced also by Bakhtin (1973). In addition, software tools may be developed for supporting chat-based CSCL, starting from the polyphonic perspective (Trausan-Matu & all, 2006, Trausan-Matu & all, 2007a; Trausan-Matu & all, 2007b).

The goals of this chapter are to analyze the particularities of discourse in CSCL conversation chats, to propose a theory for the inter-animation processes that occur and to present some tools for supporting this kind of learning. The achievement of all these goals is based on a unitary conception on linguistic interaction based on dialogism and polyphony, in conjunction with a socio-cultural perspective on learning. Moreover, the polyphonic model may be considered also as encompassing Hybrid Learning in general, because the same ideas apply not only to online chat, but also, for example, to transcripts of spoken dialogs in classrooms.

For the illustration of theoretical ideas with examples, we will use chats from two series of experiments. A first series of chats is taken from Hybrid Learning sessions performed with computer-science students in the final year at the Politehnica University of Bucharest, at a Human-Computer Interaction course, as a part of the Romanian CNCSIS K-teams (http://www.k-teams.cs.pub.ro/) and EU-FP7 LTfLL (http://partners.ltfll-project.org/) projects. As homework to the collaborative interfaces class lecture, students had to discuss using an instant messenger (chat) system about what facilities and tools should have a collaborative environment. In order to animate the discussions and to force the students to debate with arguments different collaborative techniques, each student had to take the role of a director of a software company supporting forums, chat, wiki and respectively blog. Moreover, they had to conclude their discussion with the proposal of an integrated environment, which would combine the all four techniques. All the chat groups had 4 participants, chatting either in English (as non-native language) or Romanian.

A second series of experiments from which several excerpts were taken consists in chats for mathematics problem solving, investigated in the Virtual Math Teams (VMT) project at Drexel University (http://www.cis.drexel.edu/faculty/gerry/vmt/).

The next section will make a first encounter with the particularities of chat conferences for CSCL. The third section is discussing about discourse, a major issue in both the polyphonic theory and in learning. The polyphony theory and its particularization in CSCL chats will be the subject of section four. The last section before conclusions will present also a system that is implementing the theory.

COMPUTER SUPPORTED COLLABORATIVE LEARNING THROUGH CHAT CONFERENCING

Hybrid Learning combines classroom learning with online learning. Usually, online learning is based on the idea of computer support for an individual style of learning. The student may get documents and advice via the computer. He may also be examined with, for example, online multiple answers tests, and a scheduling of the lessons he has to learn may be provided and even personalized by the computer (see, for example, Trausan-Matu & all, 2002).

In online learning, collaborative instruments are also provided, but usually are seen as auxiliary. The most popular tools are probably the email and the discussion forums. These collaboration facilities not only allow interactions among students and between students and professors, but they also extend the individual style of learning toward a social one, in which communities of students may discuss about, for example, some topics to be learned or they may jointly solve some problems. However, a disadvantage of discussion forums is their asynchronicity, which may introduce delays in interactions due, for example, to the temporarily absence of an addressee.

Another very popular collaboration media are instant messengers (chat). Their synchronous feature encourages students' involvement, inducing even a kind of a rhythm in the interactions. Nevertheless, one big problem in using instance messengers for chat conferences with several participants is that, in the absence of nonverbal cues like gazing, the addressee of some utterances might be hard to determine if, for example, several participants put a question in a short interval of time.

A solution to the addressee problem in chats is the provision of a way in the messenger system for explicitly specifying the previous utterance (by clicking on it) which is the destination of an utterance, if needed. Such a referencing facility is provided in the ConcertChat chat system (Holmer, Kienle & Wessner, 2006; see also http://www.ipsi.fraunhofer.de/concert/index_en.shtml?projects/chat), which was used in a Hybrid Learning course on Human-Computer Interaction at Politehnica University of Bucharest. The students were encouraged to use the referencing facility as much as they consider. In figure 1, showing an excerpt of a chat, the explicit students' references are indicated in the second column and, for visualizing them, curly lines were drawn between the source and destination of a reference.

The usage of the explicit referencing facility of ConcertChat, in addition to solving the addressee

Figure 1. Explicit and implicit threads of discussion

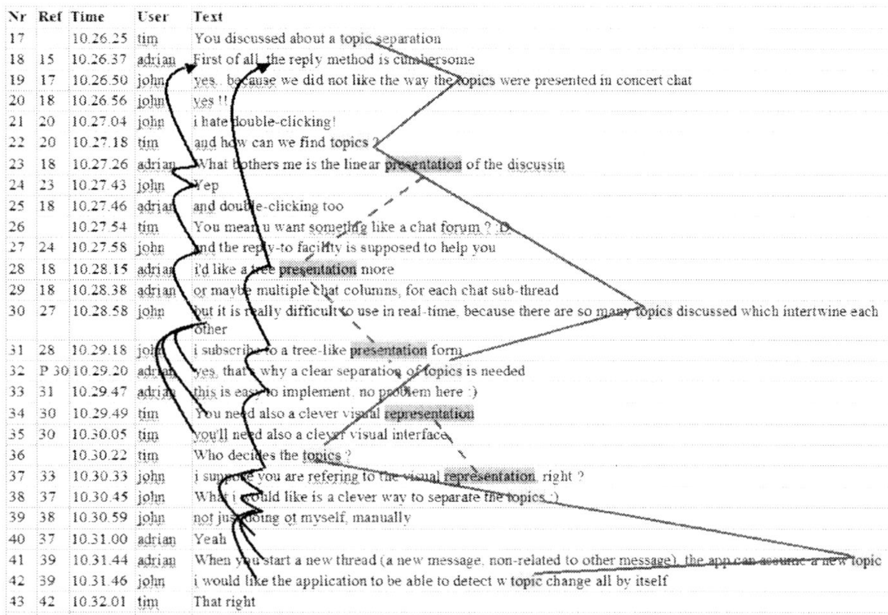

Nr	Ref	Time	User	Text
17		10.26.25	tim	You discussed about a topic separation
18	15	10.26.37	adrian	First of all, the reply method is cumbersome
19	17	10.26.50	john	yes.. because we did not like the way the topics were presented in concert chat
20	18	10.26.56	john	yes !!
21	20	10.27.04	john	i hate double-clicking!
22	20	10.27.18	tim	and how can we find topics ?
23	18	10.27.26	adrian	What bothers me is the linear presentation of the discussin
24	23	10.27.43	john	Yep
25	18	10.27.46	adrian	and double-clicking too
26		10.27.54	tim	You mean u want something like a chat forum ? :D
27	24	10.27.58	john	and the reply-to facility is supposed to help you
28	18	10.28.15	adrian	i'd like a tree presentation more
29	18	10.28.38	adrian	or maybe multiple chat columns, for each chat sub-thread
30	27	10.28.58	john	but it is really difficult to use in real-time, because there are so many topics discussed which intertwine each other
31	28	10.29.18	john	i subscribe to a tree-like presentation form
32	P 30	10.29.20	adrian	yes, that's why a clear separation of topics is needed
33	31	10.29.47	adrian	this is easy to implement. no problem here :)
34	30	10.29.49	tim	You need also a clever visual representation
35	30	10.30.05	tim	you'll need also a clever visual interface
36		10.30.22	tim	Who decides the topics ?
37	33	10.30.33	john	i suppose you are refering to the visual representation, right ?
38	37	10.30.45	john	What i would like is a clever way to separate the topics :)
39	38	10.30.59	john	not just doing ot myself, manually
40	37	10.31.00	adrian	Yeah
41	39	10.31.44	adrian	When you start a new thread (a new message, non-related to other message), the app can assume a new topic
42	39	10.31.46	john	i would like the application to be able to detect w topic change all by itself
43	42	10.32.01	tim	That right

problem, introduces a new opportunity, which is not encountered in face-to-face conferences: Having the possibility of explicitly linking utterances, multiple discussion threads may occur simultaneously, without the problem of unintelligibility due to the superimposing of the sounds of participants' voices. This phenomenon has been detected in almost all the CSCL chats we have analyzed. For example, in the chat excerpt from figure 1, several threads may be identified, from which the longest two are represented by the linked curly lines.

In addition to the explicit links, a second type of threading, starting from implicit links, is present in any linguistic artefact, including, of course, chat conversations. For example, in figure 1 are emphasized two such threads of implicit links generated by the repetition of the nouns "presentation" and "topic". In any discourse there are also implicit links generated by co-references and lexical chains (Manning & Schutze, 1999). Explicit and implicit links are the basis of the discourse formation and, meanwhile, the starting point in our polyphonic methodology.

In addition to the fact that there are several threads in parallel, even the same participant may participate to more than one discussion threads. For example, John, at utterance number 19, approves and elaborates Tim's utterance number 17. Immediately, at utterance 20, he approves Adrian's utterance 18. This phenomenon proves that there is not a situation in which several groups of participants communicate using independent threads. A normal consequence of the co-presence of multiple threads of discussions is their interinfluences. For example, the two explicit link threads from figure 1 are obviously interacting between utterance 34 (of Tim) and 30 (of John), The same interaction occurs at utterances 37 and 38. In figure 2, these interactions are represented with thick arrows.

The interactions tend many times to exhibit an inter-animation phenomenon, similar to the polyphonic music, where voices activate and enable each other. Each of the participants introduces new themes in the discourse, or they iterate an already uttered theme. For example, in figure 1, several themes may be identified: "double-clicking", the

Figure 2. Interactions among threads

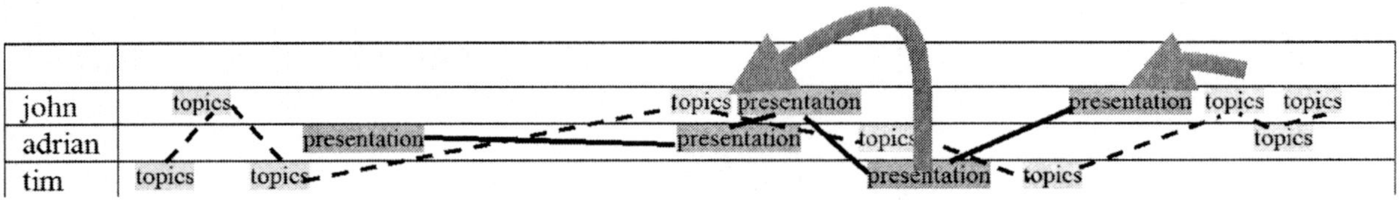

"topics" in a collaborative chat, "reply method" and ways of "presentation". Moreover, when a CSCL chat is successful, the result is the accomplishment of a coherent discursive structure. For example, when the chat was performed for solving a problem, the collaborative achievement of a solution is characterized by an elaborated collaborative discourse. If the students were supposed to discuss or to debate a topic together, a sign of their success is also the achievement of a discourse.

In order to facilitate and analyze collaborative learning, threads of discussion and interactions that weave into a coherent discourse should be identified. Moreover, different types of interactions should be discriminated and, if possible, inter-animation patterns (Trausan-Matu & all, 2007b) have to be identified. A well-suited theory for accomplishing all these desiderata is Bakhtin's dialogism and polyphony (1973). Its usage for the analysis of CSCL chats will be discussed in a further section of this chapter. In order to prepare this discussion, the next section discusses discourse, a concept that includes the threads introduced above. Implementation approaches for identifying discourse in texts will be also analyzed. A dialogistic approach on discourse, that apply to written texts, to web, to chats, to individual learning or to professor lectures will be proposed.

Discourse

In the socio-cultural paradigm (stating that learning is achieved socially), which is now gaining ground in the face of the cognitive one (focusing on the knowledge in individuals' minds), the learning goal of achieving knowledge is directed more in the direction of social interaction and less toward an individual knowledge acquisition view. In this context, negotiation and discourse have a crucial role, as Deborah Hicks emphasizes: "Learning occurs as the co-construction (or reconstruction) of social meanings from within the parameters of emergent, socially negotiated, and discursive activity" (Hicks, 1996). Moreover, Sfard sees discourse as the major factor in learning: "rather than speaking about 'acquisition of knowledge,' many people prefer to view learning as *becoming a participant in a certain discourse*" (Sfard, 2000). Therefore, discourse should be a central issue in a theory about learning.

Discourse offers coherence to any natural language communication, from written text to speech. For analyzing chat and classroom conversations in Hybrid Learning and CSCL it is extremely important to identify and analyze discourse, in order to assess the effective learning situations. Computerized tools should be developed for supporting these goals.

From a linguistics point of view, discourse analysis is an "analysis of texts beyond and 'above' the sentence – the attempt to find linguistic regularities in discourse… its main concepts are cohesion – the features that bind sentences to each other grammatically and lexically – and coherence – which is the notional and logical unity of a text" (Newmark, 1988: 54). Salkie (1995: ix) says: "text or a discourse is a stretch of language that may be longer than one sentence. Text and discourse analysis is about how sentences combine to form texts by means of cohesiveness and coherence".

Discourse in Computational Linguistics

In computational linguistics there are several theories on discourse that follow the widely used computational idea of identifying structures in the form of networks consisting of nodes and relations among them. Probably the most known theories belong to Mann and Thompson (Rhetorical Structure Theory, or RST, 1987), Jerry Hobbs (Hobbs 1985), and Barbara Grosz & all (1995). RST identifies hierarchical rhetorical structures build using a limited set of rhetorical schemas (patterns) like antithesis, elaboration etc. Each schema has one nucleus and several satellites. Jerry Hobbs' theory is based on semantic coherence relations and interpretation as abduction inferences in formal logic (Hobbs 1985).

All these theories are referring mainly to discourse in texts and not to conversations. They consider that a discourse may be divided into several segments. Among discourse segments there may be different relationships, e.g. embedding (Grosz & all, 1995) or other types of relations. As Grosz states, discourse may be segmented in sequences of utterances. However, "discourses are more than mere sequences of utterances. For a sequence of utterances to be a discourse, it must exhibit coherence. Each discourse segment exhibits both *local coherence* – i.e. coherence among the utterances in that segment - and *global coherence* – i.e. coherence with other segments in the discourse." (Grosz & all, 1995).

Coherence is obtained, in Grosz's theory, at both local and global levels, by two aspects: intentional and attentional state, that, together with the linguistic structure of utterance sequence form a tripartite organization. There is an intentional structure in each discourse, assuring that discourse is rational. This structure is built from intentions (purposes) and, sometimes, beliefs of the author of the discourse (or of each participant in a conversation) and relations among them (Grosz & all, 1995).

Each participant, at any discourse point, has a focus of attention. "Changes in attentional state depend on the intentional structure and on properties of the utterances in the linguistic structure" (Grosz & all, 1995). The centering theory is trying to explain how local coherence is obtained. Each utterance has a center, which is an entity (for example, a noun phrase) used to link that utterance to other utterances in a discourse segment. Grosz & all introduce the notion of the set of forward-looking centers and of the (single) backward-looking center for each utterance.

Grosz & all identify three types of transition relations across utterances: center continuation, center retention and center shifting. These relations follow rules (constraints) among utterances centers, like: "no element in an utterance can be realized as a pronoun unless the backward-looking center of the utterance is realized as a pronoun also" or "sequences of continuation are preferred over sequences of retaining sequences of retaining are to be preferred over sequences of shifting" (Grosz & all, 1995).

Probably the most important lack of such theories is their focus on the individual, on its intentions and the consideration of context as a list of entities. This is, we think, very well illustrated by rhetoric and even by Austin and Searle speech act theory (Jurafsky & Martin, 2000), that pays a central attention to the success of communication utterances but, as Duranti remarks, their theory is based on individual minds, is not considering collaboration (Duranti, 1997).

Computational linguistics has as the most ambitious goal the developing of computer programs for text understanding and is for some researchers a possible way to follow. However, there are very serious arguments against the feasibility of such an approach (Winograd, 1987; Winograd & Flores, 1986). Another perspective is the dialogism of Mikhail Bakhtin (1973, 1981), discussed in the following section.

Dialogic Discourse

Mikhail Mikhailovici Bakhtin was a Russian philosopher, linguist and philologist that replaced the monologic Descartes-like way of thinking with a dialogic, inter-animation paradigm. He raises the idea of dialog to a fundamental philosophical category: "... *Any true understanding is dialogic in nature*" (Voloshinov 1973, p. 102). This is in consonance with Lotman's conception of text as a „thinking device" (Wertsch 1981, p. 74), determining that: "The semantic structure of an internally persuasive discourse is not *finite*, it is *open*; in each of the new contexts that dialogize it, this discourse is able to reveal ever new *ways to mean*" (Bakhtin 1981, pp.345-346).

Bakhtin continues and extends Vygotsky's ideas (Wertsch 1991; Duranti 1997; Koschmann 1999) and dialogism may be even seen as a new philosophical paradigm that has a more large extent than dialectics (Markova, 2003). He extended Vygotsky's ideas in the sense of considering the role of discourse and language, with emphasis on speech and dialog. His basic ideas are the dialogism, the universality of the presence of multiple voices in any text, the speech genres, the polyphonic character of some texts and inter-animation.

Vygotsky has a permanently increasing influence on learning theories. He stated that learning is a social process, mediated by specific tools, in which symbols and especially human language plays a central role. However, he didn't investigate in much detail how the language and discourse is actually used in collaborative activities. It is the merit of Bakhtin to propose a sound theory of how meaning is socially constructed.

A very important idea brought by Bakhtin, related to the above communitarian characteristics of utterances, is that of speech genres, that determines "definite and relatively stable typical *forms of construction of the whole*" (Bakhtin, 1986, p. 78). Speech genres may be seen also as an additional form of coherence besides intentional and attentional states identified by computational linguistics theories like that of Grosz and al. (1986, 1995). To acquire knowledge may be seen as the ability of building a discourse in a given speech genre (e.g. mathematics, see Livingstone 1986): "to learn is to become a skilled member of communities of practice .... and to become competent at using their .... speech genres" (Stahl, 2006).

However, communities of voices, in parallel to the unity trend, have an additional differential, *unmerged*, character: "The *intersection, consonance, or interference of speeches in the overt dialog with the speeches in the heroes' interior dialogs* are everywhere present. *The specific totality of ideas, thoughts and words* is everywhere *passed through several unmerged voices, taking on a different sound in each"* (Bakhtin, 1973, p. 226). This dual nature of community and individuality of voices is expressed by Bakhtin also by the concept of *polyphony*, that he considers the invention and one of the main merits of Dostoevsky novels (Bakhtin, 1973). The relation of discourse and communities to music was remarked also by Tannen: "Dialogue combine with repetition to create rhythm. Dialogue is liminal between repetitions and images: like repetition is strongly sonorous" (Tannen, 1989, p. 29)

Utterances at Bakhtin have a wide extent, "from a short (single-word) rejoinder in everyday dialogue to the large novel or scientific treatise" (Bakhtin, 1986, p. 71). Even if they include not only spoken language, Wertsch remarked that "an utterance can exist only by being produced by a voice" (Wertsch, 1991, p. 51). Moreover, one of the main ideas of Bakhtin is that each utterance is, in fact, filled with a multitude of voices, this idea being strongly related to communities: "The very being of man (both external and internal) is the *deepest communion. To be means to communicate....* To be means to be for *another*, and through the other, for oneself" (Bakhtin, 1984). Even inner speech is, as Vygotsky also noted, a "unique form of collaboration with oneself" (quoted in Emerson, 1986, p. 33).

THE POLYPHONIC MODEL OF COMPUTER SUPPORTED COLLABORATIVE LEARNING

Polyphony in Music

Polyphony is a technique used especially in classical music (mastered, for example, by Johann Sebastian Bach in his musical fugues, but which may appear also in improvisations, for example in jazz or latino music) involving several independent participants (or "*voices*") singing simultaneously. The goal is to obtain a *coherent* framework (a nice sounding musical piece) starting from a given *theme*, even if transient deliberated *dissonances* are introduced. In order to achieve coherence, several *harmony* assuring rules should be respected, the so-called *counterpoint* rules (how notes may be used "point counter point" in the joint play of several participants):

When there is more than one independent melodic line happening at the same time in a piece of music, we say that the music is contrapuntal. The independent melodic lines are called counterpoint. The music that is made up of counterpoint can also be called polyphony, or one can say that the music is polyphonic or speak of the polyphonic texture of the music. (Polyphony, 2005).

In polyphony, the leading theme is the seed of melody that is the basis for further developments in the musical piece. A melody lasts in time and, therefore, is *longitudinal*, being characterized by duration and a sequence of notes.

When there are several voices playing in the same time, other rules apply than in the longitudinal case. These are the *transversal* rules of harmony, for example, what chords sound consonant. In polyphony, the situation is more complex because each of the voices play in paralel the same theme but they also should bring some *variations* in order to be creative, to avoid monotony. Sometimes short *dissonances* are introduced, creating a conflinct to be solved, in a kind of an inter-animation process.

The above mentioned phenomena of variation and transient dissonance bring a new, orthogonal dimension on the longitudinal-transversal axis. They are a manifestation of the *unity-difference* distinction. It may take the form of a competition similar to the one emphasized by Bakhtin in discourse in the novels. He compared the unity-difference competition to that between *centripetal* forces and *centrifugal* ones (Bakhtin, 1981). The most important fact is that this phenomena generate and maintain *inter-animation* among the participants in the chat. We can conclude that a desideratum of a successful chat for CSCL should include an important degree of inter-animation and, meanwhile, all along the chat, these developments, both longitudinal, melodic rules and transversal, harmonical rules should be respected.

A Polyphonic Perspective of Hybrid Learning

From the polyphonic perspective, we understand by a "voice" not the acoustical, physical, vocal expression of a given participant in a dialogue but, rather, a distinct position, an utterance, an event or a recurrent series of events of emitting utterances that are heard, reminded, discussed and have influence on the utterances emitted of the other voices. This perspective is a well-suited model for Hybrid Learning because it naturally allows the consideration of blending the voices of the professors in classroom teaching and the voices of the participants in dialogues, including chat collaborative activities.

In addition to the above group perspective, in our opinion, polyphony is implied also beyond group interaction. In individual learning (and, in general, in any knowledge building process) multiple voices also are implied, being, somehow, a form of internalized collaboration, as follows: Reading texts and trying to understand them implies the inner voice of the reader in a joint process with the voice of the author. There is a dialog in which the reader interprets what he reads, put questions, and try to integrate the new data in what he already knows. Solving problems is also a dialog, between the voice of the author or of the professor, who ask for the solution and the solver. Even writing is dialogic, being a classical example used by Bakhtin to illustrate how the voice of the author is melded with the voices of the potentials readers Moreover, even the activity of teaching something (even if there is no feedback from the students, in Bakhtin's terminology, even their voice is not expressed but only potentially intuited by the teacher) may determine a collaboration effect (for example, from my personal experience, I remarked that lecturing enhance knowledge building even if there is no actual dialog with the students). From another point of view, we must extend the concept of voice to the present persons, even if they do not say something.

Another extension of the polyphonic model is to class-based learning and, if we add also CSCL, to Hybrid Learning. This perspective is supported also by Bakhtin's view on utterances as encompassing more than a spoken intervention, as we discussed in the section on discourse. Therefore, we can consider *hybrid learning as a polyphony of contributions from several participants, professors and students and using different kinds of utterances, in an extended sense.*

Polyphony in Chats

The basic assumption of the usage of the polyphonic model in analyzing CSCL chats is that we can use the musical analogy of polyphony for evaluating the degree of inter-animation and the contribution of every student. By analyzing the themes of a conversation, the inter-animation patterns (Trausan-Matu & all, 2007b) and the participation of each student to this framework, we can assess the participation and contribution of each of them. Moreover, from the analysis results, feedback may be provided to the participants and suggestions may be driven for the most suitable kinds of chat sessions. In addition, for the designers of collaborative chat environments may be suggested new support tools.

Some obvious prerequisites of Computer Supported Collaborative Learning are the need that each participant involves himself/herself in the collaboration and that s/he inter-animates with the other participants in order to achieve the task they have to do. CSCL may be used according to different scenarios like problem solving (e.g. mathematics in VMT), experimenting for understanding, role-based disputes (e.g. at Politehnica University), collaborative design, etc. In all these cases, a successful learning process has as manifestation the development of a coherent and elaborated discourse (solution to a problem, explanations, justifications or designs) consisting of collaborative utterances, repetitions, difference making and other inter-animation patterns (Trausan-Matu & all, 2007b). In the following sub-sections we will illustrate with examples such classes of unity-difference along longitudinal/transversal directions polyphonic inter-animation situations. We will present several examples of good collaboration in CSCL chats and their polyphonic interpretation. Examples are taken from real chat sessions of the VMT project at Drexel and K-teams and LTfLL projects at PUB.

Collaborative Utterances

Several types of discourse may occur in CSCL chats. For example, in one of the VMT chat excerpts, from 221 to 231 there is a negotiating discourse on what problem to choose to be solved:

221 mathwhiz344: i can't think of any, but number 6 looks interesting

222 dragon: number 7

223 mathwhiz344: so which one should we do?

224 dragon: I don't know, anything that interests us I guess

225 gdog: #6 is interesting to me

226 dragon: problem is

227 dragon: there really isn't an answer to number 6 though

228 weisbari: joins the room

229 mathwhiz344: yeha

230 gdog: that's why it's interesting

231 dragon: it depends who is giving the problem

Such types of negotiating discourses appear in many collaborative situations (Stahl, 2006). From the polyphonic perspective, they may be considered as longitudinal (threads) along a transversal disaccord.

Another kind of discourse is the exploratory one. An excellent example of such a discourse is illustrated below by the co-building of knowledge about one problem they have to solve: how is changed the problem of finding the shortest path between two points on a grid if the grid is no more planar but curved. In this discourse, practically only dragon and mathwiz344 are effectively contributing (the messages preceded by "@" are references to prior utterances, provided by the ConcertChat system):

232 mathwhiz344: the grid probably extends for ever,

233 mathwhiz344: but if it's a curved space, it might meet

234 gdog: assuming if it doesn't..........

235 dragon: that would make things too complicated

236 dragon: I guess

237 gdog: y?

238 dragon: but it could work maybe

239 mathwhiz344: what if we asssumed the grid is a universe...

240 mathwhiz344: i guess your right

241 gdog: ok

242 gdog: i understand

243 dragon: well, first of all, the paper would crumple (if it were real) to form a sphere

@: Message 237:

244 mathwhiz344: why a sphere?

245 gdog: ?

246 dragon: I mean, if it were "curved" as you said before

@: Message 244:

247 dragon: like

248 mathwhiz344: oh

249 dragon: it would curve to itself

250 mathwhiz344: yeah

251 dragon: and then it would have to get smaller in some areas to fit

252 dragon: nvm

253 dragon:

It is extremely important that the utterances of the two main participants almost seem to be generated by a single person, we could say, in Bakhtin's terminology, that they inter-penetrate:

the grid probably extends for ever, but if it's a curved space, it might meet

what if we asssumed the grid is a universe...

well, first of all, the paper would crumple (if it were real) to form a sphere

why a sphere?

I mean, if it were "curved" as you said before

it would curve to itself

and then it would have to get smaller in some areas to fit

This kind of unity phenomenon is extremely important and relevant because it reflects ideal moments of collaboration, which were discussed in large also in Sacks (Sacks, 1992, pp.144-5) and in Lerner (Lerner, 1993). For example, Sacks analyzes in several instances the following fragment of conversation in which the participants emit collaborative utterances, which produce a sole sentence:

"Joe: (cough) We were in an automobile discussion,

Henry: discussing the psychological motives for

Mel: drag racing on the streets" (Sacks, 1992, pp.144-5)

Another example of collaborative utterances is:

117 ModeratorSf, 20:33 (19.05): could you guys tell templar what's going on?

118 mathpudding, 20:35 (19.05): we're experimenting with circles

119 mathman, 20:35 (19.05): and finding as many possible relations as we can

The collaborative utterances are rather rare in conversations. However, collaboration occurs very frequently under other dialogical longitudinal inter-animation schemes, like question-answering:

68 mathisfun, 20:26 (19.05): see angle alpha?

69 bob123, 20:26 (19.05): yes

70 bob123, 20:26 (19.05): what about it?

71 mathisfun, 20:26 (19.05): is that 60 degrees?

72 bob123, 20:26 (19.05): yes

73 mathisfun, 20:27 (19.05): can u use the degree, 2 length to find the last length of a triangle?

74 bob123, 20:27 (19.05): i don't get what you're saying

75 mathisfun, 20:27 (19.05): the two arrow pointed lengths and the angle can find the length A

76 bob123, 20:28 (19.05): by what?

77 mathisfun, 20:28 (19.05): the two sides and the degree

78 bob123, 20:29 (19.05): and how do you use the two sides and the degree to find the third side?

79 mathisfun, 20:29 (19.05): one moment

80 mathisfun, 20:29 (19.05): There is a fomula I think

Another example is:

83 EatUrSqRts, 20:31 (19.05): k, so add the 1/2 infinite series

84 EatUrSqRts, 20:31 (19.05): ull see it approaches 1/1 correct?

85 Jason, 20:31 (19.05): ummm lemme see

86 Jason, 20:32 (19.05): yes

87 EatUrSqRts, 20:32 (19.05): and 1/3 approaches 1/2 right?

88 Jason, 20:32 (19.05): sure

89 EatUrSqRts, 20:33 (19.05): so lets se one person

90 EatUrSqRts, 20:33 (19.05): 10/11 divide by 10 is...

91 Jason, 20:33 (19.05): 1/11

92 EatUrSqRts, 20:33 (19.05): good, so wut infinite series approaches 1/11

93 Jason, 20:33 (19.05): 1/12?

94 EatUrSqRts, 20:34 (19.05): good!

95 Jason, 20:34 (19.05)::-)

……………………..

133 EatUrSqRts, 20:47 (19.05): so, 10/12 is eaten, how much is left?

134 Jason, 20:47 (19.05): 2/12

135 FooFoo, 23:48 (19.05): 1/6

……………………..

156 EatUrSqRts, 20:54 (19.05): (collumns+1)(rows)(2)

157 EatUrSqRts, 20:55 (19.05): anyone disagree?

158 Jason, 20:55 (19.05): check it

159 EatUrSqRts, 20:56 (19.05): 56?

160 Jason, 20:56 (19.05): that can't be the area

161 EatUrSqRts, 20:56 (19.05): no, the # of short paths

Discourse in the previous examples, exhibiting moments of collaboration (Stahl, 2006), may be resembled with a collective poetry, where participants in a chat seem to enter in the rhythm of a poem. Something similar was reported also by Stahl:

Heidegger's favorite art form is poetry. Poetry makes language visible (see Heidegger ...). Poetry is a source for the creation of new expressions and new forms of speech. Poetry also opens up worlds, and it can name the elements that it brings together in those worlds. For Heidegger, language speaks (Sprache spricht). It is not so much that people use words to express their ideas, but that language speaks through us. (...) What took place there happened largely through the power of language, the mechanisms of discourse. Utterances built on each other. Words gathered richness of meaning through repetitive usage. The discourse itself provided an opportunity for all this to happen. (Stahl, 2006, p.412)

It is clear that this phenomenon in which utterances "built on each other" is extremely similar to what happens when entering a state of flow (Czikszentmihaly, 1990). Music, poetry, collaboration are probably related to this special state. In fact, polyphony may appear spontaneously in jazz music, which may be considered as entering in a group state of flow and a prototype for a successful collaboration.

Another interesting observation in the second chat excerpt from this section (utterances 232-253) is that, in addition, it seems that there are two threads of discussion between the same two participants and, something similar to a contrapunctus in a Bach fugue. In the same time with the discourse discussed above (232, 233, 239, 243, 246, 249, 251), similar to a exploratory narrative, the following discourse appear (thread of utterances 232, 233, 235, 236, 238, 240):

the grid probably extends for ever, that would make things too complicated I guess but it could work maybe i guess your right

Such a dialogue with multiple threads is specific to chats (see also the threads from figure 1). In real, face to face discussions of only two or three persons, multithreading is much more difficult to happen. In fact, this possibility of multithreaded discourse must be encouraged, humans being able to handle them. Moreover, it is possible that we maybe even need them. The examples of musical fugues, of polyphony, of movies or novels (a detailed discussion about poliphony in novels can be found in Bakhtin's writings (1973, 1981) are, in our oppinion very good illustrations of multithreaded discourse.

A third kind of discourse is determined by estrickmcnizzle, that seems to be bored and feels the need to introduce a difference, to interrupt the previous discourse. As a consequence, probably also because the other two participants feel the need to end the discourse (they could ignore estrickmcnizzle intervention), an ending discourse sequence is generated and then a fourth, negociation discourse is started:

254 estrickmcnizzle: im drinking 7 up

255 dragon: this is getting way too complicated, xp

256 gdog: dragons right @: Message 249:

257 gdog: we should probably solve another problem

258 dragon: so, do you guys think any other questions would be good to answer?

259 mathwhiz344: yeah:0

260 gdog: and drop that question

261 dragon: I like 7

262 mathwhiz344: 7's good

263 gdog: ok, we can try 7

264 estrickmcnizzle: so is 7 up

265 dragon: alright

266 dragon: lol

267 gdog: lol

268 mathwhiz344::)

As conclusion, different types of discourse may be encountered, some of them being exemplified in the above examples: openings, negotiation, exploration, solution building, conversation ending, etc. (see also Sacks, 1992). From another perspective, discourses in chats may be classified as social (openings and greetings) and mathematical (problem solving).

Repetitions

We consider that another extremely important phenomenon, related to polyphony and reflecting collaboration is repetition. For example, „two ways" is repeated several times in the following VMT chat excerpt:

160 mathisfun, 20:26 (12.05): k so there are two ways *right?*

161 bob123, 20:27 (12.05): yeah

162 bob123, 20:27 (12.05): 2c1=2

163 Marisol, 20:27 (12.05): yes, I agree there are only two ways

164 mathisfun, 20:27 (12.05): then there is a one by two

165 qwer, 20:29 (12.05): only two ways*? @: Message 158: To whole message*

166 mathisfun, 20:28 (12.05): is the one by two going to be 4 ways?

Zemel remarked that, in face-to-face collaborative problem solving, students tend also to unconsciously imitate each other's gestures, or to move together like in choreography (Zemel, 2005). We consider such phenomena as manifestations of the appearance of a state of group flow, of a collaborative moment, of a successful discourse.

69 ModeratorSf, 20:14 (19.05): you can continue the problems from last time or we can try another, what you say?

70 mathpudding, 20:16 (19.05): try another

71 TinyFryhiii12, 20:15 (19.05): another

72 mathman, 20:16 (19.05): another we came to a solution for the one last time

The relation of repetitions to music (and poetry) are remarked also by Tannen (Tannen, 1989). She considered that repetitions are sound patterns, that are used together with sense patterns as narrative, ellipsis, tropes, indirection, imagery as involvement strategies (Tannen, 1989, p.17).

An interesting repetition situation appears in another VMT chat, where an ad-hoc phrase (30/60/90) is repeated several times (including variations):

ping ponger 805 (8:24:54 PM): its a **30/60/90** *triangle SuperEvo88 (8:26:08 PM): if its equilateral its it a* **45/45/90** *triangle?*

AvrilLR (8:27:00 PM): equilateral is **60/60/60** *triangle*

AvrilLR (8:27:15 PM): not **30/60/90**

pingponger 805 (8:27:17 PM): anyone remember formula for **30/60/90** *triangle?*

AvrilLR (8:28:33 PM): so it can't be **30/60/90** *AvrilLR (8:28:39 PM): it's not a* **30/60/90** *triangle*

SuperEvo88 (8:29:04 PM): is there a formula for a **60/60/60***?*

AvrilLR (8:37:52 PM): okay it's TWO **30/60/90** *triangles*

AvrilLR (9:26:34 PM): like the ratios of the sides of a **30/60/90** *are 1/2/sqrt2 or something*

SuperEvo88 (9:30:20 PM): we detremined its a **30/60/90** *triangle*

Difference Making

Difference making has a crucial role in collaborative chats. The possibility of contemplating from a critical position the others' ideas and entering into a polyphonic framework enhances problem solving and enables learning through a trial-error process. Such processes appear also in individual problem solving but the presence of multiple participants enhance both the possibility of developing multiple threads and, meanwhile, of difference identification. The inter-animation of the multiple perspectives of the participants, the opposition as result of contemplation and the presence of a third opinion in case of conflict and sometimes the synthesis it brings are a better asset to success than a multi-voiced discourse performed by an individual, that is inherently much less critique.

For example, in the following excerpt of the collaborative solving of the "ducks problem" at Politehnica University, after a negotiation ended with an agreement, p4nzer, petry_g and tricavl enter into a dialog of longitudinal inferences (emphasized as bold) and transversal (italic) differences:

p4nzer: I'm thinking that in the shortest move sequence, "a" must ONLY move to the right and "b" ONLY to the left

p4nzer: do you agree?

tricavl: yes... you're right

petry_g: agree

tricavl: so we start with aaa_bbb

p4nzer: yes... the first move is simple...

p4nzer: it doesn't matter if we move an "a" or a "b" in the empty space.

tricavl: ok

tricavl: so aaa_bbb become aaab_bb

p4nzer: one moment thou... from what I do understand, A can only jump over B and vice-versa

tricavl: let's see!

p4nzer: so... let's say we move an a

p4nzer: we now have aa_Abbb

petry_g: ok...i think i begin to understand:))

tricavl: now what? b over a?

tricavl: aa_Babb?

p4nzer: well... if we were to move the "a" we would get stuck

p4nzer: no, that's not a valid move

p4nzer: aaba_bb is. do you understand why?

tricavl: ohh... so you moved the space twice to the right?

p4nzer: no

p4nzer: only one move

p4nzer: "b" over "a"

p4nzer: aa_aBbb -> aaBa_bb

p4nzer: get it?

tricavl: ohh... so "b" change place with the space?

p4nzer: exactly: "jumped over a into an empty space"

petry_g: yes. alex is right.

tricavl: ok. next step...

petry_g: now we can either move the "b" one space to the left or the "a" one space to the right

p4nzer: correct, no jumping moves here!

tricavl: it's the same thing

tricavl: let's move the "a"

p4nzer: aabA_bb -> aab_Abb

p4nzer: hmm... this does not look good

p4nzer: I get the feeling that if we get the sequence "aabb" we're stuck

tricavl: why? i think the algorithm here is to move the space to the righ and came back with a "b"

petry_g: "sequence "aabb" we're stuck.."..me too

p4nzer: yes, and everything we can do from here, we get an "aabb"

p4nzer: so the move aabA_bb -> aab_Abb is wrong

tricavl: ok. i think we should continue with aab_Abb -> aabbA_b

tricavl: we are using the space to control our moves.

p4nzer: ok. if you think we're wrong, what do u have in mind?

Sometimes, the participants even explicitly states that they found a difference:

p4nzer: agree with me so far?

tricavl: yes, but i did the same thing

tricavl: the difference was the place of the space:).

petry_g: and the number of moves:)

Evidence that participants permanently keep a differential position, that they do not totally enter in an unity is also provided by the usage of personal pronouns. For example, in a corpus of chats recorded in May 2005, "I" was used 727 times and "we" only 472 times. 84 times was used "me" and only 34 times "us". However, alterity is very well represented by 947 uses of "you".

A TOOL FOR THE VISUALIZATION OF THE PARTICIPATION IN THE COLLABORATIVE LEARNING CHAT

One desideratum of a successful CSCL session is a coherent and elaborated discourse, in which participants inter-animate. Such a discourse, as we have discussed in the previous sections, may be modeled as a polyphonic weaving, manifesting longitudinal/transversal and unity/difference coherent interactions. Therefore, for assessing the quality of a collaborative learning session, it is extremely important to have tools that analyze this polyphonic framework of the discourse and that provide useful abstractions to both teachers and students. Moreover, supporting tools for collaborative learning should encourage polyphonic inter-animation.

A tool was developed for the detection and the visualization of threads and their inter-animations from a polyphonic perspective (Trausan-Matu & all, 2007a). First of all, the themes (the topics) of the chat are detected. For this aim, text mining techniques (Manning & Schutze, 1999) eliminate unrelevant words and group similar nouns using the lexical ontology WordNet (http://wordnet.princeton.edu). Secondly, the links among utterances in the chat are detected. If a chat environment like ConcertChat is used, the explicit links are obviously considered. For detecting implicit links, several techniques are used, like repetition of words or patterns.

Figure 3 is a snapshot of the graphical representation of the chats and of the influence of the participant voices (Trausan-Matu & all, 2007a). For each participant in the chat there is a separate horizontal line in the graphical representation. Each utterance is placed in the line corresponding to the issuer of that utterance, taking into account its positioning in the original chat file, using the timeline as an horizontal axis. Each utterance is represented as a rectangle aligned according to the issuer on the vertical axis and having a horizontal axis length that is proportional with the dimension of the utterance. The distance between two different utterances is proportional with the time passed between them. The relationships between utterances are represented with lines that connect these utterances. The lines have different colors, according to the type of reference (explicit or implicit - Trausan-Matu & all, 2007a).

The degree in which a participant involves himself/herself and the inter-animation may be determined either by the visualization tool (using a view at a compressed ratio) or by a quantitative analysis using social network analysis algorithms (Cristea & all, 2007). For example, in figure 4a, in the middle of the conversation there is a visible rather long segment where only adrian speaks and there is no dialog. In figure 4b, several participants (tutor, TBryant) have a clearly visible very reduced participation.

In contrast, the conversation in figure 4c, displays a rather uniform distribution of utterances among participants.

At the top of the graphical representation of the conversation (see figure 3) there is a special area that represents the importance of each utterance as a rectangle, considered as a chat voice in the conversation. This importance is computed using some heuristics that consider the effects of the utterances on the rest of the conversation (Trausan-Matu & all, 2007a). Starting from the importance values, a graph that shows the contributions of every participant may be drawn (see figure 5). This graph contains on the horizontal axis the utterances in the chat and on the vertical one the value attributed to each participant in the conversation, representing the sum of each user's contributions.

Figure 3. Visualization of a chat, emphasizing the discussion threads

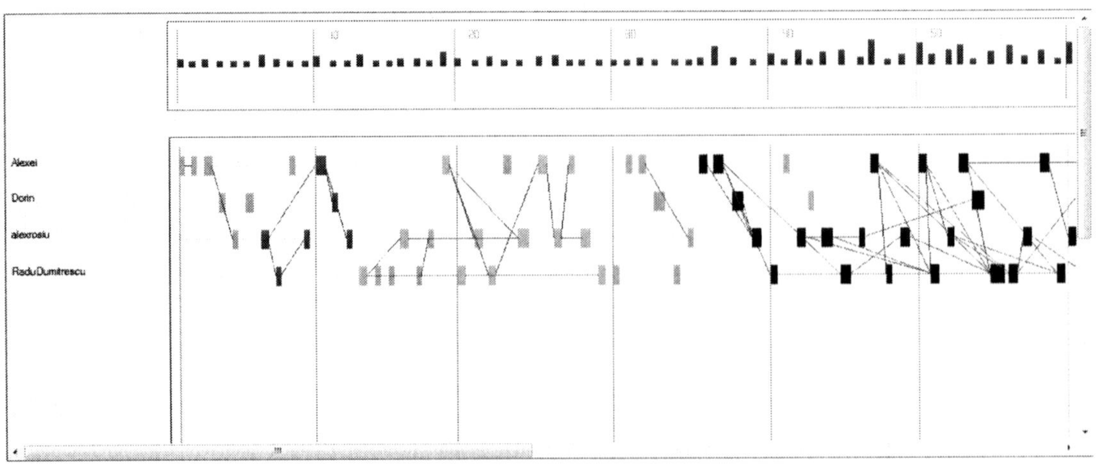

Figure 4. Global view of a chat

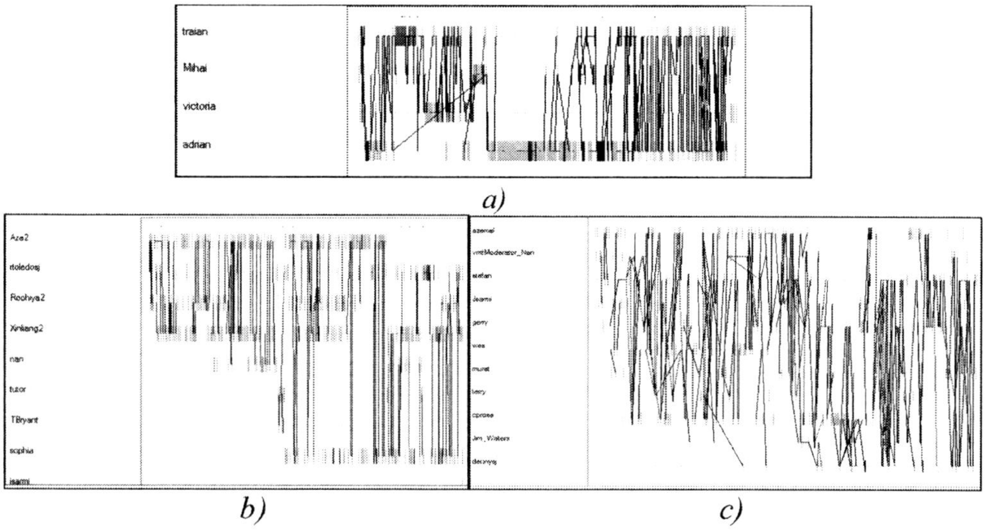

CONCLUSION

Discourse in chats and in face to face conversations is characterized by an inter-animation of multiple voices along two dimensions, the sequential, longitudinal utterance threading and the transversal, differential one. These two dimensions correspond to a unity-difference (or centrifugal-centripetal, see Bakhtin, 1981) basic feature of polyphony. The unity directed dimension is achieved at diverse discourse levels by repetitions, collaborative utterances, socializing and negotiation discourse segments.

The second, differential dimension could be better understood if we consider discourse as an artifact that, taking into account that every participant in collaborative activities has a distinct personality, is a source of a critical, differential attitude. Even if individual discourse is multi-voiced, difference and critique are possible especially in collaborative contexts.

In each dialogue, similarly to polyphonic

Figure 5. The variation of participants' contributions

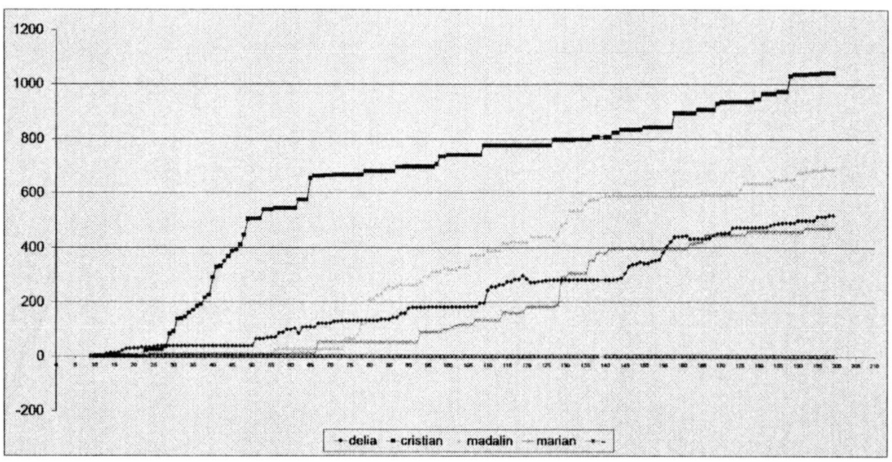

music, there are one or more themes, which are debated by the participant voices. Each theme is introduced by a voice and developed by it and/or the others. Several themes may be present in the same time in the dialogue, influencing each other.

According to Bakhtin's perspective, we may consider that the themes of a chat, during their development, are filled with the overtones of the voices (the contributions that are on a distinct position) of the participants. In addition to their sequential intertwining, voices interact transversally, they inter-animate according to several patterns, the themes weaving like in a music-like polyphony.

The polyphonic theory should be further elaborated. A three years European Union project (LTfLL - http://partners.ltfll-project.org/) has as one of its objectives to develop tools providing feedback to learners starting from analyzing the polyphonic structuring of the chats they performed. One of its side effects will be also the development of the theory.

Another interesting future issue is the extension of the polyphonic theory to encompass Hybrid Learning in general and individual learning or class-based learning in particular.

REFERENCES

Bakhtin, M. (1973). *Problems of Dostoevsky's Poetics*, Ardis, (translated by R.W.Rotsel).

Bakhtin, M. (1981). *The dialogic imagination: four essays*. Austin, TX: University of Texas Press.

Bakhtin, M. (1984). Problems of Dostoevsky's Poetics. In *Theory and History of Literature Series* (translated by C. Emerson).

Bakhtin, M. (1986). *Speech genres and other late essays*. Austin, TX: University of Texas Press.

Cristea, V., Trausan-Matu, S., Posea, P., & Gartner, A. (2007). Towards an evaluation methodology for collaborative learning. In *Proceedings of CSCS16*, Bucharest (pp.161-168).

Csikszentmihalyi, M. (1990). *Flow: The psychology of optimal experience*. New York: Harper Collins.

Duranti, A. (1997). *Linguistic anthropology*. Cambridge, UK: Cambridge University Press.

Emerson, C. (1986). The outer word and inner speech: Bakhtin, Vygotsky, and the internalization of language. In G. S. Morson (Ed.), *Bakhtin - Essays and Dialogues on His Work*. Chicago, IL: University of Chicago Press.

Grosz, B. J., Joshi, A. K., & Weinstein, S. (1995). Centering: A framework for modelling the local coherence of discourse. *Computational Linguistics*, *21*(2), 203–225.

Hobbs, J. R. (1985). *On the coherence and structure of discourse*. Technical Report CSLI-85-37, Center for the Study of Language and Information, Stanford University.

Juravsky, D., & Martin, J. (2000). *Speech and language processing: An introduction to natural language processing, computational linguistics and speech recognition*. San Francisco, CA: Prentice Hall.

Koschmann, T. (1999). Toward a dialogic theory of learning: Bakhtin's contribution to understanding learning in settings of collaboration. In C. Hoadley & J. Roschelle (Eds.), *Proceedings of the Computer Support for Collaborative Learning 1999 Conference*. Philadelphia, PA: Laurence Erlbaum Associates.

Lerner, G. H. (1993). Collectivities in action: Establishing the relevance of conjoined participation in conversation. *Text*, *13*(2), 213–245. doi:10.1515/text.1.1993.13.2.213

Livingstone, E. (1986). *The ethnomethodological foundation of mathematics*. London: Rutledge & Kegan Paul.

Mann, W. C. & Thompson, S.A. (1987). *Rhetorical structure theory: A theory of text organization*. Technical Report ISI/RS-87-190, Information Sciences Institute, University of Southern California.

Manning, C., & Schutze, H. (1999). *Foundations of statistical natural language processing*. Cambridge, MA: MIT Press.

Markova, I. (2003). *Dialogicality and social representations: The dynamics of mind*. Cambridge, UK: Cambridge University Press.

Newmark, P. (1988). *A textbook of translation*. Hertfordshire, UK: Prentice Hall.

Polyphony. (2008). Retrieved December, 1, 2008 from http://cnx.rice.edu/content/m11634/latest/

Sacks, H. (1992). *Lectures on conversation*. Oxford, UK: Blackwell.

Schegloff, E. (1981). Discourse as an interactional achievement: Some uses of 'uh huh' and other things that come between sentences. In D. Tannen (Ed.), *Georgetown University Roundtable on Languages and Linguistics 1981; Analyzing Discourse: Text and Talk*. Washington D.C.: Georgetown University Press.

Sfard, A. (2000). On reform movement and the limits of mathematical discourse. *Mathematical Thinking and Learning*, *2*(3), 157–189. doi:10.1207/S15327833MTL0203_1

Stahl, G. (2006). *Group cognition: Computer support for building collaborative knowledge*. Cambridge, MA: MIT Press.

Tannen, D. (1989). *Talking voices: repetition, dialogue, and imagery in conversational discourse*. Cambridge, UK: Cambridge University Press.

Trausan-Matu, S., Maraschi, D., & Cerri, S. (2002). Ontology-centered personalized presentation of knowledge extracted from the Web. In S. Cerri, G. Gouarderes (Eds.), *Intelligent Tutoring Systems 2002* (LNCS 2363, pp 259-269). New York: Springer.

Trausan-Matu, S., Rebedea, T., Dragan, A., & Alexandru, C. (2007a). Visualisation of learners' contributions in chat conversations. In J. Fong & P. Wang (Eds.), *Blended Learning* (pp. 215-224). Upper Saddle River, NJ: Prentice Hall.

Trausan-Matu, S., Stahl, G., & Sarmiento, J. (2006). Polyphonic support for collaborative learning. In Y.A. Dimitriadis et al. (Eds.), *CRIWG 2006 (LNCS 4154,* pp. 132 – 139*)*. New York: Springer.

Trausan-Matu, S., Stahl, G., & Sarmiento, J. (2007b). Supporting polyphonic collaborative learning. *E-service Journal*, *6*(1), 58–74. doi:10.2979/ESJ.2007.6.1.59

Turing, A. M. (1950). Computing machinery and intelligence. *Mind*, *59*, 433–460. doi:10.1093/mind/LIX.236.433

Voloshinov, (1973). *Marxism and the philosophy of language*. New York: Seminar Press.

Vygotsky, L. (1978). *Mind in society*. Cambridge, MA: Harvard University Press.

Wertsch, J. V. (1991). *Voices of the mind*. Cambridge, MA: Harvard University Press.

Winograd, T. (1987). Thinking machines: Can there be? Are we? *Report No. STAN-CS-87-1161*, Stanford, California.

Winograd, T., & Flores, F. (1986). *Understanding computers and cognition*. Norwood, NJ: Ablex.

Zemel, A. (2005). Personal communication.

KEY TERMS AND DEFINITIONS

Dialogism: A conception introduced by Mikhail Bakhtin, which considers that every human language-based artefact and activity is a dialog, including not only conversation but also written texts or even thinking.

Discourse: A human language coherent achievement starting from a theme, which is longitudinally developed in time.

Intelligent Tutoring Systems: Computer programs with artificial intelligence that can assist, as a human tutor, a student in learning. This kind of systems is based on the cognitive paradigm, and tries to build a model of the knowledge that a student have. Starting from this model and a model of the knowledge of a given domain (a knowledge base or an ontology), the system tells to the student what to do next for achieving learning.

Inter-Animation: A phenomenon specific to polyphony or to groups of collaborating people in which several voices are entering in dialog and, due to unity-difference (centripetal-centrifugal) interactions, a theme is developed.

Polyphony: A joint achievement that involves several independent participants that are collaboratively developing a time-lasting coherent framework starting from a given theme, even if transient deliberated dissonances may appear. In order to achieve coherence, several harmony assuring rules should be respected.

Utterance: An intervention using human language. It may range "from a short (single-word) rejoinder in everyday dialogue to the large novel or scientific treatise" (Bakhtin 1986, p. 71).

Voice: A distinct position, an utterance, an event or a recurrent series of events of emitting utterances that are heard, reminded, discussed and have influence on the utterances emitted of the other voices.

Chapter 29
Hybrid Teaching and Learning of Computer Programming Language

Fu Lee Wang
Caritas Francis Hsu College, Hong Kong

Tak-Lam Wong
Chinese University of Hong Kong, Hong Kong

ABSTRACT

Teaching and learning computer programming has created significant difficulties to both teacher and student. Large class size is one of the major barriers to effective instruction. A well-designed pedagogy can make the instruction most effective. Hybrid teaching and learning combines face-to-face instruction and computer-assisted instruction to maximize students' learning. This chapter will share the authors' experiences in City University of Hong Kong (CityU) as they teach computer programming courses with large class size by hybrid learning model. Evaluation has showed that hybrid teaching and learning provide great flexibilities to both teaching and learning of computer programming. The students' academic results have been significantly improved in computer programming courses.

1. INTRODUCTION

Computer programming is an essential fundamental skill required in many curriculums for higher education nowadays. It is commonly believed that the students would develop their general problem-solving skills through learning programming. Learning computer programming has been known to be difficult for high-school and university students (Boulay, 1989), and has failed to catalyze the development of higher order thinking skills (Mason, 1999). A number of challenges have been identified for both teaching and learning programming (Sleeman, 1986).

A programming course typically has a large class size. Large class size is one of the major barriers to effective instruction. It is difficult to closely monitor individual student's learning progress. The teachers do not have enough time to interact with all students in a class of hundreds of students within a few hours of lectures and tutorials each week. Teaching and learning computer programming has created significant difficulties to both teacher and student.

DOI: 10.4018/978-1-60566-380-7.ch029

Hybrid learning is to combine face-to-face instruction with computer-assisted instruction (Graham, 2005; Graham & Allen, 2005). Hybrid learning is the convergence of two representative learning environments. The traditional face-to-face learning environment has been used for centuries. On the other hand, the rapid development of technologies provides distributed learning environment as an alternative. In the past, these two environments are separated because they use different media/method combinations. Therefore, they are used to address the needs of different audiences (Graham, 2005). Traditionally, distributed learning is used as an expansion to the face-to-face learning.

Taking the university education as an example, the face-to-face learning environment is used in a teach-directed synchronous environment where the interpersonal interaction is a key component. On the other hand, the distributed learning environment is usually used in distanced learning, which focus on asynchronous self-paced learning and learning-material is the key component. The rapid development has a significant impact on the learning environment. In fact, there is an increasing trend to integrate the two learning environments as a single system. Nowadays, more and more universities conduct the learning activities under both environments.

As there is an increasing need for hybrid learning systems, efforts have been continuously devoted into the research of hybrid learning (Choy, Lam, Poon, Wang, Yu, & Yuen 2007). A number of hybrid learning platforms have been developed in real world. We have successfully implemented hybrid learning to teach computer programming courses in the City University of Hong Kong (CityU). This paper is going to share our experiences of hybrid learning. Students taking computer programming courses very often come with various backgrounds and ability levels. We have incorporated several teaching strategies in designing our teaching and learning activities for computer programming course. We combined the advantages of both learning environments to deliver computer programming courses.

Related research has showed that computer-assisted instruction (CAI) technology can be a more effective way of teaching introductory programming courses (Anderson & Skwarecki, 1986). The CAI technology allows us to have a close monitoring of student's learning progress. The CAI technology provides great flexibilities for us to render the teaching and learning of computer programming more effective. We have designed programming exercises with different levels of difficulty to fulfil the need of students with various backgrounds and ability levels. We can ensure that each step is learned by stepwise learning (Schulman, 2001). We also implemented peer learning scheme (Boud, Cohen, & Sampson, 2001). The group of more talented student will help the others to study programming. Both groups of talented and less talented student are benefited from peer learning scheme. On the other hand, we have designed programming activities in an incremental manner, so that the students gain the knowledge of large application development by implicit learning (Berry, 1997). This experience prepares the students ready to participation in a software development team.

The statistics has shown that students are greatly benefited with this mode of study. The students' academic results have been significantly improved. Students find the learning computer programming become interesting, and their programming skills are enhanced subsequently.

2. TEACHING & LEARNING PROGRAMMING COURSE AT CITYU

City University of Hong Kong (CityU) is a university financially supported by the government of Hong Kong. The university is strong in technical science. The Department of Computer Science is one of the funding departments under the Faculty of Science and Engineering. In addition to the courses offered to the students who are majored in Computer Science, the department also offers a lot of service courses to the students from other departments. Computer programming is one of the common courses offered to students from various departments. We have implemented a hybrid mode of teaching and learning programming course at CityU. We shall share our experiences in implementing hybrid learning in teaching computer Programming.

2.1 Outcomes Based Teaching & Learning

As a strategic plan, the City University of Hong Kong focuses on enhancement of teaching and learning qualities. The University has implemented Outcomes Based Teaching and Learning (OBTL), which is a student-centered approach for education. The curriculum topics in a program and the courses contained in it are expressed as the intended outcomes for the students to learn. Teaching and learning activities are designed to directly encourage the students to learn those outcomes and assessments will then be done to confirm that. It is an approach in which the students themselves are actively engaged in their learning while the teachers are trying to facilitate them to do so.

Derek Bok, President Emeritus and Research Professor at Harvard University, believes that we need a reformulation in the Undergraduate Education. He identified some core purposes of undergraduate education (Bok 2005). On the other hand, Harvard University (2004) has conducted a review of their entire undergraduate educational programs. They are going to implement a new curriculum for undergraduates. The OBTL is developed on similar concept. The university identified some core outcomes (or objectives). Those outcomes state what the students are expected to be able to do at the end of a program. Based on the program outcomes, the teachers decide the course outcomes, which state what the students are expected to be able to do at the end of a course. The OBTL has been implemented in a number of institutes over many countries.

The OBTL is developed based on the concept of constructive alignment (Biggs, 2003). The key elements of a course, such as learning activities and assessment tasks, must be aligned to each other so that the intended outcomes may best be achieved. Teaching and learning activities are designed such that the students are required to enact the learning activities and therefore they will most likely to achieve the intended outcomes. The activities can be teacher, peer, or self-initiated. The students actively gain knowledge through engaging in appropriate learning activities.

Traditional teaching starts from the perspective of the teachers. OBTL works from the perspective of the learners. Under a constructively aligned curriculum, students are actively engaged in their learning processes where the teaching are focused on what the students, rather than on what the teachers, are doing. The teacher needs to consider what outcomes have the students achieved, how to demonstrate those outcomes have indeed been achieved, and to what standards. It encourages all teachers to ask these questions by providing points for reflection on teaching. Unlike traditional teachings, the teachers have to pay a lot of efforts to design the course outcomes and related activities, instead of simply deciding on what topics to be covered.

Assessments are designed to align with the course outcomes to provide evidence on how well each student has achieved the outcomes. Such evidence could be provided by project work, case studies, assignments, examinations, laboratory work and reports, practicum, etc. With the support of technologies, the teacher is able to assess a student in multiple dimensions. The students are evaluated by their performances in each outcome. This approach not only promotes active learning, it also challenges the students to take control of their own learning.

2.2 Computer Programming Course at CityU

The traditional classroom education does not meet the requirements of OBTL. Traditionally, the learning activities are limited inside the classrooms and assessment tasks are usually in the form of examinations. In order to enhance the qualities of teaching and learning, hybrid learning is introduced to the programming courses in CityU to implement OBTL.

In the past, computer programming courses at CityU are taught in a traditional mode. The course was delivered in a mixture of large-sized face-to-face lectures and small-sized face-to-face tutorials (which might be in the form of laboratory sections). The students were evaluated by coursework and final examinations. The coursework was usually in the format of programming assignment or written quiz, and the final examination was in the format of written examinations.

Hybrid learning combines classroom education with e-learning technology. It provides a large degree of flexibilities to the teachers for course design. Activities in different formats can be provided to the students with time and geographical constraints. After implementation of Hybrid learning, the courses are delivered in multiple channels:

- The teachers present the primary course materials in the large-sized face-to-face lectures.
- Small-sized face-to-face tutorials are conducted by the tutors to allow students to do some programming practices.
- Supplementary course materials are delivered in Internet through the university e-learning platform. For example, extensive examples are provided to help students to appreciate the good programming skills.
- Computer programming clinic scheme is setup to provide consultations to students.
- Online intelligent computer-assisted instruction system is developed to provide a programming practice platform to the students.

There is one major difference between the OBTL and traditional teaching. The learning outcomes are clearly stated at the beginning of the courses. Each learning activity is aligned with the learning outcome. It provides a high level of transparency to the students. The students have a clear picture about the course structure. They know what learning activities they must enact in order to achieve the intended outcomes. On the other hand, the students are assessed by how well they have achieved the outcomes. The assessments are usually measured in multiple dimensions. In CityU, the assessments of a programming course include the followings

- Both online and offline short quizzes will be conducted to evaluate the student's performances during the semester.
- Students are required to do some programming assignments to demonstrate their programming capabilities. The e-learning platform allows a great flexibility in assignment design. For example, we provide some testing modules in the e-learning platform. This allows the student to complete the assignments stepwisely.
- The data collected in the intelligent computer-assisted instruction system may also be used to evaluate the students.
- The e-learning environment in hybrid learning makes it feasible to conduct online programming quizzes.

2.3 Computer Programming Clinic Scheme at CityU

For effective learning, it is important to provide the students with a good learning environment of computer programming. A pilot scheme of Computer Programming Clinic has been setup in CityU with the support of the Department of Computer Science.

The clinic recruits students of senior years who are good at programming as programming consultants. The consultants will share their programming experiences with students of junior years. This clinic is developed based on the idea of "help desk" system. We have setup a face-to-face clinic in the Computer Laboratory of Department of Computer Science. The junior students can visit the clinic for consultations during school hours. The consultants will perform the following tasks:

- Answer students' questions related to general programming
- Help students to identify the bugs in their program at high levels
- Help students to formulate high-level pesudocode before programming
- Suggest some appropriate readings for the students if necessary
- Demonstrate a small segment of programming code to the students to help them to understand their program if necessary
- Assign some simple tutorial problems to the students to help them to understand the programming concepts

Another obstacle for the students to learn programming is that they do not know where to seek help when they have encountered problems. Usually, the students encounter problems when they are doing some programming work after they returned home. Most students will put the problems aside and forget to solve their problems when they return to school. It greatly reduces their enthusiasm to study programming, if they lack of instant supports.

In order to provide instant supports to the students beyond normal school hours, we have setup a virtual extension of the Computer Programming Clinic in Internet. CityU has deployed the Blackboard Academic Suite (Bb) as its unified e-learning platform. To align with the e-learning strategic development of the University and to eliminate the development cost, we have implemented online clinic based on the Blackboard (Figure 1). During school hours and after school hours, consultants will be on duty to offer help to the junior students.

We devote actively in monitoring the students' learning. In addition to face-to-face and on-line consultations, the consultants will analyze the coursework submitted in the programming courses and data in the electronic systems to identify the slow learners. Moreover, the instructors of the programming courses will also refer the students who have difficulties in programming to our clinic. Corresponding personalized learning program will be provided to the students. This project will greatly enhance the learning environment of computer programming.

2.4 Computer-Assisted Instruction for Computer Programming

Instant support to the student is a critical factor to the success of teaching and learning of programming. However, it introduces a huge pressure in the resources, and it may not be affordable by some universities. It has been showed that computer-assisted instruction (CAI) technology can be a more effective way of teaching introductory programming courses - for certain populations (Anderson & Skwarecki, 1986). Programming skill has to be acquired through lots of practice (Cheang, Kurnia, Lim & Oon, 2003). With the support of CAI, we are able to provide adequate practice to students.

We have implemented a computer-assisted instruction system to supplement our supports. Figure 2 shows the Programming Assignment aSsessment System (PASS). The PASS system is a web-based computer-assisted instruction system for computer programming developed at CityU (Choy, Nazir, Poon & Yu, 2005; Yu, Poon & Choy, 2006). The PASS system is a fully automated

Figure 1. Computer programming clinic – online clinic

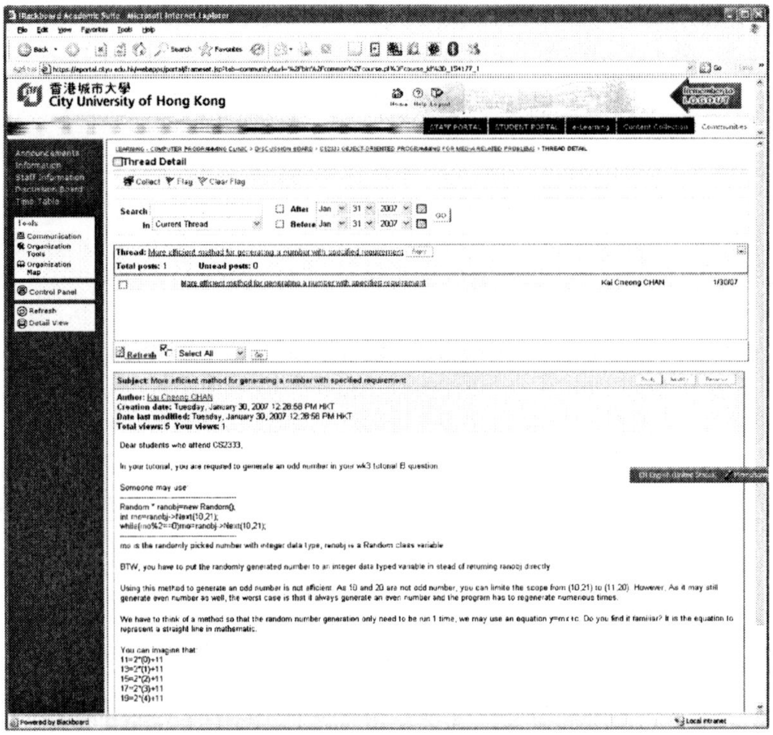

system to help students to study programming (Figure 2).

The PASS system allows the instructors to setup some tutorial problems. The instructors provide the input and the corresponding output to each test case. The students then submit their program for testing. The system automatically complies and executes the program submitted. By comparing the output generated by the students' program and the expected output provided by the instructor, the system will then provide feedbacks to the students. For example, if the student gets wrong in certain type of inputs, the system will show the attached annotation provided by the instructor to give some hints of possible mistakes to the student. The instant feedback provided by the system provides concrete assistances to students to revise their programs, and debugging will become more interesting.

The PASS system has been used in programming courses since 2003, and it has been evolved to its third version. The system is highly evaluated by both students and teachers. In the following sections, we will discuss how teaching strategies are incorporated with the intelligent computer-assisted instruction system. On the other hand, some teaching strategies are incorporated with the intelligent computer-assisted instruction system.

2.5 Programming Activity with Multiple Levels of Difficulties

Effective instruction involves working the content to provide stepwise learning which checks along the way to assure that each step is learned (Schulman, 2001). It is important to ensure that students are well-trained in the fundamentals to the extent that they can eventually consider some problems with high-level complexity. We pay extra care to design the teaching and learning activities to incorporate stepwise learning.

Figure 2. Programming assignment assessment system (PASS)

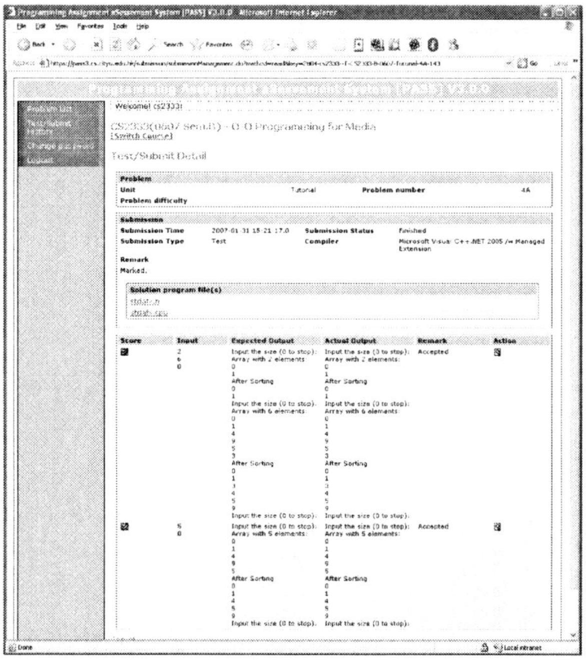

Students taking computer programming course very often come with various backgrounds and ability levels. The PASS system allows us to design exercises with different levels of difficulty to fulfil the need of students with various backgrounds and ability levels.

To illustrate the idea, we take the programming exercise of solving a quadratic equation as a running example (Figure 3). We have created a number of test cases, which are grouped into three levels of difficulty, namely, the beginner level, intermediate level and advanced level (Figure 4). The equations which have two distinct real roots are considered relatively easier; and therefore we classify the corresponding test cases as at the beginner level (Figure 4a). The test cases which correspond to quadratic equations with one repeated root or two complex roots are classified as at the intermediate level (Figure 4b). The exceptional cases (such as those corresponding to the cases when the equations become linear or identities) are classified as at the advanced level (Figure 4c).

The PASS system allows us to tell the students the level of difficulty of each exercise (Figure 5). For the same problem, students can attempt the exercises based on their capability. For example, the less talented students may design a simple program to solve the problem at the beginner level of difficulty (Figure 6a). If they submit their programs to attempt exercises at other levels of difficulty, they will fail in those test cases (Figure 6b). Instead, they must enhance their programs in order to solve the problem at the intermediate level of difficulty.

However, the talented students may work directly to solve the problem at the intermediate level of difficulty. They can even try to challenge the exceptional test cases by submitting their programs to solve the problem at the advanced level of difficulty. Eventually, they should come up with a single program which can solve the problem up to a certain level of difficulty. This approach allows the students to regulate their own learning pace. We can also cater the needs of students with various learning capabilities.

Figure 3. Programming exercise of "quadratic equation"

A Programming Exercise of Solving a Quadratic Equation

Write a program to solve a quadratic equation. The general form of a quadratic equation is $ax^2 + bx + c = 0$, where a, b, c are real numbers. When $a \neq 0$, the solution of the equation is given by the quadratic formula $x = \frac{-b \pm \sqrt{b^2 - 4ac}}{2a}$.

In this exercise, the user need to input the value of a, b and c, then the program will output the answers accordingly. We assume that all the inputs are integers, and that the outputs are to be displayed in ascending order with 2 decimal point precision.

Figure 4. Test cases of quadratic equation programming exercise at different levels of difficulty

Test Cases of Quadratic Equation Programming Exercise

(a) Test Cases at the Beginner Level of Difficulty

Input	Expected Output
$a = 1, b = -5, c = 6$	$x = 3, 2$
$a = 2, b = -7, c = -15$	$x = 5, -1.5$
$a = 1, b = 6, c = 8$	$x = -2, -4$

(b) Test Cases at the Intermediate Level of Difficulty

Input	Expected Output
$a = 1, b = -2, c = 1$	$x = 1$
$a = 1, b = 2, c = 5$	$x = -1+2\mathbf{i}, -1-2\mathbf{i}$
$a = 2, b = 12, c = 18$	$x = -3$

(c) Test Cases at the Advanced Level of Difficulty

Input	Expected Output
$a = 0, b = 2, c = 4$	$x = -2$
$a = 0, b = 0, c = 0$	x = any real numbers
$a = 0, b = 0, c = -4$	No solution

Additionally, we also require the students to study the given test cases for each exercise to figure out how we select the test cases. The students learn how to test their programs on their own by implicit learning (Berry, 1997). We teach the students how to test the program by giving examples. They will follow our approach to test the program in the future. Besides, the test cases at intermediate level and advanced level teach the student how to select boundary test value for their computer programs.

2.6 Peer Learning Scheme in Programming Course

The PASS has recorded all the program submission activities of students. The system extracts useful aggregated information based on the raw data of test/submit history. Various statistics are computed to help the teacher monitor the performance of the class.

Figure 7 shows the screen for students' performance. These data provide very useful information of students' performance. For example, we can easily know a student's progress in the course

Figure 5. Programming exercises at different levels of difficulty

Unit	Prob. No.	Problem difficulty	Prob. Type
Quadratic Equation	Beginner Level	☆☆	Practice
Quadratic Equation	Intermediate Level	☆☆☆☆	Practice
Quadratic Equation	Advanced Level	☆☆☆☆☆☆☆	Practice
Quadratic Inequality	Beginner Level	☆☆☆	Practice

Figure 6. Exercises at different levels of difficulty and sample runs of submissions in PASS

No.	Input	Annotation	Expected Output	Actual Output	Result
0	1 -5 6		2.00, 3.00	2.00, 3.00	Accepted
1	2 -7 -15		-1.50, 5.00	-1.50, 5.00	Accepted
2	1 6 8		-4.00, -2.00	-4.00, -2.00	Accepted

(a) A Sample Run of Submission to an Exercise at the Beginner Level of Difficulty

No.	Input	Annotation	Expected Output	Actual Output	Result
0	1 -5 6		2.00, 3.00	2.00, 3.00	Accepted
1	2 -7 -15		-1.50, 5.00	-1.50, 5.00	Accepted
2	1 6 8		-4.00, -2.00	-4.00, -2.00	Accepted
3	1 -2 1		1.00	1.00, 1.00	Wrong Answer
4	1 2 5		-1.00-2.00i, -1.00+2.00i	Runtime error 207 at $00401115 $00401115 $0040123E	Wrong Answer
5	2 12 18		-3.00	-3.00, -3.00	Wrong Answer

(b) A Sample Run of Submission to an Exercise at the Intermediate Level of Difficulty

based on the number of attempts to each exercise and the number of exercises completed. The summary of student performance supports fast decision making as well. We can identify the slow learner quickly and offer corresponding help.

At the same time, we have implemented peer learning scheme in programming course. We encourage the talented students to offer peer assistance to other students. We find that the talented students put in additional efforts to study all related

Figure 7. Students' performance

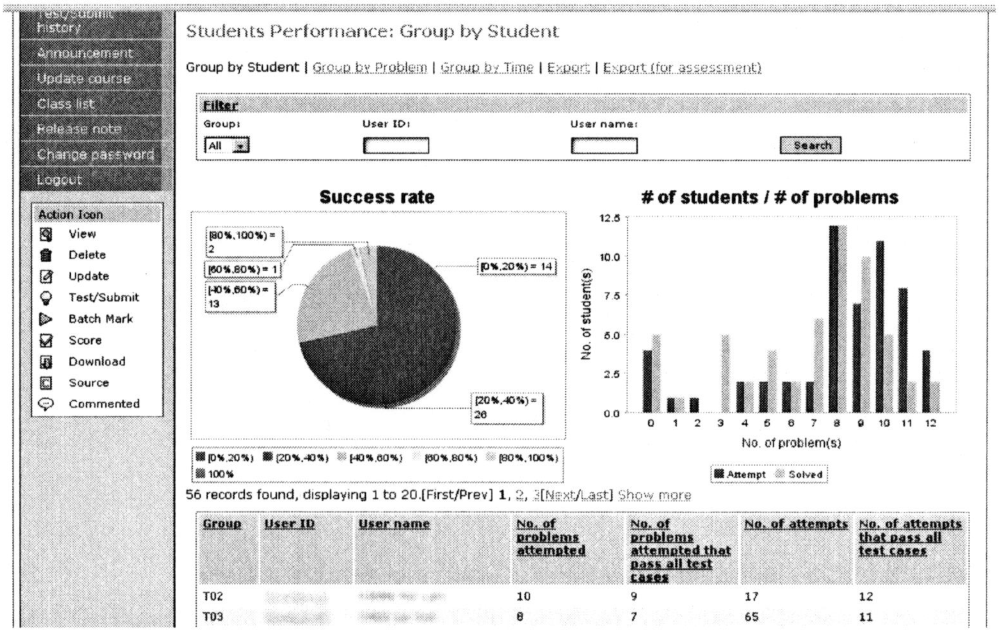

materials before they offer help. Besides, they can further enhance their understanding by explaining the programs to others.

Finally, the talented students have similar backgrounds as the other students. They understand clearly what problems their classmates are currently facing, and therefore be the most suitable persons to offer helps. Both groups of students are greatly benefited from the peer learning scheme.

2.7 Incremental Style of Programming Activity

Traditional programming course focuses on the development of small applications. Without the support of related technology, students usually develop small applications by writing the code solely on their individual effort. The student may become an analyst programmer in the future and may be involved in some large scale projects. Students often find it difficult to manage large software development jobs when they work in the industry. It is very important to provide students with experiences of software development in large scale applications while they are studying.

However, there are practical difficulties to require students to develop a large application. Traditionally, the students are required to complete a program before they can do testing. Unfortunately, students' learning motivation drops very fast as the time they have to spend on study increases. If we require the student to code a large application, they are usually unable to see their results before the completion of the whole application. They will lose their interests in programming soon after they started. Lack of motivation is one of the major resistances to learning (Atherton, 1999). As we foresee the need, we consider large application development as an essential part of an advanced programming course. Some special arrangements have to be made to keep the students' learning motivation.

Our system allows the teacher to provide the main body of the program, and students to submit their implementation of functions to the system,

Figure 8. A programming exercise based on a previously completed module

A Programming Exercise of Solving a Quadratic Inequality

Write a program to solve a quadratic inequality based on the module you developed earlier in the programming exercise of solving a quadratic equation. In general, a quadratic inequality can be written in one of the following standard forms, where *a*, *b*, *c* are real numbers:

$ax^2 + bx + c \geq 0$

$ax^2 + bx + c > 0$

$ax^2 + bx + c \leq 0$

$ax^2 + bx + c < 0$

Suppose that the equation $ax^2 + bx + c = 0$ has two real roots x_1 and x_2, where $x_1 < x_2$. If $a > 0$, the solution sets of the inequalities are, respectively, as follows.

Inequality: $ax^2 + bx + c \geq 0$. Solution: $(-\infty, x_1] \cup [x_2, +\infty)$

Inequality: $ax^2 + bx + c > 0$. Solution: $(-\infty, x_1) \cup (x_2, +\infty)$

Inequality: $ax^2 + bx + c \leq 0$. Solution: $[x_1, x_2]$

Inequality: $ax^2 + bx + c < 0$. Solution: (x_1, x_2)

or vice versa. Then, the system will integrate the source codes together as a single program. When we design a large application, we may divide the application into several modules. After the student has completed one module of the application, he/she can submit the modules to PASS. Some stubs or test drivers can be provided for testing their individual modules. This type of exercise is welcomed by the students, as they can speedily see the outcomes of their program without writing many lines of code. It is important to reinforce the student's success upon his/her completion of one module. This approach also increases the student's confidence in learning. The intermediate results can keep students' learning motivation constantly high. The students will develop the application in a progressive manner. After the students have completed the entire application, they can submit it to PASS, which will test all the modules together as a single integrated application.

This approach also supports the team-work of large scale project. The system allows the students to submit components of a program as separate files. Sometimes, the components files may be developed by different students. The system will integrate the source files together as a single project. This team-work style exercise makes the students understand the paradigm of software development. The students are exposed to programs that are built from modules so that they learn the concept of modularity of program by implicit learning (Berry, 1997). When developing an application, students will have to divide their solutions into modules as functions and classes.

Moreover, we require the students to archive all the files developed in their activities. When designing a programming activity, we intentionally require the students to make use of some modules developed in previous activities. For example, we may require students to develop a program to solve a quadratic inequality (Figure 8) based on the module developed earlier in the programming exercise of solving a quadratic equation (Figure 3).

Similarly, as before, we create exercises at different levels of difficulty (Figure 9). The least talented students can solve the inequality by using their simple programs that solve a quadratic equation, while the talented students can try some challenging test cases such as when the quadratic inequality has one solution or no solution. In this way, students will naturally acquire the concept of code reuse through their own experience of reusing the previously developed code, as con-

Figure 9. Programming exercises of "Quadratic Inequality"

Unit	Prob. No.	Problem difficulty	Prob. Type
Quadratic Inequality	Beginner Level	☆☆☆	Practice
Quadratic Inequality	Intermediate Level	☆☆☆☆☆	Practice
Quadratic Inequality	Advanced Level	☆☆☆☆☆☆☆☆	Practice

crete experience is important in the learning cycle (Kolb, 1984). On the other hand, we sometimes ask students to exchange files and develop their applications based on modules written by other students.

3. EVALUATION OF THE NEW PEDAGOGY

A number of extensive evaluations have been conducted to measure the effectiveness of our teaching model. Evaluation results have shown that the hybrid teaching and learning model is a promising approach in teaching and learning of computer programming.

3.1 Evaluation of Course Structure

It is suggested that the hybrid learning can be measured by interviews and questionnaires (Harding, Kaczynski & Wood, 2005). We have conducted both evaluations to measure the effectiveness of the hybrid teaching and learning.

A focus group session has been held with students who enrolled for any hybrid courses of computer programming in the Department. A set of interview questions are designed by professionals in education development. The students are interviewed by an independent interviewer and none of the course lecturers were presented. All the students in the focus group believe that the hybrid teaching and learning model can help them to learn the computer programming courses more effectively.

Few responses are extracted as examples:

Student 1: The programming assignment with different levels is a fresh idea. I can control my learning pace.

Student 2: My fellow classmates teach me a lot. They know clearly of my problem.

Student 3: Eventually, I can develop a computer game by myself.

Student 4: I enjoy working on programming during midnight.

...

Most of the students appreciate the flexibilities provided by the hybrid teaching and learning. The students can self-control their learning paces. The anytime/anywhere studying mode allows them to work at the time when they have the highest productivities. Moreover, the students become more independent and self-disciplined in their learning. Their time management skills are also enhanced. The preliminary results of interview suggest that hybrid teaching and learning is a good teaching and learning model.

On the other hand, all the students appreciate interactivity of the online assessment system. However, some of the students are less satisfied. They hope that the online intelligent computer-assisted instruction system can provide more feedbacks to help them to debug their programs.

Table 1. Evaluation of course design for a computer programming course

Questions	Average Score
The PASS system is useful to my study of computer programming.	7.8
The PASS system helps me to have comprehensive testing of program.	8.2
I like the programming activity with different levels of difficulty.	8.1
I like the programming activity with incremental style.	7.3
The peer learning scheme is useful to my study.	7.8
The course design helps me to control my learning pace.	6.8
The course helps me to identify weakness.	7.5
The course encourages collaborations between students.	7.6
The course is effective in learning computer programming.	7.4

This provides some directions for future enhancement of the system.

In order to get a more quantitative measurement for the course structure of computer programming courses, we have conducted a survey by questionnaires. The questionnaires are designed by professionals in education development in the similar way as (Harding, Kaczynski & Wood, 2005). The students are asked to score each dimension of the course structure on the scale from 0 to 10, where a score of 10 represents the highest satisfaction, while 0 represents the least satisfaction. 250 students have participated in the survey. The results are summarized as Table 1.

In Table 1, we can clearly see that the students are highly satisfied with the course structure. The students are happy with the flexibilities provided by the hybrid teaching and learning. They most believe that the mixture of teaching channels, such as mixture of tutorial, assignment, supplementary web and online assessment system, can effectively teach them about computer programming. They help the students to identify their weakness and control their own learning paces. Therefore, the students can achieve the intended learning outcomes effectively (Figure 10).

An ideal hybrid teaching and learning is a mixture of classroom learning and electronic learning. Self-paced learning is one of the major advantages of electronic learning (Graham, 2005). However, the students are generally less satisfied with the effectiveness of self-paced learning (Figure 10). As a result, there is potential to further blend our courses. In the future, we will investigate on how to improve the self-pace learning in computer programming courses.

3.2 Evaluation of Students' Performances

In the past, the students taking computer programming courses in CityU are assessed by coursework and final examinations. The coursework was usually in the format of programming assignments, and the final examination was in the format of written examinations. After implementation of OBTL, the students are assessed in multiple dimensions. We have compared the results of the students before and after the implementation of OBTL.

We have selected a typical computer programming course at the introductory level as an example (Table 2). Because the class size of this course is very large, the statistical information of this course is worthy trusted. On the other hand, the materials of assessment are moderated by peer review to ensure the standard of assessment. No scaling of score has been conducted in this course. The score boundary for each grade has been fixed by the department. As a result, this graded distribution

Table 2. Statistics of a computer programming course

		Year 2004	Year 2005	Year 2006
Total no. of students		277	253	251
Grade	Score Boundary	% of Students	% of Students	% of Students
A	69.5	7.94%	7.11%	26.00%
B	54.5	16.25%	17.79%	22.40%
C	39.5	35.38%	23.72%	23.60%
D	34.5	9.75%	12.65%	4.80%
F	below 34.5	30.69%	38.74%	23.20%

of students is a very important indicator to show the performances of teaching and learning.

In years 2004 and 2005, only a small percentage of students got grade "A", while a large percentage of students failed the course in these two years (Table 1). After the new pedagogy was implemented in year 2006, the percentage of grade "A" students increased dramatically from 7~8% to 26% (Table 1). At the same time, the percentage of failure decreased significantly. As shown in the table, the students' performances in the programming course increase significantly. This is a strong evidence to show the success of the new pedagogy.

4. CONCLUSION

This paper has shared our experiences in implementing hybrid learning in teaching computer programming in City University of Hong Kong. The traditional teaching model imposes a lot of constraints in implementing teaching and learning activities. In contrary, hybrid teaching and learning provides great flexibilities to both the teachers and the students. By designing exercises at different levels of difficulty, we provide stepwise learning experiences to students, such that they can solve problems pertaining to their corresponding ability levels. At the same time, it can cater students with different learning paces. Teachers can also define problems in various ways in PASS so as to make students familiar with modules programming and be prepared for large projects. The interviews and questionnaires have shown that hybrid teaching and learning is very effective in teaching and learning of computer programming. The students' performances in the assessments have further confirmed our findings. We believe that the hybrid teaching and learning can be applied to other courses in the future as well.

ACKNOWLEDGMENT

The PASS System is a System developed by C.K. Poon, Y.T. Yu, Marian Choy, Fu Lee Wang, Celine Chong, Usman Nazir, P. F. Tam, Isaac Yeung, Sam Lam and Leo Yuen at Department of Computer Science, City University of Hong Kong. The projected was substantially supported by grants from City University of Hong Kong (Project No. 6000118 & 6000144). The Computer Programming Clinic is a project lead by Fu Lee Wang, Kenneth Lee and Jiying Wang at Department of Computer Science, City University of Hong Kong. We would like to thank individuals for their significant contributions to the paper.

REFERENCES

Anderson, J. R., & Skwarecki, E. (1986). The automated tutoring of introductory computer programming. *Communications of the ACM, 29*(9), 842–849. doi:10.1145/6592.6593

Atherton, J. S. (1999). Resistance to learning: A discussion based on participants in in-service professional training programmes. *Journal of Vocational Education and Training, 51*(1), 77–90. doi:10.1080/13636829900200070

Berry, D. C. (Ed.). (1997). *How Implicit is Implicit Learning*. Oxford, UK: Oxford University Press.

Biggs, J. (2003). Teaching for Quality Learning at University (2nd ed.). New York: McGraw-Hill Education, Open University Press.

Bok, D. (2005). *Our Underachieving Colleges: A Candid Look at How Much Students Learn and Why They Should Be Learning More*. Princeton, NJ: Princeton University Press.

Boud, D., Cohen, R., & Sampson, J. (Eds.). (2001). *Peer learning and assessment*. London: Kogan

Cheang, B., Kurnia, A., Lim, A., & Oon, W.-C. (2003). On automated grading of programming assignments in an academic institution. *Computers & Education, 41*(2), 121–131. doi:10.1016/S0360-1315(03)00030-7

Choy, M., Lam, S., Poon, C. K., Wang, F. L., Yu, Y. T., & Yuen, L. (2007). Towards blended learning of computer programming supported by an automated system. In J. Fong & F. L. Wang (Eds.), *Blended Learning* (pp. 9-18). Pearson.

Choy, M., Nazir, U., Poon, C. K., & Yu, Y. T. (2005). Experiences in using an automated system for improving students' learning of computer programming. In *Proceedings of the 4th International Conference on Web-based Learning (ICWL 2005)* (LNCS 3583, pp. 267-272). Berlin, German: Springer.

du Boulay, B. (1989). Some difficulties of learning to program. In E. Soloway & J.C. Spohrer (Eds.), *Studying the novice programmer*. Hillsdale, NJ: L. Erlbaum Associates.

Graham, C. R. (2005). Blended learning system: definition, current trends, and future directions. In C. J. Bonk & C. R. Graham (Eds.), *Handbook of blended learning: Global Perspectives, local designs* (pp. 3-21). San Francisco, CA: Pfeiffer Publishing.

Graham, C. R., & Allen, S. (2005). Blended learning: An emerging trend in education. In C. Howard, J.V. Boettecher, L. Justice, & K.D. Schenk (Eds.), *Encyclopedia of Distance Learning* (pp. 172-179). Hershey, PA: Idea Group Inc.

Harding, A., Kaczynski, D., & Wood, L. N. (2005). Evaluation of blended learning: analysis of qualitative data. In *Proceedings of the Symposium of Blended Learning in Science Teaching & Learning,* The University of Sydney, Australia (pp. 56-62).

Harvard University, Faculty of Arts and Sciences. (2004). *A Report on the Harvard College Curricular Review, April 2004*.

Kolb, D. A. (1984). *Experiential Learning: Experience as the Source of Learning and Development*. Upper Saddle River, NJ: Prentice-Hall.

Mason, M. B. (1999). Outcomes-based Education in South African Curricular Reform. *Cambridge Journal of Education, 29*(1), 137–143. doi:10.1080/0305764990290111

Schulman, M. (2001). Basic understandings for developing learning media for the classroom and beyond. *Learning Technology Newsletter, 3*(1).

Sleeman, D. (1986). The Challenges of teaching computer programming. *Communications of the ACM, 29*(9), 840–841. doi:10.1145/6592.214913

Yu, Y. T., Poon, C. K., & Choy, M. (2006). Experiences with PASS: Developing and using a programming assignment assessment system. In *Proceedings of the 6th International Conference on Quality Software (QSIC 2006)* (pp. 360-365). Washington, DC: IEEE Computer Society Press.

KEY TERMS AND DEFINITIONS

Computer-Assisted Instruction: A type of Technology supported education/learning where the medium of instruction is computer technology, particularly involving digital technologies.

Hybrid Learning: A learning approach which combines face-to-face instruction with computer-assisted instruction.

Implicit Learning: A passive learning approach. Learner are exposed to information, and acquire knowledge of that information simply through that exposure.

Outcomes Based Teaching and Learning: A student-centered approach for education. The curriculum topics in a program and the courses contained in it are expressed as the intended outcomes for the students to learn. Teaching and learning activities are designed to directly encourage the students to learn those outcomes and assessments will then be done to confirm that.

Peer Learning: A kind of cooperative learning approach, which is a two-way reciprocal learning activity, i.e., learners teaching, and learning from each other.

Stepwise Learning: A learning approach which checks along the way to assure that each step is learned. It ensures that students are well-trained in the fundamentals to the extent that they can eventually consider some problems with high-level complexity.

Compilation of References

Ackhoff, R. L. (1989). From data to wisdom. *Journal of Applied Systems Analysis, 16*, 3–9.

AECT. (1972). The field of Educational technology: A Statement of Definition. *Audiovisual Instruction, 17*, 36–43.

Aguilar, G., & Kaijiri, K. (2007). Design Overview of an Adaptive Computer-Based Assessment System. *Interactive Educational Multimedia, 14*, 116–130.

Ahsan, S., & Shah, A. (2006). Data, information, knowledge, wisdom: A doubly linked chain? In *Proceedings of the 2006 International Conference on Information & Knowledge Engineering* (pp. 270-278). Las Vegas, Nevada: CSREA Press.

Alavi, M. (1994). Computer-mediated Collborative Learning: an Empirical Evaluation, Computer-mediated discussion. *Journal of Educational Computing Research, 8*, 291–309.

Alavi, M., & Leidner, D. E. (2001, March). Review: Knowledge management and knowledge management systems: Conceptual foundations and research issues. *MIS Quarterly, 25*(1), 107–136. doi:10.2307/3250961

Aldridge, S. (2008). *Proceedings of the 2008 international conference on Web-Based Education (WBE-2008)* – Innsbruck congress Center, Innsbruck, Austria. Retrieved April 18, 2008, from http://www.interlabs.bradley.edu/wbe2008/

Alexander, B. (2006). Web 2.0: A new wave of innovation for teaching and learning? *EDUCAUSE Review, 41*(2), 33–44.

Alexander, B. (2006, March/April). Web 2.0: A New Wave of Innovation for Teaching and Learning. *EDUCAUSE Review*, 33–44.

Alexander, H. (1987). *Formally-Based Tools and Techniques for Human-Computer Dialogues*. Chichester, UK: Ellis Horwood Limited.

Alfonseca, E., Pérez, D., & Rodríguez, P. (2004). Welkin: Automatic Generation of Adaptive Hypermedia Sites with NLP techniques. In *Proceedings of the International Conference in Web Engineering (ICWE)* (LNCS 3140, pp. 617-618). Berlin, Germany: Springer-Verlag.

Allan, B. (2007). *Blended learning Tools for Teaching and Training*. London: Facet Publishing.

Allen, D. (2001). *Getting Things Done: The Art of Stree-Free Productivity*. New York: Viking Penguin

Allen, I., Seaman, J., & Garrett, R. (2007). Blending In: The extent and promise of blending learning in the United States. In *Proceedings of the The Sloan Consortium*.

Althaus, S. L. (1997). Computer-mediated communication in the university classroom: An experiment with on-line discussions. *Communication Education, 46*, 158–174. doi:10.1080/03634529709379088

Alvarado, A. E., & Herr, P. R. (2003). *Inquiry-based learning using everyday objects: Hands-on instructional strategies that promote active learning in grades 3-8*. Thousand Oaks, CA: Corwin Press.

Amelung, M., Piotrowski, M., & Rösner, D. (2006). EduComponents: Experiences in e-assessment in computer science education. In *ITiCSE '06: Proceedings of the*

11th annual conference on Innovation and technology in computer science education (pp. 88–92). New York: ACM Press.

Amelung, M., Piotrowski, M., & Rosner, D. (2007). Large Scale Computer-Assisted Assessment in Computer Science Education: New Possibilities, New Questions. In J. Fong & F. L. Wang (Eds.), *Blended learning* (pp. 257-266). Singapore: Pearson Prentice Hall.

Amir, N., & Ron, S. (1998). Toward automatic classification of emotions in speech. In *Proceedings of ICSLP* (pp. 555–558).

Anderson, J. R. (1976). *Language, memory, and thoughts.* Hillsdale, NJ: Lawrence Erlbaum Associates.

Anderson, J. R., & Skwarecki, E. (1986). The automated tutoring of introductory computer programming. *Communications of the ACM, 29*(9), 842–849. doi:10.1145/6592.6593

Anderson, L. M. (1993). Auxiliary materials that accompany textbooks: Can they promote "higher-order" learning? In B. K. Britton, A. Woodward, & M. Blinkley (Eds.), *Learning from textbooks: Theory and practice.* Mahwah, NJ: Erlbaum.

Anderson, L. W., Krathwohl, D. R., Airasian, P. W., Cruikshank, K. A., Mayer, R. E., Pintrich, P. R., et al. (2001). *A taxonomy for learning, teaching and assessing: a revision of Bloom's taxonomy of educational objectives.* New York: Longman.

Anderson, T. (2004). Toward a theory of online learning. In T. Anderson & F. Elloumi (Eds.), *Theory and practice of online learning* (pp. 33-60). Athabasca, AB: Athabasca University.

Anderson, T. D., & Garrison, D. R. (1998). Learning in a networked world: New roles and responsibilities. In C. C. Gibson (Ed.), *Distance learners in higher education: Institutional responses for quality outcomes* (pp. 97-112). Madison, WI: Atwood Publishing.

Angel, M. (2006). *A Modern Approach to Improving Customer Support: Leveraging the Concepts of Web 2.0 for Self-service and in the Contact Center. KNOVA.* Retrieved April 14, 2008, from http://www.knova.com/products/learnmore.html

Anohina, A., Graudina, V., & Grundspenkis, J. (2007). Using Concept Maps in Adaptive Knowledge Assessment. In *Advances in Information Systems Development* (pp. 469-479). Berlin, Germany: Springer.

Apple. (2006). *iTunes U at Apple*. Retrieved from http://www.apple.com/education/solutions/itunes_u/

Applebee, A. N. (1986). Problems in Process Approaches: Toward a Reconceptualization of Process Instruction. In A. P. Petrosky & D. Bartholomae (Eds.), *The Teaching of Writing* (pp. 95-113). National Society for the Study of Education.

Aquino, K., & Serva, M. (2005). Using a dual role assessment to improve group dynamics and performance. *Journal of Management Education, 29*(1), 17. doi:10.1177/1052562903262482

Arbaugh, J. B. (2004). Learning to Learn Online: A Study of Perceptual Changes between multiple Online Course Experiences. *The Internet and Higher Education, 7*, 169–182. doi:10.1016/j.iheduc.2004.06.001

Arbaugh, J. B., & Stelzer, L. (2003). Learning And Teaching Management On The Web What Do We Know? In *Educating Managers with tomorrow's Technologies* (pp. 17-51).

Ardichvili, A., Page, V., & Wentling, T. (2003). Motivation and barriers to participation in virtual knowledge-sharing communities of practice. *Journal of Knowledge Management, 7*(1), 64–77. doi:10.1108/13673270310463626

Atherton, J. S. (1999). Resistance to learning: A discussion based on participants in in-service professional training programmes. *Journal of Vocational Education and Training, 51*(1), 77–90. doi:10.1080/13636829900200070

Atkinson, R. (2007). Web 2.0: Next-g, a sequel, or more of the same? *HERDSA News, 29*(2), 20–22.

Audet, R. H., & Jordan, L. K. (2005). *Integrating inquiry across the curriculum.* Thousand Oaks, CA: Corwin Press.

Ausburn, L. (2004). Course design elements most valued by adult learners in blended online education: An American perspective. *Educational Media International, 41*(4), 327–337. doi:10.1080/0952398042000314820

Ausubel, D. P. (1963). *The Psychology of Meaningful Verbal Learning*. New York: Grune and Stratton.

Aycock, A., Garnham, C., & Kaleta, R. (2002). Lessons learned from the hybrid course project. *Teaching with Technology Today, 8*(6), 9–21.

Badge, J. L., Cann, A. J., & Scott, J. (2005). e-Learning versus e-Teaching: Seeing the Pedagogic Wood for the Technological Trees. *Bioscience Educatione-Journal, 5*. Retrieved January 10, 2007 from http://www.bioscience.heacademy.ac.uk/journal/vol5/beej-5-6.pdf

Badger, R., White, G., Sutherland, P., & Haggis, T. (2001). Note perfect: an investigation of how students view taking notes in lectures. *System, 29*, 405–417. doi:10.1016/S0346-251X(01)00028-8

Bakhtin, M. (1973). *Problems of Dostoevsky's Poetics*, Ardis, (translated by R.W.Rotsel).

Bakhtin, M. (1981). *The dialogic imagination: four essays*. Austin, TX: University of Texas Press.

Bakhtin, M. (1986). *Speech genres and other late essays*. Austin, TX: University of Texas Press.

Barab, S. A. MaKinster, J. G., & Scheckler, R. (2004). Designing system dualities: Characterizing a web-supported professional development community. In S. A. Barab, R. Kling, & J. H. Gray (Eds.), *Designing for virtual communities in the service of learning* (pp. 53-90). Cambridge, UK: Cambridge University Press.

Barchino, J. M., Gutiérrez, S., Otón, J. J., Matínez, J. R., Hilera, J. A., & Gutiérrez, J. A. (2006). E-learning model for assessment. In Proceedings of the *IADIS Virtual MultiConference on Computer Science and Information Systems*, Portugal (pp. 59-63).

Barfield, L. (2004). *Design for new media: Interaction design for multimedia and the web*. Harlow, UK: Pearson Addison Wesley.

Barker, P. G. (1975). Syntactic Definition and Parsing of Molecular Formula. Part 1: Initial Syntax Definition and Parser Implementation. *The Computer Journal, 18*(4), 355–359. doi:10.1093/comjnl/18.4.355

Barker, P. G. (1996). Living Books and Dynamic Electronic Libraries. *The Electronic Library, 14*(6), 491–501. doi:10.1108/eb045515

Barker, P. G. (1997a). Electronic Libraries of the Future, In A. Kent & C.M. Hall (Eds.), *Encyclopedia of Library and Information Science* (Vol. 50, Supp. 22, pp. 119-153). New York: Marcel Dekker.

Barker, P. G. (1997b). Electronic Documents and their Role in Future Library Systems, In D. Raitt (Ed.), *Libraries for the New Millenium - Implications for Managers* (pp. 89-113). London, UK: Library Association Publishing.

Barker, P. G. (2005). Potential Uses of Weblogs in Electronic Course Delivery. In G. Richards (Ed.), Proceedings of the *E-LEARN 2005 World Conference on E-Learning in Corporate, Government Healthcare & Higher Education* (pp.515-522). Norfolk, Virginia, USA: Association for the Advancement of Computing in Education.

Barker, P. G. (2007a). *Designing and Building Electronic Books* (Research Seminar). Middlesbrough, UK: University of Teesside, Barker, P.G. (2007b). *Using PEAs and PeDALs for Personal Knowledge and Information Management* (Research Seminar). Middlesbrough, UK: University of Teesside.

Barker, P. G. (2007c). Using Wikis as a Teaching and Learning Resource. In C.P. Constantinou, Z.C. Zacharia, & M. Papaevripidou (Eds.), *Proceedings of the CBLIS 2007 International Conference on Computer-Based Learning in Science - Contemporary Perspectives in New Technologies in Science and Education* (pp. 12-23). Nicosia, Cyprus: Learning in Science Group, University of Cyprus.

Barker, P. G. (2007d). Blended Learning the Wiki Way. In *Proceedings of the 2nd International Conference on Blended Learning - Supporting the Net Generation Learner* (pp. 60-71). Hatfield, UK: University of Hertfordshire.

Barker, P. G. (2007e). *Published GPS Walking Routes*. London: Anquet Technology Ltd.

Barker, P. G. (2008). Blended Electronic Learning - Managing the Blend. In *Proceedings of the 3rd International Conference on Blended Learning -Enhancing the Student Experience* (pp. 45-53). Hatfield, UK: University of Hertfordshire.

Barker, P. G., & Jones, P. (1978). Syntactic Definition and Parsing of Molecular Formula. Part 2: Graphical Synthesis of Molecular Formula for Data Base Queries. *The Computer Journal, 21*(3), 224–233. doi:10.1093/comjnl/21.3.224

Barnes, C., & Tynan, B. (2007). The adventures of Miranda in the brave new world: Learning in a Web 2.0 millennium. *ALT-J . Research in Learning Technology, 15*(9), 189–200.

Barnes, K., Marateo, R., & Ferris, S. (2007). *Teaching and Leaning with the Net Generation*. Retrieved November 4, 2007, from http://www.innovateonline.info/

Barr, R. B., & Tagg, J. (1995). From Teaching to Learning. In D. DeZure (Ed.), *Learningfrom Change*. London: Kogan Page.

Barron, T. (2000, August). *A smarter frankenstein: The merging of e-learning and knowledge management*. Retrieved March 03, 2008, from http://www.learningcircuits.org/2000/aug2000/barron1.htm

Barsky, E., & Purdon, M. (2006). Introducing Web 2.0: Social networking and social bookmarking for health librarians. *Journal of the Canadian Health Libraries Association, 27*(3), 65–67.

Bates, A. (2005). *Technology, e-learning and distance education* (2nd ed.). Abingdon, UK: RoutledgeFalmer.

Bates, A. W. (1995). *Technology, open learning and distance education*. London: Routledge.

Bateson, G. (1973). *Steps to an ecology of mind*. London: Granada Publishing.

Bawaba, A. (2008). *Saudi Arabia's eLearning industry to touch US$125 million in 2008*. Retrieved April 30, 2008, from http://www.menareport.com/en/business/226175

Baym, N. K., Zhang, Y. B., & Lin, M.-c. (2004). Social interaction across media. *New Media & Society, 6*(3), 299–318. doi:10.1177/1461444804041438

Beard, R. M. (1969). *An outline of Piaget's Developmental Psychology*. London: Routledge & Kegan Paul.

Beckman, T. J. (1999). The Current State of Knowledge Management. In J. Liebowitz (Ed.), *Knowledge Management Handbook* (pp. 1-22). Boca Raton, FL: CRC Press.

Beldarrain, Y. (2006). Distance Education Trends: Integrating new technologies to foster student interaction and collaboration. *Distance Education, 27*(2), 139–153. doi:10.1080/01587910600789498

Bell, M., & Lafoe, G. (1998). Curriculum design for flexible delivery-massaging the model. In *Proceedings ASCITE 98 Conference* (pp. 65-73).

Bennett, J., Gräsel, C., Parchmann, I., & Waddington, D. (2005). Context-based and conventional approaches to teaching chemistry: comparing teachers' views. *International Journal of Science Education, 27*(13), 1521–1547. doi:10.1080/09500690500153808

Bennis, W., & O'Toole, J. (2005). How business schools lost their way. *Harvard Business Review, 83*(5), 96.

Bereiter, C. (2002). *Education and mind in the knowledge age*. Mahwah, NJ: Lawrence Erlbaum Associates.

Berg, J. E., Berquam, L., & Christoph, K. (2007). Social networking technologies: A "poke" for campus services. *EDUCAUSE Review, 42*(2), 32–44.

Berge, Z. L. (1999). Interaction in post-secondary web-based learning. *Educational Technology, 39*(1), 5–11.

Berkeley. (2006). *Webcast.Berkeley*. Retrieved from http://webcast.berkeley.edu/

Berry, D. C. (Ed.). (1997). *How Implicit is Implicit Learning*. Oxford, UK: Oxford University Press.

Berry, M. W., Dumais, S. T., & O'Brien, G. W. (1995). Using linear algebra for intelligent information retrieval. *SIAM Review, 37*, 573–595. doi:10.1137/1037127

Berry, R. (2003). Alternative assessment and assessment for learning. In *Proceedings of the 29th IAEA Conference, theme: Societies' Goals and Assessment,* USA.

Bersin, J. (2002). Measuring e-learning effectiveness. *e-learning, 3*(3), 36.

Beyond Distance Research Alliance. (2008). *The Beyond Distance Research Alliance, University of Leicester.* Retrieved April 11, 2008, from http://www.le.ac.uk/beyonddistance/index.html

Bhalerao, A., & Ward, A. (2001). Towards electronically assisted peer assessment: a case study. *ALT-J, 9*(1), 26–37. doi:10.1080/09687760108656773

Biass, E., & Davis, A. (2003). Building on solid foundations: Establishing criteria for e-learning developments. *Journal of Further & Higher Learning, 27*(3), 227. doi:10.1080/0309877032000098662

Bielawski, L., & Metcalf, D. (2003). *Blended eLearning: Integrating Knowledge, Performance, Support and Online Learning.* MA: HRD Press Inc.

Bielski, L. (2008). 2008: year of rich internet apps? (April 08). *ABA Banking Journal.* Retrieved January 11, 2009, from http://www.nxtbook.com/nxtbooks/sb/ababj0408/index.php?startpage=0

Biggs, J. (2003). Teaching for Quality Learning at University (2nd ed.). New York: McGraw-Hill Education, Open University Press.

Birenbaum, M., Tatsuoka, K., & Gutvirtz, Y. (1992). Effects of response format on diagnostic assessment of scholastic achievement. *Applied Psychological Measurement, 16*(4), 353–363. doi:10.1177/014662169201600406

Black, G. (2001). A Comparison of Traditional, Online and Hybrid Methods of Course Delivery. In *Proceedings of the International Conference on Teaching Online in Higher Education: "Synthesizing Online Teaching Strategies*

Blacker, D. (1995). Philosophy of Technology and Education: an Invitation to Inquiry. In . *Proceedings of the Philosophy of Education, 1994,* 320–328.

Blass, E., & Davis, A. (2003). Building on Solid Foundations: establishing criteria for e-learning development. *Journal of Further and Higher Education, 27*(3), 227–245. doi:10.1080/0309877032000098662

Bleed, R. (2001). A hybrid campus for the new millennium. *EDUCAUSE Review, 36*(1), 16–24.

Bligh, D. A. (2000). *What's the use of lectures?* San Francisco: Jossey-Bass.

Bloom, B. (1956). *Taxonomy of educational objectives: The classification of educational goals. Handbook I, cognitive domain.* New York: Longmans, Green.

Bloom, L. Z., & White, E. M. (1993). *Inquiry: a cross-curricular reader.* Englewood Cliffs, NJ: Prentice-Hall, Inc.

Blumenfeld, P. (1991). Motivating project-based learning: Sustaining the doing, supporting the learning. *Educational Psychologist, 26*(3&4), 369–398. doi:10.1207/s15326985ep2603&4_8

Boase, J., & Wellman, B. (2005). Personal relationships: On and off the Internet. In A. L. Vangelisti & D. Perlman (Eds.), *The Cambridge Handbook of Personal Relationships* (pp. 709-723).

Bok, D. (2005). *Our Underachieving Colleges: A Candid Look at How Much Students Learn and Why They Should Be Learning More.* Princeton, NJ: Princeton University Press.

Bonestroo, W., Ley, T., Kump, B., & Lindstaedt, S. (2007). Learn@Work: Competency advancement with learning templates. In *Proceedings of the 3rd Workshop on Learner-Oriented Knowledge Management & KM-Oriented E-Learning* (pp. 9-16).

Bonk, C. J., & Graham, C. R. (Eds.). (2005). *Handbook of blended learning: Global perspectives, local designs.* San Francisco: Pfeiffer.

Bonk, C. J., Graham, C. R., Cross, J., & Moore, M. G. (2005). *Handbook of blended learning.* San Francisco, CA: Pfeiffer.

Bonk, C. J., Kim, K., & Zeng, T. (2005). In C. J. Bonk & C. R. Graham (Eds.), *Handbook of blended learning: Global perspectives, local designs* (pp. 550-568). New York: Pfeiffer Publishing.

Bonk, C. J., Kim, K.-J., & Zeng, T. (2006). Future directions of blended larning in higher education and workplace learning settings. In C. J. Bonk & C. R. Graham (Eds.), *The handbook of blended learning: global perspectives, local designs* (pp. 550-567). San Francisco: Pfeiffer.

Bonk, C. J., Olson, T. M., Wisher, R. A., & Orvis, K. L. (2002). Learning from focus groups: An examination of blended learning. *Journal of Distance Education, 17*(3), 97–118.

Bonk, C., & Graham, C. (2006). *The Hand Book of Blended Learning.* New York: John Wiley & Sons.

Bonk, C., & Graham, C. R. (Eds.). (2006). *The Handbook of Blended learning: Global Perspectives, Local Designs.* San Francisco, CA: Pfeiffer Publishing.

Boora, R., Peacock, K., Davies, J., Carbonaro, M., Bainbridge, J., & Snart, F. (2005). Implementing a synchronous learning system in distance programs: Impressions from within a faculty of education. In G. Richards (Ed.), *Proceedings of the World Conference on E-Learning in Corporate, Government, Healthcare, and Higher Education 2005* (pp. 546-559). Chesapeake, VA: AACE.

Booth, A., & Hyland, P. (2000). *The Practice of University History Teaching.* Manchester, UK: Manchester University Press.

Boud, D., Cohen, R., & Sampson, J. (Eds.). (2001). *Peer learning and assessment.* London: Kogan

Bourner, J., Hughes, M., & Bourner, T. (2001). First-year Undergraduate Experiences of Group Project Work. *Assessment & Evaluation in Higher Education, 26*(1), 19–39. doi:10.1080/02602930020022264

Bouton, M. E. (1993). Context, time, and memory retrieval in the interference paradigms of Pavlovian learning. *Psychological Bulletin, 114*(11), 80–99. doi:10.1037/0033-2909.114.1.80

Boyd, D. (2007). The significance of social software. In T. N. Burg & J. Schmidt (Eds.), *BlogTalks reloaded: Social software research & cases* (pp. 15-30). Norderstedt, Germany: Books on Demand.

Boyer, E. L. (1990). *Scholarship Reconsidered: Priorities of the Professoriate.* Princeton, NJ: The Carnegie Foundation for the Advancement of Teaching.

Boyle, T., Bradley, C., Chalk, P., Jones, R., & Pickard, P. (2003). Using blended learning to improve student success rates in learning to program. *Journal of Educational Media, 28*(2-3), 165–178. doi:10.1080/1358165032000153160

Bra, P. D., Aerts, A., Smits, D., & Stash, N. (2002). AHA! version 2.0, more adaptation flexibility for authors. In *Proceedings of the AACE ELearn Conference*, Canada (pp. 240-246).

Brabazon, T. (2002). *Digital Hemlock.* Sydney: UNSW Press.

Brabazon, T. (2007). *The University of Goolge: Education in the (post) Information Age.* Hampshire, UK: Ashgate Publishing.

Brannon, T. (2005). Learner Interactivity in Higher Education: comparing face-to-face, hybrid and on-line instruction. *Distance Learning, 2*(2), 1.

Braun, S., & Schmidt, A. (2006). Socially-aware informal learning support: potentials and challenges of the social dimension. In *Innovative Approaches for Learning and Knowledge Sharing, EC-TEL 2006 Workshop Proceedings* (pp. 126-131).

Brescia, W. F. J., & Miller, M. T. (2006). What's it worth? The perceived benefits of instructional blogging. *Electronic Journal for the Integration of Technology in Education, 5*, 44–52.

Bridge, P., & Appleyard, R. (2007). A comparison of electronic and paper-based assignment submission and feedback. *British Journal of Educational Technology*, (OnlineEarly article).

Brinkerhaff, J., & Koroghlanian, C. M. (2007). Online students' expectations: Enhancing the fit between online students and course design. *Journal of Educational Computing Research, 36*(4), 383–393. doi:10.2190/R728-28W1-332K-U115

Brittain, S., Glowacki, P., Ittersum, J. V., & Johnson, L. (2006). Podcasting Lectures. *EDUCAUSE Quarterly*, (3): 24–31.

Brookshire, R. (2007). An end-user information systems curriculum for the 21st century. *Journal of Computer Information Systems, 47*(3), 81.

Brown, A. L., & Campione, J. C. (1996). Psychological theory and the design of innovative learning environments on procedures, principles, and systems. In L. Schauble & R. Glaser (Eds.), *Innovation in learning: New environments for* education (pp. 289-325). Hillsdale, NJ: Lawrence Erlbaum Associates.

Brown, J. S., & Duguid, P. (1991). Organizational learning and communites-of-practice: Toward a unified view of working, learning, and innovation. *Organization Science, 2*(1), 40–57. doi:10.1287/orsc.2.1.40

Brown, J. S., & Gray, E. S. (1995, January). *The people are the company.* Retrieved February 11, 2008, from http://www.fastcompany.com/magazine/01/people.html

Brown, R., & Murti, G. (2003). Student partners in Instruction: third level student participation in advanced business courses. *Journal of Education for Business, 79*(2), 85.

Brown, S., & Race, P. (2002). *Lecturing, a practical guide*. London: Kogan Page.

Bruffee, K. A. (1984). Collaborative learning and the "conversation of mankind. *College English, 46*(7), 635–652. doi:10.2307/376924

Bruner, J. S. (1967). *On knowing: Essays for the left hand.* Cambridge, MA: Harvard University Press.

Bruner, J. S. (1986). *Actual minds, possible worlds.* Cambridge, MA: Harvard University Press.

Bruner, J. S., Goodnow, J. J., & Austin, G. A. (1956). *A study of thinking.* New York: John Wiley & Sons, Inc.

Bruns, A., & Jacobs, J. (2006). *Uses of Blogs.* New York: Peter Lang Publishing.

Brush, A. J. B., Bargeron, D., Grudin, J., Borning, A., & Gupta, A. (2002). *Supporting interaction outside of class: Anchored discussions vs. discussion boards.* Paper presented at the CSCL 2002, Mahweh, NJ.

Brusilovsky, P. (1996b). Methods and techniques of adaptive hypermedia. *User Modeling and User-Adapted Interaction, 2-3*(6), 87–129. doi:10.1007/BF00143964

Brusilovsky, P. (2001). Adaptive hypermedia. *User Modeling and User Adapted Interaction, 11*(1/2), 87-110. Retrieved from http://www.sis.pitt.edu/~peterb/papers/brusilovsky-umuai-2001.pdf

Brusilovsky, P. (2001). Adaptive Hypermedia. *User Modeling and User-Adapted Interaction, 11*, 87–110. doi:10.1023/A:1011143116306

Brusilovsky, P. (2004). Adaptive Educational Hypermedia: From generation to generation. In *Proceedings of the 4th Hellenic Conference on Information and Communication Technologies in Education*, Greece (pp. 19-33).

Budanitsky, A., & Hirst, G. (2001). Semantic distance in wordnet: An experimental, application-oriented evaluation of five measures. In *Proceedings of the NAACL Workshop on Word-Net and Other Lexical Resources,* Pittsburgh.

Bull, S., & Nghiem, T. (2002). Helping learners to understand themselves with a learner model open to students, peers and instructors. In *Proceedings of Workshop on Individual and Group Modelling Methods that Help Learners Understand Themselves, International Conference on Intelligent Tutoring Systems*, Spain (pp. 5-13).

Bulterman, D. C. A., & Rutledge, L. (2004). *SMIL 2.0 Interactive Multimedia for Web and Mobile Device.* Berlin, Germany: Springer.

Burdescu, D. D., & Mihaescu, C. (2006). TESYS: E-learning application built on a Web platform. In *International Conference on E-Business,* Setubal, Portugal (pp. 315-319).

Burdescu, D. D., & Mihaescu, C. (2008). Blending e-learning and knowledge management for optimizing learning paths. In *Advances on Artificial Intelligence, Knowledge Engineering and Databases (AIKED08)*, Cambridge, U.K. (pp. 396-402).

Buzzetto, N. A., & Sweat, R. (2006). Incorporating the Hybrid Learning Model into Minority Education at a Historically Black University. *Journal of Information Technology Education, 5*, 153–164.

Buzzetto-More, N., & Sweat-Guy, R. (2006). Incorporating the hybrid learning model into minority education at a historically black university. *Journal of Information Technology Education, 5*, 153–164.

Cabré, M.T., Estopá, R., & Vivaldi, J. (2001). Automatic Term Detection: a review of current systems. *Recent advances in computational terminology, 2*, 53-87.

Cai, Y., Lu, B., Fan, Z., Indhumathi, C., Lim, K. T., & Chan, C. W. (2006). Bioedutainment: Learning life science through X gaming. *Computers & Graphics, 30*(1), 3–9. doi:10.1016/j.cag.2005.10.003

Caine, R. N., & Caine, G. (1991). *Making connections: Teaching and the human brain.* Alexandria, VA: Association for Supervision and Curriculum Development.

Callaghan, V., Clarke, G., & Chin, J., (2008). Some socio-technical aspects of intelligent buildings and pervasive computing research. *Intelligent Buildings International Journal*, 1(1).

Campbell, G. (2005). There's Something in the Air: Podcasting in Education. *EDUCAUSE Review, 40*(6), 33–46.

Campbell, M., Gibson, W., Hall, A., Richards, D., & Callery, P. (2007). Online vs. face-to-face discussion in a web-based research methods course for postgraduate nursing students: A quasi-experimental study. *International Journal of Nursing Studies, 45*(5).

Cantoni, V., Cellario, M., & Porta, M. (2004). Perspectives and challenges in e-learning: towards natural interaction paradigms. *Journal of Visual Languages and Computing, 15*, 333–345. doi:10.1016/j.jvlc.2003.10.002

Caplan, P. (2003). *Metadata Fundamentals for all Librarians.* Chicago: American Library Association.

Carro, R., Pulido, E., & Rodríguez, P. (1999). TANGOW: Task-based adaptive learner guidance on the web. In *Proceedings of the Second Workshop on Adaptive Systems and User Modeling on the Web en la Eight International World Wide Web Conference*, Canada (pp. 23-24).

Carter-Wells, J., Ivers, J., & Lee, J. (2003). Developing an online degree program: Design, delivery, unique features. In *Proceedings of the TECH ED Conference Presentation*, Ontario, CA.

Castaneda, D. I., & Rios, M. F. (2007). From Individual Learning to organizational Learning. *Electronic Journal of Knowledge Management, 5*(4), 363-372. Retrieved March 30, 2008, from http://www.ejkm.com/volume-5/v5-i4/v5-i4-art3.htm

Castells, M. (2004a). Afterword: Why networks matter. In H. McCarthy, P. Miller, & P. Skidmore (Eds.), *Network logic: Who governs in an interconnected world?* (pp. 221-225). London: Demos.

Castells, M. (2004b). *The network society: A cross-cultural perspective.* Northamption, MA: Edward Elgar.

CDC. (2001). Learning to learn: The way forward in curriculum development. *The Curriculum Development Council, Hong Kong SAR.*

Cercone, K. (2008). Characteristics of adult learners with implications for online learning design. *AACE Journal, 16*(2), 137–159.

Chabrow, E. (2005). Wireless revs up vehicle production. *Information Week*, p.100.

Chacón, F. (2003). Mind-mapping for web instruction and learning. *The Convergence of Learning and Technology - Windows on the Future 2003.*

Chan, A., & Lee, M. J. (2005). An MP3 a day keeps the worries away: Exploring the use of podcasting to address preconceptions and alleviate pre-class anxiety amongst undergraduate information technology students, Good Practice in Practice. In D. H. Spennemann & L. Burr (Eds.), *Proceedings of the Student Experience Conference*, Wagga Wagga, NSW (pp. 59-71).

Chan, V. (2003). Autonomous Language Learning: the teachers' perspectives. *Teaching in Higher Education*, *8*(1), 33–54. doi:10.1080/1356251032000052311

Chan, Y.-Y. (2005). Creating reusable webquest objects with webquest authoring engine. In *Fifth IEEE International Conference on Advanced Learning Technologies* (pp. 282 – 284).

Chan, Y.-Y. (2007). Teaching queueing theory with an inquiry-based learning approach: A case for applying webquest in a course in simulation and statistical analysis. In *Proceedings of the 37th IEEE/ASEE Frontiers in Education conference* (pp. F3C-1-6).

Chandler, D. (2006). *Semiotics: The Basics* (2nd ed.). London: Routledge.

Changchit, C. (2003). An investigation into the feasibility of using an internet-based intelligent system to facilitate knowledge transfer. *Journal of Computer Information Systems*, *43*(4), 91.

Cheang, B., Kurnia, A., Lim, A., & Oon, W.-C. (2003). On automated grading of programming assignments in an academic institution. *Computers & Education*, *41*(2), 121–131. doi:10.1016/S0360-1315(03)00030-7

Chen, L., & Huang, T. (2000). Emotional expressions in audiovisual human computer interaction. In *Proceedings of ICME* (pp. 423–426).

Cherry, C. (1971). *On Human Communication - a Review, a Survey and a Criticism* (2nd ed.). Cambridge, MA: The MIT Press.

Cheung, W., Mørch, A., Wong, K., Lee, C., Liu, J., & Lam, M. (2007). Grounding Collaborative Learning in Semantics-Based Critiquing. *International Journal of Distance Education Technologies*, *5*(2), 40–55.

Chew, E. (2008a). Book Review for Allison Littlejohn and Chris Pegler Preparing for Blended e-Learning: Understanding Blended and Online Learning. *Journal of World Education.*

Chew, E. (2008b). Book Review for Barbara Allan: Blended learning Tools for Teaching and Training. *Journal of Educational Technology & Society*, *11*(2), 344–347.

Chew, E., & Jones, N. (2006). Generic Model of Computation for Intelligent Computer Aided Progress Assessment (iCAP). In *Proceeding of the 10th International Computer Assisted Assessment (CAA) Conference: Research into E-Assessment*, Loughborough University (pp. 107-121).

Chew, E., Jones, N., & Blackey, H. (2006). Embedding Blended learning Across a Higher education Institution. In *Proceedings of the First Annual Blended learning Conference: Blended learning – Promoting Dialogue in Innovation and Practice* (pp. 64-73). Hatfield, UK: University of Hertfordshire Press.

Chew, E., Tuner, D., & Jones, N. (2009). In Love and War: Blended learning Theories for Computer Scientists and Educationists. In F. L. Wang, J. Fong, & R. C. Kwan (Eds.), *The Handbook of Blended learning*. Hershey, PA: Information Science Reference.

Chickering, A., & Ehrmann, S. (2007). *Implementing the Seven Principles: Technology as Lever*. Retrieved March 22, 2008, from http://www.tltgroup.org/programs/seven.html

Choy, M., Lam, S., Poon, C. K., Wang, F. L., Yu, Y. T., & Yuen, L. (2007). Towards blended learning of computer programming supported by an automated system. In J. Fong & F. L. Wang (Eds.), *Blended Learning* (pp. 9-18). Pearson.

Choy, M., Nazir, U., Poon, C. K., & Yu, Y. T. (2005). Experiences in using an automated system for improving students' learning of computer programming. In *Proceedings of the 4th International Conference on Web-based Learning (ICWL 2005)* (LNCS 3583, pp. 267-272). Berlin, German: Springer.

Christie, J. R. (2003). Automated essay marking for content - does it work? In *Proceedings of the 7th International Computer Assisted Assessment Conference*, UK (pp. 85-92).

Chung, G., & O'Neill, H. (1997). *Methodological approaches to online scoring of essays* (Technical Report 461). UCLA, National Center for Research on Evaluation, Student Standards, and Testing.

Chung, Q.B. (2005). Sage on the Stage in the Digital Age: The Role of Online Lecture in Distance Learning. *The Electronic Journal of e-Learning, 3*(1), 1-14.

Clark, D. (1999). *A Time Capsule of Training and Learning*. Retrieved March 1, 2007, from http://www.nwlink.com/~donclark/hrd/history/history2.html

Clark, D. (2003). *Blended Learning White Paper*. Retrieved January 16, 2007, from http://www.epic.co.uk/content/resources/white_papers/Epic_Whtp_blended.pdf

Clark, D., & Walsh, S. (2004). *iPod-Learning*. Epic Group Plc.

Clark, R., E. (1983). Reconsidering Research on Learning from Media. *Review of Educational Research, 52*(4), 445–459.

Clarke, A. (2004). *e-learning Skills*. Hampshire, UK: Palgrave Macmillan.

Clarke, G., & Callaghan, V. (2007). Ubiquitous computing, informatization, urban structures and density. *Built Environment Journal, 33*(2). Burns, B. (2007). *Darkstar: The Java game server*. Sebastopol, CA: O'Reilly.

Cleveland, H. (1982, December). Information as resource. *The Futurist*, 34–39.

Clyde, L. (2005). Educational blogging. *Teacher Librarian, 32*(3), 43.

Clyde, L. A. (2004). *Weblogs in Libraries*. Oxford, UK: Chandos Publishing.

Coates, D. & Humphreys, B. (2001). Evaluation of Computer-Assisted Instruction in Principles of Economics. *Educational Technology & Society, 4*(2).

Cobcroft, R., Towers, S., Smith, J., & Bruns, A. (2006). *Mobile learning in review: Opportunities and challenges for learners, teachers, and institutions*. Paper presented at the Online Learning and Teaching Conference 2006, Brisbane, QLD.

Collins, H. (2003). *Enterprise knowledge portals: Next generation portal solutions for dynamic information access, better decision making, and maximum results*. New York: American Management Association.

Collis, B. (2005). *The Contributing Student: A Blend of Pedagogy and Technology*. Paper presented at the Educause Australasia.

Collis, B., & Moonen, J. (2001). *Flexible Learning in a digital world*. London: Kogan Page Ltd.

Collis, B., & Moonen, J. (2006). The Contributing Student: Learners as Co-developers of Learning Resources for Reuse in Web Environments. In D. Hung & M. S. Khine (Eds.), *Engaged Learning with Emerging Technologies*. Dordrecht, The Netherlands: Springer.

Collis, B., & Moonen, J. (2008). Web 2.0 tools and processes in higher education: quality perspectives. *Educational Media International, 45*(2), 93–106. doi:10.1080/09523980802107179

Collis, B., de Boer, W., & van der Veen, J. (2001). Building on Learner Contributions: A Web-Supported Pedagogic Strategy. *Educational Media International, 38*(4), 229–240. doi:10.1080/09523980110105169

Collobert, R., Bengio, Y., & Bengio, S. (2004). A Parallel Mixture of SVMs for Very Large Scale Problems. In *Neural Information Processing Systems* (Vol. 17). Cambridge, MA: MIT Press.

ComputerUser. (2004). *High-Tech Dictionary: Emoticons*. Retrieved March 20, 2007, from http://www.computeruser.com/resources/dictionary/emoticons.html

Condie, R., & Livingston, K. (2007). Blending online learning with traditional approaches: changing practices. *British Journal of Educational Technology, 38*(2), 337–348. doi:10.1111/j.1467-8535.2006.00630.x

Condone, S. (2004). Reducing the distance: A study of course websites as a means to create a total learning space in traditional courses. *IEEE Transactions on Professional Communication, 47*(3), 190. doi:10.1109/TPC.2004.833692

Conlan, O. (2003). *State of the art: Adaptive hypermedia* (Technical report). Waterford Institute of Technology.

Conole, G., & Creanor, L. (2007). *In their own words: Exploring the learner's perspective on e-learning.* London: JISC.

Conrad, D. (2002). Deep in the hearts of learners: Insights into the nature of online community. *Journal of Distance Education, 17*(1), 1–19.

Conrad, D. (2005). Building and maintaining community in cohort-based online learning. *Journal of Distance Education, 20*(1), 1–20.

Conrad, D. L. (2008). From community to community of practice: Exploring the connection of online learners to informal learning in the workplace. *American Journal of Distance Education, 22*, 3–23. doi:10.1080/08923640701713414

Console, G. (2004). E-learning: The hype and the reality. *Journal of Interactive Media in Education, 12*, 1-18. Retrieved April 15, 2008, from http://www.jme.open.ac.uk/2004/12

Conway, R., & Easton, S. (2005). Strategies for Enhancing Student Interaction and Immediacy in Online Courses. *Business Communication Quarterly, 68*(1), 23. doi:10.1177/1080569904273300

Conway, R., Kember, D., Sivan, A., & Wu, M. (1993). Peer assessment of an individual's contribution to a group project. *Assessment & Evaluation in Higher Education, 18*(1), 45–56. doi:10.1080/0260293930180104

Cook, J. (2002). The role of dialogue in computer-based learning: an evolutionary approach to theory. *Journal of Interactive Media in Education, 5*, 1–28.

Cooner, T. S. (2005). Dialectical constructivism: Reflections on creating a web-mediated enquiry-based learning environment. *Social Work Education, 24*(4), 375–390. doi:10.1080/02615470500096902

Cooperrider, D. L., Whitney, D., & Stavros, J. M. (2005). *Appreciative Inquiry Handbook: The first in a series of AI workbooks for leaders of change.* Brunswick, OH: Crown Custom Publishing, Inc.

Corley, C., & Mihalcea, R. (2005). Measuring the semantic similarity of texts. In *Proceedings of the ACL Workshop on Empirical Modeling of Semantic Equivalence and Entailment,* Ann Arbor, MI (pp. 13-18). Association for Computational Linguistics.

Corsi, T. (2006). The real-time global supply chain game: New educational tool for developing supply chain management professionals. *Transportation Journal, 45*(3), 61.

Costa, M. L., Van Rensburg, L., & Rushton, N. (2007). Does teaching style matter? A randomized trial of group discussion versus lectures in orthopaedic undergraduate teaching. *Medical Education, 41*, 214–217. doi:10.1111/j.1365-2929.2006.02677.x

Costagliola, G., Fuccela, V., Giordano, M., & Polese, G. (2007). Logging and visualization of learner behaviour in Web-based e-testing. In *ICWL, International Conference on Web Based Learning,* Edinburgh, United Kingdom.

Cotner, J., Jones, R., & Kashlak, R. (2003). Effectively Integrating an International Field Study into the EMBA Curriculum. *Journal of Teaching in International Business, 15*(1), 5. doi:10.1300/J066v15n01_02

Coulthard, M. (1977). *An introduction to discourse analysis.* London: Longman Group Limited.

Cousin, G., & Deepwell, F. (2005). Designs for network learning: A communities of practice perspective. *Studies in Higher Education, 30*(1), 57–66. doi:10.1080/0307507052000307795

Craig, S. D., Driscoll, D. M., & Gholson, B. (2004). Constructing Knowledge from Dialog in an Intelligent Tutoring System: Interactive Learning, Vicarious Learning, and Pedagogical Agents. *Journal of Educational Multimedia and Hypermedia, 13*(2), 163–183.

Cristea, V., Trausan-Matu, S., Posea, P., & Gartner, A. (2007). Towards an evaluation methodology for collaborative learning. In *Proceedings of CSCS16*, Bucharest (pp.161-168).

Crook, C. (1994). *Computers and the collaborative experience of learning.* London: Routledge.

Crook, C. (2001). The social character of knowing and learning: implications of cultural psychology for educational technology. *Journal of Information Technology for Teacher Education, 10*(1&2), 19–36.

Crooks, S., Yang, Y., & Duemer, L. (2003). Faculty perceptions of web-based resources in higher education. *Journal of Educational Technology Systems, 31*(2), 103. doi:10.2190/E68Q-KW1G-JK5B-TTRM

Cross, J. (2002). *Internet Time Blog. Peter Henschel, RIP.* Retrieved April 14, 2008 from http://internettime.com/blog/archives/000228.html

Cross, J. (2005). Foreword. In C. J. Bonk & C. R. Graham (Eds.), *Handbook of blended learning: Global perspectives, local designs* (pp. xvii-xxiii). San Francisco: Pfeiffer.

Cross, J. (2007). *Informal learning: Rediscovering the natural pathways that inspire innovation and performance*. San Francisco: Jossey-Bass.

Csikszentmihalyi, M. (1990). *Flow: The psychology of optimal experience*. New York: Harper Collins.

Cucchiarelli, A., Faggioli, E., & Velardi, P. (2000). Will very large corpora play for semantic disambiguation the role that massive computing power is playing for other AI-hard problems? In *Proceedings of the 2nd Conference on Language Resources and Evaluation*, Greece.

Curriculum Development Council and the Hong Kong Examinations and Assessment Authority. (2007). *Technology Education Key Learning Area: Business, Accounting and Financial Studies – Curriculum and Assessment Guide (Secondary 4 - 6).*

Cybinski, P., & Selvanathan, S. (2005). Learning Experience and Learning Effectiveness in Undergraduate Statistics: Modeling Performance in Traditional and Flexible Learning Environments. *Decision Sciences Journal of Innovative Education, 3*(2), 251–271. doi:10.1111/j.1540-4609.2005.00069.x

D'Alessandro, D. M., Kreiter, C. D., Erkonen, W. E., Winter, R. J., & Knapp, H. R. (1997). Longitudinal follow-up comparison of educational interventions: Multimedia textbook, traditional lecture, and printed textbook. *Academic Radiology, 4*(11), 719–723. doi:10.1016/S1076-6332(97)80074-8

D'Souza, Q. (2006). *RSS Ideas for Educators.* Retrieved from http://www.teachinghacks.com/wp-content/uploads/2006/01/RSS%20Ideas%20for%20Educators111.pdf

Dai, Y. (2007, July 20). *Questions regarding Mary and Joan*. Lecture presented for the Advances in Educational Psychology Lectures in Faculty of Education, The Chinese University of Hong Kong, Hong Kong SAR.

Dalsgaard, C., & Godsk, M. (2007). Transforming traditional lectures into problem-based blended learning: challenges and experiences. *Open Learning, 22*(1), 29–42. doi:10.1080/02680510601100143

Daniels, H. (2005). *An introduction to Vygotsky* (2nd ed.). London: Routledge.

Darbyshire, P. (Ed.). (2005). *Instructional Technologies: Cognitive aspects of online programs*. Hershey, PA: IRM Press.

Davenport, J., & Davenport, J. A. (1985). A chronology and analysis of the andragogy debate. *Adult Education Quarterly, 35*(3), 152. doi:10.1177/0001848185035003004

Davenport, T. H. (1996). *Some principles of knowledge management*. Retrieved February 21, 2008, from http://www.strategy-business.com/press/16635507/8776

Davenport, T. H. (2005). *Thinking for a living.* Boston, Massachusetts: Harvard Business School Press.

Davenport, T. H., & Glaser, J. (2002, July). Just-in-time delivery comes to knowledge management. *Harvard Business Review*, 107–111.

Davenport, T. H., & Prusak, L. (1998). *Working knowledge.* Boston, Massachusetts: Harvard Business School Press.

Davies, M., Callaghan, V., & Gardner, M. (2008). Towards a mixed reality intelligent campus. In *Proceedings of IET International Conference on Intelligent Environments 2008*, Seattle (pp. 21-22).

Davies, M., Callaghan, V., & Shen, L. (2007). Modelling pervasive environments using bespoke & commercial game-based simulators. In *2nd International Conference on Life System Modelling and Simulation (LSMS'07),* Shanghai, China.

Davis, B. H., & Brewer, J. P. (1997). *Electronic Discourse: Linguistic Individuals in Virtual Space*. New York: State University of New York Press.

Davis, F. D. (1989). Perceived usefulness, perceived ease of use, and user acceptance of information technology. *MIS Quarterly, 13*(3), 319–340. doi:10.2307/249008

de Bruyn, L. L. (2004). Monitoring online communication: Can the development of convergence and social presence indicate an interactive learning environment? *Distance Education, 25*(1), 67–81. doi:10.1080/0158791042000212468

De Silva, L., Miyasato, T., & Nakatsu, R. (1997). Facial emotion recognition using multimodal information. In *Proceedings of ICSP* (pp. 397–401).

de Souza, C. S. (2005). *The Semiotic Engineering of Human-Computer Interaction*. Cambridge, MA: The MIT Press.

Dean, J., & Ghemawat, S. (2004). Mapreduce: Simplified data processing on large clusters. In *Operating Systems Design and Implementation* (pp.137-149).

Dede, C. (1996). The evolution of distance education: Emerging technologies and distributed learning. *American Journal of Distance Education, 10*(2), 4–36. doi:10.1080/08923649609526919

Dede, C. (2000). *The role of emerging technologies for knowledge mobilization, dissemination, and use in education.* [Commissioned report]. Washington, DC: U.S. Department of Education.

Deerwester, S., Dumais, S. T., Furnas, G. W., Landauer, T. K., & Harshman, R. (1990). Indexing By Latent Semantic Analysis. *Journal of the American Society for Information Science American Society for Information Science, 41*, 391–407. doi:10.1002/(SICI)1097-4571(199009)41:6<391::AID-ASI1>3.0.CO;2-9

Del Bimbo, A. (2001). *Visual information retrieval.* San Francisco, CA: Morgan Kaufmann Publishers.

Dellaert, F., Polzin, T., & Waibel, A. (1996). Recognizing emotion in speech. In *Proceedings of ICSLP* (pp. 1970–1973).

Delone, W., & Mclean, E. (2003). The Delone and Mclean model of information systems success: A ten year update. *Journal of Management Information Systems, 19*(4), 9.

Deng, L., & Yuen, A. H. K. (2007). Connecting adult learners with an online community: Challenges and opportunities. *Research and Practice in Technology Enhanced Learning, 2*(3), 1–18. doi:10.1142/S1793206807000385

Denton, P., Madden, J., Roberts, M., & Rowe, P. (2007). Students' response to traditional and computer-assisted formative feedback: A comparative case study. *British Journal of Educational Technology*, (OnlineEarly article).

Derks, D., Bos, A. E. R., & von Grumbkow, J. (2007). Emoticons and social interaction on the Internet: the importance of social context. *Computers in Human Behavior, 23*, 842–849. doi:10.1016/j.chb.2004.11.013

Desmarais, M. C., Leclair, R., Fiset, J.-Y., & Talbi, H. (1997). Cost-justifying electronic per formance support systems. *Communications of the ACM, 40*(7), 39–48. doi:10.1145/256175.256183

Dewey, J. (1933). *How we think*. Chicago: Henry Regency.

Dewey, J. (1933). *How we think: a restatement of the relation of reflective thinking to the educative process.* Boston: Heath.

Dewhurst, D. G., & Norris, T. A. M. (2003). Helping teachers to embed e-learning materials into undergraduate pharmacology courses. *Bioscience Education e-Journal, 1*(1). Retrieved January 10, 2007, from http://bio.ltsn.ac.uk/journal/vol1/beej-1-6.htm

DfES. (2007). *Thinking Skills: Glossary of Terms*. Retrieved March 7, 2007, from http://www.standards.dfes.gov.uk/thinkingskills/glossary/?view=get&index=^M

Dicheva, D., Dichev, C., & Wang, D. (2005). Visualizing topic maps for e-Learning. In *Proceedings of the Fifth IEEE International Conference on Advanced Learn-*

ing Technologies. Washington, DC: IEEE Computer Society.

Dickey, M. D. (2004). The impact of web-logs (blogs) on student perceptions of isolation and alienation in a web-based distance-learning environment. *Open Learning, 19*(3), 279–291. doi:10.1080/0268051042000280138

Dimitrova, V. (2003). STyLE-OLM: Interactive Open Learner Modelling. *International Journal of Artificial Intelligence in Education, 13*(1), 35–78.

Dodge, B. (1995). WebQuests: A technique for internet-based learning. *Distance Education, 1*(2), 10–13.

Donnelly, R. (2006). Blended problem-based learning for teacher education: lessons learnt. *Learning, Media and Technology, 31*(2), 93–116. doi:10.1080/17439880600756621

Dougiamas, T., & Trust, M. (2004). *Moodle*. Moodle Trust.

Downes, S. (2000). *Stephen Downes – Learning objects.* Retrieved April 28, 2008, from http://www.downes.ca/files/Learning_Objects.htm

Downes, S. (2004). Educational blogging. *EDUCAUSE Review, 39*(5), 14–26.

Downes, S. (2005). E-*Learning 2.0. Stephen's Web.* Retrieved April 10, 2008, from http://www.downes.ca/post/31741

Downes, S. (2008). *The OECD Schooling Scenarios in Brief. Stephen's Web.* Retrieved April 25, 2008, from http://www.downes.ca/cgi-bin/page.cgi?post=41340

Driscoll, M. (2002). Blended learning: Let's get beyond the hype. *E-learning, 3*(3), 54.

Drozd, M., & O'Donoghue, J. (2007). The use of a WebQuest to support undergraduate nurses. *Teaching and Learning in Nursing, 2*, 63–67. doi:10.1016/j.teln.2007.03.001

Drucker, P. F. (1993). *Post-capitalist society.* New York: HarperBusiness.

du Boulay, B. (1989). Some difficulties of learning to program. In E. Soloway & J.C. Spohrer (Eds.), *Studying the novice programmer.* Hillsdale, NJ: L. Erlbaum Associates.

Duffy, T. M., & Cunningham, D. J. (1996). Constructivism: Implications for the design and delivery of instruction. In D. Jonassen (Ed.), *Handbook of research for educational communication and technology* (pp. 170-198). New York: Simon & Shuster McMillan.

Duffy, T. M., & Jonassen, D. H. (1992). *Constructivism and the technology of instruction: A conversation.* Hillsdale, NJ: Lawrence Erlbaum Associates.

Duranti, A. (1997). *Linguistic anthropology.* Cambridge, UK: Cambridge University Press.

Durbridge, N. (1984). Media in Course Design, No. 9, Audio Cassettes. In *The Role of Technology in Distance Education.* Kent, UK: Croom Helm.

Dziuban, C. D., Hartman, J. L., & Moskal, P. D. (2004). Blended learning. *EDUCAUSE Center for Applied Research Research Bulletin, 2004*(7). Retrieved January 10, 2007, from http://www.educause.edu/ir/library/pdf/ERB0407.pdf

Dziuban, C. D., Hartman, J., Juge, F., Moskal, P. D., & Sorg, S. (2005). Blended learning: Online learning enters the mainstream. In C. J. Bonk & C. R. Graham (Eds.), *Handbook of blended learning: Global perspectives, local designs* (pp. 195-208). San Francisco: Pfeiffer.

Dziuban, C., & Moskal, P. (2001). Evaluating distributed learning at metropolitan universities. *Educause Quarterly, 24*(4), 60-61. Retrieved April 15, 2006, from http://www.educause.edu/ir/library/pdf/eqm01412.pdf

Ebersbach, A., Glaser, M., & Heigl, R. (2006). *Wiki Web Collaboration.* Heidelberg, Germany: Springer-Verlag.

Edelson, D. C., Gordin, D. N., & Pea, R. D. (1999). Addressing the challenges of inquiry-based learning through technology and curriculum design. *Journal of the Learning Sciences, 8*(3), 391–450. doi:10.1207/s15327809jls0803&4_3

Edirisingha, P., Salmon, G., & Fothergill, J. (2006). *Enriching a blended learning environment with podcasts and e-tivities: A case study*. Paper presented at the First International Blended Learning conference: Promoting dialogue in innovation and practice, Hertfordshire, England.

Edirisingha, P., Salmon, G., & Fothergill, J. (2007). Profcasting—a pilot study and guidelines for integrating podcasts in a blended learning environment. In U. Bernath & A. Sangrà (Eds.), *Research on competence development in online distance education and e-learning: Selected papers from the 4th EDEN Research Workshop in Castelldefels/Spain* (pp. 127-137). Oldenberg, Germany: BIS-Verlag der Carl von Ossietzky Universität Oldenburg.

Edmundson, A. (2007). Globalized e-learning cultural challenges. Arlington, VA: Information Resources Press.

Education and Manpower Bureau. (2006). *Action for the Future: further Consultation on Career-oriented Studies and the New Senior Secondary Academic Structure for Special Schools*.

Efimova, L., & de Moor, A. (2005). *Beyond personal webpublishing: An exploratory study of conversational blogging practices*. Paper presented at the 38th Annual Hawaii International Conference on System Science (HICSS'05), Los Alamitos.

Eggen, P., & Kauchak, D. (1999). *Educational psychology*. Upper Saddle River, New Jersey: Prentice-Hall.

Ehlers, U. (2007). A new pathway for e-learning: From distribution to collaboration and competence in e-learning . *AACE Journal*, *16*(2), 187–202.

Eisenstein, E. L. (1980). *The Printing Press as an Agent of Change*. Cambridge, UK: Cambridge University Press.

El Sawy, O. A., & Majchrzak, A. (2004). Critical issues in research on real-time knowledge management in enterprises. *Journal of Knowledge Management*, *8*, 21–37. doi:10.1108/13673270410548469

El-Gayar, O., & Dennis, T. (2005). Effectiveness of hybrid learning environments. *Issues in Information Systems*, *6*(1), 176–182.

ELI-Duke. (2006). *The EDUCAUSE Learning Initiative, DukeCapture: Automated Classroom Lecture Recording*. Retrieved from http://www.educause.edu/ir/library/pdf/ELI5011.pdf

Eliot, T. S. (1934). *The Rock*. London: Faber & Faber Limited.

Ellis, C. (2008). 'You Can't Do That in a Classroom!': How Distributed Learning Can Assist in the Widespread Adoption of Hybrid Learning Strategies In J. Fong, R. Kwan, & F. L. Wang (Eds.), *Hybrid Learning and Education First International Conference, ICHL 2008 Hong Kong, China, Proceedings* (pp. 1-16). Berlin, Germany: Springer.

Ellis, R. A., & Calvo, R. A. (2004). Learning Through Discussions in Blended Environments. *Educational Media International*, *41*(3), 263–274. doi:10.1080/09523980410001680879

Ellis, R. A., Calvo, R., Levy, D., & Tan, K. (2004). Learning through discussions. *Higher Education Research & Development*, *23*(1), 73–93. doi:10.1080/0729436032000168504

Ellis, R. A., Goodyear, P., O'Hara, A., & Prosser, M. (2007). The university student experience of face-to-face and online discussions: coherence, reflection and meaning. *ALT-J*, *15*(1), 83–97. doi:10.1080/09687760601130057

Ellis, R. A., Steed, A. F., & Applebee, A. C. (2006). Teacher conceptions of blended learning, blended teaching and associations with approaches to design. *Australasian Journal of Educational Technology*, *22*(3), 312–335.

Emerson, C. (1986). The outer word and inner speech: Bakhtin, Vygotsky, and the internalization of language. In G. S. Morson (Ed.), *Bakhtin - Essays and Dialogues on His Work*. Chicago, IL: University of Chicago Press.

Encyclopædia Britannica Online. (2008). Retrieved May 12, 2008, from http://www.britannica.com/

Evans, C., & Edwards, M. (1999). Navigational interface design for multimedia courseware. *Journal of Educational Multimedia and Hypermedia, 8*(2), 151–174.

Evans, P. (2006). The Wiki Factor. *Biz Ed*, 28-33.

Ewington, S. (2007). *CodeProject: Web Ink/Drawing Control*. Retrieved from http://www.codeproject.com/mobilepc/webinkctrl.asp

Falchikov, N., & Blythman, M. (2001). *Learning Together: Peer Tutoring in Higher Education*. London: RoutledgeFalmer.

Fallon, C., & Brown, S. (2003). *E-learning standards: A guide to purchasing and deploying standards-conform e-leraning*. Boca Raton, FL: St. Lucie Press.

Farmer, J. (2004). Communication dynamics: Discussion boards, weblogs and the development of communities of inquiry in online learning environments. In R. Atkinson, C. McBeath, D. Jonas-Dwyer, & R. Phillips (Eds.), *Beyond the comfort zone: Proceedings of the 21st ascilite conference,* Perth (pp. 274-283). Retrieved October 27, 2007, from http://www.ascilite.org.au/conferences/perth04/procs/farmer.html.

Feldberg, R. S. (1999). Increasing student involvement in lectures: (very) low tech innovations in a biochemistry lecture class. *Biochemical Education, 27*, 71–73. doi:10.1016/S0307-4412(98)00263-5

Ferdig, R. E. (2007). Editorial: Examining social software in teacher education. *Journal of Technology and Teacher Education, 15*(1), 5–10.

Ferris, D. R. (1995). Student Reactions to Teacher Response in Multi-draft Composition Classroom. *TESOL Quarterly, 29*(1), 33–53. doi:10.2307/3587804

Finegold, A. R. D., & Cooke, L. (2006). Exploring the attitudes, experiences and dynamics of interaction in online groups. *The Internet and Higher Education, 9*, 201–215. doi:10.1016/j.iheduc.2006.06.003

Flanagin, A. J., & Metzger, M. J. (2001). Internet use in the contemporary media environment. *Human Communication Research, 27*(1), 153–181. doi:10.1093/hcr/27.1.153

Flatley, M. (2005). Blogging for enhanced teaching and learning. *Business Communication Quarterly, 68*(1), 77. doi:10.1177/108056990506800111

Flavell, J. H. (1977). *Cognitive development* (2nd ed.). Upper Saddle River, NJ, USA: Prentice-Hall International, Inc.

Flexner, A. (1930). *Universities: American, English, German*. New York: Oxford University Press.

Foltz, P. W., Gilliam, S., & Kendall, S. (2000). Supporting Content-Based Feedback in On-Line Writing Evaluation with LSA. *Interactive Learning Environments, 8*(2), 111–127. doi:10.1076/1049-4820(200008)8:2;1-B;FT111

Foltz, P. W., Laham, D., & Landauer, T. K. (1999). The Intelligent Essay Assessor: Applications to Educational Technology. *Interactive Multimedia Electronic Journal of Computer-Enhanced Learning*. Retrieved November 21, 2008, from http://imej.wfu.edu/articles/1999/2/04/

Fong, J. (n.d.). *Welcome to Dr. Fong's education application projects*. Retrieved from http://jfong.cs.cityu.edu.hk

Fong, J., Kwan, R., & Wang, F. L. (2008). *Hybrid Learning and Education*. Berlin, Germany: Springer.

Ford. (2000). *Automated scoring of writing assessments* (Powerpoint presentation for the Assessment Council).

Foucault, M. (1972). *The Archaelogy of Knowledge* (A. M. Sheridan Smith, Trans.). London: Tavistock.

Foulonneau, M., & Riley, J. (2007). *Metadata for Digital Resources: Implementation, Systems Design and Interoperability*. Oxford, UK: Chandos Publishing.

Fowler, C. J. H., & Mayes, J. T. (1999). Learning relationships: From theory to design. *ALT-J, 7*, 6–16. doi:10.1080/0968776990070302

Frankland, S. (2009). Perspectives of Teachers and Students towards Assessment. In S. Frankland (Ed.) *Enhancing Teaching and Learning Through Assessment*. Berlin, Germany: Springer.

Frey, B. J., & Dueck, D. (2007). Clustering by passing messages between data points. *Science, 315*, 972–976. doi:10.1126/science.1136800

Frost, C. (2001). The Reporter: assessing vocational group journalism projects. *Journalism Studies*, *2*(3), 423–432. doi:10.1080/14616700120062257

Fry, H., Pearce, R., & Bright, H. (2007). Reworking resource based learning: A case study from a masters programme. *Innovations in Education and Teaching International*, *44*(1), 79. doi:10.1080/14703290601081373

Frydenberg, M. (2006). Principles and pedagogy: The two P's of podcasting in the information technology classroom. In D. Colton, W. J. Tastle, M. Hensel, & A. A. Abdullat (Eds.), *Proceedings of ISECON 2006* (§3354). Chicago: AITP.

Fullerton, K., Greenberg, J., McClure, M., Rasmussen, E., & Stewart, D. (1999). A Digital Library for Education: the PEN-DOR Project. *The Electronic Library*, *17*(2), 75–82. doi:10.1108/02640479910334279

Fyrenius, A., Bergdahl, B., & Silen, C. (2005). Lectures in problem-based learning–why, when and how? An example of interactive lecturing that stimulates meaningful learning. *Medical Teacher*, *27*, 61–65. doi:10.1080/01421590400016365

Gagné, R. M. (1985). *The conditions of learning and theory of instruction* (4th ed.). New York: Holt, Rinehart and Winston.

Gagne, R. M., Briggs, L. J., & Wager, W. W. (1992). *Principles of instructional design* (4th ed.). San Diego, CA: Harcourt Brace Jovanovich.

Garcia, E., Romero, C., Ventura, S., & de Castro, C. (2009). An architecture for making recommendations to courseware authors using association rule mining and collaborative filtering. *User Modeling and User Adaptive Interfaces*, *19*(1-2), 99–132. doi:10.1007/s11257-008-9047-z

Gardner, H. (1983). *Frames of Mind: The theory of multiple intelligences*. New York: Basic Books.

Gardner, M., Fowler, C., & Scott, J. (2003). A process to support the design of new e-learning services. In *Proceedings of Technology Enhanced learning conference (TEL)*,Turin, 2003

Garner, B. (2008). *Embedding Socratic Learning within Web-based Education (WBE)*. Hong Kong Polytechnic University

Garrison, D. R. (1993). Quality and access in distance education: Theoretical considerations. In D. Keegan (Ed.), *Theoretical principles of distance education* (pp. 9-21). New York: Routledge.

Garrison, D. R., & Anderson, T. (2003). *E-learning in the 21st century: A framework for research and practice*. London: Routledge-Falmer.

Garrison, D. R., & Kanuka, H. (2004). Blended learning: Uncovering its transformative potential in higher education. *The Internet and Higher Education*, *7*(2), 95–105. doi:10.1016/j.iheduc.2004.02.001

Garrison, D. R., & Vaughan, N. D. (2008). *Blended learning in higher education: Framework, principles, and guidelines* (1st ed.). San Francisco: Jossey-Bass.

Garrison, D., & Kanuka, H. (2004). Blended learning: Uncovering its transformative potential in higher education. *The Internet and Higher Education*, *7*(2), 95–105. doi:10.1016/j.iheduc.2004.02.001

Garrison, D., & Vaughan, N. D. (2008). *Blended learning in Higher Education: Framework, Principles and Guidelines*. San Francisco: Jossey-Bass.

Garrison, R., & Cleveland-Innes, M. (2005). Facilitating cognitive presence in online learning: Interaction is not enough. *American Journal of Distance Education*, *19*(3), 133–148. doi:10.1207/s15389286ajde1903_2

Garrison, R., & Vaughan, N. (2007). *Blended Learning in Higher Education: Framework, Principles, and Guidelines*. San Francisco: Jossey-Bass Publishers.

Gašević, D., Jovanović, J., Knight, C., & Richards, G. (n.d.) *Ontologies for effective use of context in e-learning settings*. Retrieved February 22, 2008, from http://elluminate.athabascau.ca/play/cidersession-080118.jnlp

Ghislandi, P., & Job, R. (2005). Collaborative learning for an online higher education course: a case study. In *Proceedings of the Fifth IEEE International Conference on Advanced Learning Technologies, (ICAL'05).*

Gibbs, G. (1981). *Twenty terrible reasons for lecturing.* Paper presented at the SCED.

Gibson, C. C. (1998). The distance learner in context. In C. C. Gibson (Ed.), *Distance learners in higher education* (pp. 113-125). Madison, WI: Atwood Publishing.

Gibson, S., & McKay, R. (1999). Application of brain research and constructivist theory. In *Proceedings of the 8th International Conference on Thinking*, Edmonton, AB.

Giguere, P. J., Formica, S. W., & Harding, W. M. (2004). Large-scale interaction strategies for web-based professional development. *American Journal of Distance Education, 18*(4), 207–223. doi:10.1207/s15389286ajde1804_3

Gilbert, S. W. (1995). Why distance education? A special bulletin. *American Association for Higher Education.*

Gillespie, H., Boulton, H., Hramiak, G., & Williamson, R. (2007). *Learning and teaching with virtual learning environments.* Exeter, UK: Learning Matters Ltd.

Gillmor, D. (2004). *We the media: Grassroots journalism by the people, for the people.* Sebastopol, CA: O'Reilly Media.

Gokhale, A. A. (1995). Collaborative learning enhances critical thinking. *Journal of Technology Education, 7*(1), 22–30.

Goldberg, M. (2004). Learning technologies, past, present and future. In *Tenth Australian World Wide Web Conference.* Retrieved February 22, 2008, from http://ausweb.scu.edu.au/aw04/papers/edited/goldberg/Ausweb.ppt

Goldfinch, J. (1994). Further developments in peer assessment of group projects. *Assessment & Evaluation in Higher Education, 19*(1), 29–35. doi:10.1080/0260293940190103

Gong. (2007). *The Gong Project.* Retrieved from http://gong.ust.hk

Gonzalez, C. (2004). The Role of Blended Learning in the World of Technology [Electronic Version]. *Benchmarks Online.* Retrieved November 20, 2008, from http://www.unt.edu/benchmarks/archives/2004/september04/eis.htm

Good, M. (2001). On the way to online pedagogy. In J. Stephenson (Ed.), *Teaching and learning online: Pedagogies for new technologies.* London: Kogan Page Limited.

Gouli, E., Gogoulou, A., Papanikolaou, K., & Grigoriadou, M. (2004). COMPASS: An adaptive web-based concept map assessment tool. In *Concept Maps: Theory, Methodology, Technology. Proceedings of the First International Conference on Concept Mapping*, Spain.

Gouli, E., Papanikolaou, K., & Grigoriadou, M. (2002). Personalizing assessment in adaptive educational hypermedia systems. In *Proceedings of the Adaptive Hypermedia and Adaptive Web-based Systems, Second International Conference* (LNCS 2346, pp. 153-163).

Gov, H. K. (2008). *Wi-Fi Facilities at Government Premises. Usage Guide.* Retrieved April 14, 2008, from http://www.gov.hk/mobile/en/wifi/guide/index.htm

Grabe, M. (2005). Voluntary use of online lecture notes: correlates of note use and note use as an alternative to class attendance. *Computers & Education, 44*, 409–421. doi:10.1016/j.compedu.2004.04.005

Graesser, A. (2005). Auto Tutor: An intelligent tutoring system with mixed-initiative dialogue. *IEEE Transactions on Education, 48*(4), 612. doi:10.1109/TE.2005.856149

Graesser, A. C., D'Mello, S. K., Craig, S. D., Witherspoon, A., Sullins, J., McDaniel, B., & Gholson, B. (2008). The Relationship between Affective States and Dialog Patterns During Interactions with AutoTutor. *Journal of Interactive Learning Research, 19*(2), 293–312.

Graf, H. P., Cosatto, E., Bottou, L., Dourdanovic, I., & Vapnik, V. (2005). Parallel support vector machines: The Cascade SVM. In L. Saul, B. Schölkopf, & L. Bottou (Eds.), *Advances in Neural Information Processing Systems* (Vol.17). Cambridge, MA: MIT Press.

Graham, C. (2006). *The Handbook of Blended Learning: Global Perspectives, Local Designs.* San Francisco: Pfeiffer.

Graham, C. R. (2005). Blended learning system: definition, current trends, and future directions. In C. J. Bonk & C. R. Graham (Eds.), *Handbook of blended learning: Global Perspectives, local designs* (pp. 3-21). San Francisco, CA: Pfeiffer Publishing.

Graham, C. R. (2006). Blended learning systems. In C. J. Bonk & C. R. Graham (Eds.), *The handbook of blended learning: global perspectives, local designs* (pp. 3-21). San Francisco: Pfeiffer.

Graham, C. R. (2006). Chapter 1: Blended learning systems: Definition, current trends, future directions. In C. J. Bonk & C. R. Graham (Eds.), *Handbook of Blended learning: Global Perspectives, Local designs*. San Francisco, CA: Pfeiffer Publishing.

Graham, C. R., & Allen, S. (2005). Blended learning: An emerging trend in education. In C. Howard, J.V. Boettecher, L. Justice, & K.D. Schenk (Eds.), *Encyclopedia of Distance Learning* (pp. 172-179). Hershey, PA: Idea Group Inc.

Graham, C. R., Allen, S., & Ure, D. (2003). *Blended learning environments: A review of the research literature*. Unpublished manuscript, Provo, UT.

Graham, M., & Scarborough, H. (2001). Enhancing the learning environment for distance education students. *Distance Education, 22*(2), 232. doi:10.1080/0158791010220204

Graves, W. (1999). The instructional management system cooperative: converting random acts of progress into global progress. *Educational Review, 34*(6), 32.

Gredler, M. E. (2005). Learning and instruction: Theory into practice (5th ed.). Upper Saddle River, NJ: Pearson, Merrill Prentice Hall.

Gribbins, M. L., Hadidi, R., Urbaczewski, A., & Vician, C. (2007). Technology-enhanced learning in blended learning environments: A report on standard practices. *Communications of the Association for Information Systems, 20*, 741–759.

Griffin, D.K., & Stephenson, J.E. (2005). Interactive electronic lectures on genes and chromosomes. *CAL-aborate*, 8-9.

Grosz, B. J., Joshi, A. K., & Weinstein, S. (1995). Centering: A framework for modelling the local coherence of discourse. *Computational Linguistics, 21*(2), 203–225.

Guetl, C., Dreher, R., & Williams, R. (2005). E-tester: A computer-based tool for auto-generated question and answer assessment. In *Proceedings of the AACE E-Learn Conference*, Canada.

Guldberg, K. (2008). Adult learners and professional development: Peer-to-peer learning in a networked community. *International Journal of Lifelong Education, 27*(1), 35–49. doi:10.1080/02601370701803591

Gutiérrez, K. D., Baquedano-López, P., Alvarez, H. H., & Chiu, M. M. (1999). Building a Culture of Collaboration Through Hybrid Language Practices. *Theory into Practice, 38*(2), 87–93. doi:10.1080/00405849909543837

Hacker, D. J., & Tenent, A. (2002). Self-regulated comprehension during normal reading. In D. J. Hacker, J. Dunlosky, & A. C. Graesser (Eds.), *Metacognition in educational theory and practice* (pp. 165 – 191). Mahwah, NJ: Erlbaum.

Hall, E. (1976). *Beyond culture*. New York, NY: Doubleday.

Hall, O. (2006). Enhancing management education using hybrid learning nets: A perspective from working adults. *Journal of Business Management, 12*(1), 2006.

Hall, O. P., & Dudley, T. L. (2006). The Role of Hybrid Learning Nets in Executive Management Education. *Information Systems Education Journal, 4*(26).

Hamer, J. (2006). Some experiences with the "contributing student approach". [ACM Digital Library]. *ACM SIGCSE Bulletin, 38*(3), 68–72. doi:10.1145/1140123.1140145

Hanjalic, A. (2006). Extracting moods from pictures and sounds: towards truly personalized TV. *IEEE Signal Processing Magazine, 23*(2), 90–100. doi:10.1109/MSP.2006.1621452

Harding, A., Kaczynski, D., & Wood, L. N. (2005). Evaluation of blended learning: analysis of qualitative data. In *Proceedings of the Symposium of Blended Learning in Science Teaching & Learning*, The University of Sydney, Australia (pp. 56-62).

Hardy, J., Bates, S., Hill, J., & Antonioletti, M. (2007). Tracking and visualization of student use of online learning materials in a large undergraduate course. In *ICWL 2007,* Edinburgh, UK (pp. 280-287).

Hargreaves, D. H. (2004). Networks, knowledge and innovation. In H. McCarthy, P. Miller, & P. Skidmore (Eds.), *Network logic: Who governs in an interconnected world?* (pp. 79-88). London: Demos.

Harmon, S. W., & Jones, M. G. (1999). The five levels of web use in education: Factors to consider in planning an online course. *Educational Technology, 39*(6), 28–32.

Harrington, C. F., Gordon, S. A., & Schibik, T. J. (2004). Course management system utilization and implications for practice: A national survey of department chairpersons. *Online Journal of Distance Learning Administration, 7*(4). Retrieved May 7, 2007, from http://distance.westga.edu/~distance/ojdla/winter74/harrington74.pdf.

Harris, B. (2007a, October 25). Flickr in art history class. *smARThistory* [Web log]. Retrieved November 3, 2007, from http://smarthistory.org/blog/88/flickr-in-art-history-class-how-fun/

Harris, B. (2007b). Midterm. *Art Survey: HA 112 at FIT.* Retrieved November 3, 2007, from http://smarthistory.org/artsurvey/?page_id=13

Harrison, M. (2006). *Blended learning II: Blended learning in Practice*. Brighton: An Epic White Paper. Retrieved January 14, 2007, from http://www.epic.co.uk

Hartigan, T., Hill, J., Lewis-Faupe, S., & Springsteen, A. (2006). iPods and Podcasting: Too Cool for School? In *Proceedings of the NERCOMP.*

Hartley, D., & Mitrovic, A. (2001). *The effectiveness of open student modelling on learning.* Unpublished master's thesis, Intelligent Computer Tutoring Group, Department of Computer Science, University of Canterbury, UK.

Harvard Business School (HBS). (2008). *The case method.* Retrieved May 6, 2008, from http://www.hbs.edu/case/

Harvard University, Faculty of Arts and Sciences. (2004). *A Report on the Harvard College Curricular Review, April 2004.*

Haury, D. L., & Rillero, P. (1994). *Perspectives of hands-on science teaching.* Retrieved February 1, 2008 from http://www.ncrel.org/sdrs/areas/issues/content/cntareas/science/eric/eric-toc.htm

Hawkes, M. (2006). Linguistic discourse variables as indicators of reflective online interaction. *American Journal of Distance Education, 20*(4), 231–244. doi:10.1207/s15389286ajde2004_4

Hawkins, J. N., & Su, Z. X. (2003). Asian Education, In F. R. Arnove & C. A. Torres (Eds.), *Comparative Education: The Dialectic of the Global and Local* (2nd ed.). Lanham, MD: Rowman & Littlefield Publishers.

Haythornthwaite, C., & Nielsen, A. L. (2007). Revisiting computer-mediated communication for work, community, and learning. In *Psychology and the internet: Intrapersonal, interpersonal, and transpersonal implications* (2nd ed., pp. 167-186). Amsterdam: Elsevier.

Haythornthwaite, C., & Wellman, B. (2002). The Internet in everyday life: An introduction. In B. Wellman & C. Haythornthwaite (Eds.), *The Internet in everyday life* (pp. 3-44). Oxford, UK: Blackwell Pub.

Haythornthwaite, C., Kazmer, M. M., & Robins, J. (2000). Community development among distance learners: Temporal and technological dimensions [Electronic Version]. *Journal of Computer-mediated Communication, 6.* Retrieved May 18, 2006, from http://jcmc.indiana.edu/vol6/issue1/haythornthwaite.html

Hede, T., & Hede, A. (2002). Multimedia effects on learning: Design implications of an integrated model. In *ASET Conference,* Melbourne, Australia.

Hedgcock, J., & Lefkowitz, N. (1994). Feeback on Feekback: Assessing Learner Respective to Teacher Response in L2 Composing. *Journal of Second Language Writing, 3*(2), 141–163. doi:10.1016/1060-3743(94)90012-4

Heinze, A., & Procter, C. (2004). Reflections on the Use of Blended Learning. In *Proceedings of the Education in a Changing Environment Conference,* University of Salford, Salford, Education Development Unit. iLecture. (2006). *iLecture system.* Retrieved from http://lectopia.uwa.edu.au/

Heisig, P. (2001). Business process oriented knowledge management. In K. Mertins, P. Heisig, & J. Vorbeck (Eds.), *Knowledge Managment - Best Practices in Europe* (pp. 13 - 36). Berlin: Springer-Verlag.

Heisig, P. (2005). *Integration von Wissensmanagement in Geschäftsprozesse.* Berlin, Germany: Kai Mertins.

Hellwege, J., Gleadow, A., & McNaught, C. (1996). Paperless lectures on the Web: An evaluation of the educational outcomes of teaching geology using the Web. In *Proceedings of 13th Annual Conference of the Australian Society for Computers in Learning in Tertiary education (ASCILITE '96)*, Adelaide, Australia.

Helms, D. (2007). *Group project.* Retrieved November 2, 2007, from http://www.msjc.edu/hs/hs123_group_project.html

Henderson, L. (1996). Instructional design of interactive multimedia: A cultural critique. *Educational Technology Research and Development*, *44*(4), 85–104. doi:10.1007/BF02299823

Henderson, L. (2007). Theorizing a multiple cultures instructional design model for e-learning and e-teaching. In A. Edmundson (Ed.), *Globalizing e-learning cultural challenges* (pp. 130-153). Hershey, PA: Information Science.

Hensley, G. (2005). Creating A Hybrid College Course: A Case Study and Recommendations for Beginners. *Journal of Online Learning and Teaching.* Retrieved February 22, 2008, from http://jolt.merlot.org/vol1_no2_hensley.htm

Herrington, J. (2007). *Rich AJAX slide shows with DHTML and XML.* Retrieved from http://www-128.ibm.com/developerworks/xml/library/x-ajaxslideshow/?ca=dgr-lnxw01AjaxSlid

Hey, J. (2004). *The data, information, knowledge, wisdom chain: The metaphorical link.* (I. O. Commission, Ed.). Retrieved 02 05, 2008, from http://ioc.unesco.org/Oceanteacher/OceanTeacher2/02_InfTchSciCmm/DIKWchain.pdf

Heywood, J. (2000). *Assessment in Higher Education – Student Learning, Teaching, Programmes and Institutions.* London, UK: Jessica Kingsley Publishers.

Hijón, R., & Velázquez, A. (2005). Steps towards the analysis of students' activity in e-learning platforms. E-Learn 2005. Association for the Advancement in Computing in Education. ISBN: 1-880094-57-6.

Hijón, R., & Velázquez, A. (2006a). E-Learning Platforms analysis and development of students tracking functionality. In *ED-MEDIA 2006 -- World Conference on Educational Multimedia, Hypermedia and Telecommunications (AACE)* (pp.2823- 2828).

Hijón, R., & Velázquez, A. (2006b). Web, log analysis and surveys for tracking university students. In *Proceedings of IADIS International Conference on Applied Computing* (pp. 561-564).

Hijón, R., & Velazquez, A. (2008a). How to improve assessment of learning and performance through interactive visualization. In *The 8th IEEE International Conference on Advance Learning Technologies (ICALT'08)* (pp. 472-476).

Hijón, R., Velazquez, A., Barn, B., & Oussena, S. (2008b). A comparative study on the analysis of students' interactions in e-Learning. In *The 8th IEEE International Conference on Advance Learning Technologies (ICALT'08)* (pp. 20-22).

Hijón-Neira, R., Urquiza-Fuentes, J., Domínguez-Mateos, F., & Velázquez-Iturbide, A. (2007a). Assessing the usability of a cookies-based access monitoring tool for a CMS. In *ICALT 2007* (pp.262-264).

Hijón-Neira, R., Velázquez-Iturbide, A., & Herrera-Cabanillas, V. (2007b). Blended learning tools for assessing students interactions. *CEDI 2007 II Congreso Español de informática, VIII Simposio Nacional de Tecnologías de la Información y las Comunicaciones en la Educación SINTICE 2007*, Zaragoza, Spain.

Hill, J. R. (2006). Flexible Learning Environments: Leveraging the Affordances of Flexible Delivery and Flexible Learning. *Innovative Higher Education*, *31*, 187–197. doi:10.1007/s10755-006-9016-6

Hillman, D. C. A., Willis, D. J., & Gunawardena, C. N. (1994). Learner-interface interaction in distance education: An extension of contemporary models and strategies for practitioners. *American Journal of Distance Education, 8*(2), 30–42. doi:10.1080/08923649409526853

Hilton, J. (2006). The future for higher education: Sunrise or perfect storm? *EDUCAUSE Review, 41*(2), 58–71.

Hinkel, E. (2004). *Teaching Academic ESL Writing: Practical Techniques in Vocabulary and Grammar*. Mahwah, NJ: Lawrence Erlbaum Associates, Inc.

Hirumi, A. (2002). A framework for analyzing, designing, and sequencing planned e-learned interactions. *The Quarterly Review of Distance Education, 3*(2), 141–160.

Hitz, S., & Turnoff, M. (2005). Education goes digital; the evolution of online learning and the revolution in higher education. *Communications of the ACM, 48*(10), 59. doi:10.1145/1089107.1089139

Hobbs, J. R. (1985). *On the coherence and structure of discourse*. Technical Report CSLI-85-37, Center for the Study of Language and Information, Stanford University.

Hodgson, V., & Reynolds, M. (2005). Consensus, difference and 'multiple communities' in networked learning. *Studies in Higher Education, 30*(1), 11–14. doi:10.1080/0307507052000307768

Hoffmann, I. (2001). Knowledge management tools. In K. Mertins, P. Heisig, & J. Vorbeck, *Knowledge Management - Best Practices in Europe* (pp. 74-94). Heidelberg, Germany: Springer-Verlag.

Holec, H. (1981). *Autonomy and Foreign Language Learning*. Oxford, UK: Pergamon.

Hollan, J., & Stornetta, S. (1992). *Beyond being there*. Paper presented at the ACM CHI'92 Conference on Computer-Human Interaction, Monterey, CA.

Holmberg, B. (1983). Guided didactic conversation in distance education. In D. Sewart, D. Keegan, & H. Borge (Eds.), *Distance education: International perspectives* (pp. 114-122). London: Croom Helm.

Hopkins, C. (1998). Web + qmark + humanities = ? a case study. *Computers and Texts, 16-17*.

Hopkins, S. (2005, February 8). Keeping tech jobs in the country. *ECU News Bureau*.

Hough, B. W., Smithey, M. W., & Everton, C. M. (2004). Using computer-mediated communication to create virtual communities of practice for intern teachers. *Journal of Technology and Teacher Education, 12*(3), 361–386.

Hughes, C. E., Stapleton, C. B., Hughes, D. E., & Smith, E. M. (2005). Mixed reality in education, entertainment, and training. *IEEE Computer Graphics and Applications, 25*(6), 24–30. doi:10.1109/MCG.2005.139

Hughes, G. (2007). Using blended learning to increase learner support and improve retention. *Teaching in Higher Education, 12*(3), 15. doi:10.1080/13562510701278690

Hunter, M. G., & Carr, P. (2000). Technology in Distance Education: a Global Perspective to Alternative Delivery Mechanisms. *Journal of Global Information Management*, (April-June): 50.

Hussain, R. M. R. (2004). eLearning in Higher Education Institutions in Malaysia. *E-mentor, 5*(7), 72–75.

Hybrid Learning. (2008). *Hybrid Learning*. Retrieved April 10, 2008, from http://www4.uwm.edu/ltc/hybrid/about_hybrid/index.cfm

Iannuzzi, P. (1999). We are teaching, but are they learning: Accountability, productivity, and assessment. *Journal of Academic Librarianship, 25*(4), 304–305. doi:10.1016/S0099-1333(99)80031-7

Irving, Z., & Young, P. (2004). Enabling Robert to learn like Susan: the use of lectures in undergraduate teaching of Social Policy. *LATISS: Learning and Teaching in the Social Sciences, 1*(2), 121–137. doi:10.1386/ltss.1.2.121/0

Isen, A. M. (2000). Positive affect & decision making. In M. Lewis & J. Haviland (Eds.), *Handbook of emotions* (pp. 720). Guilford, NY: The Guilford Press.

Ishioka, T., & Kameda, M. (2006). Automated Japanese Essay Scoring System based on Articles Written by

Experts. In *Proceedings of the Association for Computational Linguistics*, USA (pp. 233-240).

Issacs, W. (1999). *Dialogue: and the art of thinking together.* New York: Currency.

Issroff, K., & Scanlon, E. (2002). Educational technology: The influence of theory. *Journal of Interactive Media in Education, 6*, 1–13.

ITtoolbox. (2004, September 30). *Knowledge Management Knowledge Base*. Retrieved March 26, 2008, from http://knowledgemanagement.ittoolbox.com/documents/popular-q-and-a/knowledge-management-and-elearning-integration-2846#

Jain, A., Murty, M., & Flynn, P. (1999). Data clustering: A review. *ACM Computing Surveys, 31*(3), 264–323. doi:10.1145/331499.331504

Jameson, A. (1999). *User-adaptive systems: An integrative overview.* Tutorial presented at the seventh International Conference on User Modeling, Banff, Canada.

Jaramillo, J. A. (1996). Vygotsky's sociocultural theory and contributions to the development of constructivist curricula. *Education, 117*(1), 133–141.

Jary, D., & Jary, J. (2000). *Collins dictionary of sociology* (3rd ed.). Glascow: Harper Collins.

Jaspers, K. (1960). *The Idea of the University*. London: Peter Owen.

Jennings, A. (2005). *Implementing an Integrated Web-Based Synchronous eLearning Collaboration Platform at Tertiary Level for Part-Time Mature Evening Students*. Retrieved February 25, 2008 from https://www.cs.tcd.ie/publications/tech-reports/reports.05/TCD-CS-2005-67.pdf

Jin, R. (2008). *S. Korea's 'e-Learning' Market Tops W1.7 Tri*. Retrieved April 1, 2008, from http://www.koreatimes.co.kr/www/news/include/print.asp?newsIdx=20526

JISC. (2005). *Study of Environments To Support E-Learning In UK Further and Higher education: A Supporting Study for the Joint Information Systems Committee (JISC), Education for Change Ltd, The Research Partnership Social Informatics Unit, University of Brighton*. Retrieved January 10, 2008, from http://www.jisc.ac.uk/media/documents/programmes/buildmlehefe/elearning_survey_2005.pdf

Job-Sluder, K., & Barab, S. A. (2004). Shared "We" and Shared "They" Indicators of Group Identity in Online Teacher Professional Development. In S. A. Barab, R. Kling, & J. H. Gray (Eds.), *Designing virtual communities in the service of learning* (pp. 377-403). Cambridge, UK: Cambridge University Press.

Jonassen, D. H. (1991). Objectivism vs. constructivism: Do we need a new philosophical paradigm? *Educational Technology Research and Development, 39*(3). doi:10.1007/BF02296434

Jonassen, D. H. (1994). Thinking technology: Toward a constructivist design model. In *Educational Technology* (pp. 34-37).

Jonassen, D. H. (2002). Learning as activity. *Educational Technology, 42*(2), 45–51.

Jonassen, D. H., Davidson, M., Collins, M., Campbell, J., & Haag, B. B. (1995). Constructivism and computer-mediated communication in distance education. *American Journal of Distance Education, 9*(2), 7–26. doi:10.1080/08923649509526885

Jonassen, D. H., Peck, K. L., & Wilson, B. G. (1999). *Learning with technology: A Constructivist Perspective*. Upper Saddle River, NJ: Merrill, Prentice Hall.

Jones, N. (2006). *CELT - About Blended Learning*. Retrieved May 20, 2008, from http://celt.glam.ac.uk/Blended-Learning-at-Glamorgan/?c=about_BL

Jones, N. (2006). E-College Wales, a Case Study of Blended Learning. In C. J. Bonk, C. R. Graham, J. Cross, & M. G. Moore, *Handbook of Blended Learning*. San Francisco, CA: Pfeiffer.

Jones, Q. (1997). Virtual-communities, virtual settlements & cyber-archaeology: A theoretical outline. *Journal of Computer Mediated Communication, 3*(3). Retrieved June 4, 2006, from http://jcmc.indiana.edu/vol3/issue3/jones.html

Jones, R. H., Garralda, A., Li, D. C. S., & Lock, G. (2006). Interactional dynamics in on-line and face-to-face peer-tutoring sessions for second language writers. *Journal of Second Language Writing, 15*, 1–23. doi:10.1016/j.jslw.2005.12.001

Jorgensen, D. (2002). The challenges and benefits of asynchronous learning networks. *The Reference Librarian, 77*, 3.

Judith, B., & Lubben, F. (2006). Context-based chemistry: The salters approach. *International Journal of Science Education, 28*(9), 999–1015. doi:10.1080/09500690600702496

Juice. (2006). *Juice, Cross-platform podcatcher.* Retrieved from http://juicereceiver.sourceforge.net/

Juravsky, D., & Martin, J. (2000). *Speech and language processing: An introduction to natural language processing, computational linguistics and speech recognition.* San Francisco, CA: Prentice Hall.

Juwah, C. (2006). *Interactions in Online Education: Implications for theory and practice.* London: Routledge.

Kalkanis, X., Callaghan, V., & Gardner, M. (2008). Towards end-user physiological profiling for video recommendation. In *4th IET International Conference on Intelligent Environments (IE08)*, University of Washington, Seattle, USA.

Kandola, J. S., Shawe-Taylor, J., & Cristianini, N. (2002). Learning semantic similarity. In [NIPS]. *Advances in Neural Information Processing Systems, 15*, 657–664.

Kasvi, J. J. J. (2003). *Knowledge support in learning operative organisations.* Unpublished doctoral dissertation, Helsinki University of Technology.

Kathawala, Y., Abdou, K., & Elmuti, D. (2002). The global MBA: a comparative assessment for its future. *Journal of European Industrial Training, 26*(1), 14. doi:10.1108/03090590210415867

Kavanaugh, A., Carroll, J. M., Rosson, M. B., Zin, T. T., & Reese, D. D. (2005). Community networks: Where offline communities meet online [Electronic Version]. *Journal of Computer-Mediated Communication, 10.* Retrieved July 4, 2006, from http://jcmc.indiana.edu/vol10/issue4/kavanaugh.html

Keegan, D., Schwenke, E., Fritsch, H., Kenny, G., Kismihók, G., Bíró, M., & Gábor, A. Ó'Suilleabháin, G., & Nix, J. (2005). Virtual classrooms in educational provision: synchronous elearning systems for European institutions. *ZIFF Papiere, 126.* Retrieved February 23, 2008, from http://www.fernuni-hagen.de/ZIFF/synchronous.pdf

Keengwe, J., Onchwari, G., & Wachira, P. (2008). The use of computer tools to support meaningful learning. *AACE Journal, 16*(1), 77–92.

Keeves, J. P., & Alagumalai, S. (1999). New approaches to measurement. In G. Masters & J. P. Keeves (Eds.), *Advances in Measurement in Educational Research and Assessment* (pp.23- 48). Oxford, UK: Pergamon.

Kehrwald, B. (2008). Understanding social presence in text-based online learning environments. *Distance Education, 29*(1), 89–106. doi:10.1080/01587910802004860

Kekkonen-Moneta, S., & Moneta, G. B. (2002). E-Learning in Hong Kong: comparing learning outcomes in online multimedia and lecture versions of an introductory computing course. *British Journal of Educational Technology, 33*(4), 423–433. doi:10.1111/1467-8535.00279

Kennedy, D. M. (2005). Standards for online teaching: lessons from the education, health and IT sectors. *Nurse Education Today, 25*, 23–30. doi:10.1016/j.nedt.2004.09.008

Kennedy, T., & Slowinski, M. (2002). *SMIL Adding Multimedia to the Web.* SAMS.

Kerfoot, B., Conlin, P., Travison, T., & McMahon, G. (2007). Web-based education in systems-based practice. *Archives of Internal Medicine, 167*(4), 361. doi:10.1001/archinte.167.4.361

Kerres, M., & Witt, C. D. (2003). A didactical framework for the design of blended learning arrangements. *Journal of Educational Media, 28*(2), 101–113. doi:10.1080/1358165032000165653

Kim, A. J. (2000). *Community building on the Web.* Berkeley, CA: Peachpit Press.

Kim, B. (2001). Social Constructivism. In M. Orey (Ed.), *Emerging perspectives on learning, teaching, and technology.* Retrieved April 15, 2006, from http://www.coe.uga.edu/epltt/SocialConstructivism.htm

Kim, K., & Bonk, C. (2006). The future of on-line teaching and learning in higher education. *Educasue Quarterly, 4.*

Kim, W. (2007). Towards a definition and methodology for blended learning. In *International Workshop on Blended Learning 2007 (WBL 07),* University of Edinburgh, Scotland.

Kim, W. (2008). Using Technologies to Improve E-learning. *Journal of Object Technology, 7*(8), 51–56.

Kleiman, L., & Kass, D. (2007). Giving MBA programs the third degree. *Journal of Management Education, 31*(1), 81. doi:10.1177/1052562906286874

Klobas, J. (2006). *Wikis: Tools, Information Work and Collaboration.* Oxford, UK: Chandos Publishing.

Knight, J. K., & Wood, W. B. (2005). Teaching More by Lecturing Less. *Cell Biology Education, 4,* 298–310. doi:10.1187/05-06-0082

Knight, P. (1997). *The Half-Life of Knowledge and Structural Reform of the Education Sector for the Global Knowledge-Based Economy* [Electronic Version]. Retrieved November 20, 2008, from http://www.knight-moore.com/pubs/half-life.html

Knowles, J. (1999). *Booklet 3.* Learning and teaching on the web: Computer Assisted Assessment.

Knowles, M. (1990). *The Adult Learner: A Neglected Species* (4th ed.). Houston, TX: Gulf Publishing.

Koehler, M. J., Mishra, P., & Yahya, K. (2007). Tracing the Development of Teacher Knowledge in a Design Seminar: Integrating Content, Pedagogy and Technology. *Computers & Education, 49*(3), 740–762. doi:10.1016/j.compedu.2005.11.012

Koku, E., Nazer, N., & Wellman, B. (2001). Netting scholars: Online and offline. *The American Behavioral Scientist, 44*(10), 1752–1774. doi:10.1177/00027640121958023

Kolb, D. A. (1984). *Experiential Learning: Experience as the Source of Learning and Development.* Upper Saddle River, NJ: Prentice-Hall.

Koohang, A., & Durante, A. (2003). Learners' perceptions toward the Web-based Distance learning activities/assignments portion of an undergraduate hybrid instructional model. *Journal of Information Technology Education,* (2): 105–113.

Koschmann, T. (1999). Toward a dialogic theory of learning: Bakhtin's contribution to understanding learning in settings of collaboration. In C. Hoadley & J. Roschelle (Eds.), *Proceedings of the Computer Support for Collaborative Learning 1999 Conference.* Philadelphia, PA: Laurence Erlbaum Associates.

Kozma, R. (1994). Will Media Influence Learning? Reframing the Debate. *Educational Technology Research and Development, 42*(2), 7–19. doi:10.1007/BF02299087

Kozma, R. B. (1991). Learning with Media. *Review of Educational Research, 61*(2), 179–211.

Krogstie, B., & Bygstad, B. (2005). Introducing a virtual classroom in a master course: Lessons learned. In *Proceedings of the Third International Conference on Education and Information Systems: Technologies and Applications (EISTA),* Orlando, Florida.

Kruse, K. (2005). *Gagne's nine levels of instruction: An introduction.* Retrieved January 23, 2007, from http://www.e-learningguru.com/articles/art3_3.htm

Kukulska-Hulme, A. (2005). *The mobile language learner—now and in the future* [Webcast]. Plenary session delivered at the Fran Vision till Praktik (From Vision to Practice) Language Learning Symposium, Umeå, Sweden. Retrieved February 3, 2006, from http://www2.humlab.umu.se/video/Praktikvision/agnes.ram

Kulik, J. A. (1985). The Importance of Outcome Studies: a reply to Clark. *Educational Communications and Technology Journal, 42*(6), 437–448.

Kulm, G. (1990). New directions for mathematical assessment. In G. Kulm (Ed.), *Assessing higher order thinking in mathematics*. Washington, DC: American Association for the Advancement of Science.

Kwan, R. (1999). *A virtual laboratory in a Web-based programming course*. Missoula, MT: Montana Academy of Sciences.

Kwan, R. (2001). Using the Web to conduct computer labs. *WebNet Journal*, *3*(4), 45–49.

Kwan, R., & Fong, J. (2005). *Web-based Learning: Technology and Pedagogy*. Hong Kong: World Scientific.

Kwan, R., & Wong, T. M. (2001). Migrating to the online environment: The experience of OUHK's School of Science & Technology. In *International Conference on Learning and Teaching On-line*, Guangzhou, China.

Kwan, R., Chan, J., & Lui, A. (2004). Reaching an ITopia in distance learning—A case study. *AACE Journal*, *12*(2), 171–817.

Kwan, R., Tsang, P., & Lui, A. (2005). Presenting a course entirely through the Web. *IACIS (International Association for Computer Information Systems) Pacific 2005*, Taipei.

Kwan, T., & Lopez-Real, F. (2005). Mentors' perceptions of their roles in mentoring student teachers. *Asia-Pacific Journal of Teacher Education*, *33*(3), 275–287. doi:10.1080/13598660500286267

Laing, G. K. (1996). The Lecture A Teaching Strategy For Large Groups: A Reprise [Electronic Version]. *Faculty of Commerce - Accounting & Finance Working Papers*. Retrieved November 24, 2008, from http://ro.uow.edu.au/accfinwp/66/

Lam, G., Rossiter, D., & Cheung, R. (2006). Web Content Development and Integration Using the Gong System. In Proceedings of the *The 4th AEARU Workshop on Network Education*, Taipei, Taiwan (pp. 125-138).

Lammers, W. J., & Murphy, J. J. (2002). A Profile of Teaching Techniques Used in the University Classroom: A Descriptive Profile of a US Public University. *Active Learning in Higher Education*, *3*(1), 54–67. doi:10.1177/1469787402003001005

Landauer, T. K. (1995). *The Trouble with Computers*. Cambridge, MA: MIT Press.

Landauer, T. K., Foltz, P. W., & Laham, D. (1998). Introduction to Latent Semantic Analysis. *Discourse Processes*, *25*, 259–284. doi:10.1080/01638539809545028

Landauer, T., & Psotka, J. (2000). Simulating Text Understanding for Educational Applications with Latent Semantic Analysis: Introduction to LSA. *Interactive Learning Environments*, *25*(2), 73–86. doi:10.1076/1049-4820(200008)8:2;1-B;FT073

Landauer, T., Foltz, P., & Laham, D. (1998). An Introduction to Latent Semantic Analysis. *Discourse Processes*, *25*, 259–284. doi:10.1080/01638539809545028

Lane, L. M. (2008). Toolbox or trap? Course management systems and pedagogy. *EDUCAUSE Quarterly*, *31*(2), 4–6.

Lang, P. J. (1995). The emotion probe: Studies of motivation and attention. *The American Psychologist*, *50*(5), 372–385. doi:10.1037/0003-066X.50.5.372

LaPointe, D., & Gunawardena, C. N. (2004). Developing, testing and refining of a model to understand the relationship between peer interaction and learning outcomes in computer-mediated conferencing. *Distance Education*, *25*(1), 83–106. doi:10.1080/0158791042000212477

Larson, B., & Keiper, T. A. (2002). Classroom Discussion and Threaded Electronic Discussion: Learning in Two Arenas. *Contemporary Issues in Technology & Teacher Education*, *2*(1), 45–62.

Latham, G., Latham, S., & Whyte, G. (2004). Fostering integrative thinking: adapting the executive education model to the MBA program. *Journal of Management Education*, *28*(1), 3. doi:10.1177/1052562903252647

Laurillard, D. (1993). *Rethinking University Teaching*. London: RoutledgeFalmer.

Laurillard, D. (1996). *The Changing University*. Retrieved January 26, 2007, from http://it.coe.uga.edu/itforum/paper13/paper13.html

Laurillard, D. (2002). *Rethinking University Teaching: A Conversational Framework for the Effective Use of Learning Technologies* (2nd ed.). London: Routledge-Falmer.

Laurillard, D. (2002). *Rethinking University Teaching: A Conversational Framework for the Effective Use of Learning Technologies* (2nd ed.). London: Routledge.

Learning in Motion. (2003). *The knowledge forum*. Retrieved September 17, 2007 from http://www.knowledgeforum.com/

Leblanc, A., & Abel, M.-H. (2008). E-MEMORAe2.0: an e-learning environment as learners community support. *International Journal of Computer Science & Applications*, *5*(1), 108–123.

Lee, M. J. W., McLoughlin, C., & Chan, A. (2008). Talk the talk: Learner-generated podcasts as catalysts for knowledge creation. *British Journal of Educational Technology*, *39*(3), 501–521. doi:10.1111/j.1467-8535.2007.00746.x

Leech, G., Deuchar, M., & Hoogenraad, R. (2006). *English Grammar for Today: A New Introduction* (2nd ed.). London: Palgrave MacMillan.

Lemaire, B. (1999). Tutoring Systems based on Latent Semantic Analysis. In S. P. Lajoie, & M. Vivet (Eds.), *Artificial Intelligence Education*. Amsterdam: IOS Press.

Lemaire, B., & Dessus, P. (2001). A System to Assess the Semantic Content of Student Essays. *Journal of Educational Computing Research*, *24*(3), 305–320. doi:10.2190/G649-0R9C-C021-P6X3

Leng, J., Huang, R., & Liao, J. (2007). Research on FCA and its Application to Content Analysis of Online Learning. In *Proceedings of the E-LEARN 2007 World Conference on E-Learning in Corporate, Government Healthcare & Higher Education*. Norfolk, Virginia, USA: Association for the Advancement of Computing in Education.

Leon, E., Clarke, G., Callaghan, V., & Sepulveda, F. (2007). A user-independent real-time emotion recognition system for software agents in domestic environments. *Engineering Applications of Artificial Intelligence*, *20*(3), 337–345. doi:10.1016/j.engappai.2006.06.001

Lerner, G. H. (1993). Collectivities in action: Establishing the relevance of conjoined participation in conversation. *Text*, *13*(2), 213–245. doi:10.1515/text.1.1993.13.2.213

Lester, F. K. J., & Lambdin-Kroll, D. (1990). Assessing student growth in mathematical problem solving. In G. Kulm (Ed.), *Assessing higher order thinking in mathematics* (pp. 53-70). Washington, DC: American Association for the Advancement of Science.

Leu, D. L., Kinzer, C. K., Coiro, J. L., & Cammack, D. (2004). Towards a theory of new literacies from the Internet and other information and communication technologies. In R. B. Ruddell & N. J. Unrau (Eds.), *Theoretical Models and Processes of Reading* (5th ed.) (pp. 1570-1613). Newark, DE: International Reading Association.

Levy, Y. (2007). Comparing dropouts and persistence in e-learning courses. *Computers & Education*, *48*(2), 185–204. doi:10.1016/j.compedu.2004.12.004

Li, F., Lau, R., & Liu, W. (2007). Emerging E-Learning Technologies. *International Journal of Distance Education Technologies*, *5*(2), 2.

Liao, Y.-K. C. (2007). Effects of computer-assisted instruction on students' achievement in Taiwan: A meta-analysis. *Computers & Education*, *48*, 216–233. doi:10.1016/j.compedu.2004.12.005

Lightfoot, J. M. (2006). A comparative analysis of e-mail and face-to-face communication in an educational environment. *The Internet and Higher Education*, *9*, 217–227. doi:10.1016/j.iheduc.2006.06.002

Lim, B.-R. (2001). *Guidelines for designing inquiry-based learning on the web: online professional development of educators*. Unpublished doctoral dissertation, Indiana University at Bloomington.

Lim, B.-R. (2004). Challenges and issues in designing inquiry on the web. *British Journal of Educational Technology*, *35*(5), 627–643. doi:10.1111/j.0007-1013.2004.00419.x

Lin, F. (2005). *Designing Distributed Learning Environments with Intelligent Software Agents*. Hershey, PA: Information Science Publishing.

Lin, Y.-M., Lin, G.-Y., & Laffey, J. M. (2008). Building a social and motivational framework for understanding satisfaction in online learning. *Journal of Educational Computing Research*, *38*(1), 1–27. doi:10.2190/EC.38.1.a

Linacre, J. M. (1999). Individualized testing in the classroom. In G. Masters & J. P. Keeves (Eds.), *Advances in Measurement in Educational Research and Assessment* (pp. 186-194). New York: Pergamon.

Linacre, J. M. (2000). Computer-adaptive testing: A methodology whose time has come (memo #69). *IOM Research Memoranda, Institute for Objective Measurement, Inc.* Retrieved from http://rasch.org/memo69.pdf

Linacre, J. M., & Wright, B. D. (1994). Chi-square fit statistics. *Rasch Measurement Transactions*, *8*(2), 350.

Lisetti, C. L., & Nasoz, F. (2004). Using noninvasive wearable computers to recognize human emotions from physiological signals. *EURASIP Journal on Applied Signal Processing*, (11): 1672–1687. doi:10.1155/S1110865704406192

Lister, B., Danchak, M., Scalzo, K., Jennings, W., & Wilson, J. (1999). The Rensselaer 80:20 Model for Interactive Distance Learning. In *Proceedings of the EDUCAUSE 1999 conference presentation.* Retrieved February 8, 2006, from http://www.educause.edu/ir/library/html/edu9907/edu9907.html

Littlejohn, A. (2003). *Issues in reusing online resources. Reusing online resources: A sustainable approach to e-learning.* London: Creative Print and Design.

Littlejohn, A., & Pegler, C. (2007). *Preparing for Blended e-Learning: Understanding Blended and Online Learning (Connecting with E-learning).* London: Routledge.

Livingstone, E. (1986). *The ethnomethodological foundation of mathematics.* London: Rutledge & Kegan Paul.

Long, G. L., Vignare, K., Rappold, R. P., & Mallory, J. (2007). Access to Communication for Deaf, Hard-of-Hearing and ESL Students in Blended Learning Courses. *International Review of Research in Open and Distance Learning*, *8*(3). Retrieved November 21, 2008, from http://www.irrodl.org/index.php/irrodl/article/view/423/933

Lowerison, G., Sclater, J., Schmid, R. F., & Abrami, P. C. (2006). Student perceived effectiveness of computer technology use in post-secondary classroom. *Computers & Education*, *47*, 465–489. doi:10.1016/j.compedu.2004.10.014

Lu, E. Y., Ma, H., Turner, S., & Huang, W. (2007). Wireless Internet and Student-centered learning: A Partial Least-Squares model. *Computers & Education*, *49*(2), 530–544. doi:10.1016/j.compedu.2005.10.009

Luca, J., & McLoughlin, C. (2005a). Can blogs promote fair and equitable teamwork? In H. Goss (Ed.), *Balance, fidelity, mobility: Maintaining the momentum? Proceedings of the 22nd ASCILITE Conference* (pp. 379-386). Brisbane, Australia: Queensland University of Technology.

Luca, J., & McLoughlin, C. (2005b). Supporting collaborative learning with blogs. In P. Kommers & G. Richards (Eds.), *Proceedings of World Conference on Educational Multimedia, Hypermedia & Telecommunications 2005* (pp. 3711-3715). Chesapeake, VA: AACE.

Lui, A. K., Choy, S., Cheung, Y. H. Y., & Li, S. C. (2006). A study on the perception of students towards educational weblogs. *Informatics in Education*, *5*(2), 233–254.

Lui, A., Kwan, R., & Lai, C. F. (2004). A learning thermometer: Improving visibility of learning activities in online discussion forums. In *The Proceedings of the International Conference of Distance Education (ICDE 2004)*, Hong Kong SAR, China.

Luppicini, R. (2005). A Systems Definition of Educational technology in Society. *Educational technology & Society*, *8*(3), 103-109.

Lyotard, J.-F. (1984). *The Postmodern Condition: A Report of Knowledge* (G. Bennington & B. Massumi, Trans.). Manchester, UK: Manchester University Press.

Mackenzie, D., & Stanwell, M. (2007). QuickTrl A Visual System for the Rapid Creation of e-Assessments and e-Learning Materials. In *Proceeding of the11th International Computer Assisted Assessment (CAA) Conference: Research into E-Assessment* (pp. 301-302). Loughborough University.

MacManus, R. (2007). *e-learning 2.0: All You Need To Know. Read/WriteWeb*. Retrieved November 13, 2007, from http://www.readwriteweb.com/archives/e-learning_20_all_you_need_to_know.php

Mann, S. J. (2005). Alienation in the learning environment: A failure of community? *Studies in Higher Education, 30*(1), 43–55. doi:10.1080/0307507052000307786

Mann, W. C. & Thompson, S.A. (1987). *Rhetorical structure theory: A theory of text organization*. Technical Report ISI/RS-87-190, Information Sciences Institute, University of Southern California.

Manning, C., & Schutze, H. (1999). *Foundations of statistical natural language processing*. Cambridge, MA: MIT Press.

Manton, M., Fernandez, B., Balch, D., & Meredith, M. (2004). Forced to conform? Using common processes and standards to create effective e-Learning. *Journal of Interactive Media in Education, 14*, 1–15.

March, T. (2003). The learning power of WebQuests. *Educational Leadership, 61*(4), 42–47.

Marginson, S. (2007). *Going Global: Trends in higher education and research in the APEC region*. Retrieved from http://www.cshe.unimelb.edu.au/people/staff_pages/Marginson/APEC_HRDWG_Symposium_170407.pdf

Markova, I. (2003). *Dialogicality and social representations: The dynamics of mind*. Cambridge, UK: Cambridge University Press.

Martinello, M., & Cook, G. (2000). *Interdisciplinary inquiry in teaching and learning (2nd ed.)*. Pearson Education, NJ: Upper Saddle River.

Martinez, A. Dimitriadis, Y., Rubia, B., Gómez, E., Garrachón, I., Marcos, J.A. (2002). Studying social aspects of computer-supported collaboration with a mixed evaluation approach. In *Proc. Conf. Computer Support for Collaborative Learning (CSCL)* (pp. 631-632). Philadelphia, PA: Lawrence Erlbaum Associates.

Martínez, R. A., Mílans del Bosch, M., Henar Pérez Herrero, M., & Sampedro Nuño, A. (2007). Psychopedagogical components and processes in e-learning. Lessons from an unsuccessful on-line course. *Computers in Human Behavior, 23*(1), 146–161. doi:10.1016/j.chb.2004.04.002

Martin-Hansen, L. (2002). Defining inquiry: Exploring the many types of inquiry in the science classroom. *Science Teacher (Normal, Ill.), 69*(2), 34–37.

Marton, F., & Saljo, R. (1976). On Qualitative Differences in Learning — 2: Outcome as a function of the learner's conception of the task. *The British Journal of Educational Psychology*, 46.

Masie, E. (2002). Blended learning: The magic is in the mix. In A. Rossett (Ed.), *The ASTD e-learning handbook: Best practices, strategies, and case studies for an emerging field* (pp. 58-63). New York: McGraw-Hill.

Masie, E. (2002, July 23). *Elliott Masie's Learning Trends*. Retrieved March 27, 2008, from http://trends.masie.com/archives/2002/7/23/238-learning-on-line-vs-e-learning-a-season-of-deals-starts.html

Masie, E. (2006). Chapter Two: The Blended Learning Imperative. In C. J. Bonk & C. R. Graham (Eds.), *The handbook of blended learning: Global Perspectives, Local Designs* (pp. 22-26). San Francisco: John Wiley & Sons, Inc.

Mason, M. B. (1999). Outcomes-based Education in South African Curricular Reform. *Cambridge Journal of Education, 29*(1), 137–143. doi:10.1080/0305764990290111

Mason, R., & Rennie, F. (2006). *Elearning: The key concepts*. London: Routledge.

Master of Educational Studies FAQ. (2008). University of Alberta. Retrieved April 9, 2008, from http://www.mes.ualberta.ca/general/frequentlyaskedquestions.html#residencies

Matheos, K., Daniel, K., & McCalla, G. I. (2005). Dimensions for blended learning technology: Learners' perspectives. *Journal of Learning Design, 1*(1), 56–76.

Matsatsinis, N., Moraitis, P., Psomatakis, V., & Spanoudakism, N. (2003). An agent-based system for products penetration strategy selection. *Applied Artificial Intelligence, 17*(10), 901. doi:10.1080/714858317

Mayer, R. (2003). The promise of multimedia learning: Using the same instructional design methods across different media. *Learning and Instruction*, 125–139. doi:10.1016/S0959-4752(02)00016-6

Mayer, R. (2004). Should there be a three-strikes rule against pure discovery learning? The case for guided methods of instruction. *The American Psychologist*, *59*(1), 14–19. doi:10.1037/0003-066X.59.1.14

Mayes, J. T. (1995). Learning technologies and groundhog day. In W. Strang, V.B. Simpson, & D. Slater (Eds.), *Hypermedia at work: Practice and theory in Higher Education*. Canterbury, UK: University of Kent Press.

Mazza, R., & Dimitrova, V. (2005). Generation of graphical representations of student tracking data in course management systems. In *Ninth International Conference on Information Visualisation (IV'05)* (pp. 253-258).

McCarthy, M. (2002). *Discourse Analysis for Language Teachers*. Cambridge, UK: Cambridge University Press.

McConnell, D. (2005). Examining the dynamics of networked e-learning groups and communities. *Studies in Higher Education*, *30*(1), 25–42. doi:10.1080/0307507052000307777

McCray, G. E. (2000). The hybrid class: Merging online instruction and the traditional classroom. *Information Technology and Management*, *1*(4), 307–327. doi:10.1023/A:1019189412115

McCrory, R., Putnam, R., & Jansen, A. (2008). Interaction in online courses for teacher education: Subject matter and pedagogy. *Journal of Technology and Teacher Education*, *16*(2), 155–180.

McDuffie, R., Smith, S., & Murphy, L. (2006). Impact of an audit reporting expert system on learning performance: a teaching note. *Accounting Education*, *15*(1), 189. doi:10.1080/06939280600551585

McEvoy, S. (2003). *Fundamentals of Programming the Microsoft Windows Media Platform*. Redmond, WA: Microsoft Press. *Podcast*. (n.d.). Retrieved from http://en.wikipedia.org/wiki/Podcast

McFarlin, B. K. (2008). Hybrid lecture-online format increases student grades in an undergraduate exercise physiology course at a large urban university. *Advances in Physiology Education*, *32*, 86–91. doi:10.1152/advan.00066.2007

McGinn, R. (1978). What is Technology? *Research in Philosophy and Technology*, *1*, 179–197.

McIsaac, M. S., Blocher, J. M., Mahes, V., & Vrasidas, C. (1999). Student and teacher perceptions of interaction in online computer-mediated communication. *Educational Media International*, *36*(2), 121–131. doi:10.1080/0952398990360206

Mclaren, C. (2004). A comparison of student persistence and performance in online and classroom business statistics experiences. *Journal of Innovative Education*, *2*(1), 1. doi:10.1111/j.0011-7315.2004.00015.x

McLoughlin, C. (2002). Learner support in distance and networked learning environments: Ten dimensions for successful design. *Distance Education*, *23*(2), 149–162. doi:10.1080/0158791022000009178

McLuhan, M. (2001). *Understanding Media*. Oxford, UK: Routledge Classics, Taylor and Francis.

Media Laboratory. (1999). *Future learning environment*. Retrieved September 17, 2007 from http://mlab.uiah.fi/fle/

Media Zoo. (2008). *University of Leicester Media Zoo*. Retrieved April 17, 2008, from http://www.le.ac.uk/beyonddistance/mediazoo/

Mehanna, W. N. (2004). e-Pedagogy: the pedagogies of e-learning. *ALT-J*, *12*(3), 279–293. doi:10.1080/0968776042000259582

Mehrotra, C. M., Hollister, C. D., & McGahey, L. (2001). *Distance Learning: Principles for effective design, delivery and evaluation*. Thousand Oaks, CA: Sage.

Mejias, U. (2005). A nomad's guide to learning and social software. *The Knowledge Tree: An E-Journal of Learning Innovation, 7*. Retrieved December 10, 2006, from http://knowledgetree.flexiblelearning.net.au/edition07/download/la_mejias.pdf

Merrill, P. F., Hammons, K., & Vincent, B. R. (1996). *Computers in education*. Needham Heights, MA: Allyn & Bacon, Inc.

Meyer, D. K., Turner, J. C., & Spencer, C. A. (1997). Challenge in a mathematics classroom: Students' motivation and strategies in project-based learning. *The Elementary School Journal*, *97*(5), 501–521. doi:10.1086/461878

Meyer, K. A. (2003). Face-to-face versus threaded discussions: The role of time and higher-order thinking. *Journal of Asynchronous Learning Networks*, *7*(3), 55–65.

Milgram, P., & Kishino, A. F. (1994). Taxonomy of mixed reality visual displays. *IEICE Transactions on Information and Systems . E (Norwalk, Conn.)*, *77-D*(12), 1321–1329.

Miller, D. B. (2006, October 18). Podcasting at the University of Connecticut: Enhancing the educational experience. *Campus Technology*. Retrieved April 10, 2007, from http://campustechnology.com/news_article.asp?id=19424&typeid=156

Miller, D. B. (2007). *iCube*. Retrieved April 10, 2007, from http://icube.uconn.edu/

Miller, P. (2007). *Marc Andreesen digs into the Platform. Web 2.0 Explorer: Guest bloggers*. Retrieved April 25, 2008, from http://blogs.zdnet.com/web2explorer/?p=402

Mitcham, C. (1994). *Thinking Through Technology*. Chicago: The University of Chicago Press.

Mitchell, T., Aldridge, N., Williamson, W., & Broomhead, P. (2003). Computer based testing of medial knowledge. In *Proceedings of the 7th Computer Assisted Assessment Conference*, UK.

Mitchell, T., Russell, T., Broomhead, P., & Aldridge, N. (2002). Towards robust computerised marking of free-text responses. In *Proceedings of the 6th Computer Assisted Assessment Conference*, UK.

Mitrovic, A., & Martin, B. (2004). Evaluating adaptive problem selection. IN *Proceedings of the Adaptive Hypermedia and Adaptive Web-Based Systems conference* (LNCS 3137, pp. 185-194). Berlin, Germany: Springer-Verlag.

Miyata, H. (2008). Mobile & Collaborative Learning Development by a Concept of "Mobile-As-Participation-Platform". In *Proceedings of the 7th International Conference on Web-Based Education (WBE-2008)*, Innsbruck, Austria

Moberg, T., & Whitcomb, M. (1999). Educational technology to facilitate medical students' learning: background paper 2 of the medical school objectives project. *Academic Medicine*, *74*, 1146–1150. doi:10.1097/00001888-199910000-00020

Monash University. (2003). *The Teaching-Research Nexus: A Discussion Paper*. Monash University, Centre for Higher Education Quality.

Moore, M. G. (1993). Three types of interaction. In K. Harry, M. John, & D. Keegan (Eds.), *Distance education: New perspectives* (pp. 21-24). London: Routledge.

Morales, C., & Moses, J. S. (2006). *Podcasting: Recording, managing, and delivering the classroom experience*. Retrieved from http://www.educause.edu/LibraryDetailPage/666?ID=DEC0604

Moreno, L., Gonzalez, C., Castilla, I., Gonzalez, E., & Sigut, J. (2007). Applying a constructivist and collaborative methodological approach in engineering education. *Computers & Education*, *49*(3), 891–915. doi:10.1016/j.compedu.2005.12.004

Morrison, D. (2003). *The Search for the Holy Recipe. Library Blended learning, e-learning Centre*. Retrieved June 15, 2006, from http://www.e-learningcentre.co.uk/eclipse/Resources/blended.htm

Morrow, D. (2007). *Interactivity in an online learning environment: A case study of participant experience in professional development*. Unpublished doctoral dissertation, Griffith University, Brisbane.

Mortera-Gutierrez, F. (2006). Faculty best practices using blended learning in e-learning and face-to-face instruction. *International Journal on E-Learning*, *5*(3), 313.

Mossavar-Rahmani, F., & Larson-Daugherty, C. (2007). Supporting the hybrid learning model: A new proposition. *MERLOT Journal of Online Learning and Teaching*, *3*(1), 67–78.

Mullen, G. E., & Tallent-Runnels, M. K. (2006). Student outcomes and perceptions of instructors' demands and support in online and traditional classrooms. *The Internet and Higher Education, 9*, 257–266. doi:10.1016/j.iheduc.2006.08.005

Muller, H., Michoux, N., Bandon, D., & Geissbuhler, A. (2004). A review of content-based image retrieval systems in medical application – clinical benefits and future directions. *International Journal of Medical Informatics, 73*(1), 1–23. doi:10.1016/j.ijmedinf.2003.11.024

Muller, H., Rosset, A., Garcia, A., Vallee, J., & Geissbuhler, A. (2005). Benefits of content-based visual data access in radiology. *Radiographics, 25*, 849–858. doi:10.1148/rg.253045071

Muppala, J. K., & Ha, T. S. (1998). Effectiveness of Web-based Instructional Support in Teaching and Learning Process. In *Proceedings of the IEEE International Conference on Multimedia Engineering and Education (M2E2 1998),* Hong Kong.

Myers, M. (1986). The Teaching of Writing in Secondary Schools. In A. P. Petrosky & D. Bartholomae (Eds.), *The Teaching of Writing* (pp. 148-169). National Society for the Study of Education.

Nardi, B. A., Shiano, D. J., Gumbrecht, M., & Swartz, L. (2004). Why we blog. *Communications of the ACM, 47*(12), 41–46. doi:10.1145/1035134.1035163

Neisser, U. (1967). *Cognitive psychology.* New York: Appleton-Century-Crofts.

Neumeier, P. (2005). A Closer Look at Blended learning – Parameters for Designing a blended learning Environment for Language Teaching and Learning. *ReCALL, 17*(2), 163–178. doi:10.1017/S0958344005000224

Newell, A., & Roosenbloom, P. (1981). Mechanisms of skill acquisition and the law of practice. In J. R. Anderson (Ed.), *Cognitive Skills and their acquisition* (pp. 1-55). Hillsdale NJ: Erlbaum Associates.

Newmark, P. (1988). *A textbook of translation.* Hertfordshire, UK: Prentice Hall.

Ng, C., Yeung, A. S., & Hon, R. Y. H. (2006). Does online language learning diminish interaction between student and teacher? *Educational Media International, 43*(3), 219–232. doi:10.1080/09523980600641429

Ng, K. C. (2001). Using e-mail to foster collaboration in distance education. *Open Learning, 16*, 191–200. doi:10.1080/02680510120050343

Ng, K. C., Murphy, D., & Jenkins, W. (2002). The teacher's role in supporting a learner-centred learning environment: voices from a group of part-time postgraduate students in Hong Kong. *International Journal of Lifelong Education, 21*(5), 462–473. doi:10.1080/02601370210156754

Ng, S. C., Choy, S. O., Kwan, R., & Tsang, Y. C. (2006). Integrated assignment management system with plagiarism detection for programming courses. In *Enhancing Learning through Technology* (pp. 136 -146). Hackensack, NJ: World Scientific.

Nian-Shing, C. Kinshuk, Hsiu-Chia, K., & Taiyu L. (2004). Synchronous learning model over the Internet. *Proceedings of IEEE International Conference on Advanced Learning Technologies* (pp. 505-509). Retrieved February 25, 2008 from http://ieeexplore.ieee.org/xpls/abs_all.jsp?arnumber=1357466

Nicol, C., & Coen, M. (2003). A model for evaluating the institutional costs and benefits of ICT initiatives in teaching and learning in higher education. *Association of Learning Technology Journal, 11*(2), 46.

Nielsen, J. (1998). *Jakob Nielsen's Alertbox - "Electronic Books – A Bad Idea".* Retrieved from February 23, 2007, from http://www.useit.com/alertbox/980726.html

Njoo, M. K. H. (1994). *Exploratory learning with a computer simulation: Learning processes and instructional support.* Unpublished doctoral dissertation, Technische Universiteit Eindhoven, The Netherlands.

Nonaka, I., & Konno, N. (1998). The concept of "Ba": Building a foundation for knowledge creation. *California Management Review, 40*(3), 40–54.

Nonaka, I., & Takeuchi, H. (1995). *The knowledge-creating company.* New York: Oxford University Press.

Norman, D. A. (1993). *Things that make us smart: Defending human attributes in the age of the machine*. Reading, MA: Addison-Wesley.

Normand, C., Littlejohn, A., & Falconer, I. (2008). A model for effective implementation of flexible program delivery. *Innovations in Teaching and Education International*, *45*(1), 25. doi:10.1080/14703290701757351

Noss, R., & Pachler, N. (1999). The challenge of new technologies: doing old things in a new way, or doing new things? In P. Mortimore (Ed.), *Understanding Pedagogy and its Impact on Learning* (pp. 195-211). London: Paul Chapman Publishing Ltd.

Nübel, I. (2005). *Integration von E-Learning und Wissensmanagement*. Aachen, Germany: Shaker Verlag.

Nunan, D. (1992). *Collaborative language learning and teaching*. New York: Cambridge University Press.

O'Reilly, T. (2005). *Web 2.0: Compact Definition? O'Reilly Radar*. Retrieved April 30, 2008, from http://radar.oreilly.com/archives/2005/10/web-20-compact-definition.html

O'Reilly, T. (2005). *What is Web 2.0*. Retrieved from http://www.oreillynet.com/pub/a/oreilly/tim/news/2005/09/30/what-is-web-20.html

O'Reilly, T. (2005). *What is Web 2.0: Design Patterns and Business Models for the Next Generation of Software. O'Reilly*. Retrieved March 22, 2008, from http://www.oreilly.com/pub/a/oreilly/tim/news/2005/09/30/what-is-web-20.html

O'Reilly, T. (2005a). *Web 2.0: Compact definition?* Retrieved November 28, 2006, from http://radar.oreilly.com/archives/2005/10/web_20_compact_definition.html

O'Reilly, T. (2005b). *What is Web 2.0: Design patterns and business models for the next generation of software*. Retrieved December 15, 2006, from http://www.oreillynet.com/pub/a/oreilly/tim/news/2005/09/30/what-is-web-20.html

O'Toole, J. M., & Absalom, D. J. (2003). The Impact of Blended learning on Student Outcomes: is there Room on the House for two? *Journal of Educational Media*, *28*(2-3), 179–190. doi:10.1080/1358165032000165680

O-Bryan, A., & Hegelheimer, V. (2007). Integrating CALL into the Classroom: the Role of Podcasting in an ESL Listening Strategies Course. *ReCALL*, *19*(2), 162–180. doi:10.1017/S0958344007000523

OEDb. (2008). *100 Ways to Use Your iPod to Learn and Study Better*. Retrieved March 22, 2008, from http://oedb.org/library/beginning-online-learning/100-ways-to-use-your-ipod-to-learn-and-study-better

Olapiriyakul, K., & Scher, J. M. (2006). A guide to establishing hybrid learning courses: Employing information technology to create a new learning experience, and a case study. *The Internet and Higher Education*, *9*, 287–301. doi:10.1016/j.iheduc.2006.08.001

Olgren, C. H. (1998). Improving learning outcomes: The effects of learning strategies and motivation. In C. C. Gibson (Ed.), *Distance learners in higher education: Institutional responses to quality outcomes* (pp. 77-95). Madison, WI: Atwood Publishing.

Oliver, M., & Trigwell, K. (2005). Can "blended learning" be redeemed? *E-Learning*, *2*(1), 17–26.

Oravec, J. (2003). Blending by Blogging: weblogs in blended learning initiatives. *Journal of Educational Media*, *28*(2), 225. doi:10.1080/1358165032000165671

Oravec, J. A. (2003). Blending by blogging: weblogs in blended learning initiatives. *Journal of Educational Media*, *28*(2-3), 225–233. doi:10.1080/1358165032000165671

Ormrod, J. E. (2006). *Educational psychology: Developing learners (5th ed.)*. Upper Saddle River, NJ: Pearson Education.

Osguthorpe, R. T., & Graham, C. R. (2003). Blended learning environments: Definitions and directions. *The Quarterly Review of Distance Education*, *4*(3), 227–233.

Osswald, T., & Dugdale, T. (2006). *Podcasting: Portable Knowledge for New Opportunities in Teaching and Learning*. Retrieved from http://academictech.doit.wisc.edu/workshops/epedagogy/sessions/epedagogyPodcasting06.htm

Ouyang, L., Ou, L., & Zhang, Y. (2007). An integrated strategy for teaching biochemistry to biotechnology specialty students. *Biochemistry and Molecular Biology Education, 35*(4), 267–271. doi:10.1002/bmb.67

Page, E. (1966). *The imminence of grading essays by computer.* Phi Delta Kappan.

Page, K. (2006). A preliminary study on the current state of e-learning in lifelong learning. In *Cedefop Panorama series, Official Publications of the European Communities* (pp. 5-7).

Palloff, R., & Pratt, K. (2001). *Lessons from the cyberspace classroom: The realities of online teaching.* San Francisco, CA: Jossey-Bass.

Palmer, J. (2002). Web site usability, design and performance metrics. *Information Systems Research, 13*(2), 151. doi:10.1287/isre.13.2.151.88

Papastergiou, M. (2006). Course management systems as tools for the creation of online learning environments: Evaluation from a social constructivist perspective and implications for their design. *International Journal on E-Learning, 5*(4), 593–622.

Paredes, P. (2002). *An attempt to incorporate learning styles in adaptive web-based courses.* Advanced Studies Diploma, Escuela Politécnica Superior, Universidad Autónoma de Madrid.

Parker, J. A. (2007). Book review: Blogs, Wikis, podcasts, and other powerful tools for the classrooms. *The Internet and Higher Education, 10*(4), 289–291.

Pauca, V. P., Shahnaz, F., Berry, M. W., & Plemmons, R. J. (2004). Text mining using non-negative matrix factorization. In *Proceedings of the 2004 SIAM International conference on Data Mining (SDM 2004),* Lake Buena Vista, FL (pp. 452-456).

Pavlov, I. P. (1927). *Conditioned reflexes* (G. V. Anrep, Trans.). London: Oxford University Press.

Pawan, F., Paulus, T. M., Yalcin, S., & Chang, C. F. (2003). Online learning: Patterns of engagement and interaction among in-service teachers. *Language Learning & Technology, 7*(3), 119–140.

Payette, S., & Lagoze, C. (1998). Flexible and Extensible Digital Object and Repository Architecture (FEDORA). *Lecture Notes in Computer Science, 1513,* 41-59. Berlin, Germany: Springer-Verlag. Retrieved from http://www.cs.cornell.edu/payette/papers/ECDL98/FEDORA.html
van der Sompel, H., Bekaert, J., Liu, X., Balakireva, L., & Schwander, T. (2005). aDORe: a Modular Standards-Based Digital Object Repository. *The Computer Journal, 48*(5), 514-535.

Pearson Education. (2008). *Intelligent Essay Assessor.* Retrieved November 21, 2008, from http://www.knowledge-technologies.com/prodIEA.shtml

Pearson, J. (2006). Investigating ICT using problem-based learning in face-to-face and online learning environments. *Computers & Education, 47,* 56–73. doi:10.1016/j.compedu.2004.09.001

Pearson, J., & Trinidad, S. (2005). OLES: An instrument for refining the design e-learning environments. *Journal of Computer Assisted Learning, 21,* 396. doi:10.1111/j.1365-2729.2005.00146.x

Pedroni, M. (2007). E-learning and knowledge management: Context structuration. *Proceedings of the 2007 Informing Science and IT Education Joint Conference* (pp. 99-106).

Peled, A., & Rashty, D. (1999). Logging for success: Advancing the use of WWW logs to improve computer mediated distance learning. *Journal of Educational Computing Research, 21,* 413–431.

Pelletier, C. (2005). *New Technologies, New Identities: The University in the Information Age.* London: RoutledgeFalmer.

Perez, D., Alfonseca, E., Rodríguez, P., & Pascual, I. (2006). Willow: Automatic and Adaptive Assessment of Students' Free-Text Answers. In *Proceedings of the 22nd International Conference of the Spanish Natural Language Proceeding Society.*

Perez, D., Gliozzo, A., Alfonseca, E., Strapparava, C., Magnini, B., & Rodríguez, P. (2005). About the effects of combining Latent Semantic Analysis with other Natural Language Processing techniques for free-text assessment. *International Journal Signos, 38*(59), 325–343.

Pérez-Marín, D. (2007). *Adaptive Computer Assisted Assessment of free-text students' answers: an approach to automatically generate students' conceptual models*. Unpublished doctoral dissertation, Escuela Politécnica Superior, Universidad Autónoma de Madrid. Retrieved from http://www.eps.uam.es/~dperez/index1.html

Perez-Marin, D., Pascual-Nieto, I., & Alfonseca, E. (2007). A Study on the Impact of the Use of an Automatic and Adaptive Free-text Assessment System during a University Course. In J. Fong & F. L. Wang (Eds.), *Blended learning* (pp.186-195). Singapore: Pearson Prentice Hall.

Perkinson, R. (2006). International higher education plenary address. *The UK's International Education Conference*, Edinburgh, UK.

Perraton, H. (2000). Choosing Technologies for Education. *Journal of Educational Media, 25*(1), 31–38. doi:10.1080/1358165005000l221

Perry, B. (2006). Using photographic images as an interactive online teaching strategy. *The Internet and Higher Education, 9*, 229–240. doi:10.1016/j.iheduc.2006.06.008

Peterson, C., Caverly, D. C., & MacDonald, L. (2001). Developing academic literacy through WebQuests. *Journal of Developmental Education, 26*(3), 38–39.

Pettenati, M. C., & Ranieri, M. (2006). Informal learning theories and tools to support knowledge management in distributed CoPs. In *Innovative Approaches for Learning and Knowledge Sharing EC-TEL 2006 Workshops Proceedings* (pp. 345-355).

Pettijohn, J. (2002). Virtual Tours – A tool for enhancing and enlivening the international business class. *Journal of Business education, 75*(5), 291.

Phillips, R. (2005). Challenging The Primacy Of Lectures: The Dissonance Between Theory And Practice In University Teaching. *Journal of University Teaching & Learning Practice, 2*(1).

Piaget, J. (1970). *Genetic epistemology*. (E. Duckworth, Trans.). New York: Columbia University Press.

Piaget, J. (1985). *The equilibration of cognitive structures*. Chicago, IL: University of Chicago Press.

Picard, R. W., & Scheirer, J. (2001). The Galvactivator: a glove that senses and communicates skin conductivity. In *9th International Conference on Human-Computer Interaction*, New Orleans, LA.

Picard, R., Papert, S., Bender, W., Blumberg, B., Breazeal, C., & Cavallo, D. (2004). Affective learning - a manifesto. *BT Technology Journal, 22*(4), 253–269. doi:10.1023/B:BTTJ.0000047603.37042.33

Picciano, A. G. (2002). Beyond student perceptions: Issues of interaction, presence, and performance in an online course. *Journal of Asynchronous Learning Networks, 6*(1), 21–40.

Picciano, A. G., & Searman, J. (2007). K-12 Online Learning: A Survey of U.S. School District Administrators. *Journal of Asynchronous Learning Networks, 11*(3). Retrieved November 21, 2008, from http://www.sloan-c.org/publications/survey/pdf/K-12_Online_Learning.pdf

Pilcher, E. S. (2001). Students' evaluation of online course materials in Fixed Prosthodontics: a case study. *European Journal of Dental Education, 5*, 53–59. doi:10.1034/j.1600-0579.2001.005002053.x

Pilgrim, M. (2002). *What is RSS? O'Reillyxml.com*. Retrieved March 22, 2008, from http://www.xml.com/pub/a/2002/12/18/dive-into-xml.html

Polanyi, M. (1967). *The Tacit Dimension*. New York: Anchor Books.

Polyphony. (2008). Retrieved December, 1, 2008 from http://cnx.rice.edu/content/m11634/latest/

Postman, N. (1992). *Technopoly: The Surrender of Culture to Technology*. New York: Knop.

Poysa, J., Lowyck, J., & Hakkinen, P. (2005). Learning Together "Three"-Hybrid "Place" as a Conceptual Vantage Point for Understanding Virtual Learning Communities in Higher Education Context. *PsychNology Journal, 3*(2), 162–180.

Preece, J. (2000). *Online communities: Designing usability, supporting sociability.* Chichester, UK: John Wiley & Sons.

Price, S., & OLIVER, M. (2007). A Framework for Conceptualising the Impacts of Technologies on Teaching and Learning. *Educational technology and Society, 10*(10), 16-27.

Probst, G., Raub, S., & Romhardt, K. (1999). *Managing knowledge.* Chichester, UK: John Wiley & Sons Ltd.

Punie, Y., & Cabrera, M. (2006). *The future of ICT and learning in the knowledge society.* Luxembourg: European Communities.

Puntambekar, S. (2006). Analyzing collaborative interactions: divergence, shared understanding and construction of knowledge. *Computers & Education, 47*, 332–351. doi:10.1016/j.compedu.2004.10.012

Purdue. (2006). *Purdue University Boilercast.* Retrieved from http://boilercast.itap.purdue.edu:1013/Boilercast/

Quinlan, J. R. (1993). *C4.5: Programs for Machine Learning.* San Mateo, CA: Morgan Kaufmann Publishers.

Race, P. (1994). *The open learning handbook: promoting quality in designing and delivering flexible learning.* London: Kogan Page Limited.

Ramani, L., & Rocha, H. (2000). *Interaction map: Information visualization techniques in web-based distance education environments* (Tech. report IC-00-17). Universidade Estatual de Campinas, Brazil.

Ramirez, M. (2008). *UH report shows college students making the grade online, in class. Back to EurekAlert!* Retrieved March 30, 2008, from http://www.eurekalert.org/pub_releases/2008-03/uoh-urs032408.php#

Ramsden, P. (2003). *Learning to Teach in Higher Education* (2nd ed.). London: RoutledgeFalmer.

Ras, E., Memmel, M., & Weibelzahl, S. (2005). Integration of e-learning and knowledge management - barriers, solutions and future issues. In *WM 2005* (S. 155-164). Heidelberg, Germany: Springer-Verlag.

Rau, W., & Heyl, B. S. (1990). Humanizing the college classroom: Collaborative learning and social organization among students. *Teaching Sociology, 18*(2), 141–155. doi:10.2307/1318484

Ravenscroft, A. (2001). Designing E-learning interactions in the 21st century: revisiting and rethinking the role of theory. *European Journal of Education, 36*(2), 133–156. doi:10.1111/1467-3435.00056

Ray, B. B., & Coulter, G. A. (2008). Reflective practices among language arts teachers: The use of weblogs. *Contemporary Issues in Technology & Teacher Education, 8*(1), 6–26.

Reader, G. *(Labs)*. (2008). Retrieved April 18, 2008, from http://www.google.com/help/reader/tour2.html

Reading, J. (2008). Book Review: The University of Google: Education in the (Post) Information Age. *Ariadne, 54*. Retrieved March 3, 2008, from http://www.ariadne.ac.uk/issue54/reading-rvw/

Reffay, C., & Chanier, T. (2002) Social network analysis used for modelling collaboration in distance learning groups. In *Proc. Intelligent Tutoring System Conference* (pp. 31-40). Berlin, Germany: Springer-Verlag.

Reisetter, M., Lapointe, L., & Korcuska, J. (2007). The Impact of Altered Realties: Implications of Online Delivery for Learners' Interactions, Expectations, and Learning Skills. *International Journal on E-Learning, 6*(1), 55–80.

Reynard, R. (2007). *Hybrid Learning: Maximizing Student Engagement Campus Technology.* Retrieved February 22, 2008, from http://www.campustechnology.com/article.aspx?aid=48204

Richardson, W. (2006). *Blogs, wikis, podcasts, and other powerful web tools for classrooms.* Thousand Oaks, CA: Corwin Press.

Richards-Wilson, S. (2006). What every business school needs to know about its master of business administration. *Journal of Education for Business, 82*(2), 95. doi:10.3200/JOEB.82.2.95-100

Ridgway, P. F., Sheikh, A., Sweeney, K. J., Evoy, D., McDermott, E., & Felle, P. (2007). Surgical e-learning: validation of multimedia web-based lectures. *Medical Education, 41*, 168–172. doi:10.1111/j.1365-2929.2006.02669.x

Riffell, S., & Sibley, D. (2005). Using web-based instruction to improve large undergraduate biology courses: an evaluation of a hybrid course format. *Computers & Education, 44*(3), 217–235. doi:10.1016/j.compedu.2004.01.005

Roehler, L. R., & Cantlon, D. J. (1997). Scaffolding: A powerful tool in social constructivist classrooms. In *Scaffolding student learning: instructional approaches and issues* (pp. 6–42). Cambridge, MA: Brookline Books.

Rogers, P. C., & Wang, M. J. (2008). Cross-cultural issues in online learning. In P. Rogers & G. Berg (Eds.), *Encyclopedia of Distance and Online Learning.* PA: IGI Publishing.

Rosé, C., Gaydos, A., Hall, B., Roque, A., & VanLehn, K. (2003). Overcoming the knowledge engineering bottleneck for understanding student language input. In *Proceedings of the 11th International Conference on Artificial Intelligence in Education*, Australia.

Rose, E. (1999). Deconstructing interactivity in educational computing. *Educational Technology, 39*(1), 43–49.

Rosenberg, M. J. (2001). *E-Learning: Strategies for delivering knowledge in the digital age.* New York: McGraw-Hill.

Rosenberg, M. J. (2006). *Beyond e-learning: Approaches and technologies to enhance organizational knowledge, learning, and performance.* San Francisco: Pfeiffer.

Rosenkoetter, L. E. (2006). Moving toward online courses. *Radiography, 13*(4), 271–275. doi:10.1016/j.radi.2006.04.005

Rösner, D., Amelung, M., & Piotrowski, M. (2006): E-Learning-Komponenten zur Intensivierung der Übungen in der Informatik-Lehre – ein Erfahrungsbericht. In P. Forbrig, G. Siegel, & M. Schneider (Eds.), *GI-Fachtagung Hochschuldidaktik der Informatik.* Bonn, Germany: GI-Verlag.

Rossett, A., & Frazee, R. V. (2006). Blended learning opportunities. *American Management Association White Paper.* Retrieved from http://www.amanet.org/blended/

Rossett, A., & Schafer, L. (2006). Job aids and performance support: the convergence of learning and work. *International Journal of Learning Technology, 2*(4), 310–328. doi:10.1504/IJLT.2006.011337

Rossiter, D., & Lam, G. (2006). Integrated Learning with Podcasting Import and Export in the Gong System. In *Proceedings of the International Conference on ICT in Teaching and Learning 2007*, Hong Kong (pp. 27-36).

Rossiter, D., Lam, G., & Mak, B. (2006). Automatic Audio Indexing and Audio Playback Speed Control as Tools for Language Learning. In *Proceedings of the 5th International Conference on Web-based Learning,* Penang, Malaysia (LNCS 4181, pp. 290-299). Berlin, Germany: Springer-Verlag.

Roth, W.-M. (1998). Teacher questioning in an open-inquiry learning environment: Interactions of context, content, and student responses. *Journal of Research in Science Teaching, 33*(7), 709–736. doi:10.1002/(SICI)1098-2736(199609)33:7<709::AID-TEA2>3.0.CO;2-R

Rovai, A. P., & Jordan, H. M. (2004). Blended learning and sense of community: A comparative analysis with traditional and fully online graduate courses. *International Review of Research in Open and Distance Learning, 5*(2). Retrieved October 10, 2007, from http://www.irrodl.org/index.php/irrodl/article/viewArticle/192/274

Rowley, J. (2007). The wisdom hierarchy: representations of the DIKW hierarchy. *Journal of Information Science*, 163–180. doi:10.1177/0165551506070706

Rudd, T., Sutch, D., & Facer, K. (2006). *Towards new learning networks.* Bristol, UK: Futurelab.

Rudner, L. M. (1998). An on-line, interactive, computer adaptive testing mini-tutorial. *ERIC Clearinghouse on Assessment and Evaluation.*

Ruiz, J., Mintze, M., & Leipzig, R. (2006). The impact of e-learning in medical education. *Academic Medicine*, *81*(3). doi:10.1097/00001888-200603000-00002

Russel, J. A. (1980). A circumplex model of affect. *Journal of Personality and Social Psychology*, *39*(6), 1161–1178. doi:10.1037/h0077714

Russel, T. (1999). The No Significant Different Phenomenon. *Office of Instructional Telecommunication pg the CAM*, *36*(5), 37-41.

Russo, T. C., & Campbell, S. W. (2004). Perceptions of mediated presence in an asynchronous online course: Interplay of communication behaviors and medium. *Distance Education*, *25*(2), 215–232. doi:10.1080/0158791042000262139

Ryymin, E., Lallimo, J., & Hakkarainen, K. (2008). Teachers' professional development in a community: A study of the central actors, their networks and web-based learning. *E-Learning and Education (Eleed) Journal*, (4). Retrieved December 14, 2008, from http://eleed.campussource.de/archive/4/1251/

Sacks, H. (1992). *Lectures on conversation*. Oxford, UK: Blackwell.

Salmon, G. (2000). *E-Moderating: The Key to Teaching and Learning Online*. London: Kogan Page.

Salmon, G. (2002). *E-tivities: The Key to Active Online Learning*. London: Kogan Page.

Salmon, G. (2005). Flying not flapping: a strategic framework for e-learning and pedagogical innovation in higher education institutions. *ALT-J*, *13*(3), 201–218. doi:10.1080/09687760500376439

Salmon, G. (2005). Flying not Flapping: a Strategic Framework for e-learning and Pedagogical Innovation in HEIs. *ALT-J. Research in Learning Technology*, *13*(3), 201–218.

Salmons, J. (2007). *From working together to thinking together: Building collaborative advantage*. Retrieved March 26, 2007, from http://www.trainerspod.com/info/

Salomon, G., & Perkins, D. N. (1998). Individual and social aspects of learning. In D. P. Pearson & A. Iran-Nejad (Eds.), *Review of Research in Education* (Vol. 23, pp. 1-24). Washington, DC: American Educational Research Association.

Salter, G. (2003). Comparing online and traditional teaching – a different approach. *Campus-Wide Information Systems*, *20*(4), 137–145. doi:10.1108/10650740310491306

Salton, G., & Lesk, M. E. (1968). Computer evaluation of indexing and text processing. *Journal of the Association for Computing Machinery*, *15*, 8–36.

Saltz, J. S., Hiltz, S. R., Turoff, M., & Passerini, K. (2007). Increasing participation in distance learning courses. *IEEE Internet Computing*, *11*(3), 36–44. doi:10.1109/MIC.2007.64

Sander, P., Stevenson, K., King, M., & Coates, D. (2000). University Students' Expectations of Teaching. *Studies in Higher Education*, *25*(3), 309–323. doi:10.1080/03075070050193433

Sankey, M., & Smith, A. (2004). Multimodal Design and Hybrid Course Materials: Developing a New Paradigm for Course Delivery at USQ. In *Proceedings of the Common Ground Publishing Pty Ltd and RMIT University, International Conference on Computers in Education 2004*, Melbourne, Australia.

Sankey, M., & St. Hill, R. (2005). Multimodal design for hybrid learning materials in a second-level economics course. In *Proceedings of the 11th Australasian Teaching Economics Conference* (pp. 98-106).

Santrock, J. W. (2004). *Educational Psychology*. New York: McGraw-Hill Higher education.

Sapp, D. A., & Simon, J. (2005). Comparing grades in online and face-to-face writing courses: Interpersonal accountability and institutional commitment. *Computers and Composition*, *22*, 471–489. doi:10.1016/j.compcom.2005.08.005

Sauers, D., & Walker, R. (2004). A comparison of traditional and technology-assisted instructional methods in the business communication classroom.

Business Communication Quarterly, 67(4), 430. doi:10.1177/1080569904271030

Sawyer, R. K. (2006). Analyzing collaborative discourse. In R. K. Sawyer (Ed.), *The Cambridge Handbook of The Learning Sciences* (pp. 187 – 204). New York: Cambridge University Press.

Scardamalia, M., & Bereiter, C. (1994). *Computer support for knowledge-building communities.* Hillsdale, NJ: Lawrence Erlbaum Associates.

Schegloff, E. (1981). Discourse as an interactional achievement: Some uses of 'uh huh' and other things that come between sentences. In D. Tannen (Ed.), *Georgetown University Roundtable on Languages and Linguistics 1981; Analyzing Discourse: Text and Talk.* Washington D.C.: Georgetown University Press.

Schlager, M. S., & Fusco, J. (2003). Teacher professional development, technology, and communities of practice: Are we putting the cart before the horse? *The Information Society, 19*, 203–220. doi:10.1080/01972240309464

Schmid, F., Mitchell, T., Whitehouse, J., & Broomhead, P. (2007). Exam online: e-Enabling "Traditional" HE/FE Examinations. In *Proceeding for 11th International Computer Assisted Assessment (CAA) Conference: Research into E-Assessment* (pp. 381-396). Loughborough University.

Schmidt, A. (2005). Bridging the gap between knowledge managment and e-learning with context-aware corporate learning. In *WM 2005* (pp. 203-213). Heidelberg, Germany: Springer-Verlag.

Schmidt, A. (2008). Enabling learning on demand in semantic work environments: The learning in process approach. In J. Rech, B. Decker, & E. Ras, *Emerging Technologies for Semantic Work Environments: Techniques, Methods, and Applications.* Hershey, PA: IGI Publishing.

Schmidt, H. G. (1993). Foundations of problem-based learning: some explanatory notes. *Medical Education, 27*(5), 422–432. doi:10.1111/j.1365-2923.1993.tb00296.x

Schmotter, J. (2004). On two-plus decades: A world of difference. *Selections, 4*(1), 3.

Schulman, M. (2001). Basic understandings for developing learning media for the classroom and beyond. *Learning Technology Newsletter, 3*(1).

Schwen, T. M., & Hara, N. (2004). Community of practice: A metaphor for online design? In S. A. Barab, R. Kling, & J. H. Gray (Eds.), *Designing for virtual communities in the service of learning* (pp. 16-50). Cambridge, UK: Cambridge University Press.

SEAL. (2008). *Second Environment Advance Learning.* Retrieved April 11, 2008, from http://www.le.ac.uk/seal/

Sener, J. (2007). *University of North Carolina at Pembroke—cjencyclopedia.com: Online encyclopedia of Criminal Justice.* Retrieved March 10, 2007, from http://www.sloan-c-wiki.org/wiki/index.php?title=University_of_North_Carolina_at_Pembroke_--_cjencyclopedia.com:_Online_Encyclopedia_of_Criminal_Justice

Senge, P. M. (1995). *The fifth discipline fieldbook.* London: Nicolas Brealey Publishing. Sharma, N. (n.d.). *The origin of the "data information knowledge wisdom" hierarchy.* Retrieved February 11, 2008, from http://www-personal.si.umich.edu/~nsharma/dikw_origin.htm

Senge, P. M. (2006). *The fifth discipline.* London: Random House Business Books.

Sfard, A. (2000). On reform movement and the limits of mathematical discourse. *Mathematical Thinking and Learning, 2*(3), 157–189. doi:10.1207/S15327833MTL0203_1

Shadbolt, N., & O' Hara, K. (2008). *The spy in the coffee machine - The end of privacy as we know it.* Oxford, UK: Oneworld Publications.

Shank, P. (2007). *The value of multimedia in learning.* Preluat de pe http://www.adobe.com/designcenter/thinktank/valuemedia/The_Value_of_Multimedia.pdf

Shank, R. (Ed.). (2007). *The Online Learning Idea Book: 95 Proven Ways to Enhance Technology-based and Blended learning.* San Francisco, CA: Pfeiffer, John Wiley & Sons.

Shannon, C. E. (1948). A Mathematical Theory of Communication. *The Bell System Technical Journal, 27*, 379–423, 623–656.

Sharpe, R., Benfield, G., Roberts, G., & Francis, R. (2006). *The undergraduate experience of blended e-learning: A review of UK literature and practice*. York, UK: The Higher Education Academy.

Sharpe, R., Benfield, G., Roberts, G., & Francis, R. (2006). *The Undergraduate Experience of Blended e-learning: a Review of UK Literature and Practice*. UK: The Higher education Academy.

Sheard, J., Albrecht, D., & Butbul, W. (2005). ViSION: Visualization student interactions online. In A. Treloar & A. Ellis (Eds.), *Proceedings of the Eleventh Australasian World Wide Web Conference* (pp. 48-58).

Sheard, M., & Ahmed, J. (2007). *Engaging the 'Xbox Generation of Learners' in Higher Education* [Electronic Version]. Retrieved November 26, 2008, from http://www2.hud.ac.uk/edu/research/docs/xbox_research_report.pdf

Shearer, R. L. (2003). *Interaction in distance education*. Madison, WI: Distance Educator, Inc.

Shen, L., Callaghan, V., & Shen, R. (2008). Affective e-learning in residential and pervasive computing environments. *Journal of Information Systems Frontiers (special issue on "Adoption and Use of Information & Communication Technologies in the Residential/Household Context"), 10*(3).

Shen, L., Leon, E., Callaghan, V., & Shen, R. (2007). Exploratory research on an affective e-learning model. In *International Workshop on Blended Learning 2007 (WBL 07)*, University of Edinburgh, Scotland.

Shepherd, C. (2005). *The Blended Learning Cookbook*. United Kingdom: Saffron Interactive.

Shepherd, E. (2007). Blended Delivery Meets e-Assessment. In *Proceeding for 11th International Computer Assisted Assessment (CAA) Conference: Research into E-Assessment* (pp. 399). Loughborough University.

Shepherd, J. (2007, May 8). It's a world of possibilities. *The Guardian*.

Shi Y.C., Xie W.K, Xu G.Y., (2003). The smart classroom: Merging technologies for seamless tele-education. *IEEE Pervasive Computing, 1536-1268(3)*, 47-55.

Shih, Y. (2003). A survey of distance education challenges and technologies. *International Journal of Distance Learning Technologies, 1*(1), 1.

Shinkareva, O. (2007). The Relationship between Adult Students' Instructional Technology Competency and Self-Directed Learning Ability in an Online Course. *Human Resource Development International, 10*(4), 417. doi:10.1080/13678860701723737

Shute, V. J., & Torreano, L. A. (2002). Formative evaluation of an automated knowledge elicitation and organization tool. In *Authoring Tools for Advanced Technology Learning Environments: Toward Cost-Effective Adaptive, Interactive, and Intelligent Educational Software*.

Shyu, C., Brodley, C., Kak, A., & Kosaka, A. (1999). ASSERT: A physician-in-the-loop content-based retrieval system for HRCT image databases. *Computer Vision and Image Understanding, 75*, 111–132. doi:10.1006/cviu.1999.0768

Siemens, G. (2004). Connectivism: A Learning Theory for the Digital Age [Electronic Version]. *elearnspace*. Retrieved November 20, 2008, from http://www.elearnspace.org/Articles/connectivism.htm

Siemens, G. (2005, June). *Elearnspace*. Retrieved March 25, 2008, from http://elearnspace.org/doing/blended.htm

Sife, A. S., Lwoga, E. T., & Sanga, C. (2007). New Technologies for Teaching and Learning: Challenges for Higher Learning Institutions in Developing Countries. *International Journal of Education and Development Using ICT, 3*(2), 57–67.

Sigel, I. E. (Ed.). (1999). *Development of mental representations: Theories and Applications*. Mahwah, NJ: Lawrence Erlbaum Associates.

Simonson, M., Smaldino, S., Albright, M., & Zvacek, S. (2006). *Teaching and Learning at a distance: Foundations of distance education* (3rd ed.). Upper Saddle River, NJ: Merrill Prentice Hall.

Sims, R. L. (2003). Promises of interactivity: Aligning learner perceptions and expectations with strategies for flexible and online learning. *Distance Education, 24*(1), 87–103. doi:10.1080/01587910303050

Simsek, N. (2005). Perceptions and Opinions of Educational Technologies Related to Educational Technology. *Educational Technology and Society, 8*(4), 178–190.

Singh, H., & Reed, C. (2001). *Achieving success with blended learning* [white paper]. Lexington, MA: Centra Software.

Skill, T. D., & Young, B. A. (2002). Embracing the Hybrid Model: Working at the Intersections of Virtual and Physical Learning Spaces. *New Directions for Teaching and Learning, 92*, 23–32. doi:10.1002/tl.76

Skill, T., & Young, B. (2002). Embracing the blended model: Working at the intersection of virtual and physical learning spaces. *New Directions for Teaching and Learning, 2002*(92). doi:10.1002/tl.76

Skinner, B. F. (1954). The science of learning and the art of teaching. *Harvard Educational Review, 24*, 86–97.

Sleeman, D. (1986). The Challenges of teaching computer programming. *Communications of the ACM, 29*(9), 840–841. doi:10.1145/6592.214913

Smart, A. (2008). Tim Berners-Lee: a very British boffin. *Telegraph.co.uk*. Retrieved April 6, 2008, from http://www.telegraph.co.uk/connected/main.jhtml?xml=/connected/2008/03/30/sv_timbernerslee.xml

Smith, G. G., & Kurthen, H. (2007). Front-Stage and Back-Stage in Hybrid E-Learning Face-to-Face Courses. *International Journal on E-Learning, 6*(3), 455–474.

Smith, J. (1997). *Integrated spatial and feature image systems: Retrieval, Compression and analysis.* Ph.D. thesis, Columbia University, Graduate School of Arts and Sciences, New York.

So, P. (2008). Getting with the programme. *South China Morning Post.*

Sorel, R., Dear, R., & Edge, D. (2001). Evolution of web-based distance learning strategies. *International Journal of Educational Management, 15*(4/5), 245.

Sosnovsky, S. (2004). Adaptive navigation for self-assessment quizzes. In *Proceedings of the Adaptive Hypermedia and Adaptive Web-Based Systems* (LNCS 3137, pp. 365-371). Berlin, Germany: Springer-Verlag.

Spady, W., & Marshall, K. (1994). Light, not heat, on OBE. *The American School Board Journal, 181*, 29–33.

Spanier, G. B. (2001). *Higher Education's Biggest Unrecognized Opportunities.* Penn State College President's Speech. Retrieved February 14, 2006, from http://www.psu.edu/ur/GSpanier/speeches/FSU_opportunities_011402.html

Spatariu, A., Quinn, L. F., & Hartley, K. (2007). A review of research on factors that impact aspects of online discussions quality. *TechTrends, 51*(3), 44–48. doi:10.1007/s11528-007-0041-9

Sridharan, B., Tretiakov, A., & Kinshuk. (2004). Application of Ontology to Knowledge Management in Web Based Learning. *Proceedings of the Fourth IEEE International Conference on Advanced Learning Technologies* (pp. 663-665).

Srivastava, J., Cooley, R., Deshpande, & Tan, P. (2000). Web usage mining: Discovery and applications of usage patterns from Web data. *SIGKDD Explorations, 1*(2).

Stacey, E., Smith, P., & Barty, K. (2004). Adult learners in the workplace: Online learning and communities of practice. *Distance Education, 25*(1), 107–123. doi:10.1080/0158791042000212486

Stahl, G. (2006). *Group cognition: Computer support for building collaborative knowledge*. Cambridge, MA: MIT Press.

Stanescu, L., Mihaescu, C., Burdescu, D. D., Georgescu, E., & Florea, L. (2007). An improved platform for medical e-learning. In *Advances in Web-Learning-ICWL* (pp. 392-403).

Stanley, G. (2005). *Podcasting for ELT.* Retrieved November 10, 2007, from http://www.teachingenglish.org.uk/

Stanley, G. (2006). Podcasting: Audio on the Internet Comes of Age. *TESL-EJ, 9*(4). *The EDUCAUSE Learning Initiative, 7 Things You Should Know About Blogs.* (n.d.). Retrieved from http://www.educause.edu/ir/library/pdf/ELI7006.pdf

Stefani, L. (2001). We Might Have to Learn it but we Shouldn't have to think about it. In H. Edwards, B. Smith, & G. Webb (Eds.), *Lecturing Case Studies, Experience and Practice*. London: Kogan Page.

Stenstrom, A.-B. (1994). *An introduction to spoken interaction*. New York: Longman.

Stephens, A. C., & Hartmann, C. (2004). A successful professional development project's failure to promote online discussion about teaching mathematics with technology. *Journal of Technology and Teacher Education, 12*(1), 57–73.

Stephenson, J. E., Brown, C., & Griffin, D. K. (2006). Electronic delivery of lectures in the university environment: An empirical comparison of delivery styles. *Computers & Education, 50*(3), 640–651. doi:10.1016/j.compedu.2006.08.007

Stephenson, J. E., Rayne, R. C., & Griffin, D. K. (2007). Online assessment and feedback to facilitate higher order learning skills in classical and molecular genetics. In *Proceedings of the ECCE2007.*

Stephenson, J.E., Murray, L.A., Alberts, P.P., Parnis, N.G., Sharma, A., Fraser, J.E., & Zammit, M.J. (2008). *Educational considerations for blended learning.* West London: Brunel University.

Stiler, G. M., & Philleo, T. (2003). Blogging and blogspots: An alternative format for encouraging reflective practice among preservice teachers. *Education, 123*(4), 789–798.

Stockley, D. (2006). Building a successful e-learning strategy. *Enterprise Information, 2*(7).

Su, D. (2005). A comparative evaluation and correlation between learning styles and academic achievement on e-learning. In R. Kwan & J. Fong (Eds.), *Web-based Learning: Technology and Pedagogy, Proceedings of the 4th International Conference* (pp. 193-202). Singapore: World Scientific Publishing Co. Pte. Ltd.

Surowiecki, K. (2004). *The wisdom of crowds.* New York: Doubleday.

Swan, K., & Shea, P. (2005). The development of virtual learning communities. In S. R. Hiltz & R. Goldman (Eds.), *Learning together online: Research on asynchronous learning networks* (pp. 239-260). Mahwah, NJ: Lawrence Erlbaum Associates.

Swan, K., Shea, P., Fredericksen, E., Pickett, A., Pelz, W., & Maher, G. (2000). Building knowledge building communities: Consistency, contact and communication in the virtual classroom. *Journal of Educational Computing Research, 23*(4), 359–383.

Tabor, S. W. (2007). Narrowing the Distance: Implementing a Hybrid Learning Model for Information Security Education. *Quarterly Review of Distance Education, 8*(1), 47–57.

Tan, C., & Chan, Y.-Y. (in press). Knowledge community: A knowledge building system for global collaborative project learning. *Proceedings of the IEEE.*

Tannen, D. (1989). *Talking voices: repetition, dialogue, and imagery in conversational discourse*. Cambridge, UK: Cambridge University Press.

Tetiwat, O., & Huff, S. (2002). Determinants of the adoption of web-based educational technology: A preliminary data analysis of New Zealand tertiary educators. In *Proceedings of the International Conference on Computers in Education (ICCE).* Washington, DC: IEEE Computer Society.

The Ambulent Player demos page. (2008). Retrieved from http://www.cwi.nl/projects/Ambulant/Demos.shtml

The EDUCAUSE Learning Initiative, 7 Things You Should Know About Wikis. (n.d.). Retrieved from http://www.educause.edu/ir/library/pdf/ELI7004.pdf

The, M. I. T. Press. (2008). *WordNet: An Electronic Lexical Database*. Retrieved November 21, 2008, from http://mitpress.mit.edu/catalog/item/default.asp?ttype=2&tid=8106

THES-QS. (2007). *The World University Ranking by Times Higher Education*. Retrieved April 1, 2008, from http://www.topuniversities.com/worlduniversityrankings/results/2007/overall_rankings/top_400_universities/

Thomas, K. (2007). Methods to Enhance Student Learning: A Student Appraisal of the 2007 Annual Learning Technologies Showcase. *Library Hi Tech News*, *24*(8), 4. doi:10.1108/07419050710835938

Thomas, M., Mitchell, M., & Joseph, R. (2002). The third dimension of ADDIE: A cultural embrace. *TechTrends*, *46*(2), 40–45. doi:10.1007/BF02772075

Thomas, R. (2006). Global Trends in Higher Education. 2006 Britannica Book of the Year. In Joe (Ed.), *Encyclopaedia Britannica*. Retrieved November 7, 2007, from http://www.gather.com/viewArticlePF.jsp?articleId=281474976776571

Thomas, S. (2008). Pervasive scale: A model of pervasive, ubiquitous, and ambient learning. *IEEE Pervasive Computing / IEEE Computer Society [and] IEEE Communications Society*, *7*(1), 85–88. doi:10.1109/MPRV.2008.20

Thomas, S., Joseph, C., Laccetti, J., Mason, B., Mills, S., Perril, S., & Pullinger, K. (2007). Transliteracy: Crossing divides. *First Monday*. Retrieved March28, 2008 from http://www.uic.edu/htbin/cgiwrap/bin/ojs/index.php/fm/article/view/2060/1908

Thorne, K. (2003). *Blended learning: How to Integrate Online & Traditional Learning*. London: Kogan Page.

Thorne, S., & Payne, J. (2005). Evolutionary Trajectories, Internet-mediated Expression, and Language Education. *CALICO*, *22*(3), 371–397.

Tomaska, L. (2000). Increasing student involvement in lectures by error-prone talks. *Biochemistry and Molecular Biology Education*, *28*, 242–243.

Topper, A. (1997). *Comparing Face-to-Face and Electronic Discourse: Issues and Questions Raised in a Research Study*. Paper presented at the Annual Meeting of the American Educational Research Association, Chicago, IL.

Tormey, R., & Henchy, D. (2008). Re-imagining the traditional lecture: an action research approach to teaching student teachers to 'do' philosophy. *Teaching in Higher Education*, *13*(3), 303–314. doi:10.1080/13562510802045337

Towers, J. M. (1996). An Elementary School Principal's Experience with Implementing an Outcome-Based Curriculum. *Catalyst for Change*, *25*(2), 19–23.

Trausan-Matu, S., Maraschi, D., & Cerri, S. (2002). Ontology-centered personalized presentation of knowledge extracted from the Web. In S. Cerri, G. Gouarderes (Eds.), *Intelligent Tutoring Systems 2002* (LNCS 2363, pp 259-269). New York: Springer.

Trausan-Matu, S., Rebedea, T., Dragan, A., & Alexandru, C. (2007a). Visualisation of learners' contributions in chat conversations. In J. Fong & P. Wang (Eds.), *Blended Learning* (pp. 215-224). Upper Saddle River, NJ: Prentice Hall.

Trausan-Matu, S., Stahl, G., & Sarmiento, J. (2006). Polyphonic support for collaborative learning. In Y.A. Dimitriadis et al. (Eds.), *CRIWG 2006 (LNCS 4154,* pp. 132 – 139*)*. New York: Springer.

Trausan-Matu, S., Stahl, G., & Sarmiento, J. (2007b). Supporting polyphonic collaborative learning. *E-service Journal*, *6*(1), 58–74. doi:10.2979/ESJ.2007.6.1.59

Triantafillou, V., Markopoulos, P., Villios, K., & Ilaridis, P. (2006). Synchronous e-learning room: Scenarios, tools and usage. *Fourth International Conference on Multimedia and Information and Communication Technologies in Education, 2*, 983-987. Retrieved February 25, 2008, from http://www.formatex.org/micte2006/pdf/983-987.pdf

Tsang, H. W., Hung, L. M., & Ng, S. C. (1999). A multimedia distance learning system on the Internet. In *1999 IEEE International Conference on Systems, Man, and Cybernetics* (pp. 243-246). Retrieved February 19, 2008, from http://ieeexplore.ieee.org/xpls/abs_all.jsp?arnumber=825265

Tsankova, J., & Dobrynina, G. (2005). Developing curious students. In R. H. Audet & L. K. Jordan (Eds.), *Integrating Inquiry Across the Curriculum* (pp. 85-89). Thousand Oaks, CA: Corwin Press.

Tsoukas, H. (2003). Do We Really Understand Tacit Knowledge? In M. Easterby-Smith, & M. A. Lyles, *The Blackwell Handbook of Organizational Learning and Knowledge Management* (pp. 410 - 427). Malden, MA: Blackwell Publishing.

Tu, C. H., & McIsaac, M. S. (2002). The relationship of social presence and interaction in online classes. *American Journal of Distance Education, 16*(3), 131–150. doi:10.1207/S15389286AJDE1603_2

Tuerner, A. D. (2007). *Theory and Practice of Education.* London: Continuum International Publishing Group.

Turing, A. M. (1950). Computing machinery and intelligence. *Mind, 59,* 433–460. doi:10.1093/mind/LIX.236.433

Turner, K. (2006). JASPER (Java simulation of protocols for education and research). Retrieved May 8, 2008, from http://www.cs.stir.ac.uk/~kjt/software/comms/jasper.html

Twigg, C. A. (2002). *Innovations in online learning: Moving beyond no significant difference.* Retrieved August 2003 from http://www.center.rpi.edu/PewSym/Mono4.html

Twigg, C. A. (2003). Improving learning and reducing costs: New models for online learning. *EDUCAUSE Review, 38*(5), 29–38.

Tynan, B., & Colbran, S. (2006). *Podcasting, Student Learning and Expectations.* Retrieved November 4, 2007, from http://www.ascilite.org.au/

UM e-Learning. (2008). *Official Website for UM e-Learning.* Retrieved February 11, 2008, from http://elearning.um.edu.my/login.php

UM. (2008). *Official Website for University of Malaya.* Retrieved February 11, 2008, from http://www.um.edu.my

Umar, J. (1997). Item banking. In J. P. Keeves (Ed.), *Educational Research, Methodology, and Measurement.* New York: Pergamon Publishing.

UoL ADELIE. (2008). *ADDELIE Project in University of Leicester.* Retrieved April 15, 2008, from: http://www.le.ac.uk/adelie/

UoL. (2005). *E-Learning Strategy.* Retrieved April 15, 2007, from http://www.le.ac.uk/strategies/elearning/

UoL. (2007). *Learning and Teaching Strategy 2007.* Retrieved April 15, 2008, from http://www.le.ac.uk/teaching/strategy.html

UoL. (2008). *Official Website for University of Leicester.* Retrieved April 15, 2008, from http://www.le.ac.uk/portals/university.html

Uskov, V. (2008). *Proceedings of the 7th International Conference on Web-Based Education (WBE-2008),* Innsbruck, Austria

UW-Madison. (2006). *Podcasting at University of Wisconsin-Madison.* Retrieved from http://engage.doit.wisc.edu/podcasting/teachAndLearn/

Valenti, S., Neri, F., & Cucchiarelli, A. (2003). An overview of current research on Automated essay grading. *Journal of Information Technology Education, 2,* 319–330.

van Lier, L. (2001). Constraints and resources in classroom talk: Issues of equality and symmetry. In C. N. Candlin & N. Mercer (Eds.), *English language teaching in its social context: a reader* (pp. 90-107). London: Routledge.

Varlamis, I., & Apostolakis, I. (2006). A Framework for Building Virtual Communities for Education. *Innovative Approaches for Learning and Knowledge Sharing, EC-TEL 2006 Workshop Proceedings,* (pp. 165-172).

Vaughan, N. (2007). Perspectives on blended learning in higher education. *International Journal in e-learning, 6*(1), 81.

Vaughan, N. D., & Garrison, D. R. (2005). Creating Cognitive Presence in a Blended Faculty Development Community. *The Internet and Higher Education, 8*(1), 1–12. doi:10.1016/j.iheduc.2004.11.001

Veronikas, S. W., & Shaughnessy, M. F. (2004). Teaching and learning in a hybrid world: An interview with Carol Twigg. *EDUCAUSE Review*, *39*(4), 50–62.

Video podcast. (n.d.). Retrieved from http://en.wikipeda.org/wiki/Video_podcast

Vignare, K. (2007). Review of Literature Blended learning: Using ALN to Change the Classroom – Will It Work? In A. G. Picciano & C. D. Dziuban (Eds.), *Blended learning: Research Perspectives*. MA: The Sloan Consortium.

Voloshinov, (1973). *Marxism and the philosophy of language*. New York: Seminar Press.

Vonderwell, S., & Zachariah, S. (2005). Factors that influence participation in online learning. *Journal of Research on Technology in Education*, *38*(2), 213–230.

Vossen, P. (1998). *EuroWordNet - A Multilingual Database with Lexical Semantic Networks*. Amsterdam: Kluwer Academic Publishers.

Vygotsky, L. (1978). *Mind and Society: The Development of Higher Psychological Processes*. Cambridge, MA: Harvard University Press.

Vygotsky, L. (1978). *Mind in society*. Cambridge, MA: Harvard University Press.

Vygotsky, L. S. (1978). *Mind in society: The development of higher psychological processes*. Cambridge, MA: Harvard University Press.

Wadhwa, S., Saxena, A., & Kumar, A. (2005). A KM motivated web-based supply chain simulator: facilitating e-learning for SMEs. *International Journal of Business Performance Management*, *8*(2), 2007.

Wagner, E. (2006). On designing interaction experiences for the next generation of blended learning. In C. J. Bonk & C. R. Graham (Eds.), *Handbook of blended learning: Global perspectives, local designs* (pp. 41-54). San Francisco: Pfeiffer.

Wagner, E. D. (1997). Interactivity: From agents to outcomes. *New Directions for Teaching and Learning*, *71*, 19–26. doi:10.1002/tl.7103

Wainer, H. (2000). *Computerized Adaptive Testing: A Primer*. Mahwah, NJ: Lawrence Erlbaum Assoc Inc.

Wall, J., & Ahmad, V. (2008). Lessons learned from a case study in deploying blended learning continuing professional development. *Engineering, Construction, and Architectural Management*, *15*(2), 185.

Wallace, R. M. (2003). Online learning in higher education: A review of research on interactions among teachers and students. *Education Communication and Information*, *3*(2), 241–280. doi:10.1080/14636310303143

Wang, C.-M., & Reeves, T. C. (2007). The Meaning of Culture in Online Education: Implications for teaching, learning, and design. In A. Edmundson (Ed.) *Globalizing e-learning cultural challenges* (pp. 2-17). Hershey, PA: Information Science.

Wang, M. J. (2004). Correlational analysis of student visibility and learning outcomes in an online setting. *Journal of Asynchronous Learning Networks*, *8*(4), 71–82.

Wang, M. J. (2007). Designing online courses that effectively engage learners from diverse cultural backgrounds. *British Journal of Educational Technology*, *38*(2), 294–311. doi:10.1111/j.1467-8535.2006.00626.x

Wang, M. J., & Kang, J. (2006). Cybergogy of engaged learning through information and communication technology: A framework for creating learner engagement. In D. Hung & M. Khine (Eds.), *Engaged learning with emerging technologies*. New York: Springer Publishing.

Wang, M. J., Shen, R. M., Novak, D., & Pan, X. Y. (2008). The impact of mobile learning on learning behaviors and performance: report from a large blended classroom. *British Journal of Educational Technology*, *38*(2), 294–311. doi:10.1111/j.1467-8535.2006.00626.x

Wang, Y. (2002). Assessment of learner satisfaction with asynchronous electronic learning systems. *Information & Management*, *41*(1), 75. doi:10.1016/S0378-7206(03)00028-4

Warburton, B. (2006). Quick Win or Slow Burn? Modelling UK HE CAA Update. In *Proceeding for 10th*

International Computer Assisted Assessment (CAA) Conference: Research into E-Assessment. (pp. 425-439). Loughborough University.

Ward, J., Gordon, J., Field, M., & Lehmann, H. (2001). Communication and information technology in medical education. *Lancet, 357*, 792–796. doi:10.1016/S0140-6736(00)04173-8

Warschauer, M., & Kern, R. (2000). *Network-based Language Teaching: Concepts and Practice.* Cambridge, UK: Cambridge University Press.

Wasserman, E. A., & Miller, R. R. (1997). Wath's elementary about associative learning? *Annual Review of Psychology, 48*, 573–607. doi:10.1146/annurev.psych.48.1.573

Watson, D. (2001). Pedagogy before technology: Re-thinking the relationship between ICT and teaching. *Education and Information Technologies, 6*(4), 251–266. doi:10.1023/A:1012976702296

Webb, H. (2005). Teaching with the case method online: Pure versus blended approaches. *Decision Sciences Journal of Innovative Education, 3*(2), 223. doi:10.1111/j.1540-4609.2005.00068.x

Wee, L. C. (2006). The ORID in IS Classes. In *Proc ISECON 2006, v23 (Dallas): §3732 (refereed).* Retrieved April 25, 2008, from isedj.org/isecon/2006/3732/ISECON.2006.Wee.pdf Wenger, E. (n.d.). *Communities of Practice.* Community of Practice – a brief introduction. Retrieved April 1, 2008, from http://www.ewenger.com/theory/index.htm

Weippl, E. (2007). Dependability in e-assessment. *International Journal in e-learning, 6*(2), 293.

Wellman, B., & Gulia, M. (1999). Virtual communities as communities: Net surfers don't ride alone In M. Smith & P. Kollock (Eds.), *Communities in cyberspace* (pp. 167-194). London: Routledge.

Wenger, E. (1998). *Communities of practice: Learning meaning and identify.* Cambridge, UK: Cambridge University Press.

Wenger, E. (2000). Communities of practice and social learning systems. *Organization, 7*(2), 225–246. doi:10.1177/135050840072002

Wenger, E., McDermott, R., & Snyder, W. M. (2002). *Cultivating communities of practice.* Boston: Harvard Business School Press.

Wentling, T., Waight, C., Gallaher, J., La Fleur, J., Wang, C., & Kanfer, A. (2005). E-Learning: A review of literature. *University of Illinois National Center for Supercomputer Applications.* Retrieved November 22, 2005, from http://learning.ncsa.uiuc.edu/ papers/elearnlit.pdf

Wenzloff, J. (2005). *Furl, furled, furling: Social online bookmarking for the masses.* Retrieved July 10, 2007, from http://www.classroomhelp.com/workshop/Furl_Guide.pdf

Wertsch, J. V. (1991). *Voices of the mind.* Cambridge, MA: Harvard University Press.

Whittingdon, D., & Hunt, H. (1999). Approaches to the computerised assessment of free-text responses. In *Proceedings of the 3rd International Computer Assisted Assessment Conference*, UK.

Wiemer-Hastings, P., Wiemer-Hastings, K., & Graesser, A. C. (1999). Improving an intelligent tutor's comprehension of students with Latent Semantic Analysis. In S. P. Lajoie & M/ Vivet (Eds.), *Artificial Intelligence Education.* Amsterdam: IOS Press.

Wikipedia, Learning Styles. (n.d.). Retrieved from http://en.wikipedia.org/wiki/Learning_styles

Wikipedia. (2008). *Electronic Learning.* Retrieved March 22, 2008, from http://en.wikipedia.org/wiki/E-learning

Wikipedia. (2008). *Socrates.* Retrieved April 21, 2008, from http://en.wikipedia.org/wiki/Socrates

Williams, C. (2002). Learning online: A review of recent literature in a rapidly expanding field. *Journal of Further and Higher Education, 26*(3), 263–272. doi:10.1080/03098770220149620

Williams, J. (2003, June). Blending into the background. *E-Learning Age Magazine*, 1.

Williams, J. B., & Jacobs, J. (2004). Exploring the use of blogs as learning spaces in the higher education sector. *Australasian Journal of Educational Technology*, *20*(2), 232–247.

Williams, R. L., & Cothrel, J. (2000). Four smart ways to run online communities. *Sloan Management Review*, *41*(4), 81–91.

Williams, R. S., & Humphrey, R. (2007). Understanding and fostering interaction in threaded discussion. *Journal of Asynchronous Learning Networks*, *2*(2), 129–143.

Willis, C. L., & Miertschin, S. L. (2006, April). Mind maps as active learning tool. *Journal of Computing Sciences in Colleges*, *21*(4), 266–272.

Wilson, J., & Mosher, D. (1994). The prototype of the virtual studio classroom. *Journal of Instruction Delivery Systems*, *8*(3).

Wilson, M. (2008). Professors should embrace Wikipedia. *Inside Higher Ed*. Retrieved April 1, 2008, from http://insidehighered.com/layout/set/print/views/2008/04/01/wilson

Windham, C. (2005). The student's perspective. In D. G. Oblinger & J. L. Oblinger (Eds.). *Educating the Net Generation* (pp. 5.1-5.16). Washington, DC: EDUCAUSE.

Winograd, T. (1987). Thinking machines: Can there be? Are we? *Report No. STAN-CS-87-1161*, Stanford, California.

Winograd, T., & Flores, F. (1986). *Understanding computers and cognition*. Norwood, NJ: Ablex.

Winston, R., Moore, R., Pearson, I., Hall, W., Shadbolt, N., & Weston, J. (2008). *Skills evolution report 2008: A vision: the future of workplace skills*. Sheffield, UK: Ufi Limited.

Wise, A., Duffy, T. M., & Padmanabhan, P. (2008). Deepening online conversation: How and why to use a common reference to connect learners with diverse local practices. *Educational Technology*, *48*(4), 3–11.

Woelk, D., & Agarwal, S. (2002). Integration of e-Learning and Knowledge Management. In M. Driscoll & T. C. Reeves, *Proceedings of the E-Learn 2002 World Conference on E-Learning in Corporate, Government, Healthcare & Higher Education* (pp. 1035-1042). Norfolk, Virginia: Association for the Advancement of Computing in Education (AACE).

Wong, C. K., Lee, S. L., Lee, F. K., Cheung, K. W., Mørch, A. I., & Liu, J. (2007). A Pilot Study on the Impact of the Web-based Essay Critiquing System on Writing at the Tertiary Level. In *Proceedings of the 2007 International Joint Conference on e-Commerce, e-Administration, e-Society, and e-Education.*

Wong, K. (2000). *Web-based tool for a computerised adaptive test system.* Master Thesis, University of Victoria, Wellington, New Zealand.

Wong, K., & Kwan, R. (2002). Building a Web-based computerized adaptive testing system. In *International Conference on Information and Communication Technologies in Education,* Badajoz, Spain (Vol. 1, pp. 62-66).

Wong, K., Kwan, R., & Chan, J. (2002). A preliminary evaluation of a computerized adaptive test system on the Web. In R. Kwan et al. (Eds.), *Web-based Learning: Men & Machines* (pp. 123-134). Hackensack, NJ: World Scientific Publishing.

Wong, S. L., Ab Jalil, H., Fauzi Mohd Ayub, A., Abu Baker, K., & Sai Hong, T. (2003). Teaching a discrete information technology course in a constructivist learning environment: is it effective for Malaysian pre-service teachers? *The Internet and Higher Education*, *6*(2), 193–204. doi:10.1016/S1096-7516(03)00025-3

Woo, Y., & Reeves, T. C. (2007). Meaningful interaction in web-based learning: A social constructivist interpretation. *The Internet and Higher Education*, *10*(1), 15–25. doi:10.1016/j.iheduc.2006.10.005

Worstall, T. (2005). *2005 Blogged: Despatches from the Blogosphere*. London, UK: Friday Books.

Wright, B. D. (1996). Reliability and separation. *Rasch Measurement Transactions*, *9*(4), 472.

Wright, B. D., & Stone, M. K. (1979). *Best test design*. Chicago: MESA Press.

Xie, K., DeBacker, T. K., & Ferguson, C. (2006). Extending the traditional classroom through online discussion: The role of student motivation. *Journal of Educational Computing Research, 34*(1), 67–89. doi:10.2190/7BAK-EGAH-3MH1-K7C6

Xu, R., & Wunsch, D. (2005). Survey of clustering algorithms. *IEEE Transactions on Neural Networks, 13*, 645–678. doi:10.1109/TNN.2005.845141

Xu, W., Liu, X., & Gong, Y. (2003). Document clustering based on non-negative matrix factorization. In *Proceedings of the 26th annual international ACM SIGIR conference on Research and development in information retrieval*, Toronto, Canada (pp. 267-273).

Xu, Z. (2008). When Hybrid Learning Meets Blended Teaching: Online Computer-Mediated Communication (CMC) Discourse and Classroom Face-to-Face (FTF) Discourse Analysis. In J. Fong, R. Kwan, & F. L. Wang (Eds), *Hybrid Learning and Education* (pp. 157-167). Berlin, Germany: Springer.

Yacci, M. (2000). Interactivity demystified: A structural definition for distance education and intelligent computer based instruction. *Educational Technology, 40*(4), 5–16.

Yang, F., Han, P., Shen, R. M., Kraemer, B. J., & Fan, X. W. (2003). Cooperative learning in self-organizing e-learner communities based on a multi-agents mechanism. In *Proceedings of AI2003,* Perth, Australia (pp. 490-500).

Yang, Y., & Cornelious, L. (2005). Preparing instructors for quality online instruction. *Online Journal of Distance Learning Administration, 8*(Spring). Retrieved February 26, 2008 from http://www.westga.edu/~distance/spring81/yang.htm

Yew, J., Gibson, F. P., & Teasley, S. D. (2006). Learning by tagging: The role of social tagging in group knowledge formation. *Journal of Online Learning and Teaching, 2*(4), 275–285.

Yin, R. K. (1989). *Case Study Research: Design and Method* (rev. ed.). Newbury Park, CA: Sage Publications.

Yin, R. K. (2003). *Application of Case Study Research* (2nd ed.). Thousand Oaks: Sage Publications.

Young, A., & Norgard, C. (2006). Assessing the quality of online courses from the students' perspective. *The Internet and Higher Education, 9*, 107–115. doi:10.1016/j.iheduc.2006.03.001

Young, J. (2002). *'Hybrid' Teaching Seeks to End the Divide Between Traditional and Online Instruction: By Blending Approaches, Colleges Hope To Save Money And Meet Students' Needs*. Retrieved February 8, 2006, from http://chronicle.com/free/v48/i28/28a03301.htm

Youngblood, P., Trede, F., & Corpo, S. D. (2001). Facilitating online learning: a descriptive study. *Distance Education, 22*(2), 264–284. doi:10.1080/0158791010220206

Yu, Y. T., Poon, C. K., & Choy, M. (2006). Experiences with PASS: Developing and using a programming assignment assessment system. In *Proceedings of the 6th International Conference on Quality Software (QSIC 2006)* (pp. 360-365). Washington, DC: IEEE Computer Society Press.

Zaïane, O., & Luo, J. (2001). Towards evaluating learners□ behaviour in a Web-based distance learning environment. In *Second IEEE International Conference on Advanced Learning Technologies (ICALT'01)*.

Zang, D. (2005). Interactive multimedia-based e-learning: A study of effectiveness. *American Journal of Distance Education, 19*(3), 149–162. doi:10.1207/s15389286ajde1903_3

Zapata-Rivera, J. D. (2004). Interacting with inspectable bayesian student models. *International Journal of Artificial Intelligence in Education, 14*(2), 127–163.

Zeleny, M. (1987). Management support systems: Towards integrated knowledge management. *Human Systems Management, 7*, 59–70.

Zemel, A. (2005). Personal communication.

Zhao, C. M., & Kuh, G. D. (2004). Adding value: Learning communities and student engagement. *Research in Higher Education*, *45*(2), 115–138. doi:10.1023/B:RIHE.0000015692.88534.de

About the Contributors

Fu Lee Wang is the Head of Department of Business Administration at Caritas Francis Hsu College, Hong Kong. Prior to joining Caritas, he was a Lecturer at the City University of Hong Kong, Hong Kong. He received B.Eng. and M.Phil. from the University of Hong Kong, MBA from Imperial College London, and Ph.D. in Information Systems from the Chinese University of Hong Kong. His research interests include electronic business, information systems and e-learning. He is a member of ACM and IEEE. He has published about 50 articles in journals and proceedings of international conferences, i.e., Journal of the American Society for Information Science and Technology (JASIST), Decision Support Systems (DSS), Information Processing Letters, IW3C, SIGIR, and more.

Joseph Fong is an editorial board member of International Journal of Web Information Systems. He is a fellow of Hong Kong Computer Society, the founder chairman of the [Hong Kong Computer Society Database Special Interest Group], and the honorable founder chairman of [Hong Kong Web Society], and International Hybrid Learning Society. Fong had worked in the electronic data processing in US for 11 years, and came back to Hong Kong as an academician since 1988. His research interests are in database, data warehousing, data mining XML and Web-Based Learning. His above 100 publications include SCI Journals, Conferences, Patent (US), edited books, and an authored text book on "Information Systems Reengineering and Integration" 2nd edition by Springer in 2006. He had been a program manager of a M.Sc. of Staffordshire University hosted at City University of Hong Kong for a decade and teaches [Data warehousing and data mining], [Data Engineering], [Database Systems] and [Introduction to Database Systems]including XML technology.

Reggie Kwan, Caritas Institute of Higher Education. Reggie is the Professor and President of Caritas Institute of Higher Education. Before joining Caritas to build a Catholic university in Hong Kong, he was the Head of Computing and Mathematics at the Open University of Hong Kong. Prior to that, he was the Professor and Chair of Computer Science at Montana Tech of the University of Montana from mid-80's to late 90's. He has published six books and over 55 papers in the areas of e-learning.

* * *

Philip P. Alberts has been involved in higher education since 1981, working in the field of academic staff development and specifically teaching development. In January 2002 he started at Brunel University in the United Kingdom, working with academic staff to develop a "hybrid" approach in their teaching – combining e-learning activities with face-to-face teaching. In doing this, it was always his point of departure to facilitate judicial implementation of educational considerations and pedagogic principles. As Head of e-Learning at Brunel, Dr. Alberts oversees an e-Team to promote and support e-learning with staff and students. He is also involved in the delivery of modules of the Postgraduate Certificate in Learning and Teaching in Higher Education for staff newly-appointed at the University.

Oliver Au graduated from York University and University of Toronto with BA and MS respectively. He developed software for IBM, banks and insurance companies in Canada for over 12 years. He has taught at the Open University of Hong Kong and the City University of Hong Kong for over 4 years. Currently, he is a PhD candidate in computer science at the Loughborough University. He has an interest in software engineering and cognitive theory.

Richard G. Bagnall is Chair Professor of Lifelong Learning at the Hong Kong Institute of Education. His scholarly work is in the social philosophy of lifelong and vocational education, with particular emphasis on the ethics of educational theory, advocacy, and policy. He has published over 100 books and papers in that field, including *Cautionary Tales in the Ethics of Lifelong Learning Policy and Management: A Book of Fables* (Kluwer Academic, 2004) and *Discovering Radical Contingency: Building a Postmodern Agenda in Adult Education*, (Peter Lang, 1999). His teaching is centred on the philosophy of lifelong learning and he has supervised to graduation the doctoral studies of over 25 candidates.

Philip Barker is the *Eyetech Professor of Applied Computing* within the School of Computing at the University of Teesside in the UK. He has published numerous books, research papers and conference publications. He was appointed as a National Teaching Fellow by the UK's Higher Education Academy in 2005 for his outstanding contributions to the development of electronic learning. He has travelled the world giving lectures, workshops and keynote presentations on his research specialisms. These fall broadly into the general area of human-computer interaction and include performance support, digital knowledge management and electronic learning using mobile and hybrid learning technologies.

Raj Boora, M.Ed. Through his career, Raj has been interested in interface design, life long learning and technology integration. As the Senior Instructional Designer for the Faculty of Science at the University of Alberta, Raj is investigating integration strategies that aim to increase the role of technology in post secondary science education. Raj hopes that this work will help ensure students are able to access content via their preferred methods and increase contact time with instructional staff. Raj is also interested in course designs that incorporate elements of game based instruction to further engage students.

Wade Brown is completing his BSC, specializing in Psychology at the University of Alberta. He came to work for the Faculty of Science's Instructional Design unit, DigiTLE, through the faculty's Industrial Internship Program. This is Wade's first contribution to a scholarly publication on education, and he has enjoyed being exposed to the many facets of education and Instructional Design.

Dumitru Dan Burdescu is professor dr. eng. mat. at the Software Engineering Department, Faculty of Automation, Computers and Electronics, University of Craiova, Romania. The research activity was focused on areas like: algorithms and data structures, algorithms complexity, multimedia and e-learning. He is the author and coauthor of more than 120 scientific papers presented to conferences and published in different journals, 10 books in the computers area, member in the program committees of important conferences, member in the editorial board of international magazines. He was the director of more than 10 research grants and also the coordinator of the excellence center "Multimedia applications development".

Victor Callaghan is a full professor of Computer Science and leader of the Inhabited Intelligent Environments Group at the Essex University. His expertise concerns the creation of high-tech real and virtual environments for applications such as advanced learning environments or everyday living. Professor Callaghan has published over 100 papers on these issues and is a key member of organizational team for major conferences such as 'Pervasive Computing & Applications', 'Ubiquitous Intelligence & Computing', 'Intelligent Environments' and journals such as the Journal of Ambient Intelligence and Smart Environments, Intelligent Buildings International, Pervasive Computing & Communications, and the Journal of Ubiquitous Computing & Intelligence.

Yuen-Yan Chan is a Postdoctoral Fellow in the Faculty of Education at the University of Hong Kong and an Adjunct Assistant Professor in the Department of Information Engineering at the Chinese University of Hong Kong. Her research interests include learning sciences, engineering education, cryptography, and security education. Chan has a PhD from the Chinese University of Hong Kong, with a doctoral dissertation focused on cryptography. She's the founding chair of the IEEE Education Society, Hong Kong Chapter, and is a US National Academy of Engineering Center for the Advancement of Engineering Education new faculty fellow.

William K. Cheung received the BSc and MPhil degrees in electronic engineering from the Chinese University of Hong Kong and the PhD degree in computer science in 1999 from the Hong Kong University of Science and Technology. He is an associate professor in the Department of Computer Science, Hong Kong Baptist University. He has served as co-chairs and program committee members of a number of international conferences, as well as guest editors of internal journals in areas including artificial intelligence, Web intelligence, data mining, Web services, and e-commerce technologies. Also, he has been on the editorial board of the IEEE Intelligent Informatics Bulletin since 2002. His research interests include artificial intelligence and machine learning, as well as their applications to collaborative filtering, Web mining, distributed data mining, and Web/grid service management.

Esyin Chew is a Senior Lecturer in Learning, Teaching and Assessment at the University of Glamorgan. She has published a number of papers and book reviews related to blended learning, e-commerce and expert system and is interested in the disciplinary experiences in using educational technology in higher education. She was a software engineer, lecturer in Computer Science, reviewers of international conferences, editor of the Journal of Problem-based Learning, e-learning and e-commerce consultant. She is currently pursuing a doctoral degree in blended learning.

John Church is Associate Professor (cross-appointed) in the Centre for Health Promotion Studies and Department of Political Science at the University of Alberta. Dr. Church's research focuses on what influences policy development and the policy choices of political decision makers. He teaches public policy analysis to graduate students and Canadian health policy to undergraduates.

Myles Chykerda. Although holding an undergraduate degree in Classical Archaeology, Myles became interested in classroom applications of technology upon entering the University of Alberta's Humanities Computing program. Myles hopes to look into how archaeology sites can be linked to classroom settings without requiring massive hardware and support investment. Myles also studies the role of technology in museum presentations as well as having a strong secondary research interest in electronic gaming as well as the overall culture of gamers.

Liping Deng is an EdD (Doctor of Education) candidate at the Faculty of Education, the University of Hong Kong. Her research interests center on weblogs, online learning, learning community, teacher education and has been actively involved in several research projects on these themes in the context of higher education. She had a professional experience of working at tertiary institutions at China and United States as an instructor, educational technology specialist and researcher.

Michel Desmarais is associate professor at the Computer Engineering Department of Ecole Polytechnique de Montreal since 2002. His field of expertise is in the domains of Human-Computer Interactions, e-learning, and Artificial Intelligence. He has 15 years of experience in software project management. He was principal researcher of the Human-Computer Interaction and Computerized Learning Environments groups at the Computer Research Institute of Montreal between 1990 and 1998, where he directed a research program in HCI and computer assisted learning, and was involved in a number of research projects in close collaboration with private corporations. From 1998 to 2002, he was director of the Web services department in a private company (mvm.com) and leader of a number of R&D Web-based software projects. He is the author of over 50 papers in scientific journal, conferences, and book chapters.

Cath Ellis, BA(Hons) PhD, is course leader of a Humanities degree at the University of Huddersfield, UK. Previously at the University of Wollongong, Australia she was involved in the design, development and delivery of a degree offered across four remote campuses via Distributed Learning. At the University of Huddersfield, she leads a project which has piloted the use of Distributed Learning in curriculum delivery. She is an experienced practitioner in the use of online learning environments and videoconferencing for teaching and learning and won a University teaching award in 2003. She has published on flexible delivery and blended learning.

Sue Folley, BSc (Hons) PGCE MSc is an Academic Developer working on a project on Distributed Learning working with staff to develop materials in a pedagogically sound way for use with distributed cohorts of students. She has an MSc in Multimedia and E-learning and has previously taught Maths and IT in the FE sector, as well training staff on IT courses. Sue also works with academic staff on various teaching and learning projects, assisting with funding applications, and project management. She is currently working towards an EdD researching the use of technology in Higher Education.

Michael Gardner is Director of the Digital Lifestyles centre at the University of Essex which explores future lifestyles based around the technical vision of ambient and pervasive computing. This includes the co-creation, innovation and design of new services based on a Living Laboratory approach, combined with the development of pervasive computing technologies in inhabited and networked environments. The centre brings together the social and technical expertise of a number of research groups at the University, based on a balanced portfolio of research, teaching and commercial activities. Previously worked for Briish Telcom leading the technical R&D activities on the BT e-learning research programme

Owen P. Hall, Jr. received his Ph.D. from the University of Southern California and undertook post-doctoral studies at the Center for Futures Research. Dr. Hall is a Professor of Decision & Information Systems at the George L. Graziadio School of Business and Management, Pepperdine University. He is the recipient of a Charles Luckman teaching fellowship. Dr. Hall is the editor-in-chief of the Graziadio Business Report and a registered professional engineer, State of California. He is the author of several textbooks on computer based decision support systems and numerous technical papers on the subjects of decision support systems, distance learning systems and neural networks. Dr. Hall's current area of research includes artificial learning agents and the development of blended learning nets.

Andreas Henrich obtained the Dipl. degree in information systems in 1987 from the University of Technology Darmstadt, the Dr. rer. nat. degree in 1990 from the University of Hagen, and the Venia Legendi in 1997 from the University of Siegen. Since 1998 he has been a Professor at the University of Bamberg and since 2004 he is a full Professor for Media Informatics at this university. His research interests are especially in information retrieval, data visualization and exploration, and e-Learning.

Raquel Hijón-Neira is a graduate in Computer Science (Universidad Pontificia de Salamanca en Madrid, 1998) and she is currently finishing her PhD studies in the Universidad Rey Juan Carlos, Spain, where she is also an Assistant Professor in the Departamento de Lenguajes y Sistemas Informáticos I. She is a member of the LITE research group (Laboratory of Information Technologies in Education). She is a coauthor of the MerlinMo tracking and visualization module for Moodle LMS. Her research interest are: tracking of student activity in learning environments, data visualization and analysis, e-learning, and web 2.0.

Norah Jones is Professor of Education at the University of Glamorgan and is Head of the Centre for Excellence in Learning and Teaching. She has been involved in e-learning since 2000 when she managed the academic team in the Business School who were developing materials on-line. She has published a number of papers on the way all things 'E' are changing universities and colleges and is interested in the change of emphasis from teaching to learning. Previously, Norah was Associate Head in the Business School at the University of Glamorgan and has spent most of her career teaching Organisational Behaviour and Management. Norah has a doctorate in education management; she is a Chartered Psychologist and Fellow of the Chartered Institute of Personnel and Development.

Gibson Lam is currently a computer officer in the Department of Computer Science and Engineering, The Hong Kong University of Science and Technology, Clear Water Bay, Kowloon, Hong Kong. He received his MPhil degree in Computer Science from HKUST. His research interests include computer graphics, multimedia systems, Web services and e-learning technologies. He has been working on several education-related projects in HKUST. In the team lead by Dr. David Rossiter he recently received the HKUST Teaching Innovation Award for the innovation use of the Gong system, a Web-based voice communication tool, in language teaching.

Hiu-Fung Lam obtained her Bachelor of Science degree and the Master of Philosophy degree both from the Department of Chemistry at The University of Hong Kong. She also obtained the Postgraduate Diploma in Education and Master of Education degree from The Chinese University of Hong Kong. Lam is specialized in Curriculum Development and Science Education. She is currently a chemistry teacher at the Sai Kung Sung Tsun Catholic School (Secondary Section) in Hong Kong.

Cynthia Lee, Associate Professor at Language Centre of Hong Kong Baptist University. Her expertise is in second language teaching and learning, particularly second language pragmatics and Web-based learning.

Fion S.L. Lee is a lecturer in the Department of Computer Science at Hong Kong Baptist University of Hong Kong. Her research interests include behavior in online communities, online learning, electronic business, and information technology strategy.

Mark J. W. Lee is an adjunct senior lecturer with the School of Education, Charles Sturt University, and an honorary research fellow with the School of Information Technology and Mathematical Sciences, University of Ballarat. Previously, he worked in a variety of teaching, instructional design and managerial roles within the private vocational education and higher education sectors. Mark has published widely in the areas of educational technology, e-learning and innovative pedagogy in higher education. He is presently chair of the New South Wales Chapter of the Institute of Electrical and Electronics Engineers (IEEE) Education Society, and serves on the editorial boards of a number of international journals in the area of educational technology and e-learning.

Chi-Hong Leung is currently a Lecturer in the Department of Management and Marketing at the Polytechnic University. He graduated from the Department of Biology at the Chinese University of Hong Kong. Then he studied in the Department of Computer Science and Engineering at the same university and was awarded an MPhil degree and a PhD degree respectively. He also obtained his MBA from the University of Leicester, MEdSt from the University of Western Australia, and DBA from the University of Newcastle. His working experience covers several disciplines including engineering, education, and business.

Wang Lixun obtained his PhD (Applied Linguistics) in the UK. Since 1994, he has been doing research work in the areas of Computer-Assisted Language Learning, Corpus Linguistics, and Online Learning. At present he works as an Assistant Professor in the English Department at the Hong Kong Institute of Education.

Helen M. Madill is currently Professor and Graduate Programs Coordinator for the Centre for Health Promotion Studies in the School of Public Health at the University of Alberta. Helen has taught courses in on line and face-to-face modes and has been member of the University Teaching Services Peer Consultant team since 1996. Helen's research is in career decision-making and choice. Helen received a McCalla Professorship in 1999, the Graduate Students' Association Academic Staff Award in 2004/2005, and the Minervera Mentoring Award from the Alberta Women's Science Network in 2007.

Kai-Pan Mark is currently a Senior Research Assistant and a Master of Philosophy student in the Department of Information Systems, City University of Hong Kong. He is particularly interested in information and communications technologies in education. His current research interest is in the continuance of learning systems. He is now serving as the Vice Chairman of IEEE Education Society Hong Kong Chapter.

Catherine McLoughlin is an associate professor with the School of Education at the Australian Catholic University, Canberra. She also serves as the coordinator of the Australian Capital Territory branch of the Research Centre for Science, Information Technology and Mathematics Education for Rural and Regional Australia (SiMERR). With over 20 years experience in higher education in Europe, South East Asia, the Middle East and Australia, Catherine has experience and expertise in a variety of educational settings, with diverse students and across a wide range of cultural contexts. She is editor of the *Australasian Journal of Educational Technology* and an editorial board member of a several leading journals, including the *British Journal of Educational Technology.*

Sean McMinn is currently an instructor in the Language Centre, The Hong Kong University of Science and Technology, Clear Water Bay, Kowloon, Hong Kong. His research interests include computer assisted language learning and educational technologies, such as blogs, podcasting and wikis. He has been podcasting since late 2005, including the English One Podcast and his latest venture Campus Beat, a student group produced podcast magazine by HKUST students for their peers. He recently received the HKUST Teaching Innovation Award for innovative use of podcasting in the classroom.

Donna Morrow is a Senior Lecturer in the College of Education at the University of Canterbury, Christchurch, New Zealand. Her research interests centre on the use of information and communication technologies to support learning, with a particular focus on the use of the online environment for teaching and learning. Her research in the area of online learning has examined learner-centric interactivity, the impact of the textual environment on learners and the contributions of local learning communities as support in online environments. She has extensive experience in the design and delivery of online courses and her teaching focuses on supporting the learning process through information and communication technologies.

Jogesh K. Muppala is currently an associate professor in the Department of Computer Science and Engineering, The Hong Kong University of Science and Technology, Clear Water Bay, Kowloon, Hong Kong. He received the Ph. D. degree in Electrical Engineering from Duke University, Durham, NC, USA. His research interests include embedded systems software, high-speed networking, Web 2.0 technologies and Internet in education. Dr. Muppala is a Senior Member of IEEE, IEEE Computer Society and IEEE Communications Society, and a participating representative from HKUST with EDUCAUSE. He was awarded the Teaching Excellence Appreciation Award by the Dean of Engineering, HKUST. He recently received the HKUST Teaching Innovation Award for innovative use of Web 2.0 technologies in the classroom.

Linda A. Murray has been a Higher Education lecturer in Psychology since 1974, specialising in cognitive psychology and development with a particular interest in language and communication. This interest, combined with an increasing focus on adult learning, led to work on student learning and her current post as Director of the Learning and Teaching Development Unit at Brunel University. Dr. Murray currently has overall responsibility for the development of new academic staff, the support service for students and the implementation of e-learning at the University. In all these areas, she continues to explore the application of the psychological theories that are foundational to many aspects of higher education.

Thanh T. Nguyen is Associate Professor and Graduate Coordinator in the Instructional Technology and Design program at Bridgewater State College. She received her doctoral degree from Harvard University. Her ongoing teaching and research focuses have been on how to design a curriculum using technology as tools to reach diverse learners and to bridge the generation gap in today digital world.

Barbara O'Byrne is a professor of literacy education at Marshall University Graduate College in West Virginia. She is active in designing and evaluating blended learning courses. Her research interests include the impact of online instruction on teaching and learning, multimodal assessment practices, and the role of images in the writer's imagination, and She has recent publications in *The International Journal of Science Education, The Journal of Computer-Assisted Instruction, and The Reading Professor.*

Ismael Pascual-Nieto received the B.S. degree in Computer Science from the Universidad Autónoma de Madrid in 2005, and the M.S. degree in Computer Science and Engineering from the Universidad Autónoma de Madrid in 2007. He is currently a researcher at the Computer Science Department at the Universidad Autónoma de Madrid. His primary research is focused on the application of Natural Language Processing techniques to improve e-learning and e-assessment. He has published 10 papers in international and national journals and conferences.

Diana Pérez-Marín received the the Ph.D. degree in Computer Science and Engineering from the Universidad Autónoma de Madrid in 2007. She is currently a lecturer at the Computer Science Department at the Universidad Autónoma de Madrid. Her primary research is focused on the combination of techniques from Natural Language Processing, Student Modeling and Adaptive Educational Hypermedia fields to improve e-tutoring. She has published more than 30 papers in journals such as "Journal of Educational Technology and Society", or "Computers and Education"; and international conferences such as "Adaptive Hypermedia" (AH), "User Modeling" (UM) or "Artificial Intelligence for Education" (AIED).

Pilar Rodríguez received the Ph.D. degree in Computer Science from the Universidad Complutense de Madrid in 1990. She worked in the IBM-UAM research centre until 1996. She is a professor at the Computer Science Department at the Universidad Autónoma de Madrid. Her research comprises several fields such as Adaptive Hypermedia, visualization of information, learning styles, and application of Natural Language Processing to e-learning and e-assessment. She has published more than 60 papers in international journals and conferences. Furthermore, she has led and participated in numerous research projects on web-based education.

Jonay P. Rodriguez Martin has been a Computer Science Engineering student finishing his studies in 2008 from the Universidad Las Palmas de Gran Canaria, during his last academic year (2007-08) he has been into an exchange program (Séneca) studying at the University Rey Juan Carlos were he has been doing his final project under the tutelage of Raquel Hijón-Neira. In this project he has put into practice the integration of different technologies to improve e-learning systems. During his studies he has also worked for 2 years as web developer (J2EE, PHP, .NET). Currently he is working in Madrid developing Web applications multimodal for mobile in Solaiemes, a company that is among the 100 most innovative companies in Europe

David P. Rossiter is a Visiting Assistant Professor in the Department of Computer Science and Engineering, The Hong Kong University of Science and Technology, Clear Water Bay, Kowloon, Hong Kong. He has developed a number of educational projects, including the Gong system which may be used to develop podcasts. He has received three awards relating to teaching innovation, and four related to teaching quality.

Liping Shen is an associate professor of Computer Science and Engineering at Shanghai Jiaotong University. She has been working in e-Learning area for more than 8 years; her work and research focus on learning technology standards, personalized learning technologies and context-aware pervasive learning. When she visited Essex University in UK 2006, the affective e-learning collaboration work was reported by New Scientist http://www.newscientisttech.com/article/dn10894-emotionaware-teaching-software-tracks-student-attention.html and EuroNews (broadcast on 13th February 2007). She has peer-reviewed articles published in journals such as *Journal of Information Systems Frontiers, International Journal of Continuing Engineering Education* and *Life-Long Learning, Lectures Notes in Computer Science, INFORMATICA,* etc.

Ruimin Shen is a distinguished professor of Computer Science and Engineering at Shanghai Jiaotong University (SJTU). He is also the founder and director of the world-renowned SJTU e-Learning Lab, and the founding dean of SJTU's Network Education College (17,000 students). Winner of several national awards in innovations in distance education and e-learning, Shen's research and development specialty focus on cutting-edge technologies for "available anywhere and updatable anytime" distance education, including mobile learning, standard natural classrooms, knowledge discovery and data mining, data encoding and information retrieval. He has peer-reviewed articles published in top-tier journals such as *INFORMATICA*, *British Journal of Educational Technology*, *International Journal of Distance Education Technologies, Lecture Notes in Artificial Intelligence, Lectures Notes in Computer Science, Computers and Education*, etc.

Stefanie Sieber graduated in information systems at the University of Bamberg in 2006. She is now working on her PhD-thesis in the area of information retrieval and e-Learning.

Liana Stanescu is assistant professor at the Software Engineering Department, Faculty of Automation, Computers and Electronics, University of Craiova, Romania. She received a PhD in computer science from University of Craiova in 2002. She is the author or co-author of 7 books and more than 80 conference and journal papers on multimedia, databases, content-based visual retrieval and e-learning, reviewer, program committee member and organizer for some important conferences. The research activity carried on more than 10 research grants was directly focused on the medical domain. In the TESYS e-learning system introduced a multimedia component as an original element.

Julia E. Stephenson was awarded a BSc (Hons) in Medical Biology from Brunel University in 2002. Subsequently, she earned her doctorate from the Faculty of Science, Technology and Medical Studies at the University of Kent at Canterbury (2003-2006). Her thesis focused on different aspects of e-learning in genetics. Dr. Stephenson's work has included authoring and evaluating OnLine Assessment and Feedback (OLAAF project) in collaboration with Birkbeck, University of London; the development of electronic conference proceedings for a major international chromosome conference and also interactive karyotyping tutorials with summative and formative feedback to teach the skill of recognising chromosomally-determined infertility in boars. At present she is working at Brunel University in e-learning development from a research perspective.

Stefan Trausan-Matu, PhD, is a full professor at the Computer Science Department of the Politehnica University of Bucharest, Romania and principal researcher at the Institute of Artificial Intelligence of the Romanian Academy. He was a Fulbright post-doc at Drexel University, Philadelphia, USA, was invited professor and lectured in USA, France, The Netherlands, San Marino, Puerto Rico, etc.. His research interests are: Computer-Supported Collaborative Learning, Group Knowledge Construction, Natural Language Processing, Ontologies, Semantic Web, Human-Computer Interaction, Artificial Intelligence, and Philosophy. Prof Trausan-Matu has published 12 books, 19 book chapters and more than 160 papers. He conducted or praticipated to many international projects: LTfLL, Virtual Math Teams, EU-NCIT, Cooper, IKF, SkyNurse, LarFLaST, Poirot, PE-KADS, PAIL

Philip Tsang, Open University of Hong Kong Philip is a one of the senior academic staff of the Open University of Hong Kong (OUHK). Dr Tsang is a trained engineer and won back to back President's Award at OUHK. He is a senior member of the Institute of Electrical and Electronics Engineers (IEEE). He has been and will continue to be chair of many international conferences and he is also on a number of journals' editorial board. He is a prolific researcher and a prominent practitioner in using ICT in his teaching.

Eric Tsui is the Professor of Knowledge Management and Associate Director of the Knowledge Management Research Centre at The Hong Kong Polytechnic University. He is an Editorial Board member of the Knowledge-Based Systems, Knowledge Management Research and Practice, Journal of Knowledge Management Studies, and the Information and Knowledge Management Journal. He is also the Program Leader of Asia Pacific's very unique Master of Science in Knowledge Management, a program that is delivered via blended E-Learning and face-to-face environments. He was Chief Research Officer, Asia Pacific and Innovation Manager for CSC Australia from 2000 to 2005. He has PhD, MBA and BSc (Hons) qualifications.

David Turner is Professor of Education at the University of Glamorgan. He is a specialist on matters relating to the theory of education. His second book, *Theory and Practice of Education*, will be published in paperback in March 2009. This addresses questions of developing educational policy in complex educational settings. He is currently working on two new books, one on the theory of intelligence, and the other on quality in higher education. In both contexts he argues that educational phenomena cannot be reduced to psychology, history, economics or sociology, but that education is a distinct and complex field of understanding.

J. Ángel Velázquez-Iturbide is a graduate and PhD in Computer Science (Universidad Politécnica de Madrid, 1985, 1990). Currently, he is a Full Professor at the Universidad Rey Juan Carlos, Spain. He is the Head of the Departamento de Lenguajes y Sistemas Informáticos I, as well as the Director of the LITE research group (Laboratory of Information Technologies in Education). He is a coauthor of the WinHIPE and SRec educational systems. His research interests are: innovation for programming education, program visualization, interactive learning assistants, and tracking of student activity in learning environments.

Minjuan Wang is an associate professor of Educational Technology at San Diego State University and an adjunct faculty of Shanghai Jiaotong University. Her research specialties focus on the sociocultural facets of online learning, mobile learning, and technological interventions in language education. She has published peer-reviewed articles in prominent journals such as *IEEE Transactions on Education, Educational Technology Research and Development, Computers and Education,* and *British Journal of Educational Technology.* She has also published book chapters on engaged learning in online problem solving, Cybergogy for interactive learning online, informal learning via the Internet, and effective learning in multicultural and multilingual classrooms.

Wenhua Wang is a M.S. Candidate of Computer Science at Zhejiang University, Hangzhou, China. He received his B.S. degree from Zhejiang University in 2007. His research interests include retrieval and machine learning.

Kelvin Chi Kuen Wong is an assistant professor of computer science at Hong Kong Baptist University. He received his PhD from the University of Nottingham. His research interests include e-learning, IT in education, Web-based assessments and applications of latent semantic analysis.

Kenneth Wong, Hong Kong Institute of Education. Kenneth is an Instructor of The Hong Kong Institute of Education (HKIEd). Before joining HKIEd, Mr. Wong was an Information Technology in Education Development Officer in Education Department of the Hong Kong Government. His research and teaching expertise is in Information Technology in Education and Computer Adaptive Testing.

Tak-Lam Wong received his B.Eng., M.Phil., and Ph.D. degrees from the Chinese University of Hong Kong in 2001, 2003, and 2007 respectively. He is currently with the Chinese University of Hong Kong. His research interests lie in the areas of Web mining, data mining, information extraction, machine learning, and knowledge management. His has published papers in international journals and conferences, such as ACM Transactions on Internet Technology (TOIT), Data and Knowledge Engineering (DKE), the Annual International ACM Conference on Research and Development on Information Retrieval (SIGIR), the AAAI Conference on Artificial Intelligence (AAAI), etc.

Fei Wu received the B.S. degree from Lanzhou University, Lanzhou, China, the M.S. degree from Macao University, Macao, China, and the Ph.D. degree from Zhejiang University, Hangzhou, Zhejiang, China. His research interests include multimedia retrieval, computer animation, and pattern recognition.

Harrison H. Yang is a professor at the Department of Curriculum and Instruction, State University of New York at Oswego, US. He also served as research and teaching assistant at the College of Education in Florida A&M University; adjunct instructor and coordinator of educational technology at the Center for Instructional Technology of Florida International University. His key research interests is educational technology theory and practice.

Francis Yu, PLK Tang Yuk Tien College. Mr. Yu has been teaching in Secondary Schools for 23 years. He is currently a seconded teacher working at the Education Department of Hong Kong to help use IT in teaching and learning. Besides teaching areas such as IT, Computing and Mathematics, he is interested in conducting teaching and learning research.

Allan H.K. Yuen is an Associate Professor and Associate Dean (Learning & Teaching) of the Faculty of Education, the University of Hong Kong. His research activities focus on evaluative & comparative studies on information technology in education, learning community & knowledge building, technology acceptance & educational change, and technology & teacher education. Dr. Yuen has been engaged in more than 30 funded research projects. He is a founding member and the vice president of the Hong Kong Association for Educational Communications and Technology (HKAECT). He has also made significant contribution to local, regional and international professional organizations in educational technology.

Ly Yuen is currently a final year student in The Hong Kong Polytechnic University studying the Master of Science in Knowledge Management. She has been doing the programme since Jan 2007 with an aim to develop a life-long learning capability. During the period of study, she receives an in-depth understanding of the tools and methods in the design and implementation of KM systems. She also receives much support and gets constant inspiration from a pool of international experts and the faculty members. Her research interests include Knowledge Management Technologies, Knowledge Communities and E-Learning.

Han Wang Zhang is a B.S. Candidate of Computer Science at Zhejiang University, Hangzhou, China. His research interests include retrieval and machine learning.

Xu Zhichang is an assistant professor in the English Department of the Hong Kong Institute of Education. He had his doctoral degree in Language and Intercultural Education from Curtin University of Technology, Western Australia. His current research interests include blended teaching and learning, language education and teaching training.

Yueting Zhuang received the B.S., M.S., and Ph.D. degrees from Zhejiang University, Hangzhou, Zhejiang, China, in 1986, 1989, and 1998, respectively. Currently, he is a Professor and Ph.D. Supervisor at the College of Computer Science, Zhejiang University. His research interests include multimedia databases, artificial intelligence, and video-based animation.

Index

D

E

F

G

H

I

J

K

L

M

N

O

T

U

V